CONSPIRACY

On March 27, [...] President Roosevelt a complete physical examination at Bethesda Hospital. His medical report described a man with few life-sustaining forces left—a man who might live only a few months, possibly a year. That devastating report was suppressed. Neither Roosevelt nor his family was told that FDR was dying. Yet this ailing man—the most powerful in the world—underwent the terrible rigors of a fourth-term campaign, took part in international conferences that would alter history, and on April 12, 1945, a shocked world learned of his death. . . .

JACK ANDERSON, noted Washington columnist, says: "Bishop has long been one of my favorite writers and after reading *FDR's Last Year*, he has become my *favorite* author. I was intrigued with the mass of detail provided in the book, detail which is not available in any history book."

A LITERARY GUILD SELECTION

FDR'S LAST YEAR
was originally published
by William Morrow & Company, Inc.

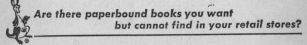

FDR'S LAST YEAR

April 1944–April 1945

By Jim Bishop

PUBLISHED BY POCKET BOOKS NEW YORK

FDR'S LAST YEAR

William Morrow edition published September, 1974

POCKET BOOK edition published September, 1975

L

This POCKET BOOK edition includes every word contained
in the original, higher-priced edition. It is printed from
brand-new plates made from completely reset, clear, easy-to-
read type. POCKET BOOK editions are published by POCKET
BOOKS, a division of Simon & Schuster, Inc., 630 Fifth
Avenue, New York, N.Y. 10020. Trademarks registered
in the United States and other countries.

Printed in the U.S.A.

Dedicated to

John Bishop, Jr.

A Brother without Envy

Contents

For the Record

TIME DEVOURS MEN AND EVENTS. ITS MOVEMENT IS steady, inexorable, merciless. It defeated the man who is the central figure of this book, and this is sad because, at the moment he was whisked away, Franklin D. Roosevelt thought he had triumphed over the calendar and the clock. He had been failing in health—dying, to be precise—for at least a year. In this he kept his counsel, refusing to discuss it with either his doctors or his family.

In the spring of 1944, FDR could taste the juices of final victory. All he asked was a little more time. The great, farseeing man had been imprisoned in a wheelchair for many years, but he had won the confidence of the American citizens for three unparalleled terms as President of the United States. He had fought the slow, agonizing battle against the great economic depression and had instilled cheer and hope in his countrymen with "Fireside Chats." He had assumed the burden of the laboring man to chart a better life and had cajoled Congress into passing reform legislation to care for the old, the infirm, the jobless.

His achievements seemed to be as inexhaustible as his energy. And that is where the President, and the people, miscalculated. He had fought a great war, had added America's material strength and muscle, its blood and its treasure, to the Allied cause. In truth, Roosevelt had achieved the impossible—fighting a two-ocean war and winning slowly, steadily on opposite sides of the world. Now, in the spring of what would be his final year, victory was assured. The Soviet legions were sweeping the Germans out of White Russia into Poland. Millions of tons of Allied shipping lay at the bottom of the seas, but German U-boats were no longer the hunters; they were the hunted. Hitler's Berlin was a shambles of masonry and smoke. Italy, as a Fascist power, was dead. Dwight D. Eisenhower was in London, amassing the greatest invasion force of men, ships and guns in the history of man. Japan had lost a decisive battle at Midway, and retreated slowly, stubbornly, before General Mac-Arthur's army and Admiral Nimitz's fleet. The General, at this moment, was planning a triumphant return to the Philippines; the Admiral aimed his task forces and fleet marines at Saipan and Guam to provide air bases within bomber range of Tokyo.

Final victory was a matter of time. As in all wars, as one side grew stronger, the other weakened. The imbalance increased every week. Mr. Roosevelt was so sure of peace to come that, as the book opens, he was charting a world organization called the United Nations, a bicameral group of nations which would debate and vote and, above all, keep the peace. Here, FDR felt that he would succeed where his idol, Woodrow Wilson, had failed in organizing a League of Nations.

The President believed his commanders in the spring of 1944 when they said that Germany would collapse "later this year" and Japan would fight to the death for another year and a half. He knew that it would not be all downhill; there would be problems, momentary defeats, heavy losses, in addition to the strident voices at home which would refer to him and his confreres as "tired, quarrelsome old men." There would be unauthorized strikes, seizures of plants which violated the War Production codes, perhaps even the failure of the first atom bomb, on which Roosevelt had secretly spent $2 billion.

The overriding concern was time. All Roosevelt asked was to live to see the final victory, the establishment of peace, the organizational meeting of his United Nations. Nothing more, nothing less. The watch on his wrist ticked more firmly than the pulse underneath. The dolorous difference between the two was that the watch could be rewound.

It was this, and more, that I had in mind when I began research on *FDR's Last Year*. Most of all, I wanted to draw a highly personal—yes, intimate—portrait of a great leader in his time of trial. It could not be done by reading, wishing, dreaming. Somewhere, somehow, a quarter of a century after Roosevelt's death, I had to find and interview those few who had once worked closely with him, those who defied time and who still remembered. Of these, only one refused permission to use his name.

In most cases, such acknowledgments of editorial assistance are buried. Here, they belong up front. Without the assistance of the Franklin D. Roosevelt people who were still alive a quarter century after his death, there would be no story to tell. Their numbers are few, their memories strong.

This is not to demean any of the books about President Roosevelt. They, too—as you will find in the Bibliography—were researched exhaustively for information embraced by the last year of the President's life.

I learned quickly that, even though Eleanor and Franklin Roosevelt are together in death, there are distinct and acrimonious camps among the living. There are "Eleanor people" and there are "Franklin people," and the contempt each reserves for the other is unremitting. There is no sign of mellowing, or forgiveness, in either camp.

This led to an additional chore: the weighing and assessing of information. Some insisted that the President would have been far less of a statesman without the counsel of his wife; others maintained that her shrill "E. R." notes, many of which were petty in character compared to the tasks which confronted him, so depressed him that he fled to Warm Springs because he knew Mrs. Roosevelt did not appreciate the Georgia hideaway and would leave him alone. A third group points out

that Eleanor was a public figure and statesman in her
own right, that she used the White House as a platform
from which to preach her personal gospel. No one—not
even the irreconcilables of the Franklin crowd—can argue
that Eleanor was not a notable public figure long after
her husband was in his grave. In my view, after almost
three years of living with this book, Mrs. Roosevelt
was a woman of lofty liberal principles and a harpy.
This would not endear me to either side, but then, I
was seeking an approximation of truth, not friendship.

The interviews constituted a race with death. How
many were left? Who would be willing to endure long
interviews and repetitive questions? There were failures.
I was hurrying toward a hospital in Wisconsin when
Leo Crowley died. He had administered Lend-Lease.

Every time I sought James Roosevelt, he was in
Switzerland. Of the four sons, the President reposed
the most confidence in Jimmy. The President's deepest
affection was reserved for his daughter, Anna. One of
the most rewarding interviews occurred in her upper
New York State home, where, in spite of the silent spinning tapes, she spoke candidly on such diverse subjects
as the Yalta Conference and the enduring role played by
Mrs. Lucy Mercer Rutherfurd in her father's life.

She imparted important insights regarding his personal
attitudes toward people and events; she remembered
what her father said, and how he said it. As an example,
Anna alone could tell how the President felt when he
was wheeled into his room after each plenary session
at Yalta, just as Alger Hiss could supplement all that
we have read about the debating sessions of Stalin,
Roosevelt and Churchill vis-à-vis the separate conferences going on among the foreign ministers, Anthony
Eden, Vyacheslav M. Molotov and Edward Stettinius.
It is difficult to believe that none of the governments at
the Yalta Conference kept an official stenographic record of the discussions. James F. Byrnes of South Carolina, who had been a court stenographer, kept personal
recollections of what was said, as did Charles Bohlen,
State Department translator. Fortunately, Mr. Hiss had

the mentality of the lawyer's lawyer, and—as we sat at dinner in the Plaza Hotel in a private room—he was willing to go over everything that transpired and impart the motivations revealed to him by Roosevelt and Stettinius.

Elliott Roosevelt was of considerable help when he was held to the things he witnessed and heard, as opposed to his conjectures. James Rowley was chief of the Secret Service when I interviewed him; he was with the President many times—Hyde Park, Warm Springs, the White House, the Second Quebec Conference, Yalta—in the last year. He and the other men of the White House detail were, for many years, almost as close to the President as his skin. To them, he often confided his innermost thoughts on diverse subjects because he knew, by their calling, that he could "sound off" without fear of being quoted. Two retired Secret Service agents, James Beary and Howard Anderson, were patient when I referred to my notebooks to ask them to recall certain situations and what—if anything—Mr. Roosevelt revealed to them about his actions. In many cases, they were able to fill the small intimate chinks which had been left open by history.

John McCormack, tall, slender wheelhorse of the Democratic party and majority leader in the House, breakfasted every ten days with FDR when the President was in Washington. Mr. McCormack, a retired Speaker of the House when I met him, was a font of information about the politics of the Presidency, and was willing to explain, not merely what FDR did, but why. Lyndon B. Johnson was Roosevelt's "favorite young congressman" in the final year of the President's life. Johnson had stepped down as President and was in the final three months of his life when he answered my questions, pertinent and impertinent. He still regarded Roosevelt as the greatest of all Presidents which, regretfully, took some of the candor out of what he gave me.

The book would be less worthy than it is were it not for the free and open discussions with Dorothy Brady and Grace Tully, FDR's personal secretaries. They knew the day-to-day, and sometimes minute-to-minute, operation of the office of the Chief Executive and were able and willing to paint a closeup portrait of the President even to such minutiae as how he transferred himself from his wheelchair to his high-backed leather chair, including the knowledge that he maintained a tilted shoe shelf under his desk for composing his lifeless legs. Louise Hachmeister was eighty years old when I reached her apartment. She had been Roosevelt's chief telephone operator. She was statuesque, incredibly handsome and, like the others, was prepared to cut in on anything I read from my notes to say, "No, no. It wasn't like that. Here's exactly what happened."

Amid the beautiful fields and horse country outside Aiken, South Carolina, a group of nuns administered a girls' school at Ridgley Hall, once the winter estate of Mr. and Mrs. Winthrop Rutherfurd. The nuns permitted Mrs. Bishop and me to examine the premises where the President often stopped secretly on his way to Warm Springs to see Lucy and her husband. The cork floor of the upstairs bathroom still bears the dimpled marks of Mr. Rutherfurd's cane. This was followed by lunch with Monsignor George Smith at the rectory of St. Mary Help of Christians Church. He was Lucy's pastor and confessor. He was more than that; the then Father Smith joined the horsey set for hunts at dawn and champagne breakfasts. He was a sly conversationalist, fencing with me about the relationship between the President of the United States and the tall, gracious society woman. He had an understandable fear that any author—at his whim—could make a sordid affair of what must stand as one of the tragic loves of history.

Frank Allcorn, one-time mayor of Warm Springs, still bald and ebullient, furnished insights to the President's semiannual retreats to western Georgia. So did Ruth Stevens, one-time manager of the Warm Springs Hotel, who prepared a Brunswick stew for the President on the day he died. In an addendum of gratitude, how could one forget Benjamin V. Cohen, the only man who begged Franklin D. Roosevelt not to run for a fourth term and who put it in writing? He sat in a booklined Massachusetts Avenue apartment tossing a rubber bone to a small terrier and recalled a great deal of Rooseveltiana. A similar interview with Thomas G. Corcoran, another member of the FDR team, did not go so well. He paced his office, insisting that it would not be proper to relate anything about the secret night automobile rides Mr. Roosevelt enjoyed with Lucy. At times he seemed more concerned with what should not be in the book than those things which should.

In Atlanta I found Brannon Lesesne of Patterson and Sons, who embalmed the President; he related the professional difficulty of treating arteries so hardened that the task required five hours. Mr. Lesesne was present when Mr. Roosevelt arrived at the Little White House with Admiral McIntire and Steve Early and had a good memory for what was said and done. In matters of settings and dialogue, my main interest centered on what the principal figures omitted from their later writings.

The luckiest thing which happened in researching this book was finding William G. Rigdon, a slightly built, modest man afflicted with declining sight. When we sat to dinner on the roof of the Washington Hotel, he told me he was a Navy lieutenant when Franklin Roosevelt appropriated him as a traveling secretary. Rigdon was a topflight stenographer. When, in the last year of the President's life, he traveled by cruiser to Hawaii and Alaska to make peace between General MacArthur and Admiral Nimitz, when the *Quincy* shoved off for Yalta, Rigdon was the man who was in daily contact with "the Boss." Rigdon was also the official historian—under the orders of Admiral Wilson Brown—of the hourly events of these voyages of high purpose. He was also the keeper of the Top Secret messages between Roosevelt and Stalin and Roosevelt and Churchill. In addition, and rather in spite of his shyness, he carried an insatiable curiosity about everything from the course and speed of the cruiser to the keeping of notes on private conversations at Yalta. Lieutenant Rigdon turned out to be a gold mine. He had boxes and dusty packages

of material about Roosevelt, and he said, "Take it all—
Xerox it or do anything you want to do—I'm not going
to write another book." My indebtedness to him, as well
as to the others, is beyond computing.

JIM BISHOP

Hallandale, Florida

FDR'S
LAST
YEAR

March 1944

THE BUZZER SOUNDED THREE TIMES. A SILENT TENSION pervaded the White House. The Boss was on his way to the Executive Wing. Major General Edwin Watson fisted a sheaf of notes and left his office. Miss Grace Tully, the dark colleen, stopped typing. Steve Early, the press secretary who often censored the President's statements with "Don't print that," walked head down to the Oval Office. Four Secret Service men took the White House stairway to reach ground level before the elevator arrived. Vice Admiral Ross McIntire, the President's physician, left his clinic against the far wall to watch the Boss go by. He would have about eight seconds in which to note the complexion, the amount of cyanosis in lips and fingernails, the mood of the man, brightness or dimness of eye.

The elevator door opened and a lightly built steel chair with wooden seat emerged. Behind it Arthur Prettyman, black valet, chief petty officer USN Retired, lifted the wheels onto the stone floor. The President was smoking. Between his strong teeth, a Bakelite holder tilted. He nodded and smiled and grasped the rims of the wheels in muscular hands. He ran the chair at speed through the lower corridor, the Secret Service men trotting ahead and behind, across the areaway past the flower conservatory and the swimming pool, making a sharp turn left toward big French doors, thence up a wooden ramp into Miss Tully's office. He nodded, made a pleasant remark about Dorothy Brady's dress and rolled on into the big august sanctum with its off-white walls, its paintings and miniatures of barkentines and frigates, to a position behind the rosewood desk.

Without assistance, Franklin Delano Roosevelt

reached for the big leather chair, pulled it diagonally toward his wheelchair and, with powerful arms supplanting useless legs, lifted himself into the chair and pulled it to the desk. Carefully, he tugged at the sharp crease in the trousers of an old gray suit and lifted one leg onto the tilted shoe rack under the desk. He lifted the other leg by the crease and placed it over the first one. Then, and then only, the most powerful man in the world looked up through rimless pince-nez at the faces of his official family. He glanced at the appointment calendar and frowned.

There was but one item on it: "Bethesda Hospital 11:00." No guests this morning, no distinguished visitors to talk of the worldwide war; no Cabinet ministers with problems of war and peace. Admiral McIntire called it "your annual checkup." The little calendar read "Monday March 27, 1944." Mr. Roosevelt nodded to Miss Tully. "Grace," he said, "To H. S. Okay. FDR." She returned to her office to write it. She and Dorothy Brady were accustomed to cryptic messages. This one was to Henry Stimson, Secretary of War. He had asked for 400 more landing craft from the Wilmington, Delaware, yards. Only he and the secretive President understood the message. "Put it in *your* files," FDR said. For eleven years he had divided the dictation and filing of messages and documents among Grace Tully, Dorothy Brady, Marguerite ("Missy") LeHand and, when traveling, Lieutenant William G. Rigdon, USN.

The files were divided among his secretaries so that none of them knew everything that he was doing, and each one knew less than half of FDR's correspondence. The President glanced up at Michael Reilly, chief of the White House detail of the Secret Service, a burly man who could, and sometimes did, lift the President fireman fashion to carry him to a chair or an automobile. "Ten-thirty," the President said, nodding. "We go to Bethesda." The things which Mike did not know he sensed with Irish deliberation. In spite of the friendly smile, he knew the Boss did not relish this physical examination. Mr. Roosevelt had neglected his body in exchange for a firm chair in the seat of power. He had been in gradually declining health and strength for years, but the Teheran Conference of four months ago precipitated an alarming loss of weight, appetite and strength. A lassitude had overcome the President and, while this was not alarming in a man sixty-two years of age who had spent twenty-three of them in a wheelchair, the oyster circles under the eyes were deepening, the mouth often hung open unconsciously, and thought processes were sometimes left unfinished, with sentences dangling. And yet, even Mr. Reilly knew that the Boss had a faculty for regathering his resources at crucial times so that, for a moment or an hour, he became his old optimistic self, a man in total command of what he was doing.

If anyone could assess Mr. Roosevelt's health, it would have to be Admiral McIntire. As a physician he had specialized in nose and throat. Years earlier, Roosevelt had been on a Navy cruiser and had had several chats with young Commander McIntire. When Roosevelt assumed the Presidency, he remembered those cordial conversations and summoned McIntire to White House duty. Within four years the commander had been promoted to the position of Vice Admiral and Surgeon General of the U.S. Navy. He had attended his august patient well, with the assistance of Dr. J. A. Tyree, Jr., and Lieutenant Commander George Fox, pharmacist and masseur.

The Admiral, in his way, was as secretive as the President. At Hyde Park in March Mrs. Roosevelt was so alarmed at the President's personal appearance that she demanded to know what could be wrong. She was told "an influenza bug." The President's daughter, Anna (Mrs. John Boettiger), had come to Washington from Seattle to visit her parents. She was the one person in the family he cherished above all others, and she begged McIntire to send her father somewhere for a thorough physical examination. She also asked the Admiral not to tell the President that she had suggested it. McIntire, who had the power to order the checkup done anywhere, selected the Naval Hospital at Bethesda and phoned a cardiologist, Lieutenant Commander Howard Bruenn, USNR, to prepare to examine Roosevelt. Young Bruenn was ordered to do a complete heart and chest cavity examination and to report his findings directly to the Admiral without explaining anything to the patient. No notice was given to Bruenn. The phone call came on the morning of the examination, and the cardiologist spent the hours between 9:00 A.M. and 11:00 A.M. clearing the area of naval patients and making the suite of rooms presentable.

As the President departed for the cavalcade of Secret Service cars on the South Lawn, McIntire asked perfunctorily how the Boss felt. This time the response was different. "I feel like hell!" Roosevelt said. The Admiral had phoned Captain John Harper, commanding officer at Bethesda, to make certain that the examination and findings would be kept private.

Anna sat beside the President. They were far out on Wisconsin Avenue when he pointed through trees to the tall, elegant buildings of the hospital. "I designed that one," he told his daughter. He hadn't, really. Mr. Roosevelt fancied himself somewhat of an architect, and he conferred with architects and submitted precise little drawings of certain public buildings. His enthusiasm matched his lack of ability. At Hyde Park he had supervised the design of a hilltop cottage to which he proposed to retire "someday." It had two bedrooms, a huge fieldstone fireplace, one bath, and no closets.

"I'll wait in the car," Anna said. Arthur Prettyman wheeled the President through the rotunda. The word had spread. Doctors, naval patients, nurses were lined on both sides of the corridor. The President smiled and waved, and they broke into applause. Inside the medical suite, Dr. Bruenn perspired. He felt an aversion to having the fate of a President, or perhaps a nation, rest in his immaculate hands. He had taken the warning phone calls from Admiral McIntire and from Captain Harper. These had led Bruenn to increased nervousness and a call back to McIntire requesting the results of previous heart and chest examinations. The Admiral wasn't certain he could find them. He would look carefully and, if he found them, would send them at once by White House messenger. He wanted such records returned after the examination, and he wanted all findings and EKGs and X rays, in addition to a fully documented, written report from Bruenn, returned at once. Softly Bruenn pointed out that, without the results of earlier examinations, he would have no point of comparison to show whether Mr. Roosevelt was doing better, worse or holding his own.

The presidential party came into Bruenn's warren. Roosevelt and Bruenn glanced at each other and smiled. The old man and the young man liked each other at once. Two male nurses and Prettyman wheeled the President into a small room. They helped undress the patient. He was given a loose gown and was lifted onto an examining table. The records were not yet in Bruenn's hands. Quickly, unostentatiously, the young doctor studied his man. There was a blue grape cast to lips and fingernails, quick, shallow respiration supine, a grayish pallor on the face and a noticeable agitation of the hands.

Mr. Roosevelt decided to talk cheerfully. As Bruenn worked, the patient chatted about small matters which held no relation to the business at hand. Nor did the President volunteer any information, such as his chronic difficulty breathing in bed; the addition of two four-by-fours at the head of his bed at Hyde Park to elevate it; the order to Grace Tully a year before to buy the Boss a coffee mug twice as big as the old one, so that he could hold it to his lips without spilling it.

The medical records arrived, and Bruenn excused himself and covered his patient so that he could glance at them. Quickly he noted a steady rise in blood pressure from 1941 onward; the electrocardiograms displayed an inversion of T waves. He returned to the examination and noted that Roosevelt was now wisecracking his way through the morning. This would indicate he had little interest in the work in progress, or he was so apprehensive that he was trying to shut it out.

Bruenn made little notations of each of his findings. Oral temperature was slightly elevated. The torso was well muscled and well nourished. The buttocks and leg muscles were flaccid to the touch and in an advanced stage of atrophy. He asked Roosevelt to breathe into a machine which registers metabolic efficiency. It was plus 15, the upper limit of normal. He asked the President to take a deep breath and hold it as long as possible. The patient expelled it after 35 seconds, which Bruenn felt was not good capacity.

The doctor asked his age. "Sixty-two and—yes, two months." Blood circulation time was recorded at 22½ seconds; it should have been 17 seconds. The interpretation was that the arteries were having difficulty pumping blood through the body. Wrist pulse was 72, and soft to the touch. Respiration was 24 to the minute. The doctor noted the cough and marked it as a finding; it was soft and persistent. From the McIntire history Bruenn made additional notes:

Severe attack poliomyelitis 1921, with severe and permanent impairment of the muscles of both lower extremities to the hips. May 1941 severe iron deficiency anemia with hemoglobin of 4.5 g/100 ml. Anemia responded to ferrous sulfate therapy. No cardiac symptoms 1941.

Additional findings, translated into layman's language, were: spasms of coughing and hypertension dating to 1937. Blood pouring through the atrium to the left ventricle of the heart was meeting with resistance. Recent influenza placed a further strain on the heart. Although no tests were available to Bruenn to ascertain generalized hardening of the arteries, the doctors felt that plaques were present in a generalized degeneration of the vascular system. The doctor noticed that any physical effort, including asking the patient to turn over, induced a marked breathlessness.

The President was carried to a Gatch bed, one which

elevates the head. The doctor noticed that the embarrassment of breathing appeared to be relieved. Examination of both eyes displayed arteriovenous nicking, that is, a lack of blood where arteries met and crossed each other. This condition is frequently followed by flame hemorrhages in both eyes. The doctor heard rales, indicating fluid in both lungs. His patient also had congestive heart failure. Under any circumstances this is a dangerous and almost irreversible condition. The lung fluid irritated the cardiovascular situation. Supine, the fluid spread the length of the posterior of both lungs. Roosevelt was breathing with half his lung power. When the bed was raised, the fluid settled in the bottom of both lungs, leaving a greater area for breathing.

The heart itself was enlarged. Listening, Bruenn found no "palpable thrills," an absence of turbulence within the organ. The left ventricle displayed more enlargement as the muscle tried to accommodate extra work in pumping. Bruenn heard a "blowing sound" which indicated that the mitral valve was not closing properly. In addition, there was a definite "blowing systolic murmur," the result of too much pressure on the aortic valve which blew open with each beat and slammed shut with violence. Normal blood pressure might be about 150/90. The President's was 186/108.

The liver was normal in size. The electrocardiogram confirmed what Bruenn's ears told him: Roosevelt had a low amplitude of T waves in areas I and V-4. Fluoroscopy proved difficult; the patient, trying to stand erect behind the fluoroscope, had to be held in place by men at both arms. This examination, in addition to chest X rays, confirmed the diagnosis of hypertension, hypertensive heart disease, failure of the left ventricle of the heart and acute bronchitis.

Dr. Bruenn waited until the President had been dressed, then extended his hand. "Thanks, Doc," Roosevelt said. He did not ask a question about the examination. Bruenn was content, because his orders were to tell the President nothing. As the wheelchair left, the doctor tried to recall some of the President's lively chatter. He could not remember a word of it. Bruenn felt that he had been exposed to a grave situation which no one knew. There was no question in the young cardiologist's mind but that he had to present a dismal report to Admiral McIntire as quickly as the notes could be collated.

He spent the afternoon and evening writing up medical tests and results, writing cool professional opinions. In the morning McIntire phoned and ordered Bruenn to the White House with his findings. Within the hour the young physician and the Admiral were in the clinic on the ground floor of the White House. The report, both written and oral, depicted a very old man with few life-sustaining forces left. He could expire at any time. And yet, with proper care—and granting that Mr. Roosevelt's mental functions were not badly impaired—he might live on for months, maybe a year or two. The prognosis would constitute a medical guessing game, but it wasn't optimistic.

At the interview McIntire did not appear to be shocked. He asked Bruenn if he would like to serve under McIntire as the President's physician-in-attendance. The implication was clear: Bruenn would be under the authority of McIntire at all times, working for McIntire, and would not be permitted to discuss Roosevelt's physical condition with the patient or the First Family. Bruenn said that he would obey orders. McIntire, with a single phone call to Captain Harper at Bethesda, had Bruenn put on detached service to the White House.

"What do you propose that we do with the patient?" the Admiral asked. The cardiologist produced a small sheet of paper. "It's written out here," he said.

The patient should be put to bed for 1 to 2 weeks with nursing care. Digitalization should be carried out: 0.4 g. of digitalis every day for five days; subsequently, 0.1 every day. A light, easily digestible diet. Portions should be small, and salt intake is to be restricted. Potassium chloride in a salt shaker could be used as desired for seasoning. Codeine, ½ grain, should be given for control of cough.

Sedation should be taken to ensure rest and a refreshing night's sleep. A program of gradual weight reduction.

It constituted a mild, cautious program, but McIntire said that the President would not submit to it. He proposed not to antagonize the patient. Better to insist on more bed rest and give Mr. Roosevelt a cough syrup containing ammonium carbonate and codeine. It amounted to a surrender to FDR's whims, in addition to McIntire's desire to go no further than to treat a cold. Although the medical report indicated a weakened heart and hardening of the arteries, the Admiral proposed to treat his patient as though there was no danger of sudden death. Whatever game of blind man's buff Roosevelt was playing with his health, the Admiral was going to play it with him.

The game was dangerously ambivalent. McIntire understood the gravity of the report and proposed to call a conference of leading doctors at the White House. Eleanor Roosevelt wrote a note:

*FDR is not well but more will be known by Monday & I think we can help keep him in good health; but he'll have to be more careful. I think the constant tension must tell & tho he has said nothing, I think he had been upset by Elliott and Ruth.**

Daughter Anna had requested McIntire to come to her rooms on the third floor of the White House before the examination. The Admiral was too stiff a martinet to submit to such orders under other circumstances, but everyone in the official family knew that the President reposed unlimited confidence in his daughter. Anna said that she was worried about her father's health, and she would like his personal physician to explain it to her. The Admiral was flushed; he did not feel responsible to anyone. Nothing to worry about, he said. Anna had

---

* Second son Elliott married Elizabeth Donner in 1931, was divorced in 1933. In the same year he married Ruth Googins and was divorced from her to marry motion picture star Faye Emerson in 1944.

been conscious of her father's soft cough for three months; she had also seen his tan complexion change to gray; the sailor's eyes had retreated in darkness. At motion pictures, she had noticed, for the first time, that her father's mouth hung open for long periods.

The Admiral said that the President had contracted influenza accompanied by a slight fever, the cough she had noticed, malaise and a thick yellowish sputum. But FDR had recovered, McIntire said. It was true that he had not recovered his former strength and there was evidence of deep fatigue, due to "night sweats and abdominal flatulence." But these were not matters to occasion worry. Everybody knew that her father had plenty of "bounce." A week or two in warm sunshine and he would be his old self again. "Why don't you do something about it?" Mrs. Boettiger asked. McIntire compressed his lips. "Do you take his blood pressure?" "When I think it necessary," he said. The young woman could not breach the medical wall. Her mother had told her that Father, in a burst of bitterness, shouted, "I cannot live out a normal life span. I can't even walk across the room to get my circulation going."

The President's family and secretaries were worried about the appearance and weakness. But their worry was not as panicky as the fear which McIntire concealed. He called a secret medical conference for the morning of March 29, 1944, and invited Harper of Bethesda; Dr. James A. Paullin of Atlanta; Dr. Frank Lahey of the Lahey Clinic in Boston; Captain Robert Duncan, executive officer of Bethesda; Captain Charles Behrens, chief of radiology at Bethesda; Dr. Paul Dickens, internist; and Bruenn. It was a formidable consultation for a "deep cold." The President was not told of the conference, before or after. McIntire candidly demanded top secrecy from all who attended. Howard Bruenn was asked to present the findings of his examination and to explain his recommendations. The deeper Bruenn got into the subject, the more faces around him seemed to harden. At the conclusion, he was saying:

Limitation of daily activities must be emphasized. Cigarette use must be curtailed. Trial of aminophylline, grains iii I tablet, enteric coated, three times a day after meals. Avoid, if possible, irritation and tensions of office. Phenobarbital grain ¼ or theodate three times a day. Period of rest for one hour after meals. Light passive massage. Dinner in quarters at the White House. A minimum of ten hours sleep. No swimming in the pool. Diet: 2,600 calories moderately low in fat. The use of mild laxatives, if necessary, to avoid straining.

Bruenn dropped the paper from which he was reading and looked around. His seniors disagreed with him at once and pooh-poohed the gravity of his diagnosis.

Everyone had an opportunity to speak. Dr. Paullin was concerned with the gaseous condition of the President's bowels; Harper and McIntire were in concert about the lack of cooperation to be expected from the patient. Someone induced smiles and chuckles when it was suggested that Bruenn had never seen FDR when he got his "Dutch up." It was noted that McIntire had been examining the President for years and had not noted any alarming pathology; it seemed hardly possible that FDR could have become gravely ill overnight. It occurred to no one to speculate why the Admiral had suddenly sent his patient to be examined by a heart specialist. Bruenn waited for a moment of silence. Softly he said that if his suggestions were not to be followed he would prefer to withdraw from the case.

Paullin and Lahey asked the young man to withhold judgment. Both planned to see the President after lunch and, if FDR agreed, would examine him. Surely Bruenn could wait until morning to hear their findings. At that moment, the only point the young man won was the installation of the Gatch bed with a raised head. Mr. Roosevelt told McIntire in the morning that he had enjoyed a "grand night's sleep." On Thursday, the thirtieth, the medical consultants met at Bethesda in secrecy. Dr. Lahey opened the discussion saying that, after "yesterday's examination," he was interested in the President's problems of digestion and elimination. After a silence he nodded toward Dr. Bruenn and said that the doctor's findings, in his opinion, were sufficiently grave to advise Mr. Roosevelt of the true state of affairs. Giving it to him bluntly, Lahey was sure, would bring co-operation from FDR.

Dr. Paullin, who wore his dignity heavily and obviously, conceded that, since examining Mr. Roosevelt he now found himself in agreement with Dr. Bruenn's findings. However, he did not believe that the President's state of health was "precarious enough to confide it to him." He went a step further. Signs of congestive heart failure, in his estimation, were so early that he did not think that digitalis was indicated. In fact, he would advocate no therapy. One after the other, they spoke of caution. In sum, they pitted their seniority against Bruenn to state that FDR's health was not as bad as he had painted it; certainly not a matter to be revealed to the President or his family.

Bruenn spoke softly. He said he must disagree. Because the President was a cripple, he said, it would be impossible to measure his myocardial reserve. The patient had given him a history of orthopnea (shortness of breath lying down) and, while erect in his wheelchair, displayed additional signs of embarrassed breathing. Bruenn reminded the eminent doctors that they had seen the X rays. There was definite enlargement of the heart shadow, and all had seen it. Further, he said, when he put the patient through a few functional tests, congestive heart failure was clearly evident and no opinion could change it. If he sensed a conspiracy of medical silence, Bruenn never mentioned it. As he moved along, Bruenn became bolder. He said he would not retreat from his position that digitalis must be prescribed to regulate the heart and to remove strain from the tortuous aorta.

The consultants had an option. They could deny Bruenn his moment of victory and send him back to Bethesda swearing him to secrecy. However, if the "patient" (their repetitive word for the President) died, Bruenn's fatal diagnosis and prognosis could create a public scandal. McIntire had opened this cardiological Pandora's box, and no amount of flattery could coax the ethical young genie back in. Paullin dwelt upon his clasped hands and was the first to capitulate. He said the digitalis could be administered to Roosevelt without the knowledge of the patient.

Dr. Bruenn said that, in addition to the digitalis, ammonium chloride could be administered followed by an injection of mersalyl, this to accelerate the accommodation of heart and lungs to their tasks. The older doctors said no, that too much medication would arouse the patient's suspicions. Digitalis and the Gatch bed should be enough for the present to make Roosevelt feel better, and they agreed that he should be requested to rest on an office couch for an hour after lunch. Bruenn had won half of what he had asked and lost half. The consultants agreed to meet in two weeks to get a progress report from Dr. Bruenn. All agreed not to discuss the case—not even with their families. In any case, as the Admiral pointed out, they were now within the ethics of doctor-patient relationship and could not mention the case, except to each other.

The parallel of helplessness between Woodrow Wilson and Franklin D. Roosevelt was obvious to Admiral McIntire. Wilson had sustained a cerebral hemorrhage which rendered him feeble and comatose. He too had an Admiral who protected him from public disclosure: Admiral Cary Grayson. Franklin D. Roosevelt had not sustained a cerebral hemorrhage, but he was a poor risk for a heart attack or stroke which would kill him outright or render him helpless without hope of rehabilitation. McIntire was the new Cary Grayson, hiding the dismal state of the President's health from the country while surrendering grudgingly to Dr. Bruenn's dark diagnosis.

The medical consensus was to proceed cautiously, medicating Mr. Roosevelt minimally, while assuring him and his family and the nation that he was suffering from a cold and required additional rest. In this, McIntire had protected his flanks by calling the secret medical consultation. If FDR expired suddenly, the Admiral could cite the mild, almost timorous, opinions of the distinguished doctors.

Bruenn became the President's personal physician because the ailment fell within his purview as a cardiologist. FDR was a docile patient. He popped the digitalis pills into his mouth, followed by a few swallows of water, without asking what they were. Whereas McIntire took the Boss's blood pressure only when he thought it necessary, Commander Bruenn was the epitome of medical conscience; he was in the presidential bedroom every morning to examine his man, to ask questions about sleep and appetite and to feel amazement that FDR never asked why he required the services of a heart specialist. In retrospect, Bruenn did not recall that Mr. Roosevelt ever asked a medical question.

Nor did the Boss protest when his desk calendar showed a decisive cut in appointments. Friday, March 31, is typical:

12:50 Commdr. Crydon M. Wassell & Mr. Cecil B. De-Mille and Mr. Steve Early   1:10
1:15 Lunch (study) Miss Grace Tully   2:00
5:50 To Drs office   6:45
7:30 Dinner—bed tray; Major Boettiger at bedside
10:50 Retired

There was a one-hour nap on a couch after lunch. He also spent fifty-five minutes in McIntire's clinic with Bruenn in attendance. When the President left to go to bed for dinner, Bruenn told McIntire that the patient's night breathing had improved and he found no evidence of venous engorgement. Rales could be heard at the base of both lungs, more in the right then in the left. The heart was still grossly enlarged to the left side of the chest. The digitalis had regulated the heart beat to 74 per minute. The apex still had a first poor sound in quality, to be followed by a systolic blow. Bruenn said he could not hear any diastolic murmurs. Due to Mr. Roosevelt's inability to stand—he had given up the use of braces about a year earlier—there was no means of weighing him. The Admiral said that in recent months Mr. Roosevelt had been weighed and his weight was down from 185 to 170 pounds.

Time magazine, as conscious of Roosevelt's health as other publications, published a small article:

Out at the Naval Hospital in Bethesda, Md., they X-rayed Franklin Roosevelt's chest. It was a mild case of bronchitis, going into its third week. To reporters, the President pooh-poohed his illness, continued to smoke from his long cigarette holder, continued to cough softly but persistently.

In the West Wing the press fretted about the President's health. Their editors gave them "hot tips" that FDR was dying and asked for health stories. They had tried, led by the short, mustached Merriman Smith of United Press, but FDR joked about his well-being. He spoke casually of "flaring sinuses" (which they had heard before) and a deep unsettling cold in the chest. Still, in the spring of 1944, the reporters who admired Roosevelt were personally worried. At press conferences they noted that his voice was weak; he was asked to repeat things he said. They too had to repeat questions because, for the first time, Roosevelt was cupping his hand behind his ear to understand questions.

Among themselves, they felt that he was weak and sick, but they had no authoritative medical opinion from McIntire. They also knew that, within four months, there would be the Democratic National Convention, and there was a good chance that Roosevelt, having won an unprecedented third term, might try for a fourth. The fillip arrived when editors pointed out that FDR had presided at more than 900 press conferences, but had stopped them abruptly three weeks ago. White House reporters began to chafe under the news tips. One had a report from his editor that Roosevelt had been smuggled out of the White House to undergo a serious operation. Merriman Smith told the press secretariat that he had two tips. One was that the President was not in the White House, he was in a Boston hospital; the other, that FDR was at the Mayo Clinic in Rochester, Minnesota. Smith said he had the names of the doctors and nurses involved. Steve Early invited Smith to phone the Mayo Clinic. There were no doctors or nurses using the names he had.

April 1944

BY THE FIRST OF APRIL PRESIDENT ROOSEVELT BEGAN TO feel better. To silence the ugly rumors regarding his health, he attended an informal dinner given by the White House correspondents. He sat in a tuxedo and black tie, smiling, smoking, nodding, exchanging quips. One thing that brought a deep guffaw from his chest was when Bob Hope took the stage as master of ceremonies, clasped his hands before him, and said, "I've always voted for Roosevelt as President. My father always voted for Roosevelt as President."

Before the extreme seriousness of his illness had been discovered, Roosevelt planned a visit to Guantanamo Bay, the U.S. naval base in Cuba. After conferring with Admiral McIntire, he canceled the visit. Dr. McIntire's reason was that the President did not enjoy flying and that high altitudes were not good for his condition. Abruptly, almost as though he had anticipated the cancellation, Mr. Roosevelt said he would go to Hobcaw Barony, a 23,000-acre estate in South Carolina owned by his friend Bernard Baruch. The old financier had invited Mr. Roosevelt several times. Three Secret Service agents, including James Beary, had been waiting at Morrison Field, Palm Beach, Florida, for ten days. The original plan had been for the President to ride his special train (code name POTUS for the President of the United States) to Palm Beach, and board a four-engine military plane at Palm Beach for the 800-mile (4-hour) run to "Gitmo." When the change in plans was flashed to

Beary, he took his men to Georgetown, South Carolina, a short distance north of Charleston, at the confluence of the Black River and the Intercoastal Waterway. The Secret Service, as always, "sanitized" the premises which, in this case, were large. They examined house, servants, grounds, river traffic—even the stables and forest reaches of the Baruch estate. For a month, these men would spend their off-duty hours living in an airless Pullman car on a siding.

They built wooden ramps for front and back staircases, built a railing on the fishing dock so that the President could not fall into the water, fashioned a canvas chute from the bedroom the President would occupy so that, in case of fire, he could be quickly shoved inside to slide down to heavy rubber cushions on the ground. Dewey Long, White House communications officer, made a special trip to Hobcaw Barony to set up three types of communication: One was a direct wire from the President's bedroom to the White House switchboard in Washington, one was a radio phone set up in a communications railroad car, and the third was two encoded wireless sets in the railroad car manned by Signal Corps specialists from the Army.

While the advance men were at work in South Carolina, the President was proclaiming to the ladies and gentlemen of his official circle that he felt well and slept well. He complained of lack of appetite and sinus headaches, but these were minor matters. Ross McIntire was writing notes in his medical diary which minimized the dangerous and deadly illness of Mr. Roosevelt: "A moderate degree of arteriosclerosis, although no more than normal in a man of his age; some changes in the cardiographic tracing; clouding in the sinuses; and bronchial irritation." The Admiral advised the President to quit smoking. At the same time Bruenn kept his personal findings up to date and, besides arteriosclerosis, they noted: "hypertension; hypertensive heart disease; cardiac failure (left ventricular) and acute bronchitis"—all of which, he wrote, "had been completely unsuspected up to this time." If Mrs. Roosevelt and Anna were told anything, it was that Admiral McIntire advised the President that "he could quite easily go on with the activities of the presidency."

Encouraged, Mr. Roosevelt returned to his chores cheerfully. He began to awaken refreshed at 8:00 A.M. and ordered bacon, eggs, toast, coffee and a muffin for his Scottie, Fala. Normally FDR was critical of White House food. The President desired to fire the White House cook, a Mrs. Henrietta Nesbitt. He could, and did, work himself up to a pitch of anger whenever White House culinary art was discussed, but he could not fire Mrs. Nesbitt because Mrs. Roosevelt forbade it. The First Lady thought that Mrs. Nesbitt was the proper person for the position. The President said he could not eat the things she cooked. Mrs. Nesbitt conceded, haughtily, that she could not make his two favorite dinner dishes, Brunswick stew and kedgeree.

When he finished breakfast, the President propped pillows behind him and held court. In Mr. Roosevelt's early days in the New York State Senate, he had learned an East Side New York device for identifying people. He would use it all his life. Harry Hopkins was Harry the Hop; Grace Tully was the Countess Abbey; Harold Ickes was Harold the Ick; Dorothy Brady became the Silly Goose; Steve Early was the Early; the late Louis McHenry Howe was Louey the How; McIntire was the Doc; Fala was Pup; his wife was Dearest Babs; Laura Delano, his confidante, was Aunt Polly; his mother, now deceased, was M'maaa—the cognomens were endless and were forms of affection.

At 10:30 A.M. he was bathed, shaved and dressed, and the bells would ring three times as he moved his wheelchair to the upstairs office or the big one downstairs. Often, when he worked upstairs next to his bedroom, he reclined on a couch and dictated to a secretary sitting at the foot of it. He had a battery of telephones on an end table to his right, also a package of Camel cigarettes and an assortment of holders. Steve Early would confer briefly with General Watson and William Hassett about the appointment calendar. Sometimes, when FDR felt fatigued early, Dorothy Brady would stand behind the President and massage the lateral muscles of his neck as she had been taught to do by pharmacist-masseur George Fox.

Rarely, Mr. Roosevelt would become affronted at a small matter. Once an usher opened the door to his office to announce, "The stenographer is here, Mr. President." "Never, never announce my stenographer. Say Miss Tully is here, or Miss Brady is here, or whoever." Usually, when someone on his staff committed a blunder or exposed him to an embarrassing situation, Mr. Roosevelt's reaction was to shake his head dolefully and try to pick up the pieces of the situation and glue them together.

When the day's work was done and he left the big main floor office, the soft bells rang thrice, and he hurried to the elevator, pausing a moment for the inevitable nose drops, and wheeling swiftly to the upstairs sitting room which was really an extension of the second floor corridor. He had a small special joy. His delight was to ask Arthur Prettyman for the cocktail table, the shaker, the ingredients for drinks and ice. The members of the White House staff who watched this little task could see the glee with which the President mixed and shook—"with the precision of a chemist"—and, sitting in his wheelchair, would shake and shake until an assortment of cold-stemmed glasses was produced.

He seldom drank more than two martinis, and sometimes varied the routine by mixing Scotch old-fashioneds, but he refused to surrender the work. From where he sat, near the big soft sofa against the crescent moon window, the President could look all the way down the broad dim corridor, with the pale lighting over the ancient frowning faces of other Presidents, down past the Lincoln Room to the window at the East Wing. "See who's home and ask them to stop in," he would tell an usher. And now, in these long and sometimes sick days of 1944, he would be told softly, "Sorry, Mr. President, there is no one home." His wife was making speeches and acting as his eyes and ears in faraway cities; his daughter was in Seattle or at Hyde Park; his four sons had been flung to the military winds; Missy LeHand was ill at the Lahey Clinic; Louis Howe was long since dead; James A. Farley had broken with his old friend; Alfred E. Smith was sick in New York; his trusted friend and former press secretary, Marvin McIntyre, was dead; Pa Watson drove home to his wife in Virginia; Harry the Hop was facing an ulcer operation; Grace Tully would have one drink and stay for dinner too if requested; Dorothy Brady had a husband and a home in Alexandria; Jimmy Byrnes was too grim for a casual cocktail and laughter; so was Secretary of State Cordell Hull.

The President would meditate on the long corridor for a moment and then he would set the unopened shaker on the end table. "Oh, never mind," he would say. "Ask Arthur to help me into bed and I'll order dinner and do some reading." The President's most pronounced characteristic was a negative one: he rarely admitted to feeling emotional or physical pain. Perhaps at some time when he was a boy—or maybe several times—he skinned a knee or cut his hand and was told that little gentlemen do not cry. Whatever the genesis, he was averse to admitting hurt. He enjoyed the company of attractive women and intelligent men and, from his early days as Assistant Secretary of the Navy in World War I, he was a thoroughgoing socializer. His heart's desire was to have cheerful people around him from the morning awakening until the final good night. And yet the White House calendar, embracing the early days of spring when he was very ill—in effect, a dying President—display a retributive vengeance on the part of his wife, who dined with friends and allowed the President to eat alone from a tray in his bed:

Sunday April 2, 1944 The President 7:15 dinner— bedtray 10:10 retired. Mrs. Roosevelt 7:30 dinner—Major Boettiger and Mr. W. L. White 11:15.

Wednesday April 5, 1944 The President dinner—bed- tray 11:15 retired. Mrs. Roosevelt 7:30 dinner—W. Hall,

Major Boettiger and Lts. Jos. D. Costello, Robert B. Schusser and Stephen Juroskie 11:00

Thursday April 6, 1944 The President 7:15 dinner —bedtray retired 10:45. Mrs. Roosevelt 7:30 dinner— Major Boettiger & Mr. F. K. O'Brien 9:30.

Perhaps the President was too sick to dine in company. The facts do not lean in that direction. He kept political and personal appointments by day, and his ingrained loneliness showed sharply in the calendar listings of "Lunch—tray—with Miss Grace Tully." It was Mrs. Roosevelt's choice to grant her husband fifteen minutes of her day, in the morning when he was breakfasting in bed. Aside from drawing a chair closer to the bedside and saying good morning and asking how he felt, the First Lady spent the remainder of the short time consulting sheets of paper and letters from citizens asking questions regarding length of service, insurance benefits, and begging leniency after courts-martial. Eleanor Roosevelt was diligent in reading these unsolicited letters, asking her secretary, Miss Malvina Thompson, to reduce them to simple questions, and then requesting the President of the United States to resolve them so that "Tommy" (Miss Thompson) could respond. Relations between Mr. and Mrs. Roosevelt from 1918 onward were cordial and, although there are photographs of them kissing at railroad terminals, the endearments were part of the front, or image, they had elected to present to the world. They never slept together, seldom dined together, but appeared to sustain mutual respect for each other. The President's goal was to leave the world in a better state than he found it; Mrs. Roosevelt had a parallel aspiration. He worked the boulevards of the broader aspects of statecraft and diplomacy; Mrs. Roosevelt was in the dingy alleys looking for the poor to feed. It was this respect that each felt for the other and the mutuality of high ideals which kept them together, not, as some have stated, his ambitions. They worked better together than apart. Whatever they amounted to as co-workers, partners, it is a surety that Franklin and Eleanor would each have been less than half of the total if they had broken the marriage in court.

The President awakened on the morning of April 5 feeling well. Prettyman propped up the pillows, Mr. Roosevelt adorned himself with pince-nez and began to read an assortment of newspapers. He had his customary breakfast ordered by the valet. It varied from fried ham and eggs to bacon and eggs, toast and coffee. Members of the secretariat claimed that the President ordered only such food as Fala enjoyed.

Someone soft of voice said, "Good morning, Mr. President." He looked over the top of *The New York Times* and saw the smiling features of Dr. Howard Bruenn. The Chief Executive cheerfully put the paper aside. He did not say that he had been reading a glowing story about his health. He did feel better, more interested in living and doing, than before the young cardiologist began to take care of him. Bruenn asked a few questions. The President said that he had slept well. The blood pressure cuff was on, the pajama sleeve rolled high. FDR thought his cough was gone. Blood pressure was 218/120. The belly area was soft, and Mr. Roosevelt said he had no gastrointestinal complaint. Both lungs were clear.

Bruenn, smiling and concerned with disturbing the Chief Executive, made a note to start phenobarbital—a quarter grain morning and noon. The apical and basal systolic murmurs were as before. The cardiologist did not expect a miracle; he would not cure this man. However, he would exhaust every ethical medical device for keeping the patient alive and feeling comfortable. Bruenn, a Republican, began to fall under the spell of Roosevelt. He admired this hearty, intelligent man, even though he could not reconcile his awe of the man's office with his duty to learn as much as possible about the President's body and how well the parts functioned.

The doctor was amazed that the patient never asked a question. As weeks and months crept by, Bruenn would expel the surprise from his mind. It was a good thing that the President did not embarrass the doctor with the endless dialogue endured now and then by all physicians. Bruenn was aware that Mr. Roosevelt knew his specialty was the human heart and once—just once—the President might have said, "Why does McIntire think I need a cardiologist unless there is something wrong with my heart?" The President spent his time talking of the Pup; how well he had slept; a trip to Hobcaw Barony, the state of the war, the tasteless meals of Mrs. Nesbitt, and the Pup's talent for pleading for food with his eyes.

Bruenn made few notes on a pad and left. Mr. Roosevelt, who knew that the Breakfast Club, consisting of Steve Early, Grace Tully, Pa Watson and others, would be in the room within a few minutes to discuss today's agenda, completed the *Times* story and managed to wander back to other pages before decision time arrived. The President was aware that the story of his health was imminent, because Steve Early would not countenance a press conference about presidential health, and Admiral McIntire would not star in it, without FDR's approval.

John H. Crider wrote:

President Roosevelt's health was reported "satisfactory" to-day [April 4] by his personal physician, Vice Admiral Ross T. McIntire. In an unprecedented report to the press on the physical check-up the President underwent a week ago in the Naval Hospital at Bethesda, Maryland, McIntire explained the results:

It had been known that Mr. Roosevelt had been suffering for about a month from a head cold and bronchitis, but Dr. McIntire said that he also had influenza or "respiratory infection" and a sinus disturbance. At one point he referred to "this acute flare-up of his sinuses and chest."

The haughty, often inaccessible Admiral wore the smile of a physician relieved of worry, "When we got through," he said, "we decided that for a man of sixty-two-plus we had very little to argue about with the exception that we have had to combat the influenza plus

the respiratory complications that came along after."
The fact that Roosevelt had not been seen around the
White House, or anywhere else, was easily covered. "I
have been completely responsible for holding him up
these last three or four days," McIntire stated. "The
bronchitis had made him a little hoarse, and I felt if we
could hold him in his study for his work, and not run
him from room to room where temperature changes occur, we would clear this thing up."

McIntire's assignment was to disarm the correspondents and, through them, the electorate of the
United States. He said that the checkup was an annual
event for the President and had been "delayed and strung
out" because Mr. Roosevelt contracted the head cold
and bronchitis in the middle of it. "They put *me* through
the jumps the other day," McIntire said, "and it's quite
comprehensive. They don't miss a thing." He paused.
A few questions were asked. "The greatest criticism
we can have," said the Admiral who had called the
secret and frightening consultations of well-known doctors, "is the fact that we haven't been able to provide
him with enough exercise and sunshine."

There were many things that McIntire did not say.
He was dispensing different diagnoses. Mrs. Roosevelt
told intimates that she heard that "Franklin had undulant
fever, probably from the cows at Hyde Park. He has
had a low fever for weeks." The diagnosis was absurd.
The therapy was not. Mr. Roosevelt was requested to
be in bed at 7:30 P.M. and he was. He ate alone and,
after reading departmental reports and making mar-
ginal notes in pencil, he extinguished the bedroom lights
at 10:40.

An article in *The Nation* brought FDR out of hiding.
The magazine wanted to know what, in particular, was
Roosevelt's foreign policy. The people were tired of
FDR's flag waving. There was a darker side to the war:
America was rife with black markets, ration stamps
for scarce commodities were stolen and counterfeited;

there was profiteering by big business and small business. The people had lost faith in Roosevelt's war.

The Boss called a press conference on April 7. The reporters stood five deep in a crescent. Mr. Roosevelt removed the cigarette holder from his mouth. Wagging his head back and forth for slow emphasis, he repeated America's war aims one at a time. "The United Nations are fighting to make a world in which tyranny and aggression cannot exist," he said. "A world based on freedom, equality and justice; a world in which all persons regardless of race, color or creed may live in peace, honor and dignity." He waved his cigarette holder at the reporters. "Some of you people, some of you who are wandering around asking the bellhop whether we have a foreign policy or not, I think that's a pretty good paragraph."

His aims were noble, but he did not realize that he had lost touch with the people. He saw the public from a train window. Most of his time was spent *inside* the White House; *inside* his home at Hyde Park; *inside* the Little White House at Warm Springs. He saw the same thirty or forty faces each week. He heard the same pleasant opinions. When he read newspapers which, in his opinion, were not fair to him, he threw them on the bedroom floor in anger.

And yet these were balmy days. This was a time when the bright warmth of spring swept up the Chesapeake to embrace the City of Washington, where topcoats were shed and secretaries stretched out on noontime grass to capture a complexion; where expert blacks shucked the succulent gray oysters fresh and glistening from their shells; where two could sit at dinner, barely hearing the string ensemble, and dream of a peaceful future in a land blessed beyond all others. In Lafayette Park, old men sat leaning on canes, watching taxicabs pick up two, three and four people all going to separate destinations. Easels and paint were in the park; the newspapers were heavy with figures on the production of bombers and fighters by the scores of thousands; of huge aircraft carriers scraping the locks of the Panama Canal on their way to the far Pacific; cruisers, battleships, destroyers, bigger tanks and more of them; tiny victory gardens producing six ears of corn, a dozen tomatoes and a hatful of beans. Victory ships were sliding down greased ways from Boston to Seattle; huge convoys loaded with Lend-Lease were shepherded, at eight knots, by swift destroyer escorts which tracked foaming furrows up and down the edges of the wandering sheep. More coal was coming; more trains were running; strikes were suppressed by executive fiat; big business guilty of unfair labor practices was seized by the army; blue stars and gold stars hung on a square of silk in windows; eleven million men and women were in uniform; enemies to the west and the east were staggering under the sledged blows of superior weaponry.

The days were warm, and becoming kinder. But the President was in trouble politically. This was an election year. If his purpose was to ask the people to return him to the White House for a fourth term, the old Roosevelt would have exuded confidence. Instead, he quarreled with the press; he picked a deliberate fight with the Congress, a fight he knew he could not win; he vetoed and canceled some of the plans of his Cabinet. Sometimes he sounded like a supreme egoist who stood on the summit of the final mountain.

He asked the Congress to pass a measure which would insure the right of servicemen and women to vote in the next election. The Senate responded like a frightened rattlesnake. It quickly passed a bill leaving the matter of soldier votes to the individual states. The House Elections Committee reported the bill to the floor favorably. Mr. Roosevelt felt stung. He penned a note in which he charged that the Congress was perpetrating a fraud on those who were fighting the war and, under state regulations, millions of men and women in the armed services would be deprived of the right to vote.

Republican Senator Robert Taft, humorless and legalistic, lost his temper. He leaped to his feet with reddened face and flailing arms and said that the President's note was "a direct insult" to Congress. The

President, he charged, preferred a national voting law to states' rights because he was lining up the soldiers, sailors and Marines to elect him to a fourth term.

In the House well, slow-speaking, rancorous old John Rankin of Mississippi, a Democrat like Roosevelt but one who enjoyed chipping away at presidential power, stood to discuss the Roosevelt bill. "Now who is behind this bill?" he asked calmly. "Who is the chief sponsor of it?" Rankin seldom had more than a nodding acquaintance with the facts. "The chief publicist is *PM,* the uptown edition of the *Daily Worker* that is being financed by the tax-escaping fortune of Marshall Field III, and the chief broadcaster for it is Walter Winchell—alias no telling what."

Michigan's Republican Clare Hoffman stood to ask a point of order. "Who is he?" he said innocently. Rankin said, "The little kike I was telling you about the other day, the one who called this body the House of Reprehensibles."

Republican floor leader Joseph Martin of Massachusetts sensed that the crude demagogic mood of the House was at the proper pitch for a roll call. He asked for it, and the House of Representatives voted down the Roosevelt bill, 224 to 168. The Rankin state measure was introduced and was passed, 328 to 69. The President had lost the sympathy and support of the Congress.

There were men with his council to whom the thought of a fourth term was anathema. Others, ambitious sycophants, urged Roosevelt to campaign once more. They told him the words he wanted most to hear: "You owe it to the country to see us through to victory and peace." The President's sorrowful response was, "All that is within me cries to return to my house in the Hudson River Valley." The Republican party painted and repainted him in the press as a rich man who had betrayed his own class with crushing taxes; a liar who had promised the mothers of America when he asked for a third term: "I hate war! I promise you, your sons will not fight on foreign soil." GOP leaders never tired of reminding the people that Mr. Roosevelt was spending

$312 million every day on the war and that it was "his war—he enticed the Japanese to attack." Mr. Roosevelt had begun to prepare the nation for hostilities in June 1940—a year and a half before the attack on Pearl Harbor and, from that time until the spring of 1944, he had spent $168 billion on defense.

One man within the Roosevelt inner council spoke up against a fourth term. He was the whispering voice, Benjamin V. Cohen. Mr. Cohen, one of Roosevelt's intellectual young Turks, was general counsel to the Office of War Mobilization, of which James F. Byrnes, the die caster from South Carolina, served as director. Mr. Byrnes was competent, but had a habit, irritating to the President, of resolving conflicts by announcing that they would be settled in his favor or he would resign and go home. Cohen belonged to that rare group which once included Rexford Guy Tugwell, Raymond Moley, Louis McHenry Howe, Thomas Corcoran and others who could heft a coin and see eight sides of it and were able to analyze all of them. In 1944 some were dead, some had fled; Cohen was still serving the President.

He dared to raise his voice. The covering letter started:

Dear Mr. President:
I thought you might be interested to read the attached memorandum of mine concerning the fourth term. It considers soberly, and possibly too gloomily, some of the difficulties which would confront the Administration during a fourth term, and it stirs the question whether there is any practical alternative.
As ever,

Yours,
Ben V.C.

The President
The White House

Attached were eight pages of political argument which, while conceding that Mr. Roosevelt could probably be

nominated by the Democratic party without a struggle
and elected too, was phrased delicately to convince the
President that he should renounce a fourth term:

*There is danger [Cohen wrote on page three] which can-
not be wholly ignored that a fourth term would be an anti-
climax. There is danger that Rooseveltian ideas, like Wil-
sonian ideas, may be discredited for a considerable period,
not because they are basically unsound but because political conditions will not permit them to be accepted or even
fairly understood. There is a question whether the influence
of Roosevelt and his ideas may not be greater in the period
following the war if there is no fourth term. If there is no
fourth term, the people will always remember that in no
crisis or emergency did Roosevelt ever let them down. Whoever succeeds the President, the common people will always be asking whether the new President is fighting for
and watching out for their interests as did Roosevelt.*

Cohen, who was a passionate and objective adherent
of Mrs. Roosevelt, marshaled his arguments to a point
where he felt it safe to beg the President to renounce a
fourth term *for a higher calling*. First, Cohen stated, both
the Democratic and Republican party leaders should
reach an agreement, presumably to be published as a
bipartisan pronunciamento, to continue to support the
Roosevelt foreign policy in the prosecution of the war
to "unconditional surrender" and to work together toward
the establishment of a United Nations. Thus, whether
the President was succeeded in office by a Republican
or a Democrat, his strong and merciless attitude toward
aggressor nations would be carried out to the letter.

*The best means of giving vitality to the agreement [Co-
hen wrote] and safeguarding its performance would be to
have both parties pledge themselves and their nominees to
the support of the suggestion that President Roosevelt accept an invitation to become the Chief Executive Officer of
the new international organization to maintain the peace.*

Thus Roosevelt would quit the presidency to serve as presiding officer of the political fetus called the United Nations.

The President's confidential response to Ben Cohen amounted to a pouting dismissal, without conceding that he already had decided to run for a fourth term:

Dear Ben:

That is a tremendously interesting analysis—and I think a very just one.

You have only left out one matter—and that is the matter of my own feelings! I am feeling plaintive.

As ever yours,

F.D.R.

Ben V. Cohen, Esq.
Office of War Mobilization,
The White House,
Washington, D.C.

The Boss was impatient with those who disagreed with him. He had inflicted a deep, suppurating wound on his party when he picked a fight with his Democratic Senate leader, Alben Barkley. The President had sent a strong new tax measure to the Congress, one designed to further his "soak-the-rich" philosophy, and Barkley, after reading it, stood in the President's bedroom and begged him to withdraw it. He reminded Roosevelt how he had fought for the President's measures down through the years, whether he believed in them or not. But this tax measure was bound to be defeated by a coalition of Republicans and reactionary Southern Democrats. The President replied stiffly that it was an equitable wartime tax measure, and that it was Barkley's duty to see it through the Senate.

Barkley fought it through the Senate cloakroom and in the senatorial walnut-paneled retreats where bourbon and branch water placed political enemies on an amiable footing. The bill was passed, but several senators appended sections to it which, in effect, exempted profitable businesses and rich men from heavy tax burdens.

Privately FDR said he would veto the bill. He sent it to the Treasury Depatment and the Office of War Mobilization. Ben Cohen wrote across a small sheet of paper: "This is a relief bill, not a tax bill. It's for the greedy, not the needy." In anger Roosevelt copied the two sentences and sent them back to Senator Barkley with the bill. The Senator assumed that these were the President's insolent impressions and announced from the Senate floor that he could no longer serve Roosevelt and would resign as party leader.

Barkley knew that, in resigning, his party in caucus would reelect him at once. Thus the resignation was a public defiance of Roosevelt by a trusted political servant. The President was shocked when Barkley shouted to the Senate, "My cup of gall runneth over." He was sure that Dear Alben was being melodramatic. Cohen wrote a confidential note to the President stating that the Barkley incident pointed up an accumulation of grievances within the party. Privately he feared that the President's obviously poor health would end in a fourth term with Roosevelt a senile cripple. And yet, it would be unpardonable to say it.

There was dissension in many places. Roosevelt had brought the stiffly starched Henry L. Stimson, Republican, in as Secretary of War and Stimson had turned out to be an excellent choice. However, after Roosevelt's eleven years in the White House, patience and understanding began to wear thin, and Stimson was carrying out the President's policy while writing in his diary that Roosevelt's "one man government" had spawned "this madhouse of Washington." Mr. Stimson was particularly outraged by the President's penchant for facing new problems by creating new governmental agencies known by their initials. He was certain that the huge monolithic structure would require decades of work to tear down into decentralized democratic government.

Nor was Stimson amused by the ring of advisers who manned the barricades in the White House corridors to keep high government officials from seeing their President. He had in mind Steve Early, Pa Watson, Grace Tully,

Harry Hopkins—and, when he sent urgent memoranda to the President, executive clerks William Hopkins and Maurice Latta regulated the channels of communication. The Secretary of War felt that they could stop a message from reaching Roosevelt's desk.

The Executive Branch of the government was spilling over in so many directions that a private directory had to be printed so that one official would have the means of reaching another. The White House personnel had seeped through the West Wing and new members were moving across the tiny private road on the west side to that Victorian pile called the State Department. On the second floor presidential assistants who seldom saw the President occupied offices called "Death Row." Among the inhabitants were Jonathan Daniels, Lowell Mellett, Lauchlin Currie and David K. Niles. Judge Samuel Rosenman was still nominally in charge of the speech-writing team, but the team had disintegrated. Harry Hopkins was in pain at the Mayo Clinic in Minnesota; Robert Sherwood, playwright, was in London.

In the East Wing of the White House, which would later be devoted to the staff of the First Lady and the Secret Service, Jimmy Byrnes ran the Office of War Mobilization, a catchall civilian agency which dealt with wages, prices, manpower and government loans. Ben Cohen worked there. Old Bernard Baruch, the good gray adviser to several Presidents, had office space although he preferred to do his thinking on a park bench; the legalistic Samuel Lubell had an office off a stairwell. Admiral William D. Leahy, Chief of Staff to the President, an unimaginative sea dog who was a pipeline from the Joint Chiefs of Staff to the President's ear, was there. In some ways Leahy was a decade and more behind the Chiefs of Staff in his thinking. He told the President that the United States, in spending $2 billion on an atom bomb, was throwing money down the drain because the bomb would never explode. It required the subservient persuasion of Admirals King, Nimitz and Edwards to convince Leahy that appropriations for 45,000-ton battleships should be cut back in favor of more Essex

Class aircraft carriers. Leahy was tractable. He endorsed almost everything the Joint Chiefs of Staff asked. He did not always subscribe to the opinions of the President or those of his immediate subordinates, but Admiral Leahy was an old-fashioned American patriot whose philosophy was to deal *generously* from a position of strength.

The air was warm, intoxicatingly clear, as the President's motorcade drove north out of Georgetown, South Carolina. Spring was alive. A few blacks fished under Lafayette Bridge. Mr. Roosevelt's eyes were heavy with fatigue, but they mirrored the small buildings of Waccamaw and the sparkling streams which seemed to flow under the wheels of the car from several directions. A few miles farther, and the wheels were on the curving driveway of Hobcaw Barony. The home of Bernard Baruch was a roomy Georgian brick structure; it had no telephone and was hardly more than a decorative pendant on the huge estate. Through all the private miles there were dirt lanes, magnolias and rhododendrons, big cypress, fernlike pine trees; spooky elms and moss hanging like the whiskers of old mandarins; the tidal flow of creeks, rivers and inlets; the coded cries of birds which, at sunset, stopped so that frogs and crickets could crouch in the recesses of the choir loft and crowd the night with atypical harmony.

The President retired to his room after spending a short time with his host. Bernard Baruch, a big man with white wavy hair and an affinity for counseling Presidents, was not well. He was accompanied by a nurse. He was a man of resources, intellectual and economic. His father, Simon Baruch, a German-Jewish surgeon, served the Confederate States Army with distinction in the Civil War. The son, as old and sturdy as some of his trees, had invited Mr. Roosevelt and his White House assistants to Hobcaw on several occasions. The President, in this matter, was the victim of gratuitous advice. Ranking members of the Government did not like Baruch; others, notably in the Roose-

velt family, admired him. Those who were suspicious of
Baruch's intentions referred to him as an inquisitive
man who would be a lavish host, but who would expect
a lot of time spent in confidential chatter. He was said
to be a man who remained outside the Government officially, but was highly regarded as the President's friend
and private counselor.

Mr. Baruch did not appear to be aware of his enemies.
Those who derided him in private greeted him with
deference. A few in the Roosevelt circle tried to drive
a wedge between the man. The male gossips wove their
webs of innuendo, but Roosevelt made a point of defending
"Barney" while, as counterpoint, he kept Baruch from
becoming too close a friend. The rich man had enjoyed
the confidence of the President's hero Woodrow Wilson,
and it implied a status of elder statesmen in dealing
with Roosevelt. All it did for the President was make
him a good listener.

The two men were to spend a month together. The
air at Hobcaw was still cool, and so were the attitudes.
As soon as the amenities were concluded, the President
went to bed. "I want to sleep and sleep," he said. "Twelve
hours every night." His fatigue was deep. For several
nights of the first week, the President slept his twelve
hours. In the White House Eleanor was hurt that her
husband did not phone in that week. Unwilling to wait
longer, she phoned him. He said he was feeling much
better, that he had slept more than usual, and had let
"the world go hang." It was a sweet figure of speech,
but untrue.

Throughout the waking hours he had Admiral William
Leahy at his side, with the latest war bulletins; he had
Admiral Wilson Brown, naval aide with shoulder four-
ragère; General Watson, military aide; Admiral Mc-
Intire; Commander Bruenn; Lieutenant William Rigdon,
USN, who acted as the President's secretary on all trips;
Dewey Long, communications officer; Mike Reilly and
the Secret Service agents; Arthur Prettyman; a few
Filipino messmen; three newspaper reporters on the

train. Most of these regarded the trip as a jail sentence; the President relaxed and enjoyed it.

Long had set two portable telephones in the President's room. One was connected to the White House switchboard. The other was used for personal calls, such as the one made almost daily to Mrs. Rutherfurd in Aiken—140 miles away. She told the President that she would drive to Hobcaw to lunch at his pleasure. He made a date and, as always, drew strength from their privacy. The rest of the time was divided into patchwork segments: 9:30 A.M. examination by Dr. Bruenn after breakfast; at 11:00 A.M. the White House pouch was brought to Mr. Roosevelt by William Hassett, newly appointed secretary who replaced the deceased Marvin McIntyre; noon, dictation of mail to Rigdon; 1:00 P.M. lunch; 2:00 P.M. drive to an inlet dock to fish all afternoon under a sun-beaten hat. Sometimes he boarded one of the two Coast Guard "six-bitters" available for fishing (the other was used by Secret Service).

He caught the warm sun of the afternoon and lifted his rod lightly and let it drop, hoping to hook channel bass. Whether he caught a fish, or sat dreaming over the sun-spangles on the water, the President enjoyed these hours and required no conversation. By sundown he was tired and taken back to the big brick home. He dined late or early as he pleased, among his admirals or with Bernard Baruch. The days were becoming warmer, and the refreshing tan was obvious in the sailor's smile. He ordered a number of current motion pictures brought with the party, but he retired early and seldom saw one.

The White House projectionist set his screen and machine in a stable. All hands were invited. Saddled horses were in the stalls. They stomped and neighed at the invasion of privacy and the laughter. It was Lieutenant Rigdon, slender, self-effacing, a man who noticed everything great and small, who saw the black horse watching the movie. Rigdon studied the horse studying the screen for two nights before he confided the secret to anyone. "Watch the black horse on the right side," he said. The unsmiling admirals thought Rigdon had been working too hard.

They watched the horse instead of the movie. All agreed that, once the picture started, the horse never took his great eyes from the screen. The other horses paid little attention to the light and sound. But Rigdon's nag studied the picture as though he wanted to see how the story ended. It led to laughter in the barn. It was, for these gentlemen, a rare sound. They were unhappy. All complained of sand fleas and mosquitoes which left welts on hands and face and neck. The Secret Service agents had to live on their Pullman at Georgetown—no pleasure as the heat increased.

One morning Mrs. Roosevelt and Anna flew down to spend the day with the President. They had word that he looked better, and they had a need to see it. The visit was pleasant. Mrs. Roosevelt asked a lot of questions about her husband's health, and she was satisfied that the rest was doing a lot of good. Consciously or unconsciously, the President felt more relaxed with Anna than with Eleanor. His wife sat with hands clasped between her knees, leaning forward to interpose a question, but the sparkling witticisms, the revealing anecdotes about fishing and "life on the farm" were reserved for his daughter. It was after this trip that Eleanor told her intimates that, when she wanted to know what the President was doing, or how he felt, she asked Anna. Alone with his daughter, he told her, "When I leave the White House, Anna, I am not going to live in the big house." The reference was to Hyde Park.

On her one-day visit Mrs. Roosevelt also brought Prime Minister and Mrs. John Curtin of Australia. Mr. Roosevelt noted that, even though Australia had to tighten its belt, it was worth it because General MacArthur and Nimitz's forces were moving up the island ladder taking the war away from the big commonwealth. When the four returned to Washington, Eleanor wrote in her diary:

F. looks well but said he still has no "pep." Dr. Mc-Intire says they will do final tests when he gets home . . . & put him on a strict regimen. He ought soon to get well. I'm trying to get him to come to Hyde Park at the end of June & only return two or three days a month during the summer months.

The President complained about abdominal gas. Dr. Bruenn could find nothing in the belly area worthy of attention. A few days later Mr. Roosevelt had a gall bladder attack. It required complete bed rest and sedatives, but it subsided and the President returned to fishing. He boasted to Bruenn that he had cut his drinking to "one and a half cocktails in the evening—and no complimentary ones—and I have cut my consumption of cigarettes from twenty to thirty a day down to five or six." The doctor may have worn an expression of disbelief. "Luckily," the President said, "they still taste rotten."

The President drove to see Belle Baruch, daughter of his host, at her home. When he tired of fishing, which was unusual, the President drove around the estate, stopping to admire the color of formal gardens. It was obvious, in early May, that he was tiring of the "farm routine." He was not accustomed to remaining for long off the edge of the world stage. And yet, as Hassett and Rigdon knew, he kept up with world affairs and signed orders, memoranda and letters, executed promotions and appointments, and still found time to sun himself.

Toward the close of the trip a Secret Service agent, Red Hepson, was making his 2:00 A.M. rounds near the main house when he saw a wild boar in a thicket. The agent in charge of the shift was Decker. Hepson hurried to him and asked what to do about the boar. The night was deadly quiet. "Shoot the son of a bitch," Decker said, shrugging. Hepson disappeared, tiptoed out to the bush with a big shotgun, and fired both barrels. The blast lit the night. Lights went on in the big house. Admiral Leahy came running out in his night-gown.

Hepson glared at Decker and said, "You told me to do it." Decker turned away. There was excitement inside the house. The noise did not lift the President out of sleep. He heard about it in the morning and roared with laughter. Mike Reilly saw no humor in it. He wanted to fire Hepson for not "using his head." Others begged him not to do it. Reilly, a callous sentimen-talist, sent Hepson back to Washington and told him not to worry about his job.

There was a war going on, and there were smaller wars among allies. Italy surrendered. Chancellor Adolf Hitler dispatched extra divisions to Marshal Kesselring, who was ordered to hold Italy if he had to kill Italians to do it. FDR said, "One down, two to go." Liaison between Germany and Japan was ineffective because each was fighting for its life a world apart. The brutal forces of geography made a worthless document of their mutual assistance pact. The Japanese military masters knew that they could help Germany by attacking the Soviet Union from Manchuria and Mongolia, but they had no intention of doing it.

Among the Allies differences of opinion led to intrac-tability and threats of unilateral action. In April 1944 the coded cables crackled between Downing Street, the Kremlin, and Washington regarding the interpreta-tion of the term "unconditional surrender." Russia and England feared, too late, that the phrase might stiffen the Germans to battle to the death. Publicly the Big Three had agreed at Teheran that "unconditional sur-render" would be demanded of the enemy. Privately Marshal Josef Stalin, at dinner with Churchill and Roose-velt, drank a toast to the summary execution of 50,000 German officers after "unconditional surrender." Mr. Roosevelt was shocked, but not for long. He drank to it.

Five months later the Allies began to worry about the phrase. The terms had been broadcast around the world many times. German Propaganda Minister Josef Goebbels rebroadcast it to the German people in another light—that Germany would be enslaved by the barbaric Russians. The phrase had the same effect in Japan, where it was cited to support the Tojo government's contention that the Americans would not be satisfied with conquest; they would kill Japanese prisoners and ravish the empire. The Big Three tried to interpret the term. Winston Churchill told Sir Alexander Cadogan, the acidulous Permanent Under Secretary for Foreign Affairs, that "unconditional surrender" meant that Germany would not be entitled to "any particular form of treatment" after the war. Cadogan replied that he wished German soldiers and civilians understood it.

The British Chiefs of Staff agreed with Sir Anthony Eden, British Foreign Secretary, that the Germans should be encouraged to have hope for their future and the future of their nation. Churchill pirouetted around the edge of the phrase by broadcasting that "unconditional surrender does not mean enslavement or destruction of the German people. If we are bound, we are bound by our own consciences to civilization. We are not to be bound to the Germans as the result of a bargain struck." The statement clarified nothing.

Nor did it impress the Germans. Their government advised them to note that Russia remained silent on the question. Roosevelt listened to the furor and said privately that, as far as he was concerned, unconditional surrender meant the same as that demanded of General Robert E. Lee by General Ulysses S. Grant at the end of the American Civil War. He recalled that as soon as unconditional surrender was tendered, Grant said that he would not want Lee's sword, and that Confederate officers should take their horses and their small arms home. It was an oversimplification in 1944; in 1918, the invading German armies had been permitted to return to the Fatherland intact. Such generosity was not contemplated in World War II.

In Great Britain Dwight D. Eisenhower and his combined staffs were working out a minute timetable for invading Europe, and Ike was uneasy about the phrase. He was Supreme Commander of Operation Overlord and he was certain that German resistance would stiffen under threat of surrender without conditions. The President said that too much was being made of the phrase. It was he who had thought of it, and he was not going to redefine what it meant.

Churchill minuted to Cadogan:

I have pointed out to the Cabinet that the actual terms contemplated for Germany are not of a character to reassure them at all, if stated in detail. Both President Roosevelt and Marshal Stalin at Teheran wished to cut Germany into smaller pieces than I had in mind. Stalin spoke of very large executions of over 50,000 of the staffs and military experts. . . . Stalin certainly said that he would require 4,000,-000 German males to work for an indefinite period to rebuild Russia. We have promised the Poles that they shall have compensation both in East Prussia and, if they like, up to the line of the Oder. . . .

Italy had surrendered while heavily occupied by the Germans. The capitulation was "unconditional," but the terms inposed by the Allies were mild. A Communist group calling itself the Political Committee for National Liberation started a revolution in Greece. Subtly, the old spheres-of-influence thinking began to dominate in London, and Prime Minister Churchill reminded the Soviet Ambassador that Greece and its friendly King Paul were in Britain's sphere; England hoped Russia would not support the revolutionaries.

The awkward phrase began to plague President Roosevelt within his Cabinet. Secretary of State Cordell Hull sent a memorandum asking for a detailed definition of "unconditional surrender." FDR tried:

It would be a mistake, in my judgment, to abandon or make an exception in the case of the words "unconditional surrender." As a matter of fact, whom do we mean those words to apply to? Evidently our enemies.

In August 1941, at the time of the Atlantic Charter, and in January 1943, at the time of Casablanca—Hungary, Bulgaria, Rumania and Finland were the Axis satellites. But they were not our enemies in the same sense that Germany and Italy were. These four little satellites were enemies under the duress of Germany and Italy.

I think it is a mistake to make exceptions. Italy surrendered unconditionally but was at the same time given many privileges. This should also be so in the event of the surrender of Bulgaria or Rumania or Hungary or Finland. Lee surrendered unconditionally to Grant, but immediately Grant told him that his officers should take their horses home for the spring plowing. That is the spirit I want to see abroad —but it does not apply to Germany. Germany understands only one kind of language.

FDR

Hull drew neither solace nor understanding from the reply. In conversations with the Joint Chiefs of Staff, the President conceded that he had in mind a harsh peace for Germany and Japan, including capital crimes trials for their leaders. Both nations, he insisted, were inherently militaristic, and both would have to be crushed brutally. In the case of Germany, he would reduce to a minimum its potential to wage war; in the matter of Japan, he proposed to disband its army and navy and to build China as a strong nation with sufficient power to subjugate Japan.

The President would not countenance a negotiated peace. He had been at the side of Woodrow Wilson in 1919 when the great powers sat around a big table at Versailles to place the responsibility for war on Germany and impose their collective will on the vanquished. It hadn't worked. Link by link, the losers cut the chains. A huge and efficient Wehrmacht had been built; a terrifying Luftwaffe had reduced cities to heaps of stone; commerce raiders and U-boats were abroad on the seas. Mr. Roosevelt would not permit it to happen again. "Unconditional surrender" meant that the Big Three would impose the conditions. For Germany and

Japan, these would be harsh. For the satellite enemies, Roosevelt was prepared to be generous, forgiving.

He could afford to be adamant. The tide of war had reached its peak at Stalingrad in the West and Guadalcanal in the East. For the axis, the tide was running out. The British-American invasion of Europe was five weeks away. Adolf Hitler, the military magician, was making monumental mistakes. FDR noted that, even though massive Russian armies had retaken the Ukraine, the Führer had insisted that the Crimea be held. The President did not pretend to understand field tactics, and made a point of not interfering with field decisions, but he could see the impossibility of holding a fat peninsula hanging off the mainland in the Black Sea.

The German 17th Army, half of which consisted of Romanians, could not hold General Tolbukhin's massive 470,000-man army, tanks and planes. Yalta, Sevastopol and Alupka fell in a month. The Germans scorched, burned and destroyed as they retreated. Strangely, they left three palaces intact (except for furnishings) at Yalta. It was said that Hitler had given one of these palaces to General von Mannstein as a postwar present. Perhaps the Germans expected to retrieve the Crimea. Sitting in his wheelchair, moving from map to map, Roosevelt felt certain of complete victory for the Allies.

The handsome, white-haired Assistant Secretary of State, Edward Stettinius, had been dispatched to London to discuss postwar problems with British and Russian experts. Stettinius not only remembered the warning FDR had given him in relation to Churchill's unquenchable thirst for more land; he had written it in his private notes:

When the President told Churchill that China does not want Indo-China, Churchill had replied, "Nonsense." The President said to him: "Winston, this is something which you are just not able to understand. You have four hundred years of acquisitive instinct in your blood and you just don't understand how a country might not want to acquire land somewhere if they can get it. A new period has opened in the world's history and you will just have to adjust yourself to it."

A new world, perhaps, but the President failed to realize that old mentalities were running it. He told Jimmy Byrnes and others in his official family that he would have to win the cordial endorsement of the Russians—not the British—before his peace plan for a world of United Nations could be realized. Stalin and Foreign Minister Molotov had been impressed at Teheran as they studied the gallant cripple in the wheelchair. Personalities and admiration, however, would have no bearing on official Soviet decisions at the peace table. FDR assumed that they would.

At almost the same time, the late spring of 1944, the Russians publicized a trial of Soviet traitors at Krasnodar. The Slavs were convicted of cooperating with the German Gestapo in the murder of 7,000 Russian Jews. The men on trial confessed, sobbing, that they had helped man the *dushegubka*—the "soul-killing" gas wagon. The Jewish world, especially those who fled Germany before the holocaust, warned that Hitler had decided to solve the "Jewish question" for all time by killing European Jews. Some spoke of large concentration camps in Poland, Germany and Austria, but the truth was too brutal to absorb. High-ranking statesmen felt that Hitler was moving Jews to concentration camps in the manner that the United States was moving Nisei from the West Coast to Montana.

The Krasnodar trial represented the first instance in which a retreating German army left evidence of genocide. There is no record of FDR's reaction. Premier Stalin milked the trial for its propaganda value but confessed privately that he thought the matter was "exaggerated." In England it aroused the Jews to an emotional pitch regarding the Balfour Declaration, the promise of a Jewish Home in Palestine. Jewish intellectuals in the United States, the Middle East and officials of the Jewish Agency in Switzerland warned that Krasnodar

was but the first of the horror camp stories; other camps
would come to light as the German armies were rolled
back toward Berlin. The stunned reaction of the Big
Three is difficult to digest; all were aware of the racial
laws passed by the German government. Adolf Hitler
did not pretend contempt for the Jews; he hated and
feared them. The world was aware of the excesses of
Kristal Nacht in 1938. Hitler stated publicly that an
international conspiracy of Jews was responsible for
Germany's problems.

The Chancellor said that 80 million Germans needed
more room, and that *Lebensraum* could be found only
to the east. Hitler had refused to permit the Jewish Agency
to buy the freedom of German Jews. Neutral states
had appealed to him to allow the unwanted to leave
the Reich. All efforts to mediate the massacre had been
declined. He could not bring himself to sell his massive
revenge.

May 1944

IN A SPACIOUS SITTING ROOM AT HOBCAW, PRESIDENT
Roosevelt composed himself behind a small desk. At
his side was Lieutenant Rigdon. In front sat Merriman
Smith of United Press, Robert G. Nixon of International
News Service and Douglas Cornell of Associated Press.
The day was Saturday, May 6, 1944. That night the
President would leave Hobcaw for the train at George-
town, South Carolina, to return to Washington.

After a month he would indulge the press. At the
White House there were always between 150 and 200
gentlemen and ladies of the press, and Roosevelt enjoyed
the informal give-and-take of conversation with reporters.
But on trips such as this, only three members of the
wire services were invited, because, most of the time,
there was nothing to report.

At the press conference the President appeared to be thinner, but his color was good and his voice was firm. At the start he bit each word carefully before spitting it out, but, as the conference progressed, his attitude softened.

Q: Would you like to sort of review your vacation?

FDR: I don't want to review it. In one word, I have rested. Had a very quiet time. Been out in the sun as much as possible. Done some fishing—some salt water fishing, some in the mouth of the river, some off the inlet and some in the ponds.

The President fell silent as the pencils continued to dance on the pads. "You know," he said, "the matter of a vacation hideout for the President is really a problem. I don't know what we are going to do about it."

Up until two years ago last December, I used to do a lot of cruising down the Potomac. Then there arose the danger of German subs, and of hostile planes flying over the Potomac. It has no antiaircraft protection. There were no other ships available, and we couldn't get a lot of escort boats for the Potomac, so the Navy stopped us. I looked around for some government property near Washington where I could spend a holiday. I tried in vain to go to Sugar Loaf Mountain. There's a place up there not far from Frederick. It belongs to a dirty rat. He's going to give it to the government some day, but he doesn't want this President going there. We found a place up on the Blue Ridge Mountains, but it is practically impossible to get to. . . .

Then I learned of this place here. I like it here. I have been very comfortable down here. I want to come back. Down here I can do a little fishing and get lots of rest. I like it around Belle Isle Gardens. It's perfectly lovely. I would like to come back down here again, but if it becomes known as one of the places where the President goes, it won't hold. So I don't think we should mention it in any of the press stories.

The press, deferential but wary, was willing to omit the geography of Hobcaw but wondered aloud whether the Charleston, Columbia and Charlotte newspapers would keep the secret. The President said that he could not guarantee what those newspapers would do. They had local information about his presence in South Carolina. He dropped into his plaintive mood:

It's a marvelous place to rest. Then, on the other hand, it's pretty difficult to go back to the same place. Really a pretty difficult thing. You know, I had thought of going to Guantanamo first, but had to rule that out. Guantanamo meant flying down from the train at Miami.

Q: Why was the naval base ruled out?

FDR: I can only tell you the reason off the record. Cuba is absolutely lousy with anarchists, murderers, et cetera, and a lot of prevaricators. They thought it a whole lot better for me to come down here.

The presence of heart disease was the true reason. And yet, assuming that the President was not aware of the gravity of his health, it is possible that his doctors used the excuse of anarchy and murder to keep him within continental United States. Admiral Leahy walked in, a formal man in full uniform, and interrupted to tell the President that he saw nothing wrong in mentioning Hobcaw, "especially if there is going to be an elapsed time of three or four months until your next visit." The Chief Executive thought about it. "I think it is all right to mention it," he said.

The distinguishing feature of practically all of Roosevelt's press conferences was his ability to talk on and on, regaling the reporters with lively and witty stories, while withholding the news they were paid to produce. On this particular day the information desired by the editors involved:

(1) The state of the President's health;

(2) Presidential comment on the successful Russian drive toward Poland;

(3) The rumor that Japan was asking a negotiated peace through Russia;

(4) Comment on the sudden death of Navy Secretary Frank Knox;

(5) The enthusiasm of the Republican right wing for General Douglas MacArthur as a candidate for President.

Roosevelt wandered on, pointing out that Hobcaw and its environs represented an "enormous amount of land vacant—no one on it." In his drives through the estate, as always "loving the trees," he felt that there was room for many homes and families and industry. "Like this thing that smells over here," he said, pointing vaguely toward a pulp mill in Georgetown.

Q: Can you smell it over here?

FDR: Yes, but don't put that in. [The President chuckled.] After the first night here, Pa Watson came in to see me at breakfast time. I asked him, "Did you do that?" He said, "What do you mean?" I told him, "That odor." He said, "I didn't do it," and I told him it must have been him, his room is just overhead.

The laughter was becoming hearty. Mr. Roosevelt went into a dissertation on the manufacture of vermouth in Italy. When he paused, a reporter decided to ask about the President's health.

Q: How are you feeling now, sir?

FDR: Fine. Really better.

Q: Any trace of your bronchitis?

FDR: I think it is all gone, but Admiral McIntire is going to put me through the usual checkup examinations when we get back, to see if it is all fixed up. Regular thing, you know.

The point was pressed no further. A second reporter cut in to ask about the government's battle with the large mail-order retailer, Montgomery Ward. The President replied, "I don't know. Once upon a time I was a lawyer. I don't know."

Q: Did you have any direct communication from General MacArthur after all this hullabaloo?

FDR: No. MacArthur was my chief of staff, and a very great friend of mine. . . . He doesn't say he will refuse. Stassen is still in.

Q: Are you going to have an announcement any time soon on Mr. Knox's successor?

FDR: No.

Mr. Roosevelt moved on to a monologue about the court-martial of a Marine lieutenant who, while on a patrol around the perimeter of the naval base at Guantanamo, Cuba, found a limping calf and ordered it shot. The lieutenant did not know whether it belonged to his government or to a Cuban farmer. He seemed fearful that the meat would rot in the heat, and ordered the calf dismembered and fed to his platoon as veal.

A solemn court-martial found him guilty and ordered his dismissal from service. The President pointed out that the sentence was reviewed all the way to the top, and confirmed. "It came on down to me. I picked it up to read it. The more I read of it, the more I laughed." On the last page, he found a place for the presidential signature over the word "Approved." FDR wrote, "The sentence is approved, but it is mitigated, so that in lieu of being dismissed the accused will be placed on probation for a year, subject to the pleasure of the President. This man must be taught not to shoot calves. Franklin D. Roosevelt."

The press conference concluded with the question, "Been getting much reading?" No, the President said, he was more interested in fishing and driving around the estate. He had seen gravestones of British officers who had fought in the Revolutionary War.

Q. Very interesting. They anticipated the war, didn't they?
FDR: I imagine they did. . . .

The press conference tailed off. In Washington or out of it, FDR tailored these story-telling bees to suit his mood. He could, at times, electrify the journalists with news; at others, he charmed them with pointless yarns.

The President was rolling through the corridors of the White House again on Sunday, May 7. He was frowning; the jolly vacation mood had been dissipated by Admiral McIntire, who said that he had called for a medical examination "and consultation" for Wednesday. Roosevelt said there was no need for a consultation. McIntire and Bruenn were sufficient to his needs. The Admiral agreed that there was probably no necessity for it, but he wanted confirmation. With reluctance Mr. Roosevelt agreed to an examination by McIntire, Bruenn, Dr. Harper, Dr. Paullin and Dr. Lahey. He would not countenance a "fuss" being made over his wasted body, nor did the proposed examination reassure him. For a man who returned from a month of sunny rest, it was a shock to learn that five physicians would be probing, listening, asking questions, organizing tests.

In collusion, the five physicians agreed not to mention heart disease or arteriosclerosis. They proposed to be cheerful. The examination was done, including gall bladder tests (a small amount of stones was discovered). Lahey told Roosevelt that he had recovered from sinus and bronchial infections and was "well and active." Paullin spoke to FDR about the future.

"Let's assume," he said, "that you're setting out on a fifty-thousand-mile trip in a brand-new machine. Good tires and the engine hitting on every cylinder. After going forty thousand miles, however, and with ten thousand miles still ahead, you find definite signs of wear and tear. There is a knock in the engine every now and then, and while the body is pretty good, the tires are not in the best of shape.

"Mr. President, the engine and the tires are your heart and arteries. I have used this story many times on men in high executive jobs, and here is this lesson to be learned: If you want to finish the journey, traveling the last ten thousand miles without mishap, you can't keep up any seventy-miles-an-hour clip. You've got to slow down to a speed that will not blow out the tires and wreck the engine. In plain words, you must live within your reserve."

The President smiled acknowledgment to a well-turned figure of speech. "Well," he said, "I'll agree to quit burning up the road. Maybe not as slow as thirty miles an hour, but much less than seventy anyway." When the visiting physicians had left, Admiral McIntire sat with the President, who, having been given a good bill of health, appeared to be tractable. They devised a daily schedule:

8:30 to 9:00 A.M.—Breakfast in quarters.

11:00 to 1:00 P.M.—Office, 2 hours.

1:00 to 2:00 P.M.—Luncheon in quarters. No business guests.

2:00 to 3:00 P.M.—Office, 2 hours.

45 minutes massage and ultraviolet light; rest before dinner, lying down.

7:30 to 8:00 P.M.—Dinner in quarters. No night work. Sleep 10 hours. Diet: smooth, 2,600 calories. High vitamin additions.

The President agreed to it, probably to please McIntire. It was the routine of a man with old and brittle arteries, out of bed no more than six hours a day, on his back eighteen. Roosevelt might have asked his favorite physician how a President could run the country and the war on a four-hour work day. It seems strange that FDR did not ask why Dr. Lahey pronounced him "well and active" if it was necessary to cut his work load to less than half, and do no work after 8:00 P.M. In a manner of speaking, the two men understood each other. The patient did not ask for precise information; the doctor did not volunteer any.

A call was put through to Seattle. Anna listened to the deep, affectionate voice. Yes, she said, if her father wanted her to live at the White House she would move. Her husband, John Boettiger, was a major on assignment

with military police. There was no reason to remain
in Seattle. But she proposed to call her mother about
it first. Anna felt that she needed Eleanor's permission.
Mrs. Roosevelt did not appreciate the presence of another
woman—even her daughter—as hostess in the White
House. Her assent was grudging and full of questions.
Anna put it on a truthful plane: Father was lonely.
The doctors were cutting the number of visitors in half.
He would be in bed having dinner at 7:30 every eve-
ning.

Dr. McIntire had assured Mrs. Roosevelt that "he
is getting better." She was also told that the doctors
"know what they are doing." And yet she worried because,
on the few occasions when he found time to see his
wife, he appeared to "tire easily"; also she noted that
he was still plagued by "indigestion." It would now
be up to Anna to see that he took proper care of himself.
A few weeks later Eleanor wrote to her son James,
"Pa is enjoying not doing things which bore him, and
he's getting so much pleasure out of having Anna
around."

After Hobcaw, the sunny mood of the White House
declined to bleak dusk. Grace Tully noticed that the
President seemed fatigued and hollow-eyed. Secretary
William Hassett kept a highly personal and gloomy diary:
"The pres. was in fine form but he is thin and although
his color is good, I feel that he has not entirely shaken
the effects of the flu followed by bronchitis, which has
bedeviled him for many weeks now."

After Anna's arrival the darkening mood embraced
her, although in her father's presence she sparkled with
family stories and brightened his day. Unknown to him,
she sorted through his night pouch, removing papers
and questions which she felt could be handled by others.
When he insisted that he wanted to further reduce his
weight (160 pounds), Anna persuaded him to eat more
and gain weight.

Dorothy Brady was taking dictation from the President
one day when he noticed she was grimly silent. He asked
why. The young secretary told him she felt hurt by

something said by a friend. He may have been thinking of himself when he said solemnly, "Child, life is very precious. Hold onto it as long as you can. Yesterday was yesterday. Today is today." The Democratic boss of the Bronx, Ed Flynn, stopped in to chat with Roosevelt after the dictation period. Flynn understood politics and the disciplines of the Roman Catholic Church. He knew nothing of medicine, but he told friends he departed "shocked" at the evident weakness of the President and the palsied tremors of his hands.

At work FDR did not stay within the bounds set by McIntire. He cut his work day a little; the secretaries and chief telephone operator Hachmeister kept the inconsequential phone calls from him and much of the unimportant mail. He was able to accomplish as much as ever by reaching decisions quickly—as though he did not have the time to weigh the problems. Within a few minutes the Boss approved an Army budget of $49 billion, of which $34 billion would come from funds allocated the previous year. He nominated James V. Forrestal to replace Frank Knox as Secretary of the Navy on May 10, the day the doctors were examining him. He ordered the National War Labor Board to go to court to force Montgomery Ward to comply with the government labor practices act.

A meeting of the Cabinet was overdue, so Roosevelt called one for May 12. Some of the more caustic members called it "a delightful social occasion." The invasion of continental Europe (D Day) was less than a month away, but the President did not mention it. As usual, he turned first to white-haired Secretary of State Cordell Hull and said, "Cordell, what's the news from abroad?" The old lion kept his head bowed toward his clasped hands on the polished table. "Not very encouraging," he said. That completed the State Department report. Hull was conscious and sensitive of the truth: that FDR was his own Secretary of State and kept Hull on the job because he had great power within the Senate. Sumner Welles, Under Secretary, was the man FDR wanted in that job; Welles was precise and analytical in his foreign reports and the President appreciated the manner in which Welles could weigh the several sides of any State Department problem, leaving it to FDR to make a choice.

Among the members who sat around the table, Henry Morgenthau was the least admired. John Garner once said that the President's personal friend and Dutchess County neighbor was "the most servile" of Roosevelt's ministers. Garner and others thought that Morgenthau purposely revealed little or nothing at Cabinet meetings about the workings of his Department of the Treasury, preferring to lunch with the President alone every Monday. FDR furthered this contempt by frequently phoning Mr. Morgenthau and shouting, "Henry, come over and hold my hand!" and hanging up.

Jesse Jones, Secretary of Commerce, incited fear in some members, who felt that his speech was too blunt and critical of the others. Henry Wallace acted the shy schoolboy and seldom spoke unless the President asked a direct question. Stimson was the only Republican left in the Cabinet. His vision was broad and he spoke his mind freely. Harold Ickes, the acidulous liberal who ran the Interior Department, often waited until the President said "yes" to a proposition, at which point he would mutter "no." Frances Perkins, still at the helm in the Department of Labor, commanded the respect of all—even those who wished to stare with jaundiced eye at a female in the Cabinet.

In May of 1944 the group was lost in a cryptogram of initials. It was difficult, almost impossible, to conduct business without a 14-page guide to the 156 agencies responsible to the Executive Branch of the government. Besides, the problems and decisions often moved over the heads of members of the Cabinet to the President's desk. Henry Wallace and Jesse Jones were in acrimonious debate about who controlled which agencies. James F. Byrnes, for example, was "assistant President" and Director of the Office of War Mobilization. The dual positions were more important to the national welfare than most Cabinet departments, and yet Byrnes was not a member of the Cabinet.

The President created bureaus to solve specific problems but failed to notify others of their existence. There was an Alaska War Council; an Interdepartmental Committee for the Voluntary Payroll Savings Plan for the Purchase of War Bonds; an Advisory Board of Just Compensation of the War Shipping Administration; a British-American Joint Patent Interchange Committee. No one person, including the Director of the Bureau of the Budget, understood all of them or their separate functions. General William ("Wild Bill") Donovan was in charge of the Office of Strategic Services and said that South America should come under its wing, but he was fought to a draw by Nelson Rockefeller, Coordinator of Inter-American Affairs.

Stimson threatened to resign as Secretary of War. "One man cannot do it all," he protested. The trouble with the President, he felt, was that Roosevelt had never learned how to say no. FDR was trying to play Daddy to everybody, coaxing, cajoling, yessing, and he was sending emissaries out to execute tasks without consulting the Cabinet members. "Everything," Stimson complained, "has to come to you." FDR agreed with Stimson as he had all the others, and the Secretary of War stayed on.

The President's attitude toward his Cabinet was that they were political consultants rather than administrative confreres. The agenda was always within his purview. When comment from Jesse Jones or Cordell Hull became critical, FDR listened gravely, nodded in agreement, and then told a story which diverted the collective thinking into more pleasant channels. He was not an autocrat, but he dominated the thinking of his top ministers by handing down policy decisions which brooked no rebellion. Further, the President consulted the assistant secretaries and under secretaries in greater depth, on a daily basis, than he did their superiors. He assumed, correctly, that the second and third echelon in each department knew more about the details of problems than the members of the Cabinet.

The day, the time, as always, was peculiar unto itself. On the best-seller list, a biography of Adolf Hitler entitled *Der Fuehrer,* written by Konrad Heiden, fought for top honors in the nonfiction field with a love letter written to the deceased John Barrymore by Gene Fowler. It was called *Good Night, Sweet Prince.* In the field of fiction, Betty Smith's *A Tree Grows in Brooklyn* was a best seller with John Hersey's *A Bell for Adano,* and *The Robe.* Books were retailing for $2.50 and $3.00.

In New York Best & Company offered women a "gamin haircut for $1.50 and complete styling—haircut, shampoo, reverse curl setting for $3.50." At Russeks a full-length Persian lamb coat sold for $595. War and chronic crises required analgesics, and Americans diverted themselves by patronizing motion pictures in greater numbers to see Barbara Stanwyck in *Double Indemnity* or Danny Kaye in *Up in Arms.* On Broadway the legitimate theater flourished with *Oklahoma!* at the St. James; Jan Kiepura and Marta Eggerth in *The Merry Widow;* and Kenny Baker, Mary Martin and John Boles sharing a good run in *One Touch of Venus.*

The alternative was to read of 600 heavy bombers raiding targets in Germany and France or Chicago *Tribune* publisher Robert McCormick warning that "the Communists not only dominate the Democratic party but are actively trying to control the Republican National Convention as the New Deal did in 1940." In London the Polish government-in-exile feared the tidal wave of Russian armies across Poland almost as much as it had the 1939 advance of the German Army.

Political and military leaders around the world remembered an old truth: the war had started over a corridor in Poland. One by one, starting with France and England, great nations had been precipitated into the holocaust because of the savage and unwarranted invasion of Poland. In London Churchill's government had suffered the Polish government-in-exile protests against realignment of its prewar borders. The question was of honor and principle, but neither Great Britain nor the United States had an inclination to discuss it. As the Russian forces swept closer and closer to Warsaw, the Poles became louder and more demanding. They asked for a clarification of Soviet postwar intentions and made it abundantly clear that they feared Communist Russia almost as much as Fascist Germany. The Soviet Union remained silent, to the embarrassment of Churchill and Roosevelt. The Free World leaders, anxious not to arouse Stalin, also remained silent on the subject. In private FDR stated that he had between five and seven million Poles as registered voters in the United States, and he would be forced to take a public stand on Poland soon.

The problem would, in time, become thorny and insoluble, leaving blood on the fingers of all who touched it. In the second week of May 1944, when Poland became newsworthy again, Roosevelt went to Shangri-La, his hideaway in the hills, for a Thursday-to-Sunday rest. Hours before FDR left the White House in a new bulletproof car to ride up to the Catoctin Mountains, Churchill had called a meeting of dominion prime ministers in London to formulate a unified empire point of view regarding a United Nations organization. Either Churchill misgauged their firm attitude about a responsible world organization, or he was trying to inoculate them with his personal views. He felt that a series of regional councils—one for Europe, one for the Americas, one for Asia, and another, if necessary, for Africa—could convene to settle problems in their individual areas, and then meet as a world group to thrash out agreements.

The dominion chiefs opposed the notion. They could no longer be limited to settling problems in a series of world enclaves. Anything which affected one part of the world to its detriment, they stated, would eventually affect all the others. Besides, the British Empire was so disparate geographically that it would be impossible to think in terms of a disjointed and separated people. Churchill insisted on a regional organization for Europe, responsible to the world body. He would like the United States, the Soviet Union and Great Britain to sit in this body.

No one, including Foreign Secretary Anthony Eden, was enthusiastic. The consensus was that Winston Churchill applied practically all of his energy to winning the war, and had given superficial time to the peace. "We have no idea of three or four Great Powers ruling the world," the P.M. wrote in his minutes. "We should certainly not be prepared to submit to an economic, financial and monetary system laid down by, say, Russia or the United States with her faggot-vote China. The Supreme World Council or Executive is not to rule the nations. It is only to prevent them from tearing each other to pieces." The Prime Minister did not confide his opinions to Roosevelt.

The President was barely behind his White House desk again when he decided to visit Hyde Park. The war was approaching a crescendo. D Day in Europe was now three weeks off. And yet his daily interest in the conduct of the war flagged. He listened to military briefings with patient courtesy but evinced little interest. He asked few questions. His candid assumption was that the Allies would win the war—he was concerned with when.

The day before he left for Hyde Park Roosevelt issued a statement on the third "Extension of the Lend-Lease Act." He was proud of it, and, for the edification of his political enemies, noted that, when he signed the first bill on March 11, 1941, Britain stood alone: "Everywhere the peace-loving peoples of the world were facing disaster." He attributed the contribution of material assistance as a major reason for the prospect of ultimate victory against the Axis Powers:

In April 1941, the first full month of the Lend-Lease program, we furnished aid valued at $28,000,000. In the month of March 1944, the Lend-Lease aid supplies amounted to $1,629,554,000. . . . Our total aid is $24,224,806,000. . . . This unity of strength, both in men and in resources, among the free peoples of the world will bring complete and final victory. That victory will come sooner, and cost less in lives and materials because we have pooled our manpower and *our material resources, as United Nations to defeat the enemy.*

At 9:00 P.M. the President signed a personal letter and said that he was ready. It was a soft evening with a warm breeze up from the Potomac. It was a night so kind to the cheek that it brought to mind a scent of forgotten friendliness. In twenty minutes he was driving out of the East Gate in a slow motorcade which turned right and moved down Fifteenth Street past the darkened shaft of the Washington Monument to the Bureau of Engraving.

As a matter of choice, Mr. Roosevelt favored the Baltimore and Ohio Railroad over the Pennsylvania when starting for Hyde Park. Some said it was because the Pennsylvania charged him a pro rata share of full fare Pullman tickets even when he occupied his special car, the *Ferdinand Magellan,* alone. The President said this was not so. He said that the Secret Service was opposed to the Pennsylvania because, when it transferred to the New York Central to get to Hyde Park, the train passed over the Hell Gate Bridge on the East River, New York. The Secret Service saw danger in it. There may have been an additional reason: the Pennsylvania seemed loath to sidetrack heavy traffic on its main line to allow Roosevelt's POTUS to pass.

Mr. Roosevelt refused to alter his orders that his train, no matter what the destination, travel at 25 to 30 miles an hour. At that speed, he claimed, he could study the farms and towns along the right of way. In truth, when his car took a turn any faster than 30 miles per hour, the shift of gravity caused sharp pain in his lower back and buttocks. A presidential special requires extra care. In front, a dead-head locomotive clanked along the right of way a mile ahead at all times. The main train, consisting of seven to seventeen Pullman cars, carried two white flags designating a special. One hour ahead of it, track crews were ordered to spike all switches in a closed position.

On a four-track mainline, this would close all traffic

on one track for at least an hour and a half as the presidential special loafed through. Railroads which were bursting with orders to move tanks, plane parts, munitions and oil kept traffic no farther apart than two towers. Closing one track for Mr. Roosevelt meant ordering war goods as well as perishable foods to sidings for an hour or two as he headed home, or back to Washington. He had a predilection for leaving the White House at night. The President slept well on a train—as he did everywhere else—and if the schedule called for an early arrival at the New York Central siding along the river near Crum Elbow and Hyde Park, he would sleep until 8:30 or 9:00 A.M., holding the train panting until he was ready to leave. Rarely, he would use the B&O and get off at Highland on the west bank of the Hudson.

The President was opposed to a bulletproof vest, a bulletproof automobile, and a bulletproof railroad car, but Mike Reilly ordered them and, with blustery charm, convinced the Boss that he must minimize his chances of being hurt. In the matter of presidential safety, Reilly was more than a Secret Service man; he was a guardian angel. He riffled through the congressional appropriations and learned that $750 was allocated for an automobile each year. On his own, he discussed the matter with Detroit automobile manufacturers, stating that it was a shame that Roosevelt had to ride around in Al Capone's old car—which, he found, had bulletproof windows but not a bulletproof body. The automobile manufacturers pooled their resources and built a bulletproof car for FDR. They leased it for a few dollars a year to the White House. It was all that Reilly expected, but the windows were so thick that, when H.M. George VI was riding to the White House on a warm afternoon, he did not have the strength to lower them and almost fell unconscious in the heat.

Reilly also conferred with the Association of American Railroads. They agreed to take the *Ferdinand Magellan* to the Philadelphia shops and have it made safe from bullets and bombs. The President heard about it and called Reilly in and said he didn't want it. The White

House Secret Service chief was tougher than the President. His clincher was: "This is not solely for your use, Mr. President. It will be used by future Presidents."

Roosevelt's opposition collapsed. The Pullman had been built in 1928. At the shops, all steel was cut off by acetylene torches. The outer shell was replaced with heavy-gauge steel. A thick metal shield was built the length of the undercarriage. Glass windows three inches thick were built. The ends of the car were armor-plated. An elevator was built into the rear platform, so that the President could stand on it, and, by pressing a button, would be lowered to ground level. Five compartments in the car were cut away and reduced to three—the largest of which was the President's lounge at the rear.

This was big enough for sofas, a desk, and wingback chairs, all secured to the floor. The four-wheel trucks were replaced by six wheels to hold the extra weight. All doors on the car were self-locking. They could be opened only from the inside. The roof had submarine escape hatches in case the car was derailed on a bridge and submerged. Among the members of the Secret Service, a strong swimmer was taken on all trips. His function was to grab the President in case of danger, in river or on the sea, and hold him aloft until assistance arrived. Reilly told the railroad executives that he hoped they would add loudspeakers on the roof so that Mr. Roosevelt could address crowds from a sitting position inside.

The *Ferdinand Magellan* had its name obliterated from the sides and left blank. The car was painted the rich kelly green of the Southern Railroad. When it was ready, it weighed 285,000 pounds empty. It was a source of irritation to two types of railroaders. Car knockers, who checked journals and identification, maintained that they had never sent a Pullman car without a name and had to be advised to list "one blank Pullman." Engineers who were told to make up the rest of the presidential specials in the Washington yards backed down slowly to the Bureau of Printing and Engraving dock, hooked up and, moving the throttle slowly forward, found that their big drivers were spinning, tossing sparks, but the train was not in motion. Until they became accustomed to the extra weight, incredulous engineers thought that the air brakes were still on. The weight situation was not improved by the car directly in front of the President's. This was operated by the Army Signal Corps and was equipped with heavy wireless sets, wireless telephone, a radio phone hooked up to the White House switchboard, cryptographic machines for deciphering messages and an imposing array of heavy batteries.

The Association of American Railroads charged the White House one dollar for its efforts.

The President, driven up the River Road to Crum Elbow in May 1944, glanced without expression at the huge and solemn trees, the sparkling stream which tumbled over smooth round stones—noisily too—down the back hill of the estate, and at last, on the final rise, he saw the flat whiteness of the building which enjoyed two wings, a majestic columned entrance facing the Hudson, and another on the opposite side. The elms and oaks, and the flowering shrubs too, were somewhat formal if they flourished close to the "Big House," but similar trees and shrubs halfway down the cascade seemed to be as healthy, even though some of the thorny shrubs were close enough to dig fingernails into each other.

Mr. Roosevelt was a sick man and looked like a sick man. He did not communicate his thoughts about the place to anyone on this day. He sat in the back right-hand seat of the limousine, the Secret Service man on that side moving forward so that the President could look out. Once he had loved this estate as though it were the only great house with character. Somewhere, sometime, he had divorced himself from Crum Elbow and the decree was absolute. Lamely, he had said to Anna: "When I leave Washington, there are lots of people who are going to drive down Route Nine and want to stop in and say hello. I propose to work with Daisy [Mrs. Margaret Suckley] on the library items, and this will take all of our time. Remember, I won't have Secret Service men

to keep people away, Sis. Everything is going to come
out of my pocket; I just can't afford it."

It is always dangerous to speculate, but the reader
cannot be stopped from asking himself why privacy would
cost so much. No one will know the true reason, except
that Elliott and Anna were aware that the President
proposed to live in his hilltop cottage without Eleanor;
his happy memories of boyhood ponies and sleigh rides
with his father seemed overpowered by recollections of
the autocratic Sara. He told friends, half amusedly, half
bitterly, about the cold day in his second term when he
drove up to the front porch and his mother, wearing a
gray shawl and a frown, emerged shouting, "Franklin,
you'll catch your death of cold. Come in this instant and
get a sweater." It was funny, and yet it did not seem
to occur to her that he could not move his legs to obey
her command. He sent a Secret Service man in for a
floppy coat, though he was about to be carried up the
porch to his wheelchair.

Sara was dead, lying up the road in Saint James Episcopal churchyard, but the austere attitude of the old lady
permeated the house. The Roosevelt children and grandchildren never touched a gold clock on a mantelpiece,
flowered shirring on a chair, a white china cat in front
of a fireplace without thinking that they were Sara's. It
was a beautiful house, exquisitely furnished, but Mr.
Roosevelt, only child, intended to gift-wrap it and give
it to the National Parks Department. As long as he
remained in office, however, he would return to this place.
Eleanor, who appeared at times to be reaching modestly
to forgive her husband, would ask in plaintive notes:
"Why don't you come to H.P. with me on Thursdays
and return to Washington Monday nights? E."

At one time Mr. Roosevelt answered his wife's notes
with dispatch. Now, gray of cheek, reading behind palsied
hands, he would turn them over and say to a secretary,
"Put this in your file." Thirty-one years had elapsed since
they had clung to each other. Whether Eleanor, as the
wronged person, was ready to spend the sunset years
hand in hand she confided to no one but Franklin. If

she made the shy approach, she was rebuffed. It seems strange that, in Washington, the gossip capital of the world, Eleanor never heard a whisper that her husband's heart was still where it was in 1913, in the snowy palms of Lucy's hands.

The majesty of Crum Elbow was spurned by both Eleanor and Franklin. None of the children could afford to keep it painted, furnished and landscaped, and none expressed a fondness for the estate. There was a richness of huge and solid furniture, valuable wall paintings, not counting the framed photographs and political cartoons which, on a single hallway wall, traced the life of Franklin D. Roosevelt. In back, the sturdy wooden ramp up and down which FDR propelled his wheelchair was scarred for lack of paint; the five steps which he could not negotiate were gleaming. In the tiny snuggery on the ground floor he had a specimen of a brand-new invention—a television set. It had not excited the President. He sat close to the small screen and watched flickering pictures come up the Hudson River Valley from New York to reset themselves into figures, faces and words he could understand, but the set was mostly used by the Secret Service detail, which took turns sneaking into the snuggery. Mr. Roosevelt was impressed the first few times he saw images, but, as he could not think of a wartime use for it, television was held to be an expensive toy.

When he retired, the President pulled himself and his chair up the dumbwaiter shaft to the second floor, and rolled down a narrow white hall, barely wide enough for his wheels. Halfway down, on his left, was the room in which he grew up. He seldom passed it without glancing in; he was never known to stop. Sara kept it as it was in 1887. The thin red and blue figured carpet did not cover all of the nine-by-twelve floor. The frail brass-plated bedstead retained its dull gold blur. The mattress was thin enough for an ascetic. The night table, one-foot lamp and Bible were intact, but someone had removed the wash basin and soap. An eight-by-ten copy of Stuart's Washington was still on the wall, and a small enclosed bulb, hanging on a wire, brightened a chest of drawers and a large mirror.

There was a window between the chest of drawers and a small homework desk, and it may be that the aging President remembered the window best of all. This was his private personal view from the front of the Big House. Here, a boy could crouch behind a lowered green shade and watch horses and carriages come small and distant through the front gates, becoming larger and more familiar as they approached the gray gravel turn of the front portico. He could spy on his elders as he could spy on the gray squirrels which scurried halfway up the eaves of the porch to pause before his private and personal view. Here, he could watch the seasons change in majestic mockery of the calendar; he could pity himself if he awakened to find rain, or he could feel that chest surge of boyish enthusiasm when he crept out of bed to find six inches of snow on the ground, the fat flakes still falling in slow pirouette. Sometimes, when lightning flashed frighteningly blue in the summer, he could block it by pulling the shade down all the way, but he could not block out the sound of thunder, which seemed to roll deep from the throat of the great river with threats from hill to hill. As a growing boy, that room had been his prison and his private world. When he departed for Groton and Harvard, Franklin D. Roosevelt left that dowdy-looking room forever. The room could not follow him, but his mother could.

The Secret Service men who, in his illness, helped propel his chair down the tight upper hall noticed that he never gave the room more than a glance as he rolled on to the far end of the south wing. There, the President of the United States had a larger, more imposingly furnished bedroom, though hardly rich. The carved walnut bed dominated with its two snowy pillows and white-fringed bedspread. At the foot a couch with a flowered cover and raised pillow almost matched the elevation of the head of the bed which enabled the sleeper to breathe more easily. On the walls were a few personal photos, facing the old fireplace which had taken the chill from the room before there was central heating.

On a cheap marble-topped washstand stood the local telephone. Above it, hanging from the wall, was the direct line to the White House. The French windows opened onto a small private porch overlooking the woods behind the house and the Hudson below. The clothes closet appeared to be an afterthought, built out from the wall. Adjoining it was the bathroom, where the lavatory, the tub and the medicine chest were at a precise height to be used by a man in a wheelchair.

The entire house was imposing; it had character. Except for the long shelves of books in the living room and the several fireplaces, the precise placing of chairs, table-cloths and bric-a-brac imposed a cold, unyielding atmosphere, as though it was like this a hundred years ago, and not counting casual breakage, would be like this a hundred years from now. When Sara Delano Roosevelt died, she mentioned in her will that she would like to have her bedroom furniture moved back to her original room and placed exactly where it had once been, because here a President of the United States had been born. FDR, at the same time, decreed that his boyhood bedroom should be reserved for the use of "the oldest son at home." In the manner of his mother the President was given to minority-of-one opinions. When he designed "Hilltop Cottage" as a post-presidential refuge, he insisted that there be no closets, no telephone and but one bathroom. "The younger generation is just washing itself away," he told Judge Samuel Rosenman. The cottage was the first house he considered his own. He never spent a night in it.

Increasingly, he spent more time in the upstairs bedroom at Crum Elbow and less on the grounds. On a rare soft day he would ask to be driven to his mother's rose garden on the north side of the house. It was a formal place of formal flowers with an acre of carefully trimmed lawn between the tall hemlock hedges. Once, he tried to drive down the back road to see the Christmas trees he had ordered to be sold at Christmastime. He felt productive about this matter, and he kept a little book of accounts numbering the trees, rate of growth, the total sales to be reported in his income tax return. This time, when he drove down with friends, the thick growth of other trees prevented him from seeing the young firs, and he would not permit himself to be carried to them. It was an unusual moment, because none present remembered the President ever calling attention to his paralyzed legs. "Now you people go in there and take a look. I can't," he said, and pointed to the legs.

The Secret Service men did not know whether to be happy or saddened that FDR no longer awakened all hands at 3:00 A.M. to get aboard a boat and go to a little island off Red Hook, there to await the first gray- and canary-colored bands in the east and be ordered to identify birds. Mr. Roosevelt sat in his wheelchair like a lonely teacher—pad and pencil on his lap—and, as each bird warbled or cheeped, asked the Secret Service men to identify it. Mr. Roosevelt, who seemed able to name all the sounds with authenticity, kept a score. When birds were soundless, the men were ordered to flush the woods. Birds would be identified by sound or sight. Reilly once asked a Dr. Brown of the New York State Forestry Service if Roosevelt really knew birds. "I ask," he said, "off the record." Dr. Brown said that the President indeed knew about as much about winged creatures as any non-professional ornithologist in the area.

Reilly was so impressed that later, when he saw FDR get into a pleasant academic argument about the precise identity of an amber-jack fish he caught at Hobcaw, Reilly bet that the President was right, even though his adversary was Dr. Waldo Schmitt of the Smithsonian Institution. The fish was sent to the Smithsonian. Mike Reilly won his bet.

There would be no more of those days. Sometimes, after lunch, the President went off to his office on the main floor of the house, there to sign decrees, promotions, presidential mail and special messages. On May 20 he announced that he was sending Vice President Henry Wallace to China, along with John Carter Vincent, chief of the State Department's Division of Chinese Affairs; Owen Lattimore, deputy director of the Office of War Information; and John Hazard, chief liaison officer of the Division for Soviet Supply in the Foreign Economic Administration. Roosevelt said:

Eastern Asia will play an important part in the future history of the world. Forces are being unleashed there which are of utmost importance to our future peace and prosperity. The Vice President, because of his present position as well as his training in economics and agriculture, is unusually well fitted to bring both to me and to the people of the United States a most valuable firsthand report.

The statement was a bland pacifier. The President, who did not confide his reasons for sending Wallace to China, may have availed himself of an opportunity to resolve a couple of dilemmas at one stroke. Lieutenant General Joseph Stilwell, Chief of Staff to Chiang Kaishek, privately advised that his problems with the Generalissimo had become insuperable. Chiang, who was leading the forces of Chinese democracy against Japan, was diverting the strength of his armies to fight Chinese Communists.

FDR saw China as the world's fifth first-class power. He expected Chiang to dominate militaristic Japan when the war was over. Henry Wallace was to confer with the Generalissimo to straighten out the goals, the primary objectives, and to maintain strong dependent ties to the United States. He was also expected to reason with Vinegar Joe Stilwell so that the American general could work with the Chinese or to recommend that Stilwell be relieved of command.

Wallace was also to estimate China's capacity for feeding its 600 million people after the war without asking for large credits from the United States. An additional reason for the assignment may have been that the Democratic party would hold its national convention in July and the Vice President had become a controversial figure. Some of the old-line Democratic bosses referred to Wallace as a "leftist," a "Communist fellow-traveler," and perhaps worst of all, a "dreamer." The journalists who covered Hyde Park hardly noticed the last sentence of the President's publicity release, which said: "He left today, and will report to me upon his return, which is expected about the middle of July." There could be a subtle reason for keeping a Vice President in China until after the convention.

It was on this trip home that the President displayed increasing faith and confidence in William Hassett, his press secretary away from the White House. Hassett was a spare New England Catholic, a sentimentalist ashamed of sentimentality. Although he was friendly and had a sense of humor, Hassett was in permanent awe of the office of President of the United States. FDR's personal liking displayed itself in his relaxed attitude with Hassett. In the morning, when he was on the bathtub board, he would summon his secretary and say, "Have a seat on the can, Bill, and remember your pants are up." Sometimes, when the secretariat was housed at the Vanderbilt estate, the President would drive up early unannounced and call loudly for "Cardinal Richelieu" (Bill Hassett) and the "Empress Josephine" (the stately and jolly Louise Hachmeister) and the "Duchess" (Grace Tully).

It was Hassett who insisted that the signature of a President of the United States was too important to be blotted, and, as FDR scrawled his name to letters and documents, Bill placed them on the rug face up around the desk and Mr. Roosevelt coined the phrase "Hassett's laundry." The secretary, who was too taciturn to be easily won as a friend, found himself becoming more and more devoted to the President. He kept a diary and his feelings of adulation began to creep into the daily entries. He worried more about FDR's health than most and was quick to jot that his boss looked "gray and drawn" or "ebullient and bright-eyed, almost his old self." He penned his resentment of politicians who took too much time with the President and, although he understood the relationship between the boss and Lucy Rutherfurd, he drove the subject from his diary and his mind except for one instance—and this he blocked out with ink.

Hassett was most impressed by the broad range of subjects which FDR could discuss with some authority. Although he did not fancy himself a tactical military expert, Roosevelt could discuss the moves and counter-moves of armies; the clamor for a unified military command distressed him because he believed that it could not be achieved in mid-war. "General Marshall knows nothing about ships," FDR said, "and Admiral King doesn't understand the Army." From there, he could turn his attention slyly to Grace Tully and announce, with solemn judgment, that he had it on good authority that the Duchess had been caught "snitching a piece of ham" on Friday. Sometimes he referred to the notes that Mrs. Roosevelt had left with information she had gleaned in her travels: not enough men in MacArthur's forces; destroyers sent to the Pacific without sound detectors or radar; the effect of strikes at home on munitions output. Almost all of these were denounced as "scuttlebutt" by the President.

Benignly and yet pontifically, the President would defend the gossip columnist Walter Winchell and indict, item by item, those newspapers which opposed him and which, FDR maintained, published military secrets. Sometimes he would wonder aloud why the Justice Department didn't prosecute those newspapers. He was convinced that he had the right enemies—the rich, the greedy and grasping—and the right friends, those patriots who placed country and, incidentally, Franklin Roosevelt above personal interests. With ease he could slip from that subject to the correctness of placing dental floss or toothpicks on a table for dining or what women proposed to do about girdles in a war in which rubber was at a premium.

The President was, as always, cheerful, optimistic, and confident. Those who spent the most time with him are convinced that this euphoria was not forced, and his mental and emotional attitude remained unchanged from "the old days." And yet, there is evidence that, like a stolid Dutch sage, he could envision his own death without flinching. In mid-war he wrote out his will, handed it to his former law partner, Basil O'Connor, and said, "Stick this in your safe." It was not a notable document, but the President expressed a wish not to be embalmed, not to be seen in an open casket, and a wish to be buried with Eleanor in his mother's rose garden. As an amateur architect, he described the color and dimensions of the headstone to mark the graves and the legends which should be engraved. It was done quickly. He forgot it and dictated another set of burial instructions. A third was written by hand and addressed to his son James. In matters of memorials, his attention was on the fieldstone Franklin D. Roosevelt Library. He had appointed Judge Samuel Rosenman, Harry Hopkins and Grace Tully as library administrators, to supervise what documents should be made available to the public, and which should be sealed for reasons of security or to forestall embarrassment to living persons. It did not occur to him that he was the first living President to design his own memorial.

He could not understand why the work did not go ahead with more speed; the cornerstone of the library had been laid five years earlier. Nor would he acknowledge that 16,000 books, 34,000 pamphlets, 15,000 photographs, 275,000 feet of motion picture film, 300 radio recordings, 14,000 filing cabinets, 12,000 museum pieces and 4,500 rolls of microfilm represented a formidable task which would require many government researchers a number of years to read, to listen to, to view in order to catalog the treasures and cross-file the subjects. He urged all hands to full speed ahead because he yearned to see the library as the treasure of twentieth-century history he knew it would be. He did little work in the library himself, pausing to visit, to study with pleasure the work which had been accomplished, returning to the Big House to spend his spare time working on his stamp collection. He seemed pleased that the aisles were wide enough for the spinning wheels of his chair.

Now and then he made suggestions about the hanging of photographs.

The librarians dared not tell the President that most of the material intended for display had to be sent to the cellar to remain piled in annotated boxes. The library's size was suited to the display of only about 10 percent of what Roosevelt had; when he learned that his across-the-river friend, Henry Morgenthau, Jr., kept a diary, FDR asked that it be sent to Hyde Park. It amounted to 840 volumes of personal and opinionated recollections. FDR insisted that everything he had saved (and he saved everything) be included, not excluding a model of the U.S.S. *Constitution* which he had purchased and rerigged himself and one of the bullets aimed at him in Miami, in 1932, recovered from the body of Mayor Anton Cermak of Chicago.

The aura of optimism still surrounded Roosevelt when he returned to the White House on May 24. He scheduled two open press conferences in his office—the 951st and 952nd. The difference between these and the wire service press conference at Hobcaw was the semantic sword play of the big ones that FDR so enjoyed. His ambition at the White House interviews was to place his impending United Nations in a desirable light to the people of the United States while at the same time dissociating it from Woodrow Wilson's abortive League of Nations.

However, while Roosevelt sat astride his prerogative as President to get in the first word, the press waited patiently to stake a claim to the last.

FDR [studying the standing group around his desk, spilling back toward the fireplace]: Everybody in? I have a number of things this morning. It has been published that we have called a meeting early in July on the monetary subject. I thought I would read you just a summary of the form of the invitation that went to the other United Nations and associated nations [tilting head back to read from sheet of paper]:

"The publication of the joint statement of the monetary experts, recommending the establishment of the international monetary fund, has been received with great gratification here as marking an important step toward postwar international economic cooperation. Undoubtedly, your people have been equally pleased by this evidence of the common desire to cooperate in meeting the economic problems of the postwar world. Therefore, I am proposing to call a conference of these nations, for the purpose of formulating definite proposals for the international monetary fund, and possibly a bank for reconstruction and development.

"It would be understood, of course, that the delegates would not be required to hold plenipotentiary powers, and the proposals formulated at the conference would be referred to the respective governments and authorities for their acceptance or rejection."

FDR: I thought I would put that in before certain agencies of information could say that I was doing this without consulting the Congress. . . . You have got the names of all the countries that have been asked to send delegates. The conference will be held at Bretton Woods, New Hampshire. . . .

Roosevelt was a practical politician and an involuntary cynic. His United Nations notion, expressed at Casablanca and at Teheran, received no applause from Great Britain and a bearish frown from the Soviet Union. FDR was moving back to his original notion of inviting the strong and the weak to have an equal vote in a sort of lower house, or assembly; the big five—Russia, Great Britain, China, France and the United States—would be a senate, with veto power over the lower house.

The President's desire to succeed where his idol, Wilson, had failed, was the thing which prompted him to ask Secretary of State Cordell Hull to draw up an international bank first, bait for potentially victorious but impoverished nations. The Russians were not prepared to accept the Bretton Woods invitation until mid-July. Axis nations and their satellites, of course, were not invited.

Q: Mr. President, you have so far received far more than enough delegates to the Democratic Convention to assure—— [President began to laugh heartily]—to assure your renomination, except for one fact, unless you refuse it. Now, not asking what your decision is, but have you reached a decision [general laughter] whether to accept or refuse?

FDR: *You know, this is good. We get a different form of it just about once a week. This is a new one. [Removes glasses to wipe eyes.] It's a brand-new one. It's awfully interesting.*

Q: What's the answer, sir?

FDR: *I am making a list of the varieties of questions.*

Q: Are you going to answer them all at once, Mr. President? [Gale of laughter sweeps the room.]

FDR: *I think I will give you a real good one. Time will tell. [More hilarity.]*

Q: Only fifty-five days of time left.

FDR [*still laughing*]: *You remember in 1940 there was some lady—at least she said she was a lady—who used to say, just after the convention, "Ninety-three days more of Roosevelt." And the second time, she put the word "only" in. "Only nine-two days more of Roosevelt." And she went right on down through [President laughs so heartily, clapping his hands, that his words are lost]. And I bet that you have all forgotten her name. . . .*

Q: Mr. President, with the time of invasion apparently drawing nearer, is there anything you can tell us in generalized terms about our preparations and the chances for the success of the operation?

FDR: *Well, that's in the first paper that I hold in my hand, thinking that somebody would use the word "invasion." There was an editorial in a certain local paper, suggesting that the word "invasion" is not quite adequate for the tremendous thing that is happening in Europe. And suggesting that instead of the word "invasion" we should call it "liberation." And I most heartily support that idea. It isn't a war of invasion—you want to get the word "invasion" out of people's heads all over the world—it's a war of liberation. This action in Europe, which is going to come sometimes this* *summer,* is intended to be a liberation and not an invasion, and I would say that all of our plans are built on that basis.*

Of course, we have got a great deal further ahead in the discussion of things at the present time than we had at what we might guess at having been a similar period in the last war. . . . We can't do them all at the same time, but we are taking up the major problems of the postwar world and talking them over, and in many cases making specific recommendations or specific determinations of what all the United Nations are going to do to seek peace and stability. In other words, we are making far greater progress in this war than we did in the last war. . . .

The President, given a proper question, could talk on and on, citing and reciting examples which would simplify his point of view. Sometimes he would interpolate: "I was reading a book the other day which coincides with my personal thinking"—even when he had not read a book in months. On some occasions there was such a book, and he may have read it years before; sometimes there was no such book, except as it existed at the moment in his mind.

The main body of the White House press corps admired FDR. In turn, the President was certain that he could bandy words with the gentlemen and ladies of the press without becoming acerbic. Sometimes he snapped, "No comment." At other times it was uttered by a press secretary, standing behind the President's chair. Like most Presidents, he was disenchanted with the Fourth Estate because he felt that the rich and powerful chain publishers—Hearst, McCormick, Gannett, Scripps-Howard—were opposed to him, while their hirelings were friends. It is an irony of journalism that most Democratic Presidents liked the press corps, but were disliked by the publishers; in the case of Republican Presidents, the opposite was true. In but one case was Roosevelt known to be crude and insolent to a reporter. John O'Donnell, Washington columnist for the New York *Daily News,*

---

* D Day was only days away.

candidly and bluntly opposed FDR. What he wrote irritated FDR to the point where he awarded O'Donnell a German Iron Cross.

Four days later another give-and-take press conference occurred in the President's office. A few of the interrogators had orders from their editors to return to the matter of the United Nations. Some believed sincerely that this global fetus was the discarded League of Nations with a new father. A world organization of nations, they feared, could not keep the peace for long unless each of the members sacrificed some of its sovereignty. Even the proponents of the United Nations were unwilling to see this nation abridge its prerogatives in foreign or domestic affairs. After World War I Senator Henry Cabot Lodge of Massachusetts aborted American participation in the League of Nations on the grounds that the United States would no longer be permitted to make its own decisions or to seek its own high destiny. Woodrow Wilson's ghosts had returned.

Mr. Roosevelt might have avoided the trap, but he chose instead to face it and talk it to death.

Today [he said] we are a little older; we have gone through some pretty rough times together. And perhaps we are not saying that we can devise a method of ending all wars for all time. Some of us—I don't think I include myself in this—are a little more cynical than we were then. Some of us—and I don't think I include myself—are a little more foolish-minded domestically than we were when we were twenty-five years younger.

And so we have an objective today, and that is to join with the other nations of the world not in such a way that some other nation could decide whether we were to build a dam on Conestoga Creek, but for general world peace in setting up some machinery for talking things over with other nations, without taking away the independence of the United States in any shape, manner or form, or destroying—what's the other word?—the integrity of the United States in any shape, manner or form; with the objective of working so closely that if some nation in the world started to run amok, or some combination of nations started to run amok, and seeks to grab territory or invade its neighbors, that there would be a unanimity of opinion that the time to stop them was before they got started; that is, all the other nations who weren't in it with them.

And, in a sense, the League of Nations had that very, very great purpose. It got dreadfully involved in American politics, instead of being regarded as a nonpartisan subject. And that is why, in this particular year, the Secretary of State and I have been working very closely together, and we have been working in conferences wtih the duly constituted constitutional machinery of government, which in this case happens to be the senators on the Foreign Relations Committee— four from each party. And, so far, the conversations with them have been conducted on the very high level of nonpartisanship. So far, they have worked very well.

The President wandered on, trying to anticipate all the arguments the opponents of the United Nations might marshal, but they were coming to mind loosely and disjointedly. He kept the floor as the correspondents copied his words, and he kept restating his case.

But let me emphasize that both the Secretary of State and I —and, I think, the senators—have been trying to look at this thing in a spirit of nonpartisanship, thinking about a hundred and thirty-five million Americans, and thinking about a great many small nations, as well as the bigger nations, who at this stage are directly involved. After we get through talking—what I call the first draft—we will talk, of course, with all the other nations of the world. . . .

Q: Mr. President, do you want this foreign policy matter eliminated from the 1944 campaign?

FDR: Well, you see, the trouble is that I do not control all the newspapers of the United States, so it doesn't make much difference whether I like it or not [laughter]. Is that a fair answer?

Q: I had in mind the Republican Party, Mr. President. [More laughter.]

FDR: Well, I see you are getting into politics again, and

the whole basis of this thing, so far, has been going along on an amazingly effective nonpartisan basis, and I don't want you or anybody else to go and gum the works intentionally. . . .

Someone in the back of the press group bailed the President out of the situation by asking a question about the Senate Banking and Currency Committee advocating a rise in price of commodities, such as cotton and textiles, and that such advocacy was strongly opposed by Roosevelt's Office of Price Administration. Once more FDR enunciated a long, wandering speech, replete with amusing anecdotes, about prices.

Well [he said], I grow lumber. I am getting twenty-nine dollars a thousand board feet—which is pretty good. Of course, thinking personally and selfishly, I would like to see lumber selling at seventy-nine dollars a thousand. Well, we have all got that streak in us. If you pick out cotton, you will have somebody else on your neck, and then you will get inflation. But if you do it for one—I suppose one out of ten —you ought to do it for almost anything that grows. . . . Which reminds me of a friend of mine, a foreman of one of the substantial trades, who came in last January, and said to me, "I have an awful time when I go home." He says, "My old lady is ready to hit me over the head with a dishpan."

I said, "What's the trouble?" "The cost of living." "Well," I said, "what, for instance?" "Well, last night I went home and the old lady said, 'What's this? I went out to buy some asparagus, and do you know what I got? I got five sticks. There it is. A dollar and a quarter. It's an outrage.'" Well, I looked at him and I said, "Since when have you been buying asparagus in January—fresh asparagus?" "Oh," he said, "I never thought of that." "Well," I said, "tell that to the old lady, with my compliments."

Q: Mr. President, is that the same foreman you mentioned in a press conference some time ago who bought the strawberries in winter? [Much laughter.]

FDR: It happened to a different one, but it's all right. Still makes a true story.

The White House press corps enjoyed the conference as much as the President. Their position was to try to stop him from diverting them with long anecdotes while pressing for current information. FDR enjoyed the respect his office engendered, while at the same time posing as "one of the boys." He often juggled several questions without responding directly to any. If he pleased, he tossed an explosive ball back to them, making headlines. Sometimes—but rarely—he became visibly angered. He knew the gentlemen and the ladies of the press, and he was conscious of the truth that those who worked for publishers opposed to the Roosevelt Administration tried hard by pitching curves to get enough material to make him look bad. The President admired the exceptions—George Durno of International News Service, Tom Reynolds of United Press—who telegraphed stories favorable to him at times, even though their publishers were enemies of the Administration.

Roosevelt found a paradox in Walter Trohan of the Chicago *Tribune*. "You know, Mike," he said to Reilly, "Trohan hates my guts; he comes to every press conference and politely spits in my eye. And yet, on trips, I enjoy chatting with him, and I must say he doesn't seem to mind when I spit back in his eyes." The President also drew enjoyment from the presence of Mae Craig, who represented a group of small Maine newspapers with the single-minded tenacity of a schoolteacher fuming at a stubborn and sly boy. At times Mr. Roosevelt's jolly attitude drew him close to revealing matters of state which were not ready for public scrutiny. In the early administrations, Marvin McIntyre and Pa Watson stood behind his chair and stopped him in mid-sentence. Often it was the belligerent Steve Early. By 1944 these had been replaced by Bill Hassett and Jonathan Daniels.

Secret Service men filtered the members of the press into the Oval Office, then stationed themselves in the group of journalists and outside the doors. As the conference droned on, and the questions and responses became more flippant and superficial, FDR would turn his eyes to the senior reporter present, who would sing out, "Thank you, Mr. President." The group hurried through the doors in awkward haste, especially those who worked for afternoon newspapers. They knew that they could make the final editions with their stories.

The news which was withheld from the press at the conference of May 30, 1944, was considerable. The massive ground, sea and air forces under the command of General Dwight D. Eisenhower crouched in silence all over the British Isles, waiting for the assault on the Normandy peninsula which would begin in seven days. Aircraft production had reached a new high—8,700 bombers, fighters, and spare parts kits in May. Brigadier General John Deane had been sent to Moscow to coordinate Russian attacks in the east with British-American attacks in the west. Deane had the unpleasant task of facing Marshal Antonov twice to tell him of D-Day postponements. The Soviets were suspicious that the Allied landings would be weak; Roosevelt feared that the Russian assault would be halfhearted, enabling Hitler to transfer German divisions from the eastern front to the west.

The President had also decided to run for a fourth term. Pa Watson was aware of it. Harry Hopkins was told about it—and applauded weakly from his sickbed. Ed Flynn was aware that his friend, his idol, required assistance to arrange a spontaneous draft at the upcoming Chicago convention, but Mr. Flynn feared that Roosevelt was dying. Mrs. Roosevelt and her secretary, Malvina Thompson, were not told. Dorothy Brady and Grace Tully were aware of the decision, but Vice President Henry Wallace was not. The party bosses made it clear that they would work loyally for an unprecedented fourth term if FDR was willing to dump Wallace. Roosevelt was not willing. Having enjoyed an unprecedented third term, he was certain that he was above party and represented the only chance of victory against a rising tide of Republicanism. Therefore, he should be permitted to choose a Vice President. Indeed, he confided to friends in Hyde Park and at the White House, he thought that

Wallace had done "a fine job" as Vice President and deserved another chance.

Party bosses such as Ed Crump, Ed Kelly, Tom Pendergast, Frank Hague and Flynn studied the accelerated decline in the President's health and felt that this time—this particular time—the Vice-Presidency might be the most important elective office in the nation; certainly too important for a philosophical dreamer such as Wallace. As the month of May expired in unseasonably hot weather, the bosses began to goad certain senators and members of the Cabinet to see Roosevelt and talk to him about the Vice-Presidency. For his part, the President had already filed Ben Cohen's analytical dissertation on why Roosevelt should *not* run for another term under the letter *C* in Grace Tully's file. There was a great deal that was not told to the press that day.

June 1944

THE FIRST WEEK OF JUNE WAS COOL. BLOSSOMS SHIVERED in silence, and silence pervaded some of the high places in Washington. The chill of weather held an expectancy. Signals between London and Washington were few in number. And yet the people of the United States acted out a noisy charade that no war was in progress. They made hit songs of "On a Slow Boat to China," "Mairzy Doats," "Green Eyes" and "A Nightingale Sang in Berkeley Square." The people dropped five billion nickels into four hundred thousand jukeboxes. Everyone who desired to work was working and earning better wages.

Night clubs flourished behind blackout curtains. Big league baseball continued even though the best talent was off beyond the horizon in military uniform. Senator Harry Truman, chairman of a hard-working committee to investigate war contracts and spending, agreed not to investigate a huge secret plant in Tennessee when the Secretary of War stated in confidence that it was the biggest, most secret project in the history of man. The people had ration books and stamps for meats, scarce edibles, gasoline and oil, for retreaded rubber tires, but they had more money to spend than before, and they found ways of buying and investing.

The expense account came into its own as a flourishing industry. Ben Hogan fired a 66 in a Chicago golf tournament. A two-year-old filly named Expression won $38,-000 in a stakes race at Arlington; William Tilden practiced for the National Singles tennis title at Forest Hills; Chester Bowles of the Office of Price Administration said that price markups of 13 percent from producer to consumer would be permitted—but no more than that. General Motors was selling at 128½ on the New York Stock Exchange.

In the bedlam of good cheer, few noticed the silence in high places. There were no fireside chats; the most exciting publicity release concerned federal aid to education. The German armies paused, in their general retreat, east of Warsaw. The Russians mounted no offensive. In the Pacific General MacArthur's troops were bypassing the Japanese on New Guinea and heading toward the Philippines; Admiral Chester Nimitz was moving toward the Japanese bastion of Saipan. The Eighth Air Force left Great Britain at dawn for a new assignment, to bomb French rail lines and communications centers.

And yet these communiqués exuded an aura of quietude, as though the contenders had paused for breath. On Sunday, June 4, General Charles de Gaulle, imperious and intractable leader of the Free French, demanded to see Prime Minister Winston Churchill. After several messages to and from the British Foreign Office, the General was sent to a small town on the southeast coast of Britain where Churchill sat in a private train. With him were General Ismay and Foreign Secretary Anthony Eden. De Gaulle wished to discuss the imminent crossing of the Channel and the liberation of France and the defeat of Germany. Churchill said that he could not oblige, that President Roosevelt had "forbidden" unilateral talks between France and Britain. Besides, the Prime Minister said, de Gaulle had signified several times that he did not wish to discuss the fate of France with Britain alone.

Loftily, de Gaulle demanded to know how the British had arranged for him to lead the forces of liberation. Churchill said that no arrangements had been made; it was too early and too dangerous. De Gaulle stated that he fully expected to be the first of the leaders of the free world to set foot in France. Irritated, Churchill found that there was a bathtub on the train and sunk his pink body into its laving water. There was but one telephone, and Eden had it to his ear for hours. It was a cheap manner in which to subvert the churlish demeanor of de Gaulle, as Sir Alexander Cadogan pointed out, but the Prime Minister was "in one" and Eden was "on the other."

The French General was aware that D Day was imminent, but he had a personality flaw which alienated those who might have been cordial. FDR could barely endure de Gaulle's presence, and referred to him as a self-appointed Joan of Arc. Churchill, who suffered de Gaulle in England throughout most of the war, lost his temper in the presence of the General on several occasions. General Eisenhower did not want de Gaulle at his headquarters at any time; he found it impossible to confide even the most minuscule military plans without sustaining the cold disagreement of the General, who was not above "correcting" the Commander in Chief in the bluntest terms. Although the Free French had no military strength, except as the United States and Great Britain succored their tattered brigades with uniforms, tanks, artillery, ammunition and air cover, Charles de Gaulle felt that the Cross of Lorraine should lead the liberation of Paris and that his government—unrecognized and nonexistent—was the proper instrument to guide, counsel and admonish all friendly troops on French soil.

The cross-Channel invasion was scheduled for dawn, June 6, 1944. In the history of man, no force matched the assemblage of ships and men waiting in chaotic order along the south coast of England. The British Home Fleet, from battleships down to tugboats; the American Atlantic Fleet, ranging from aging men of war to LSTs which swallowed tanks, armored cars and men, swung silently on the tide. Ageless British villages, adorned with leafy trees and small gardens, were hosts to almost 2,000,000 men lounging in the fields, their faces streaked with charcoal. In airports behind the coast, swift medium bombers, brand-new P-51s, and British Hurricanes and Spitfires crouched in revetments facing the exposed gliders which would be towed by C-47s to the French coast. Hundreds of small-gauge locomotives and thousands of railroad cars, shiny in new paint, waited to be carried to the far shore. Hundreds of millions of gallons of fuel were stored below ground, above ground, in camouflaged tanks, on flatcars. At dawn on Monday, June 5, the forces farthest removed from France slipped anchor and turned south from Belfast, the Orkneys, Scapa Flow and Liverpool.

In the White House, President Roosevelt, as grave of face as anyone had ever seen him, called Mrs. Roosevelt. Now, he said, he could tell her: D Day would be dawn tomorrow. She said she wished, in a way, that he had not told her because she knew she wouldn't sleep. He waved a slip of paper. He had been devising a prayer for all the gallant and frightened men on whom the fate of the free world rested. When the President noticed the downcast expressions of Eleanor and Miss Tully, he began to prattle hopefully. He said he didn't know quite what to do when Hitler was ready to surrender: "I may go to England; Winnie wants me to go." Then he said he would decline; he would rather visit American troops in Honolulu and the Aleutians, because "they are still fighting a difficult war." The President, as well as Eisenhower and all others privy to the operation called

Overlord, knew that it could fail. If it did, triumph would fall into the hands of the Russians. Their massed armies were already on Polish soil moving toward Germany. The success of Overlord would force Adolf Hitler to fight separate battles to the east and west—a division of strength, a final checkmate. Eisenhower told General Marshall that he would know, with some certainty, by June 8 whether the operation would succeed. If he could move his men inland off the beaches, reinforcements and supplies would follow. If the Germans stopped him on the sands at Normandy, it would not mean defeat, but it would set the clock of victory back at least two years. It would require that much time to reinforce General Alexander's armies in Italy and regroup for an invasion of southern France.

Radio broadcasts from Germany indicated that the Reich knew that the invasion was imminent but could not decide whether the initial landings would be a feint to draw German reserves to the west, or whether Eisenhower would be committing all his strength to one landing. Hitler, who was in East Prussia, assured Generals Keitel and Jodl that the impending landings would be designed to draw General Rundstedt's forces to the western edge of France, while the main invasion forces would land between Dieppe and Dunkirk.

British monitors were surprised to hear a German radio broadcast of a newspaper article published in the *Neueste Nachrichten* in Munich, which proclaimed that the Third Reich would have to begin to lay plans for a third world war, this one to occur at sea. Plans for the invasion of Great Britain failed, the article stated, because German seapower was less than a third of British-American power. Germany "will have no chance until such time as the Third Reich and the new Europe create superior sea power." The words were defeatist, but no more mysterious than those of Captain Ludwig Sertorius on Radio Berlin: "They are coming and it is good that they should come."

The President, who could will himself to sleep, failed on the night of June 5. He kept a pad of yellow foolscap at his bedside, and he was on and off the phone to the Pentagon until 4:00 A.M. At that time he asked chief operator Louise Hachmeister to please ask "the staff" to report to the White House at once. Harry Hopkins, who had returned after six months in a hospital, was awakened by a ringing phone. FDR knew that, at midnight in Washington, it was 5:00 A.M. in Normandy, France, and the first waves of Americans, with wire cutters and demolition charges, were wading through the surf. The White House was still gray in the pre-dawn coolness when the first dead and wounded were being lifted off the French beaches, and the first yellow bulldozers began to carve temporary landing strips inland.

By noon Washington time Prime Minister Churchill assured Roosevelt that the initial landings had been highly successful. The President called a press conference. One hundred eighty-one correspondents waited outside his office door as his assistants, including Jonathan Daniels, filed in to stand behind his chair. "My goodness!" he said. "All smiles. Just look at those two coming in." Daniels said, "You don't look so solemn yourself, Mr. President." FDR: "No. I'm not so solemn, I suppose. . . . All right. Bring in the wolves."

The President commented on the smiles of the reporters. "I think it is all right to use this," he said, "which has not been published yet. It came in a dispatch from Eisenhower on the progress of the operations, as of about twelve o'clock today. The American naval losses were two destroyers and one LST. And the losses incident to the air landing were relatively light—about one percent."

Q: That's the airborne troops, sir?

FDR: Well, air losses as a whole. And of course there are a great deal of reports coming in all the time, and it's being given out over there just as fast as it possibly can. I think the arrangements seem to be going all right. . . .

Q: Mr. President, how do you feel about the progress of the invasion?

FDR: Up to schedule. And, as the Prime Minister said, "That's a mouthful." [Laughter]

Q: Mr. President, how long have you known that this was the date?

FDR: I have known since—since—I am trying to think back—I would say Teheran, which was last December, that the approximate date would be the end of May or the very first few days of June.

Q: I was wondering if you could explain what were the elements entering into the consideration as far back as Teheran that would lead military leaders to be able to choose a date which seems to be quite far ahead.

FDR [archly]: Did you ever cross the English Channel?

Q: Never been across the English Channel.

FDR: You're very lucky.

Q: Tide? Is it a question of—

FDR: Roughness in the English Channel, which has always been considered by passengers one of the greatest trials of life, to have to cross the English Channel. And, of course, they have a record of wind and sea in the English Channel, and one of the greatly desirable and absolutely essential things is to have relatively small-boat weather, as we call it, to get people actually onto the beach. And such weather doesn't begin much before May. . . .

Q: Some reports said that the Germans were taken by surprise tactically.

FDR: I don't know—I don't know—. Perfectly frankly, I have no idea.

Q: They knew about the time and the tide too, didn't they?

FDR: They must have known whether it was raining or not [laughter] . . . The war isn't over by any means. This operation isn't over.

You don't just land on a beach and walk through—if you land successfully without breaking your leg—walk through to Berlin. And the quicker this country understands it the better. Again, a question of learning a little geography.

Q: Mr. President, could you tell us something of your hopes for the future on this great day?

FDR: Well, you know what it is; it's win the war and win it a hundred percent.

Q: One last question, Mr. President. How are you feeling?
FDR: I'm feeling fine! I'm a little sleepy.

In spite of fatigue, the President read his D-Day prayer on radio that night with ringing solemnity:

Our sons, pride of our nation . . . Lead them straight and true. Give strength to their arms, stoutness to their hearts, steadfastness in their faith. They will need Thy blessings. Their road will be long and hard. For the enemy is strong. He may hurl back our forces. Success may not come with rushing speed, but we shall return again and again. . . . Give us faith in Thee; faith in our sons; faith in each other; faith in our united crusade. . . .

There were some men in high places who, ignoring the provisions of the Constitution of the United States, said that there would be no elections in 1944. It is not an accident that most of the rumormongers were members of the Republican party. Politics, a national pastime in democracies, would continue as usual. The Republican party had been out of executive power for twelve years. Some were embittered to the point where they accused the President of staging D Day to coincide with the Republican convention in June, and the Democratic in July. Others counseled that, as the argument against a third term had borne no elective fruit, it would be witless to fight against a fourth. The target, if FDR ran again, should be that the government was in the hands of "tired, quarrelsome old men."

Wendell Willkie wanted to try again. Senator Arthur Vandenberg was willing to be nominated. Governor Thomas E. Dewey of New York and Harold Stassen of Minnesota were prepared to sacrifice themselves as nominees of the GOP. There were others—Bricker, Taft, Lowden, and, surprisingly, General Douglas MacArthur, friend of the President and subordinate to his orders. The General, who was in disagreement with the Joint Chiefs of Staff that the energies of the country should be directed against Germany first and then Japan, wrote a purposefully indiscreet letter to a Nebraska Congressman, who publicized it. The note criticized the New Deal and charged that the Roosevelt Administration had abandoned the Philippines to funnel its resources into the war in Europe.

Publication of the letter caused a furor among Republicans, who regarded MacArthur as an instant candidate for the Presidency; it enlisted the active support of the Chicago *Tribune* and the New York *Daily News,* which found themselves opposed to almost every move FDR made; it brought silence to the White House, which refused comment. MacArthur, either frightened by the publicity or cautiously optimistic, sent a second letter which was intended to clarify the first. In the second missive, the General made it clear that he would not be an active candidate, would not campaign for high office —but if he found himself drafted by the Republican party, he would serve.

And yet, within the rank and file of party workers, there was little enthusiasm. Few wanted a prima donna to lead the party to victory as a hero of the people and hold himself above the job needs of the local wheelhorses. Party politics is greed and aggrandizement and spoils. The GOP had tried field generals before—and would again—but only when it felt that the game would be lost without a medaled hero. Nor did it want Wendell Willkie. The 1940 nominee had tarnished himself with global statements which sounded like grandiloquent echoes of Franklin D. Roosevelt.

Mr. Willkie was certain that he could have the nomination for the asking. He misgauged the delegates. He was despised by congressional Republicans, and Wendell Willkie thought that he could appeal to the people over the heads of the party bosses. A month before the Republican convention he turned what rusty muskets he had left on "party reactionaries and bigots." This cost him the remainder of his support. In Wisconsin, where Willkie felt strongest, he ran fourth on the slate of primary delegates. A corporation president introduced Willkie at a party rally as "America's leading ingrate."

The insolence was insufferable. Willkie ran a stubby hand through his thick hair, grabbed the rostrum and shouted, "I don't know whether you are going to support me or not and I don't give a damn. You're a bunch of political liabilities anyway." Willkie expired politically that night.

MacArthur felt encouraged to write another letter, this to Senator Arthur Vandenberg, reiterating his decision not to campaign for any office but to submit to the will of the people if he were drafted. This time he said that Vandenberg could be MacArthur's wise "mentor" (a faint promise of party loyalty) and that there was a great deal he would like to tell the Senator which present "circumstances prevent."

The President appeared to be unconcerned about the Republican convention and its nominee. However, when he felt a summer breeze of sentiment for Douglas MacArthur, his tactical mind warned him that the General, if nominated, would publicize all the complaining memoranda he had written to the President and the Joint Chiefs of Staff, top secret material which argued that the Pentagon risked the safety of the American West Coast in the early stages of the war, left Hawaii at the mercy of the Japanese if they had had the initiative to land amphibious troops after their merciless attack on the Pacific Fleet; how Japan, if not stopped, would find rubber and oil in Borneo and Java and the Malay Peninsula—in short, Roosevelt's military policies could be made to look weak. Mr. Roosevelt did two things to counteract this: he sent word to MacArthur and to Admiral Nimitz that he would meet them at Honolulu in July to adjudicate their differences; he asked Dorothy Brady to search the presidential files for a stenographic report of a discussion between MacArthur and Admiral Thomas Hart of the Far East squadron a week before the attack on Pearl Harbor. Miss Brady found it. In it MacArthur stated without equivocation that if the Japanese attacked, he could defend the Philippine archipelago without further reinforcements. He also said, "My greatest security lies in the inability of our enemy to launch his air attack on our islands."

These were words for eating, and FDR kept them in a safe place in case he might need them. Outwardly he was as friendly to "Doug" as the General was to him. However, complaints kept pouring in from MacArthur and his Chief of Staff, General Richard Sutherland. They reiterated that MacArthur's forces had climbed a ladder of Japanese-held islands a thousand miles long, and that each time the army had fought and defeated the enemy in his strong points. It was urgent, MacArthur stated, that the military strength of the United States not be dissipated by funneling it to his one-time aide, Dwight Eisenhower, or to the Navy in the Pacific, which was leapfrogging Japanese strong points to attack advanced positions with heavy carrier task forces backed up by a fleet train, and three Marine divisions—the Third, the Fourth and the Fifth.

Didn't Admiral Nimitz understand that Admiral Yamamoto was luring U.S. carriers farther east into Japanese waters merely to catch the fleet when it was committed to a landing? Sooner or later, the Japanese Navy, depleted in carrier strength, would catch the bulk of the American fleet deployed near a Japanese-held island, and then great hosts of Rising Sun bombers, in addition to the swift heavy units of the Japanese fleet, would attack and destroy the American Navy when it was powerless to retreat from its own landing force. It was a sinister possibility; a calculated risk.

No one in military and political circles in Washington denied MacArthur's brilliance as a general. His godlike personality abraded many. The Navy was racing eastward to the heart of the Japanese perimeter—Tinian, Saipan and Guam. The Navy was gambling boldly. If the American Third and Fifth fleets could grasp and hold these islands, new long-range B-29s could nest on these islands, fly 1,500 miles to Tokyo, drop their bombs and return to the three islands without strain. Competent and personally vain, MacArthur could not bear to share credit in the Pacific with Nimitz. He felt it was his show; he had fled the Philippines without dignity, promising "I shall return," and he intended to keep that promise. In addition, the General pointed out with logic that if Nimitz knew that the three islands were a war-shortening prize, then Imperial Japanese headquarters was also aware of the islands' value. He estimated the defenders at 45,000 first-line troops. Japan had 30,000 on Saipan alone. The Japanese Emperor, noted for his august silence, sent a message to the defenders of the Marianas: "If Saipan is lost, air raids on Tokyo will take place—therefore you must absolutely hold Saipan."

The President set July for the Pacific meeting because the energies of the Allies were committed to a deep penetration of continental Europe and a twilight hour for Hitlerite Germany; also, if the Republicans nominated MacArthur in June, it would give FDR time to decide whether to postpone the Pacific meeting, whether to relieve MacArthur of his command for campaigning or whether to "chop the legs from under him" by granting most of what he asked.

The short, impeccable Governor of New York, Thomas E. Dewey, one-time choir boy, racket-busting prosecutor, a humorless perfectionist, sent his friend Herbert Brownell to pick up delegate votes before the convention. MacArthur had the glamour; the Governor had the votes. Dewey ran his office "by the book." He had no appreciation of humor, compassion or manly foibles such as poker games. He lent himself to idolatry and contempt. He was youthful, a man with a carefully trimmed dark mustache and the speaking voice of an operatic baritone. His adherents saw him as Saint George on a white charger; those who disliked him saw the Governor as a hyper-ambitious man who would step across a dear friend's body to achieve his ambitions.

It was Alice Roosevelt Longworth, dowager martinet of Washington's social set, who described Dewey as "the little man on the wedding cake." When the last of the wartime Republican conventions was gaveled to order in Chicago the last week of June, Dewey was nominated on the first ballot. The candidacies of MacArthur, Stassen, Vandenberg, Taft, Willkie won little more than applause. New York's Governor might have strengthened his ticket

by persuading one of the important losers to run for the
Vice-Presidency. But Dewey, besides being humorless,
was also unforgiving of those who opposed him. He
selected Governor John W. Bricker of Ohio, handsome,
wavy-haired, a man once cruelly described as having
a "stellar brain—a huge black void with a flew clichés
floating around."

Dewey persuaded the convention to name his friend
Herbert Brownell as Republican national chairman. The
strategy they chose to win in November was weak: to
attack Roosevelt personally, and to wear an air of self-
righteous outrage-in-restraint. In the acceptance speech
Dewey hammered at the anticipated theme: "men in
the White House who have grown old, tired, stubborn
and quarrelsome." Anne O'Hare McCormick, covering
the convention for *The New York Times,* listened to the
many speeches, and watched Dewey leave Chicago on
the Lake Shore Limited for Albany.

*The party leaders and the delegates [she wrote] tried to
convince one another that the campaign hinges on domestic
issues. They kept insisting that the war would occupy only a
part of the next term. The main job of the administration taking over next January, they argued, would be to manage and
speed up the adjustment to peace. The dominant theme was
that this process could be better carried out under the fresh,
eager, resourceful and harmonious direction of the Republicans than by the old, tired, bureaucratic and divided minds
of the Democrats. The Republican Party grew younger and
younger with every speech.*

The President became depressed in late June. There
was no discernible reason. Nor was it immediately obvious
to those around him. FDR called speech writer Sam
Rosenman into the executive office and without preamble
said that if, after his death, Washington wanted to build
a small memorial stone to Franklin D. Roosevelt, he
would like it to be situated in "the small park triangle
where Constitution and Pennsylvania Avenues cross, facing east." He was dictating mail to Grace Tully when

he said, "I told Margaret that if anything ever happened to me she is to get Fala." Miss Suckley had given the pet to the President when it was a pup. "I'm quite sure that Eleanor will be too busy to look after him and he's devoted to Margaret."

The President called Dorothy Brady in and made two small but precious gifts. The first was a used Bakelite cigarette holder with the President's teeth marks showing in white. It was enclosed in a small plush case. "For your husband," he said. The other was a fluted china jam dish resting on a blue and white saucer. "This belonged to my mother. She gave it to me. Child, I want you to have it." Grace Tully, who had access to the President's private office without knocking, found herself walking in when FDR was sleeping with a sheaf of papers in his hand. "At first I was surprised, but considered it merely a fatigue of the moment. He would grin in slight embarrassment as he caught himself. . . . As it began to occur with increasing frequency, I became seriously alarmed." (This was the third week in June.)

Admiral McIntire was called in. He was told the symptoms. The physician decided to warn the President of his state of health, without telling him how serious it was, and at the same time to assure FDR that he could continue through a fourth term if he cut his work load in half. "Well," the Admiral said, "you may feel fine, but you don't look it. Your neck is scrawny and your face is gullied by a lot of lines that have added ten years to your age." Harsh words, perhaps necessary words. "And while we're on the subject, for heaven's sake get some new clothes. That old shirt is sizes too large and the jacket hangs on your shoulders like a bat." The Admiral's denunciation induced a deep presidential laugh.

A polite letter from Congressional Librarian Archibald MacLeish referring to the "Franklin Delano Memorial Library" elicited a kidding-in-earnest response:

Dear Archie:
You have been grossly deceived. I am still alive! Why the Franklin D. Roosevelt Memorial *Library at Hyde Park? I*

*realize that I have not seen you for a century or two and, at
that time, you were intending to be a blacksmith while I was
about to join up as an able-bodied seaman with Captain
Cook.*

Thomas Corcoran, the suede glove and mailed fist
of the administration, summoned sufficient temerity to
advise Mr. Roosevelt not to run for a fourth term, but
when the President asked for reasons, Tommy the Cork
could not utter the truth: You look like a dying man.
An intimate could say that there were no more mountains
to climb; that the war was won and might drag on
another year, but that victory was certain; that twelve
years in a man-killing job was more than enough; that
the nation could use an elder statesman at Hyde Park—but
the tongue of Corcoran, the most loquacious of men,
became paralyzed.

So many dire and dismal signs of death were evident
to Miss Tully that she did not want to discuss it. She
was a religious woman and attended mass and offered
it up for the continued health of her President. Once,
when she did not get to the office until 11:00 A.M., worn
with thinking of what her world would be like without
the President, he summoned her, smiled wanly, and said,
"Grace, if anything should happen to me while I am at
sea, I want to be buried at sea. You know, it has always
seemed like home to me." Miss Tully swallowed hard
and Gaelic bluntness surfaced. "I am sorry, sir," she said,
"but I think that is one wish that will not be carried out
and I hope it won't. I personally do not like it or even
the thought of it, and I believe the people of the country
would feel as I do."

FDR's phone calls to Lucy Rutherfurd, spending the
summer at Allamuchy, New Jersey, became more frequent. If his preoccupation with death was communicated to her, she mentioned it to no one. The wife whom
he respected but did not love heard none of his doleful
premonitions. She was a practical woman, and she told
her friends that she had schooled herself, as she phrased
it, to acknowledge that some or all of her sons might

be killed in the world holocaust, and that "Franklin might be killed or die at any time." He was a poor risk. Mrs. Roosevelt knew it in spite of the assurances of McIntire that, if the Boss cut his work load in half and got ten to twelve hours of sleep, he could serve a fourth term with distinction.

There were no accurate medical tests for generalized arteriosclerosis in 1944. There was no means of measuring small cerebral strokes, except the powers of observation of a physician, who might detect the droop of a lip, a heavy-lidded eye, or a limitation of limb functions. Howard Bruenn saw no sign of strokes. As a patient, Franklin Roosevelt was an unusual person. Often, at the morning examinations, his blood pressure was high; the hollows under his eyes had deepened; frequently, while listening to conversation, the mouth slacked open unconsciously. After a hard day's work, Bruenn was surprised to find that the blood pressure had decreased, the patient was more alert, and made his good spirits known by joviality and laughter. The most mysterious quality of all was FDR's ability, when "down," to summon a reserve of energy for a Cabinet meeting, or a press conference, and to present himself as the cocky, confident man with the uplifted chin and the tilted cigarette holder. The Bradys, Watsons, Daniels and others who were at the President's side were accustomed to see him slump in deep fatigue, then roll his wheelchair into a meeting sparkling with wit and laughter.*

"I knew without asking," Mrs. Roosevelt said, "that as long as the war was on, it was a foregone conclusion that Franklin, if he was well enough, would run again." In this she stated the case succinctly. No one had the temerity to ask the President bluntly if he would run

* Since the President's death, medical articles have appeared which asserted that FDR sustained three cerebral strokes while in office. There is no competent evidence to support this. In 1972 Dr. Howard Bruenn assured me that he, as the President's personal physician, observed nothing to support the contention. He does not doubt that FDR had a generalized arteriosclerosis. Reduced nourishment to the brain limits the ability to think out complex problems. Narrowing arteries, with increased strain on the heart, would make Roosevelt less competent—an old man at sixty-three.

again, but his political friends and enemies assumed that he would. The President's friend Ed Flynn advised FDR not to run, to give it up while he still had a topflight record as a chief executive; obtusely, Flynn observed that the job was a "man killer," but the response was simply that a good soldier doesn't have the right to quit while his country is in danger.

The question of health became an issue. At least once a week the press published second-hand rumors as fact; some newspapers predicted that Roosevelt would complete his term of office as Woodrow Wilson did, an enfeebled mind encased in a useless body. *Life* magazine, as anxious as any to ascertain the truth, assigned Jeanne Perkins to write a definitive article about the Surgeon General, Admiral McIntire. *Life,* and Miss Perkins, knew that no one could write competently about the Admiral without inquiring into his relationship as the President's doctor.

McIntire, protesting proper reluctance, agreed, and Miss Perkins amassed considerable material about the doctor and his world-renowned patient. On June 6, however, D Day arrived and the editors of *Life* advised their writer to drop the McIntire story for the moment to help with the bigger article. Perkins wrote to McIntire stating that she was "awfully sorry we couldn't get together last Thursday and continue the pleasant business of reviewing your career for the benefit of *Life* readers."

On the same day, another letter went from Perkins to the Admiral's secretary, pleasant in tone, stating in part: "I would like to hear from you about the three or four questions you were going to put before the admiral [for me]." The secretary, a Miss Murphy, responded in part:

Here are the answers to your several questions in regard to the President: 1. No mention may be made of the number of cigarettes the President smokes in a day. 2. The sick days during the past twelve (12) years have been very few in number. There have been only two occasions when he has been in bed over a period of ten days during that time. If he had been operating on a Civil Service basis he would have a great backlog of sick leave.

3. The annual physical examination for the senior naval officers takes from two to four hours. The President's annual physical examination is the same as that of the senior officers. 4. The final checkup on his last physical examination is extremely satisfactory. 5. Specific figures in regard to blood pressure, eyes, ears, etc. are never given. Such matters are considered a patient's personal affair. 6. He wears glasses when he wishes to see long distances and when he is going to read for a long period of time.

7. Considering the difference in age, his past physical examination is equally as good as the one made on him twelve years ago. 8. He does not sleep with his window shut. 9. Sorry, but I cannot let you have the letter about the muskrat pelt. 10. Admiral McIntire's major concern right now is rehabilitation of the returning wounded men.

Life had touched the delicate nerve, and McIntire had anesthetized the magazine.

In spite of his afflictions, the President found time to give his personal attention to matters great and small. The world was thundering to a climactic struggle, but he remembered, on June 14, his special affection for Miss Barbara Rutherfurd. The President held all of the Rutherfurds in esteem, but there was a cuddly, almost nose-rubbing affection between the President and the youngest child of Lucy. In his own hand he wrote:

Telegram
To Miss Barbara Rutherfurd   Aiken 6/14/44
Thinking of you today. Hope you will come up and see me soon.
FDR

The year before, his birthday telegram was more imperative:

6/14/43
Telegram   Barbara Rutherfurd   Allamuchy, N.J.
It is today even more essential that you stop in Washington
to visit your
            Godfather

He also found time to laugh. One afternoon Mrs.
Roosevelt sent a wild-eyed young man to the West Wing
to see Steve Early and Sam Rosenman about "something
very important." They met in Early's office. The visitor
was emotionally disturbed. He demanded to know first
if the office was "bugged." Early and Rosenman assured
him it wasn't. He asked if the secretaries could eaves-
drop through the intercom system. They shook their
heads. Suddenly the visitor ran to a back door, and
flung it open to see if anyone was listening.

"Somone," he whispered, "is making an atom bomb
in this country." The two glanced at each other. "Du
Pont is taking control of it, so that it can harness all that
energy as soon as the war is over." Steve Early referred
the young man to the War Department to be rid of him.
As neither of them had ever heard of an atom bomb
project, they assumed that the visitor was crazy. That
afternoon, when Early was talking to the President, he
told him about the "nut." FDR laughed so hard he had
to remove his spectacles to wipe his eyes. "Imagine,"
Early said. "An atom bomb. What the hell will they think
of next?"

The bomb was in the final stages of development at
Oak Ridge, Hanford, Washington, and Los Alamos, New
Mexico. It would cost $2 billion, and, in the early years,
the President had managed to squeeze secret funds into
the War Department budget to finance the project.
However, the cost was jumping by hundreds of millions
and FDR said to Tully, "Pray God that it works. It
will save many American lives." Stimson said he could
no longer finance the matter through the War Department. Major General Leslie Groves, head of the Manhattan Project, needed $200 million at once, and some-

one would have to take Congress into this most secret of projects.

Finally, with the President's approval, Secretary Stimson, General George Marshall and scientist Dr. Vannevar Bush met with House Speaker Sam Rayburn, Majority Leader John McCormack and Minority Leader Joseph Martin. The building of the A-bomb was told to them in the most general terms; they were pledged to secrecy and entreated to pass huge sums through Congress without questions being asked. It wasn't an easy assignment, but leaders of both parties worked it out, and a short time later General Groves was pacing up and down the outer office of General Marshall waiting for the huge check.

He had not been told whether he would get the money. If he did not, the project would collapse at great expense to the taxpayer. If Groves was given the money, he was aware that there was an even chance that the bomb would not explode. The General claimed that, after pacing the floor for ten minutes, he was certain that he would not get the funds. Then the door to the inner office opened and General Marshall appeared holding the check in his hand. "Les," he said, "I'm sorry to have kept you waiting. You know that house I have in Fort Myer? Well, I've been working myself into a state because the bill for grass seed last year was twenty-three dollars; this year it's thirty-five."

The President worried about the Russian offensive along the eastern edge of Poland. Stalin had promised that it would coincide with Eisenhower's landing in France, so that Hitler could not divert forces from one front to another, but the British and Americans had been in France a week, and all was still quiet on the eastern front. Then, in mid-June, the Russian armies literally exploded along a 450-mile area. Gigantic masses of field artillery, tanks and infantry poured through the center of the German lines. In the first week a double-enveloping movement resulted in 20,000 Germans killed and 20,000 prisoners. In the second week Hitler sent an order to all troops to stand their ground and not to retreat "an inch." The Soviets captured 100,000 and sent 57,000 Germans, including generals, to march through the streets of Moscow. When the offensive gained momentum, a hole 250 miles wide had been torn in the German lines. It was, as one European writer observed, "June 1941 in reverse."

In spite of the successes, there was disagreement and suspicion among the leaders. Stalin, for example, had called Milovan Djilas of Yugoslavia to Moscow to review Tito's guerrilla campaign. The Soviet dictator said that the British and Americans were offended by the sight of a red star, and Stalin saw no reason why Tito had to flaunt his communism by copying the Soviet uniform. Djilas said that the Yugoslavs regarded the red star as a symbol of the future and would not discard it.

Stalin tried to placate him. "Perhaps you think that just because we are the allies of the English that we have forgotten who they are and who Churchill is. . . . Churchill is the kind who, if you don't watch him, will slip a kopek out of your pocket. Yes, a kopek out of your pocket! By God, a kopek out of your pocket! And Roosevelt? Roosevelt is not like that. He dips his hand in only for bigger coins."

Churchill did not trust Stalin. He told Sir Alexander Cadogan that the closer the Allies came to victory, the more they would have to worry about the Soviets over-running continential Europe. The ultimate triumph in war, he felt, was only a matter of how long and at what cost. The larger problem was that the Russians would invest Poland and a good part of Germany—and could they be persuaded to leave? The British Prime Minister viewed Roosevelt as the savior of the world but looked upon him as politically naive. The President had assured the P.M. that he could do business with Stalin by talking to him face to face. Churchill did not subscribe to this. He pointed to a host of treaties that Russia had negotiated with many nations, including Finland and Hitler's Germany, only to renounce them when it was to Russia's advantage to do so. Roosevelt admired Churchill as a gallant fellow sailor who had braved the fire of war alone and had not capitulated. But he was equally certain that his friend Winnie would not want to carve the world up among British, Russian and American interests when the conflict was over.

It is of some interest to note that, in the secret dispute between Roosevelt and Churchill, it was often the Prime Minister who responded with the soft, diplomatic argument. He did not want to offend the President, even when the disagreement involved an important matter, such as the invasion. At the winter conference in Teheran, when the Anglo-American group agreed on Overlord, the invasion of Normandy, they also agreed to use some of British General Alexander's forces in Italy, in addition to fresh American divisions, for a second invasion in the south of France, an operation to be called Anvil.

The grand design was to break Germany's defenses into three sections—the Russian front, the western front, and the Mediterranean front. This would leave the Italian front stagnated at Rome. Eisenhower, fighting for a foothold at St. Lo, kept cabling Marshall in Washington, demanding to know when Anvil would occur. He pointed to the obvious: that if Anvil started up the Rhone Valley, the German High Command could oppose it only if divisions were taken from Italy and the Normandy fronts. In irritation FDR asked Churchill when Anvil could be expected. The P.M. and his military chiefs had already decided to siphon the Anvil forces and put them on the Italian front with General Alexander. Other brigades, Churchill thought, should be transshipped to Greece, where Great Britian desired to protect its interests. The British argued that Alexander's forces, long stalled, had invested Rome and were shoving Kesselring north. Why break up a winning combination? Roosevelt replied:

My interest and hopes center on defeating the Germans in front of Eisenhower and driving on into Germany, rather than on limiting this action for the purpose of staging a full major effort in Italy. I am convinced we will have sufficient forces in Italy, with "Anvil" forces withdrawn, to chase Kesselring north of Pisa-Rimini and maintain heavy pres-

sure against his army at the very least to the extent neces-
sary to contain his present force. I cannot conceive of the
Germans paying the price of ten additional divisions, esti-
mated by General Wilson, in order to keep us out of northern
Italy. . . .

At Teheran we agreed upon a definite plan of attack. That
plan has gone well so far. Nothing has occurred to require
any change. Now that we are fully involved in our major
blow, history will never forgive us if we lose precious time
and lives in indecision and debate. My dear friend, I beg you
to let us go ahead with our plan.

Winston Churchill appealed to Roosevelt to forget
Anvil; he also appealed to Harry Hopkins. But the President saw the adventure in Italy and, more important,
the Balkans, as a Churchillian gambit to race the Russians to Vienna, thus serving political expediency at the
expense of military triumph. FDR insisted on Anvil. The
Prime Minister, pouting, finally agreed to it, with, as
he stated, the serious reservations of His Majesty's government.

In the same month the President welcomed Stanislaus
Mikolajczyk, Prime Minister of the Polish government-in-
exile. This was to be another dreary experience, and FDR
looked at it with slightly less patience than he reserved
for conferences with Charles de Gaulle. Mikolajczyk
received a state welcome and was tendered a state dinner,
but the ruffles and flourishes were meaningless. Roosevelt's public utterances about "our two great countries, our
two great peoples" were intended to be a sop to the only
minority group he feared—the seven million Polish-
Americans who, in spite of arguments to the contrary,
the President said voted as a solid unit. To his intimates
he stated that he never feared an anit-Jewish vote, anti-
Italian, anti-Irish—but Poles, he said, were cohesive even
unto the third generation.

When the President and his aides assembled with the
Poles for private conversations, FDR opened the proceedings on a jocular-defensive note. "I have studied
sixteen maps of Poland this morning," he said. "In only

three hundred years, parts of White Russia have been Polish, and parts of Germany and Czechoslovakia." He grinned. "On the other hand, parts of Poland have at times been annexed to those countries." The message was clear. It would be impossible—or at best arbitrary—to define the boundaries of Poland. "It is difficult," FDR said, "to untangle the map of Poland." The Poles, including their Prime Minister, were tactful diplomats. They did not harass the President to take a postwar position on Poland as they had with Prime Minister Winston Churchill and Foreign Secretary Anthony Eden.

They were gentle, slightly insistent at times, but acted as though the government of the United States was a firm and enduring friend of Poland. The war, they pointed out, started over Hitler's invasion of Poland. The treaties with Great Britain and France *guaranteed* the borders, and, as the war drew toward its climax and conclusion, they merely asked reassurances that those borders would be restored and that the Polish government-in-exile would be recognized. The United States, Roosevelt stated, would not desert her good friend at the peace table. In a jocular mood again, he said that the seven million Poles in America would vote *en bloc* and he did not care to risk their displeasure.

Still, Mikolajczyk asked for more substance than protestations of friendship. FDR reminded the Prime Minister that, in their conversations, he had been getting further away "from the mere questions of whether this town will be on this side of the line or that side of the line." The talks, broad and generous, resembled torrents tumbling into a funnel. Near the bottom, they had to pass the question of the Soviet Union. This worried the Poles; it worried Roosevelt too.

In a top secret message, Churchill had warned Roosevelt that the only way in which the Germans could be defeated on the land mass of Europe was for Russia and her huge armies to rout the Hitlerites across Poland and into the eastern provinces of Germany. The forces of Eisenhower, with the Americans on the right and

General Bernard Law Montgomery on the left, might be strong enough in time to defeat the Nazis alone, but it would require two years or more. However, the Russians were already on the plains of White Russia and the old borders of Poland. The problem would be that when Stalin had his armies investing all of Poland, who would have the strength to force him back to the old borders? Churchill was certain that Stalin would demand a piece of Poland pie, perhaps as much as Hitler had granted in the treaty of August 1939. If the Russians, who had taken the brunt of the German assault, suffered the most in losses of men, matériel and destruction of two-thirds of all her European cities, demanded a buffer state, who could deny them?

Roosevelt concluded the uneasy conferences by promising Mikolajczyk that he would get in touch with Marshal Stalin and try to arrange an amicable conference. The message was sent "urgent and secret." The Soviets permitted two weeks to go by before they responded, not only to Roosevelt but to Churchill. The Mikolajczyk government, Stalin said, was "ephemeral," a collection of emigré politicians with no power among the Polish citizenry and even less in other countries. Whom did they represent? Themselves. The Soviet Union, he stated, was prepared to recognize the newly formed Polish Committee of National Liberation, men of the underground who had remained in Warsaw to fight for Poland and who, more important, remained close to their people. Bluntly the Soviet Marshal concluded by saying that he would meet with Mikolajczyk and his ministers only if they approached him through the Polish National Committee.

The President breathed in impotent anger. He told Cordell Hull that the Russians were already reverting to the spheres-of-influence policy which had created war before, and would again. Hull, who had warned that the system of strong nations using smaller ones as buffer states and stepchildren was antiquated and dangerous, reminded FDR that the British also favored this policy. British Ambassador Lord Halifax had sounded out the

Secretary of State on the possibility of England having a postwar "controlling" interest in Greece, permitting Russia to exercise the same right in Romania. Hull, often jostled by FDR as an old man with rigid notions, said that the Russians were now prepared to gobble Poland, and were big enough to digest other states, too.

Stalin softened Roosevelt's anger at the right time. As the Mikolajczyk government was asking for talks in Moscow, Stalin addressed his generals in late June and, noting their objection to the second front as unnecessary, accorded enormous credit to the Allied day-and-night bombing of the heart of Germany and the "brilliant success" of the Eisenhower forces: "The history of war does not know of an undertaking comparable to it for breadth of conception, grandeur of scale, and mastery of execution."

In politics, indealism and naiveté are synonyms. The President had lived through two great wars, as an Assistant Secretary of the Navy and as President of the United States, and if he was adamantly certain of one goal, it was the self-determination of peoples great and small. When Churchill begged for FDR's support of a British adventure in Greece, the President agreed to "Ninety Days." After securing a firm and friendly Greek government, Great Britain must withdraw its forces. Churchill acknowledged the time span. The President did not appreciate Stalin's attitude of domination over Poland. It was a Roman Catholic country, and he was certain that, if free elections were held at the end of the war, Poland would vote for a democratic government and throw the Communists out. Now he was beset by the British again, who asked him to *please* invite General Charles de Gaulle to Washington.

Roosevelt refused. Eisenhower had a foothold in France and he was already asking for guidance about what type of French government to endorse. The cables made it plain that his staff had located two types of Frenchmen: Vichyites, who had worked with the Germans, and Gaullists, who had fought in the underground. In spite of all this, the President saw the high and noble aims of the war dissipated in factionalism. He became so irritated that he came close to administering a dressing-down to General George Marshall, whom the President admired. "Eisenhower evidently believes the fool newspaper stories that I am anti-de Gaulle, even the kind of story which says I hate him. I am perfectly willing to have de Gaulle made president, or emperor, or king or anything else so long as the action comes in an untrammeled and unforced way from the French people themselves."

He was silent a moment, cudgeling thoughts. "It is awfully easy to be for de Gaulle and to cheer the thought of recognizing that committee as the provisional government of France, but I have a moral duty that transcends an easy way. It is to see that the people of France have nothing foisted on them by outside powers. It must be a French choice and that means, as far as possible, forty million people. Self-determination is not a word of expediency. It carries with it a very deep principle in human affairs." General Marshall departed with the impression that FDR felt that de Gaulle's popularity with the French was weakening.

Still, Churchill, who was tired of de Gaulle's insolent and imperious attitude in private conversations, again asked Roosevelt to invite the French General to Washington. FDR said no. De Gaulle was aware of the rebuffs. They did nothing to moderate his demands upon Churchill and FDR. France had been defeated. De Gaulle wore the condescension of the victor. Eisenhower appealed again to Washington for guidance. As towns and provinces were liberated, he would have to know which Frenchmen were to administer conquered territory. The British told de Gaulle that Roosevelt desired to see him. The General knew the truth, but pretended to be pleased.

Irritably, FDR ordered guns to boom, swords to flash, colors to snap in the breeze, and a parade up Pennsylvania Avenue. The General could not complain about the public welcome. At the White House, the President

and Mrs. Roosevelt and the Cabinet waited outside the
front porte cochere, the gentlemen in striped trousers
and frock coats. FDR greeted the abnormally tall
Frenchman in French. This was followed by an assortment of dinners and state functions.

The President did not appear to be choking when,
with the aid of a Secret Service man, he stood to raise
his glass of champagne. He referred to de Gaulle as "our
friend." Mr. Roosevelt declined to have a stenographer
present at the private conversations. De Gaulle confided
to his military aides that Roosevelt was, at best, "conde-
scending." The General stated that, when Paris fell, he
would like a French division to lead the Allied forces,
and he would like to follow in a parade of liberation
under the Arc de Triomphe.

Someone would have to administer the affairs of the
French government, the General pointed out, and if not
he—who? Roosevelt nodded agreement. He said that the
United States was prepared to recognize de Gaulle as
head of the *de facto* government of France. This implied,
as the President made plain, that as soon as the Allied
forces had chased the Germans across the Rhine, Roosevelt expected free elections in France so that a permanent
government could be set up and recognized by the other
powers. De Gaulle accepted what he felt was a personal
humiliation. After he returned to Great Britain, Roosevelt said that the General had acted as though he represented the fourth great power in the world, instead
of a nation defeated ignominiously, now dependent upon
the sufferance and sacrifice of America and England to
fight her battles and strike the shackles of slavery.

In London, much of the fratricidal strife between British and Americans, between British and French, was left
in the capable hands of the Permanent Under Secretary for Foreign Affairs, Sir Alexander Cadogan, a small,
obsequious man with graying slick hair and the slightly
pained expression of one enduring tight shoes. Sir Alec
loved his wife without reservations. Beyond that, it is
doubtful if he ever permitted himself to admire anyone.

Cadogan bruised the P.M. when Churchill called Cabinet meetings for 6:00 P.M. and kept talking nonsense until after midnight. Sir Alec was certain, in listening, that Churchill had never studied Britain's position papers on the United Nations, the Dumbarton Oaks Conference, the numerous reports sent by the European Advisory Commission whose function was to decide the details of peace with each defeated nation. The Under Secretary dismissed President Roosevelt as being "somewhat insane." His heart's desire was to be named British Ambassador to Washington, but he feared that Lord Halifax would remain in that post forever—in good health, worse luck.

A week after D Day Cadogan felt that it was time for him to talk to M. Vienot, General de Gaulle's Ambassador to England. Cadogan begged "A" (Anthony Eden) and "PM" (Prime Minister) to get the talks started with Vienot before de Gaulle trooped haughtily into France and took command. "5:15," he minuted. "Talk with A and others about France. He agreed to ask PM to authorize us to begin discussion, on official level, with Vienot. This would be a *start*—and it's the only step forward I can think of. . . . We are on the beaches. Have landed over 200,000 men, (Allied total 400,000), 1,200 tanks, 30,000 vehicles, 40,000 tons of stores. A marvelous performance . . ." Entry the next day: "Some progress with de G. PM has been prevailed upon to allow conversations with Vienot. de G. to go to France tomorrow. But the Pres. is rushing to break *all* the plates at 9:45 tonight by saying that the French currency is backed by Eisenhower! On A's instructions got Chancellor to agree to try to persuade Winston to send a message dissuading Pres. Don't know if it went. Don't much care: if he makes the announcement I hope we shall dissociate ourselves from it (we weren't consulted). That will leave all the odium—and the guarantee of £400,000,000—on the cracked President!"

Shortly before daylight on the morning of June 13, Londoners in the East End were awakened by a new sound, the guttural throbbing of the motor of a small pilotless plane. Without warning, the engine died for lack of fuel, and the plane dived down with a thousand pounds of high explosive in its nose. It demolished a railway bridge at Bethnal Green. Six people were killed and nine injured. The Germans called it the V-1; the British called it the buzz bomb. It was the most impersonal weapon of World War II. It used a small ram-jet engine and rose from inclined rails between Antwerp and Dieppe and flew on a course of between 280 and 300 degrees until the last drop of fuel brought silence—and this could be anywhere between the Dover coast and the Midlands. It cared not whether it landed on a railroad depot or an empty park. The Germans had devised it as a weapon of terror. Before the first one arrived, they had a sufficient number of them on hand to bomb London eighteen hours a day for seven weeks. After that, the Nazis counted on having a supersonic pilotless missile to be called V-2.

British Intelligence was aware of V-2 before London was hit by V-1. Military intelligence on both sides of the war was a sometime thing, with predictions ranging about as high in inaccuracy as those of the meteorologists. Allied intelligence had reports on rocket tests at Peenemünde, in eastern Germany, in 1941. Little attention was paid to the original bomber photographs because Britain and the United States, both of whom had conducted such experiments, saw rockets as dangerous and uncontrollable toys. The military adage, always to impute more intelligence to your enemy than to yourself, failed miserably in World War II. The Germans, in 1944, had rockets; the Allies did not. The Germans had jet fighters; the Allies did not. Advices to the Free World in late 1940 announced that Hitler was building extermination camps for Jews and Slavs in Poland and Austria; the stories were discounted as a revival of the old "Hun" propaganda. Even the ninety-day warnings given to the Kremlin in the spring of 1941 that Russia was about to be attacked by Germany brought no military response from Stalin.

Intelligence in war is a sometime thing. As he sat in

the White House in the last week of June, Roosevelt
heard Admiral Leahy whisper to him that the U.S. Navy
had at last captured a U-boat (U-505) and that the jeep
carrier *Guadalcanal* had towed it to Hamilton, Bermuda.
Code books had been captured intact. But the President
did not see the true depth of the intelligence factor: that
the Navy would establish a Tenth Fleet—to exist solely
on paper, with no floating ships—in Washington; would
use that code book to monitor the submarines of Admiral
Dönitz and their reports and positions; and would set
up two-directional radio stations to pinpoint the U-boats
and track them down with "hunter-killer" forces.

When buzz bombs fell on England, the United States
had no information that Admiral Dönitz had appealed
to Hitler for permission to build flying ramps on German
submarines so that a wolf pack could surface off New
York harbor at night and unleash flaming destruction
on the metropolis. Hitler denied the request—not through
altruistic motives, but because he ordered Dönitz to concentrate on sinking merchant ships which were supply-
ing Eisenhower with tanks, planes, fuel and ammunition.

The sum of information which reached the President
seldom impressed him; he had a wait-and-see attitude.
In the third week of June, at Hyde Park, he appeared
to surrender, temporarily, to lassitude. He slept late,
retired early and took no afternoon drives. The old mansion was heavy with messages, ciphers, visitors, a daily
planeload of incoming mail and outgoing mail to be
dictated and signed. The deep, mottled gray under Roosevelt's eyes appeared to be blackish in certain light; the
President tired of wheeling himself from ground floor
office to upstairs room, and the work of pushing the chair
was undertaken by a Secret Service man who noted the
scrawny neck and the nodding head.

The hands, except when at rest on the edge of a desk
or table, trembled more than previously. He spent many
daylight hours in the upstairs bedroom, and rose to bathe
and shave with the assistance of Arthur Prettyman. The
secretaries, assistants and security personnel agreed that
President Roosevelt's good nature was still apparent,

that he was more and more given to discussing a subject, pausing, then grinning and saying: ". . . now what was I talking about?" He spent most of the morning of June 22, 1944, at his small rosewood desk reading his favorite piece of postwar legislation, to be known as the GI Bill of Rights. "This bill," he stated, "which I have signed today, substantially carries out most of the recommendations made by me in a speech on July 28, 1943, and November 23, 1943":

1. It gives servicemen and women the opportunity of resuming their education or technical training after discharge, or of taking a refresher or retainer course, not only without tuition charge up to $500 per school year, but with the right to receive a monthly living allowance while pursuing their studies.

2. It makes provision for the guarantee by the federal government not to exceed 50 percent of certain loans made to veterans for the purchase or construction of homes, farms and business properties.

3. It provides for reasonable unemployment allowances payable each week up to a maximum period of one year, to those veterans who are unable to find a job.

4. It establishes improved machinery for effective job counseling for veterans and for finding jobs for returning soldiers and sailors.

5. It authorizes the construction of all necessary additional hospital facilities.

6. It strengthens the authority of the Veterans Administration to enable it to discharge its existing and added responsibilities with promptness and efficiency. . . .

The bill, which involved a great deal more than these six points, stretched a long and friendly American hand to fourteen million men and women in uniform. It guaranteed their future *before* peace became a reality. It was the most far-reaching, generous and productive bill passed in the history of the United States. FDR expected unanimity regarding the GI Bill of Rights. He didn't get it. The bill was passed by both Houses, but the Republican party spokesmen saw it as an insidious device by Roosevelt to get the votes of soldiers and sailors all over the world. They asked why it had not been passed the winter before—or a year earlier. Why was it brought up for signature just before the Republican and Democratic party conventions? If the President's intention was to win a vast bloc of uniformed votes, the Republicans and the Southern Democrats coalesced to stop it. Once again a bill was introduced in the House to place the rules for military voting in the hands of the individual states, to set their own guidelines. The GOP, sharply cognizant of the fact that they were "out" and Roosevelt "in," had no desire to fight a popular—perhaps a beloved figure—on even terms. In the forthcoming campaign, if American sentiment was evenly divided, the military might tip the balance in Roosevelt's favor. Herbert Brownell, the mastermind of the Dewey campaign, could not envision millions of soldiers and sailors voting against dear old Daddy.

In the Democratic ranks, those who aspired to be President of the United States found themselves, in the third week of June, altering direction and acting as modest and shy supplicants for the position of Vice President. Once—and only once—did FDR permit himself to be opposed to a possible running mate. Jimmy Byrnes of South Carolina was still running for President. He told his friends that he had a right to the job; he had been Roosevelt's right-hand man, in effect Assistant President; he had stepped down from the Supreme Court to assume the post of economic stabilizer—no one had been as loyal or as helpful to the President.

Mr. Roosevelt heard the rumors and shook his head no. He admired the South Carolinian, but, assuming the post was open, Byrnes could not win it. He was a Southerner with the traditions of conservatism which go with the appellation. To American labor, Byrnes was anathema. To the Northern and Midwestern party bosses, Byrnes was an iron-headed snob. The President, who could seldom nerve himself to impart bad news to anyone, asked Leo Crowley, custodian of Alien Property, to tell Byrnes that the Presidency would be unavailable to him—no matter how high FDR's personal regard for him.

It was an unpalatable assignment, but Crowley carried it out. The response from Jimmy Byrnes was restrained fury. He picked up a phone and demanded to speak to the President. Crowley heard but one side of the conversation. Listening, he sensed that FDR was placating his man, trying not to offend him, but trying not to open the door to the Presidency. As in most situations of the sort, FDR weaseled. He would not say yes, and he would not say no. A few days later a second messenger was sent to the office of Jimmy Byrnes to tell him that the President trusted and respected no statesman as much as Byrnes, but FDR hoped that Byrnes would give up his ambition. He gave it up, but he also divested himself of much of the respect he had for his President.

The battle for the Vice-Presidency became the main event. The Democratic convention was to meet in Chicago July 19, and, while the Republican party was nominating Dewey and Bricker with dispatch, no Democratic leader could venture a guess about Roosevelt's running mate. There were two tumultuous currents racing against each other in the party. The first was that the bosses did not want Roosevelt to run for a fourth term. He had created enough momentum and goodwill for the party, they felt, to carry any candidate into the White House to "follow Roosevelt's policies and see the war through." The opposition was a welling, silent tide. The chairman of the Democratic National Committee, Edward Flynn, canonized Roosevelt at almost every opportunity, but his sharp eye and political friends reminded him that he was supporting a dying leader.

And yet, no one from Flynn on down through the party ranks had the nerve to bell the old cat. Instead, at a time when he had not declared for office, they found themselves begging him to run once more for the good of the party. By mail and in person, they told Mr. Roosevelt what he wanted to hear. The reasoning behind the deception was a fear of being caught on the wrong side if FDR ran again and won. He still used the phrase, when asking about a favor seeker, "Was he with us B.C.?" (Before the Chicago convention of 1932.) Roosevelt subscribed to a rigid code of political rewards and punishments. Underneath the jovial gentleman of the Hudson River Valley was a merciless and consummate politician who could dump mentors and buddies such as Alfred E. Smith, James A. Farley, John F. Curry of Tammany Hall, Senator Huey Long of Louisiana with as little regret as he now planned to drop Secretary of State Cordell Hull and Secretary of Commerce Jesse Jones. Hull, old and tired, would be allowed to plead "health reasons"; Jones, a tough Texan, would require arm-twisting, Cabinet meeting humiliation and a curtailment of personal power before he would be willing to return to the Southwest.

The silent slugging within the White House was for the Vice-Presidency. FDR made a tactical mistake by dropping a word here and there that he favored continuing the ticket as it stood, with Henry Agard Wallace. Ed Flynn hurried to the office of the President to state, with utmost candor, that the Democratic party was opposed to Wallace. The press looked upon Wallace as a leftist. The politicians found that they could not deal with him; he had no understanding of party work and patronage, and, after all, he was but one heartbeat from the Presidency. Flynn later told intimates that he felt like spelling out that the Vice-Presidency would be a more important office than ever, that Roosevelt was risking his health and life in running for one more term. But he didn't. "In any case," Flynn said, "he brings no strength to the ticket. The votes that Wallace can get are already in your pocket."

Admiral Ross McIntire stepped into the office as the conversation was waning. He heard the President say, diffidently, "If not Wallace, how about Bill Douglas?" The Associate Justice of the Supreme Court had been on the bench five years and had a good record. The President's private suggestion reached the ears of the Justice. This gave Douglas the right to feel that he had

been selected. Mr. Roosevelt was tossing names in the
air, watching to see which ones Flynn would shoot down.
The names of Jimmy Byrnes and Senator Alben Barkley
came up after Admiral McIntire had left the office. Names,
names, names. There were a dozen of them. FDR's
objection to Byrnes as well as Barkley was that they
were Southerners and would alienate the black vote.

He displayed little interest in the Republican convention—also held in Chicago. The President spent evenings
at the White House and weekends at Hyde Park working
with a magnifying glass and tweezers on his collection
of stamps. And yet, one cannot draw apathy from his
attitude. From his dinner conversations one gathers that
he was aware of everything political taking place, but
that he had reached a plateau of arrogant confidence
which led him to believe that Franklin D. Roosevelt
was the Democratic party. The Vice-Presidency was
of small moment—he could win with anyone he chose.
If there was anyone the President needed, it was Anna.
His wife burdened him with problems great and small
and seemed to have lost the capacity for the *bon mot*
and the gift of laughter. Harry Hopkins had remarried
and moved out of the White House to Georgetown.
The warm relationship between the two men began to
chill. Once, in pique over some small affront, the President
snapped, "All I need is Sis." When he felt strong enough
to dress for dinner, his daughter was his hostess. At
no point in his career was his independence of loyal
followers more arrogant. His illness may have had a
bearing on it. Two of the symptoms of hardening of
the cerebral arteries are aphasia and an irritating habit
of throwing down the gauntlet to friends and loved ones.

The President was a man symbolically cleansing old
mementos from a chest of drawers. He needed no one
but Sis. And, as he told Steve Early the winter before,
he didn't need the Presidency either. It needed him.
His attitude wasn't boastful; it was truculent. He was
tired of men fighting him in public—especially the men
of the right wing of his own party for the sheer hell
of opposing him. On the other hand, he found himself

faultless. For example, he would not permit anyone to paint him as vacillating regarding the Vice-Presidency, but he encouraged almost all comers to seek the office. They left President Roosevelt assured of his "blessing." The President's choice remained Henry Wallace. He sent a note to Convention Chairman Sam Jackson in which he stated, "I personally would vote for his [Wallace's] renomination if I were a delegate to the convention."

It was Robert Hannegan, Chairman of the Democratic National Committee, who suggested the unknown, Harry S. Truman, a Missourian who was chairman of the fact-finding committee for the Senate regarding war production costs. Mr. Roosevelt was conscious that Hannegan was a Missourian too, and that Truman was a product of Boss Pendergast. FDR again suggested William O. Douglas. There was an absence of "Dutch sense" and empirical will in the President's words. When Henry Wallace returned early from China and went off to the Chicago convention, Roosevelt said, "Henry, I hope it's the same old ticket." This was not true. FDR, with reluctance, had discarded Wallace in the face of opposition from party bosses. Mr. Roosevelt admired his Vice President but criticized him in private for not playing politics with the U.S. Senate as president of that body.

The bucolic-looking Vice President was laden with idealism, but he had no Senate vote to implement his noble thoughts. When faced with a matter of practical politics, the Vice President knew little about horse-trading for votes and less about how to control the measures which came to the floor. He was a good man for a President to send on a far-off mission because his interests and his knowledge were broad, but he could not match Harry Hopkins in bringing the mission to a profitable close. It is possible that Henry Wallace's glaring weakness was that he was an honest man.

June was drawing to a close when Roosevelt called Sam Rosenman in for a private chat. The judge was sure it would concern the fourth term and suggestions for speeches. It wasn't. Rosenman sat quietly as the

Secret Service closed all the doors. The President tapped
the ash from his cigarette and said that Gifford Pinchot
had stopped in, secretly. Pinchot was a former Governor
of Pennsylvania, a Republican. He was tall and slender,
a man with a lean face and broadly flourishing white
mustaches. He looked like a Western sheriff who had
lost his Stetson. Rosenman leaned forward in his chair
to find out why Pinchot would want to see Mr.
Roosevelt.

"The Governor," said FDR, "had a meeting with Wendell Willkie." He spoke slowly, in the manner of one
who is about to reveal a secret one shock at a time. As
he told the story, the President said that Pinchot and
Willkie were unhappy with the Republican party as it
was constituted. Willkie, the GOP standard-bearer, told
the ex-Governor that there should be a "new setup."
He pointed to the fact that Roosevelt, a liberal, could
not marshal votes or support from Southern senators and
congressmen because, by tradition, they were conservative. If the new liberal versus reactionary fronts were
able to coalesce in their proper political firmament, it
would be less divisive for the electorate.

"It was Willkie's idea," the President said when Rosenman asked who sent Pinchot to Roosevelt. "Willkie has
just been beaten by the conservatives in his own party
who lined up in back of Dewey. Now there is no doubt,
Sam, that the reactionaries in our own party are out for
my scalp too—as you can see by what's going on in the
South." He was sympathetic to Willkie. "I agree with
him one hundred percent and the time is now"—the President paused—"right after the election. We ought to have
two real parties, one liberal, the other conservative. . . .
Of course I'm talking about long-range politics—something that we can't accomplish this year. But we can do
it in 1948, and we can start building it up right after
the election this fall. From the liberals of both parties,
Willkie and I together can form a new, really liberal party
in America."

For a moment, Franklin D. Roosevelt was a colt again,
skittish and swift, nostrils flaring with delight at the

thought of hopping a high fence. He would use the South
this year for whatever votes he could get, but he would
betray it as soon as he was reelected. He was sufficiently
strong, he must have felt, to impose his will on the liberal
wing of the Democratic party. Democrats would, in time,
be asked to join ranks with liberal Republicans. He told
Rosenman that the "conservatives" could "join together
as they see fit." The jovial judge seemed relieved that
none of this grand refashioning of America's political
structure would begin until Mr. Roosevelt was safely
back in the White House.

The judge did not understand why he was being thus
indulged until the President jammed his cigarette down
into an ashtray and asked Sam to set up a secret meeting
with Wendell Willkie in New York. Rosenman must have
realized why he had been selected—instead of Harry Hopkins or anyone whose face was well known—to make the
Willkie contact. The President thought it was a splendid
idea, but Rosenman shook his head and said that Willkie
might think that Roosevelt was angling for a public endorsement. Possibly, Roosevelt said. He suggested that
Sam explain to Mr. Willkie that the projected meeting
had nothing to do with the coming campaign. It was
a matter which could have waited. The thing which made
it imperative was that the President was given to ecstatic
seizures, moments when great problems evolved to be
acted upon at once. He was the strongest man in the
strongest country in the strongest century of mankind's
dismal chronicle, but laden with the ponderous problems
of war and peace, allies who could not agree among themselves; whipping the nags of industry to grind out one
more plane, one more tank, one more ship, one more
gun; conscious of his own precarious health, he ordered
Sam to meet secretly with Willkie and to sound him out
on a political realignment which could leave more gore
in its wake since the old realignment of Whigs, Tories
and Federalists.

The meeting was arranged for noon at the St. Regis
Hotel. The judge arrived first in a private suite. A little
later, there was a quiet knock and Willkie came in alone.

Lunch was ordered. When the waiter arrived, he was received by Samuel Rosenman, although the servings were for two. The titular leader of the Republican party was in another room. When the waiter departed, Mr. Willkie emerged for food and conversation. The judge completed the small pleasantries and led delicately into the revolutionary proposition of welding two major political parties.

The President, he said, was delighted that Governor Pinchot had stopped in to explain Wendell Willkie's position. It was a matter, he delicately suggested, which would have to wait until after the elections—"after the war," Willkie said—but the President would like to have liberals of Willkie's stature join him in revamping national politics. Willkie was an exuberant eater and talker. He was behind Roosevelt a hundred percent, he stated. That is, in regard to the post-election realignment, of course. After the war, he said, there would have to be an American showdown in which the liberals and internationalists would be on one side confronting the "conservatives and isolationists" on the other. They talked on, and Rosenman began to feel confident. The Boss had been right again.

"You tell the President," Willkie said, "that I am ready to devote almost full time to this." The two men spent two hours over cold coffee evaluating a list of leaders of industry, labor, politics who might be induced to join their cause. "The only thing I insist on," Willkie said, "is that I not meet the President until after the election." The conferees reassured each other about secrecy and confidentiality. Willkie was not challenged as a "sore loser" in his own party. Both men spoke "above party," as though the ultimate division of American politics must polarize toward liberal and reactionary. They agreed that neither Willkie nor Roosevelt would mention the realignment until "around Christmas." When Rosenman told FDR what happened, the Boss said, "Fine, fine. I will see him at the proper time."

Thus the New York judge became a part of Roosevelt's partitioned filing system. The thing which Rosenman knew was known to no other in the White House—just as the secrets involved in dictation were known to Grace Tully but not to Dorothy Brady (or vice versa) while some of the errands done by Pa Watson were unknown to Marvin McIntyre or to Jonathan Daniels. It is difficult to conceive that secrets were kept from Harry Hopkins, but Ed Flynn arranged certain matters for the President which were not revealed to Harry the Hop. The pigeon-hole plotting extended to almost all areas of Mr. Roosevelt's public and private life. Secretary of State Cordell Hull might not have despised his brilliant deputy, Sumner Welles, had it not been for the Chief Executive's penchant for giving private assignments to Welles, keeping them secret from the Secretary of State.

The roses of June were dropping rusty petals when Secretary Bill Hassett opened the door to Roosevelt's bedroom at 11:00 A.M. to escort four men inside for an informal conference. They were Senator Kenneth D. McKellar, seventy-five; Hull, seventy-three; Secretary of War Henry L. Stimson, seventy-seven; and Gifford Pinchot, seventy-nine. There wasn't a smile in the group of granite faces. Roosevelt propped a pillow, jutted his jaw in a prognathous grin, and said, "Good morning, kindergarten children." This small, inconsequential portrait of the aged and infirm gave point to Governor Thomas E. Dewey's indictment of "men in the White House who have grown old, tired, stubborn and quarrelsome."

July 1944

THE SOVIETS HAD 1,500,000 MEN FACING 750,000. THE difference was greater than the disparity in manpower. The Russians had 31,000 field pieces; 5,200 tanks and self-propelled guns; and a bomber-fighter force of 6,000.

The Slavs and Tartars, from General Rokossovsky on down to the green recruits, were not content with a military triumph; they wanted revenge. The Germans in 1941 and 1942 had not only taken their land up to the high-water level of Leningrad, Moscow, Stalingrad, Odessa, but they had leveled the cities and villages and slaughtered the civilians.

In some sections the Soviets used 320 artillery pieces per mile. Josef Stalin revealed that he had sent as many as 100 trainloads of supplies per night throughout the buildup. Close behind the front, bombed buildings were reroofed and temporary shelters were fashioned into military hospitals to accommodate 294,000 wounded. When Russian divisions broke through German lines in parts of Belorussia, some soldiers burst into tears at what the Germans had done. Outside Zhlobin 2,500 Russian men, women and children reposed in an uncovered grave. The onrushing armies found no Jews; as many as 700,000 Russian partisans had been killed. All livestock had been slaughtered; spring planting had been forbidden by the Germans. General Tippelskirch, commander of the Fourth German Army, stated that special "rollers" had been devised to destroy all crops. Hitler had ordered Minsk destroyed; it was a big city, expensive and time-consuming to lay waste, to burn, to shell.

On July 3 the Soviets were certain of success. They had promised to support the American and British invasion of continental Europe and they kept their promise, and more. The strategy had been to attack with sufficient force to prevent the German High Command from transferring divisions to the west. The Soviet attack, on a broad front, was so brilliantly executed that the Russian armies achieved six breakthroughs; field commanders had no time to count the German dead. In a monotonous order of the day, Hitler ordered his divisions to hold the Berezina line and not to "yield an inch." The Soviet High Command was satisfied that he was serious. This eliminated the possibility of German fluid response. Rokossovsky and Cherniakhovsky struck hard on slants from the southeast and northeast. They bagged 100,000

Germans, killed 40,000 and ordered 57,00, including a few major generals, to the rear to be paraded through the streets of Moscow on July 17.

The press in Great Britain and the United States reported that the German armies on the Russian front had been weakened by the removal of seventy divisions railroaded 1,400 miles to the western front to confront Eisenhower. It was not true. Hitler, Keitel and Jodl were aware of the massive hordes of savage soldiers roaring out of the east. If the Germans could hold but one front, they preferred to hold the Russians while facing the British and Americans with half the number of divisions, retreating slowly across the face of France.

The President told intimates he was "down." It was, of course, psychologic rather than pathologic. Dr. Howard Bruenn conducted the morning and evening examinations and there was nothing new to report to McIntire. Mr. Roosevelt was "down" for a day or two, then "up" again. He became irritated with what he regarded as trivia, upset when decisions were made without his counsel. There were so many things he wanted to do at once; most of them had to await a propitious moment. He wanted to be rid of Cordell Hull, who chastised nations as one would naughty children. As July dawned, he was trying to coerce the United States and Great Britain to sever diplomatic relations with Argentina. The South American nation, under a military dictatorship, was defiantly pro-Axis and anti-American.

Hull was also breaking off diplomatic relations with Finland. This seemed to scar the President's sense of justice. Finland's crime was in fighting the Soviets for independence. The press, deprived of hard news, moved into the field of speculation. The *Herald-Tribune* stated that the President would not only run for a fourth term, but had plans to make his acceptance speech from the battlefields of Normandy. *The New York Times,* under the by-line of James B. Reston, angered the President by denigrating the Bretton Woods Conference, then in progress, to organize a United Nations. "The exploratory conversations between representatives of the United States, Great Britain, Russia and China on the formation of a world organization to enforce the peace have been delayed," Reston wrote, "because of their failure to reach agreement on questions of approach and procedure."

Mr. Roosevelt felt that the conference had not been delayed. Within a short time, forty-four nations at Bretton Woods had established an International Monetary Fund of almost $9 billion, with the United States contributing 25 percent; it also established an International Bank for Reconstruction and Development with a capitalization of over $9 billion. Anne O'Hare McCormick, writing in the *Times,* did not improve the President's mood. Speaking of Republican party strategy, she said: "The main job of the administration taking over next January would be to manage and speed up the readjustment to peace. . . . This process could be better carried out under the fresh, eager, resourceful and harmonious direction of the Republicans than by the old, tired, bureaucratic and divided minds of the Democrats." This, FDR said, was GOP propaganda.

Secretary Hull, with the reluctant approval of the President, sent a formal note to Finnish Chargé d'Affaires Alexander Thesleff stating that the United States was withdrawing recognition of Finland and that he was *persona non grata* in Washington. The Secretary was at some pains to explain that, in the matter of a military struggle between Finland and the Soviet Union, the United States was forced to feel sympathetic to the Russian cause, especially since Finland had entered into a pact with Nazi Germany and in the last week of June had enjoyed an extended visit from German Foreign Secretary Joachim von Ribbentrop in Helsinki. Mr. Hull said that he was sorry, but that he must freeze all of Finland's assets in the United States because any other course would be regarded as trading-with-the-enemy. Earlier, FDR had endorsed gallant little Finland for fighting mighty Russia. Now, through force of circumstances, the same scales were tilted in the opposite direction.

Another, and chronic, source of depression to the President was the huge shift of American manpower to "peacetime jobs." He decried this publicly. FDR reiterated that the war was far from over, that he felt that the most decisive battles lay ahead, that those who left war production jobs were akin to soldiers leaving the front lines. The war would continue for two, possibly three years, he said.

But the mood of the country was confident, serene, almost somnolent. America and its allies were winning on every front except at home. Skilled war workers passed the word that the military would be cutting back on defense orders soon. The families carried ration books for meats, gasoline and oil, for retread tires, but there was a flourishing black market for ration stamps and few viewed counterfeit stamps as unpatriotic. The magazines published photos of U.S. Marines floating face down in the surf off Saipan, but the odor of death was far away.

The stock market was of importance. It remained bullish in a trading day of 646,000 shares. General Motors was steady at 128½ points. In bed at the White House Mr. Roosevelt flushed with anger when he read Arthur Krock's assessment of the chances of Dewey and Bricker winning the autumn election. "A Democratic Party split . . . has impaired its chances outside the South in large states which gave their electoral votes to the President and has even threatened the loss of Southern electors. . . . Charges of maladministration of civilian affairs which, it will be said, is the consequence of inefficiency, corrupt machine politics, weariness, old age, and foreign doctrine and cannot safely be allowed to continue in the critical postwar period." Arthur Prettyman, hanging up the President's clothes, turned as Mr. Roosevelt tossed *The New York Times* on the floor. From the floor Fala cocked his head.

The home front was a disappointment to Mr. Roosevelt. The people could no longer be aroused to a fervor of patriotism. Rosy the Riveter had become an archaic character within two years of her birth. America had fourteen million men and women in uniform, but the profit motive remained the greatest goal of the greatest number. If Mr. Roosevelt was running out of patience with the people and the press, both were prepared to indulge him a little as the old man who had seen the nation through a great depression and a worldwide holocaust. The more he repeated that the final curtain had not been rung down on the action, the less attention they paid to the warnings. They bowled. They drank. They ate better than ever. They took time off from work.

Nor was this all. Roosevelt was annoyed that the pundits were assuming that he would run for a fourth term of office when he had not announced it. The President desired to surprise the nation with what he regarded as pleasant news, but the political writers assumed FDR would regard himself as indispensable to the office. Readers were told that the Democratic nominee for President was a foregone conclusion—they had better dwell upon who would be the vice-presidential candidate. There is no evidence that Mr. Roosevelt knew how sick, how weak, how old he was in the summer of 1944—it is positive that he knew he was under the daily care of a heart specialist—but he made it plain to his associates that he wanted to succeed where his old chief, Woodrow Wilson, had failed—to bring the nation to victory, to establish a peace-keeping organization. The question was: could he impose one more fighting campaign onto a body which no longer seemed to have the strength to turn the wheels of his chair?

Churchill, who was subservient to the friendly strength of the United States in 1941 and 1942, had become patronizing and empirically greedy. When Hull asked Anthony Eden to sever relations with Argentina, the Prime Minister took the matter out of the hands of his Foreign Minister and went over Hull's head to appeal to FDR: "You would not send your soldiers into battle on the British Service meat ration, which is far above what is given to our workmen. Your people are eating per head more meat and poultry than before the war, while ours are most sharply cut." England would continue

to suffer cordial relations with a Fascist government which
could supply beef. The best Churchill could do—"in view
of the pending American elections"—would be to sign
a short-term meat contract with Argentina instead of
a long one.

The President's reply was flippant:

> *The White House*
> *July 14, 1944*
>
> *To Former Naval Person:*
> *I would not do anything in the world to cut down the sup-*
> *ply of meat to England. Heaven knows that it is already*
> *quite short enough. We would do nothing to prevent your*
> *getting a new contract. . . .*

At times the personal struggle didn't seem to be worth
the effort. Politically and militarily, the war had been
triggered by the rape of Poland. Now, as the Soviet
armies approached Warsaw, the Poles under General
Bór-Komarowski made a unilateral decision to liberate
their capital before the arrival of the Russians. It was,
as FDR knew, a tragic mistake. The Russian armies
stopped short of Warsaw. This gave time to the Germans
to annihilate the flower of Polish manhood. Hitler ordered
his retreating Wehrmacht to wipe out Polish military
resistance, and made an attempt at erasing Warsaw from
the map.

Josef Stalin shed no tears. The Germans were doing
a favor for him. He wanted no opposition to his Polish
Socialist government organizing at Lublin. As Warsaw
radioed for assistance from Moscow, Stalin ordered the
northern armies to rest. He sent the southern wing into
Romania. Within three days the opportunistic King
Michael turned his back on his Nazi advisers, appointed
a left-wing government, accepted Moscow's terms for
peace and declared war on Germany. The British and
American governments were stunned at the rash action
of the Free Poles, and too timorous to beg the Russians
to go to the aid of Warsaw.

Increasingly, the President worried about the actions

of his friends and allies abroad, and at home. On Tuesday, July 11, obviously fatigued although in good humor, the President called a press conference and announced as casually as though it were not news that the United States recognized General Charles de Gaulle's French Committee of National Liberation as the *de facto* "authority" in French civil matters. It was a concession he did not desire, but it was politic to make the accord. General Eisenhower, he hastened to add, would retain complete authority in all military decisions in France. He expected that the French people, once freed, would make their choice of a permanent government at the ballot box.

Almost as casually, FDR dropped the second political shoe. He told the assemblage of reporters that copies of some correspondence between him and National Democratic Party Chairman Robert E. Hannegan would be furnished to them as they filed out. He would like to read aloud a letter he had sent to Mr. Hannegan this morning:

Dear Mr. Hannegan:

You have written me that in accordance with the records a majority of the delegates have been directed to vote for my renomination for the office of President, and I feel that I owe you, in candor, a simple statement of my position.

If the convention should carry this out, and nominate me for the Presidency, I shall accept. If the people elect me, I will serve.

Every one of our sons serving in this war has officers from whom he takes orders. Such officers have superior officers. The President is the Commander in Chief and he, too, has his superior officer—the people of the United States.

I would accept and serve, but I would not run in the usual partisan, political sense. But if the people command me to continue in this office and in this war, I have as little right to withdraw as the soldier has his post in the line.

At the same time, I think I have a right to say to you and to the delegates to the coming convention something which is personal—purely personal.

For myself, I do not want to run. By next spring I shall have been President and Commander in Chief of the Armed Forces for twelve years—three times elected by the people of this country under the American Constitutional system.

From the personal point of view, I believe that our economic system is on a sounder, more human basis than it was at the time of my first inauguration.

It is perhaps unnecessary to say that I have thought only of the good of the American people. My principal objective, you know, has been the protection of the rights and privileges and fortunes of what has been so well called the average American citizen.

After many years of public service, therefore, my personal thoughts have turned to the day when I could return to civil life. All that is within me cries to go back to my home on the Hudson River, to avoid public responsibilities, and to avoid also the publicity which in our democracy follows every step of the Nation's Chief Executive.

Such would be my choice. But we of this generation chance to live in a day and hour when our Nation has been attacked, and when its future existence and the future existence of our chosen method of government are at stake.

To win this war wholeheartedly, unequivocally, and as quickly as we can is our task of the first importance. To win this war in such a way that there be no further world wars in the foreseeable future is our second objective. To provide occupations, and to provide a decent standard of living for our men in the armed forces after the war, and for all Americans, are the final objectives.

Therefore, reluctantly, but as a good soldier, I repeat that I will accept and serve in the office, if I am so ordered by the Commander in Chief of us all—the sovereign people of the United States.

Very sincerely yours,
Franklin D. Roosevelt

The pencils and pens of almost two hundred reporters were still scribbling when someone shouted "Thank you, Mr. President" and the glut of journalists swept toward the President's office door as Secret Service men were shunted aside in the rush to get to the West Wing and put the flash on the wires. Although the news had been expected for months, still, as in pregnancy and terminal disease, the culminating event was stunning.

The letter, far from being a casual document, was as politically potent as patronage. The spurious modesty of the "good soldier"; the implied draft by the electorate; the posture, not as a candidate but as Commander in Chief; the cry to be released to return to his ancestral home; the quick switch to his as yet unfulfilled war aims —victory and a United Nations; every phrase was hand-crafted to enhance Roosevelt's indispensability to the office and to place him in a position unassailable by Thomas E. Dewey.

The twelfth was a hot Wednesday getting hotter. Herbert Brownell, Republican National Chairman, stopped at the old mansion New York reserved for its Governor to have breakfast with Dewey. These were dear friends as well as political allies, but neither of them appreciated the broad base of political infighting. Both were certain that the only way to win would be to denigrate Roosevelt personally. It did not occur to them that this man, who enjoyed the confidence of the electorate three times, could be beaten with a positive program vowing to create millions of peacetime jobs while holding inflation in check; that the best foreign policy would be to state and restate that final victory west and east was in sight and to propose to follow Roosevelt's precept in organizing a union of world states.

It was a very warm morning, and Dewey and Brownell devised a press release which would serve as a presage of what was to come:

Mr. Roosevelt is the first of thirty-two Presidents of the United States to claim the title of Commander in Chief makes him a soldier and to use that title as a pretext to perpetuate himself in political office. On November 4th, 1940, Mr. Roosevelt made this statement: "You will have a new President in 1944." When he said that, he was right.

It was Brownell who gave out mimeograph copies to the reporters. One read it and said that Dewey, in his acceptance speech in Chicago, said it was "the duty of a good American to accept the nomination for the presidency." Did this, he asked, apply to President Roosevelt? Herbert Brownell, trying to bait FDR, felt that he was being baited by journalists and his features froze. "Mr. Dewey's statement," he snapped, "speaks for itself. It is very clear and does not require elaboration by anyone else." Unconsciously Brownell had set the vicious, venomous tone of the campaign, and the President would wrap himself in his Navy cape in the posture of the citizen-soldier who walks his post.

For history's sake, it is tragic that some who might have served with distinction did not learn how to campaign. Roosevelt, who has been called the consummate politician, tailored his mock-modest role so that, if 40 percent of the nation was Democratic, and 40 percent Republican, he would devote all of his efforts to winning 11 percent of the independents. He was going to identify himself with the common soldier, and there was nothing Dewey could do to rebut it.

One night in July the President met with political advisers. The question to be decided was serious—who was to be endorsed for the Vice-Presidency? The President sat in his wheelchair behind his desk, the cigarette holder tapping against his teeth. Before him, in chairs and on sofas, sat Robert Hannegan, Postmaster General Walker, Edward Flynn, Mayor Edward Kelly of Chicago, and others. None of the men seemed surprised that the name of Henry Wallace was barely mentioned. It was obvious that Mr. Roosevelt was too tired to start another battle for his personal preference, as he had in 1940. As gently as possible, he was reminded that he had encouraged the candidacies of several aspirants, including Byrnes, Barkley, Douglas, Hull, Sam Rayburn, John Winant, Paul McNutt and Henry Kaiser.

One by one, the names were cast toward the ceiling, and shot down. Hannegan, a Missourian, said that

Senator Harry Truman had kept his nose clean; nobody disliked him and he had made a good record with his Senate committee investigating war industry costs. Yes, the President said, Truman was a good man, but so was Bill Douglas. FDR had already mailed a note to the convention chairman stating that "If I were delegate, I would vote for Henry Wallace." To further confound the situation, no one in the room that night of July 11 remembered that Senator Truman had promised to place the name of James Byrnes in nomination. Nor did anyone note that Truman would bray like a stubborn donkey when asked to go back on his word.

Mr. Roosevelt interposed to ask Sam Rosenman to meet Henry Wallace en route home from China and to put it to him gently that his name had been dropped from consideration. It would make it easier, FDR said, for him to face Wallace when he got to Washington. Someone else was delegated to reiterate bad news to Jimmy Byrnes. The President said that many of those present seemed to have decided on Truman. He sent an aide to find out the age of the Senator. He was sixty. The President asked each man present to give him a candid opinion about each name as it came up for discussion. FDR said of Truman that he had a good record as a loyal Democrat and supporter of the President's policies. Then he made a sharp conversational turn and asked what was wrong with John Winant, American Ambassador to Great Britain. The conferees, tough, practical politicos, thought that Winant and Wallace were idealistic dreamers. They wanted a partisan Democrat. Someone noted that Truman came from a doubtful state with fifteen electoral votes.

As the night hours wore on, the President murmured that it could be Douglas or Truman. Eagerly, Hannegan asked if he could have a note to that effect—something to show to state chairmen at the convention. The fight was gone from the old man. He took a sheet of White House stationery and in a bold and shaky hand he wrote:

July 19

Dear Bob:

You have written me about Bill Douglas and Harry Truman. I should, of course, be very glad to run with either of them and believe that either of them would bring real strength to the ticket.

Always sincerely,
Franklin Roosevelt

He had postdated it for the convention. Hannegan and Frank Walker, the Postmaster General, left together in a car under the north portico and Hannegan dropped into the back seat and whispered, "I got it." In the morning both men were back in the White House. Walker was there to visit Byrnes in the East Wing and convince him that he had no chance to become Vice President. Byrnes responded that Roosevelt had encouraged him and he was going to have his name placed in nomination. Roosevelt drew a promise from Hannegan that the "note" would not be used at the convention unless it was necessary. The Democratic chairman promised and asked if he could have the note typed by Grace Tully. Permission was given. Hannegan asked the handsome brunette to retype it, but to switch the names, so that it would read "Truman and Douglas." She asked if he had the President's permission to make the change and he assured her he had. Thus the convention delegates would assume that the Senator, not the Supreme Court Justice, was FDR's first choice.

Rosenman and Harold Ickes met Wallace at the Wardman Park and gave him the bad news. The Vice President did not believe it. Sourly, he said he would talk politics only with the President. When Wallace arrived at the White House, he displayed to President Roosevelt an impressive list of delegates and labor support. FDR reached up and put his arm around Wallace. "I hope it's the same team again, Henry," he said.

Byrnes phoned the President. He used his stenographic skill to take FDR's words down in shorthand: "I am not favoring anybody. I told them so. No, I am not favoring anyone." Hadn't he told Hannegan and Walker that he would run with Truman or Douglas? "Jimmy, that is all wrong. That is not what I told them. It is what they told me. We have to be damned careful about words. They asked if I would object to Truman or Douglas and I said no. That is different from using the word 'prefer.' " He saw no reason why Byrnes should not run if he felt disposed.

The guardian angel of the President, Mike Reilly, had been sent to Hawaii as advance man. FDR, who was fond of exterminating several birds with a single blow—a figure of spech he abhorred—had decided to make a spectacular trip to Hawaii and the Aleutian Islands in July and August. It would give him a chance to try out the role of Commander in Chief in the early days of the campaign; it would also depict him as interested in the outflung posts and the war in the Pacific; he could have conferences with MacArthur and Nimitz and smooth the differences between the two; he could stop surreptitiously near the Chicago convention in case anyone needed his guidance. It was also his notion of an ideal working vacation—a long slow train trip and a voyage on a heavy cruiser.

Mrs. Roosevelt told her husband that she had written a newspaper column endorsing Wallace for Vice President; the President, in mock anguish, begged her to "hold it." He had confounded the convention by nodding affirmatively to a half-dozen men; the "pols" had forced him to divide his blessings between Douglas and Truman; on July 13 and 14 he was busy reendorsing the discards. Byrnes would run. Wallace asked FDR to write a letter to the permanent chairman of the convention, Senator Samuel Jackson, personally espousing the Vice President; the Chief Executive had obliged:

. . . I have been associated with Henry Wallace during his past four years as Vice President, for eight years earlier while he was Secretary of Agriculture, and well before that. I like him and I respect him and he is my personal friend. For

these reasons I would vote for his renomination if I were a delegate to the convention. At the same time, I do not wish to appear in any way as dictating to the convention. . . .

Wallace took it to Chicago. Before he left, he asked Roosevelt what would happen to him if he lost the renomination. The President promised his friend a Cabinet post. After the Vice President departed, Dorothy Brady brought the final "Itinerary and Guest List" for the forthcoming trip. FDR could not be persuaded to leave on Friday, so Thursday at 10:45 P.M. was selected. In the stenciling and copying, no one remarked that the first stop would be Hyde Park, and Mr. Roosevelt had penciled it as a 6:00 P.M. arrival. No matter how slowly the train proceeded, it could not take nineteen and a half hours to negotiate three hundred miles.

Only D. L. Moorman, general passenger agent of the Baltimore and Ohio Railroad; Dewey Long and Major DeWitt Greer, in charge of White House communications and travel, were aware that the President proposed to stop the train at Allamuchy, New Jersey, for an all-day visit with Lucy Rutherfurd. The President had found an excuse to send Mrs. Roosevelt ahead to Hyde Park. She would join him there for the trip to San Diego.

If there was danger that the news reporters and photographers would divine his mysterious stops at Allamuchy and Aiken, Mr. Roosevelt was beyond worrying about it. Time and the subterfuges of love induce carelessness. The President seemed more interested in checking off those who would be at his side through the entire trip, and those who would make part of it.

Those who would go all the way included Admiral William D. Leahy; Vice Admiral Ross T. McIntire; Rear Admiral Wilson Brown, the President's aide and "trip historian"; Pa Watson; Lieutenant Commander Howard G. Bruenn; Lieutenant Commander George A. Fox, his masseur; the energetic secretary and "assistant trip historian," Lieutenant Willian M. Rigdon; Petty Officer

Arthur H. Prettyman, the President's valet, and, at the bottom of the list, Fala.

Among those who would make part of the rail trip were "Sis" (daughter Anna); Mrs. Franklin Roosevelt; speech writers Samuel Rosenman and Elmer W. Davis, who would frame the President's acceptance speech before he was nominated; Grace Tully; Dorothy Brady; Mrs. Roosevelt's secretary, Malvina Thompson (who would board the train at Hyde Park); Dewey Long, DeWitt Greer and Moorman. The pool newsmen were Merriman Smith of UP, Howard Fleiger of AP, Robert Nixon of INS. The photographers were Hugo Johnson, Al Oeth and George Skadding. There were others—three men in a radio pool; nine Secret Service agents, including a strong swimmer, who would make the entire trip, and five agents, including Reilly, already at Honolulu; nine more who would protect the President on the trip to San Diego and the return trip from Seattle to Washington. There were also eight Navy cooks and waiters.

At 10:30 P.M. Mr. Roosevelt was wheeled aboard his heavy private Pullman by Arthur Prettyman. The rest of the train, with its distinguished list of passengers, was backing down from the Virginia Avenue yards. Mr. Roosevelt seemed to be in good spirits and retired almost at once.

The train rocked along in the night, and those who stayed up late to play cards remarked that the train was not using Pennsylvania Railroad tracks. In the morning, with the sun barely up, it racked itself to a stop on a rusty siding. An automobile pulled up beside the last car. A few minutes later, FDR, dressed and shaved, sat in his chair on the small elevator at the rear stairway and descended slowly to the platform. A few people on the train were awakened by the jolting of the cars. One said, "Where the hell is Allamuchy?" It was assumed that one of the cars had a hot box, or that some minor trouble had caused the stop.

Among the Secret Service agents who trotted beside the automobile were Howard Anderson and Jim Griffith. They followed the sleepy, rural roads to a huge gate leading to a snow-white mansion. This was Tranquillity, once the home of Winthrop Rutherfurd, now owned by Lucy, his widow. The President entered the building, and those who accompanied him waited outside. Anderson was stationed at the front gate; Griffith was told to guard the rear of the building. He found an aged wicker rocker and sat with his back to the building.

The interior of the eighteen-car train was hot and became hotter. The engineer and fireman stood down beside the big locomotive and told newsmen that they had no idea why the train had been stopped. "Orders," that's all. The sun lifted itself above the fields of saw grass and small farms of corn and tomatoes and beans. Noon arrived and lunch was served. The afternoon was slow and distressing. Some said it was cooler to sit in the shade of the old railroad station and hope for a slight breeze; others decided to remain tieless and shoeless on the train. It was a long, long day.

In mid-afternoon the President's limousine was seen coming over a rise with Secret Service men on the running boards. The party appeared to be hot and exhausted. The train departed for Poughkeepsie, and the President knew that Mrs. Roosevelt would ask why he was on the "other side of the river" and he knew that he would tell her that the Secret Service did not like to have him chance traveling over the New York Central's Hell Gate Bridge —which in wartime might be a risk. It would satisfy her. It had before.

At 5:00 P.M. the train was pulling toward the Hudson River when, at Allamuchy, the stately Lucy Rutherfurd emerged to walk in her backyard. She saw the strange man sitting in the wicker rocker. She said, "Are you part of the President's party?" "Yes," he said, standing. "Well," she said, smiling, "they all left about an hour ago." Agent Jim Griffith uttered a polite farewell and ran, fuming, to the front of the house. They had indeed left without him. It would require the rest of the day and evening to catch up with the train.

The President's indiscretion spread to other areas. Before leaving the White House, he had sent a letter to

Wendell Willkie, in spite of his agreement with Sam Rosenman that the matter of a political realignment should not be mentioned to anyone until after the election:

Dear Wendell:

I will not be able to sign this because I am dictating it just as I leave on a trip to the westward. What I want to tell you is that I want to see you when I come back, but not on anything in relationship to the present campaign.

I want to talk with you about the future, even the somewhat distant future, and in regard to the foreign relations problems of the immediate future. When you see in the papers that I am back, will you get in touch with General Watson? We can arrange a meeting either here in Washington, or, if you prefer, at Hyde Park—wholly off the record or otherwise, just as you think best.

Always sincerely yours,

Mr. Roosevelt did not tell Sam Rosenman about the letter. Had he felt that he would not have had to defend his position in sending it, one may assume that he would have told Sam, the only person in the White House who knew about the secret lunch at the St. Regis Hotel. "I doubt that anyone knew about it," Rosenman said later, "except Grace, who typed it. . . . He seemed not to want any one person to know the whole story." Within a few days, the story of the secret letter began to "leak" to the press.

Wendell Willkie and his followers charged that Roosevelt himself had hinted about the letter at a dinner conversation. The leak, they claimed, was traceable to him. Willkie had confided the grand realignment of political power in the United States to a friend or two. When he received the letter from the President, he was overcome by panic that he was being drawn into a presidential trap which would make it appear to the electorate that he was backing FDR for a fourth term. The phrase "wholly off the record or otherwise" frightened the one-time

Republican nominee. He felt that he was being used, and was outraged.

On the Hyde Park—Chicago leg of the trip, the speech writers worked a full day with Mr. Roosevelt on his acceptance speech. Each draft was typed by Grace Tully, to be torn down by the President and redrafted by Rosenman and Elmer Davis. One of them remarked that it seemed strange to be working on such a historic document without the yeas and nays of Harry Hopkins. The President's close adviser was still ill, and the President seemed to have lost solicitude. He seldom conferred, even by phone, with Hopkins, and rarely referred to him.

Mr. Roosevelt might well have eliminated the two-hour stop in Chicago. His train was moved awkwardly from the Englewood Station to the Fifty-first Street coach yard of the Rock Island System. A phone was placed aboard. In a short time, Hannegan arrived, perspiring, with Mayor Edward Kelly. The large rear compartment of the President's car was cleared for private conversations. Hannegan stated the obvious: the convention gavel would not be heard for four days and yet the vice-presidential situation was a bedlam. Byrnes was running; Barkley might; Wallace had the CIO vote in his pocket and was claiming presidential endorsement; Truman wasn't even a dark horse because he was telling the early arrivals that he was nominating Jimmy Byrnes.

What solace Hannegan and Kelly drew from Roosevelt is unrecorded. He seemed surprised that there was any problem. He would not lend himself to a Stop Wallace movement, but he promised not to help his Vice President either. Hannegan had already corralled the bread-and-butter politicians—Mayor Kelly; Edwin Pauley, the millionaire who garnered and allocated funds for the party; Ed Flynn, who didn't want FDR to run; David Lawrence of Pennsylvania, and George Allen, secretary of the Democratic National Committee. Among them, they could marshal sufficient strength, Hannegan felt, to stop Wallace, but they would also have to start Truman. Worse, the word had got around that this was going

to be an open convention. Some state delegations were
ready to present favorite sons.

The train left the Rock Island yards moving slowly
westward. The day was July 15; the President did not
want to reach San Diego until the pre-dawn hours of the
nineteenth. This placed a burden on the divisional chiefs
of the railroads, who had to work out a right-of-way for
the presidential special, with its advance locomotive flying two white flags, and yet use the trackage allocated to
long, slow freight trains and swift passenger cars. This
time FDR insisted on such a slow rate of speed that the
train had to be placed on a siding at Fairbanks, Arizona,
to recharge all car batteries.

Senator Harry Truman had driven from Washington
to his home in Independence, Missouri, to pick up his
wife, Bess, and his daughter, Margaret. The Senator was
a firm family man and would have taken his aged mother
if she had elected to go to Chicago. He was packing suitcases in the car when the phone rang. It was Jimmy
Byrnes. He said that the President had "given me the
green light," and he wanted to make sure that Truman
would nominate him. The Senator said that he would
be proud to do it.

The phone rang again. This time it was Senator Alben
Barkley. He asked if Harry Truman would nominate
him. The Missourian said that he was sorry, but he had
been pledged to the cause of Byrnes. It did not occur
to him that there might be a reason why two candidates
for the Vice-Presidency would try to derail Truman to
the status of nominating agent.

The convention was a marvel of indecision and pressure. Hannegan was convinced that if Byrnes could be
dismissed before a state roll call, Truman could be placed
in nomination to face Wallace. In that event, Hannegan
reasoned, the old-line politicians would prevail and Truman would be nominated. On the other hand, if Wallace
fought Byrnes *and* Truman, he would divide the strength
of the city politicians and win.

On the Sunday before the convention opened, Truman
had breakfast with Sidney Hillman, longtime president

of the Amalgamated Clothing Workers and a political force in the liberal wing of the party. Truman tried to convince Hillman that Byrnes was bound to win. Sidney Hillman shook his head sadly. The nominee, he assured the bow-tied Senator, would be Wallace. Hopefully Truman asked who Hillman's second choice might be. "You," said the head of the Political Action Committee. The Senator was stunned. "Me?" he said. "I'm not running. I'm for Byrnes."

Personal and party loyalty were important to Truman. He hurried to the Blackstone Hotel to explain developments to Byrnes. The jaunty Irishman from South Carolina was unimpressed. He expected such diversionary tactics and looked upon Truman as his inalienable friend; if there was an enemy it was Wallace. It was confusion compounded; Hannegan told the party director of public relations, Paul A. Porter, "We have no candidate." In turn, Porter responded to the incisive questions of the press stating that he did not know where Robert Hannegan was. "He is probably with his wife and children."

When Hannegan was located at a dinner given for the party staff, he denied that he had any directive "or letter from the President." In another section of Chicago, Senator Samuel Jackson was impelled to release *his* letter from the President, endorsing the candidacy of Henry A. Wallace. On July 19, Governor Robert S. Kerr of Oklahoma, a suitably tough oil millionaire, made the keynote speech and the delegates paraded in a frenzy of open, sweaty faces every time Kerr referred to the "Commander in Chief."

Wallace arrived and said, "I am in this fight to a finish." Alben Barkley issued a publicity statement: "I am still very much in the race." Hannegan and his adherents were spreading the word, delegation by state delegation, that the President would be satisfied with either "Truman or Douglas" as a running mate. Of the two, the party wheelhorses preferred Truman, the regular, against Douglas the idealist. Truman votes were racked up on an adding machine. At 9:00 P.M. Wallace walked into the convention hall, and, to the consternation of the Hannegan forces, the delegates and the galleries stood to give him an ovation. The band, with no cue from the dais, began to play "Iowa, Iowa, the State Where the Tall Corn Grows" and two choruses of "My Hero."

The renomination of Roosevelt was no more important to the convention than the nightly singing of "The Star-Spangled Banner." Hannegan felt that the political world hung on Truman, and, too late, he asked the Senator to run. Truman declined. Hannegan produced his note from the President. (He now had a second copy of it, received from FDR in the Chicago railroad yards, with the choices reversed so that the Boss suggested "Truman or Douglas.") The Senator seemed to be saddened. Obstinately, he said he was pledged to Byrnes and could not be counted on to run unless Byrnes released him. In a sophisticated political world, this was innocence rampant. Truman insisted. He hurried to another suite in the Blackstone Hotel and confronted Byrnes with the news. The Southerner was shocked almost to silence. He asked that a personal phone call be put through to the President on his train. The word came back: "The President cannot speak to you at this time."

To Byrnes, this was clearly the end of the line; the last knife wound in three decades of political fighting. He glanced at Senator Truman and told him that he was released from placing the name of Byrnes in nomination. Byrnes was too numbed to congratulate his friend and supporter. The vacillation, indeed the now chronic ambivalence of the President, had become as distressing to his party affiliates as to his foreign alliances. If there was something for which even his dearest friends could not forgive him, it was his penchant for sudden, irreversible moves—such as the letter to Willkie.

The President's train was rolling slowly through the clear arid country of the Southwest when he conceived the notion of cabling Josef Stalin to ask for a summit conference. If it was politically motivated, it was poorly conceived; on the other hand, if it was designed to spare Poland (which is doubtful), it was too late:

Number 27. Top Secret and Personal
From the President for Josef Stalin

*Things are moving so fast and so successfully that I feel
there should be a meeting between you and Mr. Churchill
and me in the reasonably near future. The Prime Minister is
in hearty accord with this thought. I am now on a trip in
the Far West and must be in Washington for several weeks
on my return. It would, therefore, be best for me to have a
meeting between the tenth and fifteenth of September. The
most central point for you and me would be the north of
Scotland. I could go by ship and you could come either by
ship or by plane. [Here he dictated a sentence, later eliminated, praising Stalin's armies as "doing magnificently."]
I hope you can let me have your thoughts. Secrecy and security can be maintained either aboard ship or on shore.*

Roosevelt

On the same day the President dictated a letter to
former Senator George W. Norris in response to a
telegram from Norris stating a fear that the Democrats
would nominate Wendell Willkie for Vice President. Norris, who had six weeks to live, was the father of the
Tennessee Valley Authority and husbanded a hatred for
Willkie as its mortal enemy. Mr. Roosevelt addressed
the letter to him in McCook, Nebraska:

Dear George:

*Your telegram reached me on the train while I was only
one state away from McCook on my way to the Coast. I
don't think there is any possible danger of Willkie, though
feelers were put out about a week ago.*

*I am honestly trying to keep out of the Vice-Presidential
contest which includes a score of candidates and another
score who have their lightning rods up and would like to be
struck. . . .*

The train was in the deserts of California when Mr.
Roosevelt spoke to Hannegan at the Blackstone Hotel.
It was apparent to the President that his friends were
working for the nomination of Truman, and so it was

arranged that the Senator would be in the room with Frank Walker, Ed Flynn and Ed Kelly when the call came through. FDR played his part.

"Have you got that fellow lined up yet?" he asked. Hannegan said no. "Well, tell the Senator that if he wants to break up the Democratic party by staying out, he can. But he knows as well as I what that might mean at this dangerous time in the world. . . ." Truman capitulated. He could not understand why his chief preferred him over other, more worthy candidates, but he was willing to have his name placed in nomination.

The party chairman decided that, even with the presidential blessing, the only way in which Truman could be nominated would be to ask some favorite sons to step aside. Among these were Paul McNutt of Indiana, Senator John Bankhead of Alabama, Scott Lucas of Illinois, Alben Barkley of Kentucky and Robert Kerr of Oklahoma. Each declined to step aside on the ground that the convention was so uncertain that all favorite sons were now dark horses. It was thought that, as Alabama would be the first state in the roll call, it would have a psychological effect if the delegation opened the proceedings by voting for Truman instead of Bankhead. But Bankhead declined to step aside.

On the twentieth, as the President's train lay in the yards at San Diego, California, the delegates went through the motions of nominating him for a fourth term. The tally was Roosevelt 1,086, Senator Harry Byrd of Virginia 89. The chair recognized Henry Agard Wallace. Without permission, the Vice President moved to the podium and made an impassioned speech for the party not to desert the New Deal. It was an exciting appeal for a man who seldom displayed his feelings, and the delegates and galleries were in a frenzy. Michael Di Salle of Ohio, a young delegate, learned that thousands of counterfeit gallery tickets had been printed and distributed to vociferous young Wallace adherents. By the time the President—sitting in his railroad car in the yards at San Diego—was ready to make his acceptance speech, Hannegan and Pauley feared that they had lost control

of the convention and postponed nomination of a Vice
President until the following night.

Spotlights focused on a huge photograph of the President at the convention as he was introduced as "speaking
from a Pacific Coast naval base." The voice came into
the hall booming. What he had to say was tactful rather
than statesmanlike. He reiterated his desire to retire to
the "quiet life," but "you in this convention have asked
me to continue." He would be "too busy to campaign
in the usual sense" and he hoped for reelection on the
basis of "experience versus immaturity." His program
would be to win the war. Then he proposed to secure
peace "with force, if necessary." He would gear the
economy to attain full employment and a higher standard
of living for the people. For those voters who might be
wavering between Roosevelt and Dewey, he had a special
caution: It would be up to them to decide, in November,
whether plans already made and men already serving
to achieve victory and make the world a better place
in which to live were to be continued. Otherwise, the
grand plans would be replaced by a new administration
with no program except to "oppose."

The President sat in the presence of two sons and their
wives as he tried to bring a freshness of purpose to the
speech. As he sat, an Associated Press photographer was
allowed in to make a picture. It was published all over
the country and may have been given special prominence
because it was a bad one. Mr. Roosevelt looked haggard.
The eyes were dark sockets. The thin shoulders sagged
in an oversize jacket. The mouth hung open listlessly.
The legs under the desk were splayed awkwardly. It was
at this point that the people, rather than the politicians,
began to think of their President as a sick man.

At the end of the speech, there was thunderous
applause and a demonstration. Hannegan and Ed Pauley,
high on the rostrum, looked down at the crowd as Senator
Jackson tried to restore order. What they saw frightened
them. There were 30,000 unauthorized persons on the
floor and in the galleries, in a place designed to hold

20,000. Most of them carried photos of Wallace. They chanted, "We want Wallace. We want Wallace." Pauley called Mayor Kelly to the podium and asked if he knew of a legal reason for adjourning the session. "Sure," Kelly said, "we have fire laws." The session was adjourned, and the young Wallace people were in a fury. Pauley handed a fire axe to a man and told him to cut the cables leading to the huge theater organ which played "Iowa, That's Where the Tall Corn Grows." "If he won't stop playing it," Pauley said, "cut the cables."

The exit doors were flung open. Outside, thousands of citizens tried to force their way in as the delegates and Wallaceites crashed outward. Ribs began to crack; women fainted; snake dancers walked over fallen persons; Senator Jackson banged a gavel and shouted, "Session adjourned." No one heard him.

A tall man with the shiny dome and shiny shoes, James A. Farley, smiled good-naturedly at the will of the convention and returned to his hotel. He had cast one-half vote for Senator Byrd. At the hotel, he wrote: "Anyone with a grain of common sense would surely realize from the appearance of the President that he is not a well man and there is not a chance in the world for him to carry on for four more years and face the problems that a President will have before him; he just can't survive another term."

The delegates might have believed Hannegan, who urged them with desperation to believe that Harry Truman was FDR's choice, but, as the hot sun sank in Chicago, the voting politicians reminded each other that they had seen letters from the President confirming a number of candidates as his running mate. They had Harry Truman in Room H under the stands, shaking hands with delegates he had never met. Up on the convention floor Henry Wallace walked the aisles, shaking hands, grinning, asking for votes, and brushing the small sheaf of wheat from his brow.

The chairman had started the roll call. He announced Alabama in the proper rolling tones. At the podium Senator John Bankhead asked Ed Pauley to stop it, that he was about to release his delegates to Truman. Pauley rushed to Chairman Jackson, but it was too late. Alabama had voted for Bankhead. Wallace led in the balloting. When the vote reached Ohio, which had caucused and given a majority of its vote to Wallace, Ray Miller, chairman of the delegation, cast the entire vote for Truman. A labor delegate named Jack Kroll tried to grab the microphone from Miller. A few others joined the fray, twisting the microphone stand and tumbling with punches, and the roll call moved on to the next state.

The first ballot ended with Wallace at 429½ to Truman's 319½. The significance was not the difference in numbers, but that all the favorite sons held the balance of power—400 votes. The second roll call began. The switch to Truman was supposed to begin with Ed Kelly's big Illinois vote. However, when Chairman Jackson called Illinois, Kelly, who had worked hard for Truman, sustained a monumental memory lapse and cast all the votes for Senator Scott Lucas.

Huge electric fans were whirring steadily over the heads of the delegates, but Hannegan was dripping perspiration from his eyebrows. The first break came when Maryland switched its vote from a favorite son to Truman. Oklahoma's Governor Kerr did not propose to be caught lagging and, in spite of his personal ambitions, switched his state to Truman. Several states had passed, anxious to cast their votes for a winner. Paul McNutt of Indiana quit the race and switched his state to Truman (except two votes for Wallace). The name Truman began to echo through the floor. State chairmen who had already cast their ballots began to roar for attention. New York, which had cast 93 votes for Wallace, switched to Truman. Jimmy Byrnes, who had been sitting in a box with Bess and Margaret Truman, excused himself and hopped down onto the floor to sit with his South Carolina delegation. Massachusetts gave 34 votes to Truman. South Carolina switched 16 votes from Byrnes to Truman. But it was Kansas' 16 votes which gave the nomination to the junior Senator from Missouri. When it was announced, the scream of satisfaction came from a thousand throats. Jimmy Byrnes squeezed down in his floor chair until the back of his neck was close to the seat. The final vote: Truman 1,031; Wallace 105.

In a moment, all of the hundreds of Wallace placards vanished. Three gigantic white balloons, swaying above the convention with the demand, "We want Wallace," were cut loose and floated to the rafters, where they bumped softly against the iron of the girders. Someone remembered, and repeated aloud, Bennett Champ Clark's nominating speech for Harry Truman: "In this year of destiny, it is more than ever necessary to select a Vice President possessing all the qualities and all the qualifications desirable and necessary for a President of the United States." No convention made it more obvious that, this one time, the V.P. would be expected to be worthy of the high office of Chief Executive.

FDR spent the day watching an amphibious landing by the Fifth Marine Division. At his side was his son Jimmy. The President said he felt "thrilled," sitting on a hill in an automobile, watching the buglike approach of landing craft, the shore bombardment by cruisers and destroyers, and the thousands of small figures breaching the surf and running up the beach. The following morning he was still thinking about it as he dictated a letter to his wife, for the morning pouch to Washington:

Dearest Babs:

Off in a few minutes—All well. I might have to hurry back earlier if this German revolt gets worse! I fear though that it won't.

Yesterday a.m. Jimmy and I had a grand view of the landing operation at Camp Pendleton and then I got the collywobbles and stayed in the train, in the p.m. Better today.

Saw Carlson this p.m. and said good-bye to the chicks.

It was grand having you come out with me—and the slow speed was a good thing for us both.

Lots of love—back soon.

Devotedly

F.

His reference to the German revolt was a radio intercept from Berlin that Adolf Hitler had survived a bomb attack by German officers. In the Far East the Tojo government collapsed when U.S. Marines took the island of Saipan, which placed the new 20th Air Force within bombing range of Tokyo. The hastily formed government of Kuniaki Koiso sensed a chilling danger from Russia and opened its first session by addressing itself to Moscow rather than Washington by promising to "maintain friendly relations with the Soviet Union and exert our best efforts in order to avoid provocations."

The President's reference to "collywobbles" may have been dysentery, and may have been a malaise. Sitting with his son Jimmy, FDR's pleasant features tightened to an agonizing frown and he said, "Jimmy, I don't know if I can make it—I have horrible pains." He closed his eyes, and the young man felt that his father was beset by waves of discomfort which continued for several minutes. Colonel Roosevelt begged his father to cancel his appointments. The President declined. By collusion or by accident, neither reported the incident to Dr. Howard Bruenn. The subject of the President's health continued to be a private matter.

Within the White House there was a rumor that the President had survived a secret and major operation at Hobcaw in May. Harry Hopkins, a convalescent, told the President of a report that the Pacific trip had been canceled because of ill health; "the underground is working overtime here in regard to your health," Hopkins wrote. Sam Rosenman feared that a presidential speech—formerly a joy for FDR—now "took a day or more" out of his work schedule. Reading reports, pondering, making decisions—even on "easy days"—reduced the President to an approximation of exhaustion. Dr. Bruenn, a Republican, decided to vote for Roosevelt in November.

A mail pouch was flown to the President's train from Washington, and he buckled to the grind of dictating the last letters before leaving for Honolulu:

To Harry S. Truman:

I send you my heartiest congratulations on your victory. I am, of course, very happy to have you run with me. Let me know your plans. I shall see you soon.

Franklin D. Roosevelt

To Josef Stalin, Moscow:

Just as I was leaving on this trip to the Pacific, I received the very delightful framed photograph of you which I consider excellent. I am particularly happy to have it and very grateful to you.

The·speed of the advance of your armies is amazing and I wish much that I could visit you to see how you are able to maintain your communications and supplies to the advancing troops.

We have taken the key island of Saipan after rather heavy losses and are at this moment engaged in the occupation of Guam. At the same time, we have just received news of the difficulties in Germany and especially at Hitler's headquarters. It is all to the good.

With my very warm regards, I am

Very sincerely yours,

There was a determination within FDR to play the part of Commander in Chief. It meant more to him than a campaign slogan. In July, when he departed westward to iron the wrinkles from the disagreements between General MacArthur and Admiral Nimitz, Mr. Roosevelt did not invite General Marshall or Admiral King to accompany him. He would oversee this dispute alone, except for old Admiral Leahy. Further, he had notions about how to fight the war. He advised the Atlantic Fleet to assume more "risks" because supply tonnage was urgently needed in Normandy and North Africa.

He argued the merits of having several destroyers guard an aircraft carrier as against one cruiser. When Japanese aircraft suicide stories were brought to his attention, the President asked for high temporary masts and emergency wire tripping on flight decks. The rotation of personnel was important to his thinking and he asked Army and

Navy commanders to make certain that front-line servicemen were returned to rest areas promptly, to be replaced by fresh faces. Nor was he remiss in reviewing
courts-martial. Once in a rare while he overturned a
sentence. One concerned a Navy nurse who had gone
AWOL at Norfolk to join her sailor husband for a honeymoon. It was arbitrary for her to desert her post, the
President noted, but it was equally arbitrary to refuse
her request for shore leave to be with her bridegroom.

Purposefully, FDR assumed a double burden—as a
full-time working President and as a soldier. He was
aware, according to his son Jimmy, that he was
dangerously ill and could not execute one job efficiently;
in July 1944 he cultivated two.

The 14,000-ton cruiser *Baltimore* lay dockside at
San Diego waiting for orders. She was big, dark and
stark, with 8-inch rifles in repose. The *Baltimore* had
distinguished herself and her company in Pacific battles,
but the scuttlebutt had no notion of her newest assignment
until ships' carpenters began to build wooden ramps from
the main deck to the captain's quarters. The word was
passed: "President Roosevelt." On Friday evening, off-
duty swabs saw a Scottie trotting back and forth on the
deck plates. The word was passed: "Fala is aboard."

The big ship and her escorts were ready Friday evening
at sundown, but Mr. Roosevelt would not sail on Friday.
He had dinner with two sons and their wives, returned
to his railroad train and left shortly before midnight.
When his wheelchair was rolled up the ramp and he was
piped aboard, the order to single all lines was issued at
0013 on Saturday. Six destroyers with radar and sound
gear were outside Point Loma in the dark blue night of
the sea, waiting to escort the big ship. Mr. Roosevelt
retired at once. As a long-time sailor, he found surcease
in the slow throb of the big engines, outward bound at
6 knots.

In the morning the Chief Executive seemed rested as
he came on deck. The cruiser had been stripped of all
frills. When FDR saw Sam Rosenman reclining in a deck

chair in the sun, he burst into laughter. Ahead and flanking, the escorts dipped their bows creaming into heavy swells. Overhead, there was some land-based aircraft watching over the important voyager. One of the destroyers was detached to pick up messages from Washington and from San Diego.

She raced over the horizon, so that enemy submarines could not obtain a directional fix on the cruiser. In the afternoon the "news" came aboard. The new provisional government of Poland, organized at Lublin, issued a July manifesto which asserted that, after the war, the Polish borders would be on the Curzon Line to the east (which would give to the Soviet Union the territory gained by Adolf Hitler) at the expense of Germany in the west, where the boundary would be on the Oder-Neisse river line. It was not good news. The fears of the Polish government-in-exile, that the Slavic plain would be sliced anew for the benefit of Russia, were being realized.

A message from Stalin arrived in response to Roosevelt's request for an early, and perhaps politically motivated, summit meeting. The Soviet dictator said that it would not be feasible: "When the Soviet Armies are involved in battles on such a wide front, it would be impossible for me to leave the country. . . . All my colleagues consider it absolutely impossible." The President had no comment. He was taken to the bridge. In good weather he observed the escorts—now reduced to four destroyers—and asked about course changes (currently 243 true) and speed (22 knots).

He returned to his quarters for lunch with members of his party and took a leisurely nap afterward. In the evening, in spite of orders for a darkened ship, he sat on the quarter deck with officers and some of the 1,600 sailors and Marines to watch a movie. It wasn't until the third day that he began to notice the absence of Fala from his side. The dog disappeared below decks with monotonous regularity. In the evening the President thought he had discovered the reason.

Fala appeared to be shedding or shorn. There was

little black hair left on his back. Mr. Roosevelt ordered an aide to investigate. Within an hour he understood what had happened. Some of the sailors had coaxed Fala to the crew mess to feed him tidbits. The dog had been a conscious party to the wrongdoing. One sailor said he had a kid brother back home who would appreciate a lock of the hair of the President's dog. This led to a snip here and there a snip. Many sailors seemed to recollect the affection of loved ones for Fala. Mr. Roosevelt issued an order, through Captain Walter L. Calhoun, that the dog was not to be fed, and not to be clipped.

A coded Hawaiian alert was intercepted by the *Baltimore*. It was from Commander, Hawaiian Sea Frontier, and stated: "Possible enemy task force located 200 miles north of Oahu. Alert all activities." There was a serious question aboard the cruiser whether the task group should reverse course away from the danger. It was doubtful whether the report was valid. If true, it was even more doubtful that such a Japanese force would continue eastward and place itself between Hawaii and continental United States. Courses continued to zigzag at reduced speed. No further report was heard from Hawaii.

The President seemed concerned momentarily, though not depressed, when he learned that General "Pa" Watson was in sick bay with pulmonary edema. When the doctor assured him that "Pa" would recover, FDR nodded and moved onto other matters.

Lieutenant William Rigdon, the President's traveling secretary and an acute observer of events, was on the bridge of the *Baltimore* in strong morning light on July 26 when a chocolate mass appeared on the horizon. It was Molokai, a tall layer-cake island. Rigdon noted the event as "0900 July 26th." Mr. Roosevelt was sleeping. Rigdon remained unobtrusive on the bridge as the officers signaled for a broader zigzag as the force moved past Barber Point to the entrance of Pearl Harbor. An air escort of six PBMs and 12 SBDs roared over the *Baltimore* and awakened the President.

He had breakfast in his quarters and remained there until noon. The task group, aware that if the Japanese presented a danger, it would be at the entrance to the harbor, began churning up the sea at 25 knots. At 2:25 P.M. the destroyers dispersed as the big cruiser stopped engines in the shallows off Oahu, and admirals and generals came aboard, led by Nimitz and a harbor pilot. Mike Reilly came aboard to announce that secrecy was a fake; that half the island knew the President was coming for a visit. Dewey Long came aboard with a pouch of mail.

The harbor pilot, Mr. Otterson, said that the harbor was full of ships of the line, and sailors in whites were lining the rail from Tin Can Row to Ford's Island. Therefore, it was his opinion that the *Baltimore* might as well run up the presidential pennant. FDR agreed and his flag was hoisted at the main. The big vessel was warped toward a berth behind the aircraft carrier *Enterprise* as cheers, hand-clapping and whistles brought the President to the starboard rail to doff his fedora hat. It was as much a thrill to him as it was to the youngsters. FDR studied three battleships—*Massachusetts, Maryland* and *Oklahoma*—and saw six carriers and carrier escorts, 32 destroyers and destroyer escorts, 19 submarines—some lying-to with brooms on their conning towers—and 200 transports and landing craft. Mr. Roosevelt had always been a Navy man, but he had never seen such might as this in port in wartime. When the cruiser made fast, he had to submit to courtesy calls from many admirals and generals, including Towers, Lockwood, Pownall, McMorris, Wilkinson, Blandy, Carney, Leavey, Smith, Rowell—too many to remember.

Admiral Nimitz remained on board as the others departed. He was waiting for General Douglas MacArthur to arrive. At 3:45 P.M. the General was piped aboard wearing an open shirt and a configurated Army cap. He went to Roosevelt's quarters at once, where he conferred briefly with the President, Admiral Robert L. Ghormley, and General Robert E. Richardson, Commander of U.S. Army in the Central Pacific area. The conference was more a get-acquainted meeting than a debate of military strategy. Within a half hour FDR had the gentlemen on deck to pose for agreeable pictures to be released later in the United States.

At dockside, honors were rendered to the President by the Navy yard band and an honor guard. Within fifteen minutes he left to take up quarters in the home of the late Chris R. Holmes, a three-story building with an outside elevator on Waikiki Beach. It had been leased by the Navy for the use of pilots on rest and recreation leave. The President was alert, almost vivacious, as he took up quarters on the third floor. His cook found the kitchen and prepared dinner for 7:00 P.M. Before sundown Admiral Ghormley arrived to give the President a time schedule for conferences and inspections on his three-day stay in Hawaii.

A letter in the pouch nettled Roosevelt. It was from Prime Minister Churchill to Josef Stalin. The tone suggested that if Stalin declined a summit meeting in Scotland, Churchill and Roosevelt would meet in any case and make decisions: "I need not say how earnestly His Majesty's government and I personally hope you will be able to come. I know well your difficulties and how your movements must depend upon the situation at the front. . . . I am making preparations for the President and myself. . . ." It was dated two days after Stalin had declined the meeting. Poor communications had caused the misunderstanding, but FDR was certain that he would not meet with Churchill alone. Military victories brought new problems without solving old ones, and the three world leaders would require at least a week of talks to settle the big ones. When the President signaled Churchill that he would not attend a two-way meeting, the Prime Minister replied, with some pique: "We should feel it very much and a very dismal impression would be made if you were to visit France before you come to Britain; in fact, it would be regarded as a slight to your closest ally."

The night in Honolulu was soft and darkest blue, but the words emanating from the private quarters of Lieutenant General Robert Richardson were loud and as bright as lightning. The scorn which General MacArthur felt for his President welled up so violently that he vented his feelings to subordinates—a mistake he rarely made. He walked up and down a bedroom, the words crackling from the side of his mouth: "The humiliation of forcing me to leave my command to fly to Honolulu for a political picture-taking junket! In the First War I never for a moment left my division, even when wounded by gas and ordered to the hospital . . . In all my fighting days I have never had to turn my back on my assignment!"

He was convinced, he shouted, that Roosevelt, having been nominated in Chicago, felt it would be good politics to show himself conferring with his Pacific chiefs, intent on winning the Asian war. The General was seething with anger. A letter marked confidential was delivered to MacArthur. The sender was Admiral Ernest King, Chief of Naval Operations, who had passed through Hawaii a few days earlier. Although MacArthur and King differed on strategy and tactics, both men were jealous of their commands and would unite against a common enemy. The letter warned MacArthur against the proposed "intrusion" of the British into the Pacific conflict. It had been an American matter through the difficult days; now, wrote King, the English would await the collapse of Germany and move into Australia, using it as a base for an attack on the Dutch East Indies, still held by the Japanese. King predicted that as soon as MacArthur returned to the Philippine Islands, Lord Mountbatten would take command of Australia and the Dutch islands.

The General had disciplined his feelings—feelings which he would never voice in the President's presence—and he was eating in Richardson's quarters when an invitation arrived from FDR asking the General to join him on a tour of inspection in the morning. This would mean more picture-taking, more publicity for Roosevelt's campaign. He agreed to be present; softly he observed that he had not seen Franklin Roosevelt in seven years

and he had been shocked when he saw how old and sick
the man appeared on the *Baltimore*.

In the bright sunshine of morning, the President sat
near a picture window overlooking the tawny beach and
the deep blue ocean curling white. He dictated slowly,
as though entranced with the vision, with but half his
mind on his duties. Lieutenant Rigdon sat patiently and
enjoyed the scenery as the President murmured:

Number 32. Top Secret and Personal
For Marshal Stalin from the President
I can fully understand the difficulty of your coming to a
conference with the Prime Minister and me in view of the
rapid military progress now being made but I hope you can
keep such a conference very much in mind and that we can
meet as early as possible. Such a meeting would help me
domestically and we are approaching the time for further
strategical decisions.

Roosevelt

He read a digest of the morning news, and hurried
off to join Admiral Nimitz and General MacArthur. A
passing-in-review Army parade had been arranged by
General Richardson. The air was sparkling and cool as
Roosevelt sat in an open car and took the salute of
25,000 soldiers lining the streets. A few of the staff officers
asked the President to exclude Nisei soldiers on the
ground that one fanatical soldier might fire a shot into
his car. The President reared back in surprise. "Nonsense!" he said, and insisted that the Japanese-American
infantrymen be in the parade.

General MacArthur believed the show was a waste
of time; a titanic struggle was going on in the Far East
and he resented being summoned to Hawaii to watch
the splendor of glistening rifles and white gloves. The
message he had received from General Marshall ordered
him to report to Hawaii to meet "Mr. Big." He assumed
this would be the President, but he could not believe that
conferences would improve the position of his army. So
he used the automobile ride to needle "Mr. Big." Did

the President believe he could defeat Dewey as easily as he had beaten Willkie? The President replied that he was too busy with the war to pay much attention to politics. But MacArthur was not to be put off. Smiling solicitously, he asked the question again and again. Roosevelt, doffing his old gray fedora and waving to soldiers and citizens, said that Governor Dewey was a nice "little" man but lacking in experience.

That closed the topic. In the evening Nimitz and MacArthur and Leahy enjoyed dinner with FDR and pulled chairs up before a huge war map. This was the first of two high-level conferences. Mr. Roosevelt asked Admiral Nimitz to take the pointer and present the Navy's case first. The Admiral was a soft-spoken logician who was in command of the largest naval force known in history. The shortest cut to the Japanese homelands, he said, was straight west to Formosa. It was a big island which, once taken and secured, would place the United States squarely between Japan and the Philippines, with the coast of China within range of fast-moving carrier forces. Japan could not tolerate an untenable position of being at the mercy of huge waves of bombers, with her shipping blockaded by American submarines. In effect, the capture of Formosa would force Japan to fight her last great battle rather than keep her major army and navy units at Honshu and Hokkaido awaiting American landings on her big islands.

The Navy's position vis-à-vis MacArthur, the Admiral stated, was to wait until MacArthur was on the island of Mindanao in the Philippines with all his forces. This would leave him to clean up Mindanao and, with reduced strength, use his Fifth Air Force to neutralize Japanese air power in Luzon, while moving his divisions south to attack the Dutch East Indies. The Navy figured it would be ready to assault the beaches of Formosa in the summer of 1945.

General MacArthur was stunned. He had left the Philippines ignominiously in a PT boat at the request of his President. He had vowed "I shall return," and he had no intention of going back on that promise. He

was now aware of what this conference meant; it was
a struggle for men, weapons and supplies moving northward up a ladder of island bastions, and he had spent
a good part of the war complaining to the Joint Chiefs
of Staff that his theater of operations had been neglected
while other commanders in Europe—and the Navy—were
given all the men and weapons they asked for. Porten-
tously, he spoke of "American honor" as though the
moral values superseded the military. He reminded the
President that there were 7,000 starving American
prisoners of war on Luzon, and 17 million emaciated
Filipinos on all the islands. Was the United States prepared to abandon these people? Roosevelt knew that
the General was fond of wrapping himself in the
American flag and reserving a sense of outrage for himself.
He waited for the storm as the General accepted the
wooden pointer from Nimitz. MacArthur's tone was quiet
and intense. In deep, rolling tones he said that he could
not guarantee to neutralize all the Japanese air bases in
the Philippines. He could accept the assignment, with
reservations, only if his forces were permitted to land
on the southern part of Luzon.

His personal plan was to take Manila. From there
he could guarantee to cut Japan from its raw materials
in Indochina, Malaya, Siam, Burma and the Dutch East
Indies. From Manila MacArthur's army and air force
could join the Navy in smothering the Japanese on nearby
Formosa. In this way the two forces could join for the
attack. A little later, when the officers adjourned for
coffee, MacArthur had a few minutes alone with the
President. This time he dropped the needle for the
knife.

"You cannot abandon seventeen million loyal Filipino
Christians to the Japanese in favor of first liberating
Formosa and returning it to China," he said. "American
public opinion will condemn you, Mr. President. And
it would be justified." The President squirmed under
the attack. He argued that the Navy was not trying to
give anything to China; that Nimitz and his planning
group merely sought the most advantageous piece of real

estate, and that would be Formosa. Nimitz and Leahy returned to the room and MacArthur argued with passion that he had a plan of operation—whenever his country gave him the men and guns. His plan was foolproof. He would land in force at Lingayen Gulf and advance southward to Manila. The logistics had all been worked out. He would be in Manila, 120 miles away, within five weeks of his initial landing.

Admiral Leahy said the timetable was unrealistic. MacArthur responded haughtily that all he could do was to give a "professional" estimate. Leahy admitted that MacArthur was in a position to know what he was talking about, but the old Admiral felt he could not approve the five-week estimate. It would take a much longer time to come down in force through the jungle hills. The President sat listening until almost midnight. He was obviously fatigued, and ordered everyone to get a good night's sleep. No decision would be made now, he said. He wanted the men to arrive at his quarters in the morning for final argument; then he would make a decision favoring one of the plans and he expected everyone to abide by that decision.

It was a most unusual situation. A President of the United States, without military experience, was about to make a strategic decision binding on his commanders. He could have sought the counsel of General Marshall, Admiral King, and General Hap Arnold, but he did not invite them; he chose to decide by himself between the plans of two excellent field commanders who disagreed with each other. At 10:30 the following morning Mr. Roosevelt met with the chiefs again and reminded them that he planned to board the *Baltimore* after lunch and that General MacArthur planned to fly to Australia in the afternoon. Therefore, a decision would have to be reached at once.

Admiral Nimitz again presented his arguments for a westward assault and added a few new "convincers" he had picked up from his staff at night. MacArthur displayed little patience for the Navy plan. He stuck the pointer at the island of Luzon and said that from this point he could cut Japan off from the South China Sea and from her oil, tin, rice and rubber. The President, listening, shook his head. "But Douglas," he said, "to take Luzon would demand heavier losses than we can stand. It seems to me we must bypass it."

The General responded with the obsequious attitude of a brilliant student trying to correct his professor. "Mr. President, my losses would not be heavy, any more than they have been in the past. The days of the old frontal attack are over. Modern infantry weapons are too deadly, and direct assault is no longer feasible. Only mediocre commanders still use it. Your good commanders do not turn in heavy losses." MacArthur was at his best. Carefully, almost condescendingly, he explained that within six or nine months, he would hold the Philippines in the palm of his hand. When that happened, he would turn his Australian troops southward to attack the Dutch East Indies from the rear. Once more he spoke of American honor and swore that he would first redeem his pledge to free the Philippines. Once that was done, his Fifth Air Force would be ready to reduce the Japanese island potential to zero; then it could turn north to assist the Navy in conquering Formosa.

He remembered sharply, and with acrimony, the warning letter from Admiral King. Although MacArthur did not mention the missive, he said he hoped Mr. Roosevelt would not consider British interference in Australia and the Dutch East Indies. He had heard, he said, that Lord Mountbatten was being considered as a Far Eastern British commander, and he knew that the Australians and the Dutch would resent it. FDR said he had no intention of permitting the English to take over Dutch possessions.

It was close to lunchtime, and Roosevelt was still listening. The debaters began to repeat themselves. The General's trump card appeared when he stated that if the Philippines were left behind in the backwash of war, the Japanese Army could live off the land and would, in revenge, slaughter thousands of prisoners, including

women and children. The President waved his hands
for both sides to stop. Without comment, he said he
approved the MacArthur plan and would expect Nimitz
to assist in the recapture of Luzon and the other islands.
When the decision was made, MacArthur stood to make
a short speech praising Nimitz and the Navy for its heroic
work in reducing the outer bastions of Imperial Japan.
He took an oblique shot at the President, saying that
when the war began, he felt the sea road could have been
opened for reinforcements for his officers and men, who,
starving and unreplenished, fought a rearguard action
to Bataan and Corregidor. Had the Navy been prepared,
his forces could have been reinforced in time to spare
the Philippines from the ravages of General Yamashita.
Certainly, it would not do to bypass the islands a second
time.

The General did not wait for lunch. His plane was
ready, standing on the runway. He thanked the President
for his favorable decision, shook hands with the admirals
and left with an aide. On the way to the airstrip the
General predicted that the President would be dead
within a year.

Before departure the President held a press conference
and was introduced to Hawaiian newsmen by Nimitz's
irascible public relations officer, Commander Waldo
Drake. Mr. Roosevelt was cordial but gave little news.
He told of his delight in stopping by military hospitals
to be taken through the wards; his inspections at several
military bases; the tremendous difference between the
Hawaii he recalled on his last visit—a decade earlier—and
the bristling arsenal he had studied in the past few days.
He said good-bye to his pool reporters, who would not
accompany him to Alaska. It was 6:45 P.M. before he
was able to make his final farewell to Sam Rosenman
and Elmer Davis, who would return to the White
House.

At dockside all boilers had been lit on the *Baltimore,*
and she and her escorts were prepared for a voyage tinged
with danger to the Aleutian Islands. Mr. Roosevelt sat

in his car, chatting with Nimitz and Ghormley and Richardson. When he shook hands, grinning, Secret Service agents Mike Reilly, Rowley, Wood, Peterson and Lowery made their personal farewells. They too were heading back to Washington. Mr. Roosevelt was wheeled up a smooth ramp and into the captain's quarters to sign last-minute mail. This was entrusted to Dewey Long in a sealed pouch for delivery in Washington and subsequent mailing. Mr. Roosevelt, adjusting his glistening spectacles, barely read the mail. He was pleased with all he had seen, content that he had made a major decision in ruling for MacArthur. For a personal reason he expressed satisfaction that he had ordered himself to be wheeled slowly through hospital wards where young men had lost limbs. He wanted them to know, without stating it, that he too knew what it was like to have dead legs, and had surmounted the affliction.

As the lines were being cast off, he gave an affectionate greeting to Fala. The rule of the islands was that all dogs must serve a four-month period of isolation, so the Scottie had been confined to quarters on the *Baltimore*. Mr. Roosevelt made it obvious to his pet that he had missed him. In affection, the dog outdid his master with leaps and kisses. Mr. Roosevelt asked to be wheeled up to the bridge. It was another soft-scented evening, with the deep green of the Waiani Mountains visible behind the cruiser as she slipped slowly toward the harbor mouth. The escorting destroyers were already at sea, scouring the waters with sound gear and radar as they plunged in tight circles.

Ships at anchor were lined with men who shouted good-bye as the heavy cruiser slipped silently by. Outside the nets the *Baltimore* increased speed and made a slow turn west, past Diamond Head and up the Kaiwai Channel. At 10:35 the executive officer rang up for 22 knots speed, course 353 for the night. The escort fled far ahead, swift hunters sniffing the sea for prey. This leg of the trip, north-northwest to the island of Adak, would take the Chief Executive closer to the Japanese home islands than the inspection could be worth. The Tojo government had proved in December 1941 that its forces could foray as far east as the Hawaiian Islands and destroy the effectiveness of the U.S. Pacific Fleet with one blow. It had invested small sections of the Aleutians with diversionary task forces; two years of American blood and treasure were spent in dislodging them.

The trip to Hawaii and the Aleutians, without doubt, had political overtones. Mr. Roosevelt was, in the summer of 1944, more of a Commander in Chief than a President. Had he wished to settle the disagreement between Nimitz and MacArthur, he could have met them at San Diego at a sacrifice on their part of one day's travel. The Aleutian outposts, cold, dismal and of little strategic importance, excited his personal concern because this was the farthest west he could travel with a degree of personal safety, in addition to the fact that, as success succeeded success in France, he desired to draw attention to the fanatical, savage war being fought in the Pacific.

If the Japanese Navy had any roaming task forces in the northern latitudes between 158 and 176 degrees west longitude, there is no doubt that a battle would have ensued. As the *Baltimore* was the "big ship" of the group, she would have drawn the most firepower. As a precaution, the Navy sent out PBY-4 flying boats from Hawaii, Midway and the Aleutians to search the waters to the east of the small force. The long voyage had morale value to the sailors and soldiers—of this there is no doubt—but the attitude of the military was anything but depressed, because America was fighting a two-ocean war with success on both sides. The political advantage was good for Roosevelt, because it transmuted him from master politician to the role of soldier in the front lines, so to speak. In addition to the photographs of FDR with his top commanders, there would be a lot of pictures of him reviewing troops and visiting the wounded. Besides, the President intended, upon his return to the United States, to deliver a major speech on the state of the war.

On the second day out a long-range patrol plane came up over the horizon, was challenged by blinker and responded with the code of the day. A DD was dispatched to pick up the flotation pouch and bring it up on the lee side of the *Baltimore*. A harness was rigged and the pouch was hauled aboard. Within a few minutes Mr. Roosevelt was at a small dining-room table in the captain's quarters with Admiral Leahy and Lieutenant Rigdon, riffling through the messages as fast as Rigdon could slice the envelopes.

The messages, as always, were good and bad. His secretary for nearly twenty-five years, Missy LeHand, had died a few days before. Mr. Roosevelt sighed. The gentle woman had devoted her life to the man in the wheelchair. She had believed in him when few did; she urged him to greater deeds, high aspirations, criticized some of his works to his face, shielded him from the importunities of the famous and near famous, erected a glass barrier between him and his wife and exercised the proprietary interest of a daughter. She was gone, and Mr. Roosevelt could stare into space for a moment or two to dwell on the irrevocability of death, then turn to decisions which had to be made.

Joseph Kennedy, Jr., son of the former Ambassador to Great Britain, had been killed in a bomber laden with explosives which had blown up prematurely. The President of the Philippines, Manuel Quezon, the gallant fighter for freedom, had died. A White House message stated that the Philadelphia transit system, which served a million shipyard and war plant workers, had gone on strike when eight black employees had been promoted to the status of motormen; the white motormen protested that blacks "leave bedbugs" wherever they sit. The President passed a weary hand across his forehead and ordered Rigdon to send a message to the White House that the war effort in Philadelphia was important and that the Army should seize control of the transit system at once. If the strikers did not return to work within forty-eight hours, the leaders were to be placed under arrest, and the young strikers were to be told that their draft deferments were to be altered to A-1 status. In any case the Negroes were to retain their new positions.

The news from Poland was bad. The Russians, acting unilaterally, had not only formed and recognized a group of Communist Poles as the new Polish Committee of National Liberation, in effect rendering the government-in-exile powerless, but had locked the door on negotiation by issuing a worldwide manifesto. The Soviet statement said that the Russian Army "together with the Polish Army" was about to liberate Poland. In a subtly disarming gesture, the Russians said that their armies had but one purpose: "to smash the enemy and help the Polish people establish a strong, independent and 'democratic' nation." The manifesto further acknowledged that, since the Poles now had a provisional government of their own, the Russians would not establish a military government of occupation. All of it looked good on paper, but, in the field of *Realpolitik,* the Soviet Union had found a group of Poles who would look to Moscow for guidance politically and economically. The final paragraph stated that Russia disavowed any territorial aims in Poland —which, in translation, meant that Moscow intended to keep that eastern part of Poland which had been given to the Russians by the Germans in August 1939. For compensation, the Russian armies intended to secure German territory for the Poles.

The new Lublin government accepted its territorial losses without protest and served Moscow's purpose by denouncing its own London government as a "usurper" group which had adopted a "Fascist comstitution in 1935." In a single stroke, four centuries of fighting among Slavs had been ended on Stalin's terms. He made a promise that, whatever territory Poland might lose to Russia in the east "on ethnical grounds," she would retrieve when Soviet arms planted the Polish flag in German Silesia, along the east bend of the Oder River, Pomerania and, most of all, that old thorn in the Polish side, East Prussia.

Nothing in the pouch pleased the President. He would not respond to the Soviet *fait accompli* at once, but it seemed obvious to his advisers that no one had the diplomatic or military power to undo the rape of Poland.

It was a certainty that Stalin had declined the summit meeting—so important to Roosevelt's image in the forthcoming elections—not because of massive military activity on a broad front but rather because the Soviet Presidium had planned this political coup and required time for Poland to become a subservient power. It was also apparent why, when the Free Poles rose against the Germans, the Russian armies paused before Warsaw to grant time for the Nazis to kill the flower of the rightist Polish forces.

Mr. Roosevelt seemed subdued, if not depressed. He went on deck in the bright evening only because he had heard that the destroyers *Fanning* and *Cummings* had been detached to search for survivors of a B-24, which had been last heard in a message from 35-50 north, 159-34 west, the present position of the *Baltimore*. The force moved northward. Mr. Roosevelt watched eagerly through binoculars as the two DDs disappeared over opposite horizons at high speed. When night came, both destroyers returned and signaled that no survivors and no wreckage had been located. It was another in an assortment of disappointments.

August 1944

THE SMALL TASK FORCE BORE THROUGH HEAVY WALLS OF fog and temperature which declined one degree per hour. On August 2 the group passed through Amukta Pass, threading the vertebrae of islands into the Bering Sea. The trip to the Aleutians was pointless, except for the prospect of cheering lonely enlisted men. There was little to see, no decisions to make. Politically, it was a convenient outpost for presidential publicity. Ross McIntire, refusing to recognize the risk to his patient, found virtues in this vacuum. Writing about Roosevelt, he stated:

". . . and here again is testimony as to his fitness. At Adak even a storm did not keep him under cover and, after a morning of inspection, he lunched in a Quonset hut mess hall flanked by servicemen. As young as the youngest there, he soon had all of them talking, and I remember the way he threw his head back and laughed after one exchange—a redheaded Marine from Arkansas, asked what he missed the most, promptly shot back, 'Our girls!' "

The weather was bad; fog, force-seven winds pressed the *Baltimore* to the side of the dock. Two Navy tugs in addition to the engines of the cruiser could not lift her free, and the cruiser remained at her pier as the President sat on the quarterdeck, casting fishing lines over and catching a brace of Dolly Varden fish. His timetable was delayed by twenty-six hours and the next port of call, Dutch Harbor, was abandoned because the weather was bad—cold slanting rain, heavy fog, and a strong steady wind. At Adak Mr. Roosevelt was surprised at mess when laughter was heard as he said, "You don't realize the thousands upon thousands of people who would give anything in the world to swap places with you people. . . ."

The third stop, Kodiak Island, was reached on the morning of August 7, but the fog was too dense for safety. The *Baltimore* cruised a zigzag for four hours, then made a slow entry to harbor. As always, there were officers of rank waiting to pay duty calls on the President, and Mr. Roosevelt was waiting to make tours of inspection among the young recruits and draftees. This time he thanked the officers of the *Baltimore* and bade them godspeed as he and his gear were removed to the destroyer *Cummings*. The plan was to return the President to Bremerton, Washington, through the inside passage of Alaskan islands. For a few hours the weather cleared and a dim coppery sun lighted the landscape.

Within a few hours the inspection of a submarine base, landing strip, enlisted mess and baseball diamond had been completed, and FDR, in a greatcoat, elected to sit in a motorboat and fish before returning to the *Cum-*

mings. Two small fish were caught. The *Cummings* snubbed beside the *Baltimore* and filled her bunkers with fuel. The next stop was Auke Bay, where the *Baltimore* turned away from her escorts and fled southward at high speed. Again the Chief Executive paused to fish. Later he claimed that Governor Gruening of Alaska, who sat in a bobbing whaleboat with him, brought luck. The party caught five large salmon, two flounders, one halibut and several cod. At 8:10 P.M. the *Cummings* weighed anchor and, with *Dunlap* and *Fanning* ahead, started down the inside passage from Juneau.

The President's attitude became lethargic. He was berthed in a destroyer (DD 365) which was shaped like a pencil and accepted wind and sea with poor grace. Now and then, as in Tolstoi Bay, FDR ordered the vessel to halt, so that he could fish. In almost all cases, he sat in a driving rain. No one, including Admiral McIntire, urged him to remain in his cabin in bad weather. Often he was soaked to the skin as he sat silently on the forecastle, awaiting a nibble that did not materialize.

In the evening he wrote drafts of a speech to be delivered at Bremerton. Signals had been forwarded to Mike Reilly to find a good place for the speech, and he had tried baseball parks but at last suggested that the best place to make the talk would be the deck of the *Cummings.* FDR agreed at once. He was alone, as far as speech writing was concerned; neither Sam Rosenman nor Robert Sherwood was aboard, so he penciled his own drafts, working again and again over poor paragraphs to make them strong.

He was divorced from the news, except such items as pertained to the campaign. He did not know, for example, that Harvard University had displayed a sophisticated calculating machine to newsmen. It was invented by Professor Howard H. Aiken, and it was composed of a 50-foot panel of knobs, 500 miles of wire, three million electrical connections, and could solve any mathematical conundrum on earth; it could solve most obtuse problems within six seconds. It was the first computer, a milestone in solving equations which required weeks of work by the best mathematicians.

It was a dreary, cold and foggy voyage; certainly one of no accomplishment except for the military decision to endorse MacArthur's army against the plans of Nimitz's Navy. One day out of Bremerton Navy Yard a pouch was delivered to Mr. Roosevelt. The newspaper headlines were pleasing: "President Meets MacArthur and Nimitz in Hawaii"; "President Makes Trip in Cruiser, 'Amazed' at Hawaii Change"; "President Reviews Battle-Tested 7th"; "Roosevelt Chats With Wounded"; "Visits Hospitals, Sees Surgery." Lieutenant Rigdon typed a sheet of news from the radio shack of the *Cummings:* "Herbert Brownell, after a sweep through the Midwest, chortled happily as he announced his opinion of the Democratic Party: 'We cannot speak of them as a party anymore because they have been badly split by factionalism.' "

Cummings and her escorts threaded the Strait of Juan de Fuca and edged south past the islands of Puget Sound toward Bremerton. The shipyard workers had been asked to remain ashore to listen to the President's homecoming speech. Thousands of them lined the docks as Navy tugs warped the *Cummings* to the side of a pier. Mike Reilly and Anna boarded to great him. Mr. Roosevelt had elected to continue the role of Commander in Chief and would make his speech from above the gun mount on the foredeck of the *Cummings*. A lectern had been set up at 5:00 P.M. while the President, in his cabin, was assisted into the braces he had not worn for a year. As always, they were heavy and uncomfortable.

The speech was a mistake. A force-five wind hit the *Cummings* steadily, causing it to chafe against its mooring lines and pull away sluggishly. At 6:00 P.M. there was still sufficient daylight for Mr. Roosevelt to make his talk, but, as he grasped the lectern and heard the deep roar of cheers from docksides and tall cranes, the heavy rocking of the destroyer forced him to grasp the lectern with both hands, and he almost lost the pages of his speech. To keep from falling, he was forced to pull with his arms against the sudden leaning of the vessel. Even worse, the speech was poorly organized, rambling from one aspect of the trip to another, sometimes without point. His voice boomed from the loudspeakers, hoarse and deep, often with painful halts in mid-sentence as he struggled to right his body. In the middle of the talk, the President experienced sharp pains across his chest. These frightened him but he continued: "I have seen new type ships coming right onto the shore and heavy cruisers and battleships offshore bombarding the land. Of course, if their fire was real I would not be here to tell you about it." He recited the war record of the cruiser *Baltimore;* said he appreciated the press and radio not revealing his whereabouts. "All the battleships and smaller craft that were sunk or damaged on the seventh of December 1941 have been raised with the exception of the *Arizona.* And that's one thing I will never forget, the way the sunken fleet was set afloat again and has gone all over the world in actually carrying out the plans of war."

The rocking of the ship brought sharp pains to his thighs and knees, but he continued with the speech, telling of visits to hospitals, military airfields, reviewing the Seventh Division, describing a course in jungle warfare. "And they're proud of all this basic training and the final training of our sons." He explained in detail the visit to Alaskan outposts, the rain, the fog, the snow. Some American soldiers, imbued with the pioneer spirit, told him that they would settle in Alaska after the war. All people, he said, can be trusted except the Japanese, "because whether or not the people of Japan itself know and approve of what their warlords have done for nearly a century, the fact remains that they seem to be giving hearty approval to the Japanese policy of acquisition of their neighbors and their neighbors' lands and military and economic control of as many other nations as they can lay their hands on."

He spoke for thirty-five minutes, after which a motor drive around the Navy Yard had been arranged. The President canceled it. Assisted by two men, he left the forward gun mount tottering in pain, the windblown sheaf of papers clutched in one hand. This time he did not wave assistance aside. In the captain's cabin, he collapsed in a chair. The leg irons were beyond endurance, and the chest pains frightened the President. Howard Bruenn cleared the cabin and arranged for an electrocardiogram to be taken at once. Anna Roosevelt, along with Mike Reilly and others, remained outside the cabin. Bruenn studied the tracings and saw no changes. The EKG was similar to all the others which had been made. Bruenn's conclusion was that the rocking of the vessel weakened the President as he tried to hold himself from falling, and this induced spasm of the intercostal muscles.

The *Cummings* unmoored silently and left for Pier 91 at Seattle. There Mr. Roosevelt's train had been backed up so that he could be wheeled off the destroyer gangway and into his private car without further fatigue. The train began to move off the pier shortly before 9:00 P.M. His daughter, in addition to Dorothy Brady and Grace Tully, sat with the President, each feeling that the voyage had taxed him too much. He appeared to be tired and worn, although his attitude was cheerful. Rigdon jotted in his diary: "Total miles traveled by sea this voyage, 7248 miles."

More frequently, the President's judgment was coming to question. The trip to the Pacific did not accomplish the patriotic fervor it was supposed to engender. At his whim, Mr. Roosevelt had wrapped himself in his Navy cloak and assumed the posture of Commander in Chief of the Armed Forces, but a month of labor had accomplished little. In Washington he faced another problem of his own devising. His letter to Wendell Willkie had frightened the Republican; he felt that he was falling into a Roosevelt trap, and so he had leaked the story of the letter to the press.

At the first news conference in August a reporter asked bluntly if the President had written a letter to Willkie. Mr. Roosevelt lied; he said he had not written such a letter. When this was published, Willkie's friends threatened to reveal the text of the missive. FDR was so embarrassed that he wrote again to Willkie:

August 21, 1944

Personal
___

Dear Wendell:

A most unfortunate thing happened at my press conference on Friday. I had written to you on July thirteenth, just as I was leaving for my trip to Hawaii and Alaska—a purely personal note telling you I hoped much to see you on a non-campaign subject after I got back. Quite frankly when I was asked—in a series of questions about foreign affairs— whether I had written you to invite you to Washington, I said "No." That afternoon Steve Early said to me, "Are you sure you did not write to Wendell Willkie?" And it flashed into my mind then that I had written you before I left.

The interesting thing is how word of my note to you got out to the Press. I have been trying to find out where the leak was down here, as I regarded it as a purely personal note between you and me. As far as I can remember I said nothing about it to anybody, though it is possible that I told Leo Crowley that I was going to ask you if we could talk the subject matter over. I am awfully sorry that there was any leak on a silly thing like this—but I still hope that at your convenience—there is no immediate hurry—you will stop in and see me if you are in Washington or run up to Hyde Park if you prefer.

I hope you have had a good summer. My trip to the Pacific was extraordinarily interesting. I hope to be able to tell you about it and about how I am trying to keep China going. Our friend, Madame Chiang, is in Brazil with her sister, Madame Kung, and I hope they will both come here before they return home.

Always sincerely,
Franklin D. Roosevelt

Willkie was frightened. His early meeting at the St. Regis Hotel in New York with Sam Rosenman had been hyper-secret, and, although Willkie, rejected by the

Republican party as a despised liberal, felt that President Roosevelt's plan to coalesce liberal Democrats and Republicans into one political party, leaving reactionary Republicans and Southern Democrats to form a separate party, was healthy and imminent, he exacted a promise from Rosenman that FDR would not discuss it until after the autumn election. The July letter from the White House had pointed to an earlier meeting, and Willkie feared it would disenfranchise him from the GOP and might appear to be an endorsement of Roosevelt.

At the time of the first letter the Republican leader had written a reply, but, after several readings, placed it in his files. "I am fearful," he wrote, "that any talk between us before the campaign is over might well be the subject of misinterpretation and misunderstanding. And I do not believe, however much you and I might wish to plan otherwise, that we could possibly have such a talk without the fact becoming known. Therefore, if it is agreeable to you, I would prefer postponement of any such talk until after the November election." No response to either of the President's notes is recorded.

Mr. Roosevelt was in the White House but two days when he decided to visit Hyde Park. Before he left, he asked the White House ushers to set up a luncheon table for him and Mr. and Mrs. Harry Truman on the south lawn under the Jackson magnolia tree. August 18 was a warm, slightly breezy day, and Truman arrived expecting a discussion on campaign strategy.

Roosevelt, however, confined himself to generalities, stating that he intended to remain "above politics" and permit the electorate to decide whether they wanted to continue with an experienced administration or assume the risk of electing an inexperienced team in the closing days of the greatest war in history. At one point, Mr. Roosevelt said, "Senator, how do you propose to campaign?" Truman replied, "By plane. I can cover more states that way." Roosevelt wagged his head. "No," he said. "Make it by train all the way. This time we may need you." It was an enigmatic remark if the President did not appreciate the precarious state of his health, and a sharply pointed one if he did.

In the late afternoon FDR saw John McCormack of Massachusetts, majority leader in the House. The monologue was rambling. The President had no work for McCormack, but spoke of the state of the war. "John, I have three plans before me regarding our campaign. Two regard invasions of Asia—the other is an invasion of Japan itself. I have to make a decision. If we go in, it is going to cost one million American casualties." McCormack said he wouldn't want to make the decision. Something was mentioned about Germany. Roosevelt pounded his fist on his desk. "Hitler can win every battle until he wins the Atlantic," he said loudly, "and he still hasn't won the war."

The President spent a long, weary weekend at Hyde Park and became upset when he read a United Press story in *The New York Times* that he and Winston Churchill would have a summit meeting on French soil within a few weeks. The story stated that FDR was "already packing his bags for the trip" and would be present at the so-called triumphal march into Paris. Interior Secretary Harold Ickes, on vacation at Bar Harbor, Maine, inquired about it, stating that it would be disastrous in Russian eyes. Harry Hopkins, convalescing in Washington, phoned to say that such a meeting would give Russia the feeling that she had been "left out."

A letter went from Hyde Park to Bar Harbor referring to the article as "a boner." "I have no thought of going to London, Paris, or to any point in that direction," the President wrote. Secretly, FDR had asked Churchill to meet him in Bermuda. The Prime Minister replied that he could not do it but would meet Roosevelt in Quebec in September.

A third problem was the opening of the Dumbarton Oaks Conference—the first session of which convened on August 21. The Russian Ambassador, Andrei Gromyko, was privately agreeable to Under Secretary of State Edward Stettinius and Britain's Sir Alexander Cadogan, but, in public speeches, hewed to the Soviet line, which consisted of regarding international peace-keeping bodies as weighted heavily in favor of the United States through voting procedures—and, conversely, as threats to the Soviet Union. Nor did Roosevelt's proposed United Nations bring unity in Washington. Those opposed referred to the United Nations as the old Wilson League of Nations in modern dress. Books on the subject began to appear, and some argued that no amalgam of nations could work together for peace without surrendering individual sovereignty. Others, claiming to be realistic, said that the United Nations would work if an Executive Council composed of Britain, China, the Soviet Union and a spate of smaller nations held the reins of world government with each to have an irrevocable veto over any proposed measure. Sumner Welles, in *The Time for Decision,* went a step further and said that no action should be implemented without unanimity of the "big powers," plus a two-thirds vote of the general council. This would render the U.N. impotent in matters of aggression.

Candidate Thomas E. Dewey said that he was disturbed that the proposed world organization would "subject the nations of the world, great and small, permanently to the coercive power" of the Big Four. That, he said, would be immoral and imperialistic. Gromyko slowed possible agreement by insisting that "all four big powers" should not only be unanimous in their actions against smaller nations but in their relations with each other. This meant that no action could be taken by any group of powers without the approval of the Soviet Union.

The more a world peace-keeping establishment was discussed, the more impossible it seemed of attainment. Gromyko torpedoed any chance of agreement by demanding that each of the sixteen Soviet republics be allowed separate votes in the U.N. Assembly. When Stettinius reported this to Roosevelt, the President threw his hands up and roared, "My God!" He invited Gromyko to confer with him in the Roosevelt bedroom. As always, Mr. Roosevelt believed that, in face-to-face confrontation, all men become reasonable. He sat in a bathrobe as

Gromyko, in the dark conservative suit of the diplomat, listened to the argument against sixteen votes. The President made light, simplistic points, but could not make the Soviet Ambassador yield. FDR said that in the United States, when husbands and wives brought a dispute to court, they were permitted to testify but not to vote. FDR went into a dissertation on fair play. Gromyko was unmoved.

The President suggested a cable to Stalin, appealing the Soviet stand. Gromyko said he had no objection. Roosevelt, fearful that his dream of a world structure for peace would expire unborn, marshaled his arguments and sent them to Stalin. He waited a long week for a response. Stalin said that the entire peace-keeping structure rested on unanimity of the Big Four powers. They must be unanimous regarding all positive actions. He felt that it was not unreasonable for sixteen republics within Russia to ask for a vote apiece. He concluded by stating that he could not ignore international prejudices against the Soviet Union.

The intransigence of the Russians angered the President. His conception of what would be a fair and equitable peace-keeping organization was in conflict with the Soviet Union's paramount goal: national self-protection. In retrospect, it is conceivable that neither Stalin, nor Chiang Kai-shek, or even Churchill was interested in global peace, each confining his thinking to what Roosevelt regarded "the old spheres of influence." Peace was going to spawn problems. FDR was thoroughly frightened when the Warsaw Poles, under General Bór-Komarowski, staged a premature uprising against the Germans. The Poles appealed to the Russian armies, across the Vistula, for assistance, but Stalin ordered his forces to rest. The Germans massacred 300,000 Poles who were fighting for liberation from Germans and Russians. The President stated that American planes would drop supplies to beleaguered Polish forces if the Russians would permit the planes to land on Russian fields to refuel.

Victory was in the air everywhere, but Mr. Roosevelt

was in an agony of frustration. As the Russians moved across the Polish plains toward Germany, and British and American forces moved toward Paris, Jimmy Byrnes stopped in the President's office to ask what kind of a peace Mr. Roosevelt had in mind for Germany. The Chief Executive was harsh. He said he was tired of listening to pleas for a "soft peace" from the men in his State Department. "The German people must be taught their responsibility for this war," he said, "and for a long time should have only soup for breakfast, soup for lunch, and soup for dinner." Byrnes left for his own office and wrote in his diary that the words did not sound like President Roosevelt.

On August 20 Roosevelt and Churchill sent a joint message to Marshal Stalin asking help for the Polish insurgents: "We are thinking of world opinion if anti-Nazis in Warsaw are in effect abandoned." Two days later, Stalin cabled: "Sooner or later the truth about the handful of power-seeking criminals who launched the Warsaw adventure will be out. They . . . have exposed practically unarmed people to German guns, armor and aircraft. . . . I can assure you that the Red Army will spare no effort to crush the Germans at Warsaw and liberate it for the Poles." Angry, Churchill announced to his Cabinet: "They did not mean to let the spirit of Poland arise again in Warsaw. Their plans were based on the Lublin Committee."

It was a difficult and irritating month for the President. In the final week Paris was liberated and this brought a momentary smile to his fatigued features. It was another momentous milestone on an interminable road. Harry Hopkins, as sick as the President and weaker, reported to Roosevelt that he had made final arrangements for the Second Quebec Conference in September. The close relationship between the two men seemed to chill as the illness of both persisted. Hopkins, who had attended every major conference with FDR, was not invited to Quebec. On the twenty-eighth Hopkins sent a cable to his friend Winston Churchill:

Dear Winston: Although I am feeling much better I still must take things easy and I therefore feel that I should not run the risk of a setback in health by attempting to fight the battle of Quebec on the Plains of Abraham where better than I have been killed.

Speech writer Robert Sherwood found that "Hopkins' excuse was hardly convincing, for he had never allowed considerations of health to stop him from going anywhere. . . . The fact of the matter was that a distinct change had come about in the character of his relationship with the President." It was as though Roosevelt could no longer brook any illness other than his own. The Christmas before Missy LeHand died, he had not sent greetings to his old secretary. The specter of death was omnipresent in the White House and FDR seemed prepared to divorce himself from it. Sherwood, writing of Roosevelt and Hopkins, said: "The trouble was that he [Hopkins] has been out of commission too long and Roosevelt had of necessity lost confidence in his ability."

September 1944

THE EARLY DAYS OF SEPTEMBER WERE WARM INSIDE AS well as outside the White House. The President was prepared to leave for the Second Quebec Conference on the tenth, but his daily tasks seemed to increase in number and complexity, although his doctors had warned him to cut his appointments in half, to take afternoon naps, and to have dinner in bed. The additional tasks appeared to induce a mental depression or loneliness, and Roosevelt did not respond to Republican campaign attacks.

Thomas E. Dewey, youthful and energetic and grim, campaigned across the nation warning the electorate that the administration was old, tired and quarrelsome, and that the prospect of peace belonged in younger hands. The Republican nominee seized on anything that would help his cause, and the polls indicated that Dewey's popularity was rising, while Roosevelt's was declining. Dewey quoted a statement made by Selective Service boss General Lewis Hershey that soldiers and sailors might have to remain in uniform after the war because the economy was unprepared to absorb millions of men. The President was distressed over Hershey's statement, which was called "a boner." Roosevelt had initiated long-range plans for the reconversion of war plants to peacetime work and the sale of government industry to private business.

Clare Boothe Luce, playwright and wife of the editor-in-chief of *Time,* wrote a series of guest columns for Walter Winchell which started a fight in the House of Representatives. She wrote that the President was callous with regard to the welfare of fighting men, and said that Admiral Nimitz had tried to block Roosevelt's tour of the Pacific by warning him "that it would place a needless strain on the Air Force and naval personnel responsible for the President's safety and would accomplish nothing." Democratic Congressman Michael Brady attacked Mrs. Luce and her newspaper columns as "flippant and wise-cracking." Congressman Harold Knutson, Republican of Minnesota, defended Mrs. Luce and said that her charges did not go far enough. "She did not inform the country that the President was accompanied by a flotilla of battle-ships, cruisers and destroyers." In addition, Knutson said, there is "the rumor that Fala, that little Scotty dog, had been inadvertently left behind at the Aleutians on the President's return trip, and that they did not discover the absence of the little doggie until the party reached Seattle, and that it is rumored a destroyer was sent a thousand miles to fetch him."

The rumors, the innuendo irritated the President more than usual. He authorized his press secretary to refute the story about his dog. In the early years he had managed to ignore gossip and rumor; in 1944 the un-

truths and distortions aroused his "Dutch." They hurt—
deeply, grievously. If there was solace and a smile, it
occurred on the rare visits to Lucy Rutherfurd. He left
Washington on the night of September 1 and did not arrive at Highland, New York, until late the following
afternoon. The train stopped at Allamuchy, New Jersey.
This time the word went around the train that Mr. Roosevelt had stopped to "see an old friend, Mrs. Winthrop
Rutherfurd, whose husband had died a few months
before." He seemed no longer to care about the keeping
of an old secret.

Bill Hassett scribbled two pages about the visit in his
personal diary. Later, before the diary was published,
he obliterated both pages, noting only the train's departure from Washington at night and its arrival at Highland
late in the afternoon, instead of in the morning. It is
possible that the three pool reporters knew or suspected
the long romance between the President and Mrs.
Rutherfurd. Granting a professional sense of curiosity
about everything Mr. Roosevelt did, the three men must
have understood that the long unannounced stops at
Allamuchy and Aiken involved visits to the same
person.

In illness the President seemed not to care who knew.
It was as though he understood his own deterioration,
the disarray of heart and arteries, and decided to make
the most of what time was left. Certainly, from the spring
of 1944 onward, he was less sensitive about whose
political toes he stepped on; he was mortally tired of
the Presidency but was impelled to run once more so
that he could end the war and fashion the peace. The
only interest he evinced, for example, in Harry Truman
was that he campaign by train instead of plane because
"we might need you." When the Missouri Senator was
leaving a White House reception with Edward McKim,
his old Battery D sergeant, McKim said, "Hey, Bud,
turn around and take a look. You're going to be living
in that house before long." Truman hung his head. "Ed-
die," he said, "I'm afraid I am and it scares the hell out
of me."

At the same White House reception, Trude Pratt, a strong-willed worker at Democratic party headquarters, sat near the President. Later she wrote: "I had a long talk with the Boss, sticking my neck out—trying to convince him to speak more often, and before crowds. He said he did not want to speak, his voice was bad. I told him he had to, his ills were imaginary, and if he did not want to win he should not have run (after that I almost died)—but he said I was right."

Mr. Roosevelt was convinced that his voice was weak and hoarse. He had made his last attempt to walk when he was aboard the swaying destroyer *Cummings,* and he vowed he would speak sitting down or from the back seat of an open automobile. He said he would not stand at the forthcoming conference. For a full day before he left for Quebec (September 9) the President held military conferences and made several visits to the White House map room. At the last moment, he was brushing up on what he proposed to ask of Churchill, and what he proposed to give the Prime Minister.

The President had asked Cordell Hull, Henry Stimson and Henry Morgenthau to consider the facets of peace in Germany. They were waiting in his office and he wheeled his chair back to listen and have notes taken by Miss Tully. Stimson said that the three Cabinet secretaries had been working toward preventing a recurrence of Germany's desire to dominate the world. However, he admitted that they were in disagreement. Hull and Stimson favored a stiff peace for Germany, but Morgenthau proposed to reduce the nation to an agricultural status. FDR, far from being shocked, said he believed that three points were vital to postwar Germany: no airplanes, not even a glider; second, no one should be allowed to wear a uniform; third, no marching should be allowed. These three things, Mr. Roosevelt insisted, would do more than any other measures toward convincing the Germans that they had been defeated. The rationale was childish. Stimson, with the endorsement of the Secretary of State, attacked the Morgenthau plan. The Ruhr and Saar, vital to Germany's heavy industry, should be stripped of all existing industries, weakened and controlled to such a degree that all equipment should be destroyed, and all mines "shall be thoroughly wrecked." Stimson argued that this industry was vital to the industrial health of all Europe. It should not be destroyed, but rather internationalized, or converted to a European trusteeship. The Secretary of War was also opposed to Morgenthau's plan to put all German arch-criminals to death by military squads upon identification and without a trial. If the victorious Americans believed in a Bill of Rights, Stimson said, then they should extend the right to a fair trial to all German officers and ranking Nazis.

The President made no decision that day. He said he would think about plans for a defeated Germany and zones of occupation. When the group disbanded, he did a strange thing: He did not invite Secretary of State Hull to the Quebec Conference, or Secretary of War Stimson, but he did ask Treasury Secretary Morgenthau to join him in Canada. When the little group departed, FDR held a separate conference with the Joint Chiefs of Staff: Admiral William Leahy; General George C. Marshall; Admiral Ernest J. King; and General H. H. Arnold. Mr. Roosevelt wanted the best opinions regarding strategy west and east before the big conference. Admiral King was in favor of keeping Great Britain out of the fighting in the Far East; the United States had done well enough without assistance. The President disagreed. He felt that, after the collapse of Germany, England would want to send fleet units and planes to the Far East. King was certain that it would be another instance of too little too late, and said that the logistics of transferring a fleet from home waters to a fighting station halfway around the world were almost insurmountable. Roosevelt seldom countered the opinions of the military chiefs, but this time he tapped his cigarette holder firmly on the desk and said that Churchill was determined to take part in the Pacific War and the United States would render the British every assistance.

The eleventh summit meeting of the wartime leaders was projected to unify Britian and the United States in two areas: the shape of the peace to come in Europe and British participation in the war in the Far East. When the President's special train left the Hudson River Valley at Highland for the slow run north to Quebec, he advised his assistants that he had received a Navy signal that Prime Minister Churchill, aboard R.M.S. *Queen Mary*, had reached Halifax. Mr. Roosevelt wanted to be waiting at Quebec when the P.M. arrived there.

Sunday, September 10, was bright and summery on the Plains of Abraham. Mr. Roosevelt, in a floppy panama hat, sat in his car at Wolfe's Cove. Beside him, radiant in a flame-colored silk dress with matching hat, sat Mrs. Roosevelt. They watched smiling as a big Canadian Pacific locomotive eased into the station and came to a clanking, hissing stop. Four Royal Mounted Policemen stood beside the President's car with U.S. Secret Service agents as the familiar round figure of Churchill stepped from his car and assisted his wife, Clemmie, to the walk. The opening conversation between the leaders was almost stilted. "Hello," said FDR, raising his hat, "I'm glad to see you. Eleanor is here. Did you have a nice trip?" Mr. Churchill, wearing a blue uniform and a naval cap, reached into the car, shook hands, and said, "We had three beautiful days. But I was frightfully sick." "I've lost some weight," Roosevelt said. The P.M. grunted. "I've lost some color." Mrs. Churchill walked around to the other side of the car to engage Eleanor Roosevelt in small conversation. Fala scurried nervously about, in the car and out, sniffing people and wagging his tail. Churchill looked at the pale warm Canadian sky. "Victory is everywhere," he said.

The crowd around the station and on the high ground cheered as the aged Governor-General of Canada, the Earl of Athlone, his spouse, Princess Alice, and Prime Minister Mackenzie King joined the group to welcome the distinguished visitors. And of these there were many. Foreign Minister Anthony Eden was flying in from England with a party, and had called Sir Alexander Cadogan up from the Dumbarton Oaks Conference. Churchill brought Lord Moran, his personal physician; Lord Leathers, Minister of Transport; Lord Cherwell, British Paymaster General; Admiral of the Fleet Sir Andrew Cunningham, First Sea Lord; Field Marshal Sir Alan Brooke; Sir Charles Portal, Chief of the Air Staff; General Sir Hastings Ismay, Chief of Staff to the Minister of Defense.

Roosevelt had also brought with him Admiral William D. Leahy; Vice Admiral Ross T. McIntire; Rear Admiral Wilson Brown; Major General Edwin ("Pa") Watson; Stephen Early, press secretary; Grace Tully; Dorothy Brady; Lieutenant Commander George A. Fox; Lieutenant Rigdon; Chief Steward Arthur Prettyman; Mayor DeWitt Greer of the Army Signal Corps; Mrs. Roosevelt; her secretary, Miss Malvina Thompson; Lieutenant Commander Howard Bruenn; chief telephone operator Louise Hachmeister; twenty-eight Secret Service men; an assortment of ranking Army, Navy and Air Force officers who had flown to Quebec; and one guest who was advised to arrive a day late, Secretary of the Treasury Henry Morgenthau, Jr.

Considerations of protocol and assorted honors prevented the busy men from meeting at once. At 10:25 A.M. the parties were drawn up before the Citadel, where the American colors were hoisted on a tall staff to snap in the morning breeze beside the British and Canadian banners. The Royal 22nd Regiment Band played the anthems; Mr. Roosevelt sat in his car on the parade ground and watched detachments of the Royal Canadian Army, Navy and Air Force pass in review with arms swinging. News reporters and photographers, numbering about a hundred, were permitted to watch.

The honors concluded, the lesser members of both parties left for their quarters at the Chateau Frontenac. Before the Roosevelts departed for their quarters within the Citadel (which, for the first time in the war, was not guarded by antiaircraft guns), the President greeted General George C. Marshall; Admiral Ernest King; Air Corps

General Henry H. Arnold; Brigadier General Andrew J. McFarland, Secretary to the Joint Chiefs of Staff; Captain Edwin Graves, USN, Deputy Secretary, and their staffs of planners. The British and Americans, preparing for grave decisions at Quebec, had denuded their capitals of ranking officers and best political thinking.

Nothing, it seemed, had been left to chance. By mid-afternoon on Monday, September 11, British and American opposite numbers were conferring on large and small problems listed on a lengthy agenda. They were to bring their findings to military chiefs who, in turn, would set the matter before the President and the Prime Minister. On the first afternoon Churchill had a small elaborate replica of a quay and harbor made of sunken ships displayed to the President and Mrs. Roosevelt. It was an example of what Eisenhower's forces had used to land men and supplies at the Cherbourg Peninsula. FDR became so enamored of the exhibit that he begged Churchill for it to display at the Pentagon in Washington so that desk officers could see how the Allies had improvised to tame the English Channel.

After lunch Roosevelt, followed by Churchill, wheeled his chair into a huge map room that he had set up secretly in his suite of rooms. It was designed to show the vast areas of the Pacific War, so that British participation on a large scale could be discouraged. The Prime Minister removed his cigar to smile and remind the President that when Churchill had been at the White House, he had insisted on his own map room. Now the order had been reversed.

As was true of all the summit meetings, the honors and booming of cannon were superseded as time wasters only by the elaborate dinners, which were held every night. These colorful but unproductive events might have been harmless, except that, when dinner was over, Mr. Churchill seemed to brighten and always asked for a long private chat with the President. It was obvious to FDR's party that he was fatigued. Under normal circumstances, he had been retiring at 7:30 P.M. to 8:30. At Quebec, the dinners did not end until 11:00 P.M., at which time Churchill was ready for an exchange of dialogue. On one occasion in Washington Colonel Elliott Roosevelt watched his father's head lolling and shouted, "For God's sake, tell him you're tired. You work all day while he takes naps."

Dr. Bruenn noticed a rise in blood pressure on the second day. One evening, after Roosevelt sat through a long, dismal motion picture biography of Woodrow Wilson, with its attendant illness, helplessness and death, Roosevelt seemed depressed; his blood pressure was 240/130. His weight was down to 168 pounds, too light and weakening for his big frame.

Sir Alexander Cadogan had political blood pressure. He found Roosevelt and Churchill almost impossible to pin down to a common opinion. "P.M. Pres., A. and at intervals Morgenthau and Cherwell talked—or rambled—on a variety of things. It's quite impossible to do business this way," he wrote. "Stayed there for lunch —P.M. Clemmie, Pres. A. and Dick Law. Towards end of lunch, got on to Dumbarton Oaks. Both Pres. and P.M. rambled hopelessly. I tried to pin them down to a point, but they always wandered away. Lunch went on until 4."

In Washington State Secretary Cordell Hull, who had been told by the President that the Quebec Conference was to be military, learned that Cadogan was present, also Anthony Eden and foreign office specialists. His sense of outrage at not being invited flamed high when he learned that Treasury Secretary Morgenthau had been asked to present his views about reducing Germany to the status of a "pastoral nation." Referring to FDR, Hull roared, "In Christ's name, what has happened to the man!" The State and War Departments, in addition to the weighty personal views of Harry Hopkins and the Joint Chiefs of Staff, were as one regarding postwar Germany. All believed that the Ruhr and Saar valleys should be stripped of heavy industry and steel-making capacity and that the conquered nation should be occupied by the victorious powers until the war-making potential of Germany had been reduced to the irreducible.

It was important, however, to leave Germany sufficient industrial potential to take its place among self-supporting nations, and especially to be able to export coal to Great Britain and France from the Saar Valley.

Morgenthau was encouraged to present his radical plan. The President, who was convinced that Germany would be a long-time aggressor among nations, favored stripping the country of all heavy industry. Morgenthau made it plain that if Germany was reduced to a pastoral nation, much of the economics of heavy industry must fall to Great Britain to her ultimate profit. With little debate Churchill and Roosevelt initialed the agreement. The Prime Minister proposed the dismantling of "metallurgical, chemical and electric industries in Germany." Experience had shown, the memorandum stated, that these industries could easily be converted from peacetime to wartime pursuits:

The industries referred to in the Saar and in the Ruhr would, therefore, necessarily be put out of action and closed down. It is felt that these two districts should be placed under somebody under the world organization which would supervise the dismantling of these industries and make sure that they are not restored by subterfuge. This program for eliminating the war-making industries in the Ruhr and in the Saar is looking forward to converting Germany into a country primarily agricultural and pastoral in its character.

The decision was vital to the interests of the Soviet Union. The Morgenthau Plan was not communicated to them; in fact, FDR sent notes to Hull and Stimson to refrain from acquainting anyone with the decision. In addition to the formal luncheons, dinners, and midnight conferences, mail pouches were arriving from Washington and some of the messages required presidential responses. Stettinius wrote that Gromyko stated finally and un-equivocally that the Russian government would vote "no" on the United Nations plan to prevent members of the Security Council from voting on issues which concerned one of them. Russia proposed to hold power of veto over any problem which concerned her, even though it might involve a charge of aggression against the Soviet Union. This reduced the power of the proposed Assembly and the Security Council to prevent war, but neither the United States nor Great Britain could envision a working United Nations without Russia. Churchill did not seem to be alarmed; he was less interested in world security than in European peace and spheres of influence. In recent weeks, according to Eden and Cadogan, he was worried that the Soviet armies would sweep across the face of continental Europe and that no power could force them to retire to their homeland. A few of his subordinates felt that the Prime Minister was more worried about Russian aspirations than Hitler's Nazis.

Word reached Roosevelt that his one-time mentor, Al Smith, was dying in St. Vincent's Hospital in New York. A telegram left Quebec at once:

Dear Al: I am indeed sorry to hear that you are back in the hospital. I am thinking of you and know if you follow the doctor's orders you will be feeling yourself again. With my affectionate regards, and Winston is with me and joins heartily in good wishes.   FDR.

Smith died three weeks later.

Admiral King had prepared logistical plans designed to show the British that, after the surrender of Germany, it would require too much time for them to send a fleet to the far Pacific and engage the Japanese. The pins in the map, the around-the-world supply routes, the giant strides of the U.S. Navy in addition to MacArthur's northward climb toward the Philippines did not discourage the urbane British. Churchill pointed out that the small British command under Lord Louis Mountbatten had done herculean work in containing the Japanese in Burma and India. The Prime Minister also said that he would not be surprised, now that the American Third Army was standing on the border of Germany, if the Nazis surrendered within weeks. If so, the British expected to assume a fighting role in the Pacific no matter how difficult the road.

Admiral King went a step further. In spite of FDR's ruling that MacArthur and the Navy should combine to retake the Philippines, King again presented a plan to bypass Manila in favor of attacking Formosa. The President listened to all the presentations and again decided against Formosa. He said he hoped that the British Fleet, when freed of duty in the North Sea and the Mediterranean, would attack the Japanese garrison in the Malay Peninsula—which was British territory. Perhaps fearful that the wrong word might reach Mac-Arthur, FDR sent a "Dear Douglas" letter from Quebec in which he said:

There is no question that Mr. Churchill and the British Chiefs of Staff want to send all they can to the Malay Peninsula, etc.——Army and Navy and Air—as soon as the German war ends. In regard to our own force, the situation is just as we left it at Hawaii though there seem to be efforts to do a little by-passing which you would not like. I still have the situation in hand.

After initialing the Morgenthau Plan, the two chiefs of state and their military planners debated zones of occupation in Germany. FDR did not seem pleased when Churchill proposed that the British police the northern sector, with all its ports and industry, assigning the Americans to Bavaria and the south. The Russians, it was assumed, would prefer to police the eastern sector, though no one knew how far that would extend. Churchill's argument was that General Bernard Law Montgomery and his British and Canadian troops had fought the battle of the north, and it would be easier for allies to rest their arms where they stood at war's end than to move to other areas. Roosevelt said that the British plan would leave the American armies with no ports for supply.

Churchill pointed on the map to Bremen and Bremerhaven and said that the British would not object if the

city and port were to be manned by Americans. The
President accepted. He also suggested that a place should
be allocated to France—preferably in the western part
of Germany—to police as a victor nation. The Prime
Minister said he had no objection if the Russians would
agree to it. The question of how long the Allies would
monitor Germany was a sore point with Churchill. He
was fearful that, shortly after Germany was beaten,
Americans would lose interest in European affairs and,
as in World War I, would begin to withdraw their troops.
Thus the subjugation of Germany over a long period
would fall to Britain and Russia in the main, and Russian
strength in Army divisions would outweigh the British
at least three to one.

At the end of the conference Mr. Roosevelt seemed
to have lapsed into a depressive lassitude. At luncheon,
the Prime Minister said joyously, "Everything we have
touched has turned to gold." The President did not
respond. Before the issuance of a joint Quebec communiqué, Churchill reminded Roosevelt that Great Britain
had stood alone against the Nazis before the American
advent into the war. England was almost bankrupt. He
hoped that, when the war was over, the United States
would continue to be generous with Lend-Lease. It was
a portentous afterthought. Mr. Roosevelt noted that,
as part of the Morgenthau Plan, it had been agreed
to extend $6 billion in credits to the United Kingdom.
Churchill felt that England would need more assistance.
The President asked Mr. and Mrs. Churchill to visit
him at Hyde Park for a few days of additional talks.

The Prime Minister returned to his quarters and invited
Admiral Ross McIntire to visit. There, in obvious embarrassment, Churchill asked the President's physician to
please tell him, in confidence, the true state of Roosevelt's
health. He said he had a high personal regard for the
President and had been alarmed by reports reaching
him that FDR was a very sick man. The Prime Minister
did not say that the future welfare of Great Britain depended a great deal on United States goodwill, a matter which involved a living Roosevelt. McIntire said he

gave Churchill the results of "our June checkup" and added that the President had been under strain for more than eleven years. "If he does not overdo," McIntire said cheerfully, "there is every reason to believe he can win through." The P.M. nodded solemnly. "With all my heart I hope so," he said. "We cannot have anything happen to this man. His usefulness to the world is paramount during these troubled times."

As the summit conference closed, Churchill followed the President to Hyde Park. When the two men were alone, Churchill used much of his time persuading Mr. Roosevelt to an opinion the President already opposed. This time the secret subject was the Danish nuclear scientist, Dr. Niels Bohr. Roosevelt endorsed Bohr's views of atomic energy; Churchill opposed them unalterably. Dr. Bohr was part of the Manhattan Project, which was in the late stages of developing the first atomic bomb at Alamogordo, New Mexico. Bohr, looking ahead to the postwar world, foresaw "fateful nuclear competition" between nations. This, in turn, could lead to a holocaust.

Bohr had brought his foreboding to the White House. He was advised to fly to England and try to persuade the Prime Minister that, at the very least, the United States and Britain should share their knowledge with their ally, the Soviet Union. Bohr, a slow-speaking walrus of a man with long drooping mustaches, had an unfortunate habit of building his arguments block by block before reaching an ultimate conclusion. He managed to irritate Churchill, who closed the interview before Bohr reached his point.

In the matter of nuclear energy, Churchill was angry on two points, and he brought both before President Roosevelt at the Hyde Park hiatus. One was that the United States was not sharing its nuclear discoveries with her partner, Great Britain. (This was true.) Second, he felt that Bohr's notions of confiding atomic progress to the Russians was madness, and he wanted assurance that Bohr would be stopped. Churchill pointed out, with asperity, that while Bohr was in London the scientist had received an invitation from Soviet scientist Peter Kapitza to visit Moscow. The Russians would not be inviting Bohr, Churchill reasoned, unless they were spying on the "Tube Alloys" project and knew that Bohr had knowledge about it. The matter was embarrassing to FDR, who had long ago agreed with Bohr that the Russians would find out about the matter sooner or later, and, as a gesture of friendship, should at least be advised that the making of an atom bomb was in progress.

Somehow, on September 19, the Prime Minister destroyed Roosevelt's confidence in Dr. Bohr. Churchill's feelings in the matter were so strong that he drew up a confidential *aide-mémoire* and signed it along with Roosevelt.

1. The suggestion that the world should be informed regarding tube alloys, with a view to an international agreement regarding its control and use, is not accepted. The matter should continue to be regarded as of the utmost secrecy, but when a "bomb" is finally available, it might perhaps, after mature consideration, be used against the Japanese, who should be warned that this bombardment will be repeated until they surrender.

2. Full collaboration between the United States and the British Government in developing tube alloys for military and commercial purposes should continue after the defeat of Japan unless and until terminated by joint agreement.

3. Enquiries should be made regarding the activities of Professor Bohr and steps taken to ensure that he is responsible for no leakage of information particularly to the Russians.

The few highly placed persons in the American government who were privy to the memorandum were shocked that Churchill would propose it and stunned that the President would sign it. Mr. Roosevelt's thinking was ambivalent and vacillating. Much depended on who had his ear. Thus a humanitarian-physicist, Dr. Niels Bohr, was blackballed without charges or hearing.

In spite of Churchill's "Everything we have touched has turned to gold," most of the world was in pain and privation. East and west, scores of millions of men at war were consumers, not producers, and food shortages were common. The United States was spending $300 million each day on the war but could not supply its citizens with enough meat or grain to meet the demand. In London 1,104,000 homes had been damaged by bombing and buzz bombs by September 1944. The United States sent Britain 10,000 Nissen huts to shelter the homeless and it was not enough. Nor was the food sufficient.

In the United States the total labor force was 66 million persons, of whom only 670,000 were unemployed. The war had ended the worst economic depression in the history of the country, but the paychecks were difficult to spend. There was a thriving black market in gasoline ration stamps, retread tires, and scarce commodities including butter and sugar and oil. Military leaders could only guess at the hardships endured by enemy nations, such as Germany and Japan. In China, which Roosevelt insisted on regarding as one of the first-class powers of the world, there was widespread starvation and defeat and neglect.

American Ambassador Clarence E. Gauss, in Chungking, cabled the State Department that the capital city of Generalissimo Chiang Kai-shek was "in despair." In mid-September General Joseph Stilwell radioed General George Marshall: "The jig is up in South China." Gently and insistently, Winston Churchill kept reminding Roosevelt that, in Chiang Kai-shek, · the United States was backing the wrong horse in the Far East. FDR, who had backed General Clare Chennault and his Flying Tigers and Stilwell and his small command, signaled the Generalissimo: "The extremely serious situation which results from Japanese advances in Central China, which threatens not only your government but all that the United States Army has been building up in China, leads me to the conclusion that drastic measures must be taken immediately if the situation is to be saved." The President, in the first pale light of victory east and west, realized that the suffering giant of Asia might collapse at any time. He urged that Stilwell be placed in command of all Chinese armies—under the political guidance of Chiang Kai-shek. It was delicate face-saving, and Chiang asked FDR to send a personal representative who could adjust the acrimonious relations between Stilwell and himself. The President dispatched General Patrick Hurley, former Secretary of War under Herbert Hoover, to Chungking.

Hurley, a man of cosmopolitan knowledge everywhere but in China, tried to arrange a détente between Chiang's Kuomintang and the Communist chief Mao Tse-tung. The Reds held Yenan Province. The communes were disciplined and loyal. Hurley was impressed. Mao, however, appeared to be more interested in Roosevelt's chance of reelection to a fourth term than he was in Chiang and Chungking. "We will wait," he said. "We have had long training in patience." He wanted to know specifically if the United States would abandon China after the November election. He seemed less interested in banding with Chiang to fight the Japanese. The man with the moon face smiled and said: "We will retreat and retreat across China. But what will Chiang do?"

Roosevelt became irritated when he received no reply from Chiang. He sent a message to the Generalissimo via General Stilwell and asked the General to deliver it in person. "The action I am asking you to take," FDR wrote, "[is] at once placing General Stilwell in unrestricted command of all your forces." Vinegar Joe read the message and felt a surge of delight in delivering it to the Generalissimo. It amounted to poor tactics on the part of the President, asking a personal enemy to deliver a stinging ultimatum to a personal enemy.

Stilwell wrote in his diary: "I handed this bundle of paprika to the Peanut and then sank back with a sigh. The harpoon hit the little bugger right in the solar plexus, and went right through him. It was a clean hit, but beyond turning green and losing his power of speech, he did not bat an eye. He just said to me: 'I understand.'" The bait offered by Roosevelt for compliance was not sufficient. FDR had written: "The Prime Minister and I meeting at Quebec decided to reopen the land lines to China." It didn't work. Chiang Kai-shek told Hurley that he could not tolerate having a subordinate hand him an ultimatum. Stilwell would have to go.

Thus the matter was returned to Roosevelt's trembling hands. FDR pleaded for a subordinate command for Stilwell. Chiang said no. The President surrendered. Stilwell was ordered home. Roosevelt admitted to his military chiefs that no competent general would be placed in charge of the Nationalist Chinese armies; there would be no rapport between Chiang and Mao; the Japanese army was advancing so rapidly that Chennault was burning his airfields and supplies and running inland; the China policy was in ruins. And all of it was Roosevelt's invention.

By the time Stilwell arrived in the United States, he was blaming Roosevelt as "a weak and procrastinating politician"; a man who was "probably ill." In Chungking the Generalissimo was in a rage. He shouted to palace intimates that he did not need the help of America; if necessary he would fight the war on his own without United States aid. Sarcastically, Stilwell said that Chiang Kai-shek stationed the major strength of his armies in the north, holding Mao's Communist army at bay, while the weaker wing fled before the Japanese at Kweilin.

Sixty-three reporters clacked westward on the campaign train of Thomas E. Dewey, and they reported everything the precise prosecutor had to say. They also reported the fact that, if his train was due to arrive at a city three minutes ahead of schedule, the Republican ordered it slowed or stopped so that it always arrived on time.

"This is a campaign," Dewey said from the rear platform at Des Moines, "against an administration which was conceived in defeatism, which failed for eight straight years to restore our domestic economy, which has been the most wasteful, extravagant and incompetent administration in the history of the nation, and worst of all, which has lost faith in the American people."

The "worst" may have sounded smug and not on speaking terms with truth, but the speeches made the headlines in the nation's press. If Dewey had a weakness, it lay in the taut manner in which he controlled his campaign down to the most minute details. At each city an advance man brought six copies of the local newspapers aboard for the candidate to riffle through before speaking; the speech on the rear platform was enunciated in the self-righteous baritone which was Thomas Dewey's trademark; after the speech he led a motorcade to the leading hotel where he traded responses to the questions of the local press. After exactly one half hour he excused himself for a behind-closed-doors conference with local Republican officials, then back to the train and a great deal of staff preparation for the next stop. When he made short local speeches, he sent word how high he wanted the lectern to be.

He changed suits but once a day—brown, blue, gray, pin-striped—always with a tie of subdued hue and always with a gray homburg in his hand, never on his head. National reporters aboard the train dubbed him "Mr. Warmth." His vice-presidential candidate, John Bricker, was touring the East, and it was he who brought a solitary smile to an audience when he said, "Truman? That's his name, isn't it? I never can remember that name." In spite of this, the Republican campaign lacked color and enthusiasm. It was a one-man show, and Dewey was accused of being chilly and aloof when greeting local politicians whose task it was to reap the votes. And yet, even though the atmosphere was redolent of Boy Scouts working sincerely for merit badges, it aroused the personal ire of President Roosevelt, and he determined to step off the pedestal of Commander in Chief to make one of his old-time rousing speeches for the Teamsters Union in Washington. He would spank Dewey publicly.

In the third week of September Sam Rosenman was called to the President's White House bedroom and, on entering, was shocked to find that FDR, in his underwear, was leaning on the arm of Admiral McIntire trying to learn to walk with his braces. It was a sign that he proposed to campaign again, but the odds against walking again were almost insuperable. As a physical specimen, he was old and tired, and he had not put his braces on three times in three years. The last time, aboard the destroyer *Cummings,* proved to the President that he was unable to stand.

As he advised Rosenman of ideas he had about the Teamsters speech, he tottered back and forth in the bedroom, leaning, almost falling, as McIntire accepted the President's weight. "I am going to walk again," he said cheerfully. Rosenman knew that agreement had been reached with the Teamsters that the President would make his speech sitting at his dinner plate. The judge concluded that the Boss intended to do more campaigning, and he could not afford to be seen sitting on the rear platform of trains. The iron against both wasted legs, and the leather harness around the waist, cut deeply into flesh, but he did not wince and he kept trying.

On the evening of September 23 the President emerged in his wheelchair from draperies behind the big dais in the Presidential Room of the New Statler Hotel. Screened by Secret Service men, he was lifted up to his seat near the center of the dais and, as the friendly crowd of Teamsters and their friends roared approval, Mr. Roosevelt beamed his great smile and held both hands aloft in greeting. To his left was Daniel Tobin, Teamster president; to the right was AFL president William Green. In front of his dinner plate stood an assortment of silvery microphones. He looked old but trim in his black tie and dinner jacket. While others ate, the President barely touched dinner, working instead on the final draft of his speech with a pen.

Shipbuilder Henry Kaiser, a man with a polished dome, spent more time studying the President than speaking to his tablemates. At a place down front, Anna Roosevelt Boettiger whispered to Rosenman: "Do you think Pa will put it over? If the delivery isn't just right, it will be an awful flop." She too remembered Bremerton.

So did the crowd. Many of the diners commented that the President looked better than the photo of him made in San Diego when he delivered his acceptance speech. Like an old champion, Mr. Roosevelt had summoned all his strength, not only to deliver his first major speech of the campaign but to use ridicule for his most telling shots. The room was in breathless silence when he picked up his sheaf of papers, looked over the tops of his glasses, and grinned.

"Well," he said, "here we are together again—after four years—and what years they have been! You know, I am actually four years older"—he rolled his eyes upward in innocence—"which is a fact that seems to annoy some people. In fact, in the mathematical field, there are millions of Americans who are more than eleven years older than when we started in to clean up the mess that was dumped in our laps in 1933." There was a burst of cheers and table pounding. In mock seriousness, he said: "We all know that certain people who make it a practice to deprecate the accomplishments of labor—who even attack labor as unpatriotic—they keep this up usually for three years and six months in a row." The crowd roared approval. FDR began to sound like the Roosevelt who loved nothing better than a good fight. Continuing the feigned innocence, he said: "But then, for some strange reason, they change their tune—every . . . four . . . years—just before election day. When votes are at stake, they suddenly discover that they really love labor and they are anxious to protect labor from its old friends.

"I got quite a laugh, for example—and I am sure that you did—when I read this plank in the Republican platform adopted at their national convention in Chicago last July [with head swinging from side to side as he read]: 'The Republican party accepts the purposes of the National Labor Relations Act, the Wage and Hour Act, the Social Security Act and all other Federal statutes designed to promote and protect the welfare of American working men and women, and we promise a fair and just administration of these laws.' "

The President thrust his jaw toward the microphones.

"You know, many of the Republican leaders and Congressmen and candidates who shouted enthusiastic approval of that plank in that convention hall would not even recognize these progressive laws if they met them in broad daylight." The crowd roared with laughter, but the President maintained his mock solemnity. "Indeed, they have personally spent years of effort and energy—and much money—in fighting every one of those laws in the Congress, and in the press, and in the courts, ever since this administration began to advocate them and enact them into legislation. . . .

"The whole purpose of Republican oratory these days seems to be to switch labels. The object is to persuade the American people that the Democratic party was responsible for the 1929 crash and the depression, and that the Republican party was responsible for all social progress under the New Deal. Now, imitation may be the sincerest form of flattery—but I am afraid that in this case it is the most obvious common or garden variety of fraud." The applause was deafening. However, while deriding the Republican party in pseudo-innocence, the President did not intend to neglect the liberal wing of the GOP, a segment which he had always cultivated. "Of course," he said, "it is perfectly true that there are enlightened, liberal elements in the Republican party, and they have fought hard and honorably to bring the party up to date and to get it in step with the forward march of American progress. But these liberal elements were not able to drive the Old Guard Republicans from their entrenched positions. Can the Old Guard pass itself off as the New Deal? I think not. We have all seen many marvelous stunts in the circus but no performing elephant could turn a handspring without falling flat on his back." The Presidential Room was engulfed in laughter.

". . . What the Republican leaders are now saying in effect is this: 'Oh, just forget what we used to say, we have changed our minds now; we have been reading the public opinion polls about these things and now we know what the American people want.' And they say: 'Don't leave the task of making the peace to those old men who first urged it and who have already laid the foundations for it, and who have had to fight all of us inch by inch during the last five years to do it. Why, just turn it all over to us. We'll do it so skillfully that we won't lose a single isolationist vote or a single isolationist campaign contribution.' " Slowly, deliberately, with forceful emphasis, the President used the words of his enemies: "I think there is one thing you know: I . . . am . . . too . . . old . . . for . . . that." He was forced to wait until pandemonium died before saying, "I cannot talk out of both sides of my mouth at the same time.

"Labor-baiters forget that at our peak American labor and management have turned out airplanes at the rate of 109,0000 a year; tanks, 57,000 a year; combat vessels, 573 a year; landing vessels, 31,000 a year; cargo ships, nineteen million tons a year—and Henry Kaiser is here tonight, I am glad to say; and small arms ammunition—oh, I can't understand it; I don't believe you can either—23 billion rounds a year. But a strike is news, and generally appears in shrieking headlines, and, of course, they say labor is always to blame. The fact is that since Pearl Harbor only one-tenth of one percent of man-hours have been lost by strikes. Can you beat that? . . .

"Words come easily, but they do not change the record. You are, most of you, old enough to remember what things were like for labor in 1932. You remember the closed banks and the breadlines and the starvation wages; the foreclosure of homes and farms and the bankruptcies of business; the 'Hoovervilles' and the young men and women of the nation facing a hopeless jobless future; the closed factories and mines and mills; the ruined and abandoned farms; the stalled railroads and the empty docks; the blank despair of a whole nation—and the utter impotence of the Federal Government. You remember the long, hard road, with its gains and setbacks, which we have traveled together ever since those days.

"The opposition in this year has already imported into this campaign a very interesting thing, because it is foreign. They have imported the propaganda technique invented by the dictators abroad. Remember, a number of years ago, there was a book, *Mein Kampf,* written by Hitler himself. The technique was all set out in Hitler's book, and it was copied by the aggressors of Italy and Japan. According to that technique, you should never use a small falsehood; always a big one, for its very fantastic nature would make it more credible, if only you keep repeating it over and over and over again. Well, let us take some simple illustrations that come to mind. For example, although I rubbed my eyes when I read it, we have been told that it was not a Republican depression, but a Democratic depression from which this nation was saved in 1933; that this administration —this one today—is responsible for all the suffering and misery that the history books and the American people have always thought had been brought about during the twelve ill-fated years when the Republican party was in power.

"Now there is an old and somewhat lugubrious adage which says: 'Never speak of rope in the house of a man who has been hanged.' In the same way, if I were a Republican leader speaking to a mixed audience, the last word in the whole dictionary that I think I would use is that word 'depression.' You know, they pop up all the time. For another example, I learned, much to my amazement, that the policy of this administration was to keep men in the Army when the war was over because there might be no jobs for them in civil life. Well, the very day that this fantastic charge was first made, a formal plan for a method of speedy discharge from the Army had already been announced by the War Department, a plan based on the wishes of the soldiers themselves.

"This callous and brazen falsehood about demobilization did, of course, a very simple thing: it was an effort to stimulate fear among American mothers and wives and sweethearts. And, incidentally, it was hardly calculated to bolster the morale of our soldiers and sailors and airmen who are fighting our battles all over the world."

As he marshaled his arguments and rolled his eyes

ceilingward in disbelief, the President was working his way toward the "crusher." The paragraph, which would in time be one of the best remembered of all the Roosevelt speeches, was his own. At Quebec FDR had penned it and asked Grace Tully to mail it to Rosenman for inclusion in the speech:

"These Republican leaders have not been content with attacks on me, or my wife, or on my sons," he said sorrowfully. "No, not content with that, they now include my little dog Fala." The audience began to roar. "Well, of course, I don't resent attacks, and my family doesn't resent attacks, but Fala does resent them." Then, archly, with both brows high on his forehead: "You know, Fala is Scotch, and being a Scottie, as soon as he learned that the Republican fiction writers in Congress and out had concocted a story that I had left him behind on the Aleutian Islands and had sent a destroyer back to find him—at a cost to the taxpayers of two or three, or eight or twenty million dollars—his Scotch soul was furious. He has not been the same dog since." The surf of laughter hit a high-water mark. The President had to wait to continue. "I am accustomed to hearing malicious falsehoods about myself, such as that old worm-eaten chestnut that I have represented myself as indispensable. But I think I have a right to resent, to object to libelous statements about my dog."

The success of the speech was assured. Millions of Americans at home, listening to radios, were laughing. But the President wanted to inject one more serious note about the tasks ahead:

There is the task of finishing victoriously this most terrible of all wars as speedily as possible and with the least cost in lives. There is the task of setting up international machinery to assure that peace, once established, will not again be broken. And there is the task that we face here at home, the task of reconverting our economy from the purposes of war to the purposes of peace.

These peace-building tasks were faced once before, nearly a generation ago. They were botched by a Republican ad-

*ministration. That must not happen this time. We will not
let it happen this time.*

The speech was a resurrection of the old fighting
Roosevelt, glib of tongue, at ease in his story-telling, pretending shock at the claims of the Republican party. The
press gave it a lot of space on page one, even though
a majority of the newspapers were opposed to a fourth
term, as they had been to a third. In the Republican camp
there was more anger than dismay. Foolishly, Thomas
Dewey permitted himself to be quoted saying: "Mr.
Roosevelt designed that speech to make me angry, and
he has. The result is that I will now campaign all the
harder." Judge Samuel Rosenman, who had been writing
speeches for Roosevelt for seventeen years, shook his
head in wonderment as he left the Statler with Anna
Roosevelt and said: "I think it's the finest speech he ever
made." *Time* magazine, not a proponent of Roosevelt,
made much of the Fala story: ". . . even the stoniest
of Republican faces around U.S. radios cracked into a
smile."

On September 29 two sick men met in the Oval Office.
Secretary of State Cordell Hull, pale and unsteady, was
present to fight the Morgenthau Plan for Germany and
was not aware that Mr. Roosevelt had already discarded
it. Roosevelt sat behind his desk, patient in fatigue, trying
hard to listen to the interminable points adduced by Hull.
The Secretary had sent a paper to the President arguing
against Morgenthau; now he consulted it from behind
his glasses, rereading what the President had already
studied.

He began by reminding Mr. Roosevelt that, prior to
Morgenthau's appearance at Quebec, the President had
appointed a Cabinet *committee* to deal with postwar
matters such as Germany. This committee had reached
agreement, but had not time to prepare its findings when
the Secretary of the Treasury enunciated his own plan
to emasculate the vanquished. "The memorandum submitted by the Secretary of the Treasury," he read in a

tone close to contempt, "is decidedly at variance with the views developed in the State Department. In the meantime, I have received your memorandum of September fifteenth with the statement of views respecting the Ruhr, Saar, etc., and the conversion of Germany into an agricultural and pastoral country, which was formulated at Quebec. This memorandum seems to reflect largely the opinions of the Secretary of the Treasury in the treatment to be accorded Germany. I feel I should, therefore, submit to you a line of thought that has been developing in the State Department on this matter."

He continued at length. The President retained his composure. Hull said that the primary objective after the war was to make Germany incapable of starting another conflict. To achieve this, military occupation of the country would be necessary for an indefinite time. In addition, all war plants which could not be converted to peacetime purposes would have to be destroyed or allocated to the victors to be removed to other lands; secondly, those plants which could be converted to peacetime pursuits should be forced on Germany and the victorious powers should oversee such conversion.

The old Secretary's voice was quavering when he finished. FDR assumed an air of camaraderie and said that he had ditched the Morgenthau Plan and felt more receptive to the State Department ideas. Later the same morning the humorless Secretary of War, Henry L. Stimson, hair parted severely in the middle, arrived with the same complaint. Mr. Roosevelt was forced to sit through it again. At one point, the President interrupted the dissertation to say: "Henry, we are not far apart in our ideas." Stimson said that he hoped Roosevelt would not approve a "peace of vengeance." FDR, who was averse to admitting mistakes, told Stimson he did not know "how" he had initialed the Quebec agreement. "It must have been done," he said ruefully, "without much thought."

In the afternoon James A. Farley stopped at the State Department to pay his respects to Hull. "He was pale and drawn and nervous," Farley said. The old Tennessee judge stood behind his desk in silence, studying Farley. "Jim," he said softly, "I am through." Tears welled in his eyes. "This illness has put me out. I am going to resign as soon as possible after the election."

Farley said he was sorry that the Secretary was not well and hoped a good rest would help him to recover. Hull turned away from his future and said bitterly that he had not seen the President from before the Quebec Conference "until this morning." He said that the Cabinet committee had worked out an agreeable plan for postwar Germany, and then Morgenthau had released his bombshell at Quebec without prior consultation with other members of the Cabinet. "My first impulse was to give public expression of my opposition to the plan, which would destroy Germany and put Europe out of economic balance. Then I decided to wait and let public opinion take care of the situation."

"I could tell," Farley said, "that he resented the short-circuiting by the White House."

October 1944

THE CHILL DAYS OF EARLY AUTUMN MATCHED THE political atmosphere. The United States and Great Britain were confronted with a victorious ally, who, imploring assistance two years earlier, now assumed an independence which amounted almost to estrangement. FDR had asked Stalin for a three-way summit conference. It had been declined. The President had asked for help for the uprising of Poles in Warsaw and none had been forthcoming. As the month of October became the top sheet on the calendar, Mr. Roosevelt, head of the most powerful nation in the world, was reduced to the status of supplicant. He signaled Stalin that a summit conference had been promised, and he felt that the three great allies

must meet to discuss postwar operations. He suggested
Scotland, Stockholm or The Hague as likely places.

Knowing that Stalin often required three weeks to
respond to an urgency, the President asked Ambassador
Averell Harriman to request an interview with Josef
Stalin. The meeting was cordial. Harriman said that the
President would like to have the meeting in November
shortly after the election. There were questions, Harriman said, which involved coordination of military objectives and problems of peace which would require unanimity of purpose. Stalin agreed that a meeting was
"very desirable." However, he was now under the orders
of his doctors, who said that the dictator's health would
not permit travel. Harriman, studying his man, thought
that the short deep-chested Marshal appeared to be in
robust health. He was also in good humor.

Stalin suggested that Roosevelt and Churchill could
meet with Foreign Minister Molotov. As Ambassador,
Harriman could not decline the invitation, but he knew
that Roosevelt would, because a foreign minister would
be empowered only to participate in discussions, not to
make binding decisions. An additional block to a three-
way summit meeting was the Quebec Conference, where
Churchill and Roosevelt had reached momentous decisions. The Russians, who nurtured formidable suspicions at all times, claimed to know no more about what
transpired at Quebec than what the Russian ambassadors in Washington and London had been told. When
Winston Churchill received word that Stalin would not
participate in a summit meeting, he sent an eloquent note
to Stalin in which he stated that "on the agreement of
our three nations, Britain, United States of America, and
USSR, stand the hopes of the world." With Stalin's
permission, Churchill wrote, he would like to visit
Moscow in the near future for general discussions.

Stalin could find no way of declining to play host to
the British Prime Minister. The visit was arranged, even
though Roosevelt would not attend, and thus the agreements would be no more binding on the Big Three than
those arrived at by two men in Quebec. Privately, Win-

ston Churchill was more fretful about Russian military victories than he had been in the dark days of 1940 when Hitler defeated the Low Countries and France, and sent the remnants of the British Army fleeing from the beaches at Dunkirk. In that case, the Prime Minister seemed not to doubt the eventual triumph of British and Allied arms.

This time he was worried. The Russians were halfway across Poland, they had poured through the Balkans without let, were poised before Hungary and had decimated the flower of Germany's armies. "Winston," wrote a friend, "never talks of Hitler these days; he is always harping on the dangers of communism. He dreams of the Red Army spreading like a cancer from one country to another." Churchill's physician, Lord Moran, noted in his personal diary: "The advance of the Red Army has taken possession of his mind. Once they got into a country, it would not be easy to get them out. Our army in Italy was too weak to keep them in check." As an afterthought, Churchill told his doctor: "Stalin will get what he wants. The Americans have seen to that."

As the campaign gathered momentum, the President's health became an issue. It wasn't the innuendo of the newspapers, or even the mock pity of hard Republican campaigners who pretended to be saddened by Mr. Roosevelt's physical decay. A lot of the fear was coming from Democrats, callous city bosses who wanted to know "on the level" if Roosevelt could endure one more term. Admiral McIntire expressed himself in favor of ignoring the speculation. The President, however, saw it for what it was, a cogent concern for the nation. McIntire kept insisting to FDR that he was not sick; he was merely a sixtyish man with a crippling affliction who was "just getting over the flu and still troubled with bronchitis."

The Admiral was angered that the rumors, instead of diminishing in the face of White House silence, were becoming more outrageous. He pointed out to Bruenn that the whispers—even in Washington—were that Mr. Roosevelt was undergoing increasing incapacitation and actual collapse. He was also said to be suffering from a coronary thrombosis, a brain hemorrhage, a nervous breakdown, an aneurism of the aorta and cancer of the prostate. Some said he had been spirited to a Miami sanitarium, others that he was in a Chicago hospital where eminent specialists were considering the risk of operating. The Admiral found the boss to be "deeply angered." FDR's response was to schedule speeches in New York, in Philadelphia, Chicago and Boston. The doctor asked the President to please make such speeches in a sitting position. Roosevelt promised. McIntire told the patient that the braces would no longer help: "Standing will not exercise the muscles of your legs, as swimming did. It will merely subject them to ache and strain." He told Roosevelt that, if he used the braces, standing on them for forty-five minutes would induce the exact amount of strain "as running three miles at top speed."

For the first time, the matter got out of hand. On October 12 McIntire, who feared the press and never addressed himself to reporters unless he was under orders to do so, issued a statement: "The President's health is perfectly okay. There are absolutely no organic difficulties at all. The President is eight or nine pounds under his best weight," but that, the Admiral said, was a good sign, not a bad one. "The President is justifiably proud of his new flat—repeat, f-l-a-t tummy." Someone asked why Dr. Howard Bruenn, known to be a heart specialist, was in daily attendance on the President. The Admiral said, with asperity, that a good physician worries about such matters even when there is no reason for them. "Here is a man of sixty-two, under terrific strain for years, who has been coughing for more than two months. . . . That stout heart of his has never failed. However, the problem is to protect the President's reserve strength with constant watch on the heart. This is the business of Commander Bruenn." The Admiral lied arrogantly.

Time magazine, alert to the importance of Roosevelt's state of health, published an article three days after McIntire soothed the worries of the press and opened by quoting the New York *Sun:* "Let's not be squeamish.

It is convention not the constitution which forbids open comment on the possibility that a President may be succeeded by his Vice-President. Six Presidents have died in office." The New York *Daily News* stated it for the subway readers: "Dewey is 42; Roosevelt is 62." Every morning at 8:30, Admiral McIntire parked his five-year-old Lincoln convertible inside the west gate of the White House. A *Time* reporter, dissatisfied with the health portrait described by the doctor, waited for him to park his car and asked how healthy is healthy.

The Admiral, disarming as always, said: "I wish he'd put on a few more pounds. He hasn't been in the pool since before going to Quebec. But he's going to start in the pool again now. He is a powerful swimmer and that gives him a good workout. Nothing wrong organically with him at all. Does a terrific day's work. But he stands up under it amazingly. The stories that he is in bad health are understandable enough around election time, but they are not true."

They were true. The worst aspect of the President's illness was that McIntire and Roosevelt did not confide their apprehensions to each other, and neither man asked questions of the other. If Roosevelt's goal was victory and an enduring peace, then McIntire's was to keep his medical puppet alive and in office. If, in this election year, the Admiral and the President ever had an honest conversation about the gravity of FDR's condition, neither their wives, their secretaries, nor their confreres were aware of it.

At a Cabinet meeting, the President raised the subject. "There has been this constant rumor that I'll not live if I'm elected," he said, glowering at the faces around the table over the tops of his spectacles, "and people have been asked to believe that I'm all worn out and sick. You all know that this is not so, but apparently I have to face them to prove it." There was some unintelligible murmuring around the Cabinet table. "I'm going right after Dewey," the President said with finality, "and make this a real campaign." Later, when he sat with his son James, the name Dewey was mentioned and Mr.

Roosevelt thrust forward a pugnacious jaw. "The little man makes me pretty mad," he said.

Nor did it improve his morale when Cordell Hull stopped in to see the President and said he would have to resign as Secretary of State, that he must go to a hospital. FDR begged the old man not to quit at the moment. "Please," the President begged, "stay on until after the election." He wanted no more fuel to the fire of all the tired old men. But there were too many old men and they were being felled by the prodigious labors of the times. The President's mentor, Alfred E. Smith, died in early October. The funeral warranted the presence of Roosevelt, but he could not stand in his braces and he could not bear the overwhelming memories of the 1920s, as he explained to his wife. He delegated Mrs. Roosevelt, Grace Tully, General Watson and William Hassett to attend the services at St. Patrick's Cathedral in New York as his surrogates. Three days later, as he was working on a message to General Eisenhower, a secretary stepped into FDR's office and said: "Excuse me. It's just come over the radio that Wendell Willkie died early this morning." Roosevelt's jaw slacked; his mouth hung open. "What was the matter with him?" "Streptococcic throat and what the doctors call complications." Willkie had been a young, vigorous man.

On the night of October 2 the final broadcast of the Polish resistance emanated from Warsaw. The *Armija Krajowa* which had risen 200,000 strong to fight the Hitlerites was no more. Referring to the fearsome Russians, the male voice said: "We were treated worse than Hitler's satellites, worse than Italy, Romania, Finland. May God, who is just, pass judgment on the terrible injustice suffered by the Polish nation, and may He punish accordingly all those who are guilty." The question of Poland, and what to do with this Slavic nation over whose breast World War II began, was becoming a stain on the honor of the Allied powers. The *Armija Krajowa* (AK) claimed that it had been called out of hiding by a broadcast from Moscow to rise against the

Nazis. The broadcast was a public indictment of Josef Stalin as a traitor to the cause of Poland, and a last farewell from the democratic forces in Warsaw.

The new Polish government, sponsored and endorsed by the Russians, had been formed in Lublin. In that city, the hard-headed Communist Osóbka-Morawski issued an ultimatum of the Polish government in London: "We are willing to accept Mikolajczyk and Grabski and Popiel and one more and that is all." He issued a postscript: "They had better accept soon or the offer will not be repeated." The offer was not accepted, and not repeated. This left Poland under the domination of the Soviet Union. Within a few days, Alexander Werth, president of the Anglo-American correspondents of Moscow, managed to achieve something denied to all others: passage to the city of Lublin. "I was to stay several days in Lublin," he radioed. "The streets were crowded, which they seldom were in any newly liberated Russian town; there was also great activity in the market-place. Everywhere there were many Russian and Polish soldiers. . . . The German occupation—which had lasted five years—had left a deep mark on the people of Lublin, and the arrival of the Russians had not set their minds at rest; far from it.

"On the other hand, there were—especially among the better-dressed people—grave misgivings about the Russians and strong AK sympathies; and there was also much talk of 2,000 AK men having been arrested by the Russians in the Lublin area alone. . . . On Sunday all the churches, and there were said to be more churches per square mile in Lublin than in any other Polish city, were crowded. Among the faithful, kneeling and praying, there were many Polish soldiers. The shops were almost empty although there was a good deal of food in the marketplace. But the food was dear and there was much animosity against the peasants who were described as 'a lot of blood suckers'; there were also many stories of how the peasants 'crawled' to the Germans; a German soldier only had to appear in a Polish village and the peasants were so scared they'd bring out roast chickens and butter and eggs and sour cream. On the other hand, the Russian soldiers were given strict orders to pay for everything but the peasants weren't keen at all to give anything away for rubles."

An elderly woman, ruminating about the German occupation, stared at the street and said that, in spite of the German horrors, she was worried and uneasy about the Russian occupation. She remembered Maidanek, and the oven extermination camp built by the Germans only two miles from Lublin. There they cremated Jews and Slavs. When the wind was from the east, the Lublin pedestrians walked with handkerchiefs to their noses. She remembered the freezing freight trains, loaded with hungry children whose parents had been killed. They were on their way to Germany as slave labor. "Any German soldier," she said, "would sell you a Polish child for thirty zloty. . . . To kill a human being, it was as easy as stepping on a worm and squashing it."

In a manner of speaking, she represented Polish thinking everywhere. The nation had suffered for years under the Germans; it was now being occupied by Russian masters. Poland, proud and unwilling to bargain, demanded nothing less than complete freedom, even in Lublin. This was a chronic embarrassment to the United States government, Great Britain, and the Soviet Union, which was in poor temper to explain why the gallant Poles would remain under the Russian heel. If the alliance of the three great powers were to break, it would fall into rubble on the plains of Poland. Roosevelt and Churchill fretted about how hard to press Moscow for an equitable settlement; Stalin had to decide how to appear to yield without giving up the new satellite.

October 4, 1944

Number 76. Top Secret and Personal
From the President to Ambassador Harriman
Will you please deliver the following message to Marshal Stalin at once:
While I had hoped that the next meeting could have been between you, Churchill and myself, I appreciate that the

Prime Minister wishes to have an early conference with you.

You, naturally, understand that in this global war there is literally no question, political or military, in which the United States is not interested. I am firmly convinced that the three of us, and only the three of us, can find the solution to the still unresolved questions. In this sense, while appreciating the Prime Minister's desire for the meeting, I prefer to regard your forthcoming talks with Churchill as preliminary to a meeting of the three of us which, so far as I am concerned, can take place any time after the elections here.

In the circumstances, I am suggesting if you and Mr. Churchill approve, that our ambassador in Moscow be present at your coming conference as an observer for me. Naturally, Mr. Harriman would not be in a position to commit this government relative to the important matters which you and the Prime Minister will, very naturally, discuss.

You will, by this time, have received from General Deane the statement of our Combined Chiefs of Staff position relative to the war against Japan and I want to reiterate to you how completely I accept the assurances which you have given us on this point. Our three countries are waging a successful war against Germany and we can surely join together with no less success in crushing a nation that I am sure in my heart is as great an enemy of Russia as she is of ours.

Roosevelt

October 8, 1944

From Marshal Stalin to The President

Your message of October 5th (refer to #76) somewhat puzzled me. I supposed that Mr. Churchill was going to Moscow in accordance with the agreement reached with you at Quebec. It happened, however, that this supposition of mine does not seem to correspond in reality.

It is unknown to me with what questions Mr. Churchill and Mr. Eden are going to Moscow. So far I have not been informed about this by either one. Mr. Churchill, in his message to me, expressed a desire to come to Moscow, if there would not be any objections on my part. I, of course, gave my consent. Such is the matter in connection with Mr. Churchill's trip to Moscow. In the future I will keep you informed about the matter, after the meeting with Mr. Churchill.

Communication between the powers was poor. Churchill radioed Roosevelt that he planned to go to Moscow alone; Roosevelt waited until the trip was imminent and then tried to torpedo it by reminding Stalin that no agreements between the two would be binding on the United States. Stalin, misunderstanding the visit, had already signaled Churchill: "I share your conviction that firm agreement between the three leading powers constitutes a true guarantee of future peace. . . . Certainly I should like very much to meet you and the President . . . I wholeheartedly welcome your desire to come to Moscow in October." Nor was Stalin devoid of ideas which Churchill was pressing to discuss. Eden wrote in his diary that Churchill, in an earlier message, had wired Stalin about the necessity for discussing "both Poland and the Balkans, as well as war plans."

When Churchill was in receipt of FDR's earlier message that he could not engage in a three-way summit conference until after November, the Prime Minister sniffed that the Red Army would not stand still to await the result of an American election. The Prime Minister and his Foreign Secretary flew to Moscow for private talks on a subject to which President Roosevelt would not lend himself: a division of spoils. The foundation of the projected United Nations was the self-determination and independence of all peoples and nations. Churchill, born and raised as part of Queen Victoria's great British Empire, had an overriding interest in "spheres of influence" among great powers. The Russian, Stalin, had a strong interest in surrounding his mother country with a picket fence of smaller countries to be called satellites.

At noon of Churchill's first day in Moscow, the Soviet government sent an American automobile with bulletproof windows to the British Embassy for the private use of the Prime Minister and Foreign Secretary. Other limousines brought thirty-eight additional guests to a fourteen-course luncheon at the Kremlin.

When the principals adjourned to the great conference hall, Stalin sat prepared for an enduring and rancorous argument about every bit of land from Helsinki to Athens. He recalled that FDR had rebuffed Russian ambitions everywhere and kept reciting that the self-determination of nations large and small was the true goal of the peace. Militarily, Russia's position was now stronger than ever if there was a showdown. The Russian armies occupied Finland, Estonia, Latvia, Lithuania, half of the great Polish plain, all of Romania and Bulgaria, and were poised on the frontiers of Greece and Turkey. If there was to be an estrangement between Russia and her strong allies, Stalin could continue to occupy the major portion of the face of Europe before meeting opposition. On the other hand, no one knew better than Stalin and Molotov the price Russia had already paid in millions of military and civilian lives and the leveling of cites and towns all the way to Stalingrad.

Russia had bled; it was weak and needed help. The last ounce of strength was in the military; it had men and guns and an indomitable will and little else. Anthony Eden brought to the conference table what appeared to be the perennial thorn of Poland and encountered a chill from Molotov and Stalin, and no help from his Prime Minister. En route back to the British Embassy, the handsome Eden became almost passionate about the matter. "Poland," he said to Churchill, "is a first-class issue. If people feel that Russia is putting in puppets and that everybody who doesn't agree with her is an enemy of Poland, they will be uneasy. Poland must be allowed to settle her own affairs."

At the table with the Russians, Winston Churchill was possessed of a feeling that the Great Bear, starved and beaten for so long and now fattening up in other lands, had no wish to return to its cave. Within a few minutes, the two leaders had disposed of a great section of Europe, each getting a little more than he expected.

Speaking of cynicism, Stalin had a better eye for the future than Churchill, because he understood that the Soviet Union would eventually control Romania, Bulgaria, Yugoslavia and Hungary, leaving only the nettlesome politics of Greece for Great Britain. There could have been no doubt among the gentlemen at the table that the United States would not be a party to "spheres of influence," which Roosevelt had denounced as the breeding grounds of war when he designed the United Nations.

The heroes had become the villains. Churchill said bluntly, "The moment is apt for business." Stalin agreed, although he did not ask whether the reference was to the absence of Roosevelt. "Your armies are in Romania and Bulgaria. We have interests, missions and agents there." Then, with a large smile: "Don't let us get at cross purposes in small ways." When the matter of Poland arose again, Mr. Churchill settled the matter to the satisfaction of the Russians: the Curzon Line would be Poland's eastern boundary on the Russian border. This gave the Soviet Union exactly what Adolf Hitler had given the Russians in August 1939, with the exception of the industrial city and oil fields of Lvov, which were slightly on the Polish side of the border. Stalin decided not to press the matter but to wait for a Big Three meeting and then demand Lvov. To compensate Poland for depriving it of territory on the east, it was proposed by the Russians to grant German territory to it on the west. The line would be along the Oder River. The Russian Marshal expected no disclaimer from the Lublin government about this agreement. If there was trouble, it would come from the London Poles and the Americans. No Sunday fowl was ever carved more quickly and in such amicable circumstances than Poland and the Balkans.

The conferences continued until October 18 with increased cordiality on both sides. Rain swept Moscow the morning the British left. Josef Stalin, who had never accompanied any statesman to the airport, insisted on traveling to the plane with Churchill. He permitted photos to be taken of the two men smiling and grasping each other's hand. On the same day Stalin dutifully reported to FDR:

October 19, 1944

Secret and Personal

From Premier J. V. Stalin to President Franklin Roosevelt

1. During the stay of Mr. Churchill and Mr. Eden in Moscow we have exchanged views on a number of questions of mutual interest. Ambassador Harriman has, certainly, informed you about all important Moscow conversations. I also know that the Prime Minister had to send you his estimate of the Moscow conversations. On my part I can say that our conversations were extremely useful for the mutual ascertaining of views on such questions as the attitude toward the future of Germany, Polish question, policy in regard to the Balkan States, and important questions of further military policy. During the conversations it has been clarified that we can, without great difficulties, adjust our policy on all questions standing before us, and if we are not in a position so far to provide an immediate necessary decision of this or that task, as for example, on the Polish question, but nevertheless, more favorable perspectives are opened. I hope that these Moscow conversations will be of some benefit from the point of view that at the future meeting of three of us, we shall be able to adopt definite decisions on all urgent questions of our mutual interest.

2. Ambassador Gromyko has informed me about his recent conversation with Mr. Hopkins, in which Mr. Hopkins expressed an idea that you could arrive in the Black Sea at the end of November and meet with me on the Soviet Black Sea coast. I would extremely welcome the realization of this intention. From the conversation with the Prime Minister, I was convinced that he also shares this idea. Thus the meeting of the three of us could take place at the end of November in order to consider the questions which have been accumulated since Teheran. I would be glad to receive a message from you on this matter.

Seldom in the history of statecraft have so many words been used to reveal so little. No report exists to show what Harriman may have told FDR. Certainly the President, had he known of the agreements of mutual domination, would have been outraged. The proof of how little he knew of the agreements—and the fact that he had better prepare himself to face two votes of opposition to his one—is in the reply he sent to Stalin:

I am sure that the progress made during your conversations in Moscow will facilitate and expedite our work in the next meeting when the three of us should come to a full agreement on our future activities and policies and mutual interests.

Through all of this, the only news made public was that the Soviet Union tried to buy two million artificial legs in the United States. A canvass of American prosthetic plants showed that they could not even supply the domestic demand.

Most of the White House was in darkness. On the south side, pale light crept through the filmy curtains of the President's office. A pie-shaped wedge of light came from the Diplomatic Reception Hall on the ground floor. Mr. Roosevelt, on October 10, was about to make a fireside chat. He sat in his office until the last moment, reading a 5,000-word communiqué summing the accomplishments at Dumbarton Oaks:

(1) The new world order was officially named the United Nations.

(2) France "in due course" would become one of the Big Five entitled to a permanent seat on the eleven-nation Security Council. The other four were the United States, Great Britain, the Soviet Union and China.

(3) The Assembly, to which all peace-keeping nations may be members, would have less power than planned. It would be empowered to debate, but not to make recommendations.

(4) The United Nations should have armadas of

pooled air power to be "immediately available" to send against aggressors.

If the announcement was not electrifying, it was not publicly damaging, such as revealing the Russian demand for membership and votes for sixteen Soviet Republics. Hull, too ill to attend his duties, was in Bethesda Naval Hospital and had told Ambassador Gromyko that a demand for sixteen votes, against one for the United States and one for Great Britain, would destroy the United Nations before it was born.

The President was wheeled to the elevator with Fala and went down to the Diplomatic Reception Hall where fifty White House correspondents applauded his entry. When FDR was seated behind the microphones, he smiled up at Mike Reilly and tapped his mouth. He had remembered to bring his "pivot" tooth this time. He appeared to be weak, almost sagging toward the array of microphones, but when he spoke, his voice was strong.

It was not a great speech. FDR opened by hoping that all Americans regardless of party would register and vote. Again he accused the GOP of making it difficult for servicemen to vote: "There are politicians and others who quite openly worked to restrict the use of the ballot in this election, hoping selfishly for a small vote." If he was playing Commander in Chief, he was doing it under an old campaign hat because he charged that Thomas E. Dewey stated that the Roosevelt Administration desired to keep "the boys in uniform" because "the New Deal is afraid of the peace." "It seems a pity," Roosevelt said softly, "that reckless words, based on unauthoritative sources, should be used to mislead and weaken morale."

Somewhere in the short talk he had to deal with the accurate charge that the head U.S. Communist, Earl Browder, pledged Communist support for a Roosevelt fourth term. "I have never sought," the President said slowly, "and I do not welcome the support of any person or group committed to communism or fascism, or any other foreign ideology which would undermine the American system of government."

Then he called Fala to him, lifted himself from the desk chair to his wheelchair, and nodded good night to the reporters. Within fifteen minutes, all except the faint corridor lights of the White House had been extinguished. The President counted the short radio talk as a campaign speech, although Henry Hopkins and Mrs. Roosevelt felt that it lacked the energetic values needed to show the electorate that he was strong enough for a fourth term.

The national polls showed, in the middle of October, that the race was close with the President in the lead. If the Democratic campaign was weak and apathetic, then the Republican was strong and unrelenting. Thomas E. Dewey felt that his strongest card was to speak like a prosecutor with the President in the prisoner's pen, but this may have been a weakness. In addition, Dewey was too easily infuriated. When Roosevelt said that the machinery for keeping the peace should remain in experienced hands, the Republican nominee cried "foul" because it had been privately agreed that the United Nations was a bipartisan, not a campaign, issue. Dewey was again outraged when Roosevelt, in a press conference, announced that the Democratic party was the party "of sound money." The hard dollar had been a Republican fief for many years.

If, in October, the race was as close as the polls indicated, then it is possible that Dewey's tactics helped to reelect Roosevelt. He too seemed to tire of the phrase "quarrelsome old men" and fell into the trap of using that hoary old gambit, communism, for his final moves. In Catholic Boston Governor Dewey charged that Roosevelt was selling his party, putting it up for the highest bidder, and the Communist party was taking over the New Deal. The President, he stated, had pardoned that old-line Communist, Earl Browder, "in time to organize a fourth term election." It was difficult, even for Communist haters, to imagine FDR selling his party out to a frowzy left-wing group which didn't have the strength to elect anyone. "Now," shouted Dewey, "the Communists are seizing control of the New Deal, through which they aim to control the government of the United States." On the same day, in Worcester, Dewey said that a Republican victory "next month will end one-man government, and we can forever remove the threat of monarchy in the United States." The attack was poorly aimed and repetitious; neither Dewey nor his manager, Herbert Brownell, was willing to accept campaign counsel from their entourage. They had competent speech writers, idea men and publicity experts, but both men were convinced that name-calling would win the election.

In the Democratic camp the only response to the attacks came from Roosevelt himself. The big city and state party bosses did not fear Dewey; they were afraid of Roosevelt. By letter and by phone they begged him to take to the stumps and show himself to the people. If the voters saw and heard the President, he would win. If he sulked in the White House, he could lose. They could not bring him before the public, but Dewey did. It was the only time within the memory of the President's oldest political allies that they saw him bristle at the mention of his adversary's name. He snapped that he felt "contempt" for Dewey.

Then, after a series of consultations, Mr. Roosevelt sat at his upstairs desk and wrote on a sheet of paper:

Oct. 21—A speech on foreign policy at a dinner in the Waldorf-Astoria Hotel in New York.

Oct. 27—(Navy Day) Speech on the war at Shibe Park in Philadelphia.

Oct. 28—Speech on postwar domestic problems at Soldier Field, Chicago.

November 4—General roundup speech at Fenway Park in Boston.

November 7—The usual, short election eve Fireside Chat from Hyde Park.

He would, at last, emerge from the shell. Robert Sherwood was back from London, and FDR asked him and Sam Rosenman to get busy on the research and early drafts of all speeches. Arrangements would have to be made for him to sit in his car for the outdoor speeches at Shibe Park, Soldier Field and Fenway Park. This would entail building a sloping wooden ramp in midfield for his car to climb and for spotlights to light it. Also, electrical connections to a board holding microphones would have to be arranged so that it could rest between the two rear doors of the automobile as the President spoke. He advised the speech writers to arrange for him to speak at the Waldorf *sitting* at the head of the table. The torturous rehearsals with leg braces in his bedroom had not been successful.

The speeches were run through a literary meat grinder. Among those who worked on pages and paragraphs, phrases and particulars were Ben Cohen, Chip Bohlen, Harry Hopkins, Robert Sherwood, Archibald MacLeish, Aldolf A. Berle, Russell Davenport, Sam Rosenman, Raymond Gram Swing and Dorothy Thompson. There was more than sufficient talent in the group to ruin any assortment of speeches, but the drafts were typed, sent "upstairs," to return with Xs drawn through parts, substitute phrases written between lines, and suggestions penned in margins. Those speeches were done again and again; ideas which passed muster yesterday were excised today. An aroused President was preparing to sink his opponent with every weapon which would sound Rooseveltian. The Waldorf-Astoria speech consisted of ten separate drafts.

Mrs. Roosevelt wanted to help, but she was politely rebuffed. The President accepted the slips of paper, the notes with suggestions, and filed them. Robert Hannegan, the Democratic national chairman, did not like Mrs. Roosevelt. He called her a bearer of bad news. Once, when she cornered him, Mrs. Roosevelt said that she had spoken to Walter White of the National Association for the Advancement of Colored People and he said that unless Roosevelt underscored a civil rights stand, he would lose the Negro vote. She asked the President to see Walter White, but FDR and Hannegan knew that a public stand in favor of civil rights would risk losing the Southern states; down there whites voted; blacks didn't. Mrs. Roosevelt wrote to her son James: "I don't think Pa would really mind defeat. . . ." General Watson said that "the President just doesn't seem to give a damn." There may have been truth to these observations, but Dewey's arrogance altered FDR's attitude. The President was aroused. He not only wanted to make that foreign policy speech in New York on October 21, he insisted on a fifty-mile parade through the streets of New York. If the people wanted to see him, he proposed to make himself available for their scrutiny as a healthy man.

Roosevelt had extraordinary luck with weather. There had been times, in three earlier campaigns, when drenching rain and sleet stopped as he appeared to make a speech. It was called "Roosevelt weather." On the morning of October 21 New York was swept by a cold relentless rain which darkened the sides of tall buildings and caused millions emerging from subways to scurry for shelter. Admiral McIntire requested Mr. Roosevelt to cancel the parade. The President declined. He was helped into his voluminous Navy cape, he donned his old gray fedora and his glasses and sat in the back of the open Packard. Further, although Mike Reilly was the only person aware of it, FDR was wearing his braces in an unlocked position.

His special train had backed slowly into the Brooklyn Army base at 7:30 A.M. The people he respected—his doctor, his wife, his secretaries, all of whom except McIntire had entreated FDR to expose himself to the people—were now asking him not to leave the railroad car. The President pointed to the morning newspapers. All published maps showing the route of the presidential motorcade and the time he was expected at each place. "I'm going," he said. "Mike, get that car ready. With the top down." The same newspapers had page-one stories about the outer edge of a hurricane which was passing New York at sea. The one would not cancel the other.

The fact that it was a bad day made it a good day in FDR's opinion. He would show himself to the multitudes of New York, and, from the back of a truck preceding his limousine, newsreel cameramen would display the gallant President to scores of millions across the country. The temperature dropped; the rain was cold and heavy and would last all day. The escort of motorcycle police preceding the President hunched down in rubber jackets. Some of the Secret Service men, who spelled each other riding the running boards of the limousine and trotting beside it, wore topcoats with rain slickers over them.

Mr. Roosevelt's health risk was more in Mike Reilly's hands than in Admiral McIntire's; Reilly sent changes of clothing to various stops around the city. The motorcade departed at 9:30 and moved slowly through the Army base, where the special train waited on a siding. In spite of the downpour, reporters estimated 40,000 men stood outside barracks to cheer, as Roosevelt went by, sitting straight in the rear left-hand seat, raising and lowering the fedora in greeting.

He had promised his friend Senator Robert Wagner a boost for Wagner's reelection. This would be informal and would take place at Ebbetts Field, home of the baseball Dodgers. The motorcade moved from the Army base to the Brooklyn Navy Yard. It did not stop, but 70,000 sailors and workmen, on cruisers and carriers, paused to shout encouragement as he wended his way up and down the lanes and piers. From there FDR was driven slowly through the heavily populated Flatbush area of Brooklyn, grinning and waving, pausing to wipe rain from his glasses. Bill Hassett, who watched from the third car in the cavalcade, was ready to admit that there was indeed magic to the presence of President Roosevelt. It was Saturday, a most dismal day, and yet Bedford Avenue was lined with people who hollered and women who blew kisses.

At Ebbetts Field the car came in from a left-field

entrance and moved slowly toward second base. Crowds of Democrats in the grandstands stood to applaud and shout greetings. As the car stopped, the President saw thousands of umbrellas. The Packard was driven slowly up on a large wooden ramp. When it stopped, Roosevelt said, "Ready, Mike?" "Ready." Reilly got into the car on hands and knees and snapped the knee braces into a locked position. The car door was open. The President took his hat off and shed the big Navy cape. Then, using Reilly's strength to hoist himself into a standing position, he stepped out of the car exposed to the elements. Rain plastered his hair and ran down his cheeks.

He rocked slowly forward, an awkward doll, to the speaker's lectern. There he raised a hand in happy greeting; the crowd went wild. All they could see was the lean white face, the strong shoulders and arms. The remainder of the body was hidden by the lectern. Hassett, watching the scene of triumph against adversity, later wrote in his diary that this exhibition should still the whispers about the President's health. It was unfortunate, he felt, that the leader of the editorial pack of wolves, John O'Donnell of the *Daily News,* was in a New York hospital with an infected spleen. Mrs. Roosevelt, who had been riding at the side of the President, worried, then marveled at the apparent exhilaration of her husband. She realized, looking at the dark spots on the gray suit, that he was soaked to the skin with cold rain.

As he spoke, FDR could hear the echoes of his words bouncing from the crowded stands:

I have never been to Ebbetts Field before, but I have rooted for the Dodgers. And I hope to come back here some day and see them play. But the chief reason I am here today is to pay a little tribute to my old friend Bob Wagner. We were together in the Legislature—I would hate to say how long ago—thirty some years ago—in the Senate of the State of New York. We have been close friends ever since, I think largely because we have the same ideas of being of service to our fellow men.

*If anybody knew and could visualize all the way through
the help that Bob Wagner has been to mankind, there
wouldn't be any question about asking him to go back to
the Senate for six years more, to carry on the splendid service that he has rendered. And so I just came here to say that
word in his behalf. He deserves well of mankind. Thank you.*

The President was given a standing ovation as he
hobbled back to the car.

Mike Reilly was in charge. He ordered that the cars
speed up and, once out of the field, turn the corner to
a U.S. Coast Guard Station. There Mr. Roosevelt was
half carried from the car inside. Officers and men stood
aside as the Chief Executive was carried into a small
infirmary. Mr. Roosevelt was stripped to the skin. The
braces clattered to the floor. He was helped onto a
table. Heavy towels were used to give him a hard rubdown. A Secret Service man brought a drink of whiskey.
FDR downed it in a gulp.

Reilly asked for the change of clothes that had been
prepared. The underwear, shirt, tie, suit and shoes replaced the soggy mess on the floor. Someone in the front
office was trying to shake the rain from the Navy cape
and the old hat. Within a few minutes the President
was dressed and ready. He was helped back into the
car, and Mrs. Roosevelt asked how he felt. "Fine," he
said. "Fine." It seems like a contradiction in terms,
but he looked pale, weak and ecstatic; the more outrageous the weather, the more he appeared to gloat.
The cars wended their way slowly through Queens, thin
crowds of residents lining the curbs, watching in excitement as the phalanx of motorcycles with blinking red
lights approached from a distance. This was the President,
and the people seemed willing to brave a few minutes
of drenching to see his face and watch him lift his hat
left and right.

After Queens the cars headed across bridges to Ed
Flynn's Bronx, where ward bosses had ordered the
faithful to be on the edge of the streets. It was afternoon—and no lunch—by the time Mr. Roosevelt inched

south through the shabby streets of Harlem, waving to blacks who hung out of upper windows. It was a long, long ride—fifty-one miles on the odometer. The downpour never stopped; it seemed to intensify at times. Mrs. Roosevelt and others suggested that part of the route be abridged, but FDR would not hear of it. This was his display of defiance and he would not change it. The hat and the shoulders of the Navy cape were shiny. Sometimes, when he tipped the hat, rivulets ran off the brim onto his face.

The smile of triumph seldom left his face. Once, he was driven in out of the rain. This occurred at Hunter College, where thousands of WAVES were lined up in uniform for inspection. The car drove slowly around the inside of the armory. The President held his hat high, and left without a word. From there the slow cars moved down Broadway and Seventh Avenue. The farther south the cars went, the more the crowds seemed to increase. By the time FDR reached the garment center, his eyes beheld an ocean of newspapers held over heads. David Dubinsky and Sidney Hillman had ordered the Garment Workers Union and their friends to be present on this Saturday afternoon, and they were there. The cheers were deafening. Reporters said it was like a wall of sound, almost impenetrable. It was the biggest, and the best, welcome of the day.

The cars turned left on 34th Street, moved by the enormous Empire State Building, where the upper section was hidden in mist, turned right on Fifth Avenue and moved slowly south for the final mile and a half. Near Washington Arch the Packard stopped at a Fifth Avenue apartment building. If anyone was more elated at reaching the final stop than FDR, it was Mrs. Roosevelt. Years earlier, when the President sold the house his mother had given him on East 65th Street, he asked his wife to rent an apartment on lower Fifth Avenue. It had been done, and nicely furnished too. In spite of many entreaties, the President had never seen the place. He referred to it as "Mrs. Roosevelt's apartment."

Police held the crowds at each end of the street. Secret

Service men surrounded the President so that no one could see that he was being carried from the automobile, under a canopy, into the building. Once inside, Mike Reilly hustled his man into a bedroom. There he was again stripped. This time, the clothes, including underwear, were so soaked that they were peeled off the body. Again a vigorous head-to-toe rubdown was given. A drink of whiskey was brought in and Mr. Roosevelt drank. When he was dressed, he lay on the bed for a few moments, as though catching his breath, but the smiles from the pillow were triumphant.

He was helped into a wheelchair and propelled himself into the sitting room. He looked so well that Mrs. Roosevelt remarked that she didn't know how he survived the ordeal. Mr. Roosevelt asked for another drink—unusual for him—and asked Hassett and a few others how he had done. Everyone agreed that it had been a magnificent performance. Police Commissioner Lewis J. Valentine estimated that three million people had seen Roosevelt that day. FDR was pleased. Mrs. Roosevelt, sitting in a wing chair, said she hoped the President had noticed that there were no steps leading into the ground floor apartment, and that no ramp was required. The President nodded.

In a few minutes he was back in the bedroom, resting for the foreign policy speech at the Waldorf. Afterward, he was assisted into his dinner jacket and black tie. The President mixed cocktails before departure. He seemed giddily gay as he was assisted into a closed car and driven up Park Avenue to the Waldorf-Astoria. Beneath the basement, on New York Central tracks, the presidential special waited. The siding, originally laid out for important travelers, had been used but once before. That was when General John J. Pershing became ill and wanted to get to an Army hospital in Washington.

The Waldorf speech was important to the future of the nation and FDR. It was to be a candid monologue of the future, uttered before an audience of plutocrats, of whom about two-thirds were Republicans. It was a dollar-cigar crowd which polka-dotted the tables across the big ballroom. Many of the rich sat in a horseshoe of upper boxes. These were men who, in one form or another, understood the uses of power. They seemed also to respect one who knew how to exercise power. The two thousand diners were applying themselves to an appetizer when the President was assisted to the dais. The diners stood and applauded.

Roosevelt sat, nodding here and there to familiar faces, waving. He applied himself more to his sheaf of papers than to his dinner. Built into this speech was a pronouncement which would prove to be an ace or a deuce in foreign policy. Republican Senator Joseph H. Ball of Minnesota, a liberal courted by Dewey, withheld support of either candidate on the grounds that neither had announced his stand on whether the unborn United Nations would have the power, in the event of war, to summon the armed forces of the United States *without* a prior commitment from the Congress. This was a highly sensitive issue and a stand either way could lose big blocs of votes. Thomas Dewey determined not to respond to the question on the ground that an affirmative response would cost him the American isolationist vote. Roosevelt made up his mind to respond bluntly and affirmatively, knowing that he had already lost the isolationist vote.

The President opened the talk by reciting his Good Neighbor policy and said it would have to spread from the Americas to nations around the world. The weakness in the victory of World War I, he said, was that, having fought for liberty, the United States lost interest in the fate of the world. His recognition of the Soviet Union in 1933 had been unpopular, he said, and he knew it, but there were 180 million people there who represented a blank space on world maps. American opinion was opposed to the League of Nations; the politicians in the United States Senate turned their backs to the World Court. The Navy was scuttled by shortsightedness. Tariff walls went higher and higher, "blocking international trade." Ironically, the economic isolationists, he argued, induced American industry to invest two and a half billion dollars in defeated Germany. He was branded a "warmonger" in 1937 for asking that aggressor nations be quarantined from the human family of nations. In July 1939 he asked for a repeal of the arms embargo law so that arms could be sold to nations resisting Adolf Hitler and Mussolini. "The late Senator William Borah told a group which I called—of all parties—in the White House that his own private information was better than that of the State Department, and there would be no war in Europe. . . . A few weeks later, after Borah said that to me, Hitler brutally attacked Poland and the Second World War began."

His reading of the speech was euphoric, accompanied by elaborate gestures and facial expressions. "These days—and now I am speaking of October 1944—I hear voices in the air attacking me for my failure to prepare this nation for war, and to warn the American people of the approaching tragedy." As always, the President was impelled to throw a bone to the liberal wing of the Republican party. He spoke of the "distinguished men and women of vision and courage" and said that one was sitting "here at this table tonight, our great Secretary of War, Henry Stimson." Increasingly, FDR was interrupted by prolonged bursts of applause. "I am quoting history to you," he said. "I am going by the record." Republicans in Congress had voted against the Selective Service bill; the repeal of the arms embargo; Lend-Lease, and, four months before Pearl Harbor, voted against extension of the Selective Service Act—"voting against keeping our Army together."

As he went on, the President began to take dead aim at personalities:

If the Republicans were to win control of the Congress in this election—and it is only two weeks from next Tuesday, and I occupy the curious position of being President of the United States and at the same time a candidate for the Presidency—if the Republicans were to win control of the Congress, inveterate isolationists would occupy positions of commanding influence and power. I have already spoken of

the ranking Republican member of the Senate Foreign Rela-
tions Committee, Senator Hiram Johnson. One of the most
influential members of the Senate Foreign Relations Com-
mittee—a man who would also be the chairman of the power-
ful Senate Committee on Appropriations—is Senator Gerald
P. Nye.

Well, I am not going back to the old story of the last
presidential campaign: Martin, Barton and Fish—[laughter]
—one of them is gone. But in the House of Representatives,
the man who is the present leader of the Republicans there,
another friend of mine and who would undoubtedly be
Speaker, is Joseph W. Martin. He voted—I am just giving
you examples—he voted against the repeal of arms embargo,
he voted against the Lend-Lease bill; against the extension
of the Selective Service Act, against the arming of merchant
ships, and against the Reciprocal Trade Agreements Act,
and their extensions. The chairman of the powerful Com-
mittee on Rules is the other one and would be none other
than Hamilton Fish. . . .

Let's be fair. There have been Democrats in the isola-
tionist camp, but they have been relatively few and far be-
tween, and so far they have not attained great positions of
leadership. And I am proud of the fact that this administra-
tion does not have the support of the isolationist press. You
know, for about a half-century I have been accustomed to
naming names. I mean specifically, to take the glaring ex-
amples, the McCormick-Patterson-Gannett-and-Hearst press.

Again his hard, incisive words were greeted with
prolonged applause. At this point, he turned to the matter
of peace and the United Nations. No one who worked
close to the President in 1944 misunderstood his overwhelming desire to establish an equitable, working, peace-
enforcing international body. He was certain of military
victory—his other great goal—even though he believed
that the defeat of the Japanese Empire might require
two or more years of fighting. At times—Bretton Woods
and Dumbarton Oaks, for example—he was in such a
feverish hurry to reach agreement on the United Nations
that other nations became recalcitrant and hesitant.

Now [he said] there are some who hope to see a structure of peace completely set up immediately, with all the apartments assigned to everybody's satisfaction, with the telephones in and the plumbing complete—the heating system and the electric ice boxes all functioning perfectly, all furnished with linen and silver—and with the rent prepaid. [The last line drew a hearty laugh.] The United Nations have not yet produced such a comfortable dwelling place. But we have achieved a very practical expression of a common purpose on the part of four great nations, who are now united to wage this war, that they will embark together after the war on a greater and more difficult enterprise, an enterprise of waging peace. We will embark on it with all the peace-loving nations of the world—large and small. And our objective, as I stated ten days ago, is to complete the organization of the United Nations without delay, before hostilities actually cease. Peace, like war, can succeed only where there is a will to enforce it, and where there is available power to enforce it.

He was about to respond to Senator Ball's pertinent question, and his sophisticated audience understood it.

The Council of the United Nations must have the power to act quickly and decisively to keep the peace by force, if necessary. A policeman would not be a very effective policeman if, when he saw a felon break into a house, he had to go to the Town Hall and call a town meeting to issue a warrant before a felon could be arrested.

The cheers now were deafening. In the matter of enforcement of peace, Mr. Roosevelt had taken an unequivocal stand. As he paused and smiled over the tops of his glasses, he may have been pleasantly surprised at the reception he was getting.

So to my simple mind it is clear that, if the world organization is to have any reality at all, our American representatives must be endowed in advance by the people themselves, by constitutional means through their representatives in the Congress, with authority to act. If we do not catch the in-

ternational felon when we have our hands on him, if we let him get away with his loot because the Town Council has not passed an ordinance authorizing his arrest, then we are not doing our share to prevent another world war. I think, and I have had some experience, that the people of this nation want their government to work, they want their government to act, and not merely to talk, whenever and wherever there is a threat to world peace. . . .

We are not fighting for and we shall not attain a Utopia. Indeed, in our own land, the work to be done is never finished. We have yet to realize the full and equal enjoyment of our freedom. So, in embarking on the building of a world fellowship, we have set ourselves a long and arduous task, which will challenge our patience, our intelligence, our imagination as well as our faith. That task, my friends, calls for the judgment of a seasoned and a mature people. This, I think the American people have become. . . . We now are, and we shall continue to be, strong brothers in the family of mankind—the family of the children of God.

The President was escorted to a waiting elevator with cheers and stomping of feet ringing in the ballroom. He had had a day which can only be described as triumphant. As he stood in the elevator leaning on two Secret Service men, Grace Tully, on the arm of Bill Hassett, came running through the crowd. Later that night, as the train moved slowly along the Hudson River to Hyde Park, Bill Hassett jotted in his diary:

All that I have seen today—the President's ride through four hours of rain in an open car, his appearance at Ebbetts Field, the ovation of three million rain-drenched followers, and finally the approval of the Waldorf diners—again convinces me that the election is in the bag. Best of all, my own fears and misgivings about the President's health under the terrific load he is carrying are dissipated, vanished like the morning dew.

In the morning the President was up early to scan the

Sunday newspapers. He made all the headlines. Most of the stories credited FDR with having endured a long, dismal day in a fighting mood, akin to the Roosevelt of old. The *Daily News* managed to locate a photo of the President in his car when he was not smiling and waving his hat. The shot caught him with his gray features relaxed, a wan, sickly-looking man. In general, FDR was so pleased by what he read that he went through his morning medical examination in a teasing mood, reminding his doctor that Mayor Fiorello La Guardia, he had heard, left the parade yesterday with sniffles and a fever, and three Secret Service men had reported off duty as ill. As for him, he never felt better.

There was a pouch of mail up from the White House, but Hassett could not get the President to look at it. Work on this Sunday came under the heading of nonsense. He went out front on the gravel driveway to pose for motion picture clips with Fala. In the afternoon Roosevelt went for a drive through the autumn-clad hills. Mrs. Roosevelt, who kept her own notes, wrote: "I was really worried . . . but instead of being exhausted he was exhilarated." Grace Tully wrote: "It was the only occasion on which I knew him to have more than a couple of drinks—and the variety didn't help much either."

It was evening, bright and brisk, before the President wheeled himself to his corner desk on the ground floor at Hyde Park. There was a lengthy message from Churchill. The part which captured FDR's interest read:

October 22, 1944

Number 801. Personal and Top Secret
Prime Minister to President Roosevelt
. . . Para 8. I was delighted to hear from U.J. [i.e., Uncle Joe Stalin] that you had suggested a triple meeting to-wards the end of November at a Black Sea port. I think this is a very fine idea, and hope you will let me know about it in due course. I will come anywhere you two desire.

The President signaled Churchill at once:

October 22, 1944

Number 632. Personal and Top Secret
From the President to the Prime Minister
The selection of a Black Sea port for our next meeting seems to be dependent upon our ability to get through the Dardanelles safely as I wish to proceed by ship. Do you think it is possible to get U.J. to come to Athens or Cyprus?

Roosevelt

There was a need for a Big Three meeting, mainly to settle the disposition of the nations of Europe and to agree on a stewardship over Germany. An Allied airborne army was in Holland, the British had invaded the Greek mainland, MacArthur had landed in the Philippines and the big naval battle at Leyte Gulf was under way as the President read his mail. Mr. Roosevelt was averse to flying; he wanted to travel to the summit meeting by Navy cruiser, but the availability of safe Russian ports was confined to the Black Sea. He would have to travel through Turkish waters at the Bosporus which would entail negotiating with that government. No ranking American naval officer believed that the Turks could keep a secret. Besides, a large part of the Black Sea was a shambles of sunken merchant ships and tankers. The Navy had no up-to-date charts. Of one thing Roosevelt was certain: Stalin would not leave Russian soil even at the risk of canceling the summit meeting. As usual, he would hide behind the dictates of Kremlin doctors or plead that Russian military matters were so pressing that they required his presence in the Soviet Union.

A note of levity crept into the subject two days later when Churchill was presiding at a Cabinet meeting. A note was handed to him that the Archbishop of Canterbury had died. The Prime Minister was puckishly delighted: "There," he said, "is a total abstainer dead of gout. How right we all are!" When he read the

President's top secret message, Churchill changed his mind:

October 23, 1944

No. 804. Personal and Top Secret
Prime Minister to President Roosevelt
Para. 2. U.J.'s doctors do not like him flying and I suppose there would be the same difficulties in Russian warships coming out of the Black Sea as of American and British coming in. One way would be for Turkey to declare war, which I expect she would be very willing to do. But I am not at all sure that the Russians would welcome this at the present juncture in view of what I told you about their wish for revision of the Treaty of Montreux. Alternatively we could ask Turkey to waive the Montreux Treaty for the passage either way of the said ships. This I expect the Russians would like. But I am not sure about the Turks. From what I saw of the Crimea it seems much shattered and I expect all other Black Sea ports are in a similar state. We should therefore in all probability have to live on board our ships. I am inquiring about Athens from Eden who will be there in a day or two. Personally I should think it a splendid setting and here again we should have our ships handy. Cyprus is of course available where absolute secrecy, silence and security can be guaranteed together with plain comfortable accommodations for all principals. Will you telegraph to U.J. on the subject, or shall I? Or, better still, shall we send a joint message?

FDR sent his own message to Stalin:

October 24, 1944

Number 100. Personal and Top Secret
From the President to Marshal Stalin
. . . We all must investigate the practicability of various places where our meeting in November can be held, such as accessibility, living accommodations, security, etc., and I would appreciate suggestions from you.

I have been thinking about the practicability of Malta, Athens, or Cyprus if my getting into the Black Sea on a ship should be impracticable or too difficult. I prefer traveling and living on a ship.

We know that the living conditions and security in Malta and Cyprus are satisfactory.

I am looking forward with much pleasure to seeing you again.

Please let me have your suggestions and advice.

Roosevelt

It is indeed a dolorous footnote to history, if the leaders of the three most powerful nations on earth cannot agree on a place to meet, what chance is there that they will agree on all the momentous issues of the world facing them? The messages reveal that Churchill had thrown the problem at Roosevelt, who tossed it to Stalin, who, as the following reveals, tossed it back to Roosevelt with a hint that there might be no meeting:

Stalin to Roosevelt

If a meeting on the Black Sea coast, as suggested by you earlier, is all right with you, I should think it highly desirable to carry out that plan. Conditions are quite favorable for a meeting there. I hope the safe entry of your ship into the Black Sea will also be possible by that time. My doctors advise for the time being against long journeys so I must take their view into account.

I shall be glad to see if you find it possible to make the voyage.

It had required lots of time, energy and goading to get FDR to campaign, but, although he started late, he was more exuberant at each stop and, with the assistance of his speech writers, marshaled his arguments, pledges and predictions masterfully. If, as some wrote, this was the last guttering of an old candle, it was indeed bright in the chilly autumn of 1944.

One week after his New York parade Franklin D. Roosevelt, buoyant as ever in the back of his car. was driving through the streets of downtown Philadelphia in rain. He had survived the New York soaking downpour without sniffles or heightened temperature, and no one could dissuade him from leading the Philadelphia parade. Again he appeared to be fatigued and sallow, but his voice was strong and his smile made hosts of people look upon him as America's savior. He was, in every sense, the champion. He acted like one, spoke with assurance, unashamedly took bows for economic recovery and military success and treated Dewey's campaign statements with contempt by repeating the Republican indictments with sarcasm.

At Shibe Park the grandstands and bleachers were filled in spite of the inclement weather. His car paused on top of a wooden ramp and a battery of microphones nailed to a board was placed across the car in front of Mr. Roosevelt. The big crowd cheered before he removed his hat. As always, he opened with the two words: "My friends." People had been listening to those words for so many years on radio that they handclapped before he could proceed:

I am glad to come back to Philadelphia. Today is the anniversary of the birth of a great fighting American—Theodore Roosevelt. This day—his birthday—is celebrated every year as Navy Day, and I think that Theodore Roosevelt would be happy and proud to know that our American fleet today is greater than all the navies of the world put together. And when I say all the navies, I am including what was—until three days ago—the Japanese fleet.

Since Navy Day a year ago, our armed forces—Army, Navy and Air Forces—have participated in no fewer than twenty-seven different D days, twenty-seven different landings in force on enemy held soil. Every one of those landings has been an incredibly complicated and hazardous undertaking, as you realize, requiring months of most careful planning, flawless coordination and literally split-second timing in execution. The larger operations have required hundreds of warships, thousands of smaller craft, thousands of airplanes, and hundreds of thousands of men. And . . . every . . . one . . . of . . . these . . . twenty-seven D days . . . has . . . been . . . a . . . triumphant . . . success.

Again the nodding sitting figure in the center of the spotlight was assaulted with waves of cheers, but FDR had a double motive—to boast and to destroy Thomas E. Dewey's repeated charge that General MacArthur was not given his fair share of arms and supplies. "I wonder," the President said in puzzlement, "whatever became of the suggestions made a few weeks ago that I had failed, for political reasons, to send enough forces or supplies for General MacArthur?"

In this speech FDR concentrated on Republican campaign attacks that the Roosevelt Administration was "the most spectacular collection of incompetent people who ever held public office" and that the administration made "absolutely no military preparations for the events that it now claims it foresaw." It was easy for the President to revenge himself; he had the numbers and dates when cruisers and carriers were laid down; when fighters and bombers were built to the number of 50,000 a year. FDR spoke with lip-smacking relish about his high-ranking appointments as Commander in Chief and his apportioning of military strength between war theaters 13,000 miles apart.

Near the end of the speech, the President seemed carried away by statistics:

It has meant moving supplies along these lines at the rate of almost three million tons a month, requiring 576 cargo ships to leave our ports with supplies every month. It has meant moving more than 14 million barrels of gasoline and oil a month, requiring 156 tanker sailings each month. And all those ships and all those tankers were built in American shipyards. . . . I need not repeat the figures. The facts speak for themselves. . . . The whole story of our vast effort in this war has been the story of incredible achievement —the story of the job that has been done by an administration which, I am told, is old and tired and quarrelsome.

The speech was not as exciting or as amusing as the Teamsters talk, but Roosevelt said that he wanted to dispose of all the military attacks in the speech in

Philadelphia, and it was done. What he had to say represented a series of triumphs; it was his right and his duty to express them to the people. However, there was much that he did not, and would not, mention. His insistence on "unconditional surrender" had not only stiffened the Wehrmacht's resistance to Eisenhower and the Russians, but forced the German people, who feared Hitler, to cling to him rather than risk dismemberment and possible slavery at the hands of the Allies. He could mock the phrase "tired, quarrelsome old men," but he would not and could not report to the American people the state of his own health because he did not want to know it. Nor, for that matter, could he mention that, in a herculean effort to make China a great power, he had backed the wrong man in Chiang Kai-shek, a man whose government in Chungking was corrupt whereas the Mao government in Yenan was almost spartan in its puritanism. He had done phenomenally well in the war, and he poured the victorious statistics through the Philadelphia speech.

The President was hardly back aboard his special train, headed slowly out of the yards for an appointment in Chicago the next night (October 28), when he called his speech writers and said that he was dissatisfied with what he had read—even though he had approved the final draft at Hyde Park—and he wanted them to work on it at once. The train was running through Ohio farmland the next morning. The President slept through the clacking of typewriters. Sam Rosenman had his personal fear. The approved draft had not been checked for correct statistics. He had left a draft of the speech at the White House with Isador Lubin with orders to recheck every fact. As statements were corrected, Lubin sent them directly from the White House to the Army Signal Corps car on the train. Longer messages were sent by telegraph to be placed aboard the train as it passed way stations.

The corrections from "Lube" were formidable. In addition, Rosenman had certain doubts of his own, so he sent additional questions. The train trip required a night and a day between Philadelphia and Chicago, but Isador

Lubin, in the White House, was awake every minute of it. Two fresh drafts of the speech were typed out before the President was pleased. He had always been exacting about the content of his public talks; he insisted on a certain amount of informality and jocularity even in the most important speeches. As the train moved slowly onto a siding in the Dearborn yards, he placed one copy of the speech in his jacket pocket. Outside the window of his car, plumes of steam from other trains climbed tall, and railroad men were boxing their own ears.

FDR asked how cold it was. It was 14 degrees above, one of the coldest October nights within memory. The wind was fresh and strong across Lake Michigan. Some politicians boarded the train, including Mayor Edward Kelly of Chicago and Frank Walker, the Postmaster General. Kelly was a loyal, balding man. He assured Roosevelt that Soldier Field was already filled with 100,000 persons, and that loudspeakers had been tacked in place outside the walls to carry the speech to an additional 125,000. The President nodded and smiled; he did not believe it.

He believed it when his Packard led a twelve-car motorcade to the entrance of Soldier Field. The only place he had ever seen more people was in 1934, when he laid the cornerstone of a medical center in Jersey City. Mayor Frank Hague had between 250,000 and 275,000 up and down Montgomery Street and Baldwin Avenue, including those on rooftops and outdoor billboards. This time the car had to slow up two blocks from Soldier Field, and an array of Chicago police officers walked ahead of the car in darkness, waving the spectators back.

In the stadium the car moved along the grass toward a confluence of light aimed from the upper perimeter of the field. The two-by-four board full of microphones was placed before him, and the President was chagrined to find that the tremendous amount of candlepower was refracting from his glasses, making the script difficult to read. There was another problem: as he read slowly, he could hear his own words bounce belatedly back from the speakers in the darkness, and the whirring of newsreel cameras on the platform in front of his car annoyed him. As he said "My friends," the crowd roared approval at recognition of the familiar voice. FDR had to wait for the words to come back to midfield. Sitting next to him, Mayor Kelly developed a nervous tic. Silently, he mouthed each word with the President. The newsreel cameras were picking it up. Jim Beary of the Secret Service noticed it and knew that it would have a hilarious effect in theaters across the country.

He spoke to Mike Reilly. "Slip the mayor a note," Reilly said. Beary, beside the car, printed: "You are mouthing the words of the President. It will be embarrassing to him." Beary crouched and slipped it under the board of the microphones to Kelly. The mayor read it in the glare of lights and, while the President went on with his address, Kelly looked up frightened and slammed his mouth shut. On camera, this drew more attention to the mistake. In spite of slight adversity and intense cold, the President, bareheaded, proceeded with his speech—this time concerning himself with the future of America:

Tonight I want to talk simply to you about the future of America, about this land of ours, this land of unlimited opportunity. I shall give the Republican orators some more opportunities to say "Me too." . . . the American people are resolved that when our men and women return home from this war, they shall come back to the best possible place on the face of the earth—they shall come back to a place where all persons, regardless of race, and color, or creed or place of birth, can live in peace and honor and human dignity—free to speak, free to pray as they wish, free from want, and free from fear.

The speech, even those sections which might be termed dull, was greeted with the loudest, most sustained enthusiasm the President had experienced. When the roars of approval subsided inside Soldier Field, he could still hear the endorsement of the crowd outside. That and the echo effect slowed his delivery, but the people of Cook County did not seem to mind the cold weather, and they stopped him after each telling sentence.

Last January, in my message to the Congress on the State of the Union, I outlined an economic bill of rights on which "a new basis of security and prosperity can be established for all." And I repeat it now:

The right of a useful and remunerative job in the industries or shops or farms or mines of the nation;

The right to earn enough to provide adequate food and clothing and recreation;

The right of every farmer to raise and sell his products at a return which will give him and his family a decent living;

The right of every businessman, large and small, to trade in an atmosphere of freedom from unfair competition and domination by monopolies at home or abroad;

The right of every family to a decent home;

The right to adequate medical care and the opportunity to achieve and enjoy good health;

The right to adequate protection from the economic fears of old age, sickness, accident and unemployment;

The right to a good education.

It was a utopian assortment of rights for the masses. A practical politician would say that it was impossible of achievement. And yet the slow-moving wheel of history was destined to bring most of these "rights" within the realm of possibility, whether, in time, they might be called farm subsidies, home loans, Medicare, old age pensions and Social Security, the G.I. Bill of Rights or whatever. At the time the speech was delivered, Franklin Roosevelt's enemies called it another of his "pipe dreams," another unsigned promissory note.

Some people—I need not name them—have sneered at these ideals as well as at the ideals of the Atlantic Charter, the ideals of the Four Freedoms. They have said that they were the dreams of starry-eyed New Dealers, that it is silly to talk of them because we cannot attain these ideals tomorrow or the next day. The American people have greater faith than that. I know that they agree with these objectives— that they demand them—that they are determined to get them —and that they are going to get them. The American people have a good habit—the habit of going right ahead and accomplishing the impossible.

He was painting a bright tomorrow, a tomorrow he might not live to witness. He promised that, when peace came,

an adequate program must, and if I have anything to say about it will, provide America with sixty million productive jobs. . . . For example, business large and small must be encouraged by the government to expand its plants, to replace its obsolete equipment. And to that end the rate of depreciation on these new plants and facilities for tax purposes should be accelerated. This means more jobs for the worker, increased profits for the businessman, and a lower cost to the consumer. . . . After the war, we shall of course remove the control of wages and leave their determination to free collective bargaining between trade unions and employers.

We must continue this administration's policy of conserving the enormous gifts with which an abundant Providence has blessed our country, our soil, our forests and our water. . . . We propose too that the government will cooperate when the weather will not—by a genuine crop insurance program. . . . And after this war has ended, then will come the time when the returning servicemen can grow their own apples on their own farms instead of having to sell apples on the street corners. I believe in free enterprise —and always have. I believe in the profit system—and always have. I believe that private enterprise can give full employment to our people. . . .

I believe in our democratic faith. I believe in the future of our country which has given eternal strength and vitality to that faith. Here in Chicago you know a lot about that vitality. And as I say good-night to you, I say it in a spirit of faith

—a spirit of hope—a spirit of confidence. We are not going to turn the clock back. We are going forward, my friends, forward with the fighting millions of our fellow countrymen. We are going forward—together!

On the train out of Chicago the President was in high spirits. He thought he had laid out a blueprint for the America of Peaceful Years, and that no one in the Republican party could approach it in promise without encroaching on FDR's drafting. Frank Walker thought so highly of the speech that he requested the President to make a speech in Ohio. Robert A. Taft, a reactionary Republican, was running for reelection to the Senate, and the President might tilt the scales against Taft. He declined. He said he was happy to have made the speeches he did, and he would make one more in Boston, and that would close the campaign. Some of the secretaries drew up a sealed one-dollar pool predicting Roosevelt's winning margin in the electoral college. When he was asked to join, he waved his hands. "Not me," he said. "Not me."

November 1944

THE TIDE OF THE FOURTH CAMPAIGN OF PRESIDENT Roosevelt crested the first week in November. Thomas Dewey led the Republican speakers bureau in resorting to ridicule and contempt in most references to the administration. FDR had used the device, but he employed it in arch surprise to induce laughter. Mr. Dewey was a serious man who sounded as though he were summing up the prosecution's case for a jury. In Albany, he had a final conference with his speech writers. What he said was, "Pour it on." They did. Someone recalled that one of the President's favorite expressions was, "I will say it again . . . and again . . . and again."

The Republican nominee used it at the Memorial Stadium in Buffalo. He repeated Roosevelt's pledge of sixty million postwar jobs and said, "It is worthless." His neatly trimmed mustache bristled as he continued, "Worthless, even though it is repeated again . . . and again . . . and again." The audience was silent for a moment, as though no one would expect a sally from Tom Dewey, then it chuckled. "Your next President," Dewey said, "will never make you a promise that he does not hope with all his heart and soul to keep." It was not good enough for Dewey to feel that he represented the right, the noble and good in the campaign. Nor was it enough for him to believe his campaign advisers that he would surely win the election. A hardworking, self-righteous candidate must believe in victory. But Dewey's problem was not that he was wrong. He was a difficult person to admire.

From the White House the President decided to interpose one more fireside chat. It was scheduled for the night of November 2 and his press department tried to pass it off as an interim report to the nation. In truth, it was as much of a campaign speech as those of New York, Philadelphia and Chicago. He opened by saying that he had hoped to visit in person such places as Cleveland and Detroit "and some of my old friends in upstate New York. I am disappointed about this, but, as I told the American people a long time ago, I follow the principle of first things first; and this war comes first. That is why I have to be right here in Washington." It wasn't a clever ploy, but it probably gulled some. He was determined to play Commander in Chief while angling for votes.

FDR engaged in a dissertation on the brilliant succession of victories in far-off places

*many months ahead of our own optimistic schedule. . . .
American troops are now fighting along a battle front of
three hundred miles in northern France and Germany, and*

about a hundred miles long in Italy. . . . Then think of the tasks that lie ahead of us—all the long tough miles to Berlin, all the major landings yet to be made in the Pacific, and you will have a conception of the magnitude of the job that remains to be done.

He was, as the prime organist, pulling out all the stops. In one breath, many unexpected victories executed under his administration; in the next, insuperable battles yet to be fought, battles which would lead to ultimate victory—and who had planned and was prepared to execute them? Then the implied danger of naive hands on the wheel: "Delays in the performance of our job at home mean prolonging the war. They will mean an increase in the total price we must pay in the lives of our men. All of our able commanders in the field know this. And so do our soldiers and sailors." The President applauded the courageous women in uniform, in the WAAC, the WAVES, the Marines and Coast Guard. He had kind words for the women in the Red Cross, women working in war industries, women who kept the home fires burning while, in the front window, were "service flags with blue stars or gold stars."

The chat was wholly political.

The world is turning with hope to the future. It would be a sorry and a cynical thing to betray this hope for the sake of mere political advantage and a tragic thing to shatter it because of the failure of vision. . . . This election will not be decided on a basis of malignant murmurings, or shouts. It will be settled on the basis of the record. . . . The America which built the greatest war machine in all history, and which kept it supplied, is an America which can look to the future with confidence and faith. I propose the continuance of the teamwork that we have demonstrated in this war. . . . If in the next few years we can start that job right, then you and I know that we have kept faith with our boys.

The President imputed all the vicious aspects of the campaign to the Republicans, and tried hard to make it appear that a vote for him was a patriotic gesture, almost a matter of preservation of the United States of America. The difference in the appeals of the two men was that Dewey was heavy-handed and crude; Mr. Roosevelt was folksy and friendly in recounting the successes of America, leaving his listeners with the impression that he was the sole architect. Dewey's most formidable problem, as Governor of the State of New York, was that he had no national and international experience to which he could point as accomplishments; Roosevelt's "list of credits" was endless. It did not help the Republican party to know that Dewey's repetitious charge that the administration consisted of "tired, old quarrelsome men" was largely true. If the GOP had had any devoted adherents among the doctors at Bethesda, Tom Dewey might have uncovered the truth that the President was wasting away with heart disease and hardened arteries. It would have been a trump card, but those who didn't know didn't ask, and those who did know weren't telling.

The fatigued President, goaded into action, campaigned as relentlessly in the final weeks as he had apathetically after the July convention. He planned to leave for Boston on November 3, with rear-platform stops in Connecticut and Massachusetts; the run through the northeast would close out his appeal for votes. On the second, however, he was engrossed in sending a message to Prime Minister Churchill. Mr. Roosevelt was disturbed about the attitude of Uncle Joe Stalin, who, with bare courtesy, had tossed the problem of a place to meet in FDR's hands and said he would await the President's wishes. For a reason which has no basis in logic, FDR handed the problem to the Prime Minister, who, of course, was powerless to dictate a solution:

November 2, 1944

Number 641. Personal and Top Secret
From the President for the Prime Minister
Referring to my 635, I have received a reply from U.J. which is not very helpful in the selection of a place for our

next meeting. . . . His doctors, to whose opinion he must give consideration, do not wish him to make any "big trips."

He gave me no information as to location of the meeting, accessibility, living conditions etc., except to express a hope that it will be possible to provide a safe entrance for my ship into the Black Sea. . . . Dr. McIntire tells me that health conditions in Black Sea ports such as Odessa are very bad, and we must think of the health of our staff and our ships' crews as well as ourselves. . . .

Please give me your advice as to the best date for the meeting from your point of view, together with any information you may have in regard to a suitable place for the meeting, danger from enemy action, living conditions etc. I will take a ship to wherever we go. I fear that Uncle Joe will insist on the Black Sea. I do think it important that we three should meet in the near future. . . .

Roosevelt

The signal offered little, asked much. The presidential election was but five days off. Whether the Black Sea was sanitary or bacteria-laden, a summit meeting would have to be held after the votes had been counted. No matter how confident a President may feel, he can lose an election and, in this case, he would, as a loser, be settling the future of the world as a lame duck. And yet, in all his communications with his international peers, Roosevelt never mentioned the possibility that—after November 7—it might not be his right to hammer out far-reaching agreements if he were rejected by the American people. The indications are that he had asked for this meeting before the elections as an aid to his candidacy and prestige at home. When that proved impossible, he wanted to arrange one "soon," before the inauguration on January 20.

A few days later a studied response arrived from Churchill:

Number 814. Personal and Top Secret
From the Prime Minister to President Roosevelt

1. Your number 641. I send you in my immediately following the report which I called for from the First Sea Lord. The whole matter has been carefully studied by the Admiralty and, as you will see, every port is reported on separately. Our sailors have pretty good knowledge of these ports. On all this I consider the Black Sea out of the question and Piraeus very little better.

It became obvious to Roosevelt that Winston Churchill was entertaining romantic dreams.

I am somewhat attracted by the suggestion of Jerusalem. Here there are first class hotels, government houses, etc., and every means can be taken to ensure security. The warships could probably lie at Haifa unless the weather turns very rough, in which case they could go to Port Said or Alexandria. Alexandria would probably be a feasible proposition.

U.J. could come by special train, with every form of protection, from Moscow to Jerusalem. I am having the timetable of the journeys studied and will telegraph to you about them. I think we ought to put the proposition to U.J., and throw on him the onus of refusing. After all, we are respectable people too.

The Prime Minister must have been aware, from many conversations and messages between him and Stalin, that the Russian was loath to leave Soviet soil. In addition, the Russians attached a strong feeling of equality, if not superiority, in acting as hosts to the British and Americans. It amounted to psychological childishness, but Stalin and Molotov tried always to insist that such meeting be on or adjacent to Soviet territory. As Roosevelt read further in the Churchill message, he realized that the Prime Minister attached no more importance to a summit meeting than Stalin:

In the event of his not coming, I earnestly hope you will pay your long-promised and deferred visit to Great Britain and then visit your armies in France. The right thing would be to have the conference between us in Britain. . . . Perhaps you would send me a draft of the telegram we should send to Stalin, after considering the information I am now sending you.

The ball had been thrown back to Roosevelt.

In the morning of November 3 he attended routine business and called Rosenman and Robert Sherwood to his desk. They had written terse speeches to be delivered on the morrow from the rear of the presidential train at Bridgeport, Hartford and Springfield. The major final address would be read at Fenway Park in Boston. Roosevelt was in no mood for levity. He told his speech writers that he wanted to answer vitriol with vitriol. He said he was "fed up" with attacks and rumors, and referred to them as "below the belt." His last word to both men was that "this is the meanest campaign waged against me in my entire political life."

The two men worked all morning and all afternoon, honing their literary knives. In the evening, they were still working at typewriters—and so were secretaries who copied the passages—when word arrived that Mr. Roosevelt was nearly ready to leave for the train. They packed the sheaves of papers, and fresh linen, and hurried to Union Station. FDR was driven to the Bureau of Printing and Engraving dock and boarded the *Ferdinand Magellan* secretly. As the other Pullmans, out in the Virginia Avenue yards, were joined to his, FDR asked to see the speeches and went over them line by line. He seemed not to be aware that he was starting a trip on a Friday. No one mentioned it. In the late morning the special pulled into Bridgeport, where a crowd waited. No one in the party appeared to be surprised that, once more, he had donned the painful braces and was assisted the few steps from his easy chair to the rear platform. After the first few sentences, everyone knew that FDR's "Dutch" was up:

There are a few politicians who work themselves into such an emotional state that they say things I hope they will be sorry for before they die. In this campaign, of course, I can't talk about my opponent the way I would like to sometimes because I try to think that I am a Christian. I try to think that someday I will go to heaven, and I don't believe there is anything to be gained in saying dreadful things about other people in any campaign.

He shook his head sadly. "After next Tuesday there are going to be a lot of sorry people in the United States."

Hartford aroused him almost as much because this big city of insurance companies had denounced Roosevelt on economic charges. Executives passed the word, and printed it too, that if employees voted for the President, they would have to close up because the American dollar would have no value.

I am glad to come back here [he said, not looking at all happy]. Four years ago I was told terrible things were being circulated all over the country. People all over the United States were being told that if I got reelected, all of the Hartford insurance companies would go broke. So, coming in here, I expected to see vast empty buildings not being used and employing no people. . . . And yet they are still here. And the joke is that the insurance companies, not only of Hartford but of other places, are better off than they ever have been before. . . .

They are making the fantastic claim this year that your government is now engaged in some deep-dyed plot to take over the insurance business. . . . I know that the workers and managers in that business cannot be easily fooled by that type of propaganda. Why, the insurance policies of the United States and your savings are safer than they ever were in the history of the United States—and so is the insurance business.

In Hartford the President thanked the white-collar workers of America for patience and fortitude. The blue-collar workers, in shipyards and munitions factories, were earning high salaries. Because of wage and price controls,

the white-collar workers earned little more than they
had before the war.

*This administration has done a pretty good job [he said]
in keeping down the cost of living—in protecting the purchasing power of their dollars in terms of rent and other necessities of life. . . . I want you—as they used to say—to give
a hand to the white-collar workers of the United States.*

Boston was the last big test. Fenway Park was jammed
long before the President's automobile came in glittering
in the focus of sweeping searchlights. It was here, four
years earlier, that he had promised the believing mothers
of America that he had said before, and would say it
again and again, that he would never send their sons to
fight a foreign war. At almost the last moment, Robert
Sherwood, tall and straight and thin, leaned over to
whisper to Mr. Roosevelt and ask would he please make
reference to that statement. FDR looked up, and nodded.
He took a pen, scanned the Boston speech and found
a place for it.

At the park he opened with references to his mentor,
Roman Catholic Alfred E. Smith, and coupled it with
mockery of the whispering campaign of 1928, when
he ran for Governor, that physically Roosevelt would
be unable to do the job. Smith, he repeated, told him
that a Governor did not have to be an acrobat. He had
since learned that a President didn't either. He covered
the subject of racial and religious prejudice and moved
on to talk of the war.

*We got into this war because we were attacked by the Jap-
anese—and because they and their Axis partners, Hitler's
Germany and Mussolini's Italy, declared war on us. I am
sure that any real American—any real, red-blooded American
—would have chosen, as this government did, to fight when
our own soil was made the object of a sneak attack. As for
myself, under the same circumstances, I would choose to
do the same thing—again and again and again!*

The audience understood the reference to the 1940 campaign promise. Roars of approval came welling from the darkness. The President was careful, dwelling on the polyglot ancestry of Americans, to turn his scorn on chiefs of state rather than on the people. It was "Hitler's Nazis," never the German people; the "tyrant Mussolini" while, in the next breath, "We are made happy by the fact that the Italian people—our long-time friends—are started once again along the paths of freedom and peace."

His voice had lost much of its quavering. It was firm and optimistic and confident.

Just the other day [FDR continued] you people here in Boston witnessed an amazing demonstration of talking out of both sides of the mouth. Speaking here in Boston, a Republican candidate said—and pardon me if I quote him correctly, that happens to be an old habit of mine—he said that, quote the Communists are seizing control of the New Deal, through which they aim to control the government of the United States. Unquote. However, on that very same day, that very same candidate had spoken in Worcester, and he said that with Republican victory in November, quote we can end one-man government, and we can forever remove the threat of monarchy in the United States. Unquote. [Archly and slowly.] Now, really—which is it—communism or monarchy?

Roosevelt had always been well received in Boston. The Democratic party ground out large friendly crowds, partly by furnishing buses and trains from outlying areas. They endorsed almost everything uttered by the President with deep roars of approval. He sat in the back of his car, under a lap robe, the thinning hair flying in the gusty wind as he addressed himself to the board of microphones before him. His personal anger, often veiled behind an oblique and sarcastic reference, was vented in public this time:

I must confess that often in this campaign I have been tempted to speak my mind with sharper vigor and greater in-

*dignation. Everybody knows that I was reluctant to run for
the Presidency again this year. But since this campaign developed, I tell you frankly that I have become most anxious
to win—and I say that for the reason that never before in my
lifetime has a campaign been filled with such misrepresenta-
tion, distortion and falsehood. . . . When any politician or
political candidate stands up and says, solemnly, that there
is danger that the government of the United States—your
government—could be sold out to the Communists, then I say
that that candidate reveals—and I will be polite—a shocking
lack of trust in America. He reveals a shocking lack of faith
in democracy, in the spiritual strength of our people.*

He left Boston for his home at Hyde Park. The
purpose was always the same in a campaign year: to
visit with his Dutchess County neighbors and shake hands,
to make an election-eve fireside chat from his office on
the main floor of the mansion, and to vote. He availed
himself of two long nights' rest in the upstairs bedroom;
then, on November 6, he was helped into his hand-driven
automobile. He was a believer in tradition, and he enjoyed establishing his own. The car, guarded by Secret
Service vehicles ahead and behind, accompanied the President into Hyde Park village, where he smiled and waved,
pausing now and then when he saw a familiar face, to
talk about crops and prices and village gossip. He drove
north to Rhinebeck, turned south and crossed the bridge
to Highland, stopping and starting as old neighbors
trotted to his car to shake his hand. The small vote of
the area would have no bearing on the outcome of the
national election, but FDR believed that he was one of
the few politicians who ever won his home district and
he felt it worth the effort.

He was back in time for early dinner with Mrs. Roosevelt; Anna; her husband, John Boettiger; and their boy,
Johnny. Sitting in his mother's small, pristine dining
room, the President said he had read his fireside speech
and liked it. The reason was that most of it had been
written by Anna and her husband. Rosenman and Sherwood were in the Big House, but they contributed little.

Whatever his inner feelings about election to a fourth term, he shared them with no one—not even his family. His attitude was confident, more that of a man who knows he will win but is mystified as to the margin.

After dinner Mr. Roosevelt wheeled himself into the living room, reading until the radio time was ready. Mrs. Boettiger and her husband had drawn a good opening contrast between the America of the day and the rest of the world: "As we sit quietly in our home at Hyde Park, our thoughts, like those of millions of other Americans, are most deeply concerned with the well-being of all our American fighting men. We are thinking of our own sons—all of them far away from home—and of our neighbors' sons and the sons of our friends. In great contrast to the quiet which is ours here in America, in our own secure homes, is the knowledge that most of those fighting men of ours have no quiet times, and little leisure at this hour to reflect on the significance of our American election day, tomorrow.

Some are standing at battle stations on shipboard, tense in the excitement of action; some lie in wet foxholes, or trudge doggedly through the sticky mud, firing as they go. Still others are high above the earth, fighting Messerschmitts or Zeros." He who said that the right wing of Congress would prevent servicemen from voting now changed his mind: "Millions of these men have already cast their ballots, and they will be wondering about the outcome of the election, and what it will mean to them in their future lives." He hoped that fifty milllion Americans would go to the polls tomorrow. He mentioned new and devilish instruments of war which carried death and destruction from continental Europe to London on silent wings and, with rare clairvoyance, predicted the onslaught of intercontinental ballistic missiles which had not been invented. "No coastal defenses, however strong, could prevent these silent missiles of death, fired perhaps from planes or ships at sea, from crashing deep within the United States itself. This time," he intoned, "this time, we must be certain that the peace-loving nations of the world band together in determination to outlaw and to prevent war."

Like most politicians, he voted fairly early so that the press could use the photographs and quotations for afternoon editions. However, Hyde Park had new voting machines, and when the President got behind the curtains, he had a problem reaching up from his wheelchair to close the curtains, and even greater problems reading the local referenda. The First Lady, standing outside the curtains, was shocked to hear the best-known voice of the century shout, "Damn!"

At lunchtime, on a frosty, pale day, he was back home reminding the housekeeper that, at 9:00 P.M., he expected the dining room table to be cleared; he wanted tally sheets and pencils to be laid out and a radio set and news ticker moved into the small room. Throughout the afternoon a surge of excitement was visible in the election questions which flew back and forth across the library. Admiral Leahy sat beside the President; the Henry Morgenthaus, the Edwin Watsons, Bob Sherwood, Steve Early, Mike Reilly, Sam Rosenman, Grace Tully and Bill Hassett took turns sitting for a while, standing, pacing, asking questions about doubtful states. Mr. Roosevelt was calm and, at times, jolly. He said he hoped he was right in giving his occupation before the election board as "tree grower." He also excused his loud "Damn!" complaining that newsreel photographers had strung their wires over his voting booth, "fouling the curtains and making everything inoperable." He sent a messenger to Hyde Park to tell Elmer Van Wagner that he would receive his neighbors at the front porch "win, lose or draw" at the usual 11:00 P.M. Mrs. Roosevelt and Bill Hassett, both secret sentimentalists, wrote later of the missing faces. "The circle of New Dealers draws inward," Hassett wrote. Mrs. Roosevelt wrote about the possessive Missy LeHand sitting beside the President at all elections; about old Sara, who could not understand Eleanor's calmness in crisis; of Louis McHenry Howe, dour and forbidding as his whirling pencil sampled the early vote; of Marvin

McIntyre, holding the press from making dire predictions with his glowing reports.

Early dinner had been over for an hour when Mr. Roosevelt wheeled his chair into the dining room and moved it partly under the table on the kitchen side. From the walls the portraits of old Delanos and Roosevelts stared down from cracked canvas. His mother's silver tea service glittered from the overhead light. Toward the windows at the back there was an adjoining alcove with a small table and chairs. When there were guests in the 1880s and 1890s, young Franklin had his dinner at that table, alone except for the presence of his elders in the dining room. All of his children had eaten in that alcove. The President, busy with foolscap and tables of 1940 election results, hardly glanced at it.

The Associated Press and United Press news tickers could not be wired into the dining room, so Bill Hassett made frequent trips to the small smoking room and back, with the sheets in his hand, to be laid before the President. Grace Tully sat beside FDR with a telephone to her ear. She had a direct line to Democratic national headquarters at the Biltmore Hotel in New York, and whatever information accrued she passed quietly to the President. He ran the election guessing game himself. Now and then, Henry Morgenthau would saunter in from the library to ask, "How are things going?" Frank Walker arrived, and he too made the pilgrimage to the dining room. Some of the early returns from the New England states established no trend. It was not until after 10:00 P.M. that the Democratic majorities in the big cities of the East and Midwest began to tip the election toward Roosevelt. The tipping became more noticeable toward 11:00 P.M. The election was not "in the bag," but it began to look good for Roosevelt.

Mrs. Roosevelt came into the dining room almost timidly, her face rounded in a big smile, to tell her husband that the villagers had come in the front gate and were on the long walk toward the portico. Roosevelt backed his chair away from the table and, with help, moved it to the porch. He should have worn a heavy coat, but he didn't. In the distance he could see the black, ghostly figures of marchers approaching, hands high in the air holding red fire; a band was playing stirring music. The Boss noted at once that there were more revelers than at any previous election. And behind the locals were two busloads of girls from Vassar College, who had asked to join the parade. Plumes of steam came from the mouths of marchers as they formed ranks in front of the porch. Mr. Roosevelt, glancing sidewards, noticed that his mother's big spruce tree was full of boys.

The people fell silent when he spoke:

I see some youngsters up in a tree which reminds me of earlier days, when I wanted to get away from the discipline of the family, and I climbed that very tree up where that highest youngster is now, and I disappeared and couldn't be found. And they got everybody—I think they got the fire department up trying to find me. [The neighbors laughed.] And I realized that I was causing a good deal of commotion, so I said "Yoohoo" or something like that, and I came down. Well, I remember my first torchlight parade right here in 1892—Cleveland's election. And I was asleep, or supposedly asleep, right up in this window [pointing], in a little room at the head of the stairs. And I was listening and I didn't know what was the matter—a queer light outside the window, people coming up the drive on farm wagons, before the days of the automobile. It was Hyde Park, a large part of it, coming down here to have a Democratic celebration. And I got up and appeared down here in an old-fashioned nightgown of some kind, on this porch, and I wrapped up in an old buffalo robe that came out of a wagon. And I had a perfectly grand evening.

A voice in the crowd yelled, "Congratulations, Mr. President!" The chant was taken up by many. The President shook his head negatively and extended his arms, palms down.

The reports that are coming in are not so bad—but I can't
concede anything. Oh, I couldn't concede anything—much
too early. I can't make any statement at all. . . . We won't
get the real returns on these so-called pivotal states for, I
suppose, another hour. And they are working out all right,
so far. It looks as if I will have to come back here on a train
from Washington for four more years.

He thanked his neighbors, listened to some stirring band
music, and seemed thrilled by the red fire and the boys
in the trees.

FDR was back in the dining room before midnight,
catching up with late returns and messages. The radio
was blaring late returns from the Midwest and from scattered precincts along the Pacific Coast. He must have
known that he had been reelected, but he would not admit
it. Then the tipping of the scales became more pronounced. By 1:30 A.M. Roosevelt, still busy with pencils and sheets of paper, must have felt that the returns
were in the nature of a landslide. Shortly after 3:00 A.M.
a radio commentator said that he had heard that the
defeated Governor Thomas E. Dewey was about to leave
his New York hotel suite and make a statement. The
President set his pencils on the table and waited. At 3:16
the Republican candidate read a brief statement of defeat
to an almost empty ballroom. He had no plans to send
a telegram of congratulations to the President.

Roosevelt waited. He had been elected to a fourth
term of office, winning thirty-six of forty-eight states. His
electoral votes were 432 to 99 for Dewey; the popular
vote, totaling 48,025,684, gave FDR 25,602,505
to the Governor's 22,006,278. It was not the landslide
he had hoped for, but it was decisive. At the White House
Harry Hopkins remained out of bed long enough to pen
a message to Winston Churchill: "It's in the bag." At
Hyde Park, as the President waited for the telegram of
congratulations from Dewey, the wire which was never
sent, he penned one to Harry S. Truman at Independence,
Missouri: "I am very happy that things have gone so
well. My thanks and congratulations for your splendid

campaign. I will see you very soon in Washington. Roosevelt."

At 4:00 A.M. the President sent a telegram to Dewey: "I thank you for your statement, which I heard over the air a few minutes ago." Bill Hassett was speaking softly to Mrs. Roosevelt, who seemed never to tire, about the presidential years ahead, years which would last until the day of January 20, 1949—a long way off. Suddenly he noticed that the President was missing. Hassett excused himself and ran to the back hall in time to see the weary President wheel himself up the ramp and back onto the dumbwaiter. Hassett asked if the Boss needed any assistance. The old man shook his head no. "Good night, Mr. President," Hassett said. Roosevelt looked up. "I still think he is a son of a bitch!" he said as he closed the door.

The city of Washington was bleak with rain. It darkened the east side of buildings, monuments, trees. And yet, two days after the election, the capital stirred early. Democratic officeholders had passed the word that President Roosevelt was coming to town. Office managers, clerks and secretaries were given the day off, to form curb-line crowds in the rain. Schoolchildren had the day off, although few knew why November 9 should be a holiday. The Metropolitan Police Department shined all its buttons and shoes, pressed its uniforms and had its band with glittering instruments waiting outside Union Station at 7:30 A.M. It would be one of the rare times when FDR would arrive at the main station. By 7:30 A.M. 30,000 people were huddled and soaked in the plaza outside the terminal. On the presidential special, near Baltimore, FDR was having breakfast, staring out of the big picture windows at the slanting, staggering beads of rain.

The train stopped in Union Station at 8:28. From long experience the President knew that he could not disembark. He must always wait for the leading politicians to reassert the prerogative of coming aboard first to welcome him, congratulate him, exchange a few feeble quips and accompany him off the train. As always, Mr. Roosevelt sat in the tenth car and managed to endure the amenities with courtesy. Outside the rear platform was his limousine. In the front seat, squirming happily, was his grandson Johnny Boettiger.

The occasion was used to advantage. After speaking a few words to Truman and Wallace, the Boss said he wanted both of them to ride with him up Pennsylvania Avenue. The presence of the new Vice President and the old one in the same car would be a mark of unity. Inside the cavernous station, the police band played "Hail to the Chief." Roosevelt came down his rear platform elevator and was lifted into the car. As the automobile moved outside into the rain, the President saw the dense throng of people and ordered the procession to stop. Microphones were placed before him. He said he would always remember this particular welcome home. "And, when I say welcome home," he said laughing, "I hope that some of the scribes on the papers won't intimate that I expect to make Washington my permanent address for the rest of my life."

There was a phalanx of police motorcycles, victoriously screaming sirens, the roar of 30,000 persons who had waited patiently for a glimpse of a gray smiling face and a free hand holding the collar of a topcoat tight around his neck. At the White House staff members from the highest rank to the lowest reached to shake his hand in passing and to wish him well. He was whisked to the second floor, changed his clothes and returned to the first floor to call a press conference. It was as though he was determined to spend the last ounce of energy.

As the reporters filed in, the President nodded to the senior men in the front row. "I have no news for you this morning," he said. In unison, the oldsters said "Thank God!" and the President clapped his hands as he laughed. He looked very thin as he slouched back in his high-back chair and the baggy gray tweeds fell in wrinkles around his frame. Mr. Roosevelt said that he would now give them his pre-election guess. He searched through drawers until he found an envelope and a small sheet of paper. He had given himself 335 electoral votes, his opponent 196. His anger with Dewey remained steady; he would not mention his name. He said he guessed he had been conservative because the final tally was now 432 to 99. Paul Ward of the Baltimore *Sun* broke the conference up with one question: "Mr. President, may I be the first to ask if you will run in 1948?" Roosevelt's laughter could be heard over the crowd.

But they knew—and he did, too—that he did not have the Congress he required. The conservatives of both parties formed a majority, even though there were some faces which seemed bright and new to FDR. In the Senate there were Brien McMahon of Connecticut, William Fulbright of Arkansas, Wayne Morse of Oregon. In the House were Helen Gahagan Douglas of California; Emily Douglas, wife of the University of Chicago economics professor Paul Douglas; Adam Clayton Powell, a black preacher of New York who claimed to be a New Dealer. It was, at best, an incomplete victory; the President was a winner, but he had been placed in an arena where strong, hostile men looked upon his moves and his motivation with suspicion. Roosevelt did not see it as an "easy" term of office, and, sitting upstairs with Harry Hopkins in the afternoon, two sick men discussed the dangers and weaknesses.

Mrs. Roosevelt came into the office and sat to get into the conversation. She began to urge upon her husband the necessity to implement all his postwar promises. He had pledged sixty million jobs and he should go about getting them. If not, she said bluntly, he would lose domestic confidence. Mrs. Roosevelt urged him not to go to Great Britain and France, as the Prime Minister hoped, because it would be unseemly to the American people. Patting one palm with the other, she said that Franklin had made many campaign pledges to the people; she hoped that he would set about redeeming them. Hopkins had little to say. In the campaign surly references had been made by the opposition about Mrs. Roosevelt being the "eyes and ears" of her husband. She said that her influence over her husband was "phony." If she was anything at all, she was "the keeper and constant spokesman for her husband's conscience." There was no denial of her assertions. Before she departed, she said she had no intention of playing the part of a "Dresden doll."

The excitement of being President of the United States had long since atrophied in Roosevelt's mind. He drew little satisfaction from the interminable work and decisions, but, in all sincerity, he did not feel that anyone else was equal to the task. When he told the country on occasion that all within him cried to return to his home in the Hudson River Valley, it was discounted as cynical modesty. However, he told the same story to friends and neighbors who believed him. Physically, he was in a cycle of accelerated disintegration, and duties which he had once performed with equanimity and self-assurance now required his utmost concentration and he was given to pointless changes of mind. As an example, no one had pressed harder for a summit conference—"the earlier the better"—but in the second week of November he was cabling Winston Churchill:

The more I think it over, the more I get convinced that a meeting of the three of us just now may be a little less valuable than it would be after I am inaugurated. What do you think of postponement? It appeals to me greatly.

Privately, Churchill was pettish and irritated. Openly, he sent a petulant note: "I am very sorry that you are inclined to make no further effort to procure a triple meeting in December."

Whether Roosevelt hoped to live out his fourth term of office is problematical. In White House conversations he spoke guardedly of being present at the peace and the opening meeting of the United Nations—but seldom projected himself beyond that unknown date. Certainly he developed a lassitude about American politics, even within his own party. He could not be led into a conversation about a possible successor; he displayed little interest in intra-party disputes. From day to day he acted more as a man who has begun a gigantic work and will not be stopped before completing it to his satisfaction. None of his plans, except those proposed by the Joint Chiefs of Staff, could be called long range. In a very real sense, he was a man in a deadly race with time, and he acted as though he was aware of it. His subordinates at the White House noted that, on some mornings, the Boss looked "awful"; on others he appeared to be buoyant and bright. On some occasions he rubbed his temples with his hands and complained of headaches. Now and then, Dorothy Brady and Grace Tully had difficulty keeping his attention on his dictation. Once in a rare while, the President was found leaning back, sound asleep in his chair. Most of those in the West Wing were increasingly worried about his health and whispered behind their hands about it. In like manner, words of exultation passed from mouth to mouth when he appeared to be bright and sparkling with life.

He had been both pleased and worried about the Russian successes in Poland. He told intimates that a way must be found to coordinate the Soviet military drives with Eisenhower's plans to crush Germany from the west. The fall of Germany must not, under any circumstances, be a Russian victory. Immediately after the election, the President became apathetic on the subject. There was mounting military tension about a race to Berlin, but Mr. Roosevelt could foresee no conflict between allies. A year earlier, Henry Stimson sent a memorandum to the White House stating that if Soviet forces won the battle in Germany, "we will not be able to share much of the postwar world with him [i.e., Stalin]." To the contrary, FDR felt that Eisenhower's strong Second Front, in addition to all the Lend-Lease which had been sent to Russia under the most perilous circumstances, guaranteed America's premier place at the peace table.

The Russians said nothing, but did not subscribe to FDR's opinion. Soviet Marshal Andrei Grechko stated Stalin's opinion years later when he wrote:

*The Soviet-German Front was the most active, principal
front of the Second World War. Pinned down were seventy
percent of the total combat-worthy forces of the Fascist
bloc. It was on this Front that enemy armies sustained the
greatest losses, nearly four times as much as those incurred
on all other fighting fronts . . . Even after the Second Front
was opened in Europe in June 1944, most of the German
Fascist divisions were still on the Soviet-German Front.*

Secretly, and without conferring with Britain and the
United States, Stalin called his top marshals to Moscow
in mid-November to plan the last, the final great offensive against Germany in early 1945. He felt certain that
neither the United States nor Britain would be sufficiently
deep into German territory to threaten Berlin, and his
ardent desire was to see Soviet troops under the Brandenburg Gate.

The race for Berlin, Stalin explained, would require
forty-five days. The Soviet army groups were to chase
all Germans—even civilians—before them. This would free
the new Polish western border of "aliens." The land up
to the banks of the Oder, inside Germany, would be
Polish.

None of this was communicated to Churchill and
Roosevelt. While the Prime Minister worried about the
Soviets taking over all of Europe, FDR was busy working
out plans for his inauguration on January 20. He was
angered that Senator Harry F. Byrd of Virginia (and
his committee) had appropriated only $25,000 for the
formality. The President sat working with pen and paper,
and, when he had concluded, he called an unexpected
press conference. He said: "You know, I am terribly
concerned about dollars and cents because I am afraid
that a lot of people in the Senate—Senator Byrd is the
chairman of this committee—and what are you laughing
at?—and they have appropriated 25,000 for the inauguration. But, you know, I think I can save an awful
lot of money. And with that desire to save money, I said,
'I think I can do it for less than ten percent of that cost.
I think I can do it for less than $2,000. Give them a

light buffet luncheon, that will be the only expense.' "
There was laughter throughout the President's monologue.
"The ladies here are all fascinated over what a good
housekeeper I am." May Craig, of New England newspapers, said: "That's not what fascinates me." The President joined in the guffaw.

Privately he had been researching inaugurations of
other Presidents and he had learned that not all of them
journeyed to the Capitol to stand on the steps to take
the oath of office. The south side of the White House,
facing the Washington Monument, had once been considered the front of the executive mansion. That side
was favored with twin spiraling staircases which met at
the top on a porch behind a fence. Mr. Roosevelt
proposed to take the oath of office on the porch, with
the south grounds reserved for political and personal
friends who would be admitted by invitation. The press,
he said, would have a wooden stand immediately below
the balcony, and they could see and hear everything and
take photographs. "Now isn't that a happy thought?"
They grinned and nodded.

Q: "Are you going to parade any on inauguration
day?"

The President, shrugging: "No. Who is there to
parade?"

His thrift is suspect. His official intimates felt that the
President had tired of the trappings of office. He was
doing what pleased him, while using the stinginess of
the Byrd committee as a target for public amusement.
Privately, he was tired of pausing at each public affair
to listen to "Hail to the Chief," an assortment of ruffles
and flourishes he had heard too many hundreds of times.
Visiting Hawaii, he was disturbed by the number of
admirals and generals who had to pay courtesy calls
aboard the cruiser *Baltimore* before he could disembark
and relax in his beach house. Frequently, he wheeled
his chair around the public rooms of the White House,
demanding to know why the chief usher had ordered
so many vases of fresh flowers, and what they cost. These
rooms, he felt, were sufficiently beautiful for visitors

without flowers. As his interest in politicians and political affairs waned, so too did his daily visits to the map room to study the colored pins of victory.

The divergent viewpoints of Vice Admiral McIntire and Commander Howard Bruenn were at no point better exemplified than in mid-November. McIntire insisted that Roosevelt was in good health; Bruenn kept penning his grave findings about the President's health. On the fourteenth, McIntire wrote to Dr. Harold T. Hyman in New York: "The specific charges made as to the physical condition of the President were so numerous and so malicious that I told the newspapermen that I would not dignify them by denials for each new condition. I am glad to tell you that all of these fancy diagnostic charges are false. The President is in excellent health. . . ." On the eighteenth Bruenn, aware that the hypertensive heart disease was irreversible, was disturbed to find that Mr. Roosevelt was still losing weight and, in addition, had lost his appetite. Bruenn prescribed eggnogs to bolster intake, and noted that the Boss "looked tired." He had no difficulty lying supine, and the lungs were clear. But the apical impulse of the heart was 3 to 4 cm. to the left of the mid-clavicular line, and the first sound, at the apex, was still followed by the soft systolic murmur which disturbed Bruenn. Blood pressure was 210/112 mm. Hg—high.

As a physician, McIntire understood the situation but denied it. His daily reports from Bruenn became Navy secrets. The Admiral's dominance over the Commander was complete. McIntire could have revealed the President's grave condition to FDR in April 1944. If this had not stopped Roosevelt from running for the fourth term, the Admiral, as a physician of integrity, could have retired or requested other duty. It would have made FDR's health a public scandal. All along, the Admiral knew the President could not survive another four-year term. He might also have guessed that FDR could have added to his slender span by retiring after a third term to his library and his stamp collection at Hyde Park. McIntire was aware that the suspected generalized hardening of the arteries was exerting a greater strain on a limping heart. The researcher is left with the assumption that McIntire was lying—not only to the world but to the President himself. Clearly he was certifying untruths to Mrs. Roosevelt and Anna whenever the matter of health arose. It is callous to suggest that the Admiral's motive in not telling FDR and his family the truth was to perpetuate himself in office as Surgeon General of the United States Navy and personal physician to the White House, but there is no other option. One must be mindful of the fact that McIntire was so fearful of the physical decline of his patient that in effect he resigned and turned the work over to cardiologist Bruenn. The Admiral remained the physician-in-residence, but he treated only the sinuses and pounced on Bruenn's daily reports, read them and hid or destroyed them. To the end of his days, McIntire would assert that Roosevelt was in basic good health for a man in his sixties.

The President began to enjoy the prerogative of an on-and-off friendship with Harry Hopkins. In some matters—notably the projected summit meeting—he would ask that Hopkins be summoned to the office. In others (as examples, the impending resignation of Cordell Hull as Secretary of State and the reappointment of James Byrnes as War Mobilization Director and Assistant to the President), he would neither discuss nor share his decisions with Hopkins. The summit meeting—no place to go and no date set—plagued the President sporadically. On some days, without warning, it became of paramount interest as though FDR felt that time was a-wasting. Hopkins sat with him, skinny legs crossed, the deep-socketed eyes set in saffron skin, to state again that Uncle Joe would not leave Russian soil and was using his doctors to prop his premise. This was an assumption. Harry the Hop suggested the Crimea as a meeting place, and rarely voiced an alternative. On one occasion he suggested the French Riviera, but reminded FDR that

Cannes would be within German bombing range from northern Italy.

The President had listened to ideas from many members of his staff, and their uniform opinion was that they did not trust the Russians, and "why should the President of the United States have to cart himself all over the world to meet Salin?" Why indeed? On November 18 FDR was teetering on the point of surrender. He was about to tell Stalin that a "safe and suitable Russian port would be all right," but so many of his advisers descended upon him in the course of other duties to beg him not to go to Russia that he changed his mind and dispatched a rambling message to Stalin which resolved nothing:

Number 124. Top Secret and Personal
From the President to Marshal Stalin
My Navy people recommend strongly against the Black Sea. They do not want to risk a capital ship through the Aegean or the Dardanelles as it would involve a very large escort needed elsewhere. Churchill has suggested Jerusalem or Alexandria, and there is a possibility of Athens, though this is not yet sure. . . . What I am suggesting is that we should all meet about the twenty-eighth or thirtieth of January, and I should hope that by that time you will have rail travel to some port on the Adriatic and that we should meet you there or that you should come across in a few hours on one of our ships to Bari and then motor to Rome, or that you should take the same ship a little further and that we should all meet in a place like Taormina in eastern Sicily, which should provide a fairly good climate at that time. . . . I hope to talk over many things with you. We understand each other's problems and, as you know, I like to keep these discussions informal, and I have no reason for a formal agenda . . . My warmest regards to you.

Roosevelt

The message was neither decisive nor incisive; it was a portrait of a wandering mind. Within the hour a message went to Churchill (Top Secret No. 649) stating that a copy of the message to Uncle Joe would follow. Then:

It does not seem to me that the French Provisional Government should take part in our next conference as such a debating society would confuse our essential issues. The three of us can discuss the questions you raise in regard to turning over part of Germany to France after the collapse of Nazism and the further problems of helping to build up a strong France.

                             Roosevelt

Churchill was infuriated. He wanted a summit meeting at once. The suggestion had come from him that if Stalin could not attend such a conference in England, then Roosevelt, Churchill and Molotov could meet and decide the problems. A postponement beyond November or December was unthinkable to the Prime Minister, because the Soviet armies were pushing Hitler back to Germany and Churchill was not willing to wait until the Russians invested Germany before carving up Deutschland. In addition, England required the presence of a strong and friendly France on the continental soil of Europe as a bulwark against Russians precisely as the Soviets needed Poland as a buffer.

The Prime Minister's reply was on Roosevelt's desk the next afternoon:

Number 825. Top Secret and Personal
From the Prime Minister for the President
Naturally I am very sorry to receive your numbers 649 and 950. Your message to U.J. will, of course, make it certain that he will not come anywhere before the end of January. . . . There is, in my opinion, much doubt whether U.J. would be willing or able to come to an Adriatic port by January 30th, or that he would be willing to come on a non-Russian vessel through this heavily mined sea. However, if he accepts, of course, we shall be there. I note you do not wish the French to be present. I had thought they might come in towards the end in view of their vital inter-

*ests in the arrangements made for policing Germany, as
well as in all questions affecting the Rhine frontiers. . . .
Even if a meeting can be arranged by the end of January,
the two and a half intervening months will be a serious
hiatus. There are many important matters awaiting settlement—for example, the treatment of Germany and the future
world organization, relations with France, the position in
the Balkans, as well as the Polish question, which ought not
to be left to moulder. . . .*

The President was pondering the dilemma of the three
strongest powers in the world unable to agree on a date
or a place for a meeting, much less to reach unanimous
conclusions on sticky world problems. It was then that
Arthur Bliss Lane, former Ambassador to Poland,
stopped by to sit with the President and adopt a bellicose attitude about Russia. Lane said that the President
should *demand* the independence of Poland and said
that if the United States, now equipped with the strongest Army, Navy and Air Force the world had ever seen,
was not strong enough to make an imperative demand,
it would never be in a position to ask for anything. Mr.
Roosevelt listened, then sighed. "Do you want me to go
to war with Russia?" he asked. Lane blustered but lost
the interest of the President.

From London, Mikolajczyk wired Roosevelt begging
help for stricken Poland. He had given up asking the
British for a firm stand. He stated that the Poles would
feel betrayed if, after all their suffering and sacrifices,
they would lose nearly one-half their territory. "I retain
in vivid and grateful memory your assurances given
me in the course of our conversations in June, last,
in Washington, pertaining particularly to Lwow and
the adjacent territories." Mikolajczyk reminded the
President that Lwow and Cracow and Warsaw had been
Polish cities for over six hundred years. Would Roosevelt
please use his enormous power and prestige to appeal
to the Russians to give Lwow and the adjacent oil fields
to Poland? FDR, who was enmeshed in sending and
receiving Top Secret messages, sent one to Mikolajczyk

promising nothing. It was evasive from opening to closing.
He ended it by suggesting that Ambassador Harriman
discuss these questions with the Polish government-in-
exile "privately." Three days after receipt of this message
Mikolajczyk resigned as Prime Minister. The last bridge
between the London Poles and the Lublin government
had been cut. The Prime Minister was succeeded in
office by Tomasz Arciszewski; Churchill ignored him,
especially when he heard that the Polish Cabinet had
decided not to grant any concessions to the Soviet
Union.

Sir Owen O'Malley, British Ambassador to the Poles,
listened in disbelief as Churchill addressed Parliament on the subject and blamed the mess on Mikolajczyk.
". . . Had the Polish government agreed to give up the
disputed territory there would never have been any Lublin Committee. If Mr. Mikolajczyk had returned to Moscow in early November with power to conclude an
agreement on the frontier lines, Poland might have taken
full place in the ranks of the nations contending against
Germany and would have had the full support and
friendship of Marshal Stalin and the Soviet Government."
O'Malley could not believe the words or credit the logic.
Perhaps the only person who permitted himself a cynical smile was Stalin.

Three days later, the Marshal sent a Top Secret message
to Roosevelt. In this, he decided to test the will of the
President:

*It is greatly regretted that your naval organs doubt the
expedience of your initial supposition that the Soviet coast
of the Black Sea should be chosen as the meeting place for
the three of us. . . . I have in mind that we shall succeed
in choosing as a meeting place one of the Soviet port cities.
I still have to take into consideration the advice of the doctors about the danger of long trips. I still hope, however,
that we shall succeed, if not right now, then somewhat
later. . . .*

Stalin

The rudeness of the message upset the staff but not the President. He ordered it filed and said that he was going to Warm Springs, Georgia, for a rest. The demands of the campaign had imposed the same deep fatigue he had endured before. He found a magic in Warm Springs, a recharging of human batteries, a retreat from the world in piney woods. Mike Reilly sent an advance party of Secret Service agents to the spa. An oversized baggage car bearing the mark of the Baltimore and Ohio Railroad was backed onto a siding and a ramp was dropped. A bulletproof Packard was driven up the ramp into the recesses of the heavy railroad car. Two Secret Service convertibles followed it.

Monday the twenty-seventh was cold and rainy in Washington. As the President signed "Hassett's laundry" he frowned. A lower right molar tooth had loosened, and he felt pain. His secretaries said they could make an immediate appointment with a dentist, but he said no, the tooth could be removed as easily at Warm Springs. It is possible that Hassett, the obsequious secretary, was the most observant person in the official family. He knew that, since reelection, the President had been overworking himself again:

After a very busy day with more than an average number of callers, the President left the White House at 4:30 P.M. for the Bureau Terminal to entrain for Warm Springs—a long overdue vacation. The "tired, quarrelsome old man" has been on the job working like a Trojan ever since election day—as before—while fatigued and worn-out young Dewey has been resting for a fortnight in a $40 a day suite at Sea Island off the Georgia Coast. My guess is that he will be given ample opportunity to rest in the years just ahead. The All-American boy should be made of sterner stuff . . . we pulled out of the Bureau of Engraving and Printing at 5 o'clock.

With the President were his doctors, McIntire and Bruenn; his secretaries, Grace Tully and Dorothy Brady; his masseur, George Fox; his chief telephone operator, Louise Hachmeister; Leighton McCarthy, retiring

Ambassador to Canada and a trustee at Warm Springs; and Basil ("Doc") O'Connor, his former law partner. FDR told his staff that he would be gone three weeks—twenty-two days, in fact—before returning to Washington just before Christmas. Admiral McIntire was the only one who begged off; he would remain in Warm Springs until Friday, then return to Washington. Bruenn would remain near the President at all times.

Most important to Roosevelt was that he would have time to see Lucy Rutherfurd. With the connivance of the Secret Service and the respect of the members of the official family, the President assumed practically no risk in these visits. He brought his cousins, Margaret ("Daisy") Suckley and Laura ("Aunt Polly") Delano. Both were what were called maiden ladies, and both sympathized with the long-term romance. Both women got along well with each other, although it is difficult to imagine two more dissimilar women.

Daisy, the taller of the two, was compact in body and mind; she was the perfect choice as FDR's librarian. She was bookish and sensible. Aunt Polly was gossipy, vivacious, small and garish. She was the one who could, and sometimes did, arrive at breakfast laden with diamond rings and bracelets. Her hair had been dyed pale purple, and she painted a deep cleft of widow's peak on her forehead. Her facial makeup was flour-white. Since she had been denied the Japanese lover of her youth, she had purchased a 200-acre estate at Rhinebeck, a few miles north of Hyde Park, and spent her time raising dachshunds and Irish setters. The President was more relaxed, more jovial and more inclined to share his inner feelings with his maiden cousins than anyone else except his daughter, Anna.

And yet, in spite of the periods of long and sometimes witty conversation, Mr. Roosevelt's problems perched on his shoulders permanently. He had begged Cordell Hull to stay on until after Inauguration Day, but the old man was chronically ill and sick of the difference between the recommendations from the State Department and the President's final decisions. "Round out our third term," FDR begged, and Hull said no. Selecting a man to replace the old Tennessee judge was a delicate problem; it was not a question of pinpointing a qualified person, but rather, finding someone who would be tractable in the presence of the President's whims and who would also be acceptable to the Congress and to old man Hull. The latter seems inconsequential, but Hull commanded the respect of Congress and he would denounce any successor who did not have his approval. Therefore, the most able man, Sumner Welles, could not be chosen. Nor could Jimmy Byrnes, who would surely insist on being his own Secretary of State. James Dunn was able, but he had made potent enemies. So Roosevelt reached down into the pile of personalities and came up with Under Secretary of State Edward R. Stettinius, handsome, white-haired, one who would offend few and be admired by few.

On the train, FDR approved Stettinius' nominations for assistant secretaries—Dunn, Nelson Rockefeller and Congressional Librarian Archibald MacLeish. The President told Hassett that the only liberal in the group was MacLeish. He sent a terse personal note to the distinguished poet, congratulating him on remaining in Washington—"even though it means jumping from one mausoleum to another." In the morning, at Gainesville, Georgia, there was a pink dawn but the day became overcast, dull and threatening by the time the train made all the grades and curves into the hill country southwest of Atlanta. The gleaming special pulled into Warm Springs close to 3:00 P.M. It seemed as though the entire town had trooped down the hill to greet the distinguished patron. He disembarked, as always, surrounded by Secret Service men. When he was in the car, he waved his arm, the face lighted up every time he saw a familiar face. Tom Bradshaw, the blacksmith who had engineered Roosevelt's hand-driven automobile, received a loud "Hello!"

The weather remained chilly and rainy for a week. Each day the pouch was flown from Washington to Fort Benning, Georgia, then driven by car to the "Little

White House." The day after arrival Hassett noted with alarm: "The biggest batch of mail I ever laid before the President . . ." Lucy Rutherfurd was in the guest house. When the President was free of work, he asked Hassett to phone her and Aunt Polly and Daisy to stop in. The stone fireplace crackled with flaming logs. Outside the French doors in the back of the house the rainy wind split around the big piney branches and made a separate sighing sound. A detachment of Marines in combat boots traced and retraced the heavy foliage around the fenced-in compound. Secret Service men had small sentry boxes. When the weather was bad, they remained inside, wiping foggy condensation from the windows with kerchiefs.

The important annual Thanksgiving Dinner occurred on the thirtieth. It was held, as always, at Georgia Hall in the big dining room. Everything and everyone was in place, expectantly, when the President arrived at 7:00 P.M. There was no standing ovation because few patients could stand. The smiles and applause, however, were a welcome home. At the head table Basil O'Connor, balding, slender and businesslike, was toastmaster. Mike Reilly stood behind FDR. Even though this was Warm Springs, the habitat of helpless friends, the Secret Service had spent the day "sanitizing" the building, looking over, through, and under every piece of furniture including lamps and ashtrays.

It was a long cry from the time, back in the 1920s, when Roosevelt heard that two patients had arrived at the railroad station and went down to try to get them into his automobile to bring them up for treatment in the perennially warm pool. This time there were 110 patients sitting radiant with expectancy. Among the few who were not victims of poliomyelitis were Dr. Stuart Raper of the foundation staff, O'Connor and Commander Bruenn. As always, there was jocularity. The President's face frowned seriously only once—when he noticed that twenty of the new patients wore Army or Navy uniforms. However, his big smile returned and he carved one side of the first big bird in ceremonial gesture.

He spoke long and informally with the patients, rambling at will from old stories about the foundation to the subjects of war and peace.

FDR suffered several spasms of coughing as he spoke. To the older patients, he looked thin and tired. Ruth Stevens brightened the dinner by staging a songfest and entertainment for the diners. When it was over, and the last crusts of pumpkin pie had been lifted from the little plates, the President was moved in his wheelchair to the door. As the patients passed him on their way out, he extended a hand wearily and spoke a few words of encouragement. To some he said he would meet them at the pool when the weather became warmer. He seemed glad to get back to his little house. From day to day he invited permanent staff members to his cottage to ask about the Warm Springs Foundation. He wanted to know how it was getting on, and if patients showed any improvement. They too noticed that he had a persistent cough. "What I want to know," FDR often asked, "is—are we keeping the best of what we started with, now that we've got all the handsome architecture—the feeling and the spirit?" The President's old friend Fred Botts thought that Mr. Roosevelt looked like a tragic caricature of himself, and, when FDR coughed and the thin shoulders shook, Botts turned away. He said he could not bear to look.

December 1944

ON SUNDAY THE MORNING SUN BUTTERED PINE MOUNtain and the President was up early. He told Bill Hassett to bring the pouch up at once. He wanted to have a light lunch about noon, and then he proposed to drive Lucy Rutherfurd part way on her journey back to Aiken, South Carolina. He sent word to Georgia Hall that, if the weather remained warm and sunny, he could be expected at the pool tomorrow or Tuesday.

In the late morning FDR sat with Lucy and Daisy and Aunt Polly. At these times no one was allowed inside the gates. The President must have felt a degree of melancholy when the time arrived for Mrs. Rutherfurd to depart. With her female insight and her depth of knowledge of Franklin Roosevelt, it must have saddened her too to see what time and the duties of the Chief Executive had done to him. The four sat chatting for a while, had lunch, and FDR ordered his personal car.

With a Secret Service car in front and one behind, Mr. Roosevelt and Mrs. Rutherfurd drove from Warm Springs as nearly alone as possible. He drove slowly, carefully. To the Secret Service men ahead, the President appeared to be in a jaunty mood, talking most of the way. He turned south on Alternate Route 27, then a left onto the hills and curves of Route 41. The scenery, even in December, was a delight to the eye. The air was crisp and sparkling, the road dipped precipitously, then climbed in winding curves through hummocks of tall trees out into meadowland where farms rested under the winter sun. The distance to Talbotton was 25 miles, and Mr. Roosevelt required almost an hour to negotiate it.

He passed around the edge of Manchester, saw black children in their Sunday best coming from church, little girls with tight pigtails and shiny faces. The road wandered almost aimlessly, rising and falling into glades through a crossroads at Woodland, then straight south to Talbotton. There, where Route 208 turned east to Macon, Georgia, he parked the car at the side of the road. For a moment there was privacy; time for a farewell and a promise perhaps to meet again. There is no record of whether this was done with happy heart or the sinking despair sometimes hidden by a broad smile.

At the crossroads Mrs. Rutherfurd's car waited to take her home. He could not help her out of his car. The best he could do was to raise his hat in salute. She left, walked across the road and disappeared in her automobile. Mr. Roosevelt nodded. A Secret Service man came in and sat beside him. The three cars turned back. It can be said without speculation that the five-day visit of Lucy was as important to his well-being as his retreat from the world at Warm Springs.

Dr. Bruenn was present when the molar was removed. He also agreed that the President could revive his atrophied muscles down at the warm pool. The air held a chill, but immersion in the pool with other patients cheered Mr. Roosevelt. He played water polo as vigorously as his weakened state would permit. Afterward he had a long passive rubdown by Commander Fox. He said he felt better. Bruenn conducted a casual medical examination and was shocked to learn that Roosevelt's blood pressure had jumped to 260/150. Bruenn always wore a good professional mask. Quietly he told the President that, for a while, he should stay away from the pool. FDR said that he needed the pool exercise because his hips felt "contracted." The doctor thought that a better way of overcoming this would be to lie on his back across his single pine bed allowing his heels to touch the floor.

The President subscribed to any new magic. He tried the exercise and insisted he derived benefit from it. Bruenn told him he would feel even better if he would "start eating." To this FDR had a stock response: "Can't eat—can't taste food." The next morning the doctor made an electrocardiogram. It showed no heart changes, and Bruenn could find no trace of digitalis toxicity. However, to increase appetite, he cut the dosage of digitalis to 0.1 g. per day. The President, at 165 pounds, continued to lose weight slowly.

Problems followed the President to his retreat. The solution of perplexities, he learned, spawned unforeseen enigmas. France was free, and became an uncertain issue. Poland, almost free, became a more insuperable problem than when it was under the Nazi heel. Italy had a new government accompanied by Latin puzzles. Greece was free and started a war with itself. The

United Nations was a fetus prepared for birth, but too many mid-wives were at the accouchement. A man as well versed in statecraft as Roosevelt could not imagine that three victorious nations, working in desperate alliance, could face each other in so many diverse postures. As an idealist, FDR was pained to learn that the closer the trio came to final victory, the more each began to pursue his own path to national aggrandizement.

Even in bed in the morning he felt out of sorts. McIntire had returned to Washington and had sent a chest specialist from Bethesda, Dr. Robert Duncan, to supplement Bruenn's cardiological examinations. FDR would tolerate one morning examination, but two strained his good nature. When he learned that Duncan was a chest specialist, the President again refused to ask a question, spending the examination time in stories, recollections and witticisms. When the ordeal was over at 9:30 A.M., Arthur Prettyman helped him out of his pajamas for his morning bath and shave before dressing for the waiting delegation of secretaries and messengers in the living room. The weather was continually more threatening than fair, and Bruenn advised the President to remain away from the warm pool.

Provisional President Charles de Gaulle asked Moscow for an invitation to the Kremlin. His nation had been freed by British and United States armies but the haughty, big-nosed General did not advise them that he was making such a visit—or, of course, what he proposed to discuss. Early in December de Gaulle, carrying a bronze plaque to be presented to the citizens of Stalingrad for their stubborn, almost hopeless battle against the German Sixth Army, took off in a transport plane.

He disappeared in the mists to the east of Paris. Only a few knew his destination. His primary purpose was to prove to his Western allies that France was not their satellite. He proposed to negotiate an alliance with the Soviet Union. In White Russia he landed and was placed aboard a private train. The train roared at speed across the plains. From his window de Gaulle saw the desolation of much of European Russia. As the express slowed for the approach into Kursk station, he saw that the area was decked in Russian and French bunting. A Red Army Guard stood at attention with gleaming bayonets. A band played "La Marseillaise" and the Soviet anthem.

The area was in a roaring blizzard. From de Gaulle's car a red carpet stretched a hundred yards. On the last yard of it stood the moon-faced Commissar for Foreign Affairs, Vyacheslav Molotov, and a group of fur-hatted, booted Russian dignitaries. The General peeked out and kept everyone waiting five minutes. Then, warm in a khaki greatcoat and red cap, he detrained, saluted everyone and shook hands without a smile and spoke into a microphone: "On behalf of the people of France, I pay homage to the gallant people of the Soviet Union." That was the entire speech. Gravely, he crouched to step into the lead car. Then he was whisked off in the blinding snow to the guest house at the Foreign Office.

At conferences with Stalin and Molotov the French General assumed the posture of a victor, one who has certain rights and is slightly outraged to learn that he must demand them. Stalin pointed out that a big part of the French Resistance in the war was played by Maurice Thorez and his Communists. They too had bled and died like other Frenchmen. The Soviet Union had a stake in the survival of La Belle France. De Gaulle reminded the Russians that the *Boche* might be losing the war, but had yet to be defeated. De Gaulle and his nation would like to help bring about a just peace and would like to lend assistance in the west. He could, if he had chosen, have gone to Churchill and Roosevelt, who had troops on his soil, but he had elected to come to Moscow as a threat to the Western bloc of Great Britain and the United States.

His initial demand was for Stalin to issue direct orders to Thorez and the communists to work with the de Gaulle forces, not to provoke friction. Stalin smiled when he listened to his interpreter and ran the back of his hand over his mustache. "Please not to shoot Thorez," he said, "at least not for the present." Stalin guaranteed that the Communists would behave as loyal Frenchmen. De Gaulle had a lifelong habit of ignoring jokes unless he was telling them. He said that, in his view, within a year or two after peace had been established, the British and the Americans would go home; this would leave Russia to the east and France to the west as deterrents against Germany in the middle. Stalin said that this premise was possible but that strength in the west was now with the United States and Great Britain; he did not think that France "at present" would be a strong military ally.

Stalin tempted de Gaulle with a quasi invitation to become one of the victor nations, with full partnership rights, provided that the Frenchman would listen to logic about Poland. The status of Poland, as an independent nation working in concert with the Soviet Union, was, Stalin said, a fact of life—not negotiable. De Gaulle said bluntly that he could not subscribe to this line of reasoning. The talks were resumed day after day; Stalin was finding the Frenchman to be as difficult as Roosevelt and Churchill had said he was.

The General tried another tack. Without consulting his Western allies, de Gaulle asked for an agreement from Stalin to hand over the German Rhineland to France. Stalin began to act tough. He said no—nothing about frontiers had been decided except for Poland, and he would not come to an agreement with the French without United States and British assent. At this time (the second week of December) Stalin began to send Top Secret messages to London and Washington about the conference. In addition, Stalin tired of the haughty attitude of the General and began to speak of the prostration of France in terms of condescension. De Gaulle further alienated the Russians by saying, when he presented the plaque to the people of Stalingrad, "This is a symbol of our common victories over the enemy." By animadversion, he also seemed to blame the defeat of France on Great Britain and America: their intervention in France always seemed to arrive too late to help.

The General returned to the Rhineland question and

France's possible domination of the area by saying: "If I understand another question correctly, the German frontier will run along the Oder and then along the Neisse, that is, west of the Oder." Stalin nodded. "Yes," he said, "I think the old Polish territories—Silesia, East Prussia, Pomerania—should be returned to Poland while the Sudeten country should be given back to Czechoslovakia." De Gaulle tried to run a parallel situation along the Rhine, but the Marshal shook his head negatively: "Please understand me. We cannot settle this question of France's eastern frontier without having talked about it to the British and the Americans. This and many other problems must be decided jointly." De Gaulle left Moscow with nothing more than a treaty of alliance, such as existed between Russia and Great Britain. France, as a "victor," was also invited to membership on the European Advisory Commission, which was bogged down in what to do with great and small parcels of real estate all over Europe.

Throughout the conference Stalin sent personal messages to the P.M. and FDR. The record indicates that he sent more of them to Churchill than to Roosevelt; most of them ended with the plea: "I shall be obliged for a reply to this message and for your comments on these points." Stalin's cables to Churchill indicate that he was informing the P.M. about everything except the argument over Poland. When Britain proposed a tripartite pact among itself, France and Russia, de Gaulle denounced the proposal with indignation. The French General said that he would not sign such a pact in any case; it would make France look like a junior partner in an old alliance. De Gaulle wanted a straight French-Soviet alliance. He again reminded Stalin that Germany was always France's problem but rarely threatened Britain. De Gaulle wanted a French-Soviet pact so that, at the moment of a Germanic threat, both nations would be prepared to move against the Germans from opposite directions.

"If we shelve this" (i.e., the tripartite pact), Stalin said, "Churchill will be offended. However, since the

French are so anxious to have a straight Franco-Soviet pact, let me suggest this: If the French want us to render them a service, then let them render us one. Poland is an element in our security. Let the French accept in Paris a representative of the Polish Committee of National Liberation and we shall sign the Franco-Soviet pact. Churchill will be offended, but it can't be helped." De Gaulle was not pleased. "You have probably offended Churchill before," he said. "I have sometimes offended Churchill," Stalin replied in an offhand manner, "and Churchill has sometimes offended me. Some day our correspondence will be published, and you will see what kind of messages we have sometimes exchanged."

De Gaulle sat staring at his short Russian host without response. There was a moment of embarrassment. Stalin broke it by asking the General when he proposed to go home. De Gaulle said perhaps in two days. He said he had been impressed with the Russian aircraft factory he had been permitted to visit. Hours after the meeting broke in icy calm, Bidault called on Molotov and said that de Gaulle planned to meet with members of the Lublin committee for an exchange of political talk. Molotov was pleased. He said that the Russians could be drawing up a preliminary draft of a Franco-Soviet pact while the Polish talks were going on. The French General had superficial conversations with the Poles and came to the conclusion that they had no opinions about the future of their nation except what was told them by the Kremlin. In exchange for the Franco-Soviet pact, de Gaulle agreed to send an "unofficial French Representative" to Lublin, no more. In private, Stalin said that, even though he signed the pact, he could see no purpose in an alliance with a country which had been defeated by the Germans in five weeks. At a brilliant reception at the French Embassy de Gaulle said the difference between the French and the Russians in war was that the Russians had more room in which to run.

The French General returned to Paris ruffled in sentiment. To his provisional Cabinet he was specific: He did not appreciate the condescension accorded to him in Moscow; Stalin, personally, was a stubborn and unreasonable man; de Gaulle could not tolerate Soviet feelings that French claims upon Germany were "presumptuous." He was aware that the three great powers were prepared to accord France the honor of becoming the fourth great nation, with China as the fifth, but de Gaulle found no balm in this. He was aware that a summit meeting was in preparation and that France had not been invited; de Gaulle sent identical notes to Moscow, Washington and London stating: "The Provisional Government of the French Republic cannot consider itself bound by any of the decisions taken without it, and, consequently, such decisions lose some of their value."

Thus the truism: war brings soluble problems, victory brings the insoluble. The State Department now tossed its Italian dilemma to Roosevelt at Warm Springs. The entire north of Italy was still in the hands of Field Marshal Albert Kesselring and his German divisions, but the newly formed coalition Cabinet in Rome, headed by Premier Ivanoe Bonomi, resigned. The American State Department, under the forty-three-year-old Edward Stettinius, backed Count Carlo Sforza for the position of Premier, at exactly the time that the British in Rome announced they would not recognize an Italian government in which Sforza had a post. The British then reminded the United States that both nations had signed a military government agreement which stated that "Italian political leaders in exile should have no part in the operation or administration [of the government]."

Sforza had found sanctuary in the United States during the war. He also opposed any recognition of the House of Savoy—Crown Prince Umberto aspired to a restoration of the monarchy—while Churchill felt more at ease with a "figurehead" king of his choosing. The hot potato went to Warm Springs; the President tossed it between his hands for a day and signaled his Secretary of State not to oppose Sforza and yet settle the matter along democratic lines. On December 5, Stettinius decided to borrow his President's language:

The position of this government has consistently been that the composition of the Italian government is purely an Italian affair. . . . This government has not in any way intimated . . . that there would be any opposition on its part to Count Sforza. . . . We expect the Italians to work out their problems of government along democratic lines. . . .

Thus the potato, still warm, was hurled back to Rome. The British, unwilling to brave a breach with the United States, became sullen. The Prime Minister alone risked hot words of anger. He fired .off a cable to Roosevelt in which he referred to Count Sforza as "a dishonorable intriguer and mischief maker" and he proposed to tell the Italians this because "we have been accorded command in the Mediterranean as the Americans have command in France." FDR read the towering fury in the words but refused to conciliate. He sent a message to the P.M. stating that "Italy is still an area of combined Anglo-American responsibility." Adolf Hitler's old dream that the different political ideologies of the Allies—communism, monarchial empire and democracy— would eventually break down in disaffection seemed almost at hand.

Winston Churchill felt that, in Italy and the Balkan countries, Great Britain should make the primary decisions and Washington should support them. At the same time that the Italian political situation was mired in disagreement, Greece became a victim of street fighting. The ELAS organization, a Communist-affiliated group, had been a strong factor in the resistance battle, and knew that if it could take Athens, it would have one-third of the population and all of the government. The British were backing Premier George Papandreou and his pro-British coalition. Churchill had a commitment from Josef Stalin that Greece would be a one-hundred-percent British sphere of influence, and the Prime Minister acted promptly. He ordered reserve British troops in Italy and Sicily aboard American landing craft for a landing in Athens. He also ordered British Spitfires to strafe the streets.

Within forty-eight hours Athens was a no-man's-land.
The Germans had fled northward, their divisions intact,
through Yugoslavia. But peace had not come to the
place where democracy was born. The gutters were ruddy
with English and Greek blood, both killing in the name
of democracy. The dead could not be buried because
the ELAS was using cemeteries, with mausoleums and
headstones, as strong points. Cemeteries were promptly
bombed. At night British aerial flares revealed the ruins
of the Parthenon in a saffron glow. It was taken by
British paratroopers. The Acropolis on which it stood
had not been captured in street fighting since the Persians
achieved it in a mass assault in 480 B.C.

Two untoward events occurred within hours of each
other. The State Department leaked Churchill's Top
Secret order to General Scobie: "Do not . . . hesitate
to act as if you were in a conquered city where a local
rebellion is in progress . . . We have to hold and dominate
Athens. It would be a great thing for you to succeed
in this without bloodshed if possible, but also with bloodshed if necessary." Admiral Ernest J. King, Chief of
Naval Operations, acting on his personal initiative,
ordered Rear Admiral H. K. Hewitt, in the Mediterranean, not to use American landing craft to bring British
Army units ashore in Greece.

On December 9 Harry Hopkins was dozing in a chair
in the White House when the operator informed him
that "John Martin" was phoning from somewhere overseas. Hopkins knew that John Martin was the Prime
Minister's code name on the telephone. He asked that
the call be put through. He recognized the voice, but
the rest was an indecipherable babble of anger. The
Prime Minister mentioned the words "Greece" and
"Halifax" and "do something about it." Hopkins tried
to comprehend, but couldn't. He advised the P.M. that
he would get in touch with the British Ambassador,
Lord Halifax, in Washington at once. Halifax was out,
his whereabouts unknown.

Hopkins was disturbed because Churchill was angry.
He arose early on Sunday the tenth and phoned Halifax

for an appointment. The frail man then went to the map room to see if there had been any radical alteration of the colored pins. There was none, but in a sheaf of new documents he found King's order to Hewitt. Without further consultation, as he said later, he was certain he understood Churchill's incoherent anger. Harry Hopkins did not phone Warm Springs. He felt that too many problems which could be resolved in Washington were being flown to the presidential retreat. Instead, Hopkins, shoulders slumped, walked across the White House to the office of Admiral William Leahy.

One of Hopkins' great virtues was that he could reduce a disagreement to its basic elements. He displayed the order, a surprise to Leahy. Then he asked if it were not true that Admiral Hewitt was under the command of British General H. M. ("Jumbo") Wilson. Leahy nodded. Hopkins' second point was that the landing of troops in Greece was much more a political decision than a military one. It was agreed. Hopkins stated that Admiral King issued the order without prior consultation with the Joint Chiefs of Staff or the President; "it's like walking out on a member of the family who is in trouble," he said. Leahy, the ultraconservative Admiral who still believed in battleships in an age of aircraft carriers and who freely predicted that the atom bomb would not work, did a rare thing. He phoned King at the Pentagon, explained the situation and got an agreement that the order would be withdrawn at once. King, a starchy sundowner, assented.

At noon Lord Halifax was in the White House protesting to Hopkins. The unusually tall British Ambassador did not engage in the customary conversation of diplomacy. He told Hopkins bluntly that the P.M. was "hopping mad" and was sending a strong protest to the President. The British Chiefs of Staff had gone so far as to advise General Wilson to ignore Admiral King's order and to use Admiral Hewitt's ships. It amounted to a most disorderly contretemps between "cousins."

Hopkins was never a beggar, but this time he begged

Halifax to ask Churchill not to send the protest to Roosevelt. Harry Hopkins was sure that FDR knew nothing about the situation; it had been cleared up and corrected; it would only make the Greek situation worse because the President was not in sympathy with the British landing in Athens and the street fighting. Halifax said he would do so at once. One additional thought: Hopkins told Halifax that the American government felt that the British had made a mess of the Greek situation.

Churchill canceled his protest. However, he appeared in the House of Commons and asked for a vote of confidence in the Greek action. The cherubic face scowled as he poured the ashes of humiliation on Great Britain:

Poor old England. We have to assume the burden of the most thankless tasks, and in undertaking them to be scoffed at, criticized and opposed from every quarter, but at least we know . . . our objective. It is that these countries shall be freed from the German armed power, and under conditions of normal tranquillity shall have a free universal vote to decide the government of their country. . . . We are told that because we do not allow gangs of heavily armed guerrillas to descend from the mountains and install themselves with all the bloody terror and vigor of which they are capable, in power in great capitals, we are traitors to democracy.

The Churchill government won its vote of confidence by a resounding 279 votes to 30.

The winds of world events whirled around President Roosevelt, but he sat in the living room at Warm Springs paying scant attention; he was concerned with voting procedure in the United Nations. On December 5, when Greece hung limply in blood, FDR sent Top Secret messages to Stalin and Churchill explaining the American formula for voting in the Security Council. It was a pre-summit position paper. In it FDR bent a little. Instead of arguing that a party to an international dispute would not be permitted to vote on it, he altered the formula to say that a party to a disagreement which did not involve hostilities must refrain from voting. If war was an alternative, all members of the Security Council could vote or exercise a veto. Roosevelt didn't use the word war; he referred to any "threat to the peace." He was literally living in the future, while Churchill and Stalin were drawing closer and closer to the present.

Again, *Realpolitik* was opposed to idealism. The President wanted to avoid the impression that five great powers, plus a few temporary additions to the Security Council, would rule the world. He stated in the most positive way, "I firmly believe that willingness on the part of the permanent members not to claim for themselves a special position in this respect would greatly enhance their moral prestige and would strengthen their own position as the principal guardians of the future peace." The impression he was making in London and Moscow was one of disquietude and irritation. As Cadogan stated so simply in his personal diary: "Churchill paid a big price for Greece in his talks at Moscow." On a rainy day the President took time to write a long friendly letter to Winston Churchill which eventually got to the point where FDR said he felt sorry for Britain's problems in Greece, but that he could not endorse bloody retaliation. "Even an attempt to do so would bring only temporary value to you, and would in the long run do injury to our basic relationships."

This represented a lapse in judgment because, while British troops were killing Communists in Athens, Stalin remained silent. No protest came from Moscow. There were other miscalculations. Mr. Roosevelt still believed firmly that he could persuade Stalin to pursue the path of international righteousness in friendly face-to-face conversation. He also assumed that he had Winston Churchill's vote in his pocket. Roosevelt agreed in principle all the "wrongs"—the Russian setting up of Communist governments in Poland, Romania and Bulgaria and the British battle to impose the imperial will on Greece and Italy as "temporary." He insisted to his State Department advisers that nothing would be "permanent" until it had been agreed to at the forthcoming conference. Even the de Gaulle government, as far as FDR was concerned, remained provisional until the French people had an opportunity to vote freely and secretly. He was in the position of a pugilist who has fought too many fights and is no longer conscious of time or the additional damage inflicted by one more beating. He was becoming single-minded, a man with a limited attention span; one, sadly, who believed that Great Britain and the Soviet Union would be grateful for all the Lend-Lease material which had been shipped to them. To those who were at his side in Warm Springs—Tully and Hassett, especially—the President seemed serene in his attitude from day to day, concerned more with the peace than with the war, more certain all the time that he would succeed where his idol, Woodrow Wilson, had failed.

His attitude was but momentarily upset by a disagreeable letter he received from his wife. As Franklin's lassitude increased, Eleanor's impatience with him became more pronounced. She lost her restraint when her husband appointed James Dunn to the post of Under Secretary of State:

December 4, 1944

Dearest Franklin:

I realize very well that I do not know the reasons why certain things may be necessary nor whether you intend to do them or not to do them.

It does, however, make me rather nervous for you to say that you do not care what Jimmy Dunn thinks because he will do what you tell him to do and that for three years you have carried the State Department and you expect to go on doing it. I am quite sure that Jimmy Dunn is clever enough to tell you that he will do what you want and to allow his subordinates to accomplish things which will get by and which will pretty well come up in the long time results to what he actually wants to do.

In addition, it seems to me pretty poor administration to have a man in whom you know you cannot put any trust, to carry out the things which you tell him to do. The reason

I feel we cannot trust Dunn is that we know he backed Franco and his regime in Spain. We know that now he is arguing . . . the War Department in favor of using German industrialists to rehabilitate Germany because he belongs to the group who believe we must have business going in Germany for the sake of business here. . . .

She asked time to see her husband "before you begin to look weary." The sentence must have struck a sensitive chord because Roosevelt did not respond by inviting his wife to Warm Springs. His exhaustion was his own, but Anna believed that her mother increased his impatience. Regarding life in the White House, Anna wrote: "Although she knew the doctors had said he should have an hour of relaxation, no business, just sitting around, maybe a drink, she would come in more and more frequently with an enormous bundle of letters which she wanted to discuss with him immediately and have a decision." On one occasion: "Father blew his top. He took the bundle of letters and pushed it over to me. 'Sis, you handle this.' " It was an affront to Eleanor, the closest the President would come to a marital argument. It is doubtful that, in his lifelong habit of self-containment, he ever shouted at his wife.

Mr. Roosevelt seemed to associate tension with the White House. His calendar showed that he spent less and less time in the Executive Mansion and more and more time in Hyde Park, or, less frequently, Warm Springs, or on long trips, such as the one to the Pacific, or a lengthy rest at Hobcaw. At the White House Mr. Roosevelt was accessible and exposed to the department heads and all manner of problems which he was expected to resolve. The problems followed him no matter where he went, but he deluded himself that he was "getting away from it all." Once in a while there came an hour or a day of complete relaxation—sometimes even fun.

One such occurred on December 8. Warm Springs was electing a mayor. The contenders were Reverend W. G. Harry, who had been mayor as long as FDR had been in the White House. Opposing Harry was the rotund and naive Frank Allcorn, owner of the Warm Springs Hotel. During the day FDR phoned several times to find out how the election was going. When the last votes had been counted, it was determined that Allcorn, a native New Yorker, had won by four votes. The President said that he was surprised that a carpetbagger could be elected.

Merriman Smith of the United Press, with the connivance of the Secret Service and the Little White House staff, sat and typed a speech for Allcorn. Although the President did not attend, he was a party to the jollity. A parade of local citizenry, reporters and Secret Service men marched to the hotel and pressed the speech upon the new mayor to read. Allcorn did it without digesting its contents:

Folks—and those four voters—it is wonderful being with you tonight. The last time I stood here, I was just an humble citizen. Tonight I am just an humble mayor. I see my good friend the Reverend Harry sitting over there. You know, he had his eye on the mayor's seat—but look what I have on it. Seriously, just looking at the reverend makes me realize that there but for the Grace of God and four voters, go I. . . .

From now on, things will be different in Warm Springs. You may as well know it. I'm going to be progressive. I used to get a dollar and a half for a steak in my hotel. From now on, they will be two dollars. That's progress, Allcorn style. . . . The first thing we need is a street. What the hell good is a town without a street? And then we will need somebody to walk on it. And the first man who says that I'm coming out in favor of streetwalkers is a liar. The next thing I propose to do is to find some industry for Warm Springs to replace Roosevelt. He is fine business while he lasts, but surely this business won't last beyond 1960 and the eighth term—and we must look ahead—yes, I say, look ahead to the days when Elliott is in office and we have to change the picture in the lobby.

One of the newsmen was called in to read and mimic Allcorn for the President. There were rare guffaws of laughter in the living room that night.

Rare is the correct word. On the following day, a series of Top Secret messages began to ebb and flow from the cottage. A cynic might regard them as amusing rather than mind-boggling. Of the Big Three only Winston Churchill had the enthusiasm of a small boy to meet anywhere at any time. As Stalin was using his doctors as an excuse, Roosevelt disliked planes and flight; he also pointed out that he could not be any farther away than a ten-day response to any act of Congress. His feelings were still oscillating when he sent the following to Churchill rather than Stalin:

December 9, 1944

Number 672. Top Secret and Personal
From the President for the Prime Minister
I think I can leave after inauguration day. I had hoped that Uncle Joe would come to Rome or Malta or Taormina or Egypt but if he will not—and insists on the Black Sea— I could do it even at great difficulty on account of Congress. Harriman suggested Batum which has an excellent climate. You and I could fly there from Malta or Athens, sending ahead one of my transport flagships on which to live. Yalta is also intact, though the roadstead is open and we should probably have to live ashore.

Roosevelt

The following morning he received a message from Stalin, on another subject:

December 10, 1944

Stalin to Roosevelt
Thank you for your communication on the subject of France. General de Gaulle and I have arrived at the conclusion that the Franco-Soviet mutual aid pact will benefit both Franco-Soviet relations and European security in general. . . . As to the postwar frontier of France, examination of this question has, as I informed you, been deferred.

The President noted that Stalin omitted any reference to the conference, so he cabled Ambassador Harriman to ask Stalin about it. A few days later Harriman's coded reply arrived at Warm Springs:

Personal and Secret for the President from Harriman
I talked with Marshal Stalin this evening about the proposed meeting and explained that you wished the meeting to take place somewhere in the Mediterranean. He said he knew that and had answered you that he could not go to the Mediterranean. *He suggested Odessa where he was already having prepared suitable facilities ashore. He said if you preferred to go to the Crimea or the eastern part of the Black Sea where it was warm, anywhere down to Batum, he would be agreeable.*

The Ambassador said he had explained that Roosevelt had an aversion to flying. Stalin said that he would speak to his doctors again. . . . Stalin appeared well.

In the morning the President's mind was on another subject. He sent a message to Stalin appealing to him not to recognize the Lublin government until after the Big Three had reached agreement at the forthcoming conference. Stalin responded to this at once. He said that the London government-in-exile had turned out to be a vicious screen for criminal elements in Poland which were murdering officers and men of the Red Army. The Lublin group, he maintained, was helpful to the war effort and was already carrying out agrarian reform for the peasants. The Red Army must have a trustworthy Poland in its rear if it was expected to carry the final battle into Germany. If, Stalin pointed out, the Lublin government proclaimed themselves to be the provisional government of Poland, the Soviet Union must recognize it.

The threats were implicit and FDR required no second or third reading to appreciate them. He dispatched an urgent Top Secret message to Moscow at once, hoping to thwart trouble before it began:

*I must tell you with a frankness equal to your own that I see
no prospect of this government following suit and transferring its recognition from the Government in London to the
Lublin Committee in its present form. This is in no sense
due to any special ties or feeling for the London Government. . . . I cannot ignore the fact that up to the present
only a small fraction of Poland proper west of the Curzon
Line has been liberated from German tyranny, and it is
therefore an unquestioned truth that the people of Poland
have had no opportunity to express themselves in regard
to the Lublin Committee.*

He again asked Stalin to wait. The Soviet Marshal,
as strong a dictator as Hitler, found a device without
credibility to support his stand. His reply said that "your
suggestion is perfectly understandable to me" but that
he was powerless to implement it. The Presidium of
the Supreme Soviet, meeting in secret congress, had
already advised the Lublin Committee that Russia would
recognize it as Poland's legitimate provisional government as soon as it was formed. Churchill, who received
a copy of the message, notified Roosevelt that the
Presidium of the USSR had suddenly been brought into
the top echelon of government. On the fifteenth a message
arrived from Harriman which, by omission, indicated
that he had not been advised about the Polish situation.
He confined his cable to assuming that, although Stalin
had left the door open to a meeting in the Mediterranean,
"it was my definite impression . . . that he spoke rather
regretfully when he said he would have to consult his
doctors again . . . indicated that he was anxious to
have the meeting take place promptly after the inauguration."

Roosevelt was aware that he was about to face a
fait accompli. On the twelfth of the month he turned
away from it momentarily—he knew that the future of
Poland would plague him more than any other facet of
peace—and sent a note to Sam Rosenman to get Robert
Sherwood and start working up a State of the Union
message to be delivered to Congress on January 6. "Try

to hold it to 3,000 words," he wrote; he would deliver it standing and he hoped it would be short. Rosenman and Sherwood appealed to all Executive branches to submit drafts of their trials and triumphs of the past year and projections for the next year.

The weather at Warm Springs remained squally and chilly. Roosevelt left on December 18, waving to a small crowd at the station and promising to return as soon as his White House duties permitted. He spent the day and night in his club car, jotting topics and "catchy phrases" for his State of the Union message. Bad news had reached him two days earlier when, in a plethora of victories on the western front, Hitler ordered Field Marshal Gerd von Rundstedt to attack Eisenhower's forces. German Intelligence had learned that, from Holland south to Switzerland, the British and American army groups were strong, well supplied, and in excellent position for an advance to the Rhine River. In but one place, near Wilz in Luxembourg, was the thin line. There Major General Troy H. Middleton held the U.S. Eighth Army Corps in defensive positions.

Hitler argued that if two panzer armies and two infantry armies could thrust through the Ardennes Forest in bad weather, they could attack at the weakest point, hold the initiative and the element of surprise and move west through Saint-Vith and Bastogne; then, in a lightning move, turn north and race to Antwerp. This would accomplish two great strategic objectives: It would deny to the Allies their main port of supply for gasoline, oil and ammunition, and it would seal off thirty British and American divisions caught in Holland and Belgium. Generals von Rundstedt and Model argued that the scheme was too ambitious; they would prefer to seal off a small salient, such as the one at Aachen. The German Chancellor barely listened. He wanted no partial victory. His desire was a Dunkirk on a much larger scale. If he could take Antwerp and box 450,000 British and American soldiers behind his lines, he had a chance for a negotiated peace with the West, and could then turn all his divisions eastward to face the Russian attacks.

Hitler had his way. It was a last, and bold, throw of the dice. General Omar Bradley, in charge of the First, Ninth and Third Armies in the center of the Allied lines, received Intelligence reports that German panzer divisions were rolling up to the Ardennes Forest at night in massed formation. He conferred with General Eisenhower and General Carl Spaatz about it at SHAEF headquarters in Paris. All agreed that Germany no longer had sufficient offensive power to mount a meaningful attack. Above all, it was understood that the Germans lacked fuel, and "Rundstedt is too sensible to risk an attack." The effect of this miscalculation was shattering. When the drive began, at 5:30 A.M. on December 16, it was assessed as a limited diversion. It was not until the Fifth Panzer Army literally destroyed the American 28th and 106th divisions that SHAEF—busy with plans for the capture of Aachen and the Roer dams—realized the gravity of the situation.

When the President reached the White House on the nineteenth, he spent considerable time in the map room watching young officers move the red pins (German) westward into a deep pocket in Allied lines. The green pins (U.S.) were either in full retreat or engulfed in pockets. The Joint Chiefs of Staff could not explain to FDR why an ostensibly defeated nation would attack, but, as the hours and days clicked forward toward Christmas, the German master plan became obvious. In the small city of Bastogne, General Anthony McAuliffe and his 101st Airborne Division held out in deep snow and low gray skies. He appealed for supplies, but the Air Force found the ceilings too low for an air drop.

General Lawton Collins with his Seventh Corps was north, in the Hürtgen Forest, when Eisenhower and Beetle Smith, his Chief of Staff, ordered him west by southwest 100 miles to try to blunt the point of the panzer attack. Patton and his Third Army, close to Trier on the Moselle, executed one of the swiftest maneuvers of any army by turning northward to pinch Rundstedt at the base of his bulge. Generals Simpson, Gerow and Ridgway, on the north side, pinched southward. The four German armies were blunted 90 miles south of Antwerp. The bulge receded slowly. The President, watching from his wheelchair, displayed neither panic nor anxiety. His deep concern, however, was evident by the number of daily trips he made to the map room. He glanced at the casualty list when the battle was over, and shook his head sadly: 8,000 dead; 48,000 wounded; 21,-000 prisoners. It was an expensive miscalculation.

The Russian High Command, which watched the battle with interest, was surprised when General Eisenhower sent Deputy Commander Air Chief Marshal Tedder on a quick flight to Moscow to ask the Soviets when he could expect a Russian attack on the eastern front to relieve the pressure. He was detained in Cairo by bad flying weather. Churchill asked Moscow the question by cable. Stalin stated that the bulk of German forces was already on the Russian front, but that the "Supreme Command" planned an attack within a short time. "You may rest assured," he radioed, "that we shall do everything possible to render assistance to the glorious forces of our Allies."

Before the battle ended, General McAuliffe, holding out at Bastogne, sent a radio message to Eisenhower and Roosevelt:

We have stopped cold everything that has been thrown at us from north, east, southwest . . . Four German panzer divisions, two German infantry divisions and one German paratroop division. We continue to hold Bastogne . . . We are giving our country and our loved ones at home a worthy Christmas present.

In the German view, the battle represented the last offensive. Although no one in the armed forces was permitted to speculate on defeat, Hitler realized that his remaining strength was defensive. Poring over charts in his dungeon at Wolfschanze, he moved armies on both fronts which now existed largely on paper. As

Christmas approached, Germany had lost three million officers and men. The summer attacks in 1944 by Eisenhower on one side and Zhukov and Rokossovsky on the other had cost Hitler one million dead, wounded and missing. The great cities of Germany lay in ruins; war production and only war production was repaired and maintained; the civilian population lived like silent moles. Adolf Hitler had not fully recovered from the bomb attempt on his life in July. In bitterness, he sometimes watched the motion pictures of his plotting generals being lifted onto meat hooks. Himmler was ordered to scour Germany for the dregs of manhood to be put into uniform—25 divisions of men sixty and over, and boys as young as fifteen.

The Battle of the Bulge was at high tide when Mr. Roosevelt called a press conference the week before Christmas and said, "I haven't got any news." He added that he had uncovered a new word at Warm Springs: "contentious." May Craig, the journalistic dumpling of New England newspapers, said, "Mr. President, this is a contentious question but I would like a serious answer." There was laughter throughout the conference, a sound common when the President and the press honed their swords.

FDR: "You would find it awfully hard to get, May."

"There is a good deal of question as to whether you are going right or left politically, and I would like your opinion on which way you are going."

"I am going down the whole line a little left of center. I think that was answered, that question, eleven and a half years ago, and still holds."

"But you told us a little while ago that you were going to be Doctor Win-the-War and not Doctor New Deal."

"That's right."

"The question is whether you are going back to be Doctor New Deal after the war—"

"No, no. No. Keep right along a little to the left of

center, which includes winning the war. That's not much of an answer, is it?"

"No."

Reporter Godwin: "Mr. President, would you welcome, and do you see the prospect of an early conference with Mr. Churchill and Mr. Stalin?"

"I saw that. Yes, a highly speculative story."

"I asked if you saw the prospect of an early conference."

"I said it's highly—highly—what? What was the word I used about it? Yes, speculative."

"I would like to eliminate the speculation and go to the highest source."

"I know you would. So would I. You are not the only one."

A reporter asked what had happened to the document called the Atlantic Charter, the one which promulgated man's Four Freedoms. It had been designed by President Roosevelt and Prime Minister Churchill aboard the American heavy cruiser *Augusta* at Argentia in 1940 as the British battleship *Prince of Wales* lay anchored to windward. When the question was asked, the President launched into one of the funniest stories of his career. He said there never was a document, as such, called the Atlantic Charter. He and Churchill had dictated parts of it to secretaries. Other parts were handwritten by Under Secretary of State Sumner Welles and Foreign Under Secretary Sir Alec Cadogan.

The room was heavy with laughter as Roosevelt said that the pieces of paper were placed together. Then Roosevelt and Churchill passed the pieces and bits back and forth, altering words and phrases. "There is no copy of the Atlantic Charter as far as I know. I haven't got one. The British haven't got one." The bits of paper were sent to the radio operators aboard *Augusta* and *Prince of Wales* for transmission to the world. "The nearest thing you will get is those radio operators." Someone asked if it weren't true that, much later, in January 1942, member Allied nations signed such a document in Washington.

Yes, FDR said, that was true. What happened was that the State Department copied the phrasing from some old newspapers and made a document of it. Member nations sent their ambassadors to the White House to sign it. "We had two or three sessions that day. . . . I delivered a speech, and then asked to sign first for the United States. I then asked the signatory powers to sign. But there was nothing to sign! It was in the State Department safe and the keeper of the safe was out somewhere in Bethesda, which didn't help at all. And I said, 'All right, we haven't got the document for you to sign.' I was prepared to write out in longhand very simple words, 'We hereby approve and join in the Declaration by the United Nations'—but, before writing it, I looked for a pen and there wasn't any pen. Then someone found a pen, but it wouldn't work. I used really strong language, luckily I wasn't on the air, and I borrowed the pen of the Mexican ambassador. . . . When the document finally arrived at the White House—too late—there at the bottom it was stated 'Signed Roosevelt and Churchill.' But those words were typed."

Although the President had just arrived in Washington, he wanted to go to Hyde Park for Christmas. Long ago he had become a master of deluding the press with irrelevant stories and the 984th conference was no exception. Neither the Battle of the Bulge nor the stubborn jockeying of the summit powers for a place of meeting was discussed. It was a pleasant, innocuous morning for Roosevelt; it was a defiant one for Winston Churchill. He chose that time to desert Roosevelt and cling to Stalin. In the House of Commons, he thrust his jaw forward and said that he had come to discuss "the grim, bare bones" of the Polish question. "It was with great pleasure that I heard from Marshal Stalin at Teheran that he too was resolved upon the creation and maintenance of a strong, integral, independent Poland as one of the leading powers in Europe. I am convinced that that represents the settled policy of the Soviet Union." There could hardly have been a Member of Parliament who did not understand that this was a cynical sellout of Poland as the satellite of the Soviet Union.

They applauded the words. Isolated shouts of "Hear! Hear!" were heard, but everyone versed in foreign policy understood that Poland was being traded in return for Greece, Yugoslavia and the benevolent goodwill of Italy and France. In sum, eastern Europe would belong to the Russians; the British were satisfied with the Mediterranean, Adriatic and Atlantic areas. Russia, said Mr. Churchill, would extend her borders westward—hardly at the expense of Poland, which would be compensated by rich German territory in the west. Official Washington was shocked by the boldness of the move without consultation. FDR was stunned; he told his intimates that Britain and the Soviet Union were reverting to the crime which incited war—spheres of influence. His personal influence was waning; in a three-vote contest, he had lost his fight for Poland before the Big Three could confer.

After dinner the President decided to remain in the upstairs sitting room with his friend and former law partner, Harry Hooker, who had been goading FDR to ask Congress to pass a measure installing compulsory military service as a peacetime measure. Mr. Roosevelt wasn't sure what his position was. He was listening and sipping a cocktail. Mrs. Roosevelt came down the corridor, sat and joined the conversation. She thought her husband looked ghastly. As she wrote:

"He had rallied so often before, but this time seemed to be different. For the first time I was beginning to realize that he could no longer bear to have a real discussion such as he always had."

Rather than a discussion, she may have meant disagreement. As Hooker argued for a peacetime draft, Mrs. Roosevelt became shrill in her opposition:

I disliked the idea thoroughly and argued against it heatedly. . . . In the end, I evidently made Franklin feel I was really arguing against him and I suddenly realized he was upset . . . I had forgotten that Franklin was no longer the calm and imperturbable person who, in the past, had always

*goaded me to vehement arguments when questions of policy
came up.*

The President was aware that his wife was a politically
conscious person. In the early days he was delighted
to pit his statesmen and generals and admirals against
her clear and fair thinking, but she too was older, and
more impatient. They had walked a long road together
but they had disagreed more frequently with the advancing years on matters ranging from foreign policy to the
status of White House cooking. On his part, the President
was less certain of himself; he listened more and made
decisions out-of-hand or tucked the problems in the
back of his mind, as though he hoped that they would
dissipate. Most of his intimates knew, when they saw
his jaw fall loose, that they had lost his attention and
that his mind was "far away." The White House staff
and privileged members of Congress discussed Mr.
Roosevelt's health daily. An old friend from World War
I was passing the White House on a daily walk with
Vice President-elect Harry Truman. "Someday soon,"
the friend said, "you will be walking through the front
door of that place." Truman looked up at the pristine
columns of the building. "I hope not," he said. "I hope
not." Then he paused. "But I think you're right."

The Christmas group left the White House on Saturday
the twenty-third. Mr. Roosevelt sent a message to
Churchill, hoping to settle a place and date for the summit
meeting before his allies carved the world between them:

December 23, 1944

Number 676. Personal and Top Secret
From the President for the Prime Minister
*I am today sending to Harriman the following message
in regard to our projected three party meeting with U.J.
Please let me have your opinion as to the possibilities of
this plan from your point of view:*
*"If Stalin cannot manage to meet us in the Mediterranean
I am prepared to go to the Crimea and have the meeting at
Yalta, which appears to be the best place available in the*

*Black Sea, having the best accommodations ashore and the
most promising flying conditions. We would arrive by plane
from some Mediterranean port and would send in advance
a naval vessel to Sevastopol to provide necessary service and
living accommodations if it should be necessary for me to
live aboard ship.*

*"I would plan to leave America very soon after the inau-
guration on a naval vessel. You will be informed later of a
date of arrival that will be satisfactory to Churchill and to
me. My party will be numerically equal to that which was
present at Teheran, about 35 total."*

*I still hope the military situation will permit Marshal Sta-
lin to meet us half way.*

Roosevelt

There was both urgency and the odor of surrender
in the message. The meeting of the three war leaders
had been in the planning half a year. In other years
FDR would have pressed for a quick meeting. In 1944
he was no longer physically strong enough to cut through
Stalin's excuses and delays to insist on meeting him
on his own ground soonest. The President might not
have become aroused, even at Christmastime, if he had
not seen clearly that his partners were making momentous
decisions without him. When they advised him of some
which he regarded as reprehensible, he sent messages
agreeing to them as "temporary measures." Now, almost
too late, he agreed to fly part of the way.

Churchill responded at once, as though the matter
had been settled. The message burbled with enthusiasm.
The Prime Minister suggested that the code name for
the summit meeting be ARGONAUT. He added, "You
and I are direct descendants." In Greek mythology the
Argonauts sailed with Jason aboard the ship *Argo* in
search of the Golden Fleece. The ship was reputed to
have landed at Colchis on the Black Sea. In modern
terminology argonaut is applied to anyone who is adven-
turous and seeks something involving danger. The President was pleased with the suggestion.

In Moscow, Averell Harriman learned that he could

not get an appointment with Josef Stalin. He told Foreign Commissar Molotov that the matter was urgent and Molotov coolly assured the American Ambassador that he could speak for Stalin. The Russians expressed cordial enthusiasm for the President's suggestions but postponed a reply until after Christmas. At Hyde Park FDR waited with impatience. On the twenty-seventh Harriman assured Roosevelt that Molotov had promised a definite response by "tomorrow." He said he had discussed "in detail the arrangement for the holding of the meeting at Yalta with your ship at Sevastopol." On the twenty-eighth Churchill advised the President: "Stalin will make good arrangements ashore." A message arrived from Harriman stating that, at last, the Soviets had agreed to the site at Yalta. Since the recent evacuation of the Germans, much work had to be done to make the place habitable: "Suitable quarters and staff meeting places can be made available."

Earlier FDR decided that no problem of state would make Christmas at Hyde Park less merry than it once was. The old house was full of grandchildren and the President wore a semi-permanent smile as he wheeled here, there and everywhere to see what the little ones were doing. Colonel Elliott Roosevelt, on leave, brought his new wife, motion picture star Faye Emerson, to Crum Elbow. The First Lady played the role of grandmother magnificently and seemed at times to be towing small children through the rooms attached to her skirt. It was the first Christmas since 1932 that the Roosevelts were home. Elliott spent an entire afternoon driving his father around the estate, especially where Christmas tree cuttings had been made. Before the turkey dinner, Mr. Roosevelt sat in his favorite high-back leather chair to the right of the fireplace and called all the children—grown-ups were permitted to sit some distance away—to his feet. They crouched around him, some dreaming toward crackling logs, others leaning backward on the floor to stare at "Grandpère."

Mr. Roosevelt began a solemn and highly dramatic reading of Dickens' *Christmas Carol*. Head back to take advantage of his bifocals, he simulated the inoffensive, frightened voice of Bob Cratchit and the menacing snarl of Mr. Scrooge. About at the halfway point a three-year-old grandson noticed a tooth gap in the lower part of the President's mouth. He pointed excitedly and shouted, "Grandpère, you've lost a tooth!" Mr. Roosevelt allowed himself a brief smile and returned to the story. The little boy stood to get a better look and said, "Did you swallow it?" The President slammed the book shut and fell into a paroxysm of laughter. He had to wipe his eyes. He glanced at the adults in the far reaches of the library. "There's too much competition in this family for reading aloud," he said. Faye Emerson said, "Next year, it will be a peaceful Christmas." Eleanor Roosevelt nodded seriously. "Next year," she said, "we'll *all* be home again."

All gifts had been opened, and colorful wrapping paper was strewn on the floor, but the President told Mrs. Roosevelt that he was too busy to open his gifts. She seemed disappointed. "All right," he said. "I will open a few every day. I promise." With the glee of a youngster who knows how to surprise himself, FDR opened a few presents each evening until the second week in January. In the latter part of Christmas week he told Mrs. Roosevelt that the summit meeting would be held at Yalta and, of course, swore her to secrecy. On that day, or one shortly after, he called Anna for a private chat and revealed the place of the conference. Then, unexpectedly, he said, "Sis, will you come along with me?" Anna smiled. She was happy, touched by this mark of favor. Laughing and nodding, she said, "Father, I promise not to keep any notes and I will not write about the conference later." In a similar mood the President reminded his daughter that the trip would be made on a Navy cruiser, that women were not permitted on U.S. naval vessels. "We will have to keep you out of sight," he said, "and we can't have you going to the sailors' head."

Christmas, as always, was a different day to different people. Winston Churchill selected that day to take his

Foreign Secretary, Anthony Eden, and hop into a Coastal Command long-range plane for a flight to Athens. He argued that this was no moment to temporize. The Russians were in Czechoslovakia and Hungary with their southern wing, and they were heading for Vienna. In spite of the fact that Churchill had passed his seventieth birthday and was advised by his physician, Lord Moran, not to make the long flight, the Prime Minister landed in Athens and set about restoring order. He accomplished what his generals couldn't. Publicly, he endorsed a Greek regency under Archbishop Damaskinos, and revealed a promise by King George that he would not return to Athens unless "summoned by a free and fair expression of the national will." At Hyde Park press secretary William Hassett, alone in his room, was penning: "To me, the President seems tired and weary—not his old self as he leads the conversation. I fear for his health despite assurances from the doctors that he is O.K."

The Roosevelts were back in the White House the last day of the year. At once the President called some people to his desk. One of the early arrivals was Edward Stettinius. The Boss asked if the second- and third-echelon studies about the war, various countries and borders in Europe, world economic affairs and the Far East were in progress. The Secretary of State assured him that these matters were in hand. The young and brilliant assistant, Alger Hiss, was working up the United Nations Charter article by article and phrase by phrase.

Mr. Roosevelt leaned forward and spoke in a conspiratorial whisper. "We are going to Yalta," he said. Stettinius seemed mystified. "You had better look at the map," the President said, "but with no one else present when you do." Within a few minutes Admiral McIntire was at his desk. The President was in a mood for revealing a secret. The Admiral asked how the Boss proposed to make the trip. The answer was by ship to the Mediterranean, then fly from Caserta to Yalta. The Admiral left, consulted an atlas and came back in the office a short time later shaking his head no. Caserta was inland from

Naples, which indicated that Mr. Roosevelt proposed to land there. The Admiral pointed out that there were too many high mountains between Caserta and Yalta, and he did not recommend that the President fly high. Farther south was British Malta, a small island lying almost on the thirty-fifth parallel, with a flying route easterly over the Turkish Straits to Yalta. FDR agreed and dispatched a message at once to Churchill. Within a day the Prime Minister's silly response was in the White House: "We shall be delighted if you will come to Malta. I shall be waiting on the quay. You will also see the inscription of your noble message to Malta of a year ago. Everything can be arranged for your convenience. No more let us falter! From Malta to Yalta! Let nobody alter!" It was on Mr. Roosevelt's desk when he called Jimmy Byrnes in the East Wing and asked him to stop in the office.

The unsmiling Byrnes wished to discuss shipping problems. The Boss wanted to invite Byrnes to join him on the trip to Yalta. The Director of War Mobilization sat back in surprise. "Jimmy," the President repeated, "I want you to go with me on this trip to the Crimea." The face of Byrnes darkened. He had no desire to be a member of a large entourage around FDR. On several occasions the Boss had discussed a forthcoming meeting of the Big Three, but it had turned out to be a meandering topic with no terminal. Now the decision had been made, and approximate time, too. Byrnes did not wish to go. The President became persuasive. "You know what went on at the other meetings," he said, "and as Director of Mobilization you have acquired a knowledge of our domestic situation that will be of great service in settling the economic questions which are certain to come up." It was a long sentence, a breathless one for the President.

Byrnes was doubtful. "When you are out of town," he pointed out, "the machinery doesn't stop. Problems like the one we are now discussing constantly arise. I think I should remain here and work on those problems." The Boss became slightly more insistent. If time was a factor, he proposed to send the busy people over by special plane to Africa, then a hop to Malta and on to the Crimea. The conference wouldn't last more than several days and Byrnes could fly back. He wanted Jimmy at his side. Byrnes was blunt: "I will go," he said, "but I'm not happy."

The President had sent an assortment of recriminations to Stalin regarding Poland. It was dispatched December 30. It could have had a bearing on Stalin's willingness to arrange the Yalta Conference, because it amounted to a rebuttal of Stalin's allegations that the London Poles had set terrorists in Poland to killing Red Army men, while the Lublin Committee was forming a Polish army to assist the Russians. "I am disturbed and deeply disappointed over your message . . . in regard to Poland, in which you tell me that you cannot see your way clear to hold in abeyance the question of recognizing the Lublin Committee as the provisional government of Poland until we have had an opportunity at our meeting to discuss the whole question thoroughly. I would have thought no serious inconvenience would have been caused your government or your armies if you could have delayed the purely juridical act of recognition for the short period of a month remaining before we meet. . . ."

Stalin's response arrived on the final day of 1944. It was not a message. The Russian Foreign Office called in the newspaper correspondents in Moscow to tell them that the Lublin Committee had just announced that it was now the provisional government of Poland, and that the Soviet Union was the first to grant it official recognition. It was, in effect, a cruel answer to FDR's plea for patience; the first direct evidence that Russia proposed to surround itself with satellite nations, regardless of the wishes of its allies and most certainly in contravention of the articles of faith and independence which would be the cornerstone of the United Nations organization.

Mr. Roosevelt first read the announcement on the

wire-service news tickers. He displayed no reaction. He read it and returned to his desk to add to the list of personages he proposed to bring with him on his trip to Yalta.

January 1945

THE NEW YEAR CAME UP GHOSTLY GRAY OVER THE FACE of Europe. From the Baltic to the Adriatic the winds were gusty and cold. In many countries gray faces, matching the dawn, emerged from cellars. The struggle to the death continued; it was a world of ice and flame in its sixth year of anguish. The harsh, shouting voice of Adolf Hitler, silent since the attempt on his life the previous July, was on the radio at 12:05 A.M. His New Year greeting to his people was to boast of "millions of new soldiers and artillery corps." He had secret new weapons of a frightening character. Germany—his Germany—would never capitulate, Hitler said, because surrender would mean "enslavement" of a noble Aryan nation, and Germans preferred death to slavery. He predicted that the war would end in 1946, in victory.

Berlin was in ruins. As the dictator addressed the nation from Supreme Headquarters in the east, British bombers flew over the capital again. The beautiful Tiergarten, once a woodland for lovers and picnic parties, was a collection of blackened trunks bare in the light of the waning moon. Entire rows of buildings in all sections of the city lay in broken stone hills; the inherent industry of the people was displayed in the clearing of the piles of rubble so that ambulances and military traffic could pass through. Other parts of the city crackled with bright flames. The huge Chancellory on the edge of the Wilhelmstrasse was half gone, a section of its roof caved in; the stately marble corridors and diplomatic halls were blackened with scars. The big lush

carpeted bomb shelter under the Chancellory garden
was intact. The eminent edifice of the Brandenburger
Tor was pitted with bomb fragments; all of the animals
at the famous zoo had been removed or had died—except
one hippopotamus which wallowed serenely in its lake.

Hitler husbanded his hopes. He was certain that the
alliance of the Bolsheviks with Great Britain and the
United States would crack. Militarily, he had lost the
war, but he would demand that Germans "stand and
die" without yielding an inch. "Even now," he told the
generals on his staff, "these states are at loggerheads.
He who, like a spider sitting in the middle of his web,
can watch developments, observes how these antagonisms grow stronger and stronger from hour to
hour."

Eleven hundred miles to the east, the onion-shaped
towers around the Kremlin reposed under cocked hats
of snow. Three years earlier this metropolis shuddered
under the impact of thousands of cannon. The war, like a
dismal tide of destruction, had receded. Moscow at New
Year's was gay. Citizens coveted tickets to the concert
halls and the ballet. Fireworks burst in arcing colors
over Red Square. People at home reposed in warmth,
listening to small radios proclaim victory upon victory
by the Red Army over the dreaded "Hitlerite armies."
At the Kremlin Marshal Stalin arrived early to compose
a message to President Roosevelt. It would be received
in Washington seven hours later, still early in the morning.

1 January 45

Marshal Stalin to President Roosevelt

*I have received your message of December 30. I greatly
regret that I have not been able to convince you of the
correctness of the Soviet government's attitude toward the
Polish question. I nevertheless hope that events will convince you that the Polish National Committee has always
rendered and will continue to render to the Allies, and in
particular the Red Army, considerable assistance in the
struggle against Hitlerite Germany, whereas the émigré*

*government in London assists the Germans by creating
disorganization in this struggle.*

*I naturally fully comprehend your suggestion that the So-
viet government's recognition of the provisional government
of Poland should be postponed for a month. There is, however, a circumstance here which makes it impossible for me
to fulfill your wish. The position is that as early as December 27 the Presidium of the Supreme Soviet of the
U.S.S.R. informed the Poles in reply to an inquiry on the
subject that it proposed to recognize the Provisional Government of Poland as soon as the latter was formed. This
circumstance makes it impossible for me to fulfill your
wish. Permit me to send you my greetings for the New
Year and to wish you health and success.*

Three days later Stalin sent identical thoughts to the
Prime Minister. The cynical Churchill appreciated the
cynical Stalin resorting to the subterfuge of pretending
that his personal will could be thwarted by the Soviet
Presidium. Stalin's control over the affairs and events
of the Soviet Union was as complete and dictatorial
as Hitler's over Germany. Toward the end of the message
Stalin stated: "I am aware that the President has your
consent to a meeting between us three at the end of
this month or the beginning of February. I shall be glad
to see you and the President on the territory of our
country."

British Air Chief Marshal Tedder, dark and taciturn,
finally reached Moscow to ask the Russians for something
which had already been granted by cable: a plea from
Eisenhower and Churchill for a Russian offensive to
blunt the Battle of the Bulge in the west. Rundstedt
had already lost the engagement and was withdrawing
his forces into Germany. In a better-late-than-never
mood, Tedder walked along the corridor leading to
Stalin's office accompanied by a British Embassy admiral
and general, and two American generals. Under his arm
he carried two boxes of cigars, a gift from Dwight
D. Eisenhower. Along the corridor Russian soldiers
standing post with rifles and bayonets stared suspiciously

at the package. When Tedder arrived in Stalin's office, the Russian dictator watched the gift deposited on his desk, took an underhung pipe from his mouth and, speaking through Pavlov, his interpreter, said, "When do they go off?" Tedder didn't flinch. His sense of humor was that of the straight man. "They do not go off, sir," he said, "until I have gone." Stalin chuckled. He liked this Britisher at once.

"I know why you have come," he said. "You want to know what we are doing and what we are going to do." The dictator ordered a large map to be spread upon the table. To Marshal Tedder's surprise, there was no diplomatic fencing. Curving arrows marked the Soviet projected drives, as Stalin explained, all aimed toward the Oder River. As the Americans and British thought that Hitler was moving extra forces from the eastern front to the western to oppose them, so too the Russians thought that the Germans were moving fresh divisions from west to east, "or else," as Stalin said, "they would not resist as much as they do. In my opinion," he said gratuitously, "the war will not end before the summer. . . . We must not forget, however, that the Germans are frugal and enduring. They have more stubbornness than brains." When Stalin completed his explanation of Russian tactics, he asked Tedder to explain in detail Eisenhower's plans in the west. To Pavlov's interpretations, he kept nodding, asking a question here and there.

General Antonov of Russia's Stavka, or Supreme Headquarters, moved closer as Tedder explained Allied long-range bombing on German synthetic oil plants. The big Blechhammer (Blachownia Slaska) oil plant was still out of range of the western Allies but within range of Soviet bombers. Stalin measured the distance with his pudgy fingers and turned to Antonov with flashing irritation. Tedder did not have to understand Russian. Antonov got to his feet pale and shaking. Tedder said he felt impressed. Churchill, Harriman and Tedder had requested the Russian High Command to bomb

Blechhammer twelve weeks before; now he knew that it would be done.

Stalin turned back to Tedder, smiling again. "We are comrades," he said. "It is proper, and also sound, selfish policy, that we should help each other in times of difficulty. It would be foolish for me to stand aside and let the Germans annihilate you; they would only turn back on me when you were disposed of. Similarly, it is to your interest to do everything possible to keep the Germans from annihilating me."

In London ice and snow were not problems. Rockets and buzz bombs continued to fall sporadically on the city. Some of the weary citizens said that they preferred the rockets which exploded first, then could be heard approaching. The buzz bombs used ram-jet engines, which could be heard for miles. When they passed overhead, scores of thousands of persons paused, on streets and in homes, to listen. When the engines stopped, the bombs fell and exploded. It was a question of whether one wanted to be curious about imminent death or in ignorance of the event.

That castigating diarist Sir Alexander Cadogan, who always referred to his superior, Foreign Minister Anthony Eden, as "A," was worried that the British and American ministers and their aides would not meet (because of American refusal) before the Yalta Conference: "Had a longish talk with A. about forthcoming meetings. He agreed we must try to have a meeting of foreign ministers before the 'Big 3' meet. Otherwise, nothing tangible will be done. They dine and wine, which is all very well, but nobody (least of all themselves) knows what, if anything, has been settled."

On the same day, January 4, Eden found time to drop a melancholy thought into his personal diary: "I am much worried that the whole business will be chaotic and nothing worthwhile settled—Stalin being the only one of the three who has a clear view of what he wants and is a tough negotiator. P.M. is all emotion in these matters; F.D.R. vague and jealous of the others."

In the first days of the month, the Top Secret messages

were flying from continent to continent. Sometimes, as on the fifth, Winston Churchill dispatched one urgent message to Moscow, another to Washington.

Personal and Most Secret
From Mr. Churchill to Marshal Stalin
I thank you for sending your two messages to the President on the Polish question. Naturally I and my War Cabinet are distressed at the course events are taking. I am quite clear that much the best thing is for us three to meet and talk all these matters over, not only as isolated problems, but in relation to the whole world situation both of war and transit to peace. Meanwhile our attitude, as you know it, remains unchanged. I look forward very much to this momentous meeting and I am glad that the President of the United States has been willing to make this long journey. We have agreed, subject to your concurrence, that the code name shall be called Argonaut. . . .

The Prime Minister sat in the small brick building near Admiralty Arch, which he used as his war plans office, and composed a message to FDR:

Number 874. Your 690. PERSONAL TOP SECRET
Prime Minister to President Roosevelt
In none of your telegrams about ARGONAUT *have you mentioned whether U.J. likes this place and agrees to it and what kind of accommodation he can provide. I am looking forward to this. It has occurred to some of us that he might come back and say "Why don't you come on for the additional four hours and let me entertain you in Moscow?" However, I am preparing for Yalta and am sending a large liner which will cover all our troubles. Would it not be possible for you to spend 2 or 3 nights at Malta and let the staffs have a talk together unostentatiously? . . .*

The President was determined to have no pre-Conference conferences. To the few in the White House privy to the situation, he explained that the Russians were inordinately suspicious of any meetings between

Churchill and Roosevelt, and that included secret meetings of the staff. Roosevelt understood Stalin's point of view. The President had been worried about the conference at Quebec—and the total absence of Russian participation—but felt that he had made the thing palatable to the Soviets by explaining that the main topic would be Japan, and the Russians still adhered to a pact with Japan. It would have been dangerous for Moscow to be part of the Quebec discussions. FDR said he had kept Ambassador Gromyko informed of the agenda and the agreements. He was now steadfast in denying to the British any pre-Yalta talks. Churchill could see no wrong, and certainly no grounds for misgivings on Stalin's part, if the English and Americans met at Malta three days before departing for Yalta. He felt it would give him time to discuss the world situation with Roosevelt and come to some firm agreements, while Eden and Stettinius discussed other matters, and the Combined Chiefs of Staff agreed on tactics and dispositions of military forces.

On January 3 FDR sent a Top Secret to the P.M. It had been already stated that the parties would fly to Russia on February 2. "I will arrive at Yalta February first or second from Malta, and Chiefs of Staff will arrive at the same time, possibly from Egypt . . . it is necessary for me to postpone my projected visit to the United Kingdom until a later date." To which Churchill replied that the two could meet at Malta "unostentatiously." The President declined. He told aides that he was "personally fond" of the P.M. but was finding him to be "excitable and dangerous." At the Quebec Conference the President had said something which worried Churchill: "I know you will not mind my being brutally frank when I tell you that I think I can personally handle Stalin better than either your Foreign Office or my State Department." The words alarmed the Prime Minister. Lord Halifax sent a coded message to London that he had seen Roosevelt and did not think he "looked too good." The British Ambassador reported that FDR's main concern did not center on Yalta at all; it was on a form of suicide attack adopted by Japanese pilots which, the President claimed, was costing forty to fifty American lives for every Japanese lost.

Churchill frequently indulged himself in tantrums of irritation over his inability to convince Roosevelt of Great Britain's inherent righteousness and charged that the President was "anti-imperialist." It was a contagion of distrust. Sir Alan Brooke, British Field Marshal, damned Dwight Eisenhower as "a second rate player" after the Ardennes offensive. The British *Economist,* catching the mood, asserted that Eisenhower's sole strategic conception was that "of an elephant leaning on an obstacle to crush it." Eden complained at a Cabinet meeting that Roosevelt was chronically suspicious of the British Empire, and "he is always anxious to make it plain to Stalin that the United States is not ganging up with Britain against Russia."

The differences of opinion among the Big Three began, in some areas, to become insuperable. Churchill, who was not senile, suddenly became irresolute. He and Stalin had already carved up spheres of influence in the Balkan nations, but Churchill told Eden that "there are a lot of things which don't matter." The Foreign Secretary, who seldom contravened the Prime Minister, snapped, "Bulgaria isn't one of them." To which Churchill shrugged and said, "I had never felt that our relations with Bulgaria and Romania in the past called for any special sacrifices from us." This was the man who, six months before, had pleaded with Roosevelt to divert British and American forces from Italy and send them into the Balkans to beat the Russian armies to those countries. Recently he had fought with ardor for the freedom of Poland. At War Cabinet sessions in January he seemed to surrender Poland when he said that "quarrels between the Poles will wreck the peace of Europe." In Washington the President told Stettinius, in speaking of Poland, "When a thing becomes unavoidable, one should adapt oneself to it." Sir Charles Portal, Marshal of the Royal Air Force, summed up his Prime Minister, "Churchill will fight to the last ditch, but not in it."

Once more the Prime Minister was swinging into the fray, when, on the fifth, he signaled Franklin Roosevelt:

5 January 45

Prime Minister to President Roosevelt

Would it not be possible for you to spend two or three nights at Malta and let the staffs have a talk together . . . ? Also, Eisenhower and Alexander could both be available there. We think it very important that there should be some conversation on matters which do not affect the Russians— e.g., Japan—and also about the future use of the Italian armies. You have but to say the word and we can arrange everything.

To which Roosevelt replied:

With favorable weather at sea I can arrive Malta February second and it is necessary to proceed by air the same day in order to keep the date with U.J. That is why I regret that in view of the time available to me for this journey it will not be possible for us to meet your suggestion and have a British-American Staff meeting at Malta before proceeding to ARGONAUT. . . .

Roosevelt

Stalin cut across the several pleas and denials to send a message to Churchill (with a copy to Roosevelt): "I know that the President has your consent to a meeting of the three of us." The President interpreted this to mean that Stalin feared that no one had formally invited Winston Churchill to Yalta. It was a ridiculous situation, and FDR cabled to Harriman in Moscow: "Stalin may wish to extend an invitation to Churchill." In a skein of misunderstandings and disagreements good manners had been forgotten. On January 10 Stalin cabled Churchill: "In accordance with the proposal sent by the President, I want your agreement to Yalta as the place and February 2 as the date of the meeting."

Churchill, momentarily serene, replied airily: "Okay and all good wishes." The greater the volume of correspondence, the more difficult it became for the gentlemen to understand each other.

The Pentagon assured the President that, regardless of weather, mail pouches could be delivered to him at Yalta and returned to Washington within a span of ten days. Roosevelt said that, under law, it was imperative for him to be able to respond to acts of Congress and to be apprized of domestic and foreign situations quickly. One such situation was in the morning mail on his desk January 3. Ben Cohen's resignation as counsel to the Office of War Mobilization and Reconversion was a terse document.

The President was upset. Cohen and "Tommy the Cork" Corcoran had been members in good standing of Roosevelt's bright young brain trust for years. It was another "kitchen problem," as FDR called White House encounters of ruffled feathers and abraded feelings. He phoned Jimmy Byrnes and said that he did not want Cohen to leave and expected Byrnes to "straighten this out." Cohen had tired of working in the East Wing and hoped that he would become Counsellor to the State Department. When the appointment was not announced, Cohen felt he had been rebuked. FDR asked Stettinius to phone Cohen and explain that the new Secretary of State had not requested the appointment. Stettinius went a step further. He not only assured Cohen of the truth—that Cohen's name had not been mentioned—but further, Stettinius called a press conference and announced that this was so. In turn, this led the reporters at the White House to ask what all the gunfire was about. Byrnes's public relations man intoned: "It is true that, for reasons wholly unconnected with his work with the Office of War Mobilization and Reconversion, he [i.e., Cohen] tendered his resignation. At the request of Justice Byrnes, Mr. Cohen has now withdrawn his resignation."

There were other, more important matters to occupy

the President that morning. He gave his budget message a final scanning and sent it to Congress for reading to both Houses by a clerk. America's fiscal year ends on June 30, but the pages of history show that wise Presidents place their requests for funds before both Houses as soon as they convene after the new year. The President asked for $73 billion for the armed forces to be spent between July 1, 1945, and June 30, 1946. "I have not made in the past, and I shall not now make, any prediction concerning the length of the war. My only prediction is that our enemies will be totally defeated before we lay down our arms." Seventy-three billions of dollars was an unheard-of sum. To administer the remainder of government—i.e., the domestic front—Mr. Roosevelt asked for $13 billion, making a total of $86 billion.

Quickly he pointed out that appropriations for the fiscal year ending June 30, 1944, had reached a peak of $128 billion; the current budget was $97 billion. He acknowledged that the federal debt would, in the current year, reach an all-time high of $252 billion. Lend-Lease, he realized, was a sensitive topic to isolationist Congressmen. The message said that $36 billion in goods and services had been sent to allies; they, in turn, rendered $4.5 billion in goods and services to the United States.

The President's continuing fear of Japan emerged in the budget message: "We shall make a great mistake if, in our military and budget planning, we underestimate the task of defeating Japan. Japan now occupies twice the area which was held by the Nazis in Europe at the peak of their power, an area as large as the continental United States. The population now under the control of the Japanese is more than three times the population of the United States. The supply lines to the Pacific and Asian theater are two and three times the distance to Europe." His dread of Japan was personal. He regarded the Japanese as a race of clever, fanatical people to whom death for the empire was an honor. The President also believed the estimates of his Joint Chiefs of Staff, that it might require two or three more years after peace in Europe to subdue the Japanese, and then only by hand-to-hand fighting on the main islands.

In government circles decisions were being made without consultation with the President. These numbered in the scores of thousands, but he was not the type of Chief Executive who becomes resentful, unless, of course, the decision backfired into the press. Two decisions affecting him had already been made. The Navy, aware that a Big Three conference was under consideration, took the heavy cruiser *Quincy* out of fleet service on November 10, 1944, and cut orders for her to proceed to the Boston Navy Yard for refitting. The *Quincy* was a 14,000-ton sister ship of the *Baltimore* and had been the first ship of war to fire a salvo at the Normandy landings on D Day. In Boston a kitchen was built in the captain's quarters, strong wooden ramps had been built over the scuppers for a wheelchair. Quarters on the starboard side of the main deck had been refurbished, including new silverware.

A complicated, two-stage wooden ramp, about 30 feet long, had been built and placed aboard to be lashed on the main deck. This would be used for embarking and disembarking the President. The crew watched the work, but the scuttlebutt "Roosevelt is coming" faded as the days passed into weeks. Two elevators were installed in the superstructure: one leading from the main deck to the bridge, the second going upward to the flat bridge. On November 16 *Quincy* was ordered to proceed at best speed to Hampton Roads, Virginia. There the big cruiser was warped by sturdy Navy tugs to the south side of Pier Six. *Quincy* was still there, out of action for two months, in January. Nor was Mr. Roosevelt aware that the Air Force had redesigned a C-54 four-engine plane and placed a small elevator in the back. The elevator, strung on steel cables, lowered a cage car to the ground. The plane was ordered to proceed to Malta, find a safe revetment and await orders. It cruised at 220 miles per hour.

The President was not told of these preparations.

He could be truculent about a "fuss" being made over his comfort. Some of the extras done in his name caused him to get his "Dutch" up. He was averse to flying, and it was predictable that he would be opposed to being exposed in a cage being lowered or lifted from a plane. The Navy did not plan to tell him that a heavy cruiser had been detached from fleet fighting for over two months, just to be ready when he announced where he wanted to go and when.

From the middle of December FDR's energies had been directed toward the State of the Union message to Congress to be read on January 6. He had issued orders to Robert Sherwood, Sam Rosenman, Archibald MacLeish, Ben Cohen and Harold Smith of the Budget Bureau that he wanted it to be brief. He told Hassett he could stand long enough to read 3,000 words. Each submitted drafts at the start, and Roosevelt took a little from this one and some from that one. As the date neared, the best that could be done was to cut it to 8,000 words. He said he would not deliver it in person. Congressional leaders were told that it would be "sent and read." The final paragraph, as he approved it, stated: "We have no question of the ultimate victory. We have no question of the cost. Our losses will be heavy. We and our allies will go on fighting together to ultimate total victory." It had impact.

The message was important not only because it was his longest but because, in the main, Roosevelt was summing up what had been done against what he proposed to do. The phrases were designed to be heard and weighed in Moscow, London, Paris, Chungking, Berlin and Tokyo as well as in Salem, San Antonio and San Diego:

Always, from the very date we were attacked, it was right militarily as well as morally to reject the arguments of those short-sighted people who would have had us throw Britain and Russia to the Nazi wolves and concentrate against the Japanese. . . . In the European Theatre, the necessary bases for the massing of ground and airpower against Germany were already available in Great Britain. In the Mediterranean area we could begin ground operations against major elements of the German Army as rapidly as we could put troops into the field, first in North Africa, then in Italy. Therefore, our decision was made to concentrate the bulk of our ground and air forces against Germany until her utter defeat.

He had debts to pay publicly:

We cannot forget how Britain held the line alone, in 1940 and 1941, and, at the same time, built up a tremendous armaments industry which enabled her to take the offensive at El Alamein in 1942. We cannot forget the heroic defense of Moscow and Leningrad and Stalingrad, or the tremendous Russian offensives of 1943 and 1944 which destroyed formidable German armies. Nor can we forget how, for more than seven long years, the Chinese people have been sustaining the barbarous attacks of the Japanese and containing large enemy forces on the Asiatic mainland.

Harry Hopkins, reading the speech in London two days earlier, had begged Mr. Roosevelt to say something generous about France. Mr. Roosevelt agreed, after some foot-dragging, but decided to mention the liberation of France by the United States and Great Britain instead:

The cross-Channel invasion of the Allied Armies was the greatest amphibious operation in the history of the world. It overshadowed all other operations in this or any other war in its immensity. Its success is a tribute to the fighting courage of the soldiers who stormed the beaches, to the sailors and merchant seamen who put the soldiers ashore and kept them supplied, and to the military and naval leaders who achieved a real miracle of planning and execution. And it is also a tribute to the ability of two nations, Britain and America, to plan together, work together and fight together in perfect cooperation and perfect harmony.

He moved on to boast of an advance in the Pacific theater of 3,000 miles; the northward drive of General Douglas MacArthur from the shores of Australia to the great islands of the Philippines; stunning naval battles and victories. "Our Navy looks forward to any opportunity which the lords of the Japanese Navy will give us to fight them again." But the war was not over. It was far from over. Roosevelt asked for a military conscription law to continue into the peacetime period. He asked for more nurses, many more nurses. While some Americans were saying that the war was over after Paris had been liberated, the United States was pouring more and more men and supplies into France and turning their faces toward Germany. The Ardennes campaign by Hitler was a surprise, but he failed to obtain his objectives. He had lost a monumental gamble. The President asked Congress to enact legislation which would permit him to use men classified 4-F—not available for military service—in plants and factories where tanks, guns and shells were being made.

Without consciously taking note that Adolf Hitler had been promising his nation new secret weapons which would turn the tide, Roosevelt said:

We have constant need for new types of weapons, for we cannot afford to fight the war of today or tomorrow with the weapons of yesterday. For example, the Army has now developed a new tank with a gun more powerful than any yet mounted on a fast-moving vehicle. The Army will need many thousands of these new tanks in 1945.

Among the new weapons, of course, he did not mention the atom bomb. He had read a secret message from Major General Leslie Groves, in charge of the project, that the first atom bomb would be ready in August and would probably be fired from an artillery rifle. It would have the blast effect of 10,000 tons of TNT. The second one would be ready to fire in December. The third would be manufactured in 1946. "If we do not keep ahead of our enemies in the development of new weapons," FDR said (and he believed that he was in a race with the Germans to complete the first atom bomb), "we pay for our backwardness with the life blood of our sons."

The speech was all-encompassing. To use the patois of the times, Roosevelt "touched all the bases." It was his eleventh State of the Union message and the only one which recounted much of what the New Deal had accomplished, and pointed ahead toward an enduring peace and full employment. To some who sat in the House well listening, it sounded like the recapitulation of a bookkeeper who is about to lose his job. Of the two remaining goals of the administration, victory in war and a peace-keeping organization, Mr. Roosevelt seemed assured of the former and determined to fight to the death for the latter:

In the field of foreign policy, we propose to stand together with the United Nations, not for the war alone, but for the victory for which the war is fought. It is not only a common danger which united us but a common hope. Ours is an association not of governments but of peoples—and the peoples' hope is peace. . . . It will not be easy to create this peoples' peace. We delude ourselves if we believe that the surrender of the armies of our enemies will make the peace we long for. The unconditional surrender of the armies of our enemies is the first and necessary step—but the first step only. . . .

The nearer we come to vanquishing our enemies, the more we inevitably become conscious of differences among the victors. We must not let those differences divide us and blind us to our more important common and continuing interests in winning the war and building the peace. International cooperation on which enduring peace must be based is not a one-way street. Nations, like individuals, do not always see alike or think alike, and international cooperation and progress are not helped by any nation assuming that it has a monopoly of wisdom or of virtue. . . . I do not wish to give the impression that all mistakes can be avoided and that many disappointments are not inevitable in the making of peace. But we must not this time lose the hope of establishing an international order which will be capable of maintaining peace, and realizing through the years more perfect justice between nations. . . .

I should not be frank if I did not admit concern about many situations—the Greek and Polish, for example. But those situations are not as easy or as simple to deal with as some spokesmen, whose sincerity I do not question, would have us believe. We have obligations, not necessarily legal, to the exiled governments, to the underground leaders, and to our major allies who came much nearer the shadows than we did.

Better than anyone else, FDR knew that it would be impossible to discharge such obligations to *exiled governments* while, at the same time, appeasing the appetites of Russia and Great Britain, *our major allies*. The two were at cross-purposes. However, the President chose this paragraph to appeal again for the self-determination of small nations: "We and our Allies have declared that it is our purpose to respect the right of all peoples to choose the form of government under which they will live and to see sovereign rights and self-government restored *to those who have been forcibly deprived of them*."

The President went a step further, with an oblique pre-Conference warning to the Soviet Union: "During the interim period, until conditions permit a genuine expression of the people's will, we and our Allies have a duty, which we cannot ignore, to use our influence to the end that no *temporary or provisional* authorities in the liberated countries block the eventual exercise of the people's right freely to choose the government and institutions under which, as freemen, they are to live." The warning was not only aimed at the Soviet Union but at England interposing its will in Greece and de Gaulle sitting astride France.

The speech droned on. The attention span of some Congressmen had been exhausted. A few looked up vacantly at the clerk; some straightened paper clips on their desks; a few rolled yellow pencils back and forth.

Near the end, Roosevelt, in deference to Harry Hopkins, offered his olive branch to France without mentioning de Gaulle at all:

Today, French armies are again on the German frontier, and are again fighting shoulder to shoulder with our sons. Since our landings in Africa, we have placed in French hands all the arms and material of war which our resources and the military situation permitted. And I am glad to say that we are now about to equip large new French forces with the most modern weapons for combat duty. [French battle strength, it was obvious, rested on help from the Allies.] In addition to the contribution which France can make to our common victory, her liberation likewise means that her great influence will again be available in meeting the problems of peace. We fully recognize France's vital interest in a lasting solution of the German problem and the contribution which she can make in achieving international security. Her formal adherence to the declaration by the United Nations a few days ago and the proposal at the Dumbarton Oaks discussions, whereby France would receive one of the five permanent seats in the proposed Security Council, demonstrate the extent to which France has resumed her proper position of strength and leadership.

The President moved on to restate his economic bill of rights for all who labor to have a job, a roof and a measure of security. Then he said:

This new year of 1945 can be the greatest year of achievement in human history. 1945 can see the final ending of the Nazi-Fascist reign of terror in Europe. 1945 can see the closing in of the forces of retribution about the center of the malignant power of imperialist Japan. Most important of all—1945 can and must see the substantial beginning of the organization of world peace. This organization must be the fulfillment of the promise for which men have fought and died in this war. It must be the justification of all the sacrifices that have been made—of all the dreadful misery that this world has endured.

The message was well received by the American press. A condensed version of it was read by the President on radio. Some cynics in Washington observed that, as a document, it was designed as a last will and testament. No one will ever know. His previous annual messages had confined themselves to an audit of last year's accomplishments and aspirations for the new year. Throughout this period the President appeared to be depressed, low in spirit and agitated in body. He was physically weak, though the daily ministrations of Dr. Bruenn disclosed no alarming symptoms. The agitation of his hands became more pronounced, and Mr. Roosevelt resorted to keeping them clasped on his lap when he was "on stage" throughout calendar appointments. The wheelchair which, in eleven years, had whirled at speed along the ground floor White House corridor, now moved slowly as the patient bent to propel the wheels. At times he resigned himself to allowing Arthur Prettyman or a Secret Service man to do the pushing. A year later Admiral McIntire would write: "This period, in fact, was the most distressing in the whole of my experience as White House physician. The President did not seem able to rid himself of a sense of terrible urgency." Those words, more than anything that the Admiral said or penned, squared with rare candor. Roosevelt acted in the manner of a man who feels he is facing death but will not discuss it. Nothing in his daily attitude among intimates in the Executive Mansion indicated fear; it would be more charitable to say that Franklin Roosevelt had mentally written himself off as a dying man who had many important things to achieve as quickly as possible.

And yet, in spite of the deep skeletal lines and gray complexion which McIntire at last noted, the President still arrogated to himself the right to pull himself together on occasion and enhance animation in his features, gestures and responses. He never again looked like the vigorous Roosevelt, but he could act the part and do it well. These moments became sporadic, perhaps rare, but they had the effect of reassuring his staff so that the whisper passed from office to office: "The Boss is like his old self again." Anna was in such a state of anxiety that she asked her father, on many occasions, "to please stop working alll day and well into the night." For her he reserved the deep smile of abiding affection and said, "I have things which must be done." The sentence was incomplete. It might have continued, "but there is not enough time in which to do them."

Making plans for the inauguration, Mrs. Roosevelt observed: "Perhaps having a premonition that he would not be with us very long, Franklin insisted that every grandchild come to the White House for a few days over the twentieth." Although communication between husband and wife was cordial, it was not confidential. One evening when, to Eleanor, the President "was far from well," he chose to tell her that his hopes were pinned to the conference at Yalta. Whether he felt sick or well, he would go there and make a valiant attempt to settle the major postwar problems while the war was still in progress and to start the machinery of the United Nations organization. "He told me," Eleanor wrote, "that he intended, if possible, to see some of the Arabs and try to find a peaceful solution to the Palestine situation." At this point he was fully informed on Hitler's extermination camps for Jews but powerless to stop them. Instead, he would goad Great Britain to grant the Jewish homeland promised in the Balfour Declaration. "When he made up his mind to do something," Mrs. Roosevelt said, "he rarely gave up the idea."

Many things that happened indicate the President was aware of his own imminent demise. On January 9, a Tuesday, he was in his office working in half-hour shifts. After thirty minutes, he would pause, exhausted. In the room sat Sam Rosenman, Grace Tully, Robert Sherwood and Dorothy Brady. They spoke of the inauguration speech and, between work periods, discussed anything except the obvious. The portrait he presented was almost unbearable. He would lie on the couch, just breathing and resting, then would force himself up for a fresh session of work. His eyes fixed on Grace Tully.

"Grace," he said, "what in this room reminds you most of me?" She pointed to a painting of an old man-of-war. "The ship print." He tried to pen something on White House stationery, but the fingers trembled so that the words were illegible. He asked Miss Tully to take some dictation. He made a statement that, in the event of his death, the ship print was to be the property of Miss Grace Tully. He ordered her to go to her office and type it at once for signing. Then he smiled at Dorothy Brady—"Child." "Dorothy," he said, "I'm not even going to ask you—the John Paul Jones is to go to you." He asked her to take a note; she felt close to tears. "In the event of my death," he said, "I wish to leave to Mrs. Maurice Brady the John Paul Jones picture which hangs behind my desk in the study of the White House." In an effort to shrug off a depressed mood, Sam Rosenman told FDR that, for once, the letters should not be divided between the filing cabinets of the secretaries but placed in the White House safe. The President agreed, and moved on to other work as though nothing of moment had occurred.

Late in the same day FDR asked Edward Stettinius to come to the White House for a confidential talk. The Secretary of State was not Secretary of State. He was a handsome compromise, an optimist, a first-class publicity man who became an expert at adopting the views of the President and repeating them. Foreign ambassadors liked Stettinius personally and regarded him as a good telephone to the President's ear. He was also good at executing the will of Mr. Roosevelt.

The lunch tray was being taken away when Stettinius arrived. The President asked Grace Tully, who had shared sandwiches with him, to close the door and see that the two were not disturbed. Without preamble, FDR swore Edward Stettinius to secrecy. Then he told his Secretary of State that the United States was on the verge of perfecting an atom bomb. Stettinius appeared to be preplexed. Roosevelt said that this bomb—"I am not sure how long it will take to perfect"—if dropped at Broadway and 42nd Street in New York City, "would lay New York low." The project, Roosevelt repeated, was hyper-secret. Only a few high-ranking officials were aware of it; he had only revealed it to Jimmy Byrnes a short time ago. But, he continued, "the time has been reached for the State Department to be informed." He didn't explain why; certainly its development had no bearing on foreign relations. It was purely a military and psychological matter. The lid of secrecy had been screwed on so tight, FDR said, that appropriations from Congress could not be specified because of the "danger of a leak." Roosevelt closed the conversation by advising his Secretary of State to establish "liaison" with the War Department. There is no known reason why the State Department had to be made aware of the project, nor could Stettinius decipher a rationalization. However, he appeared dutifully at the desk of Henry L. Stimson, who summoned his assistant, Harvey Bundy. The Secretary of War enunciated a concise history of the bomb, and the work of domestic and foreign-born scientists in designing the first one. Edward Stettinius listened in awe. His contribution to the project was to say that he would appoint James C. Dunn, his new Assistant Secretary, as the liaison man between the War Department and the Department of State. If there is an irony, it is that Stettinius, whose labors were not in the field of new weapons, was now aware of an atom bomb, but the snappy little Vice President-elect, Harry S. Truman, to whom this subject might be of the utmost importance, was told nothing.

Some men are equipped with a virtue which is also a vice. The British Prime Minister was one. He used his unusual command of the English language to press on and on for an affirmative response when the situation was irrevocably lost. In the second week of January he was still asking for a pre-Conference meeting with Roosevelt, a meeting of "our foreign ministers; we can even invite Molotov"; and a one-week conference of military chieftains which could be held, he suggested, at the Pyramids or Alexandria, Egypt. His Top Secret No. 880 was long and persistent, closing on a dour note: "At the present time, I think the end of this war may well prove to be more disappointing than was the last."

Roosevelt tossed a small dry bone to the P.M.:

I have directed Marshall, King and Arnold, with their assistants, to arrive Malta in time for a conference with your staff in forenoon *of January 30. In regard to an advance conference between the foreign ministers and the Secretary of State, in view of my absence from Washington during the time required to proceed by sea to Malta, it is impracticable for Stettinius to be out of the country for the same extended period. He will join me at Malta and be with us in* ARGO-NAUT.

Roosevelt

This message was not on Churchill's desk an hour when he busied himself preparing another plea. From the testimony of those around him it can be surmised that his persistence was not predicated on fury; to the contrary he feared that the lack of a formal agenda, in addition to the President's informal manner of talking situations to a superficial conclusion—sometimes, in Churchill's view, a most anti-British solution—made a walk into the cave of the bear a dangerous proceeding. The Prime Minister was aware, both by personal observations and reports from his emissaries, that FDR was in failing health, and no one could be certain what stand he would take on any question or how or when he might change his mind while the talks were in progress. Churchill was a first-rate politician and a third-rate military tactician. He was in no mood to listen to wandering discussions of an ideal world; he would settle for a practical one. It is easy to surmise that he begged for pre-Conference talks with Roosevelt not so much to get the President's views on world affairs as to persuade him to the British view before they faced the Russians.

In Washington the President found himself short of patience. He had said the same thing in so many Top Secret messages that he was now referring to Churchill's pre-Conference plan as a "British trap." On the twelfth the Boss restated his dictum tersely with an added note:

Your 884. It is regretted that projected business here for the Secretary of State will prevent Stettinius' arrival Malta before January 31. It is my present intention to send Harry Hopkins to England some days in advance of the Malta date to talk with you and Eden.

Roosevelt

Before him the President had Churchill's No. 884. There was a tinge of sarcasm in the "Thank you very much about the Combined Chiefs of Staff's preliminary meeting." Then, as adamant as ever, the Prime Minister wrote:

Eden has particularly asked me to suggest that Stettinius might come on 48 hours earlier to Malta with the United States Chiefs of Staff so that he [i.e., Eden] can run over the agenda with him beforehand, even though Molotov were not invited. I am sure this would be found very useful. I do not see any other way of realizing our hopes about world organization in five or six days. Even the Almighty took seven. Pray forgive my pertinacity.

As the days flipped by, Churchill began to worry about technical problems which were solely within the purview of the United States. He recalled that the Montreux Convention gave the government of Turkey the right to stop all foreign vessels of war from transiting their Strait of the Bosporus. Roosevelt planned to send at least one, probably several, naval vessels, through the strait into Russia's Black Sea, and Churchill decided to query Roosevelt about it:

1. Should we not have to warn the Turks of the impending arrival of two ships? We could indeed argue that they are merchant vessels for the purpose of the Montreux Con-

vention, with purely defensive armament and not bound on any exclusively military mission. They could thus in theory arrive unannounced at the Straits; but the Turks could still insist on stopping and examining them, and in fact would be obliged under Article Three to stop for sanitary inspection, which might lead to anything.

2. Should we not tell President Inonu about them at the latest possible moment, for his own strictly personal information, and ask him to give all the orders necessary to ensure that the ships shall pass through unquestioned except by formality? There would be no need to tell him more than that there was going to be a meeting of the heads of government some day somewhere in the Black Sea.

This too irritated Roosevelt. The mention of "two ships" appeared to mean that the British intended to send one in concert with the time and course of the American supply and communications ship *Catoctin*. Also, any information about a highly secret conference in the Black Sea to Turkish President Inonu could easily leak to any pro-German embassy. From there to Berlin would be an easy, almost predictable step. It would not require much information for Hitler to divert aircraft to bomb the site of the conference—even if the pilots only had enough fuel to go one way. The President dictated:

Your 886. I have directed the State Department to take such action at an appropriate time through Steinhardt [i.e., Laurence Steinhardt, U.S. Ambassador to Turkey] with the Turkish government as is necessary to insure passage to the Black Sea without delay or interference of the "Naval auxiliary Catoctin, *not a combatant vessel" and also four smaller naval vessels which are really minesweepers and which the Navy wishes to send to the Black Sea. We will have Steinhardt give the Turks identical information regarding the passage of American airplanes to be used by my party and for daily mail trips.*

Roosevelt

This reminded the Boss to send an additional message to Harriman in Moscow: "Hope you will be able to arrange, without offending the Russians, for the setting up of my personal mess ashore and the use of my stewards and cooks. I desire this in order to maintain my usual diet. Our supplies will be obtained from the *Catoctin*."

In addition to the transatlantic cries of alarm, the President was approaching his fourth inauguration as Chief Executive with increasing disgust. He had ordered General Watson, his military aide, to head the inaugural committee, and Watson was reporting daily that more and more "important people" wanted tickets for the private ceremony. So far, he had applications from six to seven thousand persons whose wishes could not be ignored. Members of Congress, their families and political friends from back home were demanding tickets. Democratic state and county leaders submitted long lists of worthies and contributors to the party campaign fund. And there was the big Roosevelt family, each of whom had hosts of close friends; there was a separate list from Eleanor Roosevelt; the members of the Supreme Court and their families; the President's personal list of cronies and one name not on the list—Mrs. Lucy Mercer Rutherfurd.

The President sat up in his bed, scanning each lengthening list, frowning and scowling. It amounted to too many people, he said. He did not know how to cut it down, but six or seven thousand persons, in addition to the full press, cameramen, the military band and a guard of honor would cause the south grounds to bulge. Watson said that some of the more important personages insisted that they expected to be up on the portico with the President when he swore to the oath of office. "Oh, no," Roosevelt said. "There will not be more than a hundred persons up there, including my family." Watson leaned on Mrs. Edith Helm of the White House staff for assistance. Mrs. Helm had been handling these delicate situations since Woodrow Wilson's time and she remained poised and practical. She kept counseling Pa Watson that everything would be all right, and, in the end, everything was all right.

The inauguration did not occupy the President's time. His immediate concerns, in the middle of January, were the Russian offensive and, oddly, how to deliver on his campaign promise to Henry Agard Wallace—a Cabinet post now held by Jesse Jones—without alienating the slim margin of loyalists he had in both Houses. Reason would dictate that he was more concerned with the first than with the second. This is not so. His faith in the massed Russian armies in 1944 was deeper than Stalin's. FDR felt that the Soviets had "the Hun on the run." No land power could stop them. His domestic desire to fire Jones and replace him with Wallace could, if not played with finesse, add to the number of politically potent enemies he already had in the Democratic party. Roosevelt had promised Wallace that, if he lost his bid for the Vice-Presidency, he could count on a job in the Cabinet. As the inauguration came closer, the President's desk mail produced a crop of formal resignations, none of which was expected to be accepted. They are accorded to all Presidents who serve more than one term; the ritual is supposed to free him for new appointments or to endorse old ones. In this case, Roosevelt kept his own counsel, determined to dump Jesse Jones—something which, for once, he could not delegate to someone else. Jones was a bellicose Texas tiger.

The Soviet Stavka—which is to say, Stalin, supported by his staff of marshals and generals in Moscow—ordered the offensive to begin at dawn January 12. There was grumbling by Koniev and Zhukov that their army groups had expected more time to prepare for the assault and, most particularly, the weather would be bad and no air support could be expected. Stalin, in a waspish order of the day, commanded them to move forward as fast and as far as they could on the twelfth. He also added a warning. In victory, millions of Russian soldiers had been sorely tried in battle and were tired. The men in the line, he pointed out, had strong motivation for regaining their homeland from a bestial enemy who had destroyed towns, crops and unarmed civilians. They were now fighting on Polish soil, which they regarded as foreign. They could not be expected to extend themselves in battle as they had in the past. Stalin told Zhukov and Koniev to pass the word down to army commanders and divisional and regimental staffs that the U.S.S.R. could not afford to lose a battle now, or even to stalemate one. If the weather was bad, it was equally dismal for the Germans.

Hitler, on a brief visit to devastated Berlin, stopped in the gray U-shaped building at O.K.W. headquarters and announced that the eastern front would be quiet for a while because the Russians had thirty German divisions cut off in the Courland district and would chop them up and digest them first—450,000 men—before moving westward again. Military logic was on the side of Adolf Hitler, but Stalin was illogical. It was a dawn of heavy fog and whirling snow when 163 divisions (totaling 2,200,000 men), 32,134 pieces of field artillery and 6,460 tanks began moving across the Vistula, catching the German forces unprepared. Unknown to Hitler, who monotonously ordered every man to stand and die where he was, army staffs were setting up five separate redoubts for five stubborn retreats between the Vistula and the Oder. As the Germans planned it, the Russians were going to be forced to win five great successive battles—without the loss of any—to get within 50 miles of Berlin.

The German generals—apart from Hitler—were certain that the trapped divisions would be liquidated first, and the Ukrainian wing of the Red Army would move across the mountains into Hungary. It was feasible, possible, indicated, but it didn't happen. The Russians hurrying through the snowy streets of Warsaw, much too late to save the loyalist Poles, could not credit the amount of devastation inflicted by the Germans. What the Germans had once done to the huge Warsaw ghetto and its inhabitants, it inflicted on the capital city and its people. Hitler's order of October 11, 1944, to SS Obergruppenführer von dem Bach-Zelewsky was to "raze

Warsaw to the ground." The first Russian generals to tour the city estimated, in a report in Moscow, that 90 percent of the city was rubble and that at least 300,000 civilians living in the city had been killed in 90 days.

For four days hordes of Russians ran westward through snow and fog so thick that they lost contact with units to the left and right. It was like hunting for something inside a huge bottle of milk. On all sides reflections of orange-colored blasts lighted the landscape. In addition to the First Belorussian and First Ukrainian army groups, a belated starter was Rokossovsky, whose Second Belorussian group struck out along the edge of the Baltic Sea. At the end of the fourth day Generals Keitel and Jodl and their apprehensive staffs had figured out, with map pins, precisely what the President of the United States was studying in his map room with the assistance of young officers. "The picture," both sides said, "became clear." Koniev was racing through the plains of southern Poland en route to Silesia; Zhukov, with divisions racing behind massed tanks, headed toward Poznan, his groups of divisions turning outward on each side in the form of a fleur-de-lis. Rokossovsky, with the trapped German divisions far behind him in Latvia, moved on the port of Danzig, where the war had started.

For a time there was no place for the Germans to stand and give battle, because no one was certain where the opposing lines were. The Soviet soldiers moved ahead en masse, seldom pausing to capture, killing anything in uniform that moved. The German front was broken. If the Russians did not collapse from exhaustion, they might be expected to keep moving to the German border. Roosevelt smiled with satisfaction, wheeled his chair back to his office and dispatched a message to Stalin: "Your heroic soldiers' past performance and the efficiency they have already demonstrated in this offensive give high promise to an early success to our armies." To which Stalin radioed: "I am glad that this circumstance will ease the position of the Allied troops in the west." In a sense, this was gratuitous because Patton, Hodges, Simpson and others had already pinched the base of Nazi nerve at the Ardennes. Rundstedt, having lost his daring bid to cut the Allies in half at Antwerp, now had to fight the harder to keep British and American armies out of Germany, and could not spare divisions to be sent to the Russian front.

The role of the blunt-spoken Mike Reilly vis-à-vis the President has never been adequately assessed. Nominally, his position was chief of the White House detail of the United States Secret Service. He was that, and more. The President trusted Reilly more, and felt closer to the second-generation Irishman, than he did most of his Cabinet officers. When something delicate had to be done, whether it was to locate a secret health report on Senator Alben Barkley or to arrange a secret rendezvous with Lucy Rutherfurd, the President called Mike. Just as there were no bounds to the trust and confidence Roosevelt reposed in Reilly, so too there were no bounds to the overprotective attitude and affection Mike Reilly felt for his President.

This time Roosevelt asked Reilly to leave Washington on the thirteenth with a party of Secret Service agents to scout Malta and Yalta and report directly to the Boss. Reilly, bundled to the chin against intense cold, followed eight agents aboard a new C-54 and left Washington in the morning. He would miss the inauguration, which didn't please him, but the job at hand was more important. The four-engine plane was piloted by Majors Ed Coates and Dick Mitchell. It was a day and a time of short-range hops, taken one at a time with refueling stops. They made Kindler Field, Bermuda—700 miles—nonstop.

Reilly told Major Coates that the Secret Service would sleep on the plane, wherever possible, because he was in a hurry to get to Naples. The second stop was Terceira in the Azores. The third was Casablanca and the fourth was Naples. When Mike Reilly wanted information, he never hesitated to pull rank. He asked an Air Force Intelligence expert about conditions in Yalta on the Black Sea. "Well," the officer said, "I don't know much about Yalta. Nobody around here does. The Russkies won't let anybody near the place." He pondered for a moment. "The closest airfield to Yalta is at a place called Saki—200 miles away. I do know that there are no communications facilities of any kind at Yalta. You should know that the route from Malta to Yalta by air is over the Dardanelles, which are still in German hands and lousy with antiaircraft guns."

Mike was making penciled notes. "There is a narrow airway," the officer said, "east by northeast from Malta to Athens, then on to Istanbul, Turkey, and across the Black Sea. It's the long way, and reasonably safe provided the Turks don't get the idea that this is one of the days they should protect their neutrality and shoot you down—or if bad weather doesn't force you off course to the west, which puts you right in the German shooting area."

Reilly gave the officer a weary thank you. He and his party left for Naples harbor, littered with the silent steel skeletons of ships. The U.S.S. *Catoctin* was at dock. Reilly inspected it carefully. He told the captain that he did not know if the important guest would live aboard or not, but he had better prepare good comfortable quarters. The Secret Service man also ordered wooden ramps to be built and pointed to where they should be placed. He hoped that, in an emergency, the *Catoctin*'s radio equipment was strong enough to send and receive messages at Casablanca. From there they could be radioed to and from Washington. One more thing: he asked the *Catoctin* to load up with supplies and foodstuffs for a large American party, enough for a week or ten days.

He was acting far beyond the competence of a Secret Service man, but Mike had the authority to issue orders and make changes. From Naples he and his party flew out to the tiny island of Malta. He went to see the revetment at Luqa airport, examined everything including the pier where the heavy cruiser *Quincy* would dock. He knew that the Boss would feel stiff after a long voyage, so Reilly arranged a 30-mile motor tour of Valletta and the rest of the island when he disembarked. Then he ordered Major Ed Coates to load a second C-54 with long-range radio gear and for both planes to fly in tandem to Yalta. Over the Black Sea both planes were buffeted by lowering clouds and a choppy sky. Coates remained on course and fought his yoke. The second pilot elected to turn off toward Crete. German A.A. batteries almost blew his tail off.

Reilly and fright were strangers most of the time. On this flight they locked hands. The plane bounced so hard that the Secret Service men were sure the wings would break off. Complexions became green, including Reilly's. A few prayers were addressed To Whom It May Concern. Coates, also fearful, took the four-engine plane up to 15,000 feet. The wings began to ice. He could feel the sluggishness in the controls. He dropped to the "deck," 2,000 feet, and ice was still forming. Night had fallen and, looking out, he could see nothing above or below except blackness. Coates left the controls to Dick Mitchell, went into the cabin and said loudly, "We ain't gonna make it, boys. I think we'll have to ditch this thing. Anyhow, put on your parachutes."

Someone in the group said: "What the hell good will parachutes do in the Black Sea? It's ten below zero down there." Coates shrugged and returned to the cockpit. Reilly noticed a phenomenon. Whereas all the faces around him had been pale green, they were now plaster white. Reilly said later that some began to dwell upon past sins, and he wasn't so sure that being a Secret Service man wasn't one of them. All of them had been agreed that the Chief of the Secret Service, Frank J. Wilson, didn't like them. "Well, boys," one of them yelled over the steady roar of the engines, "Wilson's gonna hit the jackpot tonight." The resultant roar of laughter convinced some of the Army men aboard that the strain had driven the Secret Service mad. The flight was dangerous from start to finish, but somehow, every fifteen minutes or so, someone would think of Wilson and the jackpot and start laughing again. It turned out to be a nerve tonic.

The sky was gray with light when Saki was sighted.

Reilly struggled to a window as the C-54 made a low pass over the field for identification. Hundreds of Russian women in wool shawls and heavy coats were sweeping the snow from a metal strip invented as an improvised runway. Some of the Secret Service agents wanted to kiss the land, but they were afraid their lips would stick to it. Reilly was greeted by "my old pal," Artikov, the NKVD (secret police) chief. As the two huddled in the cold wind, the interpreter was a busy man. "Saki," said Reilly, "is absolutely and unequivocally out as a landing place for the President of the United States. This is no airport. It's a cow pasture." If Mike thought that Artikov would promise to level off a true landing strip with runway lights and safeguards, he was mistaken. "How will you get him to Yalta?" was the question.

"We'll bring him in by ship," Reilly said, pointing. "Across the Black Sea." "You can't." "Why?" "Mines." "How many?" A shrug. "Who knows? The Germans put them there. They didn't leave a map." Comrade Artikov suggested that they had other matters to discuss and a long automobile ride ahead. They piled into a group of cars, with Artikov's NKVD men, and started on the rock-strewn, shell-pocked road to Yalta. On the south side the wind seemed warm. On the other side were hills stark with blackened trees and an icy wind strumming trunks like a harp. After three hours Artikov stopped the cavalcade at a large, warm inn. Reilly gathered his "boys" around him. He explained that he had been through this before at Teheran, and it looked like a Russian party and a Russian party could mean trouble.

"Here we go, boys," he said. "They've got gallons of that rubbing alcohol. For diplomatic reasons, we have to go through with it. When any one of you thinks he's had enough, get out. Understand? Get out. They call it a party, but it's really a contest."

The food arrived late, but the vodka was early. Men of two nations, secretive by the nature of their profession, toasted the President, Josef Stalin, Churchill, Artikov, Reilly, jeeps, the waitress with the blue eyes, Eisenhower,

Zhukov, Paulette Goddard, and last but not least, an NKVD man who was the first to fall down a flight of stairs. As Reilly reported: "Early Russian casualties were heavy, but I was wondering what was keeping me up. It may have been patriotism." Russians were sliding under the table. Some Americans had reverted to green as a skin color. Artikov staggered to his feet and made a rambling jolly speech. He collapsed. Now, Mike Reilly, he said. You make a speech. Mike pulled himself up and mumbled: "You have been kind, very hospitable to us Americans. But our hearts long for one thing. We are not used to drinking from such small glasses. Don't you have bigger ones?"

The speech stunned the translator. Those Russians who were still vertical burst into applause. Larger glasses were fetched. Artikov kept the party going all night. At dawn, eight Americans got to their feet. Across the table a lone Russian got to his feet and bowed. It was Artikov. Sleepless, except for those who died early in the game, the party went on to Yalta with rocks on the road and inside heads. "It was a painful victory," Reilly wrote later. "The sight of Yalta did nothing to ease the pain." Demolition parties of retreating Germans had destroyed the town. Three Romanov palaces, along the shore road, had been left intact. One had been promised by Adolf Hitler to General von Mannstein, the young genius who devised the military tactic called *Blitzkreig*. It was evident to the Russians that, unless the Germans had faith in ultimate victory, they would have destroyed the palaces when they retreated.

Strangely, all plumbing, beds and kitchen impedimenta had been removed. "The President," said Reilly, inspecting room after room, "will be roughing it." Comrade Artikov smiled. "We'll take care of it," he said. He said that a large party of workmen was on its way south on a special train laden with rugs, chairs, beds, plumbing, silverware, place settings—even blotters, electric lights, pens and ink. Their project would be to make the three palaces habitable—luxurious, perhaps—within ten days. Even cracked windows would be replaced. Later it developed that Stalin had ordered his agents to raid the Hotel Metropole in Moscow and to bring the best of everything to Yalta.

Reilly continued to make notes. In a private chat with his Secret Service agents, he said blandly that he was certain that Artikov would bug Livadia Palace, the abode of President Roosevelt. The Americans were not to attempt to de-bug the place until the arrival of Roosevelt, when it would be too late for Artikov to replace the listening devices. He assured his men that, no matter how many they found and dismantled, there would be others they would not locate.

The Crimea, measuring about 130 miles east to west, and about 200 north to south, was a rocky ruin with four main roads. On the eastern side of the south nipple of the Crimea stood Yalta, summer resort of Nicholas II and his court. Sixty miles along the curving coast road to the west stood Sevastopol, the main port. The logistical problem of communications would be that *Catoctin* could not berth at Yalta, but could, with care, anchor at Sevastopol. All messages to and from the President would have to go by courier between the ship and Livadia Palace. The courier planes from Casablanca could land nowhere except at Saki, normally deep in snow drifts in the winter months.

Reilly thanked Artikov and flew on to Cairo, Egypt, leaving some of his men behind. He sent a lengthy secret message to the White House, reporting on everything that he had seen and heard and giving his opinion that Yalta was rough-hewn and nearly inaccessible. Although the Germans had left the Crimea, Russian antiaircraft batteries were still stationed freezing in the spindrift snow and at sight of an aircraft tended to become trigger-happy. This so disturbed Mike that he flew back to Saki to have another talk with Artikov. What could be done to protect the planes of the President and the Prime Minister? Nothing. Had Artikov any ideas? None. The Secret Service man flew back to Naples and had a conference with Air Force General Ira Eaker about it. Both agreed that the Russian gunners would be ex-

ecuted if they damaged the President's plane, but suppose
they didn't recognize it? Eaker had an idea but was
certain that the Russians would decline it: why not station
a U.S. noncommissioned officer with each Russian antiaircraft battery—for identification purposes only? Mike
Reilly liked the notion. He flew all the way back to Saki,
advising Artikov that he had a plan. In a hut off the
airstrip Reilly explained it. Artikov listened. Then he
said "No," a simple, terse word. Reilly nodded. "No
Roosevelt then," and he turned to leave. Artikov hesitated. "In a matter of this importance, I would have
to confer with Stalin himself." He was gone a day.
Reilly felt frozen, waiting. When the NKVD chief returned, his brows were arched with surprise. "Stalin says
absolutely," he said. "I have with me an antiaircraft
colonel, and he will show you where our emplacements
are. You have permission to place an American soldier
with each battery." Within a week American Air Force
sergeants were whacking mittened hands together as
they waited beside big guns with their Russian counter-
parts.

Reilly was younger, bigger and stronger than Roosevelt
but he was, in a self-imposed symbolic sense, the
President's father.

The day before the fourth inauguration snow fell on
the capital. It blotted the image of the Washington Monument from the President's upstairs office, and, while dictating mail, he wondered if it would be deep enough
to impose a hardship on the 5,000 persons expected
to stand on the south grounds in the morning. The fall
didn't amount to quite an inch, but the temperature
was low enough to preserve the grounds in percale white.
When the mail was completed, he called Sam Rosenman
in and said he had a special mission for him. Judge
Rosenman was to leave for Europe. The President had
a thought which seemed not to have occurred to his
Joint Chiefs of Staff. Allied troops, he said, had overrun
France, were in Belgium and Holland and would soon
be in Norway and Denmark. FDR, recalling Herbert

Hoover's massive humanitarian work after World War I, told Rosenman that the civilian populations of these countries were suffering privation. They needed food, coal, clothing. Roosevelt said he wanted Sam to organize a small group from the State Department, the Foreign Economic Administration and the United States Army and go to these countries as each was liberated and assess their needs. Rosenman would be expected to return with absolute figures; the President would arrange the Shipping Administration to carry the necessities to these millions of people. America had surplus food and clothing—coal, too. What it didn't have, it could buy or requisition from Great Britain and Canada.

The judge, a good lawyer, an excellent writer of speeches, wondered why he had been selected for a massive job which really required the full-time services of a specialist in population needs. He might as well have asked why a Secret Service man had been picked to be the sole advance man for a summit conference in a far-off land. The President was selecting people not necessarily qualified for specialized functions, but persons he trusted. Rosenman was ready to leave when the Boss asked him to sit for a moment more. There would be a second task. He wanted Sam to stop in England and confer with the British about the procedure for the trials of Nazi war criminals. It would be necessary to define clearly what constituted a war criminal; what type of charges and evidence would be admissible; and what kind of Allied court could best adjudicate innocence or guilt and hand down sentences ranging downward from execution to time in prison.

Some persons, regarded by the President as war criminals, had already been captured, he said. He recalled that after World War I the Allies vowed swift and terrible justice to war criminals, but, when the Treaty of Versailles had been signed, they became bogged in questions of procedure. "This time," he said, "let's get the trials started quickly and have the procedures all worked out in advance. Make the punishment of the guilty swift." Rosenman felt, with rectitude, that two enormous assignments had been thrust upon him in a few minutes. He advised the Boss that the trial and punishment of war criminals was a most complex problem involving international law—perhaps opening precedents unknown to man. Roosevelt said that this was precisely why he wanted Rosenman to start getting studied opinions from the Department of Justice, the War Department and the Navy Department. When he had digested and reconciled those, he was to take the matter up with the British. He would then return to Washington with a detailed report, and FDR would take the matter up with the Russians and the French. "Don't forget," he said, "an International War Crimes Commission has been in session in London for some time." The judge said that he was not a complete stranger to war crimes; "I have a long memorandum, which I hope you will take on your Big Three trip. It is called 'Punishment of War Criminals.'"

When Rosenman departed, the President rested awhile, leafing through newspapers. Two irritating stories caught his eye. In the first *The New York Times* headlined it "Housekeeper Vetoes Roosevelt on Menu." It stated that Roosevelt, powerful enough to "override" the wishes of Congress on occasion, had little influence with the White House housekeeper, Mrs. Henrietta Nesbitt. The Chief Executive had announced that, after his intimate inauguration, 2,000 guests would be invited to the White House for a luncheon of chicken à la king. "We aren't going to have it because it's hot," the housekeeper told the *Times* reporter, "and you can't keep it hot for all those people." Instead, she said, there would be cold chicken salad, rolls, coffee and unfrosted cake. There will be no butter for the rolls. The second story said that Colonel Elliott Roosevelt had ordered a Priority One from the Air Transport Command to ship a gift dog to his wife from England.

Mr. Roosevelt could do nothing to alter the inauguration menu, but he could do something about that dog. He asked Pa Watson to call the ATC at once and find out the facts. After a number of phone calls from base to base, it was determined that Elliott Roosevelt had not ordered a priority shipment of the dog and did not have the rank to impose a priority anywhere. Behind his desk in the Oval Office the President had a recommendation for promotion of Elliott to brigadier general He had signed many others, but he had refused to sign that one. The Pentagon had pointed out that, without his White House connections, young Roosevelt would have received the star on merit—his photo reconnaissance flights in P-38s over enemy-held land, including the oil refineries in Romania, had been superb in execution. The President asked Watson to bring the promotion upstairs for signature. "Pa" thought it was the wrong time to sign it. "Elliott on his record has earned promotion," the President said. "He did not ask that the dog be put on the plane or given high priority. I am not going to have him punished for something he did not do." It was signed.

In the eight rooms which constituted the living quarters of the First Family, there was the noise and ebullience of expectancy: children, cousins and grandchildren all present for the inauguration the next day. The house rang with historic anticipation. There was no noise from the President's office. He rang for secretaries, issued orders, paused to shake hands and exchange pleasantries with old friends and worked. He had no way of knowing it—but he would work on this night until 2:00 A.M. In the early evening he called Tully in. He was about to dictate an important letter. He asked that it be dated tomorrow—January 20—and be hand delivered to the Secretary of Commerce, Mr. Jesse Jones, at 5:15 P.M. The time would be after the inauguration, after the luncheon, and possibly at the time FDR proposed to take an undisturbed nap.

Miss Tully listened. Her dark head was down, the pencil flourished and danced and skated over the stenographic pad:

Dear Jesse:

This is a very difficult letter to write—first, because of our long friendship and splendid relations during all these years and also because of your splendid services to the government and the excellent way in which you have carried out the many difficult tasks during these years.

Henry Wallace deserves almost any service which he believes he can satisfactorily perform. I told him this at the end of the campaign, in which he displayed the utmost devotion to our cause, traveling almost incessantly and working for the success of the ticket in a great many parts of the country. Though not on the ticket himself, he gave of his utmost toward the victory which ensued.

He has told me that he could do the greatest amount of good in the Department of Commerce, for which he is fully suited, and I feel, therefore, that the Vice President should have this post in the new administration. It is for this reason only that I am asking you to relinquish this present post for Henry, and I want to tell you that it is in no way a lack of appreciation for all that you have done, and that I hope you will continue to be a part of the government.

During the next few days I hope you will think about a new post—there are several ambassadorships vacant—or about to be vacated. I make this suggestion among many other posts, and I hope you will have a chance, if you think of it, to speak to Ed Stettinius, who will not leave to join me for several days.

Finally, let me tell you that you have my full confidence and that I am very proud of all that you have done during these past years.

With my warm regards,

> *Always sincerely,*
> *Franklin D. Roosevelt*

The President and Miss Tully were sitting in the office, dwelling upon the size of the explosion which would occur about 6:00 P.M. the next day. Jones was much more the Texas fighter than thinker. He would make a public issue of being fired; he would turn his back on Roosevelt and all his works. It could also be anticipated that he would deride Henry Wallace, the liberal lamb who had literally been fired from the Vice-Presidency just as Jesse Jones was being fired from the Department of Commerce. It is possible—nay, probable—that FDR offered an ambassadorship because he knew that Jones would decline. Nor could he, as a garrulous gut fighter, imagine himself working under the orders of the smiling, supine Ed Stettinius. The delicate situation, and its portentous public recriminations, were dreaded by the President. The inauguration would be behind him when the blast occurred; he had referred Jones to Stettinius so that he would not have to face this angry man until after Yalta—if at all.

Pa Watson stepped into the office and announced that Secretary of Labor Frances Perkins desired to see the President. This was another confrontation he had avoided. Miss Perkins, who had worked well with Roosevelt in the Governor's Mansion at Albany, and who had won the admiration of American labor leaders, had been talking about resigning her post as Secretary of Labor. She pleaded that she had put enough time in government service; she would appreciate a few years of private life. FDR had jollied her away from her adamant position several times; the night before inauguration he would have to see her once more.

Mr. Roosevelt admired Perkins, not because she was a woman doing a man's job well, but because she was the best qualified person he knew. She swept in, small, pursed face under a tricorn hat, and Miss Tully departed. Perkins said that she was determined to resign and was going to do it now. The President placed his trembling arms on the desk and began to plead with her. Miss Perkins ticked off the names of Ambassador John Winant of Great Britain and others, even Jimmy Byrnes, as qualified successors. The Boss kept shaking his head negatively. "Don't you think," she said, "I had better get Steve Early to announce my resignation right now? I'll go in his office and write out the announcement." "No," the President said firmly. "Frances, you can't go now. I can't think of anybody else. Not now. Do stay there and don't say anything. You are all right." The President did something rare. He reached across the desk and pressed her hand between his. In a voice weak with exhaustion, he said, "Frances, you have done awfully well. I know what you have been through. I know what you have accomplished. Thank you." For a brief moment the ascetic Frances Perkins became a woman with pity in her eyes. Her most ardent desire was to quit. She would stay on—for the sake of this tired man.

She returned to her office and told her secretary that she was shocked at the President's appearance. Others had returned to the topic. Some said they noticed a slight droop at the corner of his mouth. Grace Tully said she worried when Mr. Roosevelt suddenly dozed over his mail. She had witnessed it several times. In chats with political friends he frequently "drew a blank" as they listened; abashed, he had to ask what he had been talking about. After a dinner of the White House Correspondents Association, reporters who personally admired him as a great President said he seemed to have developed a slight impediment in his speech. He introduced Associate Justice Robert Jackson as "the Attorney General," a position Mr. Jackson had not held for years. After dinner one evening he announced that his guests were about to see a motion picture about Yalta—a word forbidden around the White House. Anna whispered, 'No, Father, not Yalta. Casablanca." His wife wrote that this would be his last inauguration, "perhaps even having a premonition that he would not be with us long."

Arthur Prettyman, his long-time black valet, knew as well as anyone that the Boss was failing progressively. Up until recently Mr. Roosevelt had insisted on sitting astride the board in his bathtub and bathing himself, and sitting before the lowered medicine-chest mirror to shave himself. Prettyman knew in advance when the ugly brace and harness were to be worn, and when they wouldn't be. In the third term it was rare for him to be able to completely bathe or shave himself, and sometimes a year would pass before he would don the braces. On the morning of the fourth inauguration Prettyman lifted the body, knelt beside the tub and helped the President to wash. Roosevelt's hands lacked control, so Prettyman shaved him. Prettyman knew that the President was becoming lighter or the valet was becoming stronger; he carried Mr. Roosevelt from bedroom to bathroom like an aged baby.

On this particular morning the braces would go on for the final time. President Roosevelt would endure the cruel iron strain on flaccid muscles once more. Prettyman could not imagine any affair of state lying in the future which would make this man wear them again. Late in the morning Prettyman and Colonel James Roosevelt helped the President to dress. He wore his dark business suit, a white shirt, a pin-striped tie, and heavy black shoes with laces. He sat as the thinning hair was combed once more. His breathing was noisy. James filled in the embarrassment of fatigue by reminding his father that, although his sixty-third birthday would fall on January 30, "Mother has arranged to celebrate it tonight." FDR nodded.

When the time arrived, he was helped to his wheelchair and taken to the elevator. On the first floor hall, as he passed ushers, policemen and clerks, Roosevelt suddenly became Roosevelt again, the big grin, the prideful head tossed back, now and then a loud aside which brought laughter. It is doubtful he remembered that, at his third inauguration, he whispered under his breath to Chief Justice Hughes, "I don't know how you feel about this, but I'm getting sick of it." On the portico, in sweeping black robes, Chief Justice Stone waited. He was almost humorless. There would be no whispered jokes today. Nor was there humor in Colonel James Roosevelt. Anna could display affection for her father; James felt it deeply, sadly, but could not put it in words or kisses.

The President emerged on the portico, leaning on the arm of James, clumping slowly forward down the small aisle between the distinguished men of government, the family, a princess or two and a duke. The ellipse

of the south lawn was speckled with over 5,000 guests.
The snow appeared to be hard packed. The sky was
flat unmarred gray. The thermometer was steady at 33
degrees Fahrenheit, but the gusty wind out of Anacostia
Flats made it seem colder. Mr. Roosevelt nodded and
was assisted to his seat next to the lectern. Chief Justice
Stone nodded to Henry Wallace. The Vice President
stood smiling with a Bible in his hand. He held it as
Harry S. Truman took the oath of office, then shook
hands with Wallace and the President and sat.

The red-clad Marine Band played "Hail to the Chief."
The old magnolia trees to left and right of the portico
had branches heavy with snow. Beyond the invited guests,
the President saw thousands of citizens passing against
the outside of the iron fence on Constitution Avenue.
He raised both hands above his head and waved. On
both sides of the curving staircase beneath the portico
stood the thirteen grandchildren, shivering and silent.
Below, in front of the Marine Band, fifty wounded
servicemen in wheelchairs sat smiling and applauding.
A prayer was offered by Bishop Dun of the Episcopal
Church. Monsignor Ryan of the Catholic Church waited
in a rear chair to deliver the benediction.

A Secret Service man and James Roosevelt whispered
to the President and leaned down to lift him by the
armpits. FDR reached up and wrapped his locked hands
around his son's neck. One step and he was at the lectern.

Harlan Stone held the Roosevelt family Bible; the
printing date was 1686. As the President wished, it
was opened to the thirteenth chapter of the First Corin-
thians: "And now abideth faith, hope, charity; these
three, but the greatest of these is charity." The hundred
persons on the portico stood. FDR looked out beyond
the crowd and could see the Washington Monument
and the dark ribbon of the Potomac. He could not see
an individual such as Mrs. Rutherfurd, who sat in a
car with Secret Service men. But she saw him. She
remained silent. She was not a person who would trans-
mit her thoughts, pride or pity, to anyone.

The microphone glittered before the President as he

repeated, firm of voice, the words uttered by the Chief Justice. Across the nation the people were listening. His son, holding an arm, felt his father's whole body go into a spasm of shivering. He feared that Mr. Roosevelt would not be able to hold the sheet of paper with the small speech, much less read it. He kept glancing at his father, but there was no call for help in the glance he got. Anna noticed a frown of pain on her father's face. It could be the pressure of the braces. But it wasn't. The President was feeling the same spasms of pain across his chest that he had felt as he had read a speech aboard the destroyer *Cummings*. For a moment he seemed unable to bear it and unwilling to collapse. Then firmly he said:

Mr. Chief Justice, Mr. Vice President, my friends: You will understand and, I believe, agree with my wish that the form of this inauguration be simple and its words brief. We Americans of today, together with our allies, are passing through a period of supreme test. It is a test of our courage—of our resolve—of our wisdom—of our essential democracy. If we meet that test—successfully and honorably —we shall perform a service of historic importance which men and women and children will honor throughout all time. As I stand here today, having taken the solemn oath of office in the presence of my fellow countrymen—in the presence of our God—I know that it is America's purpose that we shall not fail.

It was not going to be a great speech, unless honor and goodness are, by recitation, aspirations to greatness. The President had tinkered with this speech for two weeks, overriding the phrases of his speech writers to pen his personal thoughts:

We have learned that we cannot live alone, at peace; that our own well-being is dependent on the well-being of other nations far away. We have learned that we must live as men and not as ostriches, nor as dogs in the manger. We have learned to be citizens of the world, members of the human community. We have learned the simple truth as Emerson said, that "the only way to have a friend is to be one."

Mr. Roosevelt cited that Almighty God had blessed America in many ways: "He has given to our country a faith which has become the hope of all peoples in an anguished world." His eyes were creased with pain as he looked out at the field of polka-dotted faces below.

So we pray to Him now for the vision to see our way clearly—to see the way that leads to a better life for ourselves and for all our fellow men—and to the achievement of His will to peace on earth.

The President nodded to his son. Arm in arm, the two walked back up the portico aisle, as the people stood, and hands reached out to shake his. Once inside, the Chief Executive almost collapsed in his wheelchair—the chair which, in public, always robbed him of his pride. Some of the family began to follow; Roosevelt asked his son to wheel him quickly to the Green Room. He motioned for the door to be closed. Then he sighed and rubbed his chest. The same pain he had sustained in Bremerton, he said, had hit him again "out there," although not quite so severe. "Jimmy," he said gravely, "I can't stand this unless you get me a stiff drink. You better make it straight." Colonel Roosevelt hurried and found a large tumbler. He half filled it with straight whiskey and handed it to his father. In spite of the President's agitation, he downed it at once and held the empty glass in trembling hands, head down, waiting for the pain to subside. Within a few minutes the chest pains faded. The President had to brace himself for three successive events: the cold salad luncheon for many guests; a semiformal tea at 4:00 P.M. for guests who could not be accommodated at the luncheon; and a family dinner in the evening consisting of a huge standing rib roast, a dish which FDR loved but had not seen around the White House in months. It is quite possible that, in the agonizing spasms of pain he felt on the portico, it may have passed across the President's mind that he might be the first President to drop dead at his inauguration. Certainly his manner toward his son showed fear. If so, FDR displayed enormous courage, standing hatless and coatless in the cold, to utter with fervor the few words he was prepared to leave as a legacy to America.

After the drink he could not bring himself to greet guests in the main lobby. He sent word that he thought it would be fitting for Mrs. Roosevelt and Mrs. Truman to greet the friends and members of the administration. He sent an usher for a few friends and, as his spirits rose, had luncheon with them behind locked doors in the Red Room. As on an earlier occasion, the chest pains disappeared. It must be assumed that Colonel Roosevelt suggested calling Bruenn or McIntire, although he did not mention it. The young man's sorrowful thoughts that he was losing his father, coupled with evidence of an acute chest seizure, would induce him to send an usher running for a physician. The fact that no one went for a doctor can only be attributed to the probable truth that the President declined such services. If so, he may have thought that he did not require medical help.

In the early evening Mrs. Roosevelt, knowing nothing of the seizure because the President asked his son not to mention it to anyone, visited her husband in his room. She knew that he was about to leave for a summit conference. "We discussed whether I should go," she wrote, "and he said: 'If you go they will all feel that they have to make a great big fuss, but if Anna goes, it will be simpler. Averell Harriman will bring his daughter down from Moscow.'" They had not "discussed" her attendance at Yalta; Mrs. Roosevelt put the question to him. She wanted to go. Anna was going; it looked as though mother and daughter were in competition. The President's excuse was weak. Almost as though he was placating his spouse with superficial sops, he smiled and said that, after this term, he and Eleanor might go off to the Arabian desert and show the Arabs how to cultivate it— make it bloom with food and flowers. A year and a half would be time enough, he said. Eleanor thought he was being silly. He went on suggesting a trip around the world on a slow freighter, stopping off at out-of-the-way places to use another year. She was not engaged by that idea either.

At about this time, someone—there are no identification records—called the Secret Service into conference to announce privately that the President's health was in a grave state. Extra Secret Service guards were to be assigned to Vice President Truman from now on. The Truman agents were told bluntly that "the President might go at any time." All were sworn to secrecy. It seems illogical to concede that the Secret Service would agree to increase its protection of the Vice President unless a person with strong medical credentials did it. Dr. Howard Bruenn was not permitted to discuss the President's health with anyone except Admiral Ross McIntire. The Admiral—"White House Physician"—was the only person with authority to discuss FDR's health with his family or any party outside the family.

And yet, if the public and private utterances of McIntire are scanned, it would seem that he spent considerable time sending coded messages to the fleet surgeon in the Mediterranean to get a team of doctors and medical corpsmen into Yalta at once to clean and fumigate Livadia Palace. "Admiral Olson, the officer in command," wrote McIntire, "reported to me that he threw up both hands at first sight of the palace, doubting that it could ever be made livable. The plumbing, though recently installed, functioned poorly; but worst of all was the dirt and abounding animal and insect life. . . . Every bed, piece of bedding, rug, furniture and hanging in the palace was given at least three sprayings, and then dusted with D.D.T. talcum-powder mixture."

Quietly, Mr. Roosevelt worked through the evening at his desk in the big Oval Office. There were orders, documents, promotions and letters to sign. It was Monday, January 22, 1945. The signature, once tall and legible, had become a scrawl, as though the signer was determined to write Franklin D. Roosevelt, managed to complete "Frankl" and lapsed into a series of wavy lines. At 9:45 P.M. those who would accompany him on the train ride to Norfolk were waiting in the diplomatic reception room. There were crusty old Fleet Admiral Leahy, Vice Admiral Ross McIntire, Director of War Mobilization Justice Jimmy Byrnes, dour under a snap brim gray fedora, hands deep in overcoat pockets, Edward Flynn of the Bronx, and Anna, whispering to her husband, Lieutenant Colonel Boettiger. Others, already on the train at the Bureau of Printing and Engraving, were Vice Admiral Brown, presidential naval aide; General "Pa" Watson, military aide; and Steve Early, press secretary who had told the three pool reporters that he could tell them nothing—no place, no date, no event—but that they would be taken to Casablanca, Africa, and left there until the White House had some news to reveal.

At the moment of 10:00 P.M. the President's wheelchair came into view. He was wearing his old gray campaign hat and his dark flowing Navy cape. The limousines loaded and purred softly, quietly out of the southeast gate and down past the Washington Monument, up the little hill, and down the ramp to the railroad platform. Once inside the well-lighted cars with shades drawn, the President told the conductor that he wanted to "go slow." At 10:47 the Pullmans began to move. This was the start of the most important voyage of all. The two big steam locomotives rocked slowly down silvery rails to Richmond, then on through the night to Fredericksburg, then onto the Chesapeake and Ohio tracks to Newport News, Virginia. The President chatted a little while with his daughter and Byrnes and Flynn, then retired to his bedroom.

Before leaving his office, Mr. Roosevelt had initialed two memoranda. One was a message to Stalin that he and Churchill had agreed not to have any reporters at ARGONAUT—"only Navy photographers to take a few pictures when the conference is over"; the other was an advice to all Cabinet members, most of whom did not know that he was leaving the country. It stated, in part: "If you have any urgent messages which you wish to get to me, I suggest you send them through the White House map room. However, only *absolutely urgent* messages should be sent." At the White House William Hassett kept his office lamp burning brightly as he penned his innermost thoughts. He was permitted to know that the President was en route "somewhere in the Middle-East," to meet Stalin and Churchill. Wisely, and with a degree of affection, he wrote:

Can think of only one thing as the President sets out on his momentous journey. Having achieved every political ambition a human being could aspire to, there remains only his place in history. That will be determined by the service which he renders to mankind. So F.D.R. will win his niche or pass into the oblivion which, in a quarter of a century, has swallowed all of the statesmen of the First World War —in reality only an earlier phase of this struggle.

Stalin remains an enigma; Churchill has brains, guts, courage, and a determination to preserve the British Empire. At seventy, as at every stage of his colorful career, he has everything except vision. And F.D.R., outside of his military and naval advisers, is leaning on some pretty weak reeds. But who am I to ponder the imponderable? God will give the President strength, courage and heavenly wisdom.

The train rocked easily through the countryside, through towns and over streams and into small forests where, eighty years earlier, young men in blue and in gray grappled, struggled and died in a long quest to maintain one strong nation or two weak ones. No stars could be seen. The only lights visible to the engineer of POTUS came from the fixed lanterns on the tender of the dead-heading locomotive ahead. Sometimes he lost those lights around the smooth curves of the Virginia countryside.

In New York the late-night talkers were still discussing the inauguration. James A. Farley, one-time Postmaster General, was on the phone from his Waldorf Towers suite with the one-time Secretary of State, Cordell Hull. Farley and his family had been invited to the inauguration but had declined with gratitude. Hull, in Washington, centered his soft lisping tones not on the historic importance of the occasion but on FDR's appearance. "Cordell and I agreed that he was a sick man . . . and should not be called upon to make decisions affecting this country and the world." In the late-hour bars other men of accomplishment who had attended the event centered their thoughts on Roosevelt's pallid countenance and physical weakness. Four Roosevelt proponents—Orson Welles, actor; Quentin Reynolds, Mark Van Doren and John Gunther, authors—were saddened by what they had seen. Each had participated in radio programs for the Democratic national committee. Reynolds, one-time sports writer, had stated repeatedly over the air: "You never take a pitcher out when he's ahead." Gunther summed up the collective feelings when he said: "I was terrified when I saw his face. I felt certain that he was going to die. All the light had gone out underneath the skin. It was like a parchment shade on a bulb that had been dimmed. . . . The muscles controlling the lips seemed to have lost part of their function."

The President slept well. At 6:25 A.M. shades of night still covered the choppy water of Newport News as POTUS slid slowly through the yards and under the covered Pier Six. Brakeshoes may have squealed a little, because some of the sleeping party awakened and raised drawing-room shades. The long gray silhouette of *Quincy* was moored to the southside. A deck crew in blues and peajackets stood at attention near the starboard gangway. Roosevelt sent word that he wanted no honors as Chief of State. Captain Elliott M. Senn, who had commanded this vessel since its acceptance trials, waited beside his executive officer, Commander Munroe B. Duffill. On the pier stood Brigadier General John R. Kilpatrick, commander of the port.

Someone slipped off the train and advised everyone that Mr. Roosevelt was still sleeping, that he might not embark for an hour or two. He rested until sunup. Others on the train had dressed and breakfasted, but they remained aboard. Secret Service men paced beside the train. The trains were sunken, so that the pier floor reached the top step of the Pullmans. When the President emerged, smiling good morning, he was surprised to see that the two-stage loading ramp fitted precisely to the level of the rear platform of the train and that the chair could glide easily to the quarterdeck of the cruiser. A bosun's mate piped him aboard with a shrill little whistle. Roosevelt shook hands with Senn, Duffill and a few others at exactly 8:00 A.M. and asked that the cruiser cast off as soon as possible. His chair disappeared over a starboard scupper as work parties singled up the mooring lines. Senn was on the bridge blinking messages to *Quincy*'s escorts standing out in the roads that she was casting off.

A lieutenant commander escorted Anna up one deck to flag quarters on the port side. *Quincy* received a heliograph message that there was a U-boat alert off Cape Henry. She moved slowly northeast out of the James River. As the big cruiser turned eastward in deeper water, she picked up speed. Ahead the destroyer *Satterlee* took station; Senn signaled "21 knots." Within 50 minutes both parties passed through the submarine gate and acknowledged departure. Below decks sonar men manned the listening devices but raised no bogies. Behind the bridge others manned the grip-type radar aboard and scanned the sea ahead for 50 miles. *Quincy* was lifting and falling easily in a head sea; the light cruiser *Springfield* took up station astern. At 10:32, the President came on deck with his daughter. Shielded by a side gun mount, he pointed out big estates on the distant Virginia shore. It was cold, but the sailor was again content. The destroyers *Tillman, Herndon* and *Satterlee* formed a screen ahead. From Patuxent, Maryland, small groups of PBY-4s emerged from the mists and patrolled far ahead of the task group. Below in the wardroom Secret Service men ate a late breakfast. Among them was the anonymous agent who was a strong swimmer. His function, in case of danger, was to pick FDR up, take him over the side and keep him afloat until help arrived.

In the late afternoon the task group had left the con-

tinental shelf and turned southeast on a course to bring
it a hundred miles to port of Bermuda. Captain Senn,
a seasoned sundowner, was in overall tactical command.
His course would permit him to take advantage of Patuxent air cover for 400 miles, then pick up patrol planes
from Bermuda. At sundown lights were extinguished
on all ships; radio silence was enforced. At night *Quincy*
picked up a radio relay from Washington: "If we had
spent ten years in our research we could not have found
a worse place in the world than Yalta. It is good
only for typhus and deadly lice who thrive in those parts.
The mountain drive is frightening and at times im-
passable. Churchill." In the morning *Quincy* received
an Intelligence message from Washington: the enemy
was aware of the conference and its location.

The President was committed. Nothing could turn
him back. When he learned that two elevators had been
installed and that he could enjoy the view from the
flag bridge, he seemed surprised and elated. He spent
the afternoon hours up there, propped up and belted
into an admiral's swivel chair, in silence, staring at the
sea. It changed mood from hour to hour. At one time
hundreds of feathers of foam raced toward him like
low-flying sea birds; at others there was a swell which
lifted the ship slow and high and dropped it, hissing
at the bows, into a trough. As the force passed Bermuda
to the south, Senn set course dead east and racked up
22.5 knots. Warm wind ripped and sang through the
rigging and the radar grids; a green-white bridal train
formed behind *Quincy* to the light cruiser *Springfield*.
Ahead, the three destroyers maintained station near
the horizon. Now and then, when a sonar man thought
he had made an undersea contact, one of them would
be dispatched from the formation to run it down. The
ships were running east along the thirtieth parallel.

If there was danger, it would be on this long leg between Bermuda and the Canary Islands off the African
Coast. The antidote to U-boats was speed, and Senn kept
the force moving swiftly, even when the destroyers were
shipping heavy seas over the forecastles. Far to the north,

other destroyers were assuming lonesome stations every 300 miles across the Atlantic. Their task was as rescue teams when, a few days later, the ranking members of the State Department and the Joint Chiefs and their aides would fly to Malta. The President had said his party would consist of 35 persons. It was closer to 150.

By the morning of January 27 FDR was in mid-Atlantic in bright sunlight. His personal routine aboard ship was simple: he retired early and slept late. He breakfasted with Anna, sometimes with Byrnes and Flynn. At night he watched a motion picture with a few friends in his quarters. He ate little, in spite of Admiral McIntire's pleas. He displayed an interest in watching the daily mail pouch come aboard. Far astern, radar would pick up a long-range plane, demand code-of-the-day identification and then watch it drop a flotation bag into the sea abreast of the force. Captain Senn would dispatch a destroyer aft to pick it up as the courier plane turned, heading back to Bermuda. A work party of sailors aft of the seaplane hangars would pay out a manila line from *Quincy* with a weight on it. The destroyer would creep up on it, engage and hook it and attach the pouch. It would then be hauled aboard *Quincy* and its contents brought to the President in his cabin.

In conversations with intimates, Mr. Roosevelt mentioned that the event he had tried to avoid—meeting Jesse Jones—had occurred the day before he left Washington. Mr. Jones was hopping mad. The two were alone in the President's study for forty-five minutes. It was a painful interview. "I did the talking," Jones told James Farley later in the week, "I talked for forty of the forty-five minutes I was with him." The discharged Secretary of Commerce had a lot of critical thoughts about how Roosevelt was running the government. He covered many subjects. "I told him I knew he never liked me, but was willing to forget that in the interests of service." Roosevelt, he said, should have fired him personally and "not in the backhanded way he did it. I told him what I thought of Wallace—not personally, that would have taken too long—but as Secretary of Commerce. I told him Wallace was just incompetent."

Roosevelt pleaded that he wanted Jesse Jones to remain in government and asked him please to see Ed Stettinius about an ambassadorial post. Jones scorned the offer. "The President didn't have much to say. He evaded my eyes. As I started out, he said, 'Good-bye, I'll be seeing you soon.' I looked at him and said, 'No, Mr. President. This is good-bye. I am not coming back.' " Jones returned to his large office and released the story of his firing, and his personal outrage, to the press. Even the newspapers sympathetic to Roosevelt thought that the letter firing Jones was sophomoric, poorly phrased, discharging a Secretary of Commerce to make room for a man he fired as Vice President. Jones appealed to the conservatives in Congress not to confirm the appointment unless FDR stripped the Reconstruction Finance Corporation and other governmental appendages from Commerce. It became apparent that the President would have to do this or risk a long fight on the Hill. In time Wallace won his appointment, but his department had been skeletonized.

The First Lady had reached a stage where she became more ruffled by a political affront than a personal one. Her husband had refused her plea to be taken to historic Yalta, and Mrs. Roosevelt hid whatever hurt she had felt. But the explosion of Jesse Jones was too much for forbearance; even though FDR said not to send messages unless they were urgent, she wrote: "Of course Jones has behaved horribly & your letter when published was hard on Wallace. I know you wrote it hoping to make Jones feel better but I guess he's the kind of dog you should have ousted the day after election & given him the reasons. He would not have published that letter! . . ."

Mr. Roosevelt, as Farley and Hull pointed out, was not in strong physical and mental condition to make grave decisions. Exhaustion, physical and psychological, was his companion. And yet he had to beware of the counsel given to him by friends as well as enemies. He

was on the high seas one day when the Joint Chiefs
of Staff, in secret session at the Pentagon, signed a directive for his attention stating that they were "working towards USSR entry into the war against Japan . . . Russia's
entry at as early a date as possible consistent with her
ability to engage in offensive operations is necessary
to provide maximum assistance to our Pacific operations." The ranking gentlemen could not be expected
to place the atom bomb in the scales of their thinking,
but, at the Pacific Conference the previous July, Nimitz
and MacArthur had boasted of what they had done
to defeat the Empire of Japan, and, optimistically, what
they planned to do. An official and secret report to the
President as recently as January 9 spelled out the
triumphs:

*The United States Pacific Campaign has proceeded on
schedule with clocklike precision. The successful landing
on Luzon has assured the early recapture of the Philippines
and places all of the Japanese sea communications to the
south in an almost untenable situation, both from American
Air power and American Naval power. Our submarine, air
and surface attack has continued a relentless destruction of
Japanese mercantile and naval power. The establishment of
B-29s on Saipan has brought the Japanese Homeland
within frequent heavy bomber range.*

The report did not mention that General Curtis LeMay
planned a B-29 fire raid on Tokyo which would reduce
a third of the metropolis to ashes, but it did ask for
"Russian participation . . . for a speedy kill."

Politically, it seemed not to occur to U.S. statesmen,
including the President, that Russia was eager to enter
the war against Japan just as soon as Germany fell and
army divisions could be transferred to the Manchurian
border. In retrospect it is clear that no power could
have kept the Soviets out of the Far Eastern war because
they had old scores to settle dating to their defeat in the
Russo-Japanese War of 1904. Nor did they forget that
it was another Roosevelt—Theodore—who had forced

the Russians to submit to a humiliating peace treaty at Portsmouth, New Hampshire. The Kuriles had been taken from them; rights to the warm water at Port Arthur had been denied. And yet, in the forthcoming conference, FDR wondered what concessions he would have to make to Josef Stalin to bring the Russians into a war the Americans were winning alone. It occurred to no responsible American official that the Russians would move in on Japan and China when they chose—with or without American sanction. The Pentagon and the State Department told FDR that he would have to give the Soviets something to bait them into engagement in another war. General George Marshall, most respected officer in the Allied group, was beset by a fear of the Japanese Kwantung Army, consisting of 700,000 elite troops, then stationed in China. He felt it would cost "hundreds of thousands of American lives" to invade China and defeat the Kwantung Group. He wanted Russia to do it. Marshall ignored the advice from the U.S. Navy Intelligence group operating under Captain Ellis Zacharias, which had been intercepting and decoding Japanese military messages for four years, that the Kwantung Army existed "primarily on paper"; that it had been drained by the Japanese High Command, which needed those troops as replacements on the necklace of islands invaded by the Americans. Successive victories by the Americans brought the Joint Chiefs of Staff closer to their inner, unreasoning fear of the death struggle which would take place on the big Japanese home islands. It was called Operation Olympic and successive reports to the President estimated that American forces would sustain one million casualties. Roosevelt was bringing this fear to Yalta.

British Foreign Secretary Anthony Eden, in Moscow, sent a message of warning to Churchill before the two prepared to fly to Malta:

There may be little argument about a Russian claim to recover possession of south Sakhalin, which was ceded to Japan by the Treaty of Portsmouth in 1905. The Ameri-

*cans may look more closely at any claim to take the Kuriles.
But a most difficult issue is likely to arise over Manchuria
and Korea. We do not yet know what Russian requirements
are likely to be, but their conformity with the Cairo Declaration for which we ourselves share responsibility, will be
closely scrutinized by the Chinese, the Americans, and
others; and it is possible that these requirements can only
be satisfied at the expense of incessant friction with the
Chinese, who may expect American support and expect ours
also. At all events there is a potential cauldron of international dispute. It seems advisable therefore, at this stage, to
go warily and to* avoid anything like commitments or encouragement to Russia.

Thus, before the conference opened, Churchill and FDR
were on divergent courses.

When Eden flew home to London, his deputy, Alexander Cadogan, got to the Foreign Secretary first and begged
to know what Great Britain proposed to do about Poland.
Time was running out; the Russians were investing the
nation with troops—what to do; what to do? The result
of the talk seemed hopeful to Sir Alec but, in the cold
light of history, appears to be childishly unrealistic.
"However, some sense resulted," he wrote. "Clean the
slate; remove Lublin and London 'govts.' and set up
something more generally acceptable to all. Don't know
whether Joe [Stalin] will play on this. He might."

While Great Britain and the United States were
proceeding toward Yalta with separate and, in part,
opposing world plans, Josef Stalin, whose boast was
that he always knew what he wanted, hesitated on the
Polish front for four days. The massive Soviet offensive
had broken the German lines in many places, and Russian
armies had to be detached to encircle and sweep up
German divisions left in the rear. In spite of phenomenal
success, Stalin appeared to be beset with his apprehension
of a month earlier, that the Russian soldier was tired
of fighting and would be more inclined to lose a battle
on foreign soil than on his own. On January 25 Stalin
phoned Marshal Zhukov near Poznan and asked what

his plans were. The Marshal, a short square chunk of man, said simply, "The enemy is demoralized and is no longer able to offer serious resistance." One might have expected, as Zhukov certainly did, that Stalin would say, "Well, on to Berlin or as far as you can go." To the contrary, he lied to Zhukov: "The First Ukrainian Army Group is now unable to move any farther and to protect your left flank, since it will be busy for some tiime liquidating the enemy." Zhukov knew that his left was not exposed. He asked for orders. Stalin told him to stand fast. Zhukov wrote, "I asked the Supreme Commander in Chief not to stop the advance of the army group." Stalin was adamant. This was no time to take risks. It is possible that he was making a political rather than a military decision. As his armies stood, he could go to Yalta with an array of victories to use as a dominant bargaining position. If, for any reason, his armies faltered within the next two weeks, his position would be weaker. (After the war German General Heinz Guderian acknowledged that Hitler had insufficient reserves to stage a counterattack or even to stop the forward progress of Zhukov.)

Two days later Zhukov phoned Stalin in Moscow and received permission to move on Berlin, "but he refused to assign additional forces, which were needed for the plan." Forty-eight hours after that decision Stalin gave Marshal Koniev permission to take Berlin "with his right flank"—the army which Stalin insisted, on the twenty-fifth, was "unable to move any farther." In changing his mind, Stalin and his military Stavka now ordered both Zhukov and Koniev to take Berlin, pitting two Soviet marshals in competition for a great prize.

It becomes apparent that the Big Three approached Yalta . as adversaries, each with individual goals and bargaining postures. Seldom have friends met with more surface camaraderie and subterranean suspicion. Nowhere in modern history is there an instance in which victors met, not to seek justice, but to debate until, in time, each revealed his minimum demands of the others.

The task group was in an easterly rain on the twenty-fourth in addition to a running quartering sea. The destroyer *Satterlee* reported by heliograph that she had experienced a 61-degree roll, but Captain Senn maintained course and speed. The incoming pouch was retrieved with difficulty—an airtight aluminum can was used for the mail. One of the messages was from Harry Hopkins, who had been to London and was now in Paris trying to placate the ruffled de Gaulle. The words came a long way: from Paris to London by courier, from there to the Washington map room by wireless, from there to Bermuda and thence the cruiser *Quincy* by plane:

January 24, 1945
No. 2064 to Map Room White House from Harry Hopkins
Send following to President:
Have had very satisfactory visit London. Churchill well. He says that if we had spent ten years on research we could not have found a worse place in the world than MAGNETO, but that he feels he can survive it by bringing an adequate supply of whiskey. . . .

Harry

At 10:31 P.M. *Quincy* flashed to *Satterlee* to leave formation for Bermuda. The deep, steady roll of the cruiser forced the President to hang onto both sides of his cabin table. This type of swing, on trains or ships, usually caused him excruciating pain in the hip sockets, but he did not complain.

Hopkins had sent an optimistic report to Roosevelt regarding his visit with Churchill, but he refrained from reporting on Paris until he could meet FDR at Malta. Hopkins and Ambassador Jefferson Caffery had an appointment with Foreign Minister Georges Bidault first. The Frenchman was cordial. Hopkins, making an effort to reach the nub of the problem, said he thought that official relations between France and the United States were "at low ebb." Bidault exposed the palms of his hands in a broad Gallic gesture. Hopkins said it was time to find the cause and correct it. The Foreign Minister shook his head, conceding that de Gaulle was sometimes "difficult to handle. He believes that Frenchmen always try to please the man to whom they are talking. The General thinks they overdo it and he adopts a different attitude. He make no effort to please."

The President's ailing old friend and confidant was, in most circumstances, a successful fixer. He decided he would open the interview with de Gaulle by admitting past errors and asking the Provisional President to wipe the slate clean and start anew. Three men—FDR, Churchill and Stalin—could have told Harry Hopkins in advance that the supine attitude would only induce the General to jump on his prostrate body. The interview was a disaster. Hopkins tried to concede rudeness in the past but promised cordial equality in the future. De Gaulle's face remained long and impassive. "If you really mean," he said, "that relations between the United States and France are not all they should be, why don't you do something about it?" Innocently, Hopkins asked for an instance. The austere Frenchman replied that the Big Three arrogantly refused to make the conference a Big Four, and had not sent him an invitation. Rapidly he continued, saying that he was prepared to admit that the United States had helped France "by arming and equipping our troops—but you always seem to do it grudgingly and under pressure."

Hopkins was a master at containing his emotions, which may be a reason why his ulcers flourished. He did not remind de Gaulle that America had spent enormous amounts of blood and treasure to liberate his country from a humiliating defeat. Instead, he kept speaking of goodwill and the long and natural friendship of the two countries. When de Gaulle closed the conversation by standing, Hopkins said he could feel the frost. Later Harry Hopkins suggested to Bidault that the Big Three might be willing to invite de Gaulle to the latter stages of the summit conference—"when European matters are to be discussed." Failing that, de Gaulle might wish to meet the President at some point in North Africa

on the return voyage. De Gaulle scorned both notions
out of hand. He refused to consider them and waved
Bidault away. Caffery sent a message to Stettinius: "Mr.
Hopkins made an excellent impression and was very
sympathetic. His stay here was very useful and timely."
The State Department and FDR believed it.

The President had been at sea two days when the
flying contingents left Washington for Malta. It was,
as Edward Stettinius complained, "a bitterly cold morning." The Joint Chiefs of Staff huddled in one corner
of a hangar with their fourragèred aides. The second-
echelon military were in a larger group, armed with
heavy briefcases. The State Department contingent,
mostly in homburgs, chesterfield overcoats and gloves,
nodded pleasantly to the other groups and waited in the
din for an array of C-54s to warm up. They were, for
their time, big, noisy and slow. They cruised at 220 miles
per hour and had few of the navigational aids which
would be devised later.

Stettinius and his State Department group started
down the runway at 9:00 A.M., followed closely by the
others. With him in the rear section were H. Freeman
Matthews, chief of the European Affairs Division; Alger
Hiss, the tall lean young man who had much to do with
whatever success was achieved at Dumbarton Oaks and
who now was deeply immersed in the articles and provisions of the United Nations charter; and Wilder Foote,
Assistant to the Secretary of State. Charles Bohlen, Russian language expert of the State staff, was with Hopkins
in Paris and would join Stettinius at Malta; Averell
Harriman, in Moscow, would meet the party at Yalta.

Three hours and fifteen minutes later, the C-54 swept
down to Kindler Field at Bermuda. The Secretary of
State seemed surprised to find himself perspiring in 70-
degree temperature. He stood watching the other planes
circle and come in. An officer at the airport told Stettinius
that the array of planes could not be refueled and ready
to leave for Terceira, in the Azores, until about 7:00
P.M. Some of the party boarded cars to inspect the Naval
Operating Base at Hamilton. In the evening the planes

took off one by one, planning to reach Terceira about sunup. Stettinius, who had no deep comprehension of geography, insisted they were flying over the "South Atlantic." At 10:00 P.M. the Secretary of State announced that he would retire and he asked an aide, Major Richmond, if he should undress or sleep in his clothing. "You'd better undress," the major said solemnly, "because if we hit the water, you'll freeze over quicker."

At Terceira the Secretary of State walked to where General George Marshall was standing, watching the early sun touch the steep chocolate cliffs of the island. Stettinius said he would like to have a private word with Marshall. His office was in receipt of Intelligence reports which showed that the Russians were "busy" in the western part of the United States. He wanted to know if the General thought that this indicated the Soviets had learned something of the development of America's atom bomb. Marshall, who had been opposed to revealing the secret to Stettinius and Jimmy Byrnes, said he didn't think it mattered. But, said Stettinius, suppose the Russians at the Crimean Conference asked the President about it? Shouldn't he be prepared with a response?

General Marshall hunched his chin into his fleece-lined collar. No, he said, he did not think the President should be apprised of the suspicions of the Secretary of State, and no, he did not think the United States should plan an answer for such a question. It would be better, he said, to wait and see if the question came up—*if*. Marshall was aware that it was the Secretary of State who had informed the President that the enemy knew about the Big Three Conference and its location. The two chatted for a while and reboarded for a flight to North Africa. The final leg would be to find the tiny island of Malta. Marshall, a first-class military man, knew that if Adolf Hitler was aware of the conference site and attached any military importance to the death of the President, he could order Admiral Dönitz to station a wolf pack of submarines at the narrow Strait of Gibraltar—everyone knew that Roosevelt preferred ship to plane—and, as insurance, could dispatch long-range German bombers from the north of Italy for a 500-mile bombing run on the *Quincy* at a prearranged signal from U-boats. If all of them missed, additional bomber attacks could be made in the Mediterranean as the cruiser approached Malta. Either Hitler was not aware of the place and date of the conference, or the killing of Franklin Roosevelt was not important to German plans. The Nazi Chancellor had told his staff repeatedly that he had hoped the Big Three would meet; the more they met, the more they would disagree on the spoils of the war. Two ideologies, the British Empire and the American democracy, were bound, in Hitler's estimation, to come to blows with the Russian Communists.

On Sunday, January 28, Lieutenant Duane A. Brady, Navy chaplain, conducted services on the *Quincy* amidships at 11:15 A.M. The quarterdeck aft was swept by strong winds, and as many sailors as possible crowded the center of the vessel either to pray or to see President Roosevelt or both. Mr. Roosevelt sat bareheaded in his wheelchair with Arthur Prettyman standing beside him. Some of the crew, especially firemen from below decks, had not seen FDR since the ship left Hampton Roads. They gaped and gawked. The President nodded and smiled. The most exciting event of the morning occurred as soon as the chaplain completed divine services. The U.S. Army hospital ship *Acadia* was sighted 13 miles on the horizon, heading in the same direction as the task group, but much slower.

At sea, there is something compelling about sighting another ship. FDR watched until the huge red cross amidships was barely visible astern, then he wheeled into his quarters for lunch. And thus he missed the truly exciting event: over the horizon astern came the light cruiser *Savannah,* accompanied by the destroyers *Murphy, Frankford* and *Baldwin.* At the same time Lieutenant Rigdon, Roosevelt's inquisitive seagoing secretary, sighted the oil tanker U.S.S. *Chemung* escorted by the destroyer *McCormick. Savannah* and

her terrier friends had left Virginia two days before
Roosevelt departed from the White House. They had
been told to move slowly, conserve fuel and arrange
to rendezvous with the group at 31 degrees north, 17
west, shortly after noon on Sunday. The *Savannah* and
her destroyers relieved the older escort group and took
stations. Captain Senn ordered the cruiser *Springfield*
to refuel from the tanker *Chemung* and head for duty
at the Panama Canal. The three destroyers were told to
proceed at speed to Casablanca. The *Chemung* was
ordered to sail north to the Azores. It was a magnificent
display of U.S. Navy "close-order drill."

One of the detached destroyers carried a Top Secret
from Roosevelt to Churchill:

The approaches to ARGONAUT *appear to be much more
difficult than at first reported. I will have my advance party
make recommendations as to how I shall travel after Malta.
I agree that we must notify U.J. as soon as we can fix our
schedule in the light of present information.*

Roosevelt

In the ship's log Captain Senn noted that he continued
to hold mast courts-martial. The average punishment
meted by the square-jawed, big-chested captain was
"twenty days in the brig on bread and water. A full
meal to be served every third day." The most unusual
occurrence in the log was that, in sick bay, two sailors
had been operated on for acute appendicitis in one day.
Now and then Senn had reports of U-boat echoes, but
none were found. The destroyer *Murphy* ran down
a strong underwater echo and swung at top speed toward
it. She returned to the group an hour later to report
that she had depth-bombed a huge fish. The sea was
flat and oily except for the widening furrows made by
the task group. In the calm the speed of the *Quincy*
created a 22.5-knot wind, and the President spent an
hour in sunshine screened by a gun mount.

On Monday morning Winston Churchill boarded the
four-engine Skymaster given to him by General H. H.

Arnold, U.S.A. With him was his daughter Sarah, in military uniform, and ranking members of the Foreign Office. Ahead by hours were other planes, loaded with members of the British staff. The Prime Minister's advanced age did not, in most cases, lessen his indomitability. His daily regime of rich food, brandy, an afternoon nap, frequent emotional explosions and the use of strong cigars cannot be described as medically indicated for a man past seventy. But Winston Churchill was bright of eye, pink of cheek, one whose good health seldom deserted him. On this trip he developed a high fever. Lord Moran, personal physician to the Prime Minister, could not find the cause and promised medical tests at an infirmary when they landed at Valletta, in Malta.

The plane flew all night, with one stop, and, after a sound sleep, Churchill awakened refreshed and with a normal temperature. The Prime Minister was complacent and refused medical examination; he was less worried—perhaps more fatalistic—than Lord Moran. His round face was at the window as the Skymaster approached Luqa airfield and he pointed out dozens of American aircraft already on the field. It was not until he stepped from the plane that he learned that one of his staff planes failed to find Malta in the morning mist, ran out of fuel and fell into the sea, killing all but five persons. "Such," he said, shaking his head, "are the strange ways of fate." Mike Reilly watched with interest as Churchll and Eden disembarked, to be taken off in limousines to the British cruiser *Orion,* docked in Valletta harbor. Reilly was more interested in the number of huge American and British airplanes on the field. He counted 90 and wondered how they would all manage to land on a single metal strip at Saki.

On the same morning the *Quincy* was southeast of Madeira, making a fast zigzag approach to the Strait of Gibralter. Course and speed were set for a late night passage through the narrow entrance into the Mediterranean. It was an ideal place for spies, both from the Spanish side and the Atlas Mountains of North Africa. The United States had complained that the Spanish, a few months earlier, had illuminated the American battleship *Iowa* with searchlights as she transited the strait. Captain Senn, as well as Admirals Leahy and Brown, wondered if the Spaniards would permit the *Quincy* to go through without the bright lights. Air cover for the ships came from the Azores and a "Jeep" carrier stationed 100 miles north.

Roosevelt was pained to receive a long, involved message from Sam Rosenman advising him to sign an executive order disengaging the big Federal Loan Agency from the Department of Commerce. Otherwise, he said, advocates of Henry Wallace, including Mrs. Roosevelt and Henry Morgenthau, felt that the Iowa farmer could not be confirmed as Secretary of Commerce. The President, to whom surrender was anathema, had dug this political grave. For four years Wallace, as Vice President, had been president of the United States Senate. A White House poll showed clearly that the senators would not endorse his nomination for Commerce, unless the department was stripped of the extra powers it had under Jesse Jones. A few Roosevelt protagonists felt that he should drop Wallace and nominate someone else. After considerable scowling thought, FDR decided to divorce the loan agency from the Department of Commerce and take a chance on paying off his political promise to Wallace. It worked, but it proved to the august senators that the invincible FDR could be maneuvered into a position where he would have to truckle.

The convergence at the summit meeting from many directions was remarkably efficient. The Russians, the British and the Americans each had much larger contingents of staff than had been expected. In Moscow Stavka, which did not want Stalin to risk his life in a plane, sent him south through the heavy snows in an armored train on the thirtieth. Harriman, who was supposed to have had a berth on Stalin's train, flew on ahead, inspected Yalta and then flew to Malta to greet Roosevelt. The master of all the Russias sat at a railroad car window in daylight hours and saw the desolation wrought by the German armies. By accident, the rails were following the high-tide mark of the Nazi advance; part of the way Stalin was close to the great Don River. His train, devoid of special markings but manned by troops on flatcars with antiaircraft guns, went through Veronezh, Kharkov and Dnepropetrovsk to the Crimea. He saw the blackened ruins stark against the swirling drifts of old snow, and he saw many cities where everybody was poor and cold and hungry. He did not pause, except for water and fuel; Stalin had no time for sentiment.

On the same day American generals and admirals in Cairo boarded planes for Malta. Foreign Minister Anthony Eden, comfortable aboard the British cruiser *Sirius,* was requested to get in a longboat at 6:00 P.M. and cross the harbor of Valletta for a conference with Churchill in *Orion.* Cadogan, who was left behind, said he suspected that the Prime Minister had slept all day and would confer with Eden until 3:00 A.M. Stettinius and his staff had been ordered by the President to remain at Marrakech, Africa, from January 26 to 29, so that there would be little or no time for them to confer with the English. On the twenty-ninth Ed was directed to fly to Naples to meet Harry Hopkins and obtain his report on the conferences in London and Paris. This would kill another day or two so that Stettinius could not reach Malta before the thirtieth or thirty-first.

The *Quincy* made radar contact with Tangier, 60 miles east, on the evening of January 30. The presidential group insisted that he have another birthday party because this was the true date of his sixth-third anniversary, and several hurried below to the ship's commissary to buy small gifts. Mr. Roosevelt arranged a small dinner in his cabin. Present were his daughter, Jimmy Byrnes, Ed Flynn, McIntire, Admiral Brown, Steve Early, Pa Watson and Admiral Leahy. It wasn't easy to crowd all into the small dining room. Mr. Roosevelt feigned pleasant dismay when he found that there was not one but four birthday cakes. His favorite Filipino chef baked one; the staff officers of *Quincy* had one; the warrant officers had a third; the crew baked a large square one engraved in icing "1945?" This drew the first hearty laugh Byrnes heard from the President on the voyage. FDR insisted that all four cakes be brought on deck before dark, so that motion pictures could be made of him cutting each one, with his friends, the chefs, standing behind him. Anna sat on one side, Byrnes on the other. The Director of War Mobilization was so disturbed by the haggard appearance of the President that he spoke to Anna Boettiger and McIntire about it. Byrnes said that he did not believe that Mr. Roosevelt's wasted appearance could be due to "sinus flareups" and a cold. Anna, who was chilled with worry about her father, said that his open mouth made him look bad, but that it helped him to breathe easier. "He isn't really ill," she said. McIntire pooh-poohed Byrnes's fears. He rendered the stock explanation: "a combination of sinus infection and a cold." The Admiral was sure that the President would "bounce back" with his old resilience.

On successive after-dinner occasions Byrnes and Admiral Leahy tried to engage the President in conversations about Yalta, especially the part dealing with the United Nations. They tried on at least four evenings but were met with wandering generalizations. Byrnes was fearful that Roosevelt had not studied the situation and did not know the solutions to problems which might have been anticipated. He felt that the Boss was going to Yalta with little or no preparation. Toward the end of the voyage Jimmy Byrnes asked if the State Department had furnished research material to FDR. The President nodded. "It is below decks in the custody of Lieutenant Rigdon," he said. Byrnes sought it. In his estimation, there was a wealth of material—"splendid studies." The President did not want to read it.

Fair skies made the Mediterranean appear to be cobalt blue. The weather was warmer and Roosevelt spent a little time on deck. Captain Senn hugged the African shore line, remaining as far from the European side as possible. He requested, and received, daily and nightly air cover from bases in Morocco, Algeria and Tunisia. The captain was not as relaxed as his distinguished guest;

in fact, as he turned Cape Bon on the edge of Tunisia, Senn directed his group to sail southeast, instead of east, directly to Malta.

At Naples Harry Hopkins and Ed Stettinius held a long conference before flying on to Malta. As usual, Hopkins had no time for the niceties of diplomacy. He said that Bidault did not pretend to know all that de Gaulle had in mind, but the French wanted some "special kind of control" over the German Ruhr and the west bank of the Rhine. This seemed a repetition of the French position after World War I, when poilus invested the Ruhr Valley. Hitler had abrogated that part of the Versailles treaty by ordering his legions to cross the Rhine in the French presence. He won that gamble.

Bidault said that France did not want any German territory but expected the war-producing centers to be "internationalized, with the French predominating." Hopkins doubted that de Gaulle would accept the informal invitation to Yalta "at the end of the sessions" or to chat with FDR aboard the *Quincy* in an African harbor. On the morning of the thirty-first Stettinius took Hopkins aboard his plane for the trip to Malta. It was only a three-hour flight, but "Hopkins was so sick that we put him to bed." Stettinius said that, from his observations, the frail man with the saffron skin lived on "coffee, cigarettes, an amazingly small amount of food and paregoric."

At Valletta Stettinius paid a courtesy call on Winston Churchill. In spite of Roosevelt's warnings not to discuss matters of state with the British, Stettinius asked the British Prime Minister "what he thought of our formula for voting in the Security Council." It became obvious that Churchill had not seen it. He opened a monologue saying that the United Nations should be designed for "keeping the peace." Economic and other political matters should be handled directly between governments, he said. Anthony Eden, who was present, disagreed; so did Stettinius. Later the American Secretary of State wrote: "I told him how disappointed we would be if the Economic and Social Council which we had proposed at Dumbarton Oaks did not have an important function." Churchill blinked and jammed his cigar in his mouth. The conversation was over.

The island of Malta, which had absorbed as much bombing per square foot as any battlefield in the world, consisted of large areas of ruins, with black-aproned women staring at distinguished strangers as they sorted the rubbish. The British, who were hosts, knew that there were not a sufficient number of intact buildings to furnish quarters for the visitors. Everyone was given a chit with a billet marked on it. Some were in small staterooms aboard the passenger liner *Eastern Prince;* Harriman had a cabin aboard Churchill's cruiser *Orion.* A habitable building called Montgomery House was used by Generals Marshall, Somervell and other U.S. Army brass; also by Admiral Ernest J. King and naval officers of rank. The Secretary of State found himself in a cabin aboard the British cruiser *Sirius,* directly across a corridor from Anthony Eden. The British Governor of the island gave a formal dinner for the visitors but had trouble locating them.

February 1945

THE BIG ARMORED TRAIN SWEPT SOUTH, CASTING THE snows aside like a bridal veil inlaid with diamonds. The host was aboard, and the host was going to be one day late. His guests would arrive in the Crimea at noon on February 3. On February 1 Josef Stalin radioed ahead to Foreign Minister Vyacheslav Molotov that he would arrive on the fourth. No reason was given; none asked. It is possible that he was worried rather than elated because Marshals Zhukov and Koniev were close to the edge of the Oder River in Brandenburg province. Marshal Chuikov claimed to have made several bridgehead crossings. He had been denied permission to expand them, 50 miles from the great capital on the Prussian Plain, Berlin. The order came from the armored train: turn forces north to Pomerania; assist Rokossovsky to liquidate thirty German divisions.

Millions of Russian men, guns and tanks ground to a halt on the east bank of the Oder. This would be the new border of Poland; the German land to be given in return for what Russia would take in the east. Josef Stalin proposed to take from the Poles in square miles exactly twice the amount he would compensate them with in German territory. He was a short, broad, almost austere man, given to gleaming boots, baggy pants and plain khaki blouse. He was a man of big hard hands and big hard suspicions. He had little time for the niceties of conversation or good manners.

Stalin knew that one of Churchill's objections to the transfer of a section of German territory to Poland was that there were nine million Germans living there, and the population transition would present an insuperable problem in logistics. The Soviet Army commanders had promised their millions of soldiers complete freedom of action when they reached German soil. Roadside signs proclaimed in Russian: "You are now on German soil." All the excesses began there, and Josef Stalin would not countermand the sadistic excessses. So the homes were robbed; unwary females were raped; tens of thousands of buildings were burned. What the German Army had done in the Ukraine was now being done to Germany.

The dictator was a chain smoker. He preferred American cigarettes to Russian and he was versatile in the use of his pudgy fingers. At the Kremlin he often held his cigarette between thumb and index finger and puffed with his chin in the palm of his hand. On other occasions he held it between the second and third fingers and slapped himself lightly on the lips as he puffed. It is unlikely that he thought of the antiaircraft gunners freezing on the rocking, squealing flatcars as the big train roared through forests and blackened cities. It was so

cold that the train commander relieved each group of
gunners after one hour on duty. The Supreme Commander had slightly more mercy for Russians than for
aliens. His Foreign Minister and Deputy Chief of Staff,
General Antonov, had seen Stalin, doodling during a
conference, write the figure 20,000,000 on a pad. This
was the number of Russians, military and civilian, killed
or missing in the war. Russia easily paid the highest
price in blood throughout the war.

Stalin had other plainspoken figures. At the end of
January, he estimated the German armies at 313 divisions
and 32 brigades. Of these, 185 divisions and 21
brigades were on the Russian front; Eisenhower's forces
in France and General Alexander's in Italy faced a
total of 108 divisions and 7 brigades. The weight of
war was on the Russians—ergo, the Kremlin should dictate
the European peace. Stalin's mind operated with simple
Slavic logic. He had a minuscule imagination, a broad
(as opposed to subtle) sense of humor and no tolerance
for idealism or the poetry of existence. He understood
the number 20,000,000. No nation in the history of
man had sustained those losses; no nation survived to
carry the battle to the enemy and crush him in the rubble
he created.

Among foreigners, British Foreign Secretary Anthony
Eden understood Josef Stalin as well as anyone. The
Right Honorable gentleman was suave, one with a soft
voice and elegant words, one who smiled graciously
from under a dash of mustache even when he was losing
a diplomatic struggle. Stalin and Eden were opposites
in about every way. Everything that one man was the
other was not, but they had debated several times on
grave political and military matters and each respected
the other for his stand. The Russo-German treaty of
August 1939 was as ashes in the mouth of Eden, but,
when Hitler violated the pact and attacked the Soviet
Union in June 1941, Anthony Eden waited until winter
and then flew to Moscow to ask if England could help.
It is one of the great ironies of history that, as both
nations were on their knees before the blitzkrieg and

the German armies were moving toward Moscow and Stalingrad. Stalin accepted the offer of assistance and began to outline what he expected after Russian victory.

Eden was stunned as Stalin, sitting at a polished table with his interpreter Pavlov, said that Great Britain could not *fly* military assistance to him, nor would he ask it. It would come in ship bottoms or not at all. Stalin said that when the war was over, he would like the Russian border to be based on the Curzon Line; he expected to incorporate parts of Finland and Hungary into the Soviet Union, besides which Russia would expect to "control" the Balkan states. Austria, the dictator said, should be severed from Germany and restored to an independent status; the Rhineland should be cut off from Germany and made a protectorate; East Prussia should rightfully be given to the Poles; the Sudetenland ought to be returned to Czechoslovakia; Germany should be made to pay reparations in plants, factories and tools. Money should not be involved, because that—and the exchange of the inflated German mark—was what caused German reparations payments to collapse after World War I.

Eden was shocked. German cannon were in the snows outside of Moscow. Russian urban populations were on the roads to the Urals. This man with the hair and mustache of freshly mined iron ore was dictating a peace treaty from a position of defeat. The Foreign Minister had seldom been at a loss for words. He stammered that he was not empowered to reach any postwar agreements with the Russian Marshal; he had been ordered to ask if assistance was needed now, and what kind. Besides, he said, the United States had been attacked at Pearl Harbor a few weeks earlier, and the United States would have to be a party to any agreement. "Take what I have said back to London with you," Stalin said in his soft hoarse voice. "Discuss them and communicate them to the United States."

Three interminably bloody years had followed. Stalin sat in his great train, calling aides and discussing diplomatic and military aspects of all the booty he pro-

posed to demand at Yalta. Casually, he had promised
Roosevelt and Churchill that, within three months after
victory over Germany, the Soviet Union would declare
war on Japan "and break her spine." One of the secrets
he did not reveal was that for more than a year Russia
had been moving Lend-Lease weapons to the Far East,
where they reposed along the Amur River. Stalin said
he hoped the Japanese would abrogate their mutual
alliance treaty with Russia and declare war. "If they
do attack," Stalin told Eden and Harriman, "they will
at least solve what will be my most difficult problem
with my own people. It will be obvious who is the aggressor."

Six weeks before Stalin left the Kremlin for Yalta,
he called Harriman in and showed him a map. In return
for fighting Japan, Stalin said, the U.S.S.R. expected
to get the Kurile Islands, southern Sakhalin, a lease
on the warm-water ports of Dairen and Port Arthur
and a lease on the Chinese Eastern Railroad. Averell
Harriman, like Eden, was always surprised that Stalin
could reach the nub of his desires so quickly and bluntly.
Stalin wanted Harriman to relate this to Roosevelt so
that, when they both reached the conference, they would
understand Russia's position. Russia would also expect
the maintenance of the status quo in Outer Mongolia,
where Chiang Kai-shek had little influence. Stalin was
also amenable to turning Russia's back to the pleas
of Mao Tse-tung's Communist armies; in effect, he would
render assistance to the reactionary government of
Chiang Kai-shek.

It was perfidious; it was cynical; but it was on top
of the table. It should have calmed the fears of the
Americans and the British about Russian intentions
in the Far East. Instead, it alarmed both. Churchill and
Eden felt that Great Britain had exhausted her strength
in the war against Germany and had little weight left
to bring to bear in the Orient. Three aircraft carriers
and a flotilla of cruisers and destroyers had been sent
to the Far East, but Admiral Nimitz said they had short
range and would be of little value to him. What Churchill

feared, and Eden saw clearly, was that England, as a victor, would emerge from the war as a second-class power with first-class courtesies.

Roosevelt, on the other hand, feared that Russia would not help in the war against Japan and was using all her strength to get to Berlin. In November 1943, before the Teheran Conference, he told his aides, "There will definitely be a race for Berlin." He had endorsed a hyper-secret project called RANKIN, he said: if Germany collapsed suddenly, divisions of American troops would be parachuted into the heart of Berlin. Churchill went a step further. In a top-secret order he advised Field Marshal Bernard Montgomery to keep "German arms intact," in case they had to be used to fight the Russians. Fear of Soviet strength was so poignant, Roosevelt told his intimates, that unless he and Churchill could reach broad agreements with Stalin at Yalta, Russia might overrun Europe and parts of China and set up its own spheres of influence. FDR had one additional worrisome matter; under the American Constitution, he could not sign a treaty or pact with any nation without the approval of the Senate.

Amid the ruins of Berlin, Adolf Hitler was celebrating his twelfth anniversary as Chancellor of Germany. The city was in panic. The propaganda of Hitler and Goebbels regarding the bestiality of the Russians had taken root. The roads were choked with German refugees from the eastern provinces of Germany, driving carts, pushing baby carriages laden with household effects, on bicycles, on foot—walking, creeping, freezing. Russian fighter planes strafed the crowded roads. Far to the east, the German High Command had rescued the bodies of Paul von Hindenburg and his wife and had flown them to Berlin. The hospitals and sanitaria of the capital were jammed with wounded and dying. The Allies inaugurated 1,000-plane night raids on Berlin. Dittmar, the German radio propagandist, announced to the German people: "The situation on the Eastern Front is incredibly grave."

And yet, in a manner of speaking, Adolf Hitler moved

to the radio microphones on the night of January 30 to hint at a victory no longer possible. It was the last time he would address the German people. His voice sounded old, tired and subdued, as opposed to the shrieking stridency he had employed for twelve years: "By sparing my life on July twentieth," he said slowly, "the Almighty has shown that He wishes me to continue as your Führer. German workers—work! German soldiers—fight! German women—be as fanatical as ever! No nation can do more!" He closed by prophesying that Germany would yet become the spearhead for all Europe to defeat the Russians. As he spoke, 150,000 brave Germans who had not fled from Königsberg in East Prussia were trudging the thick ice of the Bay of Danzig 80 miles to reach Danzig. Some fell, some froze, but none realized that Rokossovsky was sweeping far ahead of them in a long northerly, easterly curve to invest Danzig and capture the refugees.

Dawn was pink and warm over Malta. It was February 2, and a group of British Spitfires landed to report that the American cruiser *Quincy* was three hours off Valletta, doing 19 knots. In a Quonset hut on the airstrip Colonel Ray W. Ireland of the Air Transport Command was making his final briefing of sixty-five American pilots. They sat attentively in heavy flight clothing. Ireland had been working on Mission Number 17 for several weeks. It consisted of flying American Very Important Persons from Malta to Yalta. The colonel was obviously fatigued. Monotonously, he reviewed the facts once more. The whole flight operation would involve flying the President of the United States, General George Marshall and Admiral Ernest J. King 1,250 miles to Yalta and 1,250 miles back. It would also involve flying 135 other VIPs and 300 staff personnel to Yalta and back. In addition, Ireland's ATC group would be expected to fly people and pouches from Cairo to Yalta and from Algiers to Yalta.

The colonel and the Secret Service had already been to Yalta and had made arrangements with the Russians. Even though an American Air Force sergeant would stand beside each Russian A.A. battery, all pilots would be expected to approach the airstrip at Saki from the southeast, pass over the field for identification, and make a 90-degree turn to the left before descending on "final." The pilots could expect plenty of assistance in case of trouble. Destroyers would be stationed at intervals all along the route they would fly. A survey ship had already gone into the Black Sea from Tunis. In addition, mine sweepers, the communications ship *Catoctin* and patrol boats were already at Sevastopol harbor.

Colonel Ireland and his superiors had hand-picked these pilots. He had fourteen C-54s, including the President's new "Sacred Cow." In addition, he had six "shop planes" loaded with spare parts, in case they were needed. Sixteen swift P-38 Lightnings would fly above three planes—the Sacred Cow, Admiral King's plane, and General Marshall's—as protection against attack. Planes would depart from Malta around midnight, leaving at ten-minute intervals. Ireland expected that all throttle settings would be identical, and that each one would arrive at Saki on schedule.

He gave out individual altitudes for night flying, so that, with all planes blacked out and keeping radio silence, there would be no midair crashes. If, for any reason, a pilot felt that his plane was about to crash, there were coded minutes of latitude and longitude he could put on the air. Ireland reminded them that, after they gassed up for the flight back, they should not press the engines because the Russians used gasoline with a lower octane value. The British were furnishing five four-engine Yorks to help transport some of their people. In the audience was Lieutenant Colonel Henry Myers, newly appointed commanding officer of the Sacred Cow. Hank had never flown a President. He asked about a parachute for the President. Colonel Ireland said no. "He won't wear one for the entire trip, and, if your tail is shot off at 3,000 feet, there's no time to run back and put one on him." After the briefing the colonel advised the flight crews to get plenty of "sack time" before evening.

The sun was strong and warm in a paled-off sky when

the *Quincy* edged past the submarine nets and emerged around the stone quay, big and slow and ominous-looking, the dark gray paint peeling from her bows. She was standing down at 4 knots, the President sitting on the open wing bridge in his Navy cape as she hove into the view of the dense crowds ashore. All of Malta seemed to know that Roosevelt was coming, and, from the *Quincy*, the people looked like confetti on the docks and the hills and jetties.

There was a majesty in the arrival. British cruisers and destroyers set up a series of shrieks. A squadron of Spitfires roared low over the ship and turned into the morning sun. A dockside band struck up the American national anthem. The U.S. light cruiser *Memphis* pulled her deep-throated whistle and kept it howling. Winston Churchill stood out on the gangway of the cruiser *Orion* in a naval uniform with a double row of brass buttons. He waved a blue Navy cap. The cigar was between his teeth when President Roosevelt saw him close aboard and waved back. A company of Marines aboard *Sirius* stood at attention on the quarterdeck. The crowd of citizens roared its welcome and waved hats. A band on another cruiser struck up "The Star-Spangled Banner." A field piece at the entrance to the harbor boomed a slow-cadenced salute.

At 10:01 a Valletta harbor pilot signaled to the engine room "through with engines." The heavy hawsers were ashore on bollards. Behind the bridge a lieutenant commander jotted in the ship's log: "Newport News to Malta, 4,883 miles." When the gangway connected Dock Nine and the ship, the first men aboard were Mike Reilly, Major DeWitt Greer of the Signal Corps and three Secret Service men. For Mike FDR had a hearty greeting on the sunny bridge. He said he felt well, had slept ten and twelve hours a night, "but I'm still not slept out." The President was fatigued from his long journey, rather than rested. He told Anna that he would sit on the open bridge in the sun and receive his distinguished callers there. He had a table with two packages of Camels. He had some wicker chairs in a circular grouping, and a small end table beside his chair. It held an extra package of cigarettes. The *Quincy* had been dockside fifteen minutes when white-haired handsome Stettinius climbed the gangway, followed by Harriman and Hopkins. Behind Hopkins was his son Robert, a sergeant in the Army. His father had found him in Paris and brought him along.

The Secretary of State found the President to be bright, alert, almost chipper. Admiral McIntire told Hopkins—after a hasty look at the saffron complexion and the hollowed eyes—that he wanted to check the President's adviser over. Whatever the medical findings, McIntire wrote that Hopkins was kept alive on liver extract and plasma for the remainder of the trip.

Within twenty minutes the Stettinius group had departed. His Excellency the Governor-General of Malta, Lieutenant General Sir Edmond Shreiber, was on the bridge to welcome Mr. Roosevelt to his island. Behind him came Admiral Sir John Cunningham, Allied Naval Commander, Mediterranean. The ship had been moored an hour and six minutes when General of the Army George Marshall came aboard. Behind him was Fleet Admiral Ernest King. They sat with the President, in company with Admiral Leahy. Theirs too was a ceremonial visit, but they had had an opportunity to confer with the British High Command and they had things to reveal. Mr. Roosevelt listened and nodded. One of the items was that the British were adamant about transferring Air Chief Marshal Sir Arthur Tedder from Eisenhower's command and substituting Field Marshal Sir Harold Alexander, currently in command of the British Eighth Army and the American Fifth, in Italy, to the post of "Ground Commander" for Eisenhower. The switch would elevate Alexander to field general of all British, American and French forces in the west. The President listened, nodding vaguely. He lit a cigarette as Marshall and King discussed it with irritation, and looked down into the oily waters beside the *Quincy*. They remained thirty-five minutes, but they did not appear to dent the consciousness of the President. When they left, Marshall and King remarked to each other that the Boss didn't appear to be listening. Leahy had listened, and offered some counsel. The General and the Admiral saw FDR in a light opposite from that of Stettinius; to them he was frail, sickly and seemed unable to concentrate.

At 11:43 Admiral Harold R. Stark and Vice Admiral H. Kent Hewitt were piped aboard. Stark had been Chief of Naval Operations at the time of the attack on Pearl Harbor. Some of the blame fell on "Dolly" Stark, and he was sent to the European Theater to keep him away from the press. Hewitt was the American in command in the Mediterranean Theater. Roosevelt spent four minutes with them. At 11:48 the Prime Minister came aboard with his daughter, Section Officer Sarah Oliver of the British WAAF. Anthony Eden was not permitted to share boarding honors with Churchill, as Cadogan was fond of observing in his personal diary. Seven minutes later, Eden was aboard. The Englishmen had many things of importance which they wanted to discuss before the night takeoff to Yalta. The President was in his quiet, nodding mood.

He spoke rarely. Once he said he had trouble sleeping, which was "a new one" to him. Another time he said he had a penicillin rash, although he did not say why he needed the antibiotic. At 1:00 P.M. lunch was served in the President's cabin. It was a squeeze, but he managed to seat Churchill, Eden, the Prime Minister's daughter, Anna, Stettinius, Jimmy Byrnes and Admiral Leahy. Churchill tried to steer the conversation to affairs of state, but Roosevelt was remote. Eden pressed harder, repeating the old warning that two great powers were going to Yalta unprepared, that he barely had time to speak to "Ed" and, worst of all, the conference had no agenda. Roosevelt, either through design or unconsciously, kept the conversation on a pleasant, inconsequential plane. He was anxious to see the island of Malta, and the Governor-General would return to take him for a drive. The best that Churchill could do, flashing his apple-cheeked smile, was to draw an invitation to dinner from the President. It was something, Eden remarked on the dock. Not much. But something.

At 2:15 the Governor-General was again aboard with Mrs. Shreiber and their daughter. At the gangway Admiral Wilson Brown had been receiving the guests. He had tried to keep them coming as others left, but now, as FDR was preparing to disembark, Vice Admiral Emory Land, War Shipping Administrator, came aboard. The President had had enough. He gave Land a handshake, a greeting and a farewell. The Admiral, according to the ship's log, was gone three minutes after his arrival.

Mr. Roosevelt enjoyed the drive. He was aware that Malta was probably the most deeply punished of all Allied real estate. The little island had endured sporadic, and sometimes constant, bombing for almost four years. Many of the old buildings were in ruins, but they were "neat" ruins; the usable stones were jack-piled, the rubble had been swept away. Roosevelt sat in a car with Shreiber. In a car behind, Mrs. Shreiber sat with the President's daughter, the Prime Minister's daughter, and her own daughter. The tour moved slowly for 30 miles, touring Valletta, Mdina, Ghajn and Tuffieha. Roosevelt reminded his host that the last time he had been to this island was December 8, 1943, and Shreiber said he knew. He thanked FDR for the scroll for gallantry he had sent to the people of Malta and had the cars stop in Palace Square, where the scroll had been etched in stone.

At 4:25 P.M. Mike Reilly lifted the President from the car and placed him tenderly in a wheelchair. Roosevelt waved his thanks to the Governor-General and was wheeled aboard the *Quincy*. Anna told him he didn't have time to wash his hands: a conference with the Joint Chiefs of Staff was scheduled within five minutes. The President smiled and shook his head. It had been a tiring day, and it was getting worse. In addition, the military always arrived on time. When he reached his quarters, Leahy, Marshall and King were ready. The missing man was General of the Army H. H. Arnold, who was ill in Washington. He had sent Major General L. S. Kuter to represent him in all matters affecting the American Army Air Forces.

Ashore, Stettinius found himself at tea with a British second-echelon group. His attention was attracted to the conversation of Lord Moran, the P.M.'s notable physician, who was ever ready to confide his diagnoses to anyone who asked. The Prime Minister, he said with finality, was "very much depressed. His work has deteriorated in the past few months. He has become wordy, irritating his colleagues with his verbosity. One subject will get into his mind to the exclusion of all others— Greece, for example." He shook his head sadly and said that Churchill was a "man of waning powers." The American Secretary of State, addressing His Lordship, said that he had been pleased at the bright appearance of the President on this particular morning. The voyage seemed to have done him some good.

Moran turned on his forgiving smile. "To a doctor's eye," he said, "the President appears a very sick man. He has all the symptoms of hardening of the arteries of the brain in an advanced stage." Stettinius appeared to be dismayed. "So," said Lord Moran, "I give him only a few months to live." He shrugged. "But men shut their eyes when they do not want to see, and the Americans here cannot bring themselves to believe that he is finished." As proof, the noted physician said that, before he left England with the Prime Minister, he had received a disturbing letter from Dr. Roger Lee, president of the American Medical Association. In it Lee reported that the President had sustained an atack of heart failure eight months earlier, and he detailed FDR's personal attitude: "He is irascible and becomes very irritable if he has to concentrate his mind for long. If anything is brought up that wants thinking he will change the subject." Stettinius, who placed weight on Moran's opinion, was stunned. He had nothing to say. Later, on the evening of February 9, Lord Moran wrote, among other things, in his diary: "Everyone was shocked by his appearance and gabbled about it afterwards. The

President looked old and thin and drawn. He sat looking straight ahead with his mouth open as if he were not taking things in."

It is a medical fact that when an insufficient supply of blood reaches the brain, impaired powers of reasoning and concentration result. In 1945 there were no reliable medical tests to evaluate arteriosclerosis of the brain. Arteries carry nourishment. Brain cells cannot metabolize any food but sugar. Deprive the cerebrum of nourishment for as short a time as four minutes, and the ability to think faces irreversible damage. In human beings arteries age slowly, moderately or swiftly. In the case of President Roosevelt, a chronic wheelchair patient who could not indulge in normal exercise, the aging process was swift. Overwork, flaccidity of musculature and chronic fatigue induced a speeding up of plaques forming inside arterial walls; this reduced the amount of blood pumped by a tired heart and increased the blood pressure because of narrowed venous walls. Lord Moran may have been an alarmist, but he was making a highly educated medical guess.

Stettinius did not know what to believe, and hoped for the best. As Secretary of State, his greatest worry was that the President's foreign policy vacillated. At Teheran FDR drank to the shooting of 50,000 German officers; at Quebec he initialed the Morgenthau Plan to dismember Germany and make an agrarian state of the nation. On this day—February 2—Ed learned that the Boss would like to see Germany kept intact, but militarily powerless. Another stunning fact Stettinius had discovered in a short visit was that Roosevelt, having favored giving France a military zone to police in Germany, was now opposed to it. Before leaving Washington, FDR had explained the importance of Yalta. He would not draw up a position paper so that the State Department and the Joint Chiefs of Staff would understand the several American goals. Instead the President stressed the growing suspicion between the three great powers; his fear that the Russian armies could overrun and hold most of Europe—not counting what they could do in a drive through Manchuria and North China. If he could get Stalin to agree to a United Nations, a world peace-keeping order, the other problems would resolve themselves. Thus the "other problems"—cooperation in international war, the policing and penalties to be assessed against the vanquished, the role of an independent Poland, the re-creation of two crippled nations—China and France—to first-class status, the zones of occupation in Germany were all to be entrusted to the President's hands at the conference table. He wanted everything except the United Nations matter to be "loose," to be bargained. To some of his associates, Roosevelt approached Yalta not as a triumphant warrior, but as one in search of a détente from his friends.

As historian James MacGregor Burns wrote later, "He was staking everything on the face-to-face encounter with Stalin." In the absence of a policy directive from the President, the State Department, having pressed all its bright young men to bear down on specific problems, had a paper which would be presented to FDR after he arrived at Yalta. There was no guarantee that the Boss would adhere to its specifications; there was no certainty that he would read it, but it represented the best thinking of the Washington internationalists:

Germany: "We should favor abolition of German self-sufficiency and its position of economic domination of Europe, elimination of certain key industries, prohibition of manufacture of arms and of all types of aircraft, and continuing control to achieve these aims."

Poland: "It was decided . . . to recommend that every effort be made to secure a Polish frontier which, in the north and central areas, would run along the Curzon Line, and in the south generally follow the eastern frontier of Lwów province. This frontier would correspond closely with the Curzon Line and would leave the Polish city of Lwów and the oil fields to Poland. [In the west] we oppose extending the Polish boundary to the Oder or the Oder-Neisse line. In regard to German territory to be turned over to Poland, we favor limiting this compensation to East Prussia—except for Königsberg, which we expect the Soviet Union to request—a small salient of Pomerania, which would include an area of roughly one hundred miles west along the Baltic coast to the Polish Corridor, and Upper Silesia." Politically, Stettinius felt that Roosevelt should "insist" that Mikolajczyk "and other representative moderate Poles in London" be included in a government of national unity. "We should insist on the untrammeled right of the Polish people freely to choose their own government and, if necessary, we should be prepared to assist in the supervision of these elections."

Bulgaria, Romania, Hungary: "We recommend that our representatives be assured of the right to be consulted on policy directives to be issued in the name of the Control Commissions sufficiently in advance to enable them to communicate with Washington whenever a directive seemed to be in conflict with the general policies of the United States . . . and of the right to travel freely within the countries unaccompanied by Soviet officers."

China: "We recommend that the Soviet and British agree to the desirability of securing the maximum degree of unity in China. The Soviet Union should be urged to use its influence with the Chinese Communists to further an agreement between them and the Nationalist government . . ."

International Trusteeships: ". . . favor the inclusion of provisions for international trusteeships in the world organization. We believe this should include League of Nations Mandates established after the First World War, territories taken from the enemy during the present war, and any territories which might be voluntarily placed under trusteeships . . ."

This, of course, is a condensation of the graphic and detailed studies by the State Department. Probably the greatest hope and the deepest despair of the forthcoming conference was that it would be unlimited in scope. Three men would settle the affairs of the world. How they would do it, or what they would agree to discuss, was conjecture. So far as President Roosevelt was concerned, he would envision Yalta as three great steps:

a settlement on defeated Germany; Russian participation
in the crushing of Imperial Japan; the United Nations.
One. Two. Three. The rest would be idealistic and
visionary; worth debate to be sure, but most of it had
a surrender value to attain agreement on One, Two,
Three.

At 6:00 P.M. the American Joint Chiefs of Staff, in
conference in the President's cabin, adjourned after
pressing upon Roosevelt the military decisions which
must be made at Yalta. He had barely—and wearily—
ended the talks when the Anglo-American Combined
Chiefs of Staff met in the same cabin. The Prime Minister, who had declined the afternoon drive in favor of his
usual nap, was refreshed and ready. Sir Alan Brooke,
the British Field Marshal, sat with his opposite number,
General of the Army George Marshall; the admirals
and air marshals joined with King and Kuter; Eden
sat dejected with his hands on the table, prepared to
listen to a long exposition by Churchill. As a meeting
of the minds, it was close to a disaster.

General Bedell Smith announced that he was present
to represent General Dwight D. Eisenhower. The military
groups, almost in defiance of Roosevelt's wishes to avoid
presenting the Soviet Union with any "bilateral
decisions," had met for three days and disagreed, at
times bitterly. Bedell Smith had presented Eisenhower's
strategic plan for the defeat of Germany; on the map
it looked like open-clawed ice tongs. The northerly one,
under British Field Marshal Montgomery, bypassed the
Ruhr Valley to the north and swept through Bremen
and Hamburg to the Baltic ports; the other, under the
Americans, yawed in a southerly semicircle toward Stutt-
gart and on to Kassel. To this the British were unified
in their opposition. They pointed to the little Rhine
bridgeheads which General Smith had presented, and
scorned them. It represented, in their opinion, the
cautious, committee style of generalship imposed by
Eisenhower. They demanded a bold thrust by
Montgomery across the northern plains of Germany—an

offensive which would have to be augmented by American armies, of course—which would cut the country in halves and probably reach Berlin before the Russians.

The British had the bold ideas; the Americans had the men and the guns. The British military chiefs demanded that someone show them what good a thrust toward Kassel would do. To Marshall, Smith and Kuter, the British motivation appeared to be more political than military: it was the desire to wrap up the war against Germany under the British flag and a British general. They also desired to seal all the north German ports from Emden to Stettin before the Russians could claim anything. Again, President Roosevelt played the part of the pacifier. But the fingers pressing parts of the map on the cabin desk became white with pressure and the voices rose in decibels. Smith, normally quiet and somewhat self-effacing, stood to shout louder than the others. Churchill, waving his lighted cigar, addressed himself directly to Roosevelt. Marshall announced that, if the British plan were accepted, he had the word of Eisenhower that he would ask to be relieved of his command.

The President stood by his commander; the oral battle within a war was finally decided when Churchill said that he would accept the American plan if the northern thrust of the British was to be the stronger of the two. Sir Alan Brooke brought up the matter of the desire of his staff to get Tedder out of Eisenhower's tent as Deputy Commander and place Field Marshal Alexander in charge of all ground forces. The British lost this one too, when FDR said that Alexander was doing a superb job in Italy and Tedder was ideal working with Eisenhower. He went a step further in getting approval of Churchill to withdraw two divisions of British troops from Greece to transfer to an active theater of war. FDR, within the unseemly bedlam, moved from point to point skillfully, then went one step too far. He asked Churchill and the British chiefs why some forces could not be withdrawn from stalemated Italy and placed under Eisenhower's command. At this point, Churchill became irritable. "No," he said, shaking his head. "It is important to follow up a surrender of German forces in Italy. We can move them across the Adriatic to occupy as much of Austria as possible. It is undesirable that more of Western Europe than necessary should be occupied by the Russians."

The meeting ended at dinnertime. The President confided to Pa Watson that he considered the pre-Conference discussion dangerous. He said he did not want Stalin to think that Britain and America were "ganging up on him." He had sent messages to Churchill pleading that there would be no time for conferences, even informal ones. There had been conferences on several levels. When the Combined Chiefs of Staff left, rather "uncombined," Mr. Roosevelt had a half hour until dinner would be served. For him it had been a difficult, wearing day, a revolving sandstone of visitors abrading the cutting edge of his intellect. Arthur Prettyman wheeled FDR into his bedroom for a change of clothing, a wash and a bow tie.

He was back in the main cabin, with its dead smoke, at 8:00 P.M. Present for dinner were Anna, Sarah Churchill, the Prime Minister, Anthony Eden, Stettinius and Jimmy Byrnes. No one remembered much about the dinner—that is to say, the food served. It was a dull event, not enlivened by the Secretary of State, who kept telling the President that he and Eden agreed on almost everything. Stettinius sparkled and bubbled as though he were trying to make the Boss feel better. Perhaps the remarks of Moran were still fresh and poignant. "We agree on the military plan in the west," he said at one point. Later: "There was wide agreement on political issues." Eden did not second his friend's motion. Nor did Mr Roosevelt emerge from his lethargy except when Anna addressed him. It may have crossed Eden's mind that he had said to Harry Hopkins, earlier in the day, "We are going into a decisive conference and have so far neither agreed what we would discuss nor how to handle matters with a bear who will certainly know his mind." The President told Churchill that he thought the war in Europe would end "this year, but the war against the Japanese might go on until 1947." Churchill did not respond. He nodded. Obviously FDR did not recall having told this to Churchill before.

At 10:00 P.M. the President was alone. He summoned Captain Senn and the staff of the *Quincy* to extend his personal thanks for a pleasant voyage and said he would probably see them again on the shores of Egypt. There he expected to confer with King Ibn Saud of Arabia and young Farouk of Egypt in hopes of arranging accommodations for a Palestine homeland for the Jews of the world. It was, he said, worth the time and effort. Within a half hour he was on his way to Luqa airport. The night air was cool and pleasant. At the airport the thunder of many four-engine planes warming up and the high whine of the fighter planes caused him to observe that when the Russians saw the size of the British-American contingent, they might consider it a small invasion.

He had never seen the Sacred Cow before, and the President was not pleased. He sat before it in his car (accompanying him on Plane Number 1 were Admirals Leahy, McIntire and Brown; Anna Boettiger, General Watson, Commander Bruenn, Mike Reilly and Arthur Prettyman) and shook his head when he saw the small elevator cage descend to the ground. He demanded to know who authorized it. Mike Reilly looked away and studied the tremendous array of aircraft. Mr. Roosevelt said he wasn't aware of the elevator, or the new plane either. As the General and admirals trudged up the front staircase, FDR's wheelchair was backed into the cage and slowly lifted into the aft section. Once aboard, he said he had no desire to inspect the craft. He wanted to retire at once. Prettyman took him to the small room aft of the wing and helped the President undress and get into pajamas. He asked Reilly what time they would take off. "Not until about 3:00 A.M., Mr. President." "That's good," the President said. He was sleeping in a few minutes.

A half mile away Prime Minister Churchill was in

bed. Altogether, the fleet of aircraft carried 700 Britons and Americans. Colonel Ray Ireland, standing most of the night in the small tower, orchestrated the event flawlessly. Planes were at the head of the runway exactly ten minutes apart with silvery spinning blades and blue flames jetting from the exhausts. Ireland waved them off, one by one, and the moment each lifted from the runway, all running lights were extinguished, all shades drawn. Around 3:00 A.M. the Prime Minister's plane moved slowly down the strip and lifted into the night sky. At 3:30 the Sacred Cow was given a green light. A short time later a squadron of P-38s and Spitfires were ordered to overtake and protect the two planes.

McIntire had asked for a 6,000-foot altitude for Mr. Roosevelt's plane, and got it. Mike Reilly was too excited to sleep. He and his Secret Service contingent sat up, chatting or talking to the crew. The navigational trick was to fly east by northeast toward Crete, but not to overfly it. The Germans still held the big island. Before Crete, all the planes were to turn to port. Reilly was looking out the window at a pink dawn when he saw Athens directly below. He heard a noise from the President's cabin and opened the door noiselessly. Mr. Roosevelt appeared to be sound asleep. Later he would tell Mike that he slept "fitfully." Because of FDR's breathing problem, the plane could not go higher than 6,000 feet, but, at that altitude, it was running in and out of big white clouds which bounced the big aircraft considerably.

Out of Athens, the Secret Service stopped a fresh contingent of U.S. fighter planes climbing toward the Sacred Cow. It was a perfect rendezvous and Reilly wondered how it was possible. They moved high above the President's plane until they were black dots near the edge of the sun. At 220 miles per hour it was a long flight made longer by the fact that all timepieces had to be set two hours ahead for Yalta. After Athens the spaced-out planes made another left turn, which brought them over the Dardanelles and Turkey. After that, there was nothing but the empty expanse of the Black Sea.

At Saki the Russians had hundreds of women with brooms sweeping snow from the runway. Planes were landing, as they had departed, at ten-minute intervals. At noon local time the Soviet airport commander spotted the Sacred Cow coming in low over the water. Above it were five P-38s which, because of their high cruising speed, had trouble remaining with the DC-4. They thundered over the tower, made the 90-degree turn for identification, then came in on final approach, landing at 12:10. An hour earlier Staff Sergeant R. W. Robitalle had served breakfast, so the President was dressed and ready to step on Soviet soil. He asked Admiral Brown to find out if the Prime Minister had landed. He was told that Churchill's plane was expected in twenty minutes. He elected to wait. This incurred a small embarrassment; at the back of FDR's plane Foreign Minister Molotov, in furry Russian hat, stood in the snow with Stettinius and Harriman.

After the P.M. disembarked, Roosevelt was wheeled into his tiny elevator and slid slowly to the hard earth. Churchill was waiting. So were Molotov, Harriman and Stettinius. Russian NKVD agents explained to Mike Reilly that the President was to ride in a nearby jeep and review an honor guard. He asked about Churchill. "Him too," they said. Reilly picked FDR up, surrounded by agents Rowley, Peterson, Deckard, Campion, Savage and Griffith, and deposited him in the small vehicle. Thoughtfully, the Russians had strewn the jeep with rugs, which Reilly tucked around the frail body. Churchill decided to walk beside the car, holding onto the railing. A military band struck up the national anthem. Roosevelt, pale and thin under a gray fedora, braved the cold winds to ride slowly down lanes of picked Russian guards. The music and the red and gold uniforms made it a colorful ceremony under a bleak sky. Afterward the troops marched in review and Roosevelt watched from the parked jeep.

He wanted to be off to Yalta. Molotov, who spoke English, told the President that there were three huts—he pointed to them—with refreshments. Mr. Roosevelt said he had a late breakfast. He and Anna were taken to an American Packard automobile. The limousine had a Russian driver. Molotov asked to introduce (and reintroduce) some of his official welcoming party. He was sorry, but Marshal Stalin had been delayed and would arrive at Yalta a day late. The men he introduced would be parties to the plenary sessions: Deputy Foreign Commissar Andrei Vyshinsky, Air Marshal Khudyakov, Admiral Kuznetsov, General Antonov, and Ambassadors Gromyko and Gusev.

Roosevelt left, with U.S. Secret Service men ahead and behind. The Prime Minister availed himself of refreshments and found hot tea with lemon and sugar, vodka, brandy, caviar, smoked sturgeon, champagne, black bread, butter, cheese and boiled eggs. Unknown to his hosts, Churchill had asked his plane crew to provide him with sandwiches and brandy for the long trip to Yalta. They were in his car. As the cars left, shortly after 1:00 P.M., Anna noticed that the women with the brooms were still sweeping the runways, the big planes were still coming in regularly and the airport was surrounded by spaced soldiers carrying tommy guns on their shoulders. The President, who maintained an active interest in travel and geography, told his daughter that they were now 900 miles south of Moscow, 5,700 miles east of Washington D.C., and within 300 miles of Turkey, Romania and Bulgaria.

In the bitter coldness, the President was astonished to find Russian military sentries on both sides of the road. They were spaced about 50 yards apart, and many were portly, pink-cheeked women with old Springfield rifles slung over their shoulders. As the car came abreast of each guard, the sentry came to attention. The landscape, as they drove toward Simferopol in the center of the peninsula, was flat and bleak. There were a few blackened trees, rusting tanks and burned-out railroad cars. No one except the military was to be seen anywhere, and yet the entire road was heavily guarded, and the salutes became too much for Mr. Roosevelt. For a while he returned the salute by doffing his hat. Some of the

women soldiers became emotional and waved their hands
and handkerchiefs at him. "Oh God," he said to Anna,
"I can't keep this up." He yanked his hat down over
his forehead, pulled the rug up under his chin and took
a nap.

Somehow, Churchill and Eden had passed the Roosevelt car. Toward the center of the peninsula Molotov
had set up a cabin with refreshments and liquor. As
the Roosevelt car approached, military guards stopped
it. The President awakened and lifted his hat. "You
go in and explain that I'm not going to get out of the
car," he said. Anna felt that her father was not "up
to getting in and out." Anna found warmth and convivial-
ity inside the little house. She made her father's excuses
and returned to the car. As they started off, the President
smiled at his favorite. "Boy oh boy," he murmured, "am
I going to enjoy having a martini tonight!" Among Anna's
tasks was to write down and procure such items as gin,
vermouth and ice. Two weeks earlier FDR had told
Anna that the Russians might not have ice for drinks.
Always he asked her "write that down." Now, for a
moment before returning to his nap, he looked at her
and said: "You did remember to write that down?"
"I sure did, Father," she said. "Don't worry." She
slouched in her seat and worried about ice. She didn't
know why, but she had a feeling that the Soviets were
anti ice. It was on the early list sent to the Crimea with
the advance party. And yet . . .

The road climbed slowly. Simferopol consisted of
an assortment of streets encompassing hundreds of half
walls. A group of children stood timidly watching the
big shiny cars pass by. In one of the cars a gentleman
rolled a window down and tossed a packet of sandwiches out. The youngsters ran for it, lying in the street.
Russian sentries drove them back. They yelled in Russian after the disappearing car, "They do not need anything." The motorcade climbed higher and higher. The
snow was harder, whiter. They were breaching the
Krymskiye Gory, a range of 4,000-foot peaks which
hugged the south coast.

Abruptly, they were through the pass and the road down to the Black Sea at Alushta. All the cars turned and found themselves on a coastal road precipice with the sea, and live trees, below. Dusk fell at 5:30. Anna felt that she had been traveling for days. She understood the unspoken strain her father sustained. He did not complain. He would doze awhile, awaken to look around at the countryside and watch the saluting guards. Then he would return to sleep.

At 6:00 P.M. the car went through Yalta. Not much could be seen of it; there was a sense of desolation riding the evening air. On the far side the Roosevelt car continued south for ten minutes, then turned right onto the grounds of Livadia Palace. The British delegation passed Livadia and—fifteen minutes farther—Koreiz, a big estate with guest houses rather than a palace. It had been built early in the century by Prince Yusupov, who assassinated the monk Rasputin. Here Stalin and his Russian party would be housed. A few miles farther on, there was a town called Alupka. There on the edge of the sea was the garlanded Vorontsov Palace, high on a rock ledge. This would be Churchill's home. Stalin had managed to find a headquarters between the British and Americans.

Livadia was a fifty-room summer palace built by Czar Nicholas in 1911. The walls were of marble and limestone. At one end was a turreted tower with moorish arches. It was on an eminence over the dark tideless waters of the sea. The mountains to the north seemed more precipitous than they were. The entire range shielded the shore from the cold winds, so that, while the peaks were snowy, cypress, cedar and yew trees grew around the palace. Below in the water, dolphins played and swam in pairs. The old Russian royal family, consisting of seven persons, were maintained by a thousand servants. There were two smaller buildings on the grounds called Svitski Korpus.

The ceilings were over twenty feet high, and the palace held many bedrooms. The Russian Socialists claimed that the Czar often changed bedrooms late at night because he feared assassination. Usually he occupied a small, almost monkish bedroom on the ground floor in the left wing, facing the sea. This was to be President Roosevelt's bedroom. The Czar's study would be used by FDR for intimate meetings. There was a cool, spring-like porch where the morning sun warmed the stone. On the second floor were bedrooms for the Czarina and the four archduchesses. The imperial bedroom would be occupied by General Marshall. Someone, amusingly, assigned the Czarina's bedroom to the humorless Admiral King. In the wing opposite the President's bedroom on the main floor—"a block and a half away," as Anna said—was her bedroom.

As FDR was assisted from the car in the driveway, the main door opened and light flooded out. Standing there was Miss Kathleen Harriman. Behind her stood Commander Tyree and Major Putnam, who had set up the presidential map room and stood ready to help. The palace exuded heat, but it looked huge and barren. FDR's Filipino mess attendants had taken command of the big kitchens. Mike Reilly saw an assortment of white-coated Russian servants. "I knew the type at once," he said. "All NKVD men. I told them to leave, we had everything under control." They protested that they wanted to help, but Reilly insisted that they get out at once. Arthur Prettyman wheeled the President around the ground floor; he was interested and wanted to look in every room. "I can't understand Winston's concern," he said. "This palace has all the comforts of home." He noticed rectangular patches on the walls where paintings had been; glass and brass doorknobs had been sawed from doors, but to him these were of small moment.

FDR noticed, in his bathroom, that the toilet had been built up. He was thankful for small considerations. Anna found a full-size bed in her room with a half-size mattress. Admiral Leahy was affronted to find he had a small room in one of the towers. Stettinius had a two-room suite in the rear of the main floor. There were rooms for Hopkins, Byrnes, Harriman, Chip Bohlen and Pa Watson. The State Department delegation managed to be assigned small but livable quarters. The secondary generals found that each five would have to share one room. The Secretary of State inspected the second floor and the towers and reported to the President, "The only acute shortage is bathrooms." In all, 215 Americans would share six bathrooms. None of the gentry could appreciate the stout Russian maids who entered bathrooms and bedrooms without knocking.

Little escaped Reilly's notice. In company with two men he inspected the grounds. Behind the palace, and away from the ledge of dark rock on which it stood, he found a group of peasant huts. He knocked and looked inside. The people were uniformly meek, almost frightened by the presence of the American. In each hut, a radio hung on the wall. It had no dialing knobs. The peasants listened to Moscow only. Many of them had false teeth made of steel, which gleamed by kerosene lamp. To Mike, the teeth looked like "shiny nails."

The U.S. Army Signal Corps had achieved the improbable: setting up a telephone line from Livadia Palace to the *Catoctin,* in Sevastopol, 80 miles away. It was a herculean task. Communications experts tested the line and found, to their dismay, that voice communication was weak and erratic. It was not dependable for the President. Reilly, who appeared to embody the strength and bluntness the Russians admired, paid a visit to NKVD headquarters. He did not accuse them of tapping Roosevelt's line. All he said was that the Americans were having trouble with it, and he was going to station American sailors every hundred yards for the whole 80 miles around the clock. Almost magically, the lines became clear. Nor were Reilly and his men above looking under beds and along walls for listening devices. Anna said they found some bugs. If so, Reilly did not mention them.

Anna was asked to find Jimmy Byrnes and Ed Flynn and a few others. The President said, "Sis, we'll have cocktails in my room." Some of the Russians who had been ordered off the premises were still in the kitchen. One, who had lived in New York, was asked to "bring

a bucket of ice and some cocktail glasses." He appeared
to go into a stupor. Mrs. Boettiger watched as he started
a whispered conference with other departing Russians.
"I'm sorry," he said, "but there is no ice." "There's
got to be ice," she said. The Russian stretched himself
in dignity and said that the Soviet Union had prepared
cocktails for the presidential party. Anna reported this
to her father. The President looked crushed. "Oh God,"
he said, "what else have they got?" Whatever it was,
FDR did not want it. "All right," he said, "we'll have
bourbon and water."

After a brace of drinks, the Filipino messboys served
an American dinner to the President, Anna, Pa Watson,
Admiral Leahy and Averell Harriman. Someone pointed
out that it was thoughtful of U. J. to have arranged
for all the plenary sessions to be held in the big ballroom
at Livadia. Mr. Roosevelt, in a joshing mood, expatiated
on the truth that he was the only "chief of state" present.
"You see," he said, eyes twinkling behind his gleaming
glasses, "people are going to have to come to see *me*."
When dinner was over, the group disbanded, but Roosevelt asked Harriman to stay. He said he felt tired and
was going to retire at once. He would like Harriman
to motor down to Koreiz to discuss plans for "tomorrow" (Sunday, February 4). Also, having in mind he
was always confident he could persuade men in face-to-
face encounters, he ordered Harriman to ask if Marshal
Stalin could visit him at Livadia at "three or three-thirty"
before the plenary session.

The American Ambassador hurried off, with Russian
guards, to drive to Koreiz. He saw Molotov. Harriman
said that the President was "extremely pleased" with
the arrangements at Livadia. Molotov seemed to have
anticipated the personal chat between U. J. and FDR
because, without consulting the Marshal, he said that
Stalin would prefer to visit with the President at 4:00
P.M. and convene the first session an hour later. Harriman
invited Molotov and Stalin to dine with the President
Sunday night. The Russian Foreign Minister accepted
"tentatively." He would consult Stalin in the morning.

In matters *diplomatique,* the simplest situations become complex. FDR was pulling a fast one on Churchill by seeking to chat privately with Uncle Joe, but Stalin, who arrived secretly at the Koreiz compound, was already visiting privately with Churchill at Vorontsov Palace, ostensibly to ask if he and his party were comfortable. Churchill, who understood that his comfort was not at issue, went into a personal discussion of Germany. Stalin said the Reich was short of bread and coal. Also, its transport system had been permanently damaged by air raids. Churchill, who had heard the rumor that Hitler and his Nazis might retreat to a Bavarian redoubt or to Dresden, asked U. J. what Russia would do about it. The stocky, graying man grinned. "We shall follow him!" he said excitedly. He volunteered that the Oder River was no longer an obstacle on the road to Berlin; the Russians already had several bridgeheads. Reports on the eastern front, he said, indicated that Adolf Hitler was down to sending his *Volksturm*—ill-equipped old men and boys—into battle.

Cordially, Churchill escorted Stalin into the British map room. Field Marshal Alexander used the pointer to explain the Italian campaign. Again, Stalin was impressed by the preciseness of the presentation—as he had been by Marshal Tedder's in Moscow. The Russian dictator walked up to the map, and, through his interpreter, asked why Churchill did not divert Allied divisions across the Adriatic into Yugoslavia, in the general direction of Vienna. This was Churchill's old heartache. This was what he had begged Roosevelt to do throughout the past year, warning him that Red troops would overrun Europe if they didn't. The British Prime Minister was uncertain whether the Russian was mocking him, or making a suggestion. "The Red Army may not give us time to complete that operation," Churchill said. When Stalin had said good night, the P.M. flushed with anger, turned to Alexander and said, "It costs him nothing to say this now." He waved his hands futilely above his head. "But I make no reproaches."

The military guard outside President Roosevelt's bedroom nodded to Commander Bruenn, who stood waiting with his bag. The Boss was awake. It was not a shiny day; the sky was a solid gray canopy; the air was brisk and chill, as it sometimes is after a final snow. Bruenn knocked and was told to come in. Roosevelt exchanged greetings with his cardiologist; the two men went through the medical charade flawlessly. Neither impeded the other at work. Amiable greetings were exchanged; the questions about sleep and general disposition were undergone. Prettyman and Fox assisted with an electrocardiogram, which showed no changes in heart action. The doctor knew, as well as FDR, that the long voyage had been tiring; Bruenn realized that the conferences and extravagant dinners would impose an additional strain. The President's only untoward symptom, besides a stuffy nostril, was a paroxysmal cough. He was asked to smoke fewer cigarettes.

At 9:30 A.M. Mr. Roosevelt was on the sun porch with his military chieftains. Once more he listened to their restrained, yet desperate desire to draw Russia into the war with Japan. The Boss seemed more attentive, more willing to ask questions, than yesterday. He asked Lieutenant Rigdon to make some personal notes on the matter. FDR could see no problem in a military sense. After 10:00 the generals and admirals were preparing to leave when Stettinius led his contingent onto the porch. He too had an appointment with Roosevelt. With him were Freeman Matthews, Alger Hiss and Chip Bohlen, Assistant to the Secretary of State. Bohlen was an important man. He spoke Russian and would act as Roosevelt's interpreter as well as taker-of-notes. The awkward truth about languages was that all the conferees would have to learn to speak in bursts of one or two sentences, then stop for translation, then proceed. Bohlen was probably the only man at the conference who could listen to the Russians, whisper the sense of what was being said to Roosevelt, and then wait for the Russian interpreter to give his version of what was being said.

The Secretary of State asked the military chiefs to remain for the State Department meeting. Stettinius turned on his pearly smile; he had no secrets to be keep from the Pentagon. All hands sat on chairs and a railing as Ed presented FDR with a digest of American postures in various theaters. It consisted of seven main points. In a conference devoid of agenda, it would be necessary for Roosevelt to press for these matters:

MEMORANDUM OF SUGGESTED ACTION ITEMS
FOR THE PRESIDENT

1. International Organization. We should seek adoption of United States proposal for voting formula and agreement to announce immediately calling of general United Nations Conference. [Copies of text of United States proposal and analysis thereof are available if you wish to hand them to Churchill and Stalin.]

Argumentation: Our proposal safeguards unity of the great powers so far as is possible by any formula—enforcement action will require unanimous vote—only with respect to discussion will a party to a dispute not be able to vote. Latin America and other small powers will be disillusioned if discussion can be vetoed.

Note: If the voting issue is settled, additional points would have to be agreed to before a United Nations Conference could be called: International Trusteeships; France as fifth sponsoring power; list of nations to be invited; date of conference and its being held in the United States on behalf of other four sponsoring powers; United States to consult China and France on behalf of Britain and Russia; form of announcement of agreement on International Organization matters (we have available the necessary papers on these points).

2. Adoption of Emergency European High Commission. (Copies of draft of declaration and of accompanying protocol are available if you wish to hand them to Stalin and Churchill.)

Argumentation: Unity of great power policy with respect to liberated and Axis satellite countries is highly desirable, and France should be included as one of the great powers for this purpose.

3. *Treatment of Germany.* (a) *Final agreement should be reached with respect to control machinery and zones of occupation. Announcement should be made of such agreement and of the earlier agreement on surrender terms.*

(b) *Boundaries: It is not expected that definite, detailed commitments will have to be made at this time. However, if it proves necessary, our detailed position has been prepared and is available.*

(c) *Minorities: We should oppose, as far as possible, indiscriminate mass transfer of minorities with neighboring states. Transfers should be carried out gradually under international supervision.*

(d) *Long range economic policies: We should favor abolition of German self-sufficiency and its position of economic domination of Europe, elimination of certain key industries, prohibition of manufacture of arms and of all types of aircraft, and continuing control to achieve these aims.*

4. *Poland.* (a) *Boundaries: We favor the Curzon Line in the north and center and, in the south, the eastern line of Lwów Province, which would correspond generally with one of the frontiers proposed in 1919 to the Supreme Allied Council. Transfer of German territory to be limited to East Prussia (except Koenigsberg to Russia), a small coastal salient of Pomerania, and Upper Silesia.*

(b) *We should be prepared to assist in the formation of a new representative interim government pledged to free elections when conditions permit. We should urge inclusion in a provisional government of Mikolajczyk (Peasant Party is most important in Poland) and other moderate Poles abroad. We should not agree to recognize the Lublin "government" in its present form.*

5. *Allied Control Commission in Romania, Bulgaria and Hungary. Our representatives must be assured of:* (a) *freedom of movement, and* (b) *consultation before decisions are made by the Control Commissions.*

6. *Iran. We should seek Soviet agreement not to press*

*for oil concessions in Iran until termination of hostilities
and withdrawal of Allied troops.*

*7. China. We should seek Soviet and British support for
our efforts to bring about Kuomintang-Communist agreement. Argumentation: Cooperation between the two groups
will expedite conclusion of the war in the Far East and prevent possible internal conflict and foreign intervention in
China.*

The military and the State Department waited in silence
as the President read through the document. All of it
coincided with his personal aspirations but, as a blueprint
for the settlement of world problems, it was thin—superficial. It was an outline of an outline.

The European High Commission had been sitting
in London since 1943, debating and setting up zones
of occupation, reparations and free elections for liberated
countries. However, Harry Hopkins stated that Roosevelt did not trust the European High Commission, and
had sent an emissary to London to make certain that
it reached no decision about anything. He had no inclination to be confronted with a series of grave decisions
reached by a third-echelon diplomatic group, working
subordinately to foreign ministers. In regard to Germany,
the State Department practically warned the President
not to reach any detailed agreement: "It is not expected
that definitive, detailed commitments [regarding bound-
aries] will have to be made at this time."

On the other hand, Germany's neighbor Poland should
have its boundaries firmly aligned at Yalta—the western
edge, adjoining Germany, to consist of "a small coastal
salient of Pomerania, and Upper Silesia." The helpless
Balkans, caught in the swirl of massive Russian infantry,
were offered no protection. Romania, Bulgaria and Hungary were to be countries where "our representatives
must be assured of freedom of movement," and they
were to be consulted "before decisions are made." One
of the saddest sections concerned China, where Chinese
fought Chinese and where the corrupt government of
Chiang Kai-shek was to be elevated to "fifth great power"

status. In Section Seven, aimed specifically at the Soviet Union, the Russians were expected to betray the Chinese Communist armies (the stronger of the two factions) to "prevent possible internal conflict and foreign intervention. . . ."

The President stuck the document in his pocket. He discussed parts of it, asking for clarification. No matter where the conversation languished, he brought it back to Russian participation in the war on Japan, and the United Nations. He was worried about Poland too, not so much because of the seven million Polish votes in the United States (he knew he would not need them anymore), but because it apparently tweaked his conscience that World War II was precipitated by Poland's refusal to grant Germany a small corridor to Danzig, and the war might very well end by robbing Poland of a great deal more territory.

In many of these matters, he leaned more on the advice of Moscow Ambassador Averell Harriman than Stettinius or his predecessor, Cordell Hull. The rich, ingratiating, intelligent railroad millionaire was more than an ambassador. In Moscow he was in personal charge not only of diplomatic matters but military, War Production Board and Lend-Lease. Nor was Harriman ordered to report to the Secretary of State; his reports to his nominal superior were a matter of courtesy; Harriman dealt directly with FDR. When the President wanted to know what would be required to get the Russians into the Far Eastern war, he might have sent Stettinius, but he didn't. The President and War Secretary Stimson agreed that Harriman was the man to draw the Russians out. Before arriving at Yalta, Roosevelt, having chatted with Harriman, announced, "Good headway has been made."

At 4:00 P.M. Roosevelt was sitting in his study when Marshal Stalin arrived. It was a square room with an aura of perpetual dusk. There was a gilt-framed painting of a farmer plowing fields hung too high on one wall; an old, elaborate chandelier overhead which was lighted by electric bulbs of varying sizes and shapes; a square desk embossed with laurel wreaths; a desk lamp with fringe hanging from the round shade; two deep chairs with faded plush seats; a high-backed couch and a marble table. The front doors to the palace burst open and a group of American Secret Service men, followed by NKVD men, poured into the center hall. They were followed by the short, broad-chested man in plain khaki. At his side was his interpreter. The stride of the dictator was firm and strong; he stared at the backs of the Secret Service men.

The President sat behind the desk. A deep chair had been moved from the front of the desk to the side. Marshal Stalin shook hands vigorously and asked if FDR was "living in comfort." FDR said he was both pleased and gateful; he was happy that all the plenary sessions would be held at Livadia; under customary protocol the meetings would have moved from the American palace to the British, to the Russian and back again. They were chatting about nothing in particular when Foreign Minister Molotov arrived. Roosevelt, who believed that the polite jest moved men toward amiability, said that, on his voyage aboard the *Quincy*, he had made a bet that the Russians would be in Berlin before MacArthur reached Manila.

Stalin permitted himself one of the terse chuckles which sounded like a hollow cough. He said the President would lose his bet. His brief assessment of the Russian front was contrary to what he had told Churchill. True, he said, his armies had a few bridgeheads across the Oder, but they were meeting with fanatical German resistance which had stopped the advance. Mr. Roosevelt required a few more light-hearted observations before reducing his adversary to the man-to-man basis he desired. He said that the austere Admiral King was in the Czarina's bedroom. Stalin grinned and asked if Roosevelt knew that the Czar changed bedrooms every night. Roosevelt shook his head. Stalin said drily that the only place one could be sure to find him in the morning was in the bathroom. The two, chatting alone in the presence of a couple of aides, got to business. If Stalin noticed that the difference between FDR at Teheran and at Yalta was a cavernous pallor, he did not mention it, even to Harry Hopkins or others for whom he felt some respect. The President was tense. He lit one cigarette after another, always offering one to the Marshal. Did the Marshal recall the toast at Teheran to kill 50,000 German officers? Well, the President said, he had observed the wanton destruction on the road from Saki and he was prepared to drink that toast again.

Stalin said that the Germans did not have time to destroy the Crimea before they retreated. It would be better if Roosevelt could see the whole Ukraine, where the Hitlerites blackened and blew up everything they could not remove as they left. There they even poisoned the earth and ordered crops plowed up. It was more than war, Stalin said. It was an extreme of sadism. He asked how things were going on the western front. The President did not feel prepared to answer the question; General Marshall would give Stalin a detailed report later. FDR said that Eisenhower would begin a limited offensive "Thursday" (February 8). Another would start "a week from today." The main drive into the heart of Germany would commence in thirty days.

Stalin turned to his interpreter and, in rapid Russian, said he was pleased to hear this; Russian armies, he said, had already captured the Silesian basin, one source of Germany's coal; if the Allied forces would take the Ruhr and the Saar Valley, Hitler's last source of coal would be gone. The President appeared to be pleased with the way the informal chat was going and ventured to say that, with the Russians approaching from the east and the Americans and British from the west, perhaps it was time for the two forces to establish daily communication. Stalin said yes, it was time. The tenor of the remainder of the conversation, initiated by Roosevelt, would indicate that he was consciously trying to prove to his host that the Americans, British and French were not acting as a coalition against the mighty Soviet Union.

He asked how Stalin got along with de Gaulle. The shoulder boards on the Marshal's uniform shrugged as he said that the French provisional leader was a rather complicated man who was completely "unrealistic" about the French contribution to victory. The President said that he had found de Gaulle to be a stiff, stubborn man prone to compare himself to Joan of Arc. The President moved on to state that there were disagreements between the United States and the United Kingdom over how to treat France and the question of zones of occupation in Germany.

This matter would be debated at a plenary session, and Stalin did not propose to settle it in private. He asked Roosevelt if he thought that France should be awarded a zone of occupation among the victorious nations, and if so, why. Roosevelt, embarrassed, made an ambivalent reply—arguing for and against France. He could not afford to tell the Russian the truth, that the people of the United States, and the Congress, expected their soldiers to come home after the war. America did not want to police Europe or Asia for a long time. Privately Roosevelt had told aides that he was prepared to maintain a considerable force of American soldiers in Germany and in Japan for "two years." Beyond that time, he hoped that the British, Russians and French would patrol Germany, and he hoped that Chiang and his Chinese would keep the peace in Japan. Molotov saw FDR's perplexed expression and said that the question properly should be debated by the three great powers, but he and Stalin were opposed to French participation.

The sky was darkening when Molotov suggested that the leaders move to the main ballroom for the first plenary session. It was 5:00 P.M. The room was about 50 by 30 feet with a half dozen arched windows on each side. The ceiling was embossed with plaster octagons; at one end was a walnut double door; at the other, a huge conical fireplace aflame with crackling logs. Near the fireplace a large round table had been set up with white tablecloths covering it, draped to the floor. Around it seventeen wooden straight-backed chairs had been set. Near the fireplace were additional chairs for aides who would sit behind the leaders to whisper counsel. Stalin made no pretense to arrange seating except regarding the chair closest to the fireplace. He waved the President to it. The seating arrangements of the first meeting became permanent. If the table may be considered a clock, FDR sat at twelve o'clock, Churchill at four o'clock, and Stalin at nine. The men who were present to settle the affairs of the world—again reading clockwise—were:

For the U.S.: President Roosevelt, Charles E. Bohlen, James F. Byrnes. For Great Britain: Sir Alexander Cadogan; Anthony Eden; Prime Minister Winston Churchill; Major Birse, Churchill's interpreter; Sir Edward Bridges; Sir Archibald Clark Kerr. For the Soviet Union: F. T. Gusev, Soviet Ambassador to Great Britain; Andrei Vyshinsky, Deputy Foreign Minister; V. M. Molotov, Foreign Minister; Marshal Stalin; I. M. Maisky; Andrei Gromyko, Soviet Ambassador to the United States. For the U.S: Admiral William Leahy and Edward Stettinius. Between Ed and FDR, a man sat sidewards, head bowed, a cigarette in his hand. This was Harry Hopkins, who insisted on getting out of bed for the historic meeting.

Stalin opened the session by speaking with a cigarette jutting from his mustache. He welcomed Russia's friends to the Crimea and said that the deliberations should be called the Crimean Conference. Without pause, he said that, as host, he had the right to name the presiding officer, and that would be Franklin D. Roosevelt. Molotov waved a photographer in to make a picture and leave. The conferees chatted as the tripod was set up; only Winston Churchill turned his puckish face to the camera. It seemed remarkable, to the diplomats, that there was no official stenographer—no stenographer at all. Anthony Eden, looking around the table, had an additional fault to find. Major Birse, Churchill's aide, and Bohlen, the President's aide, would listen to each sentence or two uttered by their leaders and translate it to Russian. Pavlov would translate Stalin's and Molotov's monologues into halting English. The British Foreign Secretary, with irritation, felt that the languages had been reversed. Pavlov should translate all English into Russian for his masters;

Bohlen and Birse could digest all Russian and give it to FDR and the P.M. in English.

When the camera was removed, and the doors closed, there was a moment of hush. The three delegations looked to President Roosevelt as the presiding officer. The President, who had an acute sense of drama, permitted his eyes to roam the entire table without uttering a word. Because the fate of Germany would be under discussion, each delegation had brought its military leaders to sit in second-row chairs—not only to listen but to discuss tactics. From this day onward, the warriors would meet each morning bringing up questions which concerned them and report back to their leaders with such solutions as might be agreed upon. At noon the three foreign ministers would meet each day to debate points which the Big Three could not resolve, or matters which were the proper province of foreign ministers. They too would report back to the Big Three each day with results at 4:00 P.M. All plenary sessions would begin promptly at 5:00 P.M.

This was the conference blueprint. The President opened the proceedings by stating that he was honored to open "this great conference." He would like to express his gratitude to his hosts, he said, for the "splendid arrangements" made for the comfort of all. He clasped his whitish hands on the table before him and said he knew everyone desired peace and wanted the war to come to an end as quickly as possible. Stalin listened to the remarks with stony face turned toward Roosevelt. Churchill doodled with a pencil and pad. Eden crossed his arms and leaned back in his chair. An important thing, Mr. Roosevelt said, was that "we" understood each other much better than in the past. The plenary sessions, therefore, would require no formality. He proposed that the talks be informal so that each of the three delegations could be candid. The room remained silent. After a moment Mr. Roosevelt said that he had discovered, after long experience, that the best manner in which to conduct business lay in open discussion. He continued, cheerful, nodding his head vigorously and turning the famous

Roosevelt smile to all sides of the table. He knew that this conference could be expected to range the entire surface of the world, he said, but he thought that the three powers should discuss the military situation in Germany first. FDR made a gracious gesture to Stalin, and said that the people of America and Great Britain had been thrilled by the advance of the Russian armies into Germany and would appreciate a report from the Soviet Union.

Stalin looked at Colonel General Antonov, Deputy Chief of Staff, who stood and read from a paper. It described in glowing terms the Russian winter offensive, which began on January 12. The general advance was along a 500-mile front, and, in the first eighteen days, averaged 19 miles a day. He singled out each army for special mention, from Rokossovsky to Zhukov to Koniev. Two of the armies, he said, had pressed on into Germany, and one had reached the banks of the Oder River slightly to the north of Frankfurt. The concluding paragraphs asked the British and Americans to speed up their offensive on the western front. He asked Russia's allies to take "severe air action" on the French and Italian fronts to keep the Germans from shifting divisions to the eastern front. The gallant Soviet troops, he said, had destroyed 45 German divisions.

He sat. The President thought he should submit to some questions. He asked Antonov if, when the Russians found themselves on German soil, they had changed the narrow-gauge tracks to the broad gauge of the Russian railroads. To the assemblage, the question bordered on the asinine. The General stood to say that what German rolling stock they could find had been destroyed. To bring Russian supplies into parts of Germany, it had been necessary to widen the tracks on a few main rail lines. The width of tracks would appear to be a tactical question for field commanders to ponder, but the President pursued it. Speaking directly to Stalin, he said that the Combined Chiefs of Staff should decide now what to do if and when they approached tracks of various widths. Most of the tracks in Germany, Stalin responded, were standard width, and Russia lacked equipment to

alter them. His voice came from deep in his chest. Before
the first two sentences could be translated, Stalin arose
to speak louder and lean with his knuckles on the table.

Without preamble Stalin veered from railroads. He
said that there were broad statements around that he
was presenting the current Russian military situation
because of demands from President Roosevelt and Prime
Minister Churchill. This was not so, he said loudly.
He said that Antonov's presentation had been made
because Stalin had ordered it to be done. The sense
of camaraderie and cheer around the table expired.
Churchill had a cigar drooping from the center of his
mouth. Roosevelt was attentive, but slack-jawed. Stettinius reasoned that Stalin had come under pressure
from the Soviet Politburo and had been charged with being tractable to his allies. The outburst ended as quickly
as it began, and Stalin resumed his chair.

Churchill suggested to Roosevelt that General Marshall should now present the British and American
strategy. Marshall, who could inspire respect without
being stiff, stood with no notes and gave a concise account
of all the action on the western front. Hitler's offensive
in the Ardennes, he said, had slowed the Allied advance,
but the price to German strength was more than they
could afford. The salient had been pinched off, and,
in some areas, the British and Americans were further
advanced than they had been before Rundstedt's gamble.
Within a month, he said, Eisenhower hoped to have
Montgomery and other forces across the Rhine into
the heart of Germany. He would guess the date to be
shortly after March 1. Gigantic American Eighth Air
Force raids by day had reduced German industry to
rubble. British night raids had destroyed many great
cities. The American Ninth Air Force, a tactical group,
was intent on destroying German transport behind the
Nazi lines. Heavy bombers were now employed to reduce
rail communications and assembly yards—which, Marshall might have added, made the question of broad-
versus narrow-gauge railroads academic. He felt certain,

he said, that German oil production was only 20 percent of what it had been.

The Russians seemed electrified at the report. They listened avidly to the translator; a few made notes. The General said that the Germans had mastered some technological aspects of U-boat problems, and he expected a renewed battle at sea. And yet, the best Intelligence estimate he could give at present was that there were between 30 and 35 German submarines at sea. When General Marshall sat, Prime Minister Churchill reminded his confreres that Danzig, as well as Kiel and Wilhelmshaven, were great U-boat bases. The Russian armies were approaching Danzig, and the P.M. hoped that they would hit the U-boat base hard.

Stalin asked Marshall whether the Allies had sufficient manpower for the big offensive of early March. It was obvious that he was trying to get an estimate of strength. Marshall got to his feet to say that, on March 1, British and American forces would come to 89 divisions. What was more important, he thought, was that one out of every three would be a heavy tank division. Abruptly, Stalin asked: "How many tanks?" The General, who seemed able to respond to almost any question precisely, said: "Nearly 10,000 tanks and 4,000 heavy bombers." Stalin's face reflected an appreciation. However, he pointed out that Russia had 180 divisions against Hitler's 80 on the eastern front. Churchill removed the cigar from his mouth to observe that Great Britain and the United States had never had superiority in manpower over the Germans; they were fighting Hitler man-for-man. "Our superiority," he said, "rests on our advantage in bombers and tanks."

The conversation moved to an aura of affable caution. No one dared offend with a question too incisive; yet the atmosphere was hardly one of allies, men who had pledged their young men and their treasure to the cause of liberty and peace. It was an adversarial relationship; each of the three was concerned with what he might have to give, balanced against what he might get. Night fell and the overhead chandeliers shone with diamond brilliance. At one point Stalin moved a step further; he asked his allies their wishes in regard to the Red Army. Churchill, smiling agreeably, said he hoped the Red Army would continue its attack. The Russian dictator bristled. The current Soviet offensive, he said, not loudly but abrasively, was not the result of any wishes of Russia's allies. His country was not bound by any agreement to conduct a winter offensive. Again the Foreign Office experts felt that he was speaking in response to accusations he may have faced in the Politburo. In spite of what *some* people thought, he said, no demand or request for a winter offensive had come from the President of the United States or the Prime Minister of Great Britain. Stalin knew that FDR and Churchill were aware of Tedder's trip to Moscow and his appeal for help. The Marshal denied that there had been any plea.

As quickly as Stalin denied the obvious, he turned in the opposite direction and—for the Russian notes being taken by aides—appeared to be painting himself into a corner. Air Chief Marshal Tedder had visited the Kremlin, he said. He shrugged as though it was of no import. Tedder had asked that the Russians *continue* their offensive, if possible. His remarks died in silence. "I mention this," he said, "to show the spirit of the Soviet Union, which is to fulfill not only formal obligations but to go further." The President nodded. The only agreement made at Teheran, as he recalled, was that each partner would move forward as quickly as he could. At that time FDR could not plan far ahead or make long-range agreements for his country because he faced an election. The armies of the Allies had been separated by over a thousand miles. The situation was vastly different. Between them, they were crushing a strong enemy. It was time, Roosevelt said, for the Allies to coordinate their plans.

Stalin appeared to have mollified himself with his defense against coercion. Churchill said that he and the President—and he was sure he could speak for the President in this matter—had the utmost confidence in the spirit and efficiency of the Marshal, his people, and their armies. Now, however, these gigantic forces of justice were barely 400 miles apart, not much more than an hour's flying time; it was time for the staffs of the three great powers to coordinate their blows against Germany. As an example, the P.M. said, if the Soviet offensive came to a halt because of bad weather or logistics it should be agreed by all that the British-American forces in the west should increase their hammer blows.

The Russian became contemplative. His hands were closed before him on the table, and he opened and folded his thumbs as he spoke. He agreed with Churchill. The staffs must speak, must coordinate all plans and then submit them to a plenary session. He was in favor of that. But he proposed that they speak not only of a spring offensive but of a summer one as well. He was not at all sure that the Hitlerites would collapse soon. They could hope, but that was not enough. Stalin proposed to Roosevelt that the Chiefs of Staff be ordered into continuing sessions beginning in the morning. At 6:45 P.M. the first plenary session, a short one, was adjourned. While most of the men sat around the table chatting for a moment, Josef Stalin disappeared. Two NKVD men, assigned to guard him in a room among allies, became alarmed. They dogtrotted through the departing groups, running back and forth, shouting to each other. The Soviet Marshal reappeared. He explained that he had hurried off to the lavatory.

The President was wheeled to his bedroom. George Fox and Arthur Prettyman undressed the Boss and placed him on the small high bed. Fox gave him a lengthy passive massage, rubbing the pungent unguents on the palms of his hands and, with a towel on his shoulder, placing the President's instep there and working slowly up and down the bony legs. Once in a while the Boss would admit to Fox that he felt "pretty well fagged," but he would not complain of pain or the sore buttocks from sitting for long periods. The massages refreshed the President; they were followed by a wash-down bath, and Mr. Roosevelt had a deep gratitude for the strong

Lieutenant Commander who made him feel stronger for a moment.

Considering the strong ethnocentricity of the Big Three, in addition to the suspicions that foreigners reserve for foreigners, it becomes understandable—almost forgivable—that the great powers would misunderstand each other from the start. For example, Chip Bohlen's personal notes give a glowing report of General Marshall's presentation but barely summarize Antonov's. The Russian notes barely mention Marshall's talk but detail everything uttered by General Antonov. The Russian notes go further. Where Marshall said that German oil reserves were down to 20 percent, Soviet notes depict him as saying down to 40 percent; where Marshall enumerated 32 German divisions facing Alexander on the Italian front, the Russian notes say 27. Where Marshall claimed that the Germans had made a breakthrough in U-boat warfare with a new device calculated to keep the boats under the surface for long periods, the Russian notes indict America for incompetence in war at sea. In addition, there were errors in translation. Churchill, at one point, asked what superiority the Russians had over the Germans on their front. Stalin replied that the Soviets had a superiority of 100 divisions to 80. Churchill's interpreter—also Bohlen—misunderstood. Soviet superiority was 100 divisions, but the correct count was 180 divisions to 80.

Stalin got into his black Packard sedan and drove back to his villa. The British, in several cars, drove behind him. When Sir Alec Cadogan reached the privacy of his room, he penned notes in his diary:

Pres. presiding. He looks rather better than when I last saw him. But I think he's woolier than ever. Stalin looks well—rather grayer—and seemed to be in very good form. I don't think they told us an awful lot that we didn't know. . . . It's always the same with these conferences: they take days to get on the rails. The Great Men don't know what they are talking about and have to be educated, and made a bit more tidy in their methods. . . . Anthony is flapping

in and out and dropping papers all over the place. . . .
This [building] was hardly damaged or looted [by the Ger-
mans]. Some of the decorations and furniture could do
with a little of both.

The President rested an hour, then dressed for a small
dinner to which he had invited a select group. When
he left the bed, Fenya came into the room—as always,
without knocking. She had served most of her life as
a maid in the Hotel Metropole in Moscow; she was
old and efficient and she remade the bed, stealing looks
at the President as she rolled up the pillows and rearranged the silken ochre counterpane. Later, she wept
and said, "Such a sweet and kind man, but so terribly,
terribly ill." FDR was in a good mood. He felt that, even
though no earth-shaking agreements had been reached,
the first plenary session had been cordial, and he enjoyed his role. It is strange that he did not see himself as
the chief representative of one of the three great powers
but as a mediator between Stalin and Churchill. As
he explained to his aides, he was keeping peace at the
peace conference.

Dinner was arranged for 8:30 P.M. It did not occur
to FDR there would be thirteen guests around the table:
Stalin, Churchill, Stettinius, Eden, Molotov, Harriman,
Clark Kerr, Gromyko, Vyshinsky, Byrnes, Bohlen, Major Birse and Comrade Pavlov. The President's messboys
cooked the dinner, which had strong overtones of Russian
delicacies: caviar, sturgeon, beef and macaroni, layer
cake, tea, coffee, vodka and an assortment of wines.
Most of the dinner was spent in good-humored banter.
Eden marveled that British Air Marshal Portal had admired a fish tank, but noted that there were no fish in it.
That had occurred yesterday. This afternoon an assortment of goldfish were swimming in the tank. Someone else remarked that, as the British could not find
any lemon peel for preprandial cocktails, the magical
Russians might bring a lemon tree. It was a jest, but
two days later a growing lemon tree stood in the hallway
of the British villa.

Stalin told his host that the Soviet Union was doing well, considering the devastation of almost all of White Russia. "We lack only tin, rubber and pineapples," he said in an offhand way. As always, the toasts in vodka were plentiful if not memorable. Once, at Teheran, Churchill drank to a Persian waiter and Stalin ordered the frightened man to drink to the Big Three. Again, tongues were loosened, although few noted that Stalin diluted each toast with water from a carafe. Gruffly, he told Roosevelt that, had he known how tired the President was, he would have agreed to leave Soviet territory and go somewhere more agreeable to his friend. The President said he was glad to be in the Crimea; he had a lifelong interest in places new to him.

All of them sat in straight-backed chairs with cracked leather seats at a table plainer than that depicted by Leonardo in *The Last Supper*. The Big Three sat together on one side, passing victuals and bottles. Roosevelt said, "What will happen when we two are gone?" Josef Stalin looked up from his plate. In his case, he said, the decision had already been made. The Americans, he supposed, would hold an election. In the Soviet Presidium, such natural contingencies as death had long been considered and decided. The President did not ask who Stalin's successor might be. Instead, he said that Ed Stettinius had an urgent desire to visit Moscow. The President noted that Molotov was listening: "Do you think Ed will behave in Moscow as Molotov did in New York?" It was one of the few times that Pavlov, the interpreter, chuckled before rendering the words into Russian. Molotov, humorless and ascetic, was known in Washington as "Stone Ass." Stalin smiled and said, "He could come to Moscow incognito." In a mood of camaraderie, FDR said: "There is one thing I want to tell you. The Prime Minister and I have been cabling back and forth for years now. We have a term of endearment by which we refer to you and that is 'Uncle Joe.'" Stalin bristled. He glared at the President and said he found it unfriendly. Jimmy Byrnes leaned forward to explain that it was intended in the same sense as Ameri-

cans use "Uncle Sam." The Marshal was not mollified.
He half stood. Stiffly, he told Roosevelt it was time for him
to leave. The President looked hurt, alarmed. Excitedly,
he ordered more champagne. "Please stay," he said.
Molotov shook his head. Wearily, he said in English:
"He is just pulling your leg. We have known this for
two years. All Russia knows you call him 'Uncle Joe.' "
Stalin sat. He said he would remain until 10:30 P.M.
He didn't depart until a short time before midnight.

Winston Churchill cut into the tension with a toast.
"The whole world will have its eyes on this conference,"
he said, standing. "If it is successful, we will have peace
for a hundred years. Only the great powers who have
fought the war and shed the blood can maintain the
peace." Stalin drank with enthusiasm. There was a hint of
anti-United Nations spirit in the thought; Stalin believed
that the Big Three should administer the affairs of the
world. Stalin drank and addressed the dinner: only the
great powers who had fought the battles and crushed
the oppressors should have the *unanimous* right to make
the peace and keep it, he said. The outspoken policy
of some, he said, that the big nations had shed their
blood to free the small ones was ridiculous. Already
some of them were reproving their liberators for not
respecting their rights, he said. He used little Albania
as an example. He called the provisional government
a "Socialist upstart." Who, he asked, could imagine little
Albania having an equal voice in world affairs with the
Big Three? The Soviet Union was prepared, with the assistance of the United States and Great Britain, to protect
the small nations from aggression. But he, Stalin, would
never permit Big Three policies to be submitted to small
nations for approval. Both Churchill and Roosevelt hastened to agree to all that Stalin had said. The P.M. said
that there would never be a question of the small countries dictating to the large. Stalin was irritated again. He
said he had in mind the *opposite;* the big nations had
a duty to dictate to the small. On the opposite side of
the table, Andrei Vyshinsky was into a dispute with
Chip Bohlen. Churchill said, "The eagle should permit

the small birds to sing, and care not wherefor they sang."
In translation, this must have lost something because
Stalin demanded of Roosevelt: "Do you want Albania
to have the same status as the United States?" Vyshinsky
said that under no cicumstances would Russia agree
to permit the small nations an equal vote with the Soviet
Union. Bohlen, in an attempt to be temperate, said that
the people of the United States had the rights of small
powers in mind, and the Big Three would be expected
to exercise judicious restraint in the world organization.
"The American people," Vyshinsky snapped, "should
learn to obey their leaders." Bohlen, losing control, said
he would be happy to have Vyshinsky come to America
and explain that to the people. Vyshinsky said he would
be happy to make the visit and tell the people.

The informal dinner was askew. Roosevelt looked
stunned. Stalin was silent for a while, then found another
bruising topic. Among all the nations in the Western
Hemisphere, only Argentina had proved unfriendly to
the Allies. He would like to know if anything was being
done to punish Argentina. Obviously, the military were
in control there and they were pro-Axis. Roosevelt replied
lamely that the Argentine people were good, but "there
are some bad men in power at the moment." Stalin
acted as though this was beyond his comprehension.
"If Argentina was in this section of the world," he said,
"I would see that she was punished." FDR tried to get
away from South America. The problem of dealing with
smaller nations, he said, was going to be complex, but
worth the effort. Again he said: "We have seven million
Poles in America—people who are vitally interested in
the future of Poland." Obviously, this was designed
to make Stalin defensive about his position in Slavic
Europe. "Of your seven million Poles," he said loudly,
"only seven thousand vote." The President looked incredulous. "I looked it up," Stalin said, "and I know
that I am right."

Once more Churchill tried to stem the loud disagreements which distressed Roosevelt. He proposed
a toast to the proletarian masses of the world. As ad-

dendum, he noted that, of the three men, he was the only one who could be voted out of office at any time. Stalin smiled and noted that the Prime Minister seemed to fear the impending British elections. To the contrary, Churchill said, he gloried in the fact that the English people could change their government. The Russian dictator altered his mood. He asked the President, in mock-serious vein, whether he had wired Moscow for 500 bottles of champagne. FDR said he wasn't certain. That would be all right, Stalin said, because he was willing to extend a credit for them to thirty years. Conversation de-escalated to a one-to-one basis. The President said that Churchill arises late in the morning, works hard until mid-afternoon, goes to bed for a pre-dinner sleep, and then sits up half the night talking. Stalin nodded. His schedule, he said, and this included all his generals and admirals, was to work until 5:00 A.M. every night. Then to bed, and up at 10:00 A.M. It was not an easy life, but he and his staff exercised it seven days a week.

For a third time, Andrei Vyshinsky repeated that the Soviet leaders were sorry to depart, but that Stalin must. The Soviet dictator raised his voice and told Roosevelt that the little birds had better be careful where they sang. (Or according to another translation, "Little birds should be careful where they walk.") The Americans felt that it was a good, rousing informal dinner. Churchill felt that he sided with Stalin—the Big Three should arrange the affairs of the world in unanimity, even if they had to abrogate the rights of small nations. Eden returned to his room and wrote with some bitterness:

Dinner with Americans; a terrible party I thought. President vague and loose and ineffective. W., understanding that business was flagging, made desperate efforts and too long speeches to get things going again. Stalin's attitude to small countries struck me as grim, not to say sinister.

The morning was warm and gray. At 7:30 Secret Service men admitted the first White House courier to

Livadia. All of the mail was dated January 31, indicating that a round trip would require ten days. Lieutenant Rigdon, the perpetually smiling secretary, had a pouch of mail signed by the President to be delivered to the White House. The courier departed at 8:00, dashing off to Saki airport. There were a few hangovers and an irritated queue of towel-holders lining up outside the bathroom doors. There had been parties and informal conferences at the three villas the night before. The Roosevelt group had always been a drinking—not drunken—crowd. At the White House it was common to see bottles of liquor rolling in bottom desk drawers.

Each of the Big Three spent the morning hours administering to the affairs of his nation. Matters military and domestic had top priority. Not until lunchtime each day—and frequently later—were they willing to emerge to discuss conference matters. The generals and admirals met late each morning with their mutual problems, pouring over maps, and either reaching agreements which would have to be endorsed later at the plenary sessions or closing in disagreement and tossing the problems back to the conferees. The daily problem with the foreign ministers was similar: they met each day at a different villa at lunch, engaged in numerous toasts, and wrestled with decisions of national policy until 3:30 P.M. or later. Their agreements, or lack of them, were also returned to their superiors at the conference for ratification or resolution. Molotov, Stettinius and Eden had the assistance of Vyshinsky, Gusev, Matthews, Hiss and Cadogan. Frequently, military problems and political overlapped; in such cases the generals and admirals referred the problem to the foreign ministers. However, whether the decisions were going upward or downward, all reached the plenary sessions. The soluble problems and the insolubles seemed to journey on elevators.

Never, in the history of man, had so many highly placed gentlemen assembled to spawn chaos. Jimmy Byrnes, for example, spent the morning of February 5 working out a declaration of policy for liberated countries. The subject was not within his purview as Director of War Mobilization, but he had heard that the President did not like the draft presented by the State Department. Byrnes had taken the time to read it; then he discussed it point by point with Roosevelt. After that he used his knowledge of stenography to work quickly on an acceptable draft. Cadogan, who had a personal respect for Hopkins, spent the morning visiting the sick man in his room. "I felt good," Hopkins said wryly, "until I went to Rome and was introduced to the Pope." General Bedell Smith had a military problem. His boss, Dwight D. Eisenhower, had been telling the President for two years that there should be no zones of occupation in Germany; that the three powers should invest the defeated nation and occupy all of it randomly. General Smith's current assignment was to assure Roosevelt that Eisenhower felt his forces were about to penetrate deeper into Germany than the previous estimates. He hoped that FDR would postpone the zones of occupation decision at Yalta and wait until Germany collapsed to see where the contending armies stood. To complicate it, none of the parties seemed to recall that the Big Three had set up an Allied Control Commission in London to decide this question, among others. The commission, among whose members was John Winant, Ambassador to Great Britain, had decided to give the northern side of Germany to Great Britain, the southern to the United States (except for one port on the North Sea) and the eastern part of Germany to Russia. The Soviet zone of occupation would be in addition to the territory to be ceded to Poland, so Russia would patrol about 40 percent of Germany.

Smith worked hard on his written plan. Roosevelt would not give it a hearing because he said he felt honor bound to adhere to the Allied Control Commission zones. In addtion, Churchill desired a fourth zone for France. Privately, FDR was prepared to give the French a section of the American zone, which would lessen U.S. responsibility in Germany. Unknown to all except the American Joint Chiefs of Staff, Winant had been asked to demand 46 percent of German territory as the American zone, and cut the Soviets to 20 percent. Ambassador Winant argued himself into a *cul de sac*. When pressed, he could think of no reason why the American Joint Chiefs of Staff suddenly desired to police almost half of Germany. George Kennan of the State Department had brought this delicate matter directly to the attention of the President, who laughed, and said, "Why, that's just something I drew on the back of an envelope." Evidently he had drawn the diagram in the presence of Marshall or King, and it had become "official." Winant, disgusted and with little influence, told the President it was possible that the Russians might reach the edge of their zone of occupation and keep right on going because zones had not been agreed to. At that point FDR agreed to the decisions of the Allied Control Commission. This did not settle the matter because, although Russian and British members of the commission had concurred, Stalin and Churchill had not. Eden, Molotov and former Secretary of State Hull had submitted the London decisions to their superiors but were unaware that the reports remained undigested. Cadogan complained often that Winston Churchill seldom read any Foreign Office policy papers, preferring to sit with Eden and others and discuss each subject as it came to mind, without reference to what had already been accomplished. Roosevelt was almost as poorly informed, and seldom read "lawyer-phrased" agreements at length. He too preferred to sit and discuss the matter with the concerned officials and hear a digest of agreement from "the horse's mouth." There are few records concerning Stalin's attitude toward Foreign Office decisions, but Molotov and Vyshinsky often reminded him, in whispers, that decisions had already been made in matters he proposed to broach.

The official attitude of the United States, which the State Department enjoyed calling "elastic," was confused and ambivalent. Unknown to Roosevelt, Stettinius arrived at Yalta with two position papers on postwar Germany. One was called "Economic Policies Toward Germany"; the other "Reparation and Restitution Policy

Toward Germany." The first envisioned a self-sustaining Germany shorn of war-making capabilities. In this, reparations, or payments of restitution, were placed at the bottom of priorities. In the second, the State Department acknowledged that the Soviet Union would insist on reparation payments in addition to slave labor from Germany to rebuild the ruin of Russian cities. "There is no compelling reason for the United States to oppose such claims," it concluded. Also, it would not argue with the Soviet Union in the matter of "labor service within reasonable limits." The phrase "within reasonable limits" was the benign trap down which Roosevelt and his State Department would fall. One paper favored the dismemberment of Germany; the second stated that "imposed dismemberment would create difficulties and disrupt the German economy."

If there was a person at the conference who was clear and unequivocal in his judgment of Germany, it was Ivan Maisky, Assistant Commissar for Foreign Affairs. At successive meetings of the foreign ministers, Maisky, when permitted to speak, stated that the first consideration of Russia in regard to Germany was "security." Twice in less than thirty years the German hordes had raced savagely through Poland and across the scarred face of White Russia. The Soviet Union, first of all, required barriers to prevent Germans from doing it again.

Second, Germany had heavy industry. This had a war-making potential. Russia proposed to strip it down and ship it to Soviet cities. Third, Russia was not so much interested in cash reparations because she was aware of the Germany of World War I, which had paid and paid until her currency was worthless and the nation collapsed. Maisky said that reparations, in the main, should come from German labor shipped to Russia; as Cordell Hull once phrased it, Maisky said, "the first priority should be for damage caused by enemy action." Maisky added his own blunt phrase: "Those who have done the most fighting should get the most." His last point was not Kremlin-inspired; Maisky thought he was conceding to Roosevelt's view when he said that perhaps Germany should be dismembered: make independent nations of the Ruhr, the Rhineland, the Catholic south. In sum, Germany should be permitted sufficient strength only to live and pay for her imports.

At lunch that day of February 5 the handsome, engaging Averell Harriman announced casually that MacArthur had retaken the city of Manila. Molotov toasted the "Allied armies" and this, to the dismay of the Americans, led to a series of twelve toasts in vodka which left everyone amiably disposed and slightly blurred. When the last glass had been drained, Molotov suggested that the conference achieve an official name: "The Crimean Conference." This hardly seemed a serious piece of business, especially as Stalin had suggested it, but all hands agreed. Eden asked Molotov what questions the Russians proposed to broach at the plenary session. Great Britain would like to be prepared. The Soviet Foreign Minister shrugged. "Any question the United Kingdom or the United States desires." It has been said that no answer is an answer. The dapper Eden said that the problem was that German problems had been discussed for years on a "technical level," but that Churchill had not studied the decisions. The Soviet Foreign Minister was in favor of discussing German matters and bringing "proposals to the Big Three in a few days." Stettinius cut in, saying that the United States was interested in German viability as a nation. Molotov said the Russians had a similar interest, even though his country proposed to strip Germany. Without pause he asked Stettinius for long-term credit loans from the United States. Although the words "Lend-Lease" were not mentioned, both Molotov and Stettinius knew that, under an Act of Congress, Lend-Lease would end when the war ended. It did not seem to Stettinius to be a proper subject for a peace conference. "We can discuss it here, or in Moscow," he said, "or in Washington later."

The Russian Foreign Minister, a realist among idealists, stated that there wasn't much to discuss. The subjects treated at yesterday's plenary session had been general, and no problems had been referred to the foreign ministers. "Yesterday," said Maisky, who spoke good English, "they spoke of military matters. This went to the chiefs of staff this morning." On the second as well as the first day, there was nothing to discuss on the foreign ministers' level.

The morning meeting of the military chiefs was cordial and unproductive. Soviet Air Marshal Sergei Khudyakov made a speech extolling Soviet air power. General Marshall and Field Marshal Alexander extolled Anglo-American air power as the only field in which they held superiority over the Germans. The British and Americans had 14,000 war planes. General Antonov was unimpressed. He knew that a realistic appraisal of the military situation—east and west—could be used to prove beyond doubt that the Soviet Union had borne the brunt of German resistance and was crushing it. Casually he cited the fact that the Soviet Union had begun its spring offensive in the dead of winter to keep Hitler from transferring the Nazi breakthrough in the west at Ardennes. Now he would like to know what offensives his western friends planned along the Rhine and in Italy to prevent German divisions from being transferred to the eastern front.

Marshall and Sir Alan Brooke hid their embarrassment. Each kept repeating that they were fighting the Germans "even"; on the other hand, Kesselring could release 10 divisions in Italy for service in the east. General Marshall reversed the Russian plea: he asked that the Russians push their offensive to the fullest while Eisenhower was trying to cross the Rhine. Antonov said, perhaps with veiled contempt, that the enormous Allied superiority in planes could be felt only when the "weather is good." He promised that the Russians would continue pressure against the Germans to the limit of Soviet strength, but he still expected cooperation from his allies. Brooke admitted that, in Italy, Alexander was expected to transfer some of his strength to Eisenhower's western front, which seemed to worry Antonov. This would free Kesselring to do the same.

The Russian staff showed its disappointment. They had hoped, Antonov said, that Alexander would be able to push northward in Italy, then turn a large force eastward through the Yugoslavian Ljubljana gap and join up with the Russian armies on their left flank to take Vienna and drive northward into Germany. This, of course, was the old Churchillian dream which Roosevelt and the Joint Chiefs of Staff had vetoed. Had it been possible, Germany would have been encircled when Montgomery began his northern march along the Baltic. General Antonov decided to settle for less. His main concern, he said, was troop transfer to the eastern front. Did the generals think it possible to prevent the Germans from withdrawing divisions from Norway and Denmark? No. The admirals said that German troops in the north would be moved by sea, and Britain and America would be hampered by mines. Antonov surrendered.

He and his subordinates discussed field artillery techniques with their western friends. Marshall introduced the subject of liaison and cooperation between the two fronts. He reminded the staffs that the Big Three had brought the matter up at the first session. Antonov was almost curt. It was out of his hands, he said. The Soviet military system was one of escalating echelons leading directly to Moscow. A field general was not permitted to make decisions. Soviet Marshal Tolbukhin explained that each objective of his forces had been given to him in an order from Moscow, where, he said, the Stavka led directly to Stalin himself. Additional forces and weapons would be sent to him. He would prepare for the tactics he proposed to employ; this would be sent to Moscow for approval. When approval arrived, he moved with the forces given to him. As soon as the objective was seized, his extra forces and reserves were transferred from his command—he did not know where.

Fleet Admiral Leahy had a solution. There was a Joint Military Mission in Moscow; why not negotiate all liaison and tactical problems through the mission? General Marshall objected. He would like to see radio contact between commanders in the field. There had already been a clash in the sky over Italy between American and Russian planes. Antonov said that this was a result of a navigational error on the part of the Soviet Air Command; there would be no necessity for field commanders to cooperate. The orders would come from Moscow. Air Marshal Sir Charles Portal—he of the long nose and memory—said that Antonov was suggesting long-range "strategic" liaison but not day-to-day "tactical" exchanges. The Soviet General shrugged. If his friends wanted, he said, they could draw a line across Germany and agree not to bomb beyond that line, and there would be no more air clashes. Portal and U.S. General Kuter said they would want to think about it. General Antonov's final word should have been his first: he had discussed these matters with Stalin, and Russia had no intention of altering its chain of command to effect day-to-day coordination of attack with their allies.

The President was seated in his appointed chair, with his back to the fireplace, at 3:45 P.M. He looked tired this time because he had to read and digest all the mail (with its concomitant problems) from Washington and had dictated to Lieutenant Rigdon almost all morning. After that he conferred with Leahy, Marshall, King and Kuter regarding their "empty" conference with the Russians; at 3:00 P.M. he had received Stettinius to get a report on the foreign ministers' luncheon. It had been a busy day, all of it leading to this moment.

Mr. Roosevelt, exhibiting a hacking cough, tilted his head and read from a sheet of paper that, as presiding officer of the conference, he proposed they discuss the occupation of Germany and the French desire for a zone of occupation. He seemed startled when Stalin picked up a paper and said that *he* proposed to discuss: (1) the partition of Germany; (2) would the Big Three establish a government of their own in postwar Germany? (3) he would like the Big Three to spell out the terms of unconditional surrender; (4) what kind of reparations and what amount? In one day the Yalta Conference had risen from no agenda to two. Eden and Roosevelt tumbled over each other to assure Stalin that his questions grew out of zones of occupation, which would have to be settled first. The Soviet Marshal refused to be put off on the grounds of logic or good manners.

He moved off into a monologue about Roosevelt, at Teheran, proposing that Germany should be divided into five separate states, about Churchill more recently in Moscow suggesting two states. He would like a unanimous decision now. Churchill interposed, as he always did when the contentions became heated, to suggest a postponement. "We are all agreed on dismemberment of Germany," he said. But boundaries involved the complexities of history, geography and economics, and no man could expect to settle so much in so little time. The Big Three should appoint a special committee to study the matter. The Soviet and American leaders realized they were overburdened with committees, whose findings and decisions no one was bound to accept unless there was one more summit conference. Roosevelt, who seemed to be fighting rearguard actions with his two powerful friends, tried again to save the day. Why not, he suggested, ask the foreign ministers to discuss this matter tomorrow and bring solutions to another plenary session? Stalin nodded. Churchill agreed.

The bugaboo of Germany's future was tossed into a dark closet. This was to be the *modus operandi* of the entire conference whenever tempers became short or academic disagreements too long. "Refer it to the foreign ministers" became the mood of the conference, although the three leaders realized that their seconds-in-command disagreed as adamantly as they because each had to parrot the will of his superior. Stalin looked genuinely puzzled, and turned to his aides for assistance when Churchill said that most of the details of these matters had already been decided by the three governments. So far as the Prime Minister knew, only the zones of occupation remained to be settled. He would like to remind his confreres that, in zones of occupation, the

French should be consulted. It was obvious to all at the table that Stalin knew nothing of the decisions of the European Advisory Commission in London.

The Russians whispered among themselves. Stalin asked if it would not be wise to inform Germany that part of unconditional surrender would mean dismemberment. Churchill became vehement. It would not be necessary to discuss any decisions with the Germans, he said. Roosevelt, again the mediator, asked if the conference should not decide on Marshal Stalin's question about whether there should be dismemberment of Germany. Stalin, using the awkward terms of diplomacy, said that he wanted it settled in principle, not specifics. FDR said it was clear to him that Churchill was not prepared to discuss boundaries. He suggested that they were talking about the same thing. The matter was referred to the foreign ministers. Stalin insisted that it was not necessary to tell the Germans now; he wanted dismemberment to be part of the surrender document so that "those in power in Germany" would know what they were signing.

The British Prime Minister begged to disagree. Dismemberment would make Germany more determined to resist defeat, he said. Roosevelt said that Intelligence reports showed that the German people had suffered so much already nothing would restore the will to fight on. Churchill dropped his argument and asked about granting France a zone of occupation. This zone, he said, would be taken from British and American zones and would not affect the Soviet Union. Stalin exhibited a shrugging interest in the matter. He reminded Churchill that it was France which had "opened the gates" to the German armies. It was France which had surrendered and enabled Hitler to turn eastward to fight Russia. It was France which had but eight divisions of soldiers now—all of them uniformed and equipped by the Americans. If this entitled them to a zone of occupation, it might open the door for other states to ask for zones.

However, he hastened to add, he would not object, so long as the British and the Americans were giving

France pieces of their share. His objection, he said, was that the recognition of France as among the victorious powers would give her a voice on the Allied Control Commission for Germany. No one would give her a zone of occupation and deny her a voice in the administration of the country. Instead of a three-power subject, this would make it a four-power deal. The British Prime Minister acknowledged this. He reminded Stalin that Great Britain required the presence of a continental power in the west with an army sufficiently strong to hold off attack until Great Britain could mobilize. Stalin could have enjoyed a riposte by reminding Winston Churchill that this is the role France failed to achieve—and Britain, too—in the current war. Instead, he asked, why not give small zones of occupation to France, Holland and Begium, but no rights in the control machinery?

Churchill declined to respond. Instead, glancing toward Roosevelt, he said no one had any idea how long the United States would maintain troops in Germany; the history of the country showed that they tended to bring their sons home shortly after victory. If Russia cared to share her burden with other nations, Churchill would not argue against it. Stalin asked FDR how long the United States would remain in Europe. This too was an embarrassment. "I can get the people and Congress to cooperate fully for peace but not to keep an army in Europe. Two years would be the limit." Stalin surprised Churchill. "I agree," he said, "that France should become strong." But not, of course, have an equal voice in the control machinery. Stalin turned on his rare smile in the recesses of his mustache. France, he said, could hardly expect to join a club as exclusive as this one. Membership required five million soldiers. The Prime Minister said, "Three million: We have suffered badly from German robot bombs. After the Americans have gone home we are going to have to think seriously of the future." The Marshal said he understood; the future was a grave problem for all. He would not object to France patrolling a zone, but he would object to her having a voice in control of postwar Germany.

Again Roosevelt, finding Stalin and Churchill on opposite sides, did not cast a two-to-one vote. He could have used the majestic unimpaired power of the United States to force a decision on those who had been bled white in the war, but he chose instead to postpone. Perhaps the edge of his contempt for the arrogance of de Gaulle was showing when he stated that France should have a zone of occupation, "but I agree with the Marshal that France should not take part in the control machinery." This startled the British delegation, which had counted on his support. FDR seemed to parrot Stalin when he suggested that if France had a vote in postwar Germany, other nations might request the same right. Holland, he said, had sustained tremendous damage when the Germans opened dikes and dams and flooded vast areas with salt water. Might she not ask for a seat on the Control Commission?

Eden, who had been silent, exposed the fallacy of Allied thinking. If France were to have a zone, he asked, how could the operation of her zone be controlled if she had no voice in control? Stalin snapped that France would be responsible to the powers which gave her the zone. Anthony Eden shook his head dolefully. The French, he said, would never submit to it. He asked Stalin if de Gaulle himself had not brought up the question of a voice in control of Germany on his recent visit to Moscow. Stalin, of course, did not know whether de Gaulle had told the British what had been discussed. He said yes, the matter had come up, and he had told the General that it was something that could only be settled by the Big Three.

To American and British observers, it seemed that Stalin was trying to reach rapport with Roosevelt, not Churchill. He responded to the P.M. with asperity, but appeared to be overly cordial to the President. It was agreed, the Russian said, that France should have a zone of occupation; the matter of membership on the Control Commission was referred to the foreign secretaries. Nor did it matter whether they agreed or not; the situation had to be resolved at a plenary session.

It might not be difficult to persuade Roosevelt to vote for France, but for Russia to share control of Germany with three powers, rather than two, was anathema. The Yalta Conference had no rules; two of three votes could not decide anything. The Russians had three firm conditions preset for this meeting: it had to be on Russian soil; it had to be done without an agenda; decisions had to be unanimous.

As it would each afternoon, darkness overtook the big ballroom. The President did not appear to be any more fatigued than when the session convened. Harry Hopkins sat behind him, in profile, head bowed as in prayer. Churchill lit a fresh cigar and wore an air of equanimity. Stalin might have been a statue of himself. To some, FDR, hollow-cheeked with glistening pince-nez, began to resemble his old hero, Woodrow Wilson. He raised the next question, German reparations. Addressing himself to the Soviet delegation, he said that the United States could not use reparations in the form of forced German labor, and he believed that he also spoke for his colleagues in the British delegation.

Marshal Stalin nodded to Ivan Maisky, former Ambassador to Great Britain, one who spoke English well. As deputy to Molotov, he had correlated all the facts his country wanted to adjudicate here and now. Normally, he was jolly in attitude; his voice, speaking English, was strident today. His pointed beard quivered as he said that his country had two ideas in mind: reduce German capability to make war; repay Russia in part for damage done by the Germans. Both objectives could be attained in one gambit—within two years after the collapse of Germany, remove heavy machinery, factories, machine tools, rolling stock, aircraft and steel plants and German investments abroad. For a period of ten years Germany should be forced to make additional reparations in merchandise or "in kind."

The total cost to Germany, Maisky said, would come to about $20 billion. Of this, the Soviet Union wanted half, which, he said, would not repay her losses. On the 20 percent of industry not carried off to the Soviet

Union or elsewhere, Germany should be able to live spartanly. The British Prime Minister had said, the day before, "Let us discuss Germany's future—if she has a future." To which Marshal Stalin had replied, "Germany has a future." Maisky said that a viable Germany was important to all of Europe; Russia had no intention of crushing her, but believed that strict tripartite control would be required to make her pay. Maisky hoped that Russia's allies realized that the mother country's losses to the Germans were so astronomical that no nation could recompense her. A system of priorities for repayment from Germany, on a reduced scale, would have to be arranged, according to the size of the contribution made by each country to the war effort. A reparations commission should be set up in Moscow, he said, to arrange priorities.

Roosevelt's advice from Intelligence sources was that Russia's losses amounted to $20 billion; she was willing to settle for half. When Maisky concluded, Stalin looked around the table for opposition. It came again from Churchill. He felt that Russian economists were naive; they did not understand war. He said that after World War I, a heavy load had been saddled on the German back. What payments had been made to victorious powers came largely from American loans to Germany. In time, the nation collapsed economically and a billion Reichsmarks could not buy a loaf of bread. And yet, he said, no one could doubt that the Soviet Union had sustained savage damage. He would favor total removal and shipment to Russia of "some plants and equipment." On the other hand, Great Britain had suffered greatly and had bled longer than anyone at the table. Thousands of homes, plants and docks had been destroyed in bombing raids and V-1 attacks, and Britain, which had lost so much of her shipping, would have to export or die. No victorious country, he said with some eloquence, would emerge from this conflict so destitute as Great Britain. If there were to be reparations from Germany, he would be glad to accept them for England, but history had shown that to destroy a vanquished nation was

to eliminate a customer from the family of nations and
upset the economic balance of all. Who, he asked, would
pay for food for a phantom, starving Germany? To
make a horse pull a wagon, it had first to be fed.

Stalin, who enjoyed homilies and rural aphorisms,
said that he would not object to feeding the horse, but
he would take care to see that it did not kick him. Churchill said he would like to continue his peroration. He favored setting up a reparations commission in Moscow to
study how much Germany could pull in the wagon, and
how much she would have to be fed. The United States,
Roosevelt said, paid far more to Germany after the
last war, as loans, than it had received in reparations.
Speaking for his country, he said that America would
want no more from Germany after the war than the
property Germany owned in the United States. In addition, he said, in spite of his nation's known generosity
toward others, it would not finance Germany again.
To comprehend the situation in its most favorable light,
he argued, Germany would have to be placed in a position
where she could pay the Soviet Union in factories,
products, tools and machinery, while permitting her
to retain sufficient purchasing power to remain a customer
for British exports. Maisky responded that the problem
after World War I was that the victor nations asked
for cash reparations; the Soviet Union did not ask for
money. Germany should be left with a fair standard
of living, he said, but it should not be above Poland,
Hungary, Czechoslovakia and other neighbors.

The session was moving toward 8:00 P.M. Stalin said
that the Big Three should have first claim on Germany.
France should not be considered because she had not
exerted a determined will to stop the Nazis. Churchill
pulled the cigar from his rosy lips and said, "Each according to his *needs*." The President settled the matter by
stating that a reparations commission comprised solely
of the Soviet Union, the United Kingdom and the United
States would be created in Moscow to consider the manner, form and substance of German reparations. It was
accepted unanimously, and Roosevelt adjourned the

session. He was wheeled from the room. On the way, the bright gleaming smile fell from his face. He paused to ask Anna to invite a few friends to dinner: Marshall, Leahy, King, Admirals McIntire and Wilson Brown, Byrnes, Steve Early, Harriman and his daughter Kathleen and Ed. In the President's bedroom, Fox and Prettyman waited for the evening rubdown. It was 8:00 P.M., a long session.

Everyone complimented Roosevelt on his rapport with Stalin. No one asked why he had agreed to refer so many pertinent problems to other bodies for study—the foreign ministers, commissions in London and Moscow. As the most powerful of the principals, the politician within FDR must have asked himself why three brothers-in-arms could not agree. Why had he been so certain that he could "handle" U.J.? At times, in the first two sessions, he could not handle his dependent—Winston Churchill. Still, it was only Monday night and Roosevelt had until the end of the week to settle major problems. Harry Hopkins returned to his bed. On his note pad were two lines of interest. "That guy can't be much interested in the peace organization" and a quotation from Stalin: "We are interested in decisions, and not discussions."

History never learned to keep a secret. The well-hidden, elaborately camouflaged meeting of the Big Three was out. It started in London with a terse dispatch on February 1: ". . . the three leaders of the major powers in the alliance against Adolf Hitler will sit down at a table and hold a kind of ex-parte peace conference in the absence of the defendant, Germany." The next day the item had crossed the Atlantic and was in *The New York Times*. White House correspondents asked Assistant Press Secretary Jonathan Daniels about it and he said, "Again I have no news." Three days later, the *Times* took another swing at the story: "President Roosevelt is reported by various sources to be conferring with Stalin and Churchill." On the morning of the sixth, Naval Intelligence radioed Yalta a copy of a fresh and stronger story in the *Times:* "London—Informed quarters in London expressed belief that Roosevelt and Churchill and Stalin might already have tackled the involved problem of halting future aggression. The White House declined comment today on the statement of Sir Walter Citrine that the Big Three were meeting. Jonathan Daniels, an assistant to the President, opened his daily meeting with newsmen by saying 'Again, I have no news . . .' " In Chicago, John S. Knight, president of the American Society of Newspaper Editors, discussed the open secret and claimed that the press was carrying its self-imposed censorship too far. It was silly to cloak the meeting with such secrecy, he said. The departure of the President had been open gossip at bars, clubs and restaurants, Mr. Knight said. Radio Berlin responded to the flurry of speculation by stating that a meeting of Stalin, Roosevelt and Churchill was under way either aboard a warship in the Black Sea or in a Black Sea port. The French Telegraph Agency, which was under the censorious thumb of de Gaulle, said that the summit meeting was being staged at Sochi, on the far eastern shore of the Black Sea.

The President read it in his study and called Stettinius. "Ed," he said, "the German radio is sending a lot of stories about a Big Three meeting. I wish you and Anthony and Molotov would draw up some kind of a safe publicity release. Try to have it ready for the session this afternoon." The statement is not worthy of comment, except to say that it was the only thing that all three foreign ministers agreed upon without alteration, and the only item sanctioned by Stalin, Roosevelt and Churchill without argument. It stated, fairly succinctly, that the Big Three, accompanied by their military chiefs of staff and their foreign secretaries, "are now meeting in the Black Sea area." It emphasized "complete agreement" in the final phase of the war against Nazi Germany. "Discussion of problems in establishing a secure peace have also begun . . . Meetings are proceeding continuously."

This was a warm sunny day. The sea was soft and spangled. From the palace above the strand and the rocks it was a broad, royal blue mirror. Anna was so pleased, sniffing the day at the window, that she told her father she would like to pack a lunch basket and ask Sarah Churchill and Kathleen Harriman to join her on a drive to Sevastopol. The President glanced from his study window and said, "Yes, Sis. It's a good idea; a grand day." He asked Mike Reilly to arrange for a car, security protection and an English-speaking Russian guide. The roads beyond the mountains were treacherous and icy and he advised the party to return to the palace before dark.

The increasing pallor and gauntness of the President were evident to all except the President. Literally, he was working himself to death, but, in spite of weakness, he was a man in a hurry. He held so many short conferences that Rigdon did not mention some in his daily calendar. People were in and out of FDR's study sometimes at ten-minute intervals. He sat, he listened, he sipped water and smoked cigarettes, he coughed and offered an opinion and waited for the next visitor. The pouch from Washington had been speeded to four days' travel time. At breakfast he read the mail and bills, dictated responses to America's domestic problems, and then hurried to informal, though important, lunches down the corridor. From there to the plenary session, with its accusatory disputes, its "agreements in principle," and then a quick rubdown and dressing for long wordy dinners and hurrying to bed at midnight. Those who were close to Roosevelt this week were certain that he regarded Yalta as the culmination of his life's work, a harmonic orchestra of the world, with him holding the baton.

The foreign ministers were at lunch, trying to reach agreement on matters which must, in a few hours, be brought to the attention of the plenary session. Molotov reminded his confreres that the Big Three had decided yesterday on the dismemberment of Germany and this would have to be publicized in the final statement at Yalta. Stettinius, watching a dispute grow between Molotov and Eden, decided to imitate the role of FDR and walk a chalk line between them. Eden suggested the elimination of the word "dismemberment" because it would further stiffen Nazi resistance. In Article 12 of the surrender terms, he suggested using the words "and measures for the dissolution of German unitary state."

The bland face of Molotov kept shaking negatively. Dismemberment was the word used by the Big Three, and Churchill himself had agreed to it. The British Foreign Minister was aware that the Prime Minister had dragooned himself into agreeing, because Stalin and Roosevelt favored it. Eden would like to soften the phrasing, even though the result would be the same. Molotov would not hear of it. Stettinius came off his chalk line to suggest that the single word "dismemberment" be placed in Article 12 of the surrender terms, and to drop the matter there. The Russian asked the Briton if he was aware that, should the word dismemberment be omitted, Stalin was prepared to ask for harsher phrasing. Eden said no. Molotov thereupon said that the words should read: "In order to secure the peace and security of Europe they will take measures for the dismemberment of Germany."

Anthony Eden decided to ask for a diplomatic postponement. He suggested that dismemberment would require further study by the three nations. Yes, Molotov said, there would be much study required about how to break Germany into weak sections, but first it must be agreed that the premise of dismemberment had been endorsed and would be carried out. The method, how many separate states, borders, could and would be thrashed out later. Stettinius offered a bright, false hope: "How about 'including dismemberment to the degree necessary to safeguard the peace and security'?" Molotov agreed. Eden became irritated. The Russian decided to retreat an inch. Why not mention dismemberment, he said, without spelling out how much and without the phrase "for the future peace and security"? The Briton said no. At that point Molotov appeared to be in relentless pursuit of Anthony Eden, reminding him again and again that Churchill had already agreed to dismemberment. Tensions mounted. Yet they had to report back with some conclusion, so all three finally settled on the word "dismemberment," to be inserted in Article 12, and that the Prime Minister should be asked how the word should be used.

The Russian Foreign Minister had a suspicion—shared by Stalin and Vyshinsky—that the British did not want to crush postwar Germany; England aspired to do business with the vanquished. They were also in agreement that Roosevelt did not sincerely care what happened to Germany; he would waver to whichever side presented the stronger case. Great Britain, they felt certain, wanted a militarily weak and an economically strong Germany; the Soviet Union felt the terms were contradictory. To the dismay of Stettinius, Molotov said he would press for adoption of the American's second suggestion: "including dismemberment to the degree necessary to safeguard future peace and security." The Secretary of State later told the President that the words were too strong, and he was sorry the suggestion had fallen from his lips.

At noon Harry Hopkins dragged himself from his bed. The President had ordered luncheon to be served in a small sun-room. He had invited the P.M., Sir Alexander Cadogan, Jimmy Byrnes and Averell Harriman. Cigarettes and coffee had been Hopkins' nutrition, but he forced himself to bathe and dress for this meal because he knew that Churchill would use the time to advance Britain's cause and try to convert FDR as an advocate. The repast continued for two hours, from 1:00 P.M. until 3:00. The conversation was secret: Rigdon was not invited to make notes. Churchill insisted that "Poland is the reason why all of us are here." He would like a firm stand on the part of FDR that the United States would back Britain in demanding no less than an independent coalition government in Poland and free elections "as soon as possible." Otherwise, he insisted, Britain had gone to war to no purpose. Mr. Roosevelt listened, nodded and admitted that something would have to be done to win the intractable Russians to Churchill's thinking; what, he did not know. His vacillation vexed Cadogan, who felt that Roosevelt could not make up his mind, that he had *no* U.S. policy. FDR felt that this was untrue; he wanted to keep the Americans out of the British camp and remain "flexible." In their lofty conversations each leader had a dream isolated in a cocoon: Stalin felt that the Big Three should dominate the world of nations, and should be permitted to surround themselves with vassal states as security; Churchill, leader of a gallant and exhausted nation, wanted to keep the British Empire intact and, at the same time, exercise its prerogative as the dominant force in western Europe; Roosevelt feared alienating the Russians—his goals were to bring the Russians into war with Japan and to set up a United Nations. The leaders, in effect, were using separate games and goals, trying to fit them together on a common table to form an attractive picture.

As the luncheon ended, the President called Mike Reilly in and bade him a temporary farewell. Reilly, along with Commander Tyree, Major Greer and two Secret Service agents, was leaving for Cairo. The P.M. said he didn't know that Roosevelt was going to Suez. The President said that when the conference was over, he was going to fly there to meet with young King Farouk of Egypt and Ibn Saud of Arabia. He would like to come to an agreement with them regarding a Jewish homeland in Palestine. He proposed to offer American services to irrigate their deserts and produce crops—make them self-sufficient. Churchill pulled on his long cigar and drily wished FDR good luck on both projects. In fact, he said, he might join the President there. England had a primary interest in the Suez Canal, in the Balfour Declaration which had promised the Jews of the world a homeland and, of course, in Arabian oil. If duty did not call elsewhere, the Prime Minister would join FDR at Alexandria.

The gentlemen stood. Churchill looked at his watch. It was 3:00 P.M. and the plenary session would convene at 4:00. It was time for his afternoon nap, but it would be a waste of time to return to his villa down the coast and make the return trip so soon. Harry Hopkins said, "Don't go. I'll get a room for you." He shuffled out. There was a bedroom on the ground floor at Livadia, shared by General Pa Watson and Admiral Wilson Brown. The General was on the palace sick list. Bruenn, examining FDR's friend, said that he too had hypertensive heart disease, and a prostate block.

Without knocking, Hopkins opened the door to find Watson in his underwear. Hopkins said that the Prime Minister needed the room for a nap. Watson said that was too bad; he proposed to take a nap himself. Quietly, Hopkins said, "Get out." Two pink spots began to glow in Watson's cheeks. He was sick, he said; Churchill was not. Go find another room for him. Hopkins was aroused. He ordered Watson out of his room. The General suggested that Hopkins give up his room. The words escalated into shouts. Two sick men lost their tempers. Hopkins went into the room and slammed the door. Watson, he said, would leave that room or someone would be called to escort him from it. Lieutenant Rigdon, passing, stood outside the door and heard vulgar name-calling. Pa clutched his chest. Hopkins was bent forward with pain. It ended with the General grabbing his khaki trousers and tunic and stomping out. Watson, the genial, jovial raconteur, lost control of his temper and could not seem to recover from his exasperation. Hopkins sent word to Churchill that the room was ready. The P.M., who was unaware of the dispute, closed the door and dropped onto the bed.

The great hall, shouldered by white Corinthian columns, was bright with sunshine. So was the President. He sat with his back to the crackling birch logs. At his side and behind him were Ed Stettinius and Chip Bohlen and Alger Hiss. He wore his faded gray suit and his head was tilted with a gleaming smile. Churchill was in the deep blue uniform of a colonel, wearing half-spectacles which slid down his nose so that he appeared to be pouting and forbidding as he spoke over their tops. Marshal Stalin addressed himself to a desk pad with a pencil and doodled. He wore his khaki uniform with a single big star on the shoulder boards and a silver star decoration on the tunic. Hopkins limped in late.

The President opened the meeting by asking for a foreign ministers' report from Edward Stettinius. Quickly and informally the United States Secretary of State said that they had agreed on the use of the word "dismemberment" in the case of Germany, but that Mr. Molotov was desirous of adding a few additional phrases. As the Big Three waited for the translation of each sentence, Molotov stood and announced brusquely that he was withdrawing his amendment. Eden and Stettinius exchanged glances. Obviously, Stalin was satisfied with the single word "dismemberment." Churchill, looking up from his penciled notes, said that he hadn't obtained permission of his War Cabinet in this matter. However, he would be glad to accept the word. In this, the conferees detected the note of nitpicking; each of the Big Three used his government "back home" as an excuse for evading agreement in matters small and large, and all three, when in doubt, had freely shied from decision by referring such questions to their foreign ministers.

Stettinius continued. The foreign ministers, he said, would like to have more time to discuss the role of France on the Allied Control Commission—if any. Two days earlier France had no status except in Britain's view. It did not seem to surprise Stalin that France had moved forward and upward, from the position of a powerless power to one which would be accorded a zone of occupation, and now a full vote on the Allied Control Commission in postwar Germany. The P.M. said that the importance of France in the postwar world had been boosted by Roosevelt's declaration that the United States had no intention of policing Europe for more than two years. Someone would have to guard the western approaches against a revitalized Germany, and it could not be Britain. It would have to be France.

Roosevelt tried to correct that statement. Yesterday, he said, he had spoken about the American attitude

regarding "current conditions." If there was to be a
United Nations, an international peace-keeping force,
then the American people would change their attitude
and might keep troops in Germany for an indefinite
period. Stalin remained silent, sketching penciled figures
on his pad. The President said they might as well proceed
to a discussion of the U.N., especially the original agreements arrived at in the Dumbarton Oaks Conference.
Churchill waved him off. He would like the conference
to understand the importance of France to the future
of Europe, he said. Germany, he prophesied, would
surely rise again, a phoenix from its own ashes.

"The American can always go home," he said, "but
France will have to live next door to Germany." France,
no matter what her contribution to the war—or lack of
it—was absolutely vital to western Europe and to England.
"She alone can deny coastal rocket sites to the Germans;
she alone can build up an army to contain Germany."
There was an opportunity for the gentlemen to go all the
way—give France a zone of occupation and a full vote
on the commission—but once more Roosevelt permitted
the subject to slide off the table and back to the foreign ministers. He nodded to Ed to stand and deliver
a polemic on the United Nations. Stettinius held a sheaf
of documents. Most important, he knew that what he
was about to propose had already been incorporated
in a letter from FDR to Stalin and Churchill on December
5, 1944. At that time Roosevelt knew that a summit
meeting was impending, and he wanted to acquaint his
adversaries with his arguments, while at the same time
pulling the props from under theirs.

Briefly, the proposal envisioned a world organization
of two houses—a large Assembly and a small Security
Council. Alger Hiss, the President's architect, had outlined an Assembly of small and large nations which
could discuss differences and agreements and vote. The
upper house would consist of seven members, four of
them "permanent"—the United States, Russia, Great Britain and China. The other three would be periodically
elective. In matters of procedure, all seven members

must favor the motion. In cases regarding the admission or expulsion of nations from the Assembly and the suppression of international disputes or mediation of them, the sending of United Nations "forces" to troubled countries—the Big Four members would have to vote unanimously. Any of the four could exercise a "veto" to kill the proposed motion, whatever it might be. If a dispute could be settled by peaceful means, Mr. Roosevelt proposed that such a motion would require all seven Security Council votes; however, if one of the Big Four was involved, that nation could discuss the problem but would not be permitted to vote on it. The veto insured that the power of any alliance of a Big Three or Big Two could not be turned against a permanent member.

The Stettinius reading was long and legalistic. The slow translation sounded pontifical. Stalin looked up from his paper and said he feared that any conflict "will destroy our unity." He directed himself to Roosevelt. Before the President could reply, Churchill was staring at Stalin over his spectacles, nodding. He said he could understand *that* argument, but he had no hope that the United Nations would ever eliminate disputes between powers. He would like the Soviet Marshal to recall that most disputes would continue to be handled by ambassadors and by diplomats in the Foreign Office. Thus there would be two avenues for redress. Stalin became surly. He said that he and his Soviet colleagues would never forget that, in the Russo-Finnish War of 1939, England and France had induced the old League of Nations to expel the Soviet Union. "You even went so far," he said, "as to speak of a crusade against us."

Roosevelt was upset. He had hoped, publicly and privately, that the new world organization would not founder on the rocks of the old. He tried to speak. The P.M. said that, at the time of the Russo-Finnish War, England and France were "very angry at you." However, if Stalin had read the Dumbarton Oaks minutes, and Roosevelt's letter of December 5, he must be aware that this could not happen again. It became obvious, without an open acknowledgment, that Stalin had not read Dumbarton Oaks or Roosevelt's letter. He was not prepared for this discussion. Stalin said he was not thinking of Russia being expelled but of the marshaling of world opinion against Russia.

The British and American delegations were surprised. Their experience had been that world opinion meant little to the Russians. Churchill blamed himself when he said that this would not happen again; he doubted that Roosevelt or Stalin would lead a savage attack against his country, and this would apply to the other two. Stettinius was still standing when Roosevelt interrupted to observe that he had before him a copy of the Big Three pledge at Teheran: "We recognize fully that supreme responsibility resting upon us and all the United Nations to make a peace that will command the good will of the world and banish the scourge and terror of war for many generations." He said he did not think the proposed organization could keep the peace forever, but if it could maintain a degree of serenity in the world for only fifty years, the U.N. was worth consideration.

Churchill decided to back up toward the United Nations. He said Britain could see no danger in it. However, he worried lest the world think that the Big Three were ruling the world. A small smile came to Stalin's lips when he asked Churchill what he would do if Egypt, as a member nation, asked for control of the Suez Canal. The P.M. said that Great Britain had no fear of small powers airing their grievances. The Empire could nullify any complaint by use of the veto. Someone asked what would happen if a "great power" like China demanded Hong Kong back from the British. China, he replied, would be content to express its opinion.

Stalin admitted that he had not studied the President's letter. He would study it, but he did not feel encouraged by what he had heard at the table about the United Nations. The Prime Minister returned to the speculative, saying that he wasn't at all worried about the present, but he was fearful of what would happen to the world organization after "the three of us are gone." The world was safe under these three men, but "we might be gone

in ten years." What would happen then? Agreement
now, said Stalin, among the Big Three was what worried
him. He asked Roosevelt to table the matter until tomorrow; he would be prepared to discuss it then. The President said that he would like to read a list of proposed
member nations—"charter members"—and he reminded
the gathering that any nation friendly to the Big Three
would be eligible for membership if the appplication
was filed no later than the final day of the Yalta Conference.

He read his list. Stalin kept interrupting. "What about
Argentina?" The President did not want to discuss it.
As he concluded his reading, Stettinius said the United
States would like to make a minor clarification of Chapter
Eight, Section C, of the U.N. charter. Stalin and Molotov
objected. They tumbled over each other's words as all
their suspicions surfaced. What changes? How minor?
These articles had been drawn up some time ago. Everyone had a copy. Why would the Americans wait until
they came to Yalta to suggest alterations? Stettinius
tried to interrupt the interrupters. He failed. It was Hiss
or Matthews who whispered that Gromyko should be
allowed to tell the Russians what it entailed, because
he was acquainted with the change. The Russian Ambassador obliged. As Bohlen listened, Andrei Gromyko
explained to Stalin that it consisted of four words: "under
the second sentence." It amounted to nothing, but it
carried Soviet hostility to the top of the table. Stalin
was not mollified. He scowled at Churchill and said
he had noted that the Prime Minister stated that if the
American voting plan was not endorsed, then it was
possible some power was trying to dominate the world.
"Who?" Stalin said. "Which one?" He turned to Roosevelt. Could it be the United States? Stalin would doubt
that. Could it be the United Kingdom? he asked Churchill.
The P.M. shrugged. This left only the Soviet Union,
Stalin said. "So Russia is striving for world domination?"
he asked. For a reason which no one present understood,
the conference broke into laughter. Stalin continued
his assault on the valorous and vainglorious figure of

Churchill. "Could it possibly be China?" he asked mock-ingly. He received no response. Stalin dropped the sub-ject, but small wounds began to bleed.

The Soviet Marshal nodded agreeably. Churchill was right in stating that there is a problem, he said. It was graver than the right of the small and weak to express opinions freely. The real question was how to preserve peace. The present leaders, he said, could rely upon each other. But what about the next generation? And the one after that? As stiff and stubborn and suspicious as he had been a moment before, now he was generous, pleasant, apologetic. He was sorry that he had not read the U.N. proposals. All he could plead was that he had other, more immediate things on his mind. He would surely study tonight. He startled everyone by stating he believed China should be accorded a seat on the permanent Council. Churchill said he would like to sec-ond that motion and include France too. No one re-sponded to that.

"I should like to bring up Poland," The President said. The three leaders had settled into a repetitive mold. Stalin would continue to focus his suspicions on Churchill and his benevolence on Roosevelt. The President would continue to be shocked at the bursts of anger from the Russians and would phrase his opinions to keep from offending Uncle Joe. Churchill's first and last aspirations were identical: to keep the Empire intact and to maintain Great Britain as a first-class power. "I come from a great distance," Roosevelt said, shuffling papers before him, "and therefore have the advantage of a more distant point of view of the problem." At this point, he may have forgotten what he had said so many times before: "There are six or seven million Poles in the United States." It was a hoary chestnut. There is a possibility that the President feared to incur Russian anger. He seemed timid, tentative and rambling in his discourse. The Poles, he said, like the Chinese, attach importance to saving face. The conferees looked at each other blankly.

"Whose face?" Stalin demanded. "The Lublin gov-

ernment or the emigré government?" FDR glanced
up and returned to his papers. The Russians should
modify the eastern boundary of Poland at the Curzon
Line, he said. Poland should be given the oil-bearing
area around Lvov. Before any challenge could be voiced,
FDR tried a "however." "However," he said, the question
of boundaries was not nearly so important as the question
of free and independent government for Poland.
Churchill decided to cast himself, momentarily, as
mediator. He and Eden had been attacked in England,
he said, for agreeing to the Curzon Line as the eastern
boundary, but, after reflection, he thought that the boundary was based on Russian right rather than Russian
might. After all, it was Russia who had freed Poland
in blood and battle. On the other hand, he continued,
the world would regard it as a "magnanimous gesture"
if Russia gave Lvov to a weaker power.

The President and the Prime Minister, in an obvious
attempt to put a friendly face on their opinions about
Poland, kept cutting across each other's speeches. To
an observer, it would appear that both men realized
that the settlement of the Polish question would be the
high point for the Russians at Yalta; if anything would
cause them to quit, to go it alone gobbling all they could
in Europe, to create an eastern world of their own—this
would be the question. It was the Americans and the
British who would have to save face, not the Poles.
Had the conference been held before the Battle of Stalingrad, Churchill and Roosevelt would have told the
Soviets what they would get from Poland—if anything.

"What people want," Roosevelt said, "is the creation
of a government of national unity to settle their internal
differences. A government which would represent all
five major parties" (he named them) "is what is wanted."
To disavow a personal stake in the matter, FDR said:
"It may interest Marshal Stalin that I do not know any
members of the London or of the Lublin government.
Mikolajczyk came to Washington and I was greatly impressed . . ."

"I," said Churchill, "am more interested in the question

of Poland's sovereign independence and freedom than in particular frontier lines. . . . This is what we went to war against Germany for. Everyone here knows that it nearly cost us our life as a nation." To Britain it was a question of honor. Poland needed only an interim government pending free elections. "His Majesty's Government cordially support the President's suggestion and present the question to our Russian allies."

Stalin asked for a ten-minute recess. He departed stiffly with his staff, his boots clumping on the parquet floor. To the Soviets, every question which came before the conference had an additional side—the Soviet view. For example, the Russians, with some justice, saw the United Nations as an organization weighted heavily toward the West. Britain, America and China would vote as a unit on the Security Council. Before Yalta, Stalin gave little study time to the organization because he did not plan to have Russia participate. Without Russia the United Nations would not represent world power. He was convinced that, militarily, the West should take greater risks in France and Germany; that they were deliberately holding back so that the Soviet Union would bleed a little more. The military commitments now pledged by the West were, in Stalin's opinion, minimal. The United Nations might be worth studying only because Roosevelt and Churchill had both pledged that the Soviet Union could veto any action on their part, or on the part of any smaller nation against the interests of Russia. Now, listening to them discuss the fate of Poland had caused the Marshal to become so pent up that he had asked for a recess. He did not require ten minutes to ask Molotov and Vyshinsky their opinions regarding the fate of Poland; that had been decided long ago. He was interested in controlling himself, in making an effort to keep from saying something which would break up the conference.

There were unmentionable wheels within wheels. Stalin knew that Churchill feared that Roosevelt, in his quest for the independence of small nations, might break up the British Empire. The President had mentioned, more than once, that when China sat on the Security Council, she might ask for Hong Kong. Churchill had no intention of giving it back. There was India, a great subcontinent. The President wanted independence for so many places, or at least to make "trusteeships" of them. The P.M. told Eden he had learned to hate the word. There would be no British Empire trusteeships as long as he was Prime Minister. The Soviets felt they should have begun by asking that Poland be returned as a Russian province, as it had been under the Czars. Diplomatically, they could have retreated from the demand to a pseudo-independent Poland under a Lublin sort of government. They hadn't. They had said flatly that Poland should be free and independent, in a sphere of Russian domination. Poles should run Poland, but the London Poles had already been characterized as "bandits," and Stalin was not going to renegotiate them back into existence. Even though victory was in sight, the Soviet leaders saw Germany as the most formidable enemy of the future. The subtle connivance of Britain, which feared Russia as the primary enemy of the future, would reawaken the clanking giant, Germany. Then too, although the Russians had one sixth of the land surface of the world, they saw themselves as a nation isolated from all others and viewed with hostility. Thus, in spite of their enormous size, they wanted Poland, Romania, Finland, Estonia, Latvia, Czechoslovakia, Hungary and Bulgaria as a *cordon sanitaire* to the west and south. Whoever attacked Russia in the future must overrun those countries first. To the Muscovites these were not satellites of the Soviet Union; they represented "collective security."

The air in the Livadia ballroom was full of questions never asked, aspirations never enunciated. At the Kremlin there was a secret Russian document to be presented to the United States asking for a reconstruction loan of $7 billion; it had been there since December 1943, and none except the Soviet masters knew of it. There was also an economic paper showing the advantage to the Soviet Union of controlling export trade in the several

small countries around it. These agreements had not
been broached to Estonia or Bulgaria or any other nation,
but, in time, the "economic treaty" would be presented
to each one, not for discussion, but for signature. One
more thing: the Soviet Embassy in Washington had
made Stalin aware that the United States military and
the politicians were speaking seriously of keeping American forces intact for a showdown with Russia.

The big room was quiet. The President looked at
his watch and said it was late. When Stalin returned,
he would adjourn the meeting. However, the Russian
dictator stalked back into the ballroom with as much
clumping of boots as when he left, but with a deeper
frown. He sat and began to speak. The interpreter was
faster than usual because the words were coming
faster than usual. "The Prime Minister has said that
for Great Britain the question of Poland is a question
of honor," he said. "For Russia it is not only a question
of honor but of security." Breathing heavily, Stalin stood.
He got behind his own chair and spoke in short, sarcastic
bursts, his knuckles white against the back of the chair,
the dark eyes glancing from Churchill to Roosevelt.
"During the past thirty years our German enemy has
passed through this corridor twice. This is because Poland
was weak. It is in the Russian interest as well as that
of Poland that Poland be strong and powerful and in
a position, in her own and our interests, to shut the
corridor by her own forces."

Hopkins, Stettinius and Hiss watched in fascination.
Obviously, the man was angry. No one had seen this
side of Stalin, at least no one in the American contingent.
He wasn't loud, as Churchill could be loud. The tone
was soft and swift and insidious with threat. "The corridor
cannot be shut from outside by Russia. It can be shut
from inside only by Poland. It is necessary that Poland
be free, independent and powerful . . ."

There was a pause. The President began to say something. Stalin held up a staying hand. "The Prime Minister
thinks we should make a gesture of magnanimity. But
I must remind you that the Curzon Line was invented

not by Russia but by foreigners—by Curzon, Clemenceau and the Americans in 1918–19. Russia was not invited and did not participate . . . Lenin opposed that line." He flung his hands high. "Now some want us to be less Russian than Curzon and Clemenceau. What will the Russians say at Moscow—and the Ukrainians? They will say that Stalin and Molotov are far less defenders of Russia than Curzon and Clemenceau." He breathed deeply, almost snorting. "I cannot take such a position and return to Moscow. I prefer that the war continue a little longer and give Poland compensation in the west at the expense of Germany." Bohlen and Birse had difficulty keeping up with the rush of words. Stalin said that the Prime Minister had proposed the creation of a new Polish government at Yalta. "I am afraid," he said, "that was a slip of the tongue. Without the participation of the Poles we can create no Polish government. They all say that I am a dictator but I have enough democratic feeling not to set up a Polish government without Poles." He cited the "sins" of the Czars in brutally absorbing Poland into Russia; the Soviet Socialist Republicans, Stalin asserted, were trying to atone for the sins of the dead kings of Russia; Poles would administer the affairs of Poland; Poland would be Poland and not part of Russia; the Soviet armies were liberating Poland and they proposed to compensate the blond Slavs with German territory all the way to the Oder and Neisse rivers. Incidentally, he said, there had been grumbling from Russia's western friends about that line too. He would like to remind his audience that none other than their favorite, ex-premier Mikolajczyk, approved that boundary. If it was agreeable to London Poles, and to Lublin Poles, why then should Britain and the United States disagree?

Who would want to back the London Poles now? Which came first, the freedom of their land from the Hitlerite heel, or the murder of Russian soldiers trying to liberate Poland? He would like an answer to this. The Russian Army could not operate at its best unless its rear and supply and communications lines to Moscow were intact. So far the London Poles had fomented insurrection to the rear of the Russian armies and had killed 212 Russian officers and men. Stalin did not propose to accept those murders without retribution. The discussion of a new, enlarged government, with London Poles added to Lublin Poles, was without merit, he said. The Lublin group, which Stalin proposed to refer to in the future as the "Warsaw government," would no longer discuss matters with the London traitors. He had a sudden thought in mid-anger. Would Roosevelt and Churchill like to have the Warsaw government come to Yalta, within a few days, to discuss the future of their nation? It might be arranged, he said. Or perhaps his allies would rather have Polish discussions resumed in Moscow? It could be arranged either way. Of one thing he was certain, he said: Britain and the United States realized that Russian military operations required peace and serenity to the rear; he knew that they would grant that. This was the reason why Russia had no choice but to back the Warsaw government. "Such is the situation," he said, shrugging, and sat.

There was a silence. The President coughed and said that he would adjourn this session. Churchill began to speak. Apparently he had not been awed by anger. He thanked the Marshal for his remarks. The P.M., however, said he doubted that the Lublin government represented one third of the Polish people. Assuming that Stalin felt so strongly about democracy, surely he would want an expanded Polish government which would represent all, or nearly all, Polish factions. There were 150,000 Polish soldiers fighting on the Italian and western fronts. Someday soon they would be home. Would they subscribe to the Lublin government? No, "they will feel betrayed." Churchill would not debate the new western border, but he warned Stalin against "stuffing the Polish goose so full of German food that it will get indigestion."

Roosevelt addressed himself to Molotov. "How long ago were these lands Polish?" he asked. "Very long ago," the Foreign Minister replied. "In that case," Roosevelt said, "this might lead the English to ask for a return of the United States to Great Britain." On that note, he declared the meeting adjourned. Roosevelt was wheeled back to his room. No one told him that Watson was ill in his room as a result of the argument with Harry Hopkins. It is doubtful that, considering the fatigue in which Roosevelt found himself that evening, he would have been able to visit his old friend. In his room Mr. Roosevelt was given a massage and McIntire's nose drops. He could spare thirty minutes to lie on the bed before dressing for dinner.

Mr. Byrnes stopped in. To him, Roosevelt looked exhausted. "The long meetings," FDR said, "are really Winston's fault because he makes too many speeches." "Yes, he does," Byrnes said, "but they are good speeches." The President smiled. "Winston doesn't make any other kind." Byrnes departed when Rigdon came into the room with fresh mail from the White House. Mr. Roosevelt sat up, pulled a robe around himself and perused it. "Later," he said.

Dinner had been scheduled for 8:30. The President was late. Whatever inner magic he possessed was brought into play again. He wheeled himself into the small dark dining room, nodding and smiling to his guests, and accepted a kiss from Anna. It was an informal meal. Among the guests were Byrnes, Leahy, Harriman, Harriman's daughter, Steve Early and Edward Flynn. FDR was bright and witty. He had been thinking of some reason why a Bronx politician should be at the conference and he thought he had it. Flynn was a strong Roman Catholic; the Boss proposed that, soon after the conference closed, Flynn should go to Moscow to make friendly arrangements between the atheistic government of Russia and its Catholic population. Then he should go to Rome and consult the Pope about it. Some of the guests grinned. Roosevelt was serious. The main thing he had in mind, he said, was that while eating he wanted a full report from Anna and Miss Harriman on their trip to Sevastopol.

He sipped a few cocktails. He smoked a few cigarettes.

He ate a little. Afterward, he excused himself and was wheeled to his study. There, he dictated a long letter to Stalin, marking a carbon copy to be sent to Winston Churchill. Once more, he was determined to cut through diplomatic debate by making a direct and personal appeal:

My dear Marshal Stalin:

I have been giving a great deal of thought to our meeting this afternoon, and I want to tell you in all frankness what is on my mind.

In so far as the Polish Government is concerned, I am greatly disturbed that the three great powers do not have a meeting of minds about the political setup in Poland. It seems to me that it puts all of us in a bad light throughout the world to have you recognizing one government while we and the British are recognizing another in London. I am sure that this state of affairs should not continue, and that if it does it can only lead our people to think that there is a breach between us, which is not the case. I am determined that there shall be no breach between ourselves and the Soviet Union. Surely there is a way to reconcile our differences.

I was very much impressed with some of the things you said today, particularly your determination that your rear must be safeguarded as your army moves into Berlin. You cannot, and we must not, tolerate any temporary government which will give your armed forces any trouble of this sort. I want you to know that I am fully mindful of this.

You must believe me when I tell you that our people at home look with a critical eye on what they consider a disagreement between us at this vital stage of the war. They, in effect, say that if we cannot get a meeting of the minds now when our armies are converging on the common enemy, how can we get an understanding on even more vital things in the future?

I have had to make it clear to you that we cannot recognize the Lublin Government as now composed, and the world would regard it as a lamentable outcome of our work here if we parted with an open and obvious divergence between us on this issue.

You said today that you would be prepared to support any suggestions for the solution of this problem which offered a fair chance of success, and you also mentioned the possibility of bringing some members of the Lublin Government here.

Realizing that we all have the same anxiety in getting this matter settled, I would like to develop your proposal a little and suggest that we invite here at Yalta at once Mr. Bierut and Mr. Osóbka-Morawski from the Lublin Government and also two or three from the following list of Poles, which, according to our information, would be desirable as representatives of the other elements of the Polish people in the development of a new temporary government which all three of us could recognize and support: Archbishop Sapieha of Cracow, Wincenty Witos, Mr. Zurlowski, Professor Buyak, and Professor Kutzeba. If, as a result of the presence of these Polish leaders here, we could jointly agree with them on a provisional government in Poland which should no doubt include some Polish leaders from abroad such as Mr. Mikolajczyk, Mr. Grabski and Mr. Romer, the United States Government, and I feel sure the British Government as well, would then be prepared to examine with you conditions in which they would disassociate themselves from the London government and transfer their recognition to the new provisional government.

I hope that I do not have to assure you that the United States will never lend its support in any way to any provisional government in Poland that would be inimical to your interests.

It goes without saying that any interim government which could be formed as a result of our conference with the Poles here would be pledged to the holding of free elections in Poland at the earliest possible date. I know this is completely consistent with your desire to see a new free and democratic Poland emerge from the welter of this war.

Most sincerely yours,
Franklin D. Roosevelt

Before writing it, the President had some consultive assistance from Harry Hopkins. In retrospect it is a rambling document, written like a series of postscripts. But its diplomatic virtues outweigh its literary vices. It was a direct appeal from a chief of state to a dictator to find a way out of an interminable European dilemma. It requires no reading "between the lines" to see that Roosevelt was trying to solve the Polish crisis by permitting *both sides* to emerge from it with a whole skin. Neither he nor Churchill could return home and concede that they had sold Poland to the Russians. The old Bolsheviks could not return to Moscow and admit that the Western Powers had foisted an independent and antagonistic Poland on them. The way out would be for Stalin to bring men from both sides to Yalta, knock their heads together and order them to form a government subservient to the Soviet Union but free on the surface. All afternoon long the Big Three had been describing a "free, independent and democratic" Poland to each other. It became a monotonous cliché. In the last sentence of the letter Poland is described as "free and democratic" but not independent. The bait was large, the hook small; if the suggestion was followed, FDR could prove that he had brought the dissident Polish statesmen together, and that out of argument and mediation had come a free choice to serve the Soviet Union.

The President was at breakfast—a late breakfast—when a Secret Service man informed him that Mr. Stettinius was outside. "Come in, Ed!" Mr. Roosevelt shouted. The Secretary of State said that he had received an early morning radio from Washington that the Soviet Ambassador to Mexico, Konstantin A. Oumansky, had been killed in a plane crash. He offered a sheet of paper. "I have taken the liberty of writing a letter expressing your condolences to Stalin, and offering to fly the body back to Moscow." The President adjusted his spectacles and read it. "Yes," he said. "Yes, Ed. That's a good gesture. Get it off by messenger." It arrived at Stalin's desk almost as soon as he had heard the news. The Russians expressed gratitude and accepted the offer.

Stettinius departed from Livadia Palace at 11:00 A.M., accompanied by Hiss and Matthews. The meeting of the foreign ministers, achieved on a rotating basis, was to be at Koreiz, the Russian villa. It was a warm, well-lighted day, but Stettinius wore a heavy black coat and a homburg. Byrnes and Hopkins stopped him before he left. They had conferred alone and decided that the United Nations voting formula was the most important question to be discussed. They advised Ed to press hard for one vote per nation in the Assembly, and to fight the Soviet proposal to place their sixteen so-called Republics in it with a vote apiece. As Roosevelt said, if the Russians were going to pretend that they had sixteen independent Republics, then the United States should ask one vote for each of its states—forty-eight. Second, he must remind and keep reminding Molotov that the Security Council had been made secure for the Soviet Union. No group of nations in the Big Four could gang up on the Russians at any time, because Moscow could exercise its veto to stop action—although not debate—at any time. In spite of the fact that there would be three additional (and temporary) members elected from the Assembly, power would remain in the hands of the Big Four—Russia, China, United States and Great Britain. Stettinius said Eden was bound to bring up a permanent seat for France, making a fifth power. Hopkins and Byrnes reminded the Secretary of State that the U.S. government had no position on France, and he was not empowered to agree with Eden.

Stettinius went to the meeting with iron instructions—not from the Boss but from advisers. He paused outside Koreiz to admire it. The villa was smaller than the other two. It sat high above the dark rocks, like a pale gem in an onyx setting. The curving gravel walks were lined with statuary. There were pine, maple and oak trees standing as sentinels, and behind the villa was a snowy mountain. Inside, in addition to Molotov, there were Maisky, Vyshinsky and Pavlov. It was the dour Maisky who was known to the Western Powers as the iron-clad intractable. He was the unreconstructed Bolshevik. Once, at a plenary session, Stalin enunciated one of his rare witticisms: "Yes," he said to Molotov, "you can convince the United States and Great Britain and the Soviet Union, but can you convince Maisky?"

When the Russians were hosts at a meeting or a luncheon they were so painfully correct that the foreign ministers and their advisers felt that the Russians had devoured a book on social intercourse. The table, the goblets, the carafe, plates and service were precisely arranged, including the flowers set in vases around the room. Comrade Molotov wore his diplomatic smile, Maisky nodded curtly, Vyshinsky projected a tired hand, and Pavlov sat in a chair behind Molotov's ear.

Before lunch, drinks were served, and Stettinius opened the talk by stating that the conference seemed to be in agreement on voting procedures in the United Nations, and he would be happy to answer questions. Molotov referred to a typewritten sheet in front of him and shook his head negatively. No, he said, the foreign ministers were not empowered to discuss the world peace organization because it had not been referred to them. Before him, he said, he had a list of proper subjects for this meeting. Eden, sitting with Cadogan, Clark Kerr and interpreter Major Birse, looked gloomy as he sipped a drink. It was going to be a stiff meeting with few off-the-cuff pleasantries.

The Russians asked for the creation of a subcommittee to redraft Article 12 of the surrender terms, adding the word "dismemberment" in regard to the disposal of Germany. This was agreed to. Proposal number two was the creation of a special commission to study how best to break up Greater Germany. This provoked a dispute. Molotov said that the commission should be kept small—Anthony Eden plus the Soviet and American ambassadors to Great Britain. No, Stettinius said. That would not do. The President had become irritated with the creation of new committees and new commissions. He said the European Advisory Commission already existed for this purpose and had been studying it for a year. France was a member of the EAC, and Stettinius understood that Molotov wanted to create a new body to eliminate France.

Eden suppoted Stettinius. France, he said, had been working on this problem with the Big Three in London, and Great Britain would not consider Molotov's proposed commission complete without France. The Soviet Foreign Minister was troubled. His government had been fighting the resurrection of France as a great power. It was true that France was already a party to the EAC, and he knew it. However, neither Britain nor America would vote for his new commission without including France. The Russian shrugged. Russia was more interested in the procedure of the group in dismembering Germany than in a roll call of its membership. Stalin, he said, would like to know *how* such a group—EAC or new commission—would tackle such an enormous problem as the best way to carve a country into separate entities. In any case, Molotov said, retreating into limbo, the foreign ministers had not received instructions to form a new commission, such as he had proposed.

The British Foreign Minister acted like a hound who has discovered a fox in a large open field. He was in swift pursuit. To the contrary, he said, the foreign ministers did have the power to recommend such a commission. Further, he would like to have it understood that Great Britain would not agree to the creation of any international commission unless France was on it. The first course of lunch was served. Molotov made a few comments on Russian food and said that the question of participation by France should be left to the commission—if it was ever created. Eden nodded. So did Stettinius. Thus the insolubles of Yalta filtered down from President and Prime Minister to foreign secretaries, down to commissions uncreated. This would be the hallmark of the Yalta Conference.

The Soviet minister then proposed, through a cloud of steamy soup, that he and his confreres consider the role of France in relation to the Allied Control Commission. This was indeed a big question. Granting de Gaulle a zone of occupation in Germany was one thing; placing France as the fourth power among the victors to govern a defeated Germany was bound to arouse antagonisms. Molotov knew that Roosevelt was opposed to granting France equal status. Ergo, Stettinius would be opposed. So the Russian proposed that France be given a zone of occupation to be carved out of the American-British sector, as agreed, and that the French zone should come under the domination of the Control Council—the U.S., U.K. and U.S.S.R. Eden, the only one at the table in favor of France, tried to negotiate. France, he said, would have to be granted membership on the Allied Control Council. It would not be logical, and the Russians and Americans knew it, to ask her to patrol a sector over which she had no governing rights. As a sop, Eden said that Britain would not favor admitting France to any conferences such as Yalta. He was almost certain that de Gaulle would refuse to accept a zone unless France was on the commission.

The tone of voice of the adversaries remained polite and academic. It was decided by the three men to toss the problem back upstairs to the Big Three. They had agreed to give France a zone of occupation; they were at loggerheads—two to one—regarding the admission of France as a fourth governing power in defeated Germany. Eden, who feared that if France got a zone, the Russians might propose Poland as a long-suffering nation deserving a zone, said that if France was admitted to the Control Commission, the three should agree now that no other nation should be invited to patrol an area of occupation. Molotov was acidulous. There would not be time, he said, to discuss *that* question.

He consulted his typewritten sheet. The next problem, he said, was German reparations. He turned to Ivan Maisky. As the gentlemen buttered rolls and ate lunch, Maisky read a statement. It was written like a school examination; as always, it had its ones, twos and threes. One, he said, reparations from Germany should be first received by those nations which had borne the burden of war and had organized the victory; other victorious nations should receive reparations after the first group. Two, all discussions regarding the usage of forced German labor should be postponed, to be discussed later; estimates of reparations should be about $10 billion for the Soviet Union, $8 billion to be divided between Great Britain and the United States, smaller sums for smaller powers.

No cynical smiles came from Stettinius and Eden. The British Foreign Minister addressed himself to his lunch and asked Maisky, in an offhand manner, how he arrived at the sums to be allocated in goods and machinery. He did not mention that Great Britain and the United States had not asked for reparations from Germany; he proposed to play Maisky's game and act as though all of this was agreeable, but could Germany endure it and live? Maisky consulted another sheet of paper, laden with figures. Germany's prewar national wealth, he said, amounted to about $125 billion. The war had reduced this to $75 billion. The Soviet Union, he said, proposed to claim for itself and its allies only 30 percent of what was left—perhaps $22 billion. This, he said, would not inflict hardship on a defeated nation. It could live—and thrive. Was anyone in favor of a better standard of living for the Germans than the Russians enjoyed? No. The 30 percent payment had been carefully thought out.

Of course, Eden said, much depended on which 30 percent was removed from the animal. If it was a matter of vital organs, it could kill him. Molotov said that a reparations committee should be established in Moscow, and it should be commissioned in writing now. The American and British ministers agreed to this without argument but wanted it understood that no guidelines had been designated at the plenary sessions. After hesitation, Molotov nodded and said that he would present the agreement to the plenary session "this afternoon." In typical Russian style, having gained a little advantage in one matter, he proceeded at once to a greater one. The United States and Great Britain, he said, should decide how much reparations they wanted from Germany—and do it soon.

This induced a dual smile from the other side of the table. The Soviet Union, in spite of crude and unpredictable diplomacy, was inwardly sensitive to world opinion. The Kremlin did not want to be alone in taking wealth from Germany. It desired partners. The largest share should go to the Soviet Union, but England and the United States should share a share. Stettinius and Eden said that they would consult about the reparations. Lunch was over; liqueurs were served. Molotov snapped his fingers and a staff member brought copies of a document entitled "Basic Principle of Exaction of Reparation from Germany." The British and American ministers appeared to be startled. The Russians were so certain of agreement that they had the paper ready for signature. Eden balked. So did Stettinius. They would have to consult their superiors first. Molotov said he already had the assent of Stalin. The meeting closed, as most of them did, with no specific agreements, but with a few questions referred back up to the Big Three, or down to commissions and subcommittees for study.

At 4:10 P.M. President Roosevelt entered the ballroom. He was followed by Stettinius, Leahy, Hopkins, Byrnes, Harriman, Matthews, Hiss and Bohlen. The other delegations nodded and smiled as he transferred his body from his wheelchair to his place at the table. On the way in he had hoped aloud that this would be a short meeting. He leaned back, lighted a cigarette and scanned the faces. He was less interested in tracing Polish borders, he said, than in the problem of finding a representative Polish government. Molotov interrupted to say that there was a Warsaw government. The President said he did not attach importance to the legality or continuity of any Polish government since, in his opinion, there had been no Polish government for a number of years. Before returning to the subject of Poland, however, he would like to hear a report from the foreign ministers. Molotov asked the interpreter,

Pavlov, to pass copies of the minutes, written in Russian and English, around the table. Summarized, the Soviet Foreign Minister stated that Vyshinsky, Cadogan and Matthews had been appointed to redraft Article 12 of the German surrender document to include the word "dismemberment." The geographical dismemberment was a study entrusted to Anthony Eden, American Ambassasor to Great Britain John Winant, and Soviet Ambassador F. T. Gusev. France, it was agreed, would be given a zone of occupation. Regarding inviting France to be a member of the Control Commission, Molotov and Stettinius felt it desirable to refer the question to the European Advisory Commission. Mr. Eden, to the contrary, felt that the question should be solved now. Also, reparations from Germany would be studied and detailed by a reparations committee which would meet continuously in Moscow. This committee, in the opinion of the foreign ministers, should begin its work as soon as organized. This and the matter of exacting reparations from Germany should be decided at the Crimean Conference.

The President and the Prime Minister expressed their gratitude to Molotov, as host Foreign Minister, for "productive work." Churchill said he would like time to study the English translation because, with one exception, he agreed with the findings. The one exception, he said, was the matter of giving France a zone without a vote on the Allied Control Commission. He realized that this was a sensitive subject, but he pointed out that it would be useless to refer it to the European Advisory Commission, now working in London, because after all arguments were in, the four parties would line up with the British and French on one side and the Soviets and the Americans on the other. That, he asserted, would amount to a deadlock. Would it not be better to settle it now, at Yalta? His voice assumed the low bulldog growl he had used to tell the Germans, in late 1941, that Great Britain would never surrender to the heel of the tyrant. He lowered his head and glanced from Stalin to Roosevelt and back again as he announced that the British people would "never" accept a situation in which questions affecting France were not settled with France in attendance. It did not follow, as Comrade Stalin had suggested, that France would demand a partnership with the Big Three. "This," he repeated, "is a very exclusive club. The entrance fee being five million soldiers or the equivalent." Stalin said that, no matter what Churchill's intentions or promises, France would eventually demand a full partnership. He rambled about his conferences in Moscow with de Gaulle. "The General," he said, "is very unrealistic. France has not done much fighting in the war, yet de Gaulle has demanded equal rights with the Soviets, the British and the Americans."

Roosevelt said his opinion was not to give France a seat on the Allied Control Commission. He bowed to no one in his admiration for France and its people, but he could not be convinced that France had earned a seat on the Control Commission. As the debate escalated, Roosevelt said that he would like to "consider further" the entire matter, and, as presiding officer, he would ask the conferees to move on to another question until he had time to restudy his position. The President had a device he used whenever tempers began to flare: introduce an innocuous but sensible subject unrelated to the matter at hand. He began to speak of Iran, claiming that 99 percent of the tribes were in bondage to one percent. It was a "very, very backward nation." If such poor nations were to initiate a plan requiring five years, or even ten, and allow the 99 percent to purchase small pieces of property, to farm them and be permitted to sell produce; if the rulers would study the American plan of the Tennessee Valley Authority, which displayed in grandeur what could be done to store water and manufacture cheap rural electricity, these backward countries would, in time, become good customers for other nations. In fact, he said, wandering on in his thesis, there were parallels in Europe where some progressive nations had cheap water power and electricity while—"fifty miles away"—others had neither. The Soviet Union, he said, was a good example of a nation willing to consider the problems of an entire province, or even a republic, "as a whole." The interpreters labored slowly through this, but it was Roosevelt's way of returning the tempers of the members to normal.

Molotov said he would like to get back to the subject of Poland. Churchill cut in to warn that if the question of France was not settled "here," it would be very difficult to settle it when they had all left Yalta. The Soviet Marshal, unimpressed, said that the Big Three had been able to settle many things by correspondence. It was a dismissal of the question. Stalin then said he had received a letter from the President, a letter which suggested inviting Poles who represented various interests to Yalta. He said he had attempted to telephone the Poles at Lublin, but had not reached them. This was difficult to countenance. The Americans and British believed that the Lublin Poles danced to Stalin's tune, and, had he wished, his military men could have located and flown them to Yalta without delay. It seemed obvious to the British and Americans that Stalin did not want either the Lublin Poles or the emigrés at the conference. It is possible that he did not want to appear to truckle to Roosevelt's wishes. It is equally possible that he feared that the friendly and unfriendly Poles might, under American prodding, reach an agreement. It is even more logical to assume that he wanted to keep Poland completely subservient to Moscow. He closed his remarks by stating that Molotov was working on a paper in response to President Roosevelt's suggestions, and that it was being typed. While this was done, he recommended that they return to the problem of voting in the Security Council. "We might talk of Dumbarton Oaks," he said.

An insistent bell rang in the President's mind. He glanced sharply at Stettinius. Just before this session had convened, Winston Churchill had stuck his head into the President's study, where FDR and Ed were conferring, and announced airily, "Uncle Joe will take Dumbarton Oaks." Then he disappeared. There was a feeling in the American delegation—suspicion is too strong a word—that the Prime Minister had driven several times to Koreiz from Vorontsov Palace for informal chats with the Russian. He had become a man with advance information. At lunch Churchill told FDR that Stalin had asked him what was happening in Greece. What was happening was that British soldiers were beating down a Communist uprising. Before Churchill could respond, Stalin said, "I don't want to criticize anything or to interfere. I'm quite content to leave it to you." The P.M. said he interpreted that to mean that Uncle Joe was willing to stand back from Greece and permit his Red allies to cry vainly for assistance because the Russians wanted a similar free hand in Bulgaria and Romania. The agreement of fifty-fifty influence in those countries, the cynical Churchill informed FDR, was dead; "he'll let his people be beaten up in Greece for the sake of his larger plans." This day Churchill had said Uncle Joe will take Dumbarton Oaks, and now the matter was on the table.

Stettinius, who had just completed a lunch with Molotov, was the most surprised man at the table when the Russian Foreign Minister stood to announce that the Soviet Union had studied the American voting plan for the United Nations and was now "happy" to accept it. The Soviet government was certain that the United Nations "guaranteed the unity of the great powers." Molotov said that the Russian delegation had been particularly impressed with "what Churchill told us." The Americans and the British regarded this as a major concession. Only the President's face showed no joy. He looked intently at Molotov and Stalin, as though expecting something distasteful or unacceptable to go with this sudden agreement. The Russians had fought and negated the United Nations as much as possible. Now came acceptance—complete acceptance. Roosevelt, who had questioned Soviet intentions to preserve the unity of the Big Three, now heard his own words echo back from another direction: "In the light of these explanations," Molotov said, "we believe it would se-cure the *unanimity* of the three powers in guaranteeing peace and security after the war." Without pausing for breath, the Soviet Foreign Minister read his paper. The Soviet Union had requested sixteen seats for Soviet Socialist Republics at the United Nations. This was a legitimate request because they were separate republics; some even conducted their own foreign affairs. However, the United States had declined the extra votes. Russia would now be satisfied with votes for a few republics —Ukrainia, Belorussia and Lithuania. If necessary, Molotov added, it might be reduced to two extra votes.

FDR scribbled on a sheet of paper and wrote to Stettinius: "This is not so good." He realized that his whole scheme for a United Nations would fail to get Senate support if Russia had three votes and the United States one. "Excuse me," he said, "are these votes in the Assembly only? They are not Security Council votes?" Molotov said, "Assembly." He wanted to continue. The President decided to talk him into silence. Those two extra votes could doom his most noble aspiration. He stated he was glad that the Soviet Union would be a charter member of both the Security Council and the Assembly. These great nations, working in harmony, could achieve—nay, impose—a lasting peace on the world. He would like to get to the subject of which nations to invite to the first U.N. meeting. He would also like to arrange to call that meeting, in some city to be decided, as soon as possible. A month, perhaps.

Churchill spoke while Molotov stood waiting to read his papers. He said he approved heartily of all that had been said, but this agreement was to be considered "in principle." He was opposed to staging a first meeting of the United Nations so quickly. Yes, he would have to oppose that because the British would have to assign delegates and would have to study the procedures of the Security Council and the Assembly. In addition, he would have to face up to problems of the British Empire; there were dominions to be notified and consulted; India, for example. The problems of the United Kingdom, he said, were different from those of the other powers. He wanted time. Hopkins wrote to Roosevelt:

"There's something behind this talk—we do not know of its basis. Perhaps we had better wait until later tonight to find out what is on his mind. Harry." FDR wrote back: "All this is local politics." Hopkins was puzzled. He wrote: "I'm quite sure now he is thinking about the next election in Britain. Harry." It was true, England anticipated an election in the spring or early summer. Was Churchill worried that he might lack authority to make lasting commitments?

When Churchill stopped, Roosevelt said that the matter of the extra votes for Belorussia and the Ukraine could easily be settled by the U.N. Assembly. Stalin began to frown. It was obvious to all that he saw himself as the person making the big concessions, but Roosevelt and Churchill seemed unwilling to accept the gift. The Prime Minister began to espouse the Russian line, which was that Belorussia, the Ukraine and Lithuania had fought valiantly in the war and had given freely of their blood to achieve victory. For this they deserved recognition and a vote. Churchill, possibly unthinkingly, said, "We have four self-governing dominions who, during the past twenty-five years, have played a notable part in the international organization for peace which had broken down in 1939. When the United Kingdom declared war on Germany, all of them sprung to arms, although they knew how weak we were. We had no means of compelling them to do this. . . . For these reasons, I cannot but hear the proposals of the Soviet Government with a feeling of profound sympathy. My heart goes out to mighty Russia, bleeding from her wounds but beating down the tyrants in her path." He said further that he appreciated Roosevelt's desire to have the first U.N. meeting in March, but he thought "the battle against Germany will then be at its height. For the time being, I let this pass."

Hopkins wrote: "Deal with this quickly, as the Russians have given in so much at this conference. Harry." The President said that each of the Big Three was different in structure. The British Empire consisted of some large countries such as Canada and Australia; the Soviet system included sixteen individual republics; the United States had one language and one foreign minister. He would like to suggest that Molotov's suggestion about two extra votes would have to be studied. Otherwise, other nations with one vote might protest big nations having more than one. Roosevelt was stalling for time. Unexpected acceptance had left him more worried than pleased. He suggested that the foreign ministers study the question of Soviet votes "tomorrow," and also recommend a date and a place for the first meeting. The British Prime Minister expected extra votes for Canada, India and Australia. He was willing to grant Russia three votes without debate if the British Empire could have four or five. "I should be very disappointed," said Churchill, "if the settlement of membership of the Assembly was postponed until a new meeting of the United Nations can be held." All three agreed to refer it to the foreign ministers.

The President asked for, and got, a ten-minute recess. He was fatigued and looked bewildered. Events were moving too swiftly for him to absorb them, and there was evidence that there was a union between Russia and England against him. When he returned, Molotov said that he had not finished his paper. Magically, the typed draft of the Russian proposals regarding Poland had arrived. Stalin was horse-trading; he had agreed to the American voting procedure in the United Nations (which at no time prejudiced Soviet independent action in the world) in return for British and U.S. concessions regarding Poland. The Soviet Foreign Minister said that the new agreement took into consideration early conference objections, particularly those in President Roosevelt's letter:

1. It is agreed that the line of Curzon should be the eastern frontier of Poland with a digression from it in some regions of 5–8 kilometers in favor of Poland.

2. It is decided that the western frontier of Poland shall be traced from the city of Stettin (German) and farther to the south along the River Oder and still farther along the River Neisse, western branch.

3. It is deemed desirable to add to the Provisional Polish Government some democratic leaders from Polish emigré circles.

4. It is regarded as desirable that the Provisional Polish Government, enlarged as is mentioned above in paragraph 3, shall as soon as possible call the population of Poland to the polls for organization by general voting of permanent organs of the Polish Government.

5. V. M. Molotov, Mr. Harriman and Sir Archibald Clark Kerr will be entrusted with the discussion of the question of enlarging the Provisional Polish Government and submitting their proposals to the consideration of the three governments.

As a document, it was simple, concise and brutal. On the surface, it appeared to be equitable. In its depths, it took a large part of eastern Poland from its people—in fact, Stalin was taking what the Germans had given him in August 1939. As a sop, he was giving a huge area in the west and northwest, which belonged to Germany and in which six million Germans lived. In Article 3 the Provisional Government was not disbanded so that a democratic government could be formed; Stalin proposed to "add to it." Article 4, asking for a general election, stated that it was "desirable," neither imperative nor necessary. The nomination of Molotov, along with the American and British ambassadors, entrusted them with "discussion," with no power to order an enlargement of the Lublin government. They would be permitted to "submit" their proposals to Russia, Britain and the United States. The worst aspect of the Molotov proposals is that the Russians later acknowledged that they thought Churchill and Roosevelt were merely trying to save face at home. It is doubtful that the Soviet hierarchy intended to implement the six-point project. It was something for the Americans and British to wave to the world and say, "See? We did our best."

Molotov said that communications experts at Koreiz

had been trying to get a telephone connection with the members of the Polish Provisional Government, but that some were in Cracow and some elsewhere. The Foreign Minister doubted that there would be time to summon them to Yalta before the conference closed. Still, he said unctuously, the document went a long way toward meeting Mr. Roosevelt's ideas. No one could pretend to read the faces of the Big Three, but Stalin looked impatient, Churchill appeared to be re-reading the English translation and Roosevelt seemed more puzzled than before. Hopkins passed another note: "Why not refer to Foreign Ministers for detailed discussion and report tomorrow or next day. Harry." The President smiled. Well, he said, progress was certainly being made. If he had to quarrel, it would be about the use of the word emigré. It seems strange that he did not ask Stalin how the Russians could invent a new government and election for a people without the presence of those people. But he didn't. He said the word emigré, to his way of thinking, connoted French royalty fleeing the Revolution; it described people who run away.

Roosevelt meandered onward, in the manner of a man thinking aloud. Molotov, who spoke English, said that the word could be changed. The President suggested that it might be changed to read Poles overseas, or Poles outside Poland—although he would insist that Poles from within Poland—the archbishop, for example—should be included. He was appreciative, he said, of Russia's willingness to have a free election soon, because that coincided with his belief in the self-determination of peoples large and small. The enlargement of the government, and subsequent elections, did indeed represent a great step forward. Molotov said that the Soviets would appreciate his acceptance of the draft, that it had come a long way toward responding to his suggestions and, though he did not mention Russian willingness to repress its suspicions in accepting the U.N. voting proceedure, most of the Americans and British who were present understood that the Russians expected some reciprocation.

Churchill, who correctly assessed himself as a master

of language, suggested that, instead of emigré, the phrase "Poles temporarily abroad" be used. The Russians agreed at once. He was worried, he said, about that western border. The British had had some experience in the transfer of populations, and it was a difficult and complex business which left no one content. Stalin asked, "What about the Germans?" The P.M. said that, since the conference began, the three of them had been talking about nations and areas without atlas or map, but his recollection was that there were six million Germans between the present Polish border and the western Neisse. To lift them physically from what would now be Poland westward to Germany would be a heart-wrenching task. Stalin smiled. "There are no Germans there," he said. As the Russian armies advanced, the civilian German families fled. The homes, the factories, the farms were empty. Churchill said that this made everything a lot easier. Stalin told him that the roads westward were choked with Germans. The P.M. began to enthuse. He had been vexed, he admitted, about the problem, but if his computations were correct, Germany had lost six or seven million persons in the war, and the influx from East Prussia and Upper Silesia would balance those who had been lost. Between this conference, he said, and the end of the war—who knows? The Germans might lose another million. Stalin grinned. "One," he said, "or two?"

It didn't matter, the Prime Minister said. He would not propose a limit on the destruction of Germans. Roosevelt suggested putting the Soviet draft aside for further discussion. Stalin shrugged. It was agreeable to him. Churchill said he would like to see the words "and Poles from inside Poland" included in paragraph three. The Soviet Marshal ordered Molotov to do it. Roosevelt suggested a recess after a session almost five hours long. The Russians departed with the feeling that they had made a compromise solution on Poland, and that it had been accepted. There had been no challenges to the document, only the substitution of a few words.

The President's strength was drained. Howard Bruenn

studied his distinguished patient with increasing anxiety. The morning examination disclosed nothing alarming, but the educated eye disclosed things hidden to instruments. Roosevelt was spent, physically and mentally. He was a man who seemed to have worked all his life toward this one supreme meeting, and, now that he was in it, he found himself embattled and his ideals assailed by his friends. The consummate politician knew that the more he compromised here, the bolder the opposition he could expect back home. Bruenn promised himself that, if Mr. Roosevelt looked no better tomorrow, he would insist on an evening medical examination. The doctor was treating Pa Watson for hypertensive heart disease, and Harry Hopkins for postoperative ulcers and an almost total absence of nutrition.

The dinner was *en famille.* The mood of the President was somber. He spoke engagingly about Stalin's concession to the United Nations and Poland, but he was enough of a realist to wonder if the Soviets would honor their pledges, or find a way of weaseling out of them. Stettinius sat on the President's left and did most of the talking. He thought it had been "a most fruitful day." As Secretary of State, he would like to know the Boss's feeling about those two extra votes in the Assembly. The feeling was one of dejection. Roosevelt knew of no way he could go back to the U.S. Senate and explain that the Russians had three votes, the United States one. He might tell them that Churchill would like to have extra votes for dominions such as Canada and India, but that wouldn't help. He would be accused of selling out to the Russians *and* the English.

Stettinius, finding he had not improved the mood, moved on to ask the composition of the first American delegation to the United Nations. Ed had given it some thought; he knew Roosevelt had wanted it to be bipartisan; Stettinius thought it might be a good idea to have a woman on it, too. He suggested Senators Tom Connolly and Arthur Vandenberg, Representatives Sol Bloom and Charles Eaton, Dean Virginia Gildersleeve of Barnard College and a liberal Republican Midwesterner, Harold Stassen. The President looked up from his dinner and said that a place should be found for Republican Senator Warren Austin, who had supported Roosevelt's foreign policy. Yes, said Ed, but we should use the senior members of the Senate Foreign Relations Committee from both parties—that meant Vandenberg rather than Austin. The President had no comment. He was listening, thinking, wondering.

Anna and Kathleen Harriman kept the conversation light and bright. At one point the President told Stettinius that he did not believe there was "anything preposterous" about the Soviet Union asking for two extra votes. The Russians had experienced difficulty hanging onto the Ukraine. In the winter of 1941, Roosevelt heard that, if Hitler won, the Ukraine would defect from Mother Russia and set up an independent nation. FDR could now understand, he said, why Stalin had extended himself to win the loyalty of a few of the "Republics." In addition, he said, it would be difficult to oppose the Soviet request now, because the British would back Stalin. When the United Nations convened, there would be about fifty votes in the Assembly, the President said. It would grow to a greater number, but three votes out of fifty were not that important. He sounded like a man trying to convince himself. "The real power," he said, "is in the Security Council." He sipped hot coffee. The priorities, as Roosevelt now saw them, he said, were to maintain the unity of the Big Three, defeat Germany, get the powers around a table to work together for peace, and defeat Japan. Any situation which threatened those priorities, to the extent to which they were endangered, was to be avoided.

Thursday, February 8, represented the fifth day of conferences. In retrospect the gentlemen could see that they had started slowly, politely, cautiously; men afraid of each other, fearful to take a long, venturesome step. Agreement on important matters appeared to be possible. No one could get all that he asked but, on paper at least, no one was giving up more than he could afford.

It was a low, misty morning, with wisps of fog outside the tall windows of Livadia, the shrubs and trees glistening with moisture. After breakfast the President became pleasantly excited because a messenger from Koreiz brought a note stating that Stalin and Molotov would like to see Mr. Roosevelt before the plenary session to discuss Far Eastern matters.

FDR called a noon meeting in his study with Hopkins, Harriman, Byrnes and Bohlen. He acquainted them with the contents of the note. Once more, he wanted to go over what he should ask in a war against the Japanese Empire and what he should give. It might have been proper to ask Churchill and Eden to attend—Britain, too, was at war with Japan—but Stalin saw the Far East as an extension of American influence and he asked only to speak to Roosevelt. The President did not invite Stettinius to either meeting. Ed was urged to go on to Vorontsov Palace, where Eden was host at a daily meeting of foreign ministers, and not to mention the afternoon session with Stalin. "You have enough to do, Ed," the President said to his Secretary of State, "with that agreement on Poland, the United Nations, and the problems of small nations."

Stettinius motored to Vorontsov Palace where he was impressed by the fact that Stalin had sent the British delegation to an estate featuring a huge stone lion with one eye half open and the other closed. He did not see the stone staircase on the sea side, with its three pairs of lions ascending. The lowest pair slept on their paws, the second pair stared and the top pair bared their fangs to roar. Stettinius felt comfortable with Eden. The British Foreign Secretary had arranged an impressive table for discussions before lunch. Ed noted that Molotov was smiling, and this boded well. Ed opened the meeting by extending a formal invitation to "their great allies" to hold the first U.N. meeting in the United States. Molotov asked where. Stettinius said that he had suggested a dozen or more cities to the President at dinner last night, but the Boss declined all.

Smiling, he said that he hoped that "no one was

shocked" when FDR suggested the charter meeting for next month. Stettinius said that he had been thinking of April all along. In any case, he assured them, the session would be arranged to suit their convenience. Stettinius had disinclination for the unpleasant. Looking at Molotov, he said that Andrei Gromyko would recall that, at Dumbarton Oaks, they had all wondered whether to admit, as U.N. members, all countries who had broken off relations with the Axis powers but had not declared war. Before the Russian Foreign Minister could respond, Ed said he was now of the opinion that they should admit, as charter members, only those who had declared war and had signed the United Nations Declaration. There was vague talk around the table, but no agreement.

The American Secretary of State moved on to another, more important matter. Regarding the Soviet proposal to admit two or three of its republics to membership, Stettinius said he was puzzled, because the articles of the United Nations clearly stated each "sovereign state" should have one Assembly vote. On the other hand, he had spoken about it to the President at dinner, and FDR said the subject "deserves sympathetic consideration." Molotov was an old hand at the shredding and reassembling of diplomatic phrases. He said he had expressed his views yesterday and would rather listen to Mr. Eden.

Eden spoke as though he had not heard the question. He was delighted to accept the American invitation. Half in jest, he said he was jealous at not having a big conference of foreign ministers in London. Molotov said it could be arranged. Stettinius seconded the motion. For a half hour it appeared that Eden and Molotov were playing table tennis with Stettinius. However, before lunch was served, all three agreed that the first meeting should be held somewhere in the United States on Wednesday, April 25. The British Secretary said he was also favorably inclined toward granting Molotov's proposal for three Russian votes. He said he would say so "at the appropriate time." Molotov nodded. "The sooner the better," he said.

Well, whom to invite? Stettinius pulled a list of nations from his breast pocket. It was passed around.

The United States of America
The United Kingdom of Great Britain and Northern Ireland
The Union of Soviet Socialist Republics

China	*El Salvador*	*New Zealand*
Australia	*Greece*	*Nicaragua*
Belgium	*Guatemala*	*Norway*
Canada	*Haiti*	*Panama*
Costa Rica	*Honduras*	*Poland*
Cuba	*India*	*South Africa*
Czechoslovakia	*Luxembourg*	*Yugoslavia*
Dominican Republic	*Netherlands*	

Except for the Big Four, it was a weak organization. If Norway was on it, why not Denmark? Where were Mexico, Brazil, Columbia, Venezuela, Ethiopia, Spain, Turkey, France—among others? Molotov saw but one country, Poland. "Which Poland?" he asked Stettinius. Ed didn't know. He and Eden might have told Molotov that the new, enlarged Polish government would be invited but they didn't. Stettinius merely said that the list had been made out based on those countries which had signed the U.N. Declaration on or about January, 1942. That Polish government was chaired by Mikolajczyk. Eden thought the list was out of date. Why not draw up a fresh one which would admit the two extra Soviet Republics, and all those who signed the Declaration by March 1—three weeks hence? This was agreed, but Molotov suggested that the three foreign secretaries state that they recommended invitations to the Ukraine and Belorussia.

Stettinius said he was impressed but would have to discuss it with the President. "I expect that the United States may be able to give a favorable reply today," he said. It was a bold statement, because he had nothing more formal than a tired man's conversation at a dinner. He said he would "check." The three appointed a subcommittee to draft a report on invitations. Abruptly, they moved on to a discussion of Iran, which was not relevant, but came under the "small nations rights" enunciated by Roosevelt. Eden said he had two distinct feelings about Iran. He realized that there was some alarm about the Soviet Union and its oil concessions in Iran, but, as Iran and Russia had a common border, he could see no reason why the Soviet Union should not be a major oil customer. His other view was that Iran should be the sole master of its own house and should not have to brook interference. Each of the Big Three, he said, had troops in Iran to protect the wartime flow of oil to the Allies, but they could demonstrate good faith by withdrawing their soldiers before the end of the war. The Russians had a constitutional fear of evacuating their troops from any piece of territory. Molotov said the oil concessions were one question, withdrawal was another. The Soviet government would require time to study it. As far as oil was concerned, the Iranians were friendly one moment, unfriendly the next. They had entered negotiations about oil, but Iran stated that, as long as the war endured, no one would get oil concessions. Molotov thought that the best procedure would be to permit Iranian matters to take their course for the present. Stettinius said that U.S. oil companies had been busy trying to secure oil leases, but had dropped all negotiations. In addition, U.S. troops were in Iran for one purpose: to guard the oil route to the Soviet Union. This appeared to have no impact on Molotov. It would be better, he said, if the British, Americans and Russians treated the matter of Iran "as an exchange of views"—one more diplomatic euphemism for let's-not-do-anything.

They agreed to adjourn early, so that a report would be ready for the plenary session, scheduled for 4:15 P.M. Molotov did not mention Stalin's projected secret visit to Roosevelt at 3:45 P.M. Neither did Stettinius.

Eden suggested that all countries which signed the declaration and also declared war on the Axis by March 1 should be invited to the United Nations. It was agreed. All three asked assistant secretaries to hurry with the typewritten report of the meeting. The Big Three would want to scan this one before convening. The completed report stated that, regarding Belorussia and the Ukraine, the Soviet Union and the United Kingdom endorsed inviting both as members; the Americans looked with sympathy toward the idea. This was hardly in harmony with Roosevelt's thinking. He would say privately that he felt the two Soviet Republics should be granted the *rights* and *privileges* of members, but that Russia was entitled to one delegation at the United Nations. This was incomprehensible to the Russians, the British and the American delegation. Even Byrnes and Hopkins, who were close to the President and his political thoughts, did not pretend to understand what it meant. Churchill and Stalin asked later how FDR could invite six South American "associated nations," which were aligned with American foreign policy, but had not signed the U.N. Declaration, as charter members, while denying membership to two Soviet Republics which had sustained the scourge and ashes of war. Churchill was so disappointed that he said he would protest his friend's "rationale." In his own behalf, the President prophesied that there would be "howls of protest" in the American Congress. He was a man racing at top speed to set up a peace-keeping organization while the war was still on; he was so close to success that he could not contain his fear that the United Nations concept could be wrecked at Yalta or in the halls of Congress.

The President was in his study with James Byrnes of South Carolina. The two men were wrestling with a word problem. Byrnes, after lunch, told the President that he had read several of Bohlen's summations of the conference, and it seemed to him that the Big Three were "agreeing" on matters involving their countries. Roosevelt hoped they could agree more. It was the word "agree" which bothered Byrnes. When the conference was over, he said, the Big Three would have to sign something binding them and their unified wishes. It could not be a treaty, although the Russians would think of it as a treaty. An American President cannot sign a treaty without ratification by the U.S. Senate. It was, said Byrnes, a matter of constitutional law. This also applied to the word "pact," as it did to "agreement." It had not occurred to the President. Byrnes said Roosevelt would have to find a way around the law or go home and fight the same futilities which had wrecked Wilson's League of Nations.

The President said he wanted Alger Hiss. Hull and Stettinius had found the tall young man to be a lawyer's lawyer. Hiss had redrafted the entire U.N. Charter, all 111 articles of it. Roosevelt found him of assistance at the plenary sessions in matters of intricate law and national rights. The State Department official was brought in. The three went into a silent thinking session. FDR, sitting behind the small ornate desk, dropped his head. Alger Hiss thought the Boss was exhausted; he was meditating. Once in a while, Byrnes would say all the words it could not be. Hiss worked hard to think of a way out of the dilemma, but every word that came to mind equated with "treaty." He was standing near the desk, with an unread copy of the foreign secretaries' minutes in his hand. Roosevelt lifted his head. "I've got it," he said. The others waited. "We will make this a *statement* of the three heads of state here, and then, within the text, we will say we are *agreed,* but mostly it will be a statement of three leaders." Hiss nodded. Legalistically, the President had found a loophole. Everyone would realize that the statement would be a *de facto* treaty, a document which would oblige three nations to abide by its text. "A statement," the President said, amending himself, "agreed to by three people—not three leaders." He was happy with himself.

Roosevelt said that he had some things to do before Stalin arrived. Byrnes returned to his room. Hiss stood in the big concave corridor reading the foreign secretaries' minutes. As a member of the subcommittee, it was part of his work to supervise what went into these daily worksheets. As he read, he was stunned to see that one of the notes said that the three secretaries had agreed to two extra votes for Russia. Hiss knew this was not true. He looked for Edward Stettinius, but missed him by a moment; Ed had gone to the President's study to brief him on the minutes. Hiss, assailed by the rigidity which hits calm cool men in panic, saw Anthony Eden coming in. The British Foreign Secretary listened to Hiss. He was not alarmed. "But you don't know what has taken place," Eden said.

There was a great deal of excitement and a number of Russians swelling through the corridor. Hiss had to hurry. In the throng he saw the snow-white hair of Stettinius. Quickly Hiss pointed to the grievous error. The Secretary of State was crestfallen. He said he was inside, explaining the agreements to FDR, and when he came to the extra votes for Russia, he was in the process of saying, "We have reached agreement on everything except for the extra votes." What emerged from his mouth was, "We have reached agreement on everything—." The door to the study swung open, and a voice announced, "The Soviet Marshal!" Ed was waved aside as the short chunky Russian came in the door and shook hands with the seated President. As Stettinius backed toward the door, he heard the President say to Pavlov, the Russian interpreter, "I have just heard that the foreign ministers agreed on everything." Stalin listened, lifted his brows, and said, "On the extra votes, too?" Roosevelt grinned. "On the extra votes, too." A monumental, historic mistake had been impaled on an unfinished sentence.

Stalin sat in a box chair beside the desk. Molotov, Harriman and Chip Bohlen came in. The Big Two had given themselves thirty minutes to discuss weighty matters. Bohlen sat with his legs crossed, a pad of yellow foolscap on his knee. He, as usual, would interpret for the President and would also write sketchy notes. Stalin had both arms on the wings of the chair. He nodded agreeably and flapped his hands for the President to commence.

The fall of Manila, FDR said slowly, directing his eyes to the Marshal and his words to Pavlov and Bohlen, had brought the Pacific War into a new phase. The United States was bearing the brunt of a war in opposite parts of the world. And, fortunately, winning. His country hoped to establish forward bases at the Bonin Islands and some near Formosa. He hoped it would not be necessary to invade the mainlands, and he did not propose to order it unless "absolutely necessary." American Intelligence estimated that the Japanese, in spite of successive defeats, still had four million men under arms. He would like to try massive bombing before thinking of invasion.

Stalin said he would like to make it plain that the Soviet Union had no objection to the Americans establishing air bases at Komsomolsk or at Nikolaevsk. These were near the mouth of the Amur River close to the northern reaches of Sakhalin. They may have been requested by the American Air Force General Kuter; both were in the remote fastness of eastern Siberia; Nikolaevsk was 1,150 miles north of Tokyo, both were on the 140th parallel. The Americans were building huge bases for the new heavy B-29s at Saipan and Tinian, 1,500 miles south of Tokyo. It did not seem likely that Roosevelt, even without the use of an atlas, would become enthused about sending thousands of Seabees and supplies to build air bases so far north of Tokyo. Further, it is possible that the military reports had not been digested by the President. He was absorbing as much as his flagging strength would permit from reports of the daily foreign secretaries' meetings and the oral swordplay at the plenary sessions.

He thanked Stalin. The Marshal said that a request had been made for an air base on Kamchatka. He would have to decline this at present because Russia was at peace with Japan, and there was a Japanese consulate on Kamchatka. One phrase in the President's personal note regarding the Soviet entrance into the Japanese war was unclear to Stalin. What did Roosevelt mean by "commercial routes"? The President explained that the Soviet Union expected arms and supplies—additional Lend-Lease—after Germany was defeated, and he was wondering how he could get supplies to the Russian armies to the north of Japan. "It is going to become very important," he said, "but also very difficult." Stalin nodded. He understood. It would not be feasible to cross the Atlantic and the northern reaches to Murmansk, then to reload on trains and move every bullet, gun and grain of wheat across the face of Russia. The Americans could have air and naval bases on the Amur River, if it would help.

Roosevelt picked up a paper and gave it to Stalin. "I think the Soviet staff should be instructed to start planning talks with the United States staff," he said. Stalin handed the paper to Molotov. "I will give instructions," he said. The President said he had two more questions of a military nature. Both related to Europe. He handed Stalin two small papers and apologized because they had been written in English. The first, Roosevelt said, involved permission to use airfields around Budapest. This concerned the big B-24 fleet staged on a complex of fields at Foggia, Italy. They made long runs to bomb Germany, and long runs back. If they could bomb central Germany and then, instead of flying back to Foggia, could go on and land, refuel and rearm at Budapest, the Americans could establish what they called "shuttle bombing."

The second request was for a team of U.S. Air Force experts to survey American bomb damage in southeastern Europe. The Americans had already surveyed the bomb damage at the Romanian oil fields in Ploesti; they had learned a great deal of what was effective and what wasn't. The President asked that these Americans be granted permission to proceed at once. "We want our people to survey the damage while the evidence is fresh and the inhabitants who lived through them are still on the spot." Stalin said he could see no objection to either request. He would consult with his military staff about both items.

Roosevelt then began a speech about trusteeships. In the case of areas too small or too weak to govern themselves at once, he would like to establish trusteeships. The British, he said, still thought in terms of mandates and colonies and dominions, but he preferred a temporary international group to supervise the welfare of the helpless. Stalin nodded. Roosevelt was encouraged. He would need this vote to counteract Churchill. In Korea, he said, he counted on a trusteeship composed of one American, one Russian and one Chinese—assisted, of course, by staffs. Before Stalin could respond, FDR said the United States had had some experience in these matters; the Philippines was a good example. The United States did not want the Philippines and it had required fifty years to get those people ready for self-government. Korea might take twenty years, maybe thirty. The Marshal said he agreed; "the shorter the time, the better." Will there be any foreign troops involved in Korea? No, Roosevelt said. "Good," Stalin replied.

The two men were moving swiftly in thirty minutes. It seemed to those who listened that they barely broached a subject, then found themselves in broad agreement and ready to move on to another one. FDR said that, in the case of Korea, he proposed not to invite the British, and he wondered if they would be offended. Stalin said, "They will be offended. In fact, the Prime Minister might kill us." FDR fell into hearty laughter. He removed his glasses and wiped his eyes. "The British should be invited," Stalin said.

Roosevelt diverted Stalin's attention to Indochina. He had asked Chiang Kai-shek about Indochina, and China didn't want it. And yet, he felt it was a potential trouble spot. "The people are of small stature, like the Javanese and Burmese, and not warlike." France, which had ruled in eastern Indochina for a long time, had done nothing to improve the country. FDR said he had a message from General de Gaulle asking for ships to transport French forces all the way to Indochina. Stalin did not smile. "Where," he said, "will de Gaulle get the troops?" Roosevelt chuckled. De Gaulle said he would find the troops when Roosevelt found the ships. Stalin shrugged. He had no comment on Indochina.

Roosevelt, who had turned in his chair to face Stalin, moved the fringed table lamp back and away from their eyes. He would like to talk about China. He shook his head negatively. For some time, he said, he had been trying to keep China alive. This was an unusual statement from one who had elevated China to the status of first-rank power, with a permanent seat on the Security Council.

Stalin made it gruffly plain that he was not backing the Communists in China, as he had told Churchill he would not help them in Greece. It was a gentlemen's agreement about spheres of influence—a phrase Roosevelt despised—but Stalin and Churchill regarded the great sleeping giant of Asia as America's "baby." The Soviet dictator was more interested in specifics: how would Russia obtain the use of Port Arthur, for example? Port Arthur was of utmost importance to the Soviet Union. It would be the only warm-water port in the whole Asian area of Russia. The President would not discuss Port Arthur without working something out for the port of Dairen, only 30 miles away on the Liaotung Peninsula at the foot of Manchuria. The Soviets could, FDR said, obtain an outright lease of Port Arthur, or make Dairen a free port under an international commission. Personally, he would prefer the second method. It had a relationship to British interests in Hong Kong; he hoped Churchill would give Hong Kong back to the Chinese and make it an international free port. However, he felt the Prime Minister would object to this.

The Marshal had no interest in Hong Kong. He brought the President back to the subject of Port Arthur and Dairen by reminding him that the Russians had to find a means of bringing their products to and from either of the ports. This would involve use of the Manchurian railways. The Japanese had stolen these railways from

China. After the war Chiang would expect them to be returned. The Czars, he recalled, had the use of the rail lines from Lupin south to Harbin and on to the two ports. The use of the rail lines as well as the ports was most important to the future of the Soviet Union. How could this be managed with Chiang? Roosevelt, who had been aware of this problem since the Teheran Conference, conceded that he had not consulted the Generalissimo about it. He did not know China's wishes in this area. However—optimistic as ever—he told Stalin there were two ways of solving it: to lease port and railroad under Soviet direction and pay the Chinese or operate both under a Sino-Russian directorate of one man each.

It was too simplistic. Molotov listened to the two men, perhaps wondering why his opposite number, Edward Stettinius, had not been invited. Throughout all the secret conference, Roosevelt had been gifted with simple solutions to complex problems. Chiang, who was weak without American assistance, was imperious with it. He hated and feared communism more than the Japanese. And yet the President of the United States was virtually committing China to a course of action in her internal affairs; this ran counter to what he had been preaching. Stalin frowned. "It is going to be difficult for Molotov and me to explain to the Russian people why they are leaving one great war to enter another." The people knew that the Soviet Union was at peace with Japan. On the other hand, if he could tell them of the political and industrial gains to be made, they would understand that it was in the national interest to engage in another war. Russia could be ready for that "other war" ninety days after Germany collapsed.

The threat was vague, almost conciliatory. Roosevelt had no doubt that the political considerations could be met, but he told Stalin that the reason he had not consulted Chiang about the Soviets declaring war on Japan was because it was a well-known fact that "anything said to them is known to the whole world in twenty-four hours." Russia agreed to that, Stalin said. He would go a step further. He asked Roosevelt not to speak to the Chinese yet. It would be better to leave Yalta with a secret agreement signed by the United States, Britain and the U.S.S.R. Roosevelt nodded. "This could be done," he said. It amounted to the betrayal of an ally. Secrecy was required. Still, the Big Three kept secrets from each other. The Japanese Ambassador to Russia had asked the Soviet Union to intercede with the United States to arrive at a formula for peace, but the Kremlin declined. No word of the peace feeler reached Roosevelt. The President, on the other hand, volunteered no information about his atomic bomb, which was five months away from an awesome and successful test.

There were a few minutes of time left. Stalin continued his use of carrot and stick; FDR was granting concessions freely. Stalin said that in late spring it might be possible to remove 25 divisions of troops from the western front to the Maritime Territory. Perhaps it would be wise to talk to Chiang then, after the Russo-Manchurian border had been fortified. "We will not be difficult," he said bluntly, "about a warm-weather port. And we have no objection to internationalizing such a port. It does not have to be reserved solely for Soviet use." Of course he would expect Japan to return the southern half of Sakhalin and other territory she had taken from Russian in the war of 1904.

The President was agreeable. As time ran out for the two men, Stalin ticked off the riches in territories and privileges Russia expected after a victory over Japan, and he assumed that the President could persuade his friend Chiang to accept these conditions. Roosevelt was not in doubt. As a realist, he knew that once the Soviet armies swept south through Manchuria, the Chinese had no more chance of evicting them than FDR had of getting the Russians out of Poland. Stalin said he could not understand the battle between Nationalist forces and Communist armies in China. Chiang, he said, was the natural leader for both. In the name of Russian aggrandizement, he would turn his back on Chinese Communists.

The two had redesigned part of the world in twenty minutes. They had ten left. Stalin said that Stettinius had mentioned that the United States might have surplus shipping after the war. The Soviet Union would need a great number of cargo vessels. Roosevelt said this too might be arranged. It would require changes in congressional legislation, but he felt that, when the war was over, whatever surplus United States shipping was not needed by America or Britain could be transferred to the Soviet Union. He worked out a deal at once. After World War I, he said, the mistake had been to make a fixed charge on each vessel, and then charge interest. Nations close to bankruptcy could not pay the interest, and the debts became impossible. He proposed to transfer vessels to the U.S.S.R. on credit without interest. The price of each ship would be based on original cost, less depreciation in wartime. The payments could be made over twenty years. The Marshal beamed with pleasure. Even Harriman had seldom seen him so happy. The President's words, Stalin said, would greatly ease the tasks of the Soviet Union after the war. FDR responded that he hoped Russia would interest itself "in a large way in the shipping game."

Stalin launched into a laudatory speech about the great value of Lend-Lease. It was, he said, "a remarkable invention"; without it, victory would have been delayed. In former wars, he said, the strong sometimes helped the weak, but when hostilities were over the weak resented the assistance. Lend-Lease, however, was such an equitable arrangement that it induced no rancor on either side.

The secret meeting was over. Stalin, Molotov and Pavlov stood. The President wanted to refresh himself for a moment before riding into the ballroom. The net effect of the conversations—pleasant and informal in character, but gigantic in their sweep of Asian problems —was that France and Britain were to be excluded, except for Hong Kong and Burma, from mainland Asian policy. Outer Mongolia would be left undominated, but Manchuria would be a Russian "sphere"; the rest of China, and Japan as well, would be an American theater. Roosevelt thought he had won the thirty-minute Battle of Smiles because he had a firm commitment for Russia to come into the war ninety days after Germany surrendered. Even with Russia at his side, Roosevelt's Joint Chiefs of Staff figured that Imperial Japan could not be beaten in less than eighteen months after the defeat of Germany. Stalin, on the other hand, felt that Soviet interests had been well served by Roosevelt: she would enter the war after the Americans had practically won it; Moscow would get southern Sakhalin, the Kuriles, railway and port rights in Manchuria, and whatever Japanese booty could be shipped back to Russia. They would also get continued Lend-Lease and, presumably, surplus United States ships.

The President was on his way to the ballroom when Lieutenant Rigdon tendered a message from Patrick Hurley:

> *Chungking, February 8 1945*
> *Top Secret. From Hurley for the eyes of the President alone. Information eyes alone Secretary of State*
> *From the Ambassador in China to the President*
> *NCR 4501. It has been suggested that if the President and his staff and Prime Minister Churchill and his staff could visit Delhi and invite the Generalissimo and his staff to meet them there it would be a great morale builder in this theater. It would also afford an opportunity to clarify policies and strategy. Delhi is suggested rather than any place in China for two reasons: (1) security and (2) accommodations. A meeting at Delhi would probably make unnecessary Wedemeyer's proposed conference at Washington. If there is a possibility of such arrangement, please advise me earliest convenience.*

Mr. Roosevelt handed the message to Stettinius. The President would send a response to Hurley stating that time and distance would not permit the visit. He was already farther from Washington than he desired to be. Except for a short stay at Suez when this conference was over, FDR would go home. He would not travel to India to see Chiang, nor would he welcome an offer from Chiang to meet him at Cairo. Whether one considers it diplomacy or deception, there was too much that Roosevelt could not discuss with the Generalissimo. Most of it concerned the disposition of China.

The fifth plenary session was called to order. Eden was asked to present a summary of the meeting of foreign ministers. When he concluded, the conference was stunned when Roosevelt rephrased the agreement to admit Belorussia and the Ukraine as separate members. "Paragraph two," he said crisply, "is that it will be for the conference to determine the list of the original members of the organization. At that stage, the delegates of the United Kingdom and the United States will support the proposal to admit to original membership two Soviet Socialist Republics." Eden stared at Churchill. Stettinius studied his hands. Molotov and Stalin glanced at each other. All of these people understood clearly that FDR had agreed to invite the two countries to charter membership. He had said yes to it forty-five minutes earlier. The new words from his mouth sounded equivocating. If all understood him, FDR was saying that the two would be invited, but it would be up to the original nations to vote acceptance to the Assembly. Stalin asked that the question be settled at the conference; Roosevelt said it was settled.

Byrnes and Admiral Leahy, hearing it for the first time, were shocked for different reasons. They were sure that the Boss would deny extra votes to Russia. Byrnes, in an aside, had even warned the President that the rock on which the original League of Nations had foundered was that the Senate believed Great Britain and its dominions would have five votes to one for the United States. Stalin spoke. "The conference," he said with ponderous patience, "has accepted the report of the foreign ministers. As I see it, Mr. Stettinius maintains that all the nations which have declared war on the Axis by March first, in addition to all which have signed the United Nations Declaration by that time, including such Central and South American countries as the United States called 'Associated Members,' will be invited to join the United Nations Assembly. I think I can assure the President that we can get the signatures of the governments of Belorussia and the Ukraine by March first." Molotov said it might be achieved before the Yalta Conference closed.

The President said the two republics represented a "technical" question; one involving three votes for a conglomerate of republics regarded as one country. The President was either bold or forgetful. For the first time, Stalin looked puzzled. Instead of resorting to anger, which came easily to him, he said softly, "I do not want to embarrass the President, but if he will explain his difficulties we will see what can be done." The President was not embarrassed. Carefully, he explained to Stalin that invitations to membership would be extended by the membership. He tried to reassure Russia by stating again that her contest for three votes would be fully supported by the United States and Great Britain. The Soviet Premier might have complicated the conundrum by asking how a membership can invite a membership unless one starts with a membership. Stalin said, "We can get their signatures." It wasn't necessary, the President said. It wouldn't overcome the difficulty, which was technical. Stalin shook his leonine head from side to side. He would withdraw the question, he said. Roosevelt smiled and thanked him.

Eden took the floor and openly opposed FDR's position. The foreign ministers had concurred in endorsing charter membership for Belorussia and the Ukraine, and he would not turn his back on that concordance. Further, he said, he could not understand the position of the President in inviting all those small nations which had remained neutral until they were certain which side would win. Compared to the enormous devastation of the Ukraine and White Russia, ravaged to the ground, what right had those who had not sacrificed for the victory to become charter members while the Soviet Republics waited outside the door to be asked to enter?

Mr. Eden said the original membership should be restricted to those who had borne the agony of the conflict.

Stalin agreed. He said he had studied the names of those invited, and he found ten who did not recognize the Soviet Union. How could the President expect harmony in the United Nations if that many countries would not acknowledge the existence of Russia on the Security Council? He was sorry, he said, but the restrictions on membership should be more stringent. Roosevelt began to wallow in words. The disagreements of Eden and Stalin represented the sharpest exchange at the conference. "These nations," FDR said, "want to establish relations with the Soviet Union, but they have not got around to it." The rebuttal was weak and illogical. FDR had explicitly agreed to the extra votes. (Eden's statement to the harried Hiss, "You don't know what has happened," seemed to imply that Roosevelt agreed to it by phone with the Prime Minister or Eden—and now, less than an hour later, he was weaseling from the agreement.) "Some countries," he said with resignation, "follow the line of the Roman Catholic Church." Meaning, one supposed, that the Church opposed communism. Besides, he said, looking at Stalin, your emissaries have already met with those countries and worked with them at Bretton Woods and the U.N. Relief and Rehabilitation sessions.

The President was in an unhappy position. Nothing mollified the Russians and the British, so he tried pleading. The United States, he said, was in a most embarrassing position. It had advised some of the Central and South American nations *not* to declare war. In conflict, they might have been more a liability than an asset. Now the Crimean Conference would penalize them for accepting leadership. "Today we ask them to do the opposite. They would be in good standing if they had not accepted our advice." He was assuming the blame for the behavior of others. Stalin raised both hands. "What principle do we use to invite nations to become members?" Membership among those who signed the U.N.

Declaration, or, as Roosevelt said, "Associated Nations." This would not do, Stalin said. What did "associated" mean? To the Marshal, it meant countries like Argentina and Turkey, which sat on the sidelines watching a world in flames. Those who had fought, he said, would resent sitting beside those who had "associated" themselves.

The President recalled the agreement of the foreign ministers on this matter. He asked Stalin, "as a personal favor," to help him. "My idea," he said pleadingly, "and it would save my life, would be to invite those who are on the list who have helped us on condition that they declare war by March first." Eden would not stand to help him. Churchill puffed his long cigar in silence. Molotov blinked through his glasses, studying the face of the President. Stalin said softly, "I agree." The silence of the P.M. was broken when the deadlock was broken. Even at this late hour in the war, he said, there was a hidden advantage in having more countries declare war on Germany and Japan. Hitler would feel the increase in pressure. Molotov said it would be just to legitimize the list of nations to be invited with those who had fought.

As the conference had no agenda, so too it now had no criteria for membership in the United Nations. As the day flagged, Russia kept insisting that it was understood by all that Belorussia and the Ukraine had been invited. The President did not respond directly. He moved off on a tangent and said he would like to invite Iceland. The Prime Minister said that if Iceland was in, then Egypt should be invited because her *nonbelligerency* had been a big help to the British. Someone said that Iceland belonged to Denmark, but had divorced itself from the motherland after the Nazi invasion. This led Churchill to ask whether Denmark had acknowledged the independence of Iceland. Stalin said, "No." Churchill relented sufficiently to state that any nation declaring war in the next few weeks could be invited "to the party." To this, the Russians nodded agreement. Roosevelt, in a self-designed morass, vacillated between that doc-

trine—to which he agreed—and the list of nations the
United States had drawn up, some of which were only
"associated countries." This gave FDR two sets of criteria. He had told Stalin the two extra votes had been
agreed; nervously, he dissented from his own agreement.

The Soviets, whispering, decided to use the easier
set of rules. If charter membership was to be based
on signing the U.N. Declaration, they would get two
extra signatures at once. The President began to say
things his supporters could not believe. We should keep
the list we have, he said. (No one but FDR had compiled
a list.) If the doors of the United Nations were opened
too quickly, he warned, tiny countries like Andorra and
San Marino would demand membership. It would be
better, he thought, just at the start, if the Big Three stuck
to his list of belligerents, associated nations, and Turkey.
Churchill returned to the fray and said that under
any set of criteria the two Russian Republics would
have to be invited. "Original membership," he said, "is
going to be supported at the first U.N. meeting by the
Big Three." Stalin was losing patience. He proposed that
the two republics be invited to the Crimean Conference
and sign the Declaration "here." Even with the support
of the Big Three, he said, would it not be awkward
if the two republics did not sign? Stettinius tried to
help the faltering President. All parties, he said, could
take the President's word. The Socialist Republics would
have seats at the United Nations. Churchill said that
if they signed, no one would have to give his word or
guarantee membership. It would be automatic, under
Roosevelt's rules. FDR was becoming signally distressed.
He said that not signing would not damage the status
of the republics in question. He just required time to
arrange it. Stalin said he would again withdraw his motion
for immediate membership but would insist that the
foreign minister's report on these countries be made
part of the final report of the conference. All three agreed
to this. Later the contretemps would reach an almost
pathetic stage when Roosevelt would ask privately for

three votes for the United States. At that time, Stalin and Churchill would say, "Yes"; Roosevelt would thereupon retreat to one vote.

The consideration of the plenary session was diverted to Poland. The President's voice was low in volume; sometimes Pavlov and Major Birse cupped their ears to hear him. The pitiless man, Josef Stalin, looked at FDR and was moved to pity. Later, he would say to the British delegates, "If I had known how tired that man is, I would have agreed to meet along the Mediterranean." Roosevelt, taking the initiative as presiding officer, said he would like to bring the attention of all to Poland. This morning, he said, he had sent a new proposal, or perhaps a counterproposal, to Comrade Stalin and Mr. Churchill.

The United States, he said, had reviewed Mr. Molotov's proposals and found no objection to Point One, the eastern boundary of Poland. He agreed that territorial compensation should be given to Poland from Germany in the west, up to the line of the Oder River. He did not agree that the line should reach to the western Neisse River. Regarding the new broad-based government of Poland, FDR said that it should be placed in the hands of Molotov, Harriman and Clark Kerr. These men should invite to Moscow Mr. Bierut, Mr. Osóbka-Morawski, Archbishop Sapieha, Mr. Wincenty Witos, Mr. Mikolajczyk and Mr. Grabski to form a body to be known as the Polish Government of National Unity.

Roosevelt felt that three men, rather than one, should form a "Presidential Committee." These men should be Bierut, Grabski and the archbishop. These "presidents" should, as Point Two, invite leaders from the present Polish provisional government in Warsaw, from dissident democratic elements inside Poland, and lastly, from Polish leaders from abroad. This government, interim at best, should pledge itself to "the holding of free elections" as soon as conditions permit. A constituent assembly should write a new Polish constitution under which a permanent government would be elected. Point Four: "When a Polish Government of National

Unity is formed, the three governments will then proceed to accord it recognition as the Provisional Government of Poland."

Molotov became bland. "After recognition of the Government of National Unity," he said, "will the London government disappear?" Churchill stepped into the breach and said recognition would be withdrawn from the London exiles. Stalin asked what would happen to the property and resources of the London group. The question seemed extraneous and caught Roosevelt by surprise. After thought, he guessed it would go to the new government. It was obvious that Roosevelt was at the point of exhaustion. A short recess was called. Two men had disposed of most of Asia in a half hour; it appeared that three men could not resolve the problem of the Polish plains in five windy days.

When the session reconvened, Churchill confounded the meeting by offering his proposals for Poland. It looked as though, with differences of opinion between the United States and United Kingdom, the U.S.S.R. could watch them fight it out and reassemble the pieces to its own liking. The Prime Minister's minutes differed little from Roosevelt's. He saw Molotov, Harriman and Clark Kerr not as mediators but as supervisors. "[They] should talk with these [Polish] leaders and submit their proposals to the consideration of the three governments." At the secret elections "all democratic parties should have the right to participate and run candidates." This was anti-Soviet. The population of Poland, in the main, feared the Russian Bear. In a free and secret election, as every diplomat knew, it would be impossible to elect a Pole who was friendly to Moscow. Ergo, any true secret election would give birth to a government opposed to Russia.

The Russians were not able to discern whether Roosevelt and Churchill had surrendered Poland to the Soviets, and were asking a more democratic government to "save face," or whether they believed what they were saying, which was that they proposed to deprive the Soviet Union of its buffer state.

Molotov said that the mistake in both new proposals was that they ignored the presence, on Polish soil, of the existence of the Warsaw government, formed in Lublin. This group had been formed by Poles who remained in their motherland throughout the war and did not flee to safer shores. What did Roosevelt and Churchill propose to do with the Warsaw government? In the present dilemma, Molotov said, "We wish to achieve a practical result. The only point—and it consists of one point—is to enlarge the Warsaw government." The three of us, he continued, wish to hold free elections. Why not accept a government in existence and broaden its base to accommodate other elements? He was pleased, he said, that the Americans and the British accepted the eastern boundaries. In spite of disagreements on the western edge of Poland, he said he knew that the Polish provisional government would accept no less than territory to the edge of the western Neisse.

The Russian Foreign Minister was also looking for a glib way out. Instead of a presidential council of three, he suggested, why not invite three men from the Warsaw government and two from the President's list to come to Moscow and sit with him and Harriman and Clark Kerr and set up a new body? He was uncertain, he said, about inviting Mikolajczyk. Molotov felt that if he and Harriman and Clark Kerr were able to sit and discuss an enlarged government with five Poles, the decisions could be relayed rapidly to the Big Three. Stettinius scribbled to FDR: "Mr. President: Not to *enlarge* Lublin, but to form a *new* Gov. of some kind."

Churchill launched into one of his colorful speeches. "We have now reached the crucial point of this great conference," he said. "If we separate still recognizing different Polish governments, the world will find *us* wanting." The consequences of a breach between Great Britain and the United States, on one hand, and the Soviet Union on the other, would be historically lamentable. The British, he said, had information that Lublin was not supported by the great mass of Poles who had suffered ravagement as opposing armies fought across her plains. "There will be an outcry in Britain, if our government simply brushed the London Poles aside." The word for it would be "betrayal." The people would say, in any case, that the British government has "given way completely to the Soviet Union on the question of frontiers." If Great Britain accused the government of forsaking Poland, he warned, followed by debates in Parliament, this would risk an overriding danger to Allied unity.

The only path toward abandonment of the London government, he said, would be to make it abundantly clear that both sides had agreed to a fresh start on equal terms. He reached his peroration. Before London could transfer recognition, he admonished, His Majesty's Government would have to be convinced that the new government would be representative of all the Polish people, and it had been created by them at an election based on a secret ballot, universal suffrage and the right of all parties to nominate their candidates for office. When this was achieved, Great Britain would disregard the Polish London government and salute the new one. Mr. Roosevelt gave his concurrence, and said that since the Big Three had agreed on the necessity of free elections, the question was academic: how to govern Poland until the elections were held.

Stalin, deriding Churchill's information about what was going on inside Poland, said that Churchill had complained to him that "he has no information about what is going on in Poland." Stalin would like to assure everyone that the Lublin leaders were very popular with all Poles. They had not fled; they fought on and emerged to the top from the underground resistance. The people's sympathies were with these men, not with those who had left their people to live in luxury in London. The Polish people were, in fact, surprised that the so-called London government had not even participated in the recent liberation of Poland. As he spoke, he too began to reach for the harsh realities of the situation. "Poland," he said, "has been liberated by the Red armies." In the past, Poles hated Russians with good reason. The

Czars had maintained Poland in serfdom, and had absorbed Polish provinces at will. These historical events, Stalin said, reverting to the use of a word he may not have used since his seminary days, "were a sin. We propose to correct these past sins of Russia, to do penance for them." The old resentment against Russia is disappearing, he said, as the Red armies advanced. There was goodwill toward Russia, which freed Poland from the Hitlerite heel.

The Soviet dictator became sarcastic. Churchill, he said, was worried that "we might leave the conference in disagreement." Stalin proposed that, since he and Churchill had different and opposing information about Poland, they talk to Poles from different groups. Why had the United States and the United Kingdom so readily recognized the de Gaulle government? Who elected him? "The three of us deal with de Gaulle. Why could we not deal with an enlarged Polish government?" It would be better and easier to enlarge a government than to try to organize a new one. It would be even better, as far as he was concerned, if free elections could be held at once. Until now, the storms of war had prevented it.

Roosevelt asked how long it would take for free elections to be held. "A month," the Soviet Marshal said quickly. "I am assuming no military reversals." The President's resolve to fight for a free and independent Poland weakened. Once again he proposed that the matter be referred to the foreign ministers "for further study." Speaking of the three foreign ministers, Churchill said, he expected that the world of diplomacy would continue in spite of the ideals of the United Nations, and he proposed that the foreign ministers of the Big Three meet regularly, every three months, the first meeting to be held in London. Eden suggested that it be called the Council of Foreign Ministers. Stalin and Roosevelt concurred. The statesmen were easily diverted from topic to topic.

Stalin, who never indulged a derisive tone when he was being cynical, said he was wondering what was preventing the formation of a unified government in Yugoslavia. This led to a noisy shuffling of papers in three delegations. The Russian was leaning on both elbows. "I would also like to know what is going on in Greece," he said. "I am not criticizing the British. Merely asking for information." Both were questions regarded as sensitive because, in a manner of speaking, both would expose a Poland in reverse. Marshal Tito's Yugoslavian partisans had been coerced into coalescing with the London Yugoslavs-in-exile, headed by King Peter. Tito, an independent Communist who told the world that Yugoslavia could dispense with Russian guidance, surprised Moscow by agreeing to a suggestion of Churchill that he consider a coalition government. The interim government would be headed by Tito as Premier, with Dr. Ivan Subasitch of the London group as Foreign Minister.

Tito would not accept a return of King Peter, but did agree to appoint a regent for the king. This too, to Moscow, was inconsistent socialism. The United States had lost the initiative in Yugoslavia by backing the wrong horse—an enemy of Tito. Churchill was equally inconsistent. He aspired to restore a king in Italy and one in Greece, but he told Peter of Yugoslavia, "The three powers will not lift one finger nor sacrifice one man to put any king back on any throne in Europe." The response to Stalin's questions was subdued. King Peter had agreed to a regency, Churchill said. Dr. Subasitch was either leaving London or had left to form a Yugoslavian government. There were, he admitted, two slight amendments to the original agreement between Subasitch and Tito which Eden would explain to Molotov. On the other hand, Churchill said, if Marshal Stalin said two words to Tito, it would have settled the problem.

Stalin shook his head negatively. Tito was a proud man, the head of a popular government, a man who would resent advice. Churchill felt that the great Marshal could risk the displeasure of Tito. Stalin said he would not be afraid to counsel Tito.

The Russians urged the Prime Minister to move on

to Greece. There was little to tell, he said. He was hopeful for peace. He did not think that a government of all
the Greek parties could be established because they
hated each other. The Greeks, Stalin observed, were
not accustomed to discussion in modern times; they
preferred to cut each other's throats. In a sense, the conversational ploy was Poland with Britain as the defendant. Mr. Churchill said he sent five British trade union
leaders to Athens to help the Greeks organize themselves
industrially, and "they had a difficult time." He felt very
much obliged to the Soviet Marshal for "not taking too
great an interest in Greek affairs." The remark induced
no laughter. Stalin said he had no intention of criticizing
British action in Greece, no matter what happened, and
he had no intention of interfering.

Roosevelt adjourned the session. As he departed,
nodding and smiling, his face was gray and almost hollow.
He was wheeled back to his room. Dr. Bruenn and Commander Fox were waiting. To some, they looked like
a trainer and a second waiting for a fighter to return
to his dressing room after a bad mauling. Admiral Leahy,
in full uniform, accompanied Roosevelt to the door.
He was always a dignified old salt, a patriot to his toes.
"Mr. President," he said, "this compromise formula
on Poland is so elastic that the Russians can stretch
it all the way from Yalta to Washington without even
technically breaking it." The Boss shook his head in
sorrow. "I know, Bill," he said. "I know. But it's the
best I can do for Poland at this time." It was the best
and the worst. Time would not improve the American
betrayal.

No one—including the Russians—was willing to place
the truth on the table. Russia, with its vast sweeping
armies, held the fate of Europe in its hairy hands. No
one could take from Russia what it did not want to
relinquish. The Red armies could race for Berlin and
engulf as much of Germany as military logistics would
permit—and stand fast *alone* on that line. It no longer
needed partners in Europe. Churchill's fear that the
Red tide could reach as far west as Hamburg, Magdeburg,

Leipzig, Munich and most of Austria was not an unfounded terror. It was an assessment. There were many
who would not forgive Roosevelt for "selling" parts of
China to Stalin, but the President knew that when the
Russian armies turned eastward, they could literally walk
through Manchuria, taking whatever they wanted in territory and loot. The President thought he had done his best
to hold Russian demands down to the return of territory
taken by Japan, the use of the Chinese railway to Dairen and Port Arthur and a lease on the ports. He told
confidants that he had "held Stalin to his minimums."

The President was accustomed to seeing Commander
Fox in the bedroom after the plenary sessions. He was
surprised to find Bruenn waiting. Both men continued
to play their long-term game. Roosevelt asked no questions; Dr. Bruenn did his work. The young Commander
found FDR "obviously fatigued." Color was "poor,
gray." Lungs were clear and the heart sounds were "of
good quality—regular in rhythm and 84 to the minute."
There was something new, *pulsus alternans*—a pulse
which skipped beats. No matter what the technical terms,
it was a syndrome of senility—a gallant old man trying
to cope gaspingly with forces beyond his strength. Admiral McIntire, who often stopped by in the evening
to speak to the President about the day's work, was
not present. Dr. Bruenn told the President that he was
working too hard and was obviously tired. He told him
that he must have more hours of rest. He would have to
stop all morning conferences: "please do not see anyone
before noon." Roosevelt would also have to get rest
in bed of one hour before each plenary session. The
Boss agreed to the restricted routine without argument.

At 9:00 P.M. Marshal Stalin was host at a dinner
for President Roosevelt and Prime Minister Churchill.
The cordiality of the atmosphere at Koreiz Villa may
be gauged by a disagreement: James Beary of the United
States Secret Service said that there were thirty-eight
toasts; Chip Bohlen said there were forty-five; Cadogan
said fifty; the Russians abstained from guessing. It was

the biggest, loudest, most extravagant dinner of the Yalta Conference. Stettinius wrote himself a note: "20 courses, 45 toasts; it lasted until 1:00 A.M."

The party which left Livadia in the chill of the night included the President, Anna, Stettinius, Leahy, Jimmy Byrnes, Ed Flynn, Averell Harriman, Kathleen Harriman and Chip Bohlen. There were some angry faces behind windows at Livadia after 9:00 P.M. The invitation list did not include Admiral King, General Marshall, General Kuter, Pa Watson, Admiral McIntire, Admiral Brown, Matthews and Hiss. It did include Harry Hopkins. Churchill brought with him Anthony Eden, Field Marshal Sir Alan Brooke, Chief Air Marshal Sir Charles Portal, Admiral of the Fleet Sir Andrew Cunningham, Sir Alexander Cadogan, Field Marshal Alexander, Sir Archibald Clark Kerr, General Sir Hastings Ismay and Churchill's daughter, Mrs. Sarah Oliver.

The host included the regulars on his team of negotiators: Molotov, Vyshinsky, Admiral Kuznetsov, General Antonov, Air Marshal Khudyakov, Gromyko, Gusev, Maisky, Pavlov and one extra—the chief of the Soviet secret police, Comrade Beria. When Mr. Roosevelt saw the array of drinks and the joyful attitude of Stalin and his entourage, he cupped his hand beside his mouth and shouted down the table to Anna, "Put it in the potted palm, Sis." No one was in a mood for discarding the first round of drinks. If there was anything which detracted from the hilarity of the evening, it was an assortment of insects which crouched under the table, and walked up the shoes of the diners to bite their ankles. There was considerable swatting while drinking. Chip Bohlen and Major Birse of the British contingent tried to make meager notes as the dinner progressed, but the shouted words slammed into walls of other shouts.

The Prime Minister delivered the first toast in the stilted, halting way the Big Three had learned to use to accommodate the interpreters. "It is no exaggeration or compliment of a florid kind," he said, standing and pouting his pink lips, staring owlishly over his half-spectacles, "when I say that we regard Marshal Stalin's life as most precious to the hopes and hearts of all of us. There have been statesmen [cries of Hear! Hear!] and most of them threw away the fruits of victory in the troubles which followed their wars. I earnestly hope that the Marshal may be spared to the people of the Soviet Union and to help us all move forward to a less unhappy time than that through which we have recently come. I walk through this world with greater courage and hope when I find myself in a relation of friendship and intimacy with this great man, whose fame has gone out not only over all Russia, but the world."

Someone shouted "Drink it down!" Everyone except Roosevelt stood and drank. The President had had his two cocktails at Livadia, and he knew that this would be a formidable night. So he sipped each toast, rendered some himself, and often refilled his small glass with water. Stalin stood, and someone rapped a glass with a piece of cutlery. "I propose a toast," he said in a growling, almost chuckling manner, "for the leader of the British Empire, the most courageous of all prime ministers in the world, embodying political experience with military leadership, who, when all Europe was ready to fall flat before Hitler, said that Britain would stand and fight alone against Germany, even without any allies. Even if the existing and possible allies deserted her, he said, she would continue to fight. To the health of the man who is born once in a hundred years and who bravely held up the banner of Great Britain. I have said what I feel, what I have at heart, and of what I am conscious."

As that drink disappeared, moon-faced Molotov, more ebullient than usual, popped like a jack-in-the-box and shouted: "I propose a toast for the three representatives of the Army, Air Force and Navy of the country which went to war before we did. . . . I wish them success so that the victorious armies of the Allies may enter Berlin and hoist their banner over that city!" He was barely back in his seat when Stalin got up, walked around the table and clinked glasses with President Roosevelt: "I toast the health of the President of the United States!

In Great Britain and the Soviet Union, Prime Minister Churchill and I had simple decisions. We fought for our very existence against Hitlerite Germany. But there is one man whose country had not been seriously threatened with invasion, but who has a broader concept of national interest and has been the chief forger of the instruments which have led to the mobilization of the world against Hitler."

The big table, heavy with steaming food, became an assortment of jolly men who took turns jumping to their feet to propose new toasts to new victories and peace. The Russian waiters hovered close, pouring vodka and whiskey as fast as the small cut-glass goblets emptied. FDR held his glass aloft, and those who vied for the next toast sat and waited. He said he would like to characterize this dinner as that of a family; great changes had come to the world; great changes were to come. There were still vast areas in the world where people had little opportunity and little hope—"our objectives here are to give every man, woman and child on earth the possibility of security and well-being!" The table resounded with shouts as the men drank it down, some trotting around the table to touch glasses with the President. Miss Harriman arose, and the strong men waited respectfully. She said that, speaking for the three ladies present, she would propose a toast to all those Russians who "have worked so hard for our comfort, and having seen the destruction wrought by the Germans, we realize what our hosts have accomplished." Gallantly, Stalin, Molotov and Vyshinsky stood and hurried to Miss Harriman to clink glasses. Jimmy Byrnes said, "I toast the common man. We toast our leaders and this is well, but we should never forget the common man who lives on this earth."

Churchill raised his glass to the Soviet armies: "The men who have broken the back of the German war machine!" Some were eating; some were not. Many were talking; the sound was incoherent gabbling. Small conversations began. Stalin told Churchill how the war with Finland started—a misunderstanding over proper boundaries and opposing guards firing at each other. Molotov, inexhaustible, devised separate toasts for each diner. Some began to sit through the toasts. A few, who drank each toast to the full, began to doze. Stalin, standing stockily in his baggy uniform and khaki tunic, was teetering a little when he stood, grinning, and said: "I talk too much—like an old man. But I want to drink to our alliance. In our alliance the Allies should not deceive each other. Perhaps this is naive? Experienced diplomatists may say: 'Why should I not deceive my ally?' But I, as a naive man, think it best not to deceive my ally even if he is a fool. Possibly our alliance is so firm because it is not so easy to deceive each other? I drink to this!"

Before midnight the gentlemen made a contest of gallantry. The toasts became more outrageously flattering. The Prime Minister, who was never a man to surrender the field of articulate expression to anyone, pushed his chair back, raised his glass, and said: "My hope is in the illustrious President of the United States and in Marshal Stalin, in whom we shall find the champions of peace, who, after smiting the foe, will lead us to carry on the task against poverty, confusion, chaos and oppression. I propose a toast to the broad sunlight of victorious peace!" The diners broke into applause. Stalin ridiculed Gusev, who drank mechanically and never smiled. He mimicked the diplomat, but there was no response. The President glanced at his watch. The time was 12:30 A.M. He had had a long day. Winston Churchill must have seen the slight gesture, because he became erect and proposed a last toast. Like an overdone soufflé, the mood fell from gaiety to somber resolution as he slowly intoned:

I must say that never in this war have I felt the responsibility weigh so heavily on me, even in the darkest hours, as now during this conference. But now, for reasons which the Marshal has given, we see that we are on the crest of the hill and there is before us the prospect of open country. Do not let us underestimate the difficulties. Na-

*tions, comrades in arms, have in the past drifted apart
within five or ten years of war. Thus, toiling millions have
followed a vicious circle, falling into the pit, and then by
their sacrifice raising themselves up again. We now have a
chance of avoiding the errors of previous generations and
of making a sure peace. People cry out for peace and joy.
Will the families be reunited? Will the shattered dwellings
be rebuilt? Will the toiler see his home? To defend one's
country is glorious, but there are greater conquests before
us. Before us lies the realization of the dream of the poor—
that they shall live in peace, protected by our invincible
power from aggression and evil. . . . The Marshal spoke
of the future. This is the most important of all. Otherwise,
the oceans of blood shed will have been useless and outrageous.*

At 1:00 A.M. the President's car was heard crunching
the gravel at Livadia. The automobiles returned one
by one. There was the sound of doors slamming and
hurried goodnights. Lights were flicking out in corridors
and on in bedrooms. Stettinius retired with his mind
racing. For months the State Department had been trying
to think of a host city for the first meeting of the United
Nations. The President had discarded all suggestions
out of hand: Atlantic City, New York, Philadelphia,
Chicago, Cincinnati, Miami, French Lick, Hot Springs,
Pinehurst. Now, seeking repose, the Secretary of
State could not free his mind of the municipal shackles.
The requirement was that the city be able to accommodate
4,000 to 5,000 delegates, advisers, secretariat and newspaper correspondents. It must have ample auditoriums,
conference rooms, radio, cable and mail communications centers and a first-class airport.

Ed had a short conversation with the Boss that day
about a city. "Go back to work, Ed," the President
said. "We haven't hit it yet." Now, in bed, Stettinius
was lulled into a state approaching sleep without quite
achieving it. He could not understand why he was not
thinking about the Russian dinner. Instead, he saw a
vague map of the United States. At 3:00 A.M. he sat

up in bed and consulted the small clock on his night table. He had it. Why hadn't he thought of it before? San Francisco! In his mind, he said later, he could see Nob Hill, the Opera House, the Veterans Building, the Pacific Union Club, the Mark Hopkins, the Fairmont, the St. Francis Hotel, the golden sunshine and the fresh breezes from the Pacific Ocean cupping the round hills.

San Francisco. He had it.

The President had been told to be in bed early, sleep late, see no one until noon and take a one-hour nap in the morning. On February 9 he was up and bathed at 9:00 A.M. It was not that he spurned the counsel of Dr. Bruenn. To the contrary, he had great faith in his young physician. It was that there were so many things which had to be done and only so many hours in which to do them. As the Yalta Conference approached a crest of productivity, he felt more and more impelled to ride that wave until it crashed on the sand in peace. He emerged from the bedroom and asked Rigdon for the daily calendar. It didn't look formidable:

Friday Feb. 9th:

1230: The President will attend a plenary meeting of the Combined Chiefs of Staff at Livadia. Present:

For the U.S.:	For Great Britain:
The President	The Prime Minister
Admiral Leahy	Field Marshal Brooke
General Marshall	Air Marshal Portal
Admiral King	General Ismay
General Kuter	Admiral Cunningham
General McFarland	Brigadier Cornwall-Jones

1330: Lunch at Livadia: The President, the Prime Minister, Mrs. Boettiger, Mrs. Oliver, Mr. Harriman, Miss Harriman, Admiral Leahy and Justice Byrnes.

1600: The President, the Prime Minister and Marshal Stalin and members of the American, British and Soviet Delegations will meet in the courtyard of Livadia where they will sit for still and motion pictures.

1615: The Sixth Formal Meeting of the Crimea Conference will convene in the grand ballroom of Livadia. Present:

For the U.S.:	For Great Britain:	For the U.S.S.R.:
The President	The Prime Minister	Marshal Stalin
Mr. Stettinius	Mr. Eden	Mr. Molotov
Admiral Leahy	Mr. Cadogan	Mr. Vyshinsky
Mr. Hopkins	Mr. Clark Kerr	Mr. Maisky
Justice Byrnes	Mr. Jebb	Mr. Gusev
Mr. Harriman	Mr. Bridges	Mr. Gromyko
Mr. Matthews	Mr. Wilson	Mr. Pavlov
Mr. Hiss	Mr. Dixon	
Mr. Bohlen	Major Birse	

2030: Dinner at Livadia: The President, Mrs. Boettiger, Major General John E. Hull, Major General Kuter, Fleet Admiral Leahy, Vice Admiral C. M. Cooke.

An average day. Or so it seemed. The President and the day were optimistic. Slowly, inexorably, the sunshine and warmth were coming. There was action all over Livadia that morning. Generals and admirals, with towels limp on their arms, stood outside the few bathrooms. Admiral Ernest King was joshed again about sleeping in the Czarina's boudoir. His face remained as expressionless as his bald head. Harry Hopkins and Pa Watson remained in bed, both too ill to dress. The Secretary of State was hurrying up and down the staircase saying that San Francisco would be the ideal city for the first U.N. meeting. General Marshall dwelled on it. He said he was thinking of all the Army and Navy operations around San Francisco Bay, but the congestion there was similar to all other port cities. Ed hurried to Admiral King, who gave it thought and said it was a good choice. He would like to see more people thinking about the war in the Pacific. In an earlier, private conversation, Anthony Eden had said he had never seen the Pacific coast of the United States.

The Secretary of State asked to see the President. He was back in his bedroom, looking in his luggage for something. Ed told him about San Francisco and all the consideration which went into it. "It sounds most interesting, Ed," he said, "but we have called off all unnecessary movements of people, conventions and so forth. What about transporting these people two or three thousand miles unnecessarily? Ask Jimmy Byrnes about it." The problem of transportation was within the purview of the director of the Office of War Mobilization. Byrnes listened. He thought San Francisco a good choice. The charter meeting would be of historic importance no matter where it was held, and, no matter where it was held, it would involve the transportation of thousands of people coming in from the west and the east. "I can tell you, Ed," he said, "if it is held in San Francisco it isn't going to cause criticism." Back to FDR. He heard the Byrnes opinion and said: "Well, that's encouraging. I'm beginning to see your picture clearly." It wasn't official yet, but San Francisco was the choice.

The noon meeting of the Combined Chiefs of Staff was sufficiently important to bring Roosevelt and Churchill. Each agreed, however, that no votes would be taken. No one, except those present, would be permitted to discuss the decisions made. The best thinking of the military was that Germany would surrender on or about July 1, 1945. Japan would surrender eighteen months later—about January 1, 1947. The Prime Minister made a strong speech asking that, after the demise of Germany, England be permitted to send land forces and its fleet to the Far East to collaborate in the final effort against Japan. The Japanese war had become an American preserve. Admirals Leahy and King were opposed to having the British Fleet act in concert with the U.S. Navy. General Marshall thought the offer involved too little too late. Roosevelt wavered. He said the United States would need all the help it could get. On the other hand, he saw the British offer as an attempt to regain some of her old colonial treasures: Burma, Hong Kong, Singapore, and possibly to help France regain control of Indochina. The other question, the one which troubled General Bedell Smith—subordination of British Field Marshal Bernard Law Montgomery's northern forces to Eisenhower's overall strategy—was resolved in favor of the Americans. Nor would General Alexander be placed in charge of Allied ground forces.

At the meeting of the foreign ministers Stettinius was the gracious host. They used the huge round table in the grand ballroom for their conversation and lunch. Ed opened it with an unusual, and mystifying, wedge. He had spoken to the President in the morning, he said, and Roosevelt asked him to state that, unless the Polish question was settled amicably, American public opinion was so strong on Poland that it might "jeopardize America's participation in a world organization." Molotov and Eden appeared to be puzzled. The United Nations was a purely American invention; the United States was threatening to withdraw from something it had dragooned the other two partners into joining. Having said it, Stettinius did not wait for a response; he said the United States agreed with Molotov that a Polish presidential committee of three men was unnecessary. America would withdraw that. From mystification, the Soviet Foreign Minister's expression expanded into a smile.

"I believe that, with this change," said Stettinius, "our three positions are not far apart. . . . Mr. Molotov spoke of the reorganization of the Polish Government. The British formula suggests the establishment of a fully representative Provisional Polish Government. We speak of a Government of National Unity. All of us agree that only the Poles can definitely decide this. . . ." The United States, threatening to secede from the unborn United Nations, emphasized that all three governments were close to agreement on Poland. Stettinius then offered a "new formula." It was the same old device of enlarging the Lublin government to accommodate distinguished expatriates and hold free elections soon. If there was dynamite in it, the explosion was imminent in the final sentence: "The ambassadors of the three powers in Warsaw, following such recognition, will be charged with the responsibility of observing and reporting to their respective governments on the carrying out of the pledge in regard to free and unfettered elections."

Molotov was abrupt. He could not respond, he said, until he read the formula in Russian. Eden said that the Churchill government was in trouble "at home" on the Polish question. Members of the War Cabinet had already disassociated themselves from any agreement to a frontier on the Curzon Line. Eden said he feared Poland would become "a source of difficulty between the Soviets and the British." Addressing Molotov with some passion, the British Foreign Secretary admitted he might be wrong, but hardly anyone in Britain believed that the Lublin government represented a free choice of the people. That's why he had asked, yesterday, for a *new* government, a fresh start, rather than adding men to the Lublin group.

The Soviet Foreign Secretary said he agreed that the holding of elections by the people of Poland was the prime requisite. In this he was taking advantage of the implication in the new American formula that the interim government would function briefly, for perhaps a month, and its composition was unimportant. He played off Stettinius against Eden. The Russophile composition of the temporary government was important only to the Russian Army, he said. Stalin had repeated, several times, that the Soviet armies had to be certain that there would be no problems along their lines of communications and supply. If the Big Three did not take that into consideration, Molotov said, "an impossible situation will arise." Anthony Eden, in the manner of a man pleading for a point already lost, said he hoped that his confreres understood that it would be much easier for the people of the United Kingdom to understand dropping recognition of an old government for a new one, but difficult for them to sympathize with abandonment of a pro-Allied one for a pro-Soviet one.

Molotov worked craftily to drive the wedge between the British and Americans a little deeper. He recalled, he said, that President Roosevelt called the Polish government situation "temporary." Russia believed that free elections were the important matter, the current composition of the Polish government minor. Marshal Stalin said elections could be held in a month. The Prime Minister said two. Either way, Russia's main concern was to prevent the election of a purely anti-Soviet government standing in power to the rear of the Russian armies. Eden, said Molotov, wanted Mikolajczyk in the government. The Soviet Union did not regard him as a friend, but if the Poles wanted him in the new government, there would be no objection. Having said it, the Soviet Foreign Minister retreated. The composition of the government, after all, was a matter for Poles. Eden interposed to say that if the elections were controlled by the Lublin government, Great Britain, for one, would not regard them as "free and unfettered elections." Stettinius said the United States would side with Britain. Molotov said that the final sentence of the Stettinius formula would surely offend all Poles. They would resent the presence of three foreign ambassadors to oversee and report on sovereign Polish elections.

As host, it would be the duty of Stettinius to report to the plenary session. The three men were splitting two votes to one on different issues, and nothing had been settled. Poland was becoming an exhausting chore, a *Mitteleuropäisch* conundrum. The Secretary of State said that, instead of tossing it back up to the Big Three once more, he would rather say "we have not yet reached an agreement and we have decided to continue discussions at a later date." Stettinius said that the lunch was running late and he would like to discuss a paper on German reparations.

The paper, which had been suggested by Roosevelt, was close to the Russian proposal, but more specific.
1. Reparations are to be given first to nations which

have borne the main burden of the war. 2. The use of German labor is to be set aside "for the moment"; there would be two types of payment: (a) removal in a single payment from Germany of equipment, rolling stock, machine tools, ships, German investments abroad, shares of industrial transport—"these removals to be carried out chiefly for the purpose of military and economic disarmament of Germany"; (b) annual deliveries of commodities for ten years after the war. The total reparations should be the subject of study by the Moscow Commission, appointed to oversee reparations. The commission should consider the Soviet government's suggested total of $20 billion.

Maisky had been listening. Now he entered the conversation. He could see no objection to the American proposal except the matter of $20 billion. After study in Moscow, "it might be a little more, or a little less." It appeared to Stettinius and Eden that the Soviets had been surprised at quick Allied acceptance of $20 billion and, on second thought, would try to raise the amount. Stettinius said that the figure was arbitrary; the President said that no one knew how much wealth was left in Germany. It might be far less than $20 billion. Molotov asked if it would be better only to mention the Soviet share—say $10 billion, the remainder to go to other nations. Stettinius explained that it would be better to say that 50 percent of whatever the Germans could pay should go to Russia. The Soviet Foreign Minister had no objection, although he would have preferred a specific sum.

The American Secretary of State posed a proper question. What price index would Russia use to measure the worth of merchandise? Molotov said 1938, prices of the year before the war started. Stettinius pressed. Was he sure? Molotov floundered like a man who had dug his own pit. His government, he said, would probably have to add 15 to 20 percent to cover present-day values of reconstruction. Ed asked if Molotov had thought of the dismemberment of Germany; how much of Germany would be left to pay reparations? Maisky said he had thought of that. The partitioning of Germany would not affect the reparations because the Soviet Union expected to collect from "inside Germany and outside Germany." The United States and the Russians agreed. Eden said he could not; he would have to consult with Churchill.

The foreign secretaries moved on, in the remaining minutes, to a discussion of invitations to nations for the first meeting of the United Nations. Stettinius said, "It is my understanding that the United States, consulting with its allies, the Soviet Union and the United Kingdom, would also consult with China and France as the fourth and fifth sponsoring powers." If Ed had expected an explosion, it didn't come. Eden said that Great Britain still looked upon China as a sleeping giant; it was now a first-class power and a permanent member of the Security Council. Russia scorned the lack of valor in the French, but permitted Britain to raise her friend to the status of China and other first-class powers.

Eden looked at his watch and reminded everyone of the picture-taking ceremony. Molotov said he wanted a brief discussion of Yugoslavia. The country was unstable, unsettled politically, he said. The Russians and the British had agreed on an interim government there with the Communist Tito as its head, and Dr. Subasitch of the liberal group as Foreign Minister. Both sides were working to keep King Peter out of the country. Now, Molotov complained, the British, instead of sending Subasitch to Yugoslavia to implement the agreement, proposed to form an interim Assembly of National Liberation. The British desired to invite all prominent Yugoslavs who had not collaborated with the enemy—to wit, friends of Great Britain. Eden said this was not so, that the Prime Minister had asked for a broad representative assembly to enable Tito and Subasitch to function at the head of a government. Stettinius had little interest in Yugoslavia. When Eden and Molotov could not agree, he suggested that both men appoint representatives to "draft a statement." This was passing the problem downstairs. This "passing" of problems up to the plenary sessions and down to subcommittees embodied the character of the whole Yalta Conference—most especially Poland. There, the Russians insisted on a subservient satellite; the British begged for the inclusion of London Poles; FDR pleaded forlornly for "free elections" because he knew that Russian armies had invested Poland, and no combination of powers was strong enough to drive them back. Hitler's attack on Poland had precipitated World War II; Roosevelt and Churchill dreaded to go home to admit that they had taken the nation from Germany and given it to Russia. The problem would not be resolved, even though it was discussed exhaustively every day.

Stettinius wanted to discuss international trusteeship of weak nations. Eden became angry. He and Churchill were convinced that Roosevelt's idealism of multinational supervision was a subtle design to rob the United Kingdom of its colonies and dominions. He would not discuss the subject. Ed said that the President would bring it up at the plenary session. The President, of course, was not aware that Churchill and Stalin had already carved "spheres of influence" at their autumn meeting in Moscow.

Although the calendar did not mention a 3:30 P.M. meeting between Stalin and Roosevelt, one occurred in the President's study. The picture-taking was scheduled for 4:00 and the Russian Marshal arrived early. It had become the custom of the two men to discuss Far Eastern matters without consulting Churchill. He was made aware of all discussions, but was not present at any of them. Further, he concurred with unusual placidity to anything the other two agreed upon. Harry Hopkins dressed for this private meeting. Stalin brought Vyshinsky and Antonov. The Russian chief said that their two military staffs had had productive talks about the Far East, and he would like to review a few points. Antonov said that the Americans had asked if the Soviets wanted an American supply line for Lend-Lease across the Pacific. The answer was yes. The Russians, he said, were aware that the Japanese could disrupt the Trans-Siberian Railway with air attacks. Sea and air routes across the Pacific would have to be established.

FDR was agreeable. Antonov said that Stalin had approved U.S. bases at Komsomolsk and Nikolaevsk or "any area which would not hamper Russian military operations." The U.S. Chiefs of Staff requested weather information for these areas. Antonov passed a paper to the President. "This will tell you," he said, "the most favorable times of the year for sea as well as air." General Marshall asked if the Russians required help in defending the huge Kamchatka Peninsula, and Stalin said the answer was yes. It was impossible, he continued, to state how much help, or what kind, at the moment. It would require study. Also there was a question of when, precisely, the Americans could move in and start building bases without prematurely alarming the Japanese. Stalin indicated that if Japan knew Soviet intentions, the Imperial government would order a preemptive attack now, when the Soviet Union was weak on the Manchurian border.

Roosevelt was doing considerable listening. Hopkins sat with his head near his knees. Stalin said he would approve an American "survey party" to go to Siberia secretly and agree on locations for U.S. bases. The big island of Sakhalin abuts the northern Japanese island of Hokkaido. Antonov said that General Marshall and Admiral King wanted to know if the Russians could capture this island when they entered the war. The answer was yes. They would do this without American assistance. Stalin seemed calm and pleased with the reaction of Roosevelt, who nodded agreeably. Antonov, however, showed anger when he repeated a question of General Marshall: "Are we assured that *combined* planning in Moscow will be vigorously pursued?" The Russian General said that this implied that the Soviet General Staff had no real interest in coordinating blows against the Japanese Empire. Antonov told Marshall that there could be no combined planning until the Russians got to the Far East. To the contrary, said Marshall, the planning could begin at once. Marshall, the Russian

General said, wanted specific data on Russian Army strength, tactical plans and air action. Antonov said he personally felt insulted at the questions. However, Marshal Stalin had empowered him to reply that "we promise to do our best to improve combined planning in Moscow."

The unpleasantness melted when Stalin said he had agreed to American air bases in the Budapest area for bombing missions out of Italy. He also approved Roosevelt's request to permit an American Air Force team access to survey parts of southern Europe which the United States had bombed. The only condition, Stalin said, was that Soviet Air Marshal Sergei Khudyakov insisted that Soviet bomb survey experts accompany the Americans. The President had no objection. Hopkins, listening, got the impression that Roosevelt's man-to-man diplomacy worked. Stalin and Roosevelt were able to reach agreements within minutes when they were alone. In the big ballroom, surrounded by experts, they questioned phrases and facets of propositions, and were prone to lapse into argument, ending by referring the questions down to the foreign ministers, who met and admitted to each other they were powerless to make decisions.

The Soviet Union, which seemed to equate suspicion with intelligence, was worried about China. Stalin stated candidly that he could not visualize China as a first-class power. But he was willing to cooperate with Roosevelt, who saw this vast divided land as a giant keeper-of-the-peace in the Orient. The Marshal had no guarantee that Chiang Kai-shek would agree to Russia's postwar demands on Manchuria—use of the Chinese Eastern Railroad and the South Manchurian Railroad, the internationalization of the port of Dairen, and a Russian naval base at Port Arthur. The Soviet Union did not want to go to war with Japan and learn later that her "just demands" would not be met. Chiang had not been told what he was giving up, nor would he, until much later. Therefore, the Soviet Marshal asked that a secret protocol be added to the statement of the

Crimea Conference, reading: "The Heads of the Three Great Powers have agreed that these claims of the Soviet Union shall be unquestionably fulfilled after Japan has been defeated." The President meditated. It amounted to twenty-five words. He found it reasonable for the United States and Britain to concede extraterritorial rights in China. He said he would sign, and he felt that Churchill would, too.

Three chairs and a loose assortment of rugs had been arranged in the courtyard for the photographers. The Prime Minister, in a khaki overcoat and a Russian caracul hat on his lap, sat beaming for the lenses in the left-hand chair. In the middle was Roosevelt in a loosely knotted Navy cape. The eyes were deep set, the face gaunt. Stalin sat on the right side, in an Army overcoat and cap, the sleeves inching down over his hands. Eden, Stettinius and Molotov stood behind the three chairs. Behind them, in disarray, groups of Russians, Americans and British stood in attitudes of conversation. Still and motion pictures were made, and the Big Three moved indoors for the sixth plenary session.

It was a dark, chill day and the crackling birch in the fireplace lent an aura of warmth to the big room. Roosevelt called on Ed to deliver the foreign ministers' report. The face of Stettinius lit up as he read, starting with Poland. He made the conclusions sound not as bitter disagreements but as cordial lack of agreements. Stalin said the Americans and the British had never suffered an invasion by the Germans. "It is not like warfare," he said. "When they come across Poland toward us, it is like an incursion of Huns." No matter the agreements or disagreements at Yalta; the Soviet Union demanded nothing less than "a strong and friendly Poland" on her borders. Stalin insisted that the Soviet Union had no intention of interfering in Poland's internal affairs; "it will live under a parliamentary system like Belgium and Holland; any talk of trying to Sovietize Poland is stupid." Even the Communists in the Polish government were opposed to Soviet influence in internal affairs because there were aspects of Russian government with which the Poles were out of sympathy—collective farms, for example.

Stalin felt unspoken criticism of Soviet action in setting up an interim government, but, he said, he would like to point out that the Lublin government restored order, whereas the British government in Greece did not. At this time, without emphasizing the point, he laid down Soviet conditions for agreement. The Warsaw government had eighteen Cabinet departments. There would be room for four or five "outside" Poles. Molotov whispered to Stalin, and the Marshal said he meant "four." The Warsaw Poles, he said almost apologetically, "will not accept more than four." Winston Churchill, slouching, listening and doodling, looked up to say that before Stettinius proceeded, he thought that a full discussion of Poland should take place. The subject was a suppurating sore.

Molotov said that the Russians and Americans were in accord on Poland. Except for a few alterations of phrases and intent, he said, the two nations were as one. The inference was that Churchill was standing alone. Before the British Prime Minister could state his case, Molotov moved to the attack. He switched from Poland to Yugoslavia and accused the British of delaying a settlement with Tito. "The carrying out of the Yugoslav settlement has been delayed," he said. "Since Mr. Churchill agreed on this settlement we feel that it should be carried out immediately." FDR could have ruled Molotov out of order, but he said nothing. Churchill became caustic. The conference, he said, would discuss one problem at a time. He became so emotional that he began to mix his metaphors; he didn't think that, just because the conference had one foot in the stirrup, it should gallop off wildly because such an agreement might prevent the ship from being brought safely into port.

Molotov, chastened, returned to Poland. What he wanted to tell the conference, he said, was that he had conferred with his governement on the American proposals and, as everyone had a copy, he suggested they follow the changes the Soviets had in mind: instead of a "fully representative government based on all democratic forces in Poland . . . and abroad," it should read, 'the present provisional government of Poland should be reorganized on a wider democratic basis with the inclusion of democratic leaders from Poland itself and from those living abroad." Also, instead of calling it the "Provisional Government of National Unity," the Soviet preferred the "National Provisional Government of Poland." He would like the words "non-Fascist" and "anti-Fascist" including among those permitted to nominate candidates. Russia accepted the right of Harriman, Clark Kerr and Molotov to *consult in Moscow* about the Polish government and Polish elections, but would delete Roosevelt's last sentence, asking them to "observe and report." This, said Molotov, would offend the Poles; besides, it is the duty of ambassadors to observe, not to dictate.

The subject of Poland had become enervating. Everyone was weary of wrangling. The President suggested that Stettinius be permitted to finish reading his report, at which time he would call a half-hour recess so that "all may study the Soviet proposals." Stettinius consulted his paper, and said that the foreign ministers, in the matter of German reparations, were in agreement on two points—which countries should receive payment, and the form it should take. They were in disagreement on Point Three—that $20 billion should be the basis for discussion, and that 50 percent of this should go to the Soviet Union. Well, not quite in disagreement. Mr. Eden had reserved his position on the third point. There was no comment from the British. Somewhat uneasily, the Secretary of State continued. He said that there had been agreement that the five governments on the Security Council of the United Nations should consult with each other about trusteeships and dependent areas before the first meeting at San Francisco.

Winston Churchill exploded. There is no modifying word for it. He came up off his chair in fury. Sir Alexander Cadogan had complained that the Foreign Office could not persuade him to read papers prepared on British political positions, and, even after agreements had been made, the Prime Minister swore that he knew nothing of them and that no one had told him about them. Churchill bore out his Under Secretary's lament. "I absolutely disagree!" he shouted. Roosevelt said, "Winston, you have not allowed Ed to finish the sentence." Stalin smiled and studied his hands interlocked on the table. "I will not have one scrap of British territory flung into that area," the Prime Minister said. Anthony Eden tried to explain. Churchill pushed him away. "After we have done our best to fight in this war and have done no crime to anyone!" Churchill roared. He spread his hands on the table and sat. "I will have no suggestion that the British Empire is to be put into the dock and examined by the grubby hands of forty or fifty nations to see if it is up to their standard." Roosevelt was trying to say something, but the rage was towering. "No one will induce me, as long as I am Prime Minister, to let any representative of Great Britain go to a conference where we will be placed in the dock and asked to justify our right to live in a world we tried to save."

Stalin surprised the whole table by rising, walking up and down and applauding. No one understood why he did it, least of all Roosevelt, who seemed mortally embarrassed by the rude display of temper. The President turned several times to Churchill, but his words could not be heard. "The trusteeship report does not cover the British Empire," he said at one point. Churchill shook his head violently from side to side. "Never. Never. Never," he kept saying. He turned to Roosevelt, his tormentor. "If we are out," he said, "I have nothing to say. As long as every bit of land over which the British flag flies is to be brought into the dock, I shall object as long as I live."

Stettinius waited for a moment of silence. When he had it, he said, "We have had nothing in mind with reference to the British Empire." The Prime Minister kept murmuring, "Never. Never." The Secretary of State got a nod from Roosevelt and continued to read. Stalin sat, still smiling. Stettinius stated that trusteeships would apply only to territory formerly held by the common enemy and such islands and places as had been mandated to it. The Prime Minister listened. "I have no objection to enemy territory coming under trusteeship," he said, "but I think it would be wise to state once and for all that these trusteeships have nothing to do with the British Empire." He did not apologize. Stalin's cynical smile caught his eye. "How would you feel," he asked, "if the international organization decided to turn the Crimea into a holiday resort?" The Marshal shrugged. "We would be delighted," he said, "to have the Crimea available for three-power conferences."

Before Roosevelt called a half-hour recess, Churchill obtained an agreement that the word "trusteeships" should apply only to formerly enemy-held territory, territory held under former League of Nations mandate and territories which asked for a trusteeship. As the groups left the ballroom, Stettinius grabbed Hiss and said, "Write out a quick memorandum on the trusteeship issue." The sheet was typed so quickly and so concisely that, while the session was still in recess, Jimmy Byrnes was able to give it to Churchill and sit with him and go over it point by point. Stettinius and Hiss sat, ready to placate the Prime Minister if another eruption impended. He was mollified. When the conference reconvened, the P.M. was his cherubic self again; it was FDR who appeared aged and worn.

Having said he had misunderstood, Churchill listened to Stettinius hurry on to a discussion of Yugoslavia. This time the Russians interrupted. They complained to Roosevelt that the Tito-Subasitch agreement had been in effect, but not implemented by Great Britain. Churchill said that the delay was normal, that Eden had two small amendments. Molotov said that if the British wanted to cater to "the whims of King Peter," that would be their business, but if they procrastinated with amendments, the Soviets would add a few of their own. Churchill told Stalin that Tito was a dictator. The Marshal said he was a hero of the resistance. The

British amendments were of no importance—procedural in character—but Eden said that if Molotov would allow him, Subasitch would leave for Yugoslavia at once. Stalin made a counteroffer. If Subasitch left London at once and helped Tito form a responsible government, the Soviets would press for adoption of the two amendments. Both sides agreed.

With relief, Roosevelt announced that the parties were close to a complete agreement on Poland; it was now a matter of a few phrases and drafting. America, he said, would find it difficult to swallow the words "provisional government" because no one but the Russians recognized this government. He would suggest they use "the government now operating in Poland." He referred once more to the millions of unhappy Poles in America. A few State Department men winced; he had used that argument so many, many times. What was more to the point is that neither Stalin nor Churchill cared what the American Poles thought about it. The President saw that he was getting a respectful hearing, but his words carried little weight. He tossed the question back to the limbo of the foreign ministers' meetings and suggested that they meet that night to devise a draft which would meet the approval of all. This was impossible. Churchill was more conciliatory to the Russians. He too favored the night meeting, but he thought that the reason Poland required a broad-based government was that, since the formation of the Lublin group, almost all of Poland had been liberated by the Red Army, and these sections of Poland deserved recognition. The broad-based government might be no more "than an ornament," he said, seeking understanding from Stalin, but "nevertheless an *important ornament.*" Hurrying on, he made a plea for retention of the last sentence, ordering the three ambassadors to observe and report on free elections.

The dual speeches appeared to confuse the Russians. The President seemed the epitome of sincerity in asking for free and unfettered elections; the Prime Minister took on the aura of a clever cynic who was asking the

Soviets to go through the *motions* of having free elections but ending with a government which would be no more than "an ornament." Churchill implied that the new government would need some guidance. He had heard that the Lublin group planned to try the officers of the Polish Home Army as traitors because they were loyal to the London government. He hoped that Great Britain's anxiety on this question would be relieved by "Marshal Stalin's usual patience and kindness." In any other nation, this remark might have induced derisive laughter. Stalin accepted it with grace.

Churchill said that, before the conference proceeded to other questions, he would like to say that Tito would have no objection to Soviet, United States and British observers of elections in Yugoslavia. He, as Prime Minister, would welcome Big Three observers at Italian and Greek elections. Observers were important, he said. In Egypt whatever government called for an election won it. Stalin said that he had heard that Egyptian politicians under Farouk made a career of buying each other out. But then, the Marshal said, one could not compare Egypt with Poland because there was a high percentage of literacy in Poland. Churchill asked if Mr. Mikolajczyk would be permitted to be a candidate in the Polish elections. Stalin replied that since Mikolajczyk was a member of the Peasant paty, which was known to be anti-Fascist, he could take part in the elections. The President said that free elections were the crux of the matter, and he hoped the foreign ministers would write something which would guarantee them.

The conference began a discussion called "Declaration on Liberated Europe." The Marshal, who was irritated at being trapped into admitting that Mikolajczyk *could be* a candidate, said that the American draft of a policy regarding liberated Europe—a document which followed the idealistic phrasing of the original Atlantic Charter and the Four Freedoms—had "good words in it." He had read it, he said, with favor because it asked the eradication of fascism and Nazism in Europe, and that, he said, was precisely what the Soviet troops were doing in Poland. Pleased, FDR said the Polish elections must be the first expression of the Declaration on Liberated Europe. In the manner of a schoolteacher, he leaned forward and looked through the tops of his glasses and said, "Like Caesar's wife, they must be above suspicion." Stalin listened to the interpretation and grunted. "Caesar's wife had that reputation," he said, "but I understand that she was guilty of a few sins."

He was smiling, and he said, on the subject of Poland, the Soviet Union would accept Roosevelt's suggestion to call the current government "The Provisional Government now functioning in Poland." This led Molotov to say that a few other items lent themselves to compromise. After days of dispute, the Russians capitulated to the "American formula" in everything except permitting Harriman and Clark Kerr to be "observers" at the elections. The Soviet position was solid: the Poles would regard it as an insult.

The conference returned to a terse discussion of the Declaration on Liberated Europe. As originally drafted by the State Department, it called for the appointment of a European High Commission to insure order, stability and free elections in countries liberated and nations which had been Axis satellites. FDR didn't like the draft and disapproved of the High Commission. The responsibility, he said, would repose with the Big Three. He gave it to Jimmy Byrnes, who spent time reworking it to the President's liking. The first three paragraphs were idealistic nosegays, citing the rights and goodnesses of national life and a principle of the Atlantic Charter, which guaranteed the right of all peoples to choose their form of government.

Churchill and Stalin had studied it, and watched Roosevelt as he read it aloud. The pertinent paragraph reads: "To foster the conditions in which the liberated peoples may exercise these rights, the three governments will jointly assist the people in any European liberated state or former Axis satellite state in Europe where, in judgment, conditions require (a) to establish conditions of internal peace; (b) to carry out emergency measures for the relief of distressed peoples; (c) to form interim governmental authorities broadly representative of all democratic elements in the population and pledged to the earliest possible establishment, through free elections, of governments responsible to the will of the people; and (d) to facilitate where necessary the holding of such elections." In the document, Russia, America and Great Britain agreed to consult with each other whenever any of these conditions arose and further, to "consult the other United Nations."

Like the U.N. declaration, the Atlantic Charter and other Roosevelt declarations, it was an expression of his liberal idealism. The inherent father image which it projected over the welfare of smaller nations was, he believed, temporary. Stalin said he would like to add one sentence to paragraph four: "In this connection, support will be given to the political leaders of those countries who have taken an active part in the struggle against the German invaders." Impishly, he advised Churchill that this would not apply to Greece. Huffily, the Prime Minister said that Greece would welcome a Soviet observer at elections there. "It would have been very dangerous," Stalin said mischievously, "if you had allowed any but British forces to go into Greece."

Roosevelt, who kept dragging Poland around like a child with a rag doll, watching everyone step on it, said that the declaration "will apply not only to Poland but to any area or country where it was needed." Churchill, who had arrived at the conference as an internationalist, was becoming more and more a defender of his homeland. This document, he said, does not apply to the British Empire. "I have told the House of Commons," he said, "that the Atlantic Charter itself has already been applied to us."

The President said that France had been mentioned in an early draft, but had been taken out because she had no representative at the conference. "Better three powers than four," said Stalin. Churchill had been prodded with a fresh thought. "It might be possible to ask France to associate herself with this document," he said.

The foreign ministers could discuss that, FDR said. He turned to Stalin and said he would be opposed to the original suggestion of adding a sentence weighted in favor of those who had fought fascism, because the entire tone was "self-determination of small nations." It was getting late, the P.M. said, and he would like to get to the matter of German war criminals before the session recessed.

He reminded the conferees that it was he who had drawn up the original document on German war criminals and German atrocities. "It is an egg," he said solemnly, "which I have laid." He would favor all three parties drawing up a list of major war criminals. At the end of hostilities the persons on the list should be hunted down and killed without trial. The Marshal, who enjoyed goading Churchill, asked what would be done with Rudolf Hess, who had fled to England in 1941. Events would catch up with Mr. Hess, the P.M. said. Thinking about it caused him to have a complete change of mind. War criminals, he said, should be given a judicial trial. This surprised everyone because, at previous meetings, Churchill had been no less bloodthirsty than Stalin and Roosevelt.

Churchill was in retreat. The Crimea Conference should not draw up a list of war criminals, he suggested. "We should merely exchange views on this subject," he said. As President Roosevelt called the meeting closed, Stalin asked Churchill if the western offensive had begun. The Prime Minister lighted a fresh cigar. Yes, he said, 100,000 British soldiers had launched an attack on the Germans yesterday. The second wave, the American Ninth Army, would move forward tomorrow. Soon, he said, the whole front would erupt in intensity. The Russians looked pleased.

The President was taken to his bedroom. Fox was ready for the rubdown. Bruenn examined his patient and was pleased to find an absence of *pulsus alternans*. As he had not told the President about the missing pulse beats, so he did not explain that the pulse was normal again. The examination was over; the rubdown was in full swing when Admiral McIntire came in. He seldom spoke as a physician; he asked how the conference was going. The President, with a towel across his middle, turned face up and smiled. "I've got everything I came for," he said, "and not at too high a price." McIntire was eager for the news. The President was obviously satisfied with the progress of the conference. He explained that Russia would enter the Japanese war at an early date. Stalin had agreed to the U.N. Charter and the Soviet Union would be a full partner. San Francisco would be the host city for the first meeting. The Admiral said that this pleased him, because he and Steve Early thought that San Francisco would draw added attention to the war in the Pacific. Mr. Roosevelt shrugged. The one nettlesome problem, he said, was Poland. "The settlement that we have in mind," he said, "leaves much to be desired." The thorny question of China, he said, had been settled amicably. Russia would negotiate a treaty of friendship with Chiang Kai-shek. He did not mention that Chiang had not been consulted, nor had he been told how much he would give for Russia's friendship. It was evidence of Russia's intent, Roosevelt said, that she acknowledged that Manchuria would remain a Chinese possession. In addition, Stalin had agreed to noninterference in Chinese internal affairs, which meant that the Soviet Union would remain neutral in Chiang's battle with Mao's Communists. There was a rotten situation, as he called it, in Yugoslavia, but this had been corrected by forcing Tito to accept a coalition government.

In sum, it was a triumph for righteousness. Roosevelt excused himself. He wanted a hot bath, "a good soaking." He would follow doctors' orders, he said as McIntire left, by having a small private dinner party. At 7:30 P.M., while Roosevelt was resting, Navy Lieutenant W. K. Kloock arrived at Livadia with a pouch. The young man established a new record: three days from Anacostia Field, Washington, to Saki and on to Livadia. Mr. Roosevelt was awakened by Arthur Prettyman. FDR wanted to reach what was in the pouch before dinner.

He called Rigdon for dictation. His self-imposed work schedule was not "following doctors' orders." It was more like flogging a tired horse on an icy hill.

Dawn came up clear and unseasonably warm in London. A U.S. C-54 came down from Prestwick, Scotland, and made a visual-approach landing at Gatwick. Aboard were Judge Samuel Rosenman and a group of experts whose function was to inventory food and civilian supplies in England for possible use in liberated portions of the continent. A lorry took the group to an apartment house near Grosvenor Square. Rosenman felt exhilarated about his work because the feeding and clothing of people under the Nazi yoke for six years seemed like a euphoric humanitarian assignment.

He was in the apartment ten minutes, the suitcases still on the bed, when he phoned Ambassador John Winant. "Don't unpack," Winant said. "I can't talk with you about it over the phone. Better come around to the embassy." Rosenman was in the Ambassador's office in a few minutes. There was a message for the speech writer:

February 9, 1945

PERSONAL AND TOP SECRET

The President wants you to meet him about February fifteenth in the Mediterranean area. You are to proceed to Naples and there communicate with the Commander of the United States Eighth Fleet, Admiral Hewitt. He will arrange for your transportation to meet the President. The President wishes you to assist in preparation of speech to be delivered on his return. As soon as the President gets home, you may return to Europe on your mission. Communicate through Map Room, White House.

Wilson Brown (Naval aide to the President)

A few hours later Rosenman was flying to Naples. It was a day flush with bright promise at Yalta. The President, ignoring medical orders, arose early and conferred with Admiral King, General Marshall, General

Kuter, Jimmy Byrnes and Averell Harriman. He personified a man content, and more than content. The conference, he said, was over. He had been at Livadia a week, had attended conferences on the record and off the record; the chiefs of staff and the foreign secretaries had thrashed out their problems, and the Big Three meeting had been a resounding success. Those who pleaded that they should return to Washington at once—King, Marshall, Jimmy Byrnes, staff men—he advised to leave "today." He confided that he expected to leave this night. He was unrealistic.

He was at breakfast when Harry Hopkins and Edward Stettinius stopped to chat. Hopkins marshaled his thoughts to convert Roosevelt's anti-de Gaulle posture to pro-French. His attitude was that, in spite of the General's desire to crucify himself on his own Cross of Lorraine, Great Britain and the United States were going to need a strong continental power in the west to contain Germany and restrain the ambitions of the Russians. England couldn't do it. France was weaker, but could be made strong. Hopkins realized that putting France on the Security Council was illusory, but if she was on it, she also belonged on the Allied Control Commission. Roosevelt was opposed to giving France any more than token support as a "great power." Stalin, he said, was also opposed. In a war involving hundreds of divisions of troops, France had but eight, and they had been outfitted at United States expense. Hopkins facetiously asked how long the American military presence would remain in Germany. A year? Two?

As Americans hurried home to their hearths and their peacetime jobs, France would be growing stronger along the Rhine. The two men argued without rancor for fifteen minutes; it seemed obvious that the President wanted to surrender his position, but didn't relish facing Stalin with it. To the contrary, Hopkins said, the Russians might welcome a strong power on the opposite side of Germany. The warm, victorious mood was still upon FDR when he said all right; he would propose France for the Allied Control Commission at the final plenary session.

Hopkins had insight about when to depart. He left for the warmth of his bed. Stettinius suggested that Cordell Hull be invited to San Francisco as Senior Delegate and Senior Adviser. The President thought it was a splendid idea. "Invite him," he said. FDR said his sole worry was Poland. Ed said the Russians balked firmly about that last sentence stating that United States, British and Russian ambassadors would "observe and report" on Polish elections. The President dwelled on it. At last he said, "If the statement of this fact irritates the Russians, we can drop the statement, but they must understand our firm determination that the ambassadors will observe and report on the elections in any case." He was willing to capitulate to the Russians, provided they agreed, *ex officio,* that the Americans would watch the elections.

The Boss looked at his watch and told Ed that he would have to see him later. FDR had scheduled an important meeting with Anthony Eden, Churchill, Stalin and Molotov. If it seemed awkward to Stettinius that there were so many unscheduled meetings with Eden and Molotov present—but not Stettinius—he kept his counsel. He left, saying that he would bring up the Polish matter one final time at the foreign secretaries' final session at noon. Neither knew that, shortly before 10:00 A.M., Stalin and Molotov had arrived at the Vorontsov Palace for a "final" discussion on Poland with Eden and Churchill. The Prime Minister had given up pleading the justice of Poland's cause. He dwelt at length on the embarrassing position in which Stalin had forced him; there was a British election coming up and he would have to explain to a hostile House of Commons what he had done to protect Poland's right to independence. Churchill asked Stalin how he could report when England had no representatives in Poland. "We do not know what is going on," he said. Stalin nodded sympathetically. "After the new Polish government is recognized," he said, "it would be open for you to send an ambassador to Warsaw." This was a high price to pay for information; if Great Britain *recognized* the expanded Lublin government without knowing of what it consisted or how it acquired governmental status, then Churchill could send an emissary who could "observe" too late. The price was exorbitant, humiliating. The P.M. agreed to pay it. At Livadia Palace the gentlemen assembled. The President said he had called the group because he wanted to tie some loose ends to the agreements. First, he wanted the parties to sign a secret agreement regarding Soviet entry into the Japanese war, stipulating the price. FDR reminded Stalin that T. V. Soong, Chinese Foreign Minister, would pay a state visit to Moscow soon; would Stalin like to approach him with the story about the return of Sakhalin, the Kuriles, the Russo-Chinese use of the Manchurian railways and the use of Port Arthur and Dairen? No, said Stalin. "I am an interested party. I would prefer to have you tell Chiang later—when I tell you." Churchill said that the United Kingdom had not been consulted about these matters but would sign anyway. He announced that he had a cable from his War Cabinet, which "practically instructed" him not to sign any agreement mentioning $20 billion as reparations from Germany. The President nodded. He told Stalin that he too was opposed to mentioning a specific sum.

The Soviet Premier became angry. He acted as though his two friends had waited until the last moment to thwart Soviet desires. Molotov snapped that $20 billion would not cover Russian losses; it was a sum to mention, the final awards might be greater or smaller. Either way, FDR was opposed to a specific amount. Stalin lost patience with his "sick friend." He stood and shouted and pounded the back of his chair. Anthony Eden said Great Britain would not sign the agreement. Churchill stated that he was opposed to specific amounts, but would sign in any case. Eden said he would respectfully advise his Prime Minister not to sign. Stalin said that $20 billion in itself was not a great deal of money. He was more interested in what he regarded as a new discovery; that Britain did not want to crush Germany, did not want to dismember the nation. She was looking for a prosperous postwar Germany as a business ally. The Prime Minister said this wasn't so; that no one, not even the Russians, had fought Nazism as long as the British. Now that victory was within their grasp, they had no intention of making Germany a prosperous power. Eden said that if Germany was bled white by the agreement, she would be unable to pay future debts and would collapse, as she had in the Weimar Republic.

Eden went a step further. He had scanned the Russian-U.S. agreement on China, and called it a "discreditable byproduct of the Conference." Roosevelt and Stalin were giving parts of China away without consulting Chiang Kai-shek. Churchill pooh-poohed his Foreign Minister. Great Britain, he said, still had some prestige in the Far East. It would protect what was left by signing the agreement. The gentlemen were still arguing when Stalin walked out into the hall with Harriman. He said he was willing to meet the President halfway on the Chinese agreement to reach accord on Germany. This, by implication, gave credence to the thought among British statesmen that Stalin would declare war on Japan merely to protect the spoils he sought. They had said it would not be necessary to give him anything, but the President had given all Russia asked. After a great deal of discussion, the Big Three agreed that the $20 billion could be mentioned, provided that it was to be used as a flexible figure, depending upon Germany's ability to pay.

Churchill returned to Vorontsov Palace and said to Lord Moran, "The President is behaving very badly. He won't take any interest in what we are trying to do." Whatever was left of loose diplomatic ends, the foreign ministers met shortly after noon to resolve them. Anthony Eden was the unhappy one because he said he was certain that Churchill and Roosevelt were succumbing to Soviet demands solely for the sake of reaching agreements. Stettinius spent most of his time teetering atop a wave of optimism. It was a long session of refashioning battered phrases.

The American delegation, Stettinius announced, was working up a draft of a communiqué to be released to the world press when the conference adjourned. Eden said he had a few ideas about the United Nations. He proposed that the United States, as host nation, should communicate all its decisions regarding the new peace-keeping organization to the Soviet Union, the United Kingdom, China and France as original signatories. Also, Eden had a draft of an invitation to be sent to other countries to participate at San Francisco.

At times, Averell Harriman, American Ambassador to Russia, was closer to acting as Roosevelt's Secretary of State than Stettinius. The President had several private conferences with Harriman. Unostentatiously and informally, Harriman often approached Stalin and Molotov to acquaint them with FDR's wishes and asked their confidential responses. The two men cooperated, but the President in effect made secretaries of state of both. When Stettinius could not wrench an agreement from Molotov, the Boss sent Harriman to Stalin. "The left hand kneweth not . . ." At 1:30 P.M. Stettinius was sent to Koreiz to get an English translation of the secret Far Eastern pact from Molotov. Ed read it and nodded. It stated the proper conditions for war, but the President would like to include three specific amendments. One was to spell out that the Manchurian railways would be operated by one Chinese and one Russian; second and third, Dairen and Port Arthur would become free ports.

None of it represented an insurmountable problem, even though Stalin felt it would be better if the Soviet Union leased the facilities at Port Arthur for the Russian Pacific Fleet. Harriman added one gratuitous statement, to which Molotov gave thought: "In addition, I feel sure that the President wouldn't wish to dispose of these matters in which China is interested without the concurrence of Chiang Kai-shek." The Soviet Foreign Minister, after some cogitation, disagreed. His response consisted of friendly circumlocution, but it melted down to a suspicion that the United States might agree to these conditions and Chiang might renounce them. Harriman pointed out that the Big Three had "guaranteed" the postwar land grants and leases. Then too, he said, pointing to the agreement, the United States had designated Sakhalin, the Kuriles, and the railways as Russian "rights." The Japanese had taken these from Russia in the war of 1904; that was a long time ago and the matter of "rights" was debatable. In effect, the United States was assuming that the Soviet Union was only retrieving what belonged to it.

Molotov's position was weak; he was aware that Stalin had agreed to most of these conditions. He said he "guessed" that the Marshal would agree to all of it except Port Arthur; it would have to be "leased" for Russian naval vessels. Harriman suggested that Uncle Joe talk to the Boss about it. At the meeting of the foreign ministers Stettinius had been unable to persuade the Russians to grant first-class power status to the French. Harriman decided to place a few more cards face up on the table. "The President," he said, "has reversed his stand on France." There had been a chat with Harry Hopkins and, although Mr. Roosevelt had personal reservations, he now felt that it would be in the interests of all the Allies to give France a full vote on the Allied Control Commission. If de Gaulle was not granted this privilege, France, the traditional adversary of Germany, might assume a defensive posture. In that event, Germany would not fear an enemy in the west—only in the east.

Molotov said he would have to discuss it with Stalin. Harriman left. Within an hour Roosevelt had word from Stalin that if a full partnership was to be granted to France, the Soviet Union would follow the President's leadership. In fact, an off-the-record meeting was held in Roosevelt's study at 4:00 P.M.—even though the official Yalta calendar states that the final plenary session was called to order at that time. Molotov and Stalin were joined by Churchill and Eden. The President had Stettinius, Harriman and Chip Bohlen with him.

The Russians were overly solicitous and sympathetic to Roosevelt. He looked gray and exhausted. When they disagreed with the President, they tried to persuade him; when they ran counter to Churchill, they attacked. No one in the small room missed the friendly smile and the palsied hands as Roosevelt announced that he had a few "small gifts"; specially engraved fourth-term medallions for Stalin, Churchill, Molotov and Eden, and a book prepared by General H. H. Arnold called *Target Germany*. The book was for the Marshal, and contained many photographs of damage inside Germany. The President discussed the terms under which Russia would fight Japan. Listening, one of the surprised men in the room was Stettinius, to whom all of it was new. When the reading had been completed, Anthony Eden again spoke up and said that Great Britain should not sign. His position was rigid. The P.M., smiling, said that the British would welcome a Russian fleet in the Far East. One may surmise that his interests were more nationalistic than international; the United States was the dominant power in the Pacific, the Russians after the war would be a strong power; British influence, except in Burma, was waning. The arguments of Admirals King and Leahy against dispatching British task units to the Far East were not lost on Churchill. And so, to remain in the game, he was going to sign.

Eden became so irritated that he sent for Sir Alexander Cadogan, who listened and counseled the Prime Minister not to sign. In retrospect, it seems incredible that no one brought up the agreement made with Chiang at Cairo in November 1943, which specifically guaranteed China's territorial integrity, including ports, railroads and rolling stock. This involved American honor. In addition, the President was slipping into a field of diplomacy he had declared was dead—spheres of influence. He had said frequently that neither the British, the Americans, nor the Russians and Chinese could exercise predominant rights over smaller nations or territories "except under a United Nations trusteeship, which is a temporary affair." He was giving Poland to the Russians, because he had no power to stop them; he was lifting battered France to the status of first-class power so that it could be a continental bulwark for the English; he turned his back to the British assault on Greece and the Russo-British agreement to divide influence in the Balkans; he was giving away land and rights which belonged to America's friend, China; he asked for, and received, the assurance of the Soviet Union that they would violate a pact of friendship with Japan and go to war; he grudgingly abandoned the Polish government-in-exile; he retreated from pressing the Russians to leave Iran; although the Russian armies were in Hungary, FDR did not ask whether the little nation, as well as Romania and Czechoslovakia, would be free of alien boots when the war ended.

He was a ghost of a great statesman laboring harder than he had ever worked in one week; his mind was obsessed now with Russian participation in the Japanese war; the formation of the United Nations; and, as a matter of principle, the future of Poland. The rest was haggling, bargaining, reasoning. The gentlemen talked until 4:45 P.M. Lofty principles and ideals were being chipped away, and the President wanted to close the conference after the plenary session. He shocked diplomats when he announced that he planned to leave Yalta "tonight." Stalin and Churchill begged the President to stay one more day. He must realize, they said, that there were a few items still under discussion, and some agreements to sign, in addition to approval of a Crimea Conference communiquè. He hesitated. Molotov said that the President had worked so hard for unity, and it was so close, that one more day could bring everything together on all major issues.

Roosevelt agreed. He was tired, but wouldn't use that as an excuse. He reminded his friends that he had been away from Washington a long time—since January 22. He planned to stop at Suez, he said, to see "three kings"—Ibn Saud, Farouk and Haile Selassie. Churchill, who had heard about this visit but placed little credence in it, quickly announced that he and Eden planned to fly to Athens, but he thought now they would leave there and join the President at Suez. The British, who regarded the Arab world as their sphere, would want to know what Roosevelt might propose for Saudi Arabia, Egypt and Ethiopia.

The plenary session was called to order at 4:50 P.M. FDR was wheeled in first. He conferred with Hopkins and Stettinius, while waiting for Stalin and Churchill to refresh themselves. Churchill arrived, bent over the President and said, "I believe that I have succeeded in retrieving the situation." FDR nodded. He did not ask *what* situation, or *how*. Stalin arrived, clumped around the table to Roosevelt and apologized gruffly for being late. All of the men knew that this would be a long and probably painful session. All that had been thrashed out before would be revitalized and debated as though this were the first time the Big Three had met. Stalin kept his head cocked close to Pavlov's mouth. He wanted to hear every word. Churchill leaned forward, elbows on the table, watching the whispering of Roosevelt and his subordinates. Anthony Eden was asked to render the minutes of the foreign ministers' meeting.

He began with a formula for Poland. The first sentence amounted to studied cynicism: "A new situation has been created in Poland as a result of her complete liberation by the Red Army." The diplomatic excuse for new and secret elections was that western Poland had recently been freed by the Soviets. The provisional government should be expanded to include all democratic elements, in Poland and from abroad. The Crimean Conference empowered Messrs. Molotov, Harriman and Clark Kerr to "consult in *Moscow* with members of the present Polish government and candidates from abroad." *After* the elections, the Soviet Union, the United Kingdom and the United States would accord recognition of the new government, "and will exchange ambassadors by whose reports the respective governments will be kept informed about the situation in Poland."

It was a victory for Stalin. The British and Americans would be kept out of Poland, and could neither observe nor report until after they had recognized the newly

elected government. The President remained silent after
the reading. Churchill said feebly that the document
did not mention borders. "There will be some criticism,"
he said, "but I think there should be some mention
of the territorial settlement." Stalin said nothing. Stettinius scribbled a note and slipped it to Roosevelt: "Eden
told me Churchill received a *bad* cable from the War
Cabinet warning that he was going too far on Poland."
FDR read it; another note was slipped under his arm
from Hopkins:

Mr. President:

*I think you should make it clear to Stalin that you sup-
port the eastern boundary but that only a general statement
be put in communiqué saying we are considering essential
boundary changes. Might be well to refer exact statement
to foreign ministers.*

Harry

This was hardly the issue. Eden's paper would keep
all foreign observers out of Poland, except Russians,
until after the elections. The President, seizing on the
feeble and uncontroversial matter of borders, spoke up
and said the Polish government—the soon-to-be-elected
one—should be consulted about a western frontier before
the Big Three made a decision. This was agreeable to
the Russians, whose concern was the border in the east.
They got what they wanted, the Curzon Line and the
Lvov oil fields. They felt little concern with how much
compensation the Poles would get in German territory
to the west. Stalin said he agreed with Churchill, that
some mention should be made of the final western border. Roosevelt said that Churchill should draft a sentence
or two guaranteeing Poland some territory in the west
and north. Molotov, who did not wish to alter a word
of the agreement, suggested that it would make "a good
last sentence." Churchill said it would be a good evening
for tea, and when that time arrived, they could recess
for fifteen minutes and add a few words to the settlement.
It was obvious that Roosevelt was throwing his support

to Churchill on the matter of a western boundary because the Prime Minister had received "a bad cable."

The second item was President Roosevelt's Declaration on Liberated Europe. This was another of the President's idealistic aspirations; it committed the Big Three to assist, feed, restore order and supervise free elections in such states as might need it or those who asked for it. Eden and Molotov had a mild disagreement on how vaguely to phrase the implementation of such services. Molotov wanted his phrasing; Eden wanted his. The Big Three listened. Stalin tipped the balance in favor of Eden's version: they "shall consult together on the measures to discharge the joint responsibilites set forth in this Declaration." The document depicted intent, nothing more. At one point Churchill asked wearily how a group of nations could agree to consult about a consultation. He was frowned down. Churchill said that, speaking of liberated areas, he would like France to be a prime signer of this document. Roosevelt, a bit late on cue, told Stalin that he had changed his mind about the status of France. Of course he had already spoken to the Russian about his change of heart, but at the conference table he stated it again. The Marshal said he had no objections and would follow the President's lead. FDR proposed France for a place on the Allied Control Commission. Stalin uttered two words: "I agree."

Churchill looked elated. He suggested that the conference send a telegram to General de Gaulle informing him of the momentous decisions. The other parties gave assent. FDR could not resist telling Stalin that he would find the French easier to deal with in the Control Commission than outside. Eden was still on his feet, shifting and waiting. When he had attention, he read the text of a telegram to Tito and Subasitch suggesting that they form a Yugoslavian government at once. Roosevelt said he had made up his mind to stay out of the Yugoslavian situation, but, if the telegram meant what he thought it did, then he could sign. However, there was some dispute between Stalin and Churchill on the phrasing. When it was resolved, all three signed.

Eden said the meeting was moving along splendidly. It shrieked to an abrupt stop as he mentioned German reparations. Churchill said the matter was out of his hands. His War Cabinet *ordered* him not to sign an agreement which mentioned a fixed sum of money. The British people would not stand by while the Soviet Union rifled the German treasury. The President said that he was in a similar position. All patriotic Americans wanted fascism crushed everywhere, but they remembered that they had to lend money to bankrupt Germany after the last war. Stalin, aroused, got out of his chair and stood behind it, the words hissing like summer rain. He said that both of his friends knew that this was not true; that the $20 billion mentioned was an arbitrary amount, and did not represent cash but rather goods and services to that amount. He turned to Maisky and whispered loud enough to be heard, that he was very tired of hearing what British and American public opinion would do to this conference. If the British felt that the Soviet Union should receive no reparations for the ruination of their heartland, he said, he wished they would clarify their position now.

Churchill cut in to state that, in reparations, the Soviet Union deserved first consideration. Molotov and Gusev admitted later that they had the feeling that Roosevelt was deserting them to stand behind Churchill. That foulest and most unfounded of human emotions, suspicion, was easily awakened in the Russians. To them, it was obvious that FDR and Churchill had spent a week bargaining for good terms from the Soviet Union. Now, on the last day, both would slam the door on Russian needs. Stalin appeared to have a right to his whispering anger. He held up two stubby fingers. The conference, he said, would have to agree "in principle" that Germany should pay reparations; two, that the Reparations Commission should "fix the amount," taking into consideration the "American-Soviet proposal that there should be twenty billions."

Roosevelt had spent a week smoothing troubled

waters. He said the word "reparations" was too sharp. Perhaps "compensation for damages caused by Germany in the war" would sound better. Churchill made a long, eloquent speech, acknowledging Russian rights to repayment for losses, but said the British government could not, and would not, commit itself to a specific figure. "No commitment is involved," Stalin said, still gripping the back of the chair. The $20 billion would be "utilized as a basis" for discussion. Mr. Roosevelt said that compensation assumed many forms. "For instance, the United States cannot take manpower as the Russians can." Ivan Maisky made a note. There had been a three-way reluctance to mention German slave labor, but now it was on the table. To the Russians it sounded as though FDR was making a suggestion. Stalin had taken no notice of it. He demanded that Churchill be "honest" about his intentions toward Russia. Then he turned to the President and reminded him that the amount of money had American endorsement; "are you withdrawing from this agreement?" The Marshal glared around the table. Roosevelt smiled. "I am completely in agreement," he said. To him, it was a matter of avoiding offensive words. He just didn't like "reparations." "It implies money." Facetiously, Stalin said the agreement would not be published. In a gesture of resignation, he said he would accept substitute words: "compensation for losses."

As he sat, Eden and Churchill vied with each other to denounce the substitution. It is difficult to divine which one said what, but the substance was that it mattered not that Roosevelt accepted substitute words; Britain could not sign the agreement. Great Britain insisted that postwar Germany be able to stand on her economic feet, to import, to export, to pay her bills. At this point, Stalin—and perhaps Molotov—appeared to realize that Churchill was not bargaining at his personal whim; he was *under orders* from his Cabinet not to cripple Germany. The conference was at an impasse. Stalin said that the $20 billion was not a final figure. Let his friend Winston Churchill suggest a figure. "It is necessary that things move forward." The President was obviously upset and nervous. The way out of such enigmas was always to delegate them somewhere else. Why not let the Allied Commission review it later? he asked. The P.M. looked up, smiling. Molotov said no, and he said it loudly. Shuffling papers, he produced the text of yesterday's foreign ministers' meeting and proved that Stettinius had agreed to the sum. Maisky asked what use there would be sending the problem to the Allied Commission if the Big Three could not settle it now. Argument around the big round table became acrimonious. The Russians charged that the British were making progress by backtracking. Suddenly, Stalin surrendered. He held his hands up for silence and asked Churchill if it would be fair to state that the Big Three agreed that Germany "should pay compensation for damages incurred in the war, and secondly, that the Moscow Reparations Commission be enpowered, later, to determine the amount." Churchill slapped the table. "I agree," he said. The President, somewhat surprised, said, "Judge Roosevelt approves and the document is accepted."

In politics, the world of fantasy and the world of realism dream together. It did not occur to the British or the Americans that when the Soviets assumed control over their large slice of Germany, they would take what they pleased in machinery, factories, tools, merchandise, slave labor, scientists, cash and foreign investments. The men around the table acted as though their documents were precise instruments of justice—bibles of war to be consulted again and again to ascertain truth. The Big Three had accomplished nothing; they had postponed the precise nature and quantity of reparations and tossed it downward to another body; they refused to face the question of dismemberment of Germany—apparently because no one had studied its consequences. The Americans wanted to break Germany into weak military fragments; the Russians wanted enough left of Germany to loot; the British switched from their bloodthirsty attitude at Teheran to a position where they were applying artificial respiration to an old customer. Frequently,

when FDR was pressed for an opinion, he used a
hackneyed phrase: "We would like to maintain freedom
of action."

Roosevelt asked for a fifteen-minute adjournment
for tea. Servants were summoned. Trays on wheels rolled
around the table, and the men sipped from glasses encased
in silver holders. Stettinius, who felt that Roosevelt
had sustained the rigors of the conference well, now
wrote that "he shows fatigue." Some of the men stood
and carried their steaming glasses to the big arched
windows where the sea, in spite of the recent thunder
and flame of war, was serene. Roosevelt asked Matthews
how much was left to discuss. The session was reconvened with Stalin saying he would like to introduce the
Turkish Dardanelles and the Montreux Convention.

The treaty was old, he said. Outmoded. The Montreux
Convention gave the Turks the right to close the straits
between the Aegean and the Black seas in time of war
and at times when the Turkish nation felt there was
danger of war. The Soviet nation, he pointed out, could
get from Black Sea ports to the Mediterranean only
at the whim of the Turks. The Russians wanted to build
a Black Sea fleet in the postwar world, but if Ottoman
guns closed the Greek Hellespont, such a fleet would
be bottled. He understood, Stalin said, that the British
had assisted the Japanese in working up the Montreux
Convention, but times had changed. The English, he
hoped, no longer desired to strangle Russia. And yet,
a small nation like Turkey now had one hand at Russia's
throat. The treaty, he said, should be revised or abrogated,
but it should not harm the legitimate interests of Turkey.
"I suggest that the first foreign ministers' meeting to
occur after this conference consider this matter."

The Marshal brought the matter to the table, and
abruptly deferred it to a lesser body. If he feared that
the British wished to dominate the Mediterranean alone,
he was mistaken. Churchill said he had discussed the
Montreux Convention with Stalin at Moscow. The British
were in sympathy. He had asked Stalin for a formal
note on the subject, but none had been received. Eden

said that the subject had been discussed with the Turkish Ambassador at London several times. The President did not like fortifications between nations at any time, he said. Canada and the United States had shared a 3,000-mile border for over a hundred years, he said, and there wasn't a gun on it. The Prime Minister thought that Stalin's decision to pass this problem to the foreign ministers was "a wise one." Russia, he said, was too mighty a power to be "dependent on a narrow exit." And yet, he felt the foreign ministers should assure Turkey that her national integrity would continue to be respected. The Marshal said gloomily, "It is impossible to keep anything from the Turks."

The hour was late. Roosevelt mentioned something about the Four Freedoms, and, mischievously, Churchill said he often intended to ask the President about Freedom From Want. "I suppose," he said, "it means privation and not desire." The meeting was ready for closing, but Roosevelt said he wanted to explain his position on Poland. Stalin, glancing around the table, asked who was recording the decisions. It was the seventh plenary session, and his alarm elicited some chuckles. Eden said the foreign ministers and their assistants had been taking notes since the conference opened. Belatedly, the Foreign Minister said he now had Russian and English translations of the final paragraphs of the Polish statement. He began by saying, "The three governments recognize . . ." FDR said no, that would not do. In America the Senate was an important part of treaty making and international agreements. That opening would have to read, "The heads of the three governments feel . . ." The rest of what they "felt" was recognition of the Curzon Line in the east and compensation in land to the west.

The mood became light. The men were like schoolboys who had worked hard all term and had a vacation in sight. They hoped they would get good marks, but they weren't certain. Molotov had a last-moment amendment. In that final paragraph, he would like a part of it to read "with the return to Poland of her ancient frontiers in East Prussia and on the Oder." Roosevelt knew that the Foreign Minister was using the same ploy as the Soviets had in the "return of their rightful islands and lands in the Far East." He rubbed his forehead as though thinking. "How long ago were these lands on the Oder Polish?" Molotov, without a smile, said, "Very long ago." FDR beamed at Churchill. "Perhaps you would want us back?" America, said the Prime Minister, would be as indigestible to Great Britain as Germany would be for Poland.

The last sentence in the Polish agreement read: ". . . the final delimitation of the western frontier of Poland should thereafter await the Peace Conference." In his hand Roosevelt crumpled a piece of paper which read: "Mr. President: You get into trouble about your legal powers & what senate will say. Harry." He smiled benignly at the men around the table, thanked them for their hard work and said that he would be leaving Livadia at "three-thirty tomorrow afternoon." There was a babel—especially from the second-echelon statesmen—that the final communiqué of the conference, in addition to the various agreements, would not be ready for signature at that time. The President seemed unaffected. He would leave at 3:30. Cadogan, barely concealing his exasperation, asked, "Why three-thirty?" Stettinius assured the gentlemen that the remaining work could be "finished off in an hour." FDR, amiably disposed, said he would leave at 6:00 P.M. instead of 3:30. In case a small dispute arose, he would be available until evening.

He left the ballroom at 8:00 P.M. The Prime Minister was to be the host at the final dinner at 8:30. No one except the British could hope to be at Vorontsov Palace within a half hour. Mr. Roosevelt, who needed a rubdown badly and some bed rest, skipped both to go to his study, where he dictated a letter to Rigdon. "This," he said, "is to be hand delivered to Marshal Stalin at once."

Dear Marshal Stalin:
I am somewhat concerned lest it be pointed out that the United States will have only one vote in the Assembly. It

*may be necessary for me, therefore, if I am to insure whole-
hearted acceptance by the Congress and people of the United
States of our participation in the World Organization, to ask
for additional votes in the Assembly in order to give parity
to the United States.*

*I would like to know, before I face this problem, that
you perceive no objection and would support a proposal
along this line if it is necessary for me to make it at the
forthcoming conference. . . .*

The last-minute letter may have been generated by
fear of repercussions in the United States when, at San
Francisco, it must be announced that the Soviet Union
had three votes. Whatever the reason, it was something
the President had mentioned before, as though he hoped,
by demanding parity, that Russia would return to one
vote and Churchill would not ask for additional votes
for British dominions. In any case, Rigdon presented
it for signature and a messenger drove off with it. Unless
Roosevelt was frightened, the note was without point.
He had been assured privately, both by the British and
the Russians, that if the United States wanted extra
votes in the Assembly, the British and the Russians would
propose them at the charter meeting.

When the Prime Minister and his group arrived at
Vorontsov Palace to freshen before dinner, Churchill
was surprised to find the doorways and corridors lined
with Red Army soldiers. They were completing a search.
Although the dinner was intimate—only nine persons—the
Red officers locked the dining room after searching under
tables and overturning chairs and chests. The military
chieftains and many of the under-secretaries had left
Yalta. Churchill's invitation list for dinner was the Big
Three, their foreign ministers and three interpreters:
Pavlov, Major Birse and Bohlen. The parties did not
arrive until 9:00 P.M. Churchill had arranged for a large
rib roast and had the chef prepare Russian favorites
as well. Chip Bohlen managed to make terse notes. There
was some general conversation; everyone was glad the
conference had been held, and glad it was over. They

commented on the amount of work and the number and range of decisions. Churchill stood and said he proposed a toast to the King of England, the President of the United States, and Comrade Kalinin, President of the Supreme Soviet of the Soviet Union. Before anyone drank, the P.M. said that he would like Roosevelt, as the only head of state present, to respond.

Roosevelt sat in the portable wheelchair he always carried in his automobile. He was slumped forward, smiling. Rather than propose a toast, he would tell a little story. A long time ago his wife had gone down in the country to open a school, and on the wall was a huge map of the world. Between Europe and the Pacific Ocean there was a big blank space. Mrs. Roosevelt asked about it. The teacher said that it was forbidden in the school to discuss this place, the Soviet Union. The President said he was serving his first term, as he recalled, and he determined to write to President Kalinin and ask him to send an emissary to the United States to open negotiations for the establishment of diplomatic relations.

The group drank to that. Marshal Stalin stood. He would propose a toast, he said. In general, he said, he had always been opposed to kings and he was on the side of the people and not beside any king. However, in this war he had learned to honor and esteem the British people, who honored and respected their king. "I would propose the health of the King of England," he said. The nine men drank. Only Churchill was dissatisfied with what he had heard. He turned to Molotov and said to tell Stalin that, in future, he could remain faithful to his scruples by toasting the three heads of state and leave the King of England out of it. It was near hilarious to hear Molotov explain to Stalin in Russian the dressing down he had just received, and, at the same time, listen to Churchill's toast to Stalin:

". . . There was a time when the Marshal was not so kindly disposed towards us, and I remember that I said a few rude things about him, but our common dangers and common loyalties have wiped all that out.

The fire of war has burnt up the misunderstandings of the past. We feel that we have a friend whom we can trust, and I hope he will continue to feel the same about us. I pray he may live to see his beloved Russia not only glorious in war but also happy in peace." The men drank again. It was Roosevelt's turn, but Stalin stood and gruffly proposed a toast, "To the three heads of state."

As always, the toasts continued. The men ate well, and fractioned into conversational groups of two or three. Churchill may have felt that he had been harsh, because he spoke directly to Stalin and explained that he must soon face an election. The Marshal could not see what could worry Churchill: "The people know they need a leader and who could be a better leader than he who had won the victory?" It wasn't quite like that, the P.M. explained. "We have two parties. I belong to only one of them." Stalin raised his bushy brows in mock alarm. "One party is much better," he said. Roosevelt said that Winston was always talking about the British Constitution, what it allowed and what it didn't allow, but he assured Stalin there was no British Constitution. And yet, he said, he thought an unwritten one was better than a written one.

It was like the Atlantic Charter. The document did not exist, and the whole world understood it and appreciated it. He said he had found one copy of it among his papers, and it was signed "Winston Churchill" and "Franklin D. Roosevelt," but, when he studied the signatures, the President realized they were both in his handwriting. Churchill smiled. "The Atlantic Charter is not a law," he said. "It's a star." Stalin said he could never comprehend the sense of discipline in the German mind. It was beyond him. When he was very young, he said, he had traveled by train all across Russia and Poland with 200 young Communists to attend a meeting in Leipzig. When they arrived on the station platform, no one was present to take their tickets. All 200, with their German Communist friends, stood on the freezing platform for two hours waiting for a station master. All of them missed the Young Communist meeting.

The President held his glass up and a waiter filled it. He would propose another toast. "You see, Winston," he said slowly, almost gently, "there is something here that you are not capable of understanding. You have in your veins the blood of tens of generations of people accustomed to conquering. We are here at Yalta to build up a new world which will know neither injustice nor violence, a world of justice and equity." In translation, the toast appeared to move Stalin close to tears. He drew a kerchief, blew his nose and wiped his eyes. It may be that he, of the three, realized how noble, how impossible the dream was. Or he may have been more intoxicated.

Stalin drank, then said he feared to return to Moscow. He did not know how he would tell the Russian people that they would not get reparations from Germany because the British forbade it. Bohlen, across the table, was listening. He felt that the only reason a discordant note had been introduced was because Molotov and Vyshinsky questioned Stalin's agreement to accede to the British at the final session. Churchill said that this question had been misunderstood many times. He was not opposed to Russia getting reparations. He hoped the Soviet Union would receive them in large measure. But, he said, no one knew how much wealth was left in Germany. Day and night air raids, the hammering of the Russian armies had taken their toll. If no one knew yet what was left worth taking, how could anyone say "20 billions of dollars"? It might be much more; it might be far less. He wanted Stalin to know that Great Britain did not want to be a party to bankrupting Germany so that she would no longer be self-supporting.

It is doubtful that Stalin understood any more—or desired to understand any more—than was encompassed in the arguments at the ballroom. But he suggested at the dinner that Churchill and Roosevelt should add something to the communiqué about making Germany pay for the damage caused to the Allied nations, and also some reference, however vague, about the Reparations Commission to be set up in Moscow. Both Churchill and FDR agreed to do it. Stettinius stood and proposed a toast to Cordell Hull, who was "an inspiration to us all . . . a great American and a great statesman."

Roosevelt said he had a toast. He said he had been twenty-eight years old when he entered political life, but, even then, Winston Churchill was well known to the world and "had long experience in the service of his country." The President moved on, hesitating a little, to recall that often Churchill was in office, and often he was out. Roosevelt, holding his glass high, said that Churchill "had been of greater service to Great Britain when he was not in the government because he had forced people to think." The diners didn't know whether it was a compliment or criticism. FDR tried to impress Stalin that the President and the Prime Minister were not "partners." Stalin growled that too many people worried about political left and political right. Who, he said, could say which was which today? Daladier was a French Radical Socialist, but he dissolved the trade unions in France. Churchill was a Tory in England but had "never molested the unions." Who was left or right of whom?

The President recalled that, in 1940, France had three prime ministers in one week. There was an organization in the United States, he explained, called the Ku Klux Klan. It was opposed to Roman Catholics and Jews and Negroes. Once he had been a guest speaker at a Chamber of Commerce in a small southern town. He said that on one side of him was an Italian Catholic; on the other, a Jew. Roosevelt had asked the president of the Chamber of Commerce if they were members of the Ku Klux Klan. The young man said yes, they were members. It was all right because everybody in the town knew them. The President remarked that this was the key to all prejudice—to get to know people.

The Prime Minister appeared to be slightly depressed. He kept returning to the British elections as though, inferentially, he was sure to lose, and therefore this would be the last time the Big Three would clink glasses. Whatever the result of the election, he said, he and Mr. Eden would continue to support the United States and Russia no matter who was in power. The air in the room may have become slightly atomized with wine, because much of the conversation was irrelevant. Churchill told Stalin that he had had a lot of trouble with Mr. Gallacher, a Communist Member of Parliament, but that he had sent the man a letter of sympathy when he lost two foster children in the war. One more non sequitur.

Stalin said he didn't think the Labour party could form a government in England. "Is there any labor party in the United States?" he asked FDR. The President said that labor was very powerful in his country, but there was no labor party. The Marshal did not seem to understand. He said that more time was needed for the conference. FDR said he was sorry; he had three kings waiting for him in the Near East. The Marshal said that he would like to say a word about the Jewish question. "The problem is a very difficult one," he said. The Russians had established a Jewish Home in Birobidzhan, but the people remained only two or three years and then scattered to the cities. The President said he was a Zionist and asked if Stalin was one. Gruffly, the Marshal said he was a Zionist "in principle, but I recognize the difficulty."

The conversation rambled onward. Again the hour was late. Stalin got up and stood behind the President's wheelchair. He asked him to stay one more day. Churchill heard it and said, "Franklin, you cannot go. We have within reach a very great prize." The President shook his head dolefully. "Winston," he said, "I have made commitments and I must depart tomorrow . . ." Stalin said that all of them needed just a little more time to complete their business. He did not believe that everything could be completed by tomorrow. FDR disagreed. He said that all necessary business would be finished by tomorrow, but if necessary, he would stay over until Monday. He and Stettinius left the dinner first, with Bohlen. Stalin asked if the President planned to discuss a Jewish homeland with King Ibn Saud. FDR said he would review the entire "Palestine question." This irritated Churchill, who lapsed into silence. A Jewish homeland was a British matter, a promise made in the Balfour Declaration. The British could not understand why Roosevelt would immerse himself in their problem. What could he promise?

As Stalin left with his booted guards, the British staff assembled in the corridor. Winston Churchill led them in three rousing cheers and a hip! hip! hooray!

The Russians were up early. Some stared sleepily from the large windows at Koreiz and opened them wide. The dawn was alight with a fan of pink ribbons. The timid breeze was warm. "Roosevelt weather," one of them said, and the joking phrase spread through the diplomatic corps. The charts showed cold and rain when the President arrived, eight days earlier. A few days had been misty, but all of them had been warm. Even Stalin smiled at the words "Roosevelt weather." The Crimea had indeed been kind to old bones. It also had a subtle narcotic effect on three delegations, each of which had come to this most monumental of all conferences certain that the other two were adversaries—each was prepared to leave counting triumphs and defeats. It would possibly occur only to Roosevelt that a nationalistic gain had to be a collective defeat. At Livadia and Vorontsov, the lesser gentlemen, in bathrobes, stood outside their bathroom door, some yawning, some with towels over an arm. Suitcases reposed on unmade beds. Stout Russian women, their heads wrapped in kerchiefs, wielded feather dusters, punched pillows, exchanged shy morning smiles with distinguished foreigners and swept rugs as white-coated men carried trays of steaming breakfasts from room to room. Everyone seemed swifter of step, perhaps lighter. The machinery for winning a long, dreadful war and imposing a peace on the weaker nations of the world had been concluded. Oh, there would still be disputes about words, but the edifice of world order had been hammered together. What did it matter if one of the doors opened in or out? The building was up, and the carpenters were pleased.

For once, 9:00 A.M. seemed late. At that time the foreign ministers and their staffs assembled around the big ballroom table. Comrade Molotov passed out Russian and English copies of "Protocol of the Proceedings of the Crimea Conference." This was the agreement, the document which would bind the Big Three. To some, it seemed strange that it would not be signed by Roosevelt, Stalin and Churchill. The signatories would be Stettinius, Molotov and Eden. The Crimea Communiqué, a publicity release to the world, would bear the names of the Big Three. They would sign other documents too—the one involving German reparations and the secret agreement which would bring the Soviet Union into war with Japan. Secrecy is often hypocritical; it was so in this case. The Russians would continue friendly relations with Tokyo, as Japan had once continued cordial conversations with Washington until the morning of December 7, 1941. None of the parties at Yalta looked upon himself as a hypocrite; a statesman, yes. A diplomat by definition.

Molotov presided at the meeting and he reminded the men that they should read each word carefully because this would be the last opportunity—except one—to alter any of it. There was shuffling of papers around the huge table, some whispering and nodding, now and then a question asking for clarification. The protocol was legalistically precise, but it came to 2,700 words, some of which could have precipitated a dispute. It was not a treaty, and yet it was binding. The preamble stated that the heads of three governments had met in the Crimea between February 4 and 11 and "came to the following conclusions." The first item was World Organization, which would include "United Nations as they existed on the 8 February 1945" and other countries which declared war on the Axis countries on or before March 1, 1945. The first meeting would be held "in the United States of America" Wednesday, April 25, 1945. It provided that the United States, on behalf of the Big Three, would consult China and the French provisional government apprising them of decisions taken at Yalta. The United States also agreed to support a proposal "to admit to original membership two Soviet Socialist Republics, i.e., the Ukraine and White Russia." The Security Council could not make political decisions without the concurring votes of *all* permanent members.

The Trustee section came next. This worried Churchill so much that the final draft, in effect, was declarative and then apologized for it. The provision would apply to (a) mandates of the old League of Nations; (b) territories detached from enemy nations; and (c) territories which desired to be placed under trusteeship; also (d) "no discussion of actual territories is contemplated at the forthcoming United Nations Conference . . . and it will be a matter of subsequent agreement which territories within the above categories will be placed under trusteeship."

Then the Declaration on Liberated Europe. This was designed to assist peoples who had lived under the yoke of fascism and who, for a moment in time, had neither subsistence nor authority. The wording is important to an understanding of this section because it was the only one with an aura of altruism. "The establishment of order in Europe and the rebuilding of national economic life must be achieved by processes which will enable the liberated peoples to destroy the last vestiges of Nazism and fascism and to create democratic institutions of their own choice. This is a principle of the Atlantic Charter—the right of all peoples to choose the form of government under which they will live . . .

". . . the three governments will jointly assist the people in any European liberated state or former Axis satellite state in Europe where in their judgment conditions require (a) to establish conditions of internal peace; (b) to carry out emergency measures for the relief of distressed peoples; (c) to form interim governmental authorities broadly representative of all democratic elements in the population and pledged to the earliest possible establishment through free elections of governments responsive to the will of the people; and (d) to facilitate where necessary the holding of such elections . . . the three powers express the hope that the Provisional Government of the French Republic may be associated with them . . ." These high-flown sentiments would apply to Poland, Hungary, Czechoslovakia, Austria, Bulgaria, Greece and France itself, where de Gaulle had imposed himself on the people. It was impossible to apply this doctrine to war-exhausted nations when two of the signatories, Churchill and Stalin, had already agreed to divide the helpless between them. President Roosevelt, in a euphoric daze at Churchill's final dinner, stated in his rambling toasts that he believed in the freedom and self-determination of small peoples and nations, but his friends could not do more than to drink to it.

The section on Germany was less than Stalin demanded, and more than Churchill wished to acknowledge. It provided for complete disarmament, demilitarization and "the dismemberment of Germany as they deem requisite for future peace and security." The statement was a suspended sword: ". . . as they deem requisite." Germany might or might not be chopped into sections. Section IV agreed that the French would have a zone of occupation "formed out of the British and American Zones." France was also "invited" to become a member of the Allied Control Council for Germany. The Russians won two valuable points in this section. One was the formal mention of $20 billion with 50 percent going "to the Union of Soviet Socialist Republics." The other was that, as part of its reparations, Germany would have to furnish "use of German labor." The British conceded defeat on both issues, but had to bring something face-saving to Britain, so a paragraph was added stating: "The British delegation was of the opinion that pending consideration of the reparations question by the Moscow Reparation Commission no figures of reparation should be mentioned." This did not deny the claim of the U.S.S.R. to $10 billion. Nor would postponing it until the Moscow Commission met help Churchill. There, Clark Kerr would be faced with the overriding votes of Molotov and Harriman.

The subject of Major War Criminals, which had aroused volcanic ire at Teheran, was at Yalta chilled in thirty-three words: "The Conference agreed that the question of major war criminals should be the subject of enquiry by the three Foreign Secretaries for report in due course after the close of the Conference." Obviously, the words "should be the subject of enquiry . . . report in due course" were designed to lull ranking Nazis from fanatical fighting as though they were on the edge of an historical *Götterdämmerung,* as indeed they were. If the softened semantics were intended to encourage defections from Hitler's policies, the words failed. The ranking statesmen and generals were conscious of the merciless crimes committed against helpless civilians in several countries, and, from postwar statements, it seems logical that few of the German leaders hoped to escape punishment.

Poland was covered by the Declaration on Liberated Areas but, to show that this country, crushed and plundered by two armies, needed special mention, the longest section of the protocol was devoted to a Declaration on Poland. It restated, in stilted language, the establishment of a broad-based government to supplement the Lublin group; Harriman, Clark Kerr and Molotov were authorized to consult with all Polish candidates "in Moscow"; the Big Three agreed to recognize the new Polish government and exchange ambassadors with Warsaw. Russian phrasing dominated this area and undermined the sympathetic approach of the United States and Great Britain. After recognition, the newly appointed ambassadors would report on conditions in Poland, and "respective governments will be kept informed about the situation in Poland." The Russians, without consulting the Poles, whose opinions they pretended to solicit, insisted that a new eastern boundary be mentioned, but that the western boundary should "await the peace conference." The tortuous and sometimes rancorous debate had a melancholy aspect: the Soviet Union, either as friend or enemy of Poland, held the country in its military fist before and after Yalta. Roosevelt and Churchill were aware that Stalin had two hidden and unplayed cards: he could denounce the Yalta Conference and depart to pursue his national goals, or he could risk a military confrontation with his western allies somewhere in Germany. The cards were not turned face up on the table.

Yugoslavia was dismissed with a declaration that Tito and Dr. Subasitch should form a provisional government composed of Slavs who had not "compromised themselves by collaboration with the enemy." The Italo-Yugoslav border was ordered to hang in the limbo of diplomatic statecraft. Section X, dealing with a proposed treaty between Yugoslavia and Bulgaria, ordered both countries to postpone the pact because "Mr. Eden suggested that . . . this could not be approved." Both nations were functioning under armistice agreements; the British contended that this rendered them powerless to enter into alliances.

Hurriedly and perhaps foolishly, the protocol revealed as much of the disagreements between the Big Three as unanimity. For example, the British were permitted to write, as Section XI, an incomprehensible dictum about southeast Europe: "The British delegation put in notes for the consideration of their colleagues on the following subjects: (a) The control commission in Bulgaria; (b) Greek claims on Bulgaria, more particularly with reference to reparations; (c) oil equipment in Romania." The protocol does not state what the British asked in a, b, or c, or what weight, if any, their "colleagues gave them. The same enigmatic manner of mentioning a subject without resolving it was repeated in the Iranian section. In two sentences, the protocol said that the foreign ministers "exchanged views" and agreed to discuss the fate of Iran "through the diplomatic channel."

More space was devoted to an agreement that the

three foreign ministers should "meet as often as necessary, probably every three or four months." As an evidence of good faith, the first meeting of the ministers in London pledged itself to discuss Russia's claim to access through the Turkish Dardanelles: "The Turkish Government should be informed at the appropriate moment."

A separate one-page Top Secret Agreement enunciated the conditions under which Russia would fight Japan. The President read it and said to Harry Hopkins: "When we get back, this goes into the White House safe." It gave to Stalin all he had asked. Near the end, it stated that "the President" would take measures to obtain the concurrence of Chiang Kai-shek. In case he was unable to wheedle compliance from the Chinese to give land, ports and railroads to the Russians, the succeeding paragraph said: "The heads of the three great powers have agreed that these claims of the Soviet Union shall be *unquestionably fulfilled* after Japan has been defeated." In return, Russia offered China "a pact of friendship and alliance."

The battle of ideals and words was over. The time was noon of Sunday, February 11. The foreign ministers and their staffs, laden with copies of the protocol, hurried to the ballroom for the final reading of the protocol, the secret agreement on Japan, and a conference communiqué, which was being hammered out and typed by the Americans. These would be read in silence and without photographers. The Big Three were seated with their interpreters. The President said that he had been so busy all week that he had not had time to see the grounds at Livadia. The morning had been so warm and sweet that he had taken a ride in a jeep with his daughter and enjoyed the formal gardens, the exalted view of the Black Sea and the mountains. Stalin said that the Soviets had maintained Livadia, Vorontsov and Koreiz as sanitaria for tubercular patients. After the conference, the sick would again be brought to the sunny mildness of the palaces. The President said that while he was on his short motor tour he inspected a guard of United

States sailors. He had not known that they had been outside Livadia since his arrival.

In painful slowness, the protocol was presented sentence by sentence. The final draft had been executed by Molotov, so he read it, even though copies were before each listener. The few suggested alterations were so minor that the proposers withdrew them. The foreign ministers were empowered to sign for their governments. When Molotov, Stettinius and Eden completed signing a dozen copies, the mood of the conference became expansive. The change was magical. Suddenly everyone—even the dour Gusev—grinned as though the Big Three had settled the affairs of all nations in matters of war and peace. There were smiles and sighs. The conversation became complimentary. The President said he felt "ecstatic," a word which became difficult to translate. He asked that the draft of the Crimea Communiqué be read by Edward Stettinius. This, the statement to the world, had been drawn up by an American who wasn't even listed as a member of the delegation, Wilder Foote, assistant to the Secretary of State.

It began: "For the last eight days, Winston S. Churchill, Prime Minister of Great Britain, Franklin D. Roosevelt, President of the United States, and Marshal J. V. Stalin, Chairman of the Council of People's Commissars of the Union of Soviet Socialist Republics, have met with the Foreign Secretaries, Chiefs of Staff, and other advisers in the Crimea.

"The following statement is made—"

Stalin asked Stettinius to stop reading. "It would be good," he said, "to list the members of each delegation by name immediately after that paragraph." There was no objection. Stettinius asked if the names could be added later, so that the signing would not be delayed. "The following statement is made by the Prime Minister of Great Britain, the President of the United States of America, and the Chairman of the Council of People's Commissars of the Union of Soviet Socialist Republics on the results of the Crimea Conference: . . ."

The communiqué, by its nature, would differ from

the protocol. The sentiments to be thrown to the world would be defined in stronger words, the war would sound akin to a holy crusade and, above all, the unanimity of Russia, the United States and Great Britain—which was, in fact, an impossibility—would be stressed as though the three nations were blood brothers. The three military staffs had met daily and coordinated "even more powerful blows to be launched by our armies and air forces . . . Nazi Germany is doomed. The German people will only make the cost of their defeat heavier to themselves by attempting to continue a hopeless resistance." Agreement had been reached about the future of Germany after "unconditional surrender . . . These terms will not be made known until the final defeat of Germany." Headquarters of the occupying forces would be in Berlin. France would be invited, "if she should so desire" to occupy a zone and become the fourth member of the Council Commission. Most language experts agree that "never" is a traitorous word, but the Big Three agreed to "ensure that Germany will never again be able to disturb the peace of the world." The following sentence would hearten the world, but could have no effect on the German people except to strengthen their will to resist: "We are determined to disarm and disband all German armed forces; break up for all time the German General Staff that has repeatedly contrived the resurgence of German militarism; remove and destroy all German military equipment; eliminate and control all German industry that could be used for military production; bring all war criminals to just and swift punishment and exact reparation in kind for the destruction wrought by the Germans; wipe out the Nazi party, Nazi laws, organizations and institutions, remove all Nazi and militaristic influences from public office and from the cultural and economic life of the German people. . . ."

Swiftly, almost carelessly, the communiqué lightly touched the subject of German reparations. Nowhere was there mention of removal of German factories, tools, dies, railroad stock, scientists and forced labor. "A Commission for the Compensation of Damage will be established. The Commission will be instructed to consider the question of the extent and methods for compensating damage caused by Germany to the Allied countries. The Commission will work in Moscow."

The formation of a United Nations in San Francisco was trumpeted with brave notes. "We are resolved upon the earliest possible establishment with our allies of a general international organization to maintain peace and security." China and France would be asked to sponsor this organization with Great Britain, the United States and the U.S.S.R. "As soon as the consultation with China and France has been completed, the text of the proposals on voting procedure will be made public." Three votes for Russia was a wound which Roosevelt would have to sustain in secret for a while. Nothing was mentioned about the right of any of the five sponsoring powers (permanent members of the Security Council) to veto any action proposed by the rest of the world. In sum, five nations proposed to rule by negation—three of them, France, Britain and China, weakened by war to the point of exhaustion. Nor of course did the Big Three discuss the matter of an international military force which, by its power, could enforce peace in any part of the globe. Peace would remain an abstract philosophy.

The Declaration on Liberated Europe—utopian or cynical, depending upon the signer—was treated in a more flamboyant manner than in the protocol. It pledged "our determination to build in cooperation with other peace-loving nations a world order under law, dedicated to peace, security, freedom and the general well-being of all mankind."

The Polish nation required a special section. The Big Three decided to start it with a problem and close with an agreement. "We came to the Crimean Conference resolved to settle our differences about Poland. We discussed fully all aspects of the question. We affirm our common desire to see established a strong, free, independent and democratic Poland. As a result of our joint discussions we have agreed on the conditions in which a new Polish Provisional Government of National Unity may be formed in such a manner as to command recognition by the three major powers. . . ."

The reading of the "broad-based democratic government" continued, but was stopped by Churchill. He said he had been paying attention to the documents, and was tiring of the use of the word "joint" in conjunction with agreements and declarations. To his way of thinking, the word "joint" signified a family roast of mutton. He would prefer a word like "united" or "common" or even "combined." Hopkins whispered to Stettinius, "This is the day we all prayed for so many years." Leahy, as formal as ever, murmured, "This gives one a feeling of great hope." Stettinius asked his colleagues to make a note of the objection to the word "joint" and assured them that the communiqué could be amended at lunch time.

Yugoslavia was mentioned as a Crimean Conference "recommendation" to Tito and Dr. Subasitch to form a government. "There was also a general review of other Balkan questions." It was followed by the revelation that the three foreign ministers would consult regularly. The document ended with

Victory in this war and establishment of the proposed international organization will provide the greatest opportunity in all history to create in the years to come the essential conditions of such a peace.

SIGNED:
Winston S. Churchill
Franklin D. Roosevelt
J. V. Stalin

February 11, 1945

The President said that he would like the communiqué to be sent in code to Moscow, London and Washington and released simultaneously. If it was agreeable to his colleagues, he proposed "tomorrow at four P.M. Washington time." Some countries had advanced their clocks and were on war time, others were not. As FDR figured, the release of the communiqué—"if strictly adhered to"—would be 4:00 P.M. in America, 11:00 P.M. in London and 2:00 A.M. in Moscow. Roosevelt had been betrayed several times by the British in matters of public relations. The signatories agreed on the exact time. Stalin, thinking aloud, referred to Iran and said that any nation which kept its oil in the ground "is working against peace." No one responded.

Lunch at Livadia was almost over when the final draft of the communiqué arrived and the Big Three signed. They had talked world politics throughout the meal, but neither Bohlen nor Harriman took notes. There was a fruit dessert in syrup. Before it was served the President's luggage and his party were on the gravel drive waiting. Admiral McIntire had the mistaken notion that the party would drive 80 miles to Saki airport. Roosevelt planned to spend the night aboard the *Catoctin* at Sevastopol. He needed a night's rest before the flight to Egypt, and he wanted to see the communiqué encoded and sent to the big U.S. radio station at Oran, thence to be transmitted to the U.S. Navy at Washington.

After dessert, a general brought some plush boxes to the President. He wore the smile of a grandfather on Christmas morning. He told Marshal Stalin that he would like to confer U.S. decorations on certain Soviet officers. After this ceremony the Marshal waved over his shoulder and two servants arrived with packages. There was vodka, wine, caviar, butter, oranges, tangerines. Other servants had presents for Stettinius, Bohlen, Leahy and Hopkins. In passing, Stalin said he would like to send the desk from the Livadia study to Roosevelt because he had worked so hard there. FDR was delighted. He clapped his hands and said he had additional gifts for the NKVD men who, with Mike Reilly's group, had guarded the conference site so well.

The President turned his wheelchair away from the table and waved good-bye. Churchill, Molotov, Eden and Stalin arose and crowded around him. Churchill said later that he thought Roosevelt was "anxious" to meet the potentates of the Middle East and "hurry home."

Personally, he said to FDR, he and his daughter Sarah would drive to Sevastopol "this afternoon, and I shall sleep aboard the *Franconia* tonight." Outside, the President was placed in the lead Packard, with Anna beside him. Mike Reilly was up front with the Russian driver. The motorcade climbed toward the mountains as the Russians and British stood in the driveway waving.

The Americans were in two parties. FDR was being driven (with Averell Harriman and his daughter) along the rocky coast road west and then north to Balaklava where, almost a century before, the British and the Russians had fought a great battle. The legendary charge of the Light Brigade had occurred. The main part of the American group, including Harry Hopkins and his son, were in limousines threading the passes through Krymskiye Gory toward Simferopol, a railroad town in the center of the island. The Russians said they had a heated train waiting at the station. The Americans could sleep in the cars—ornate because they had last been used by the royal Romanovs in 1913. Before dawn the train would take them to Saki. There they could rejoin the President.

Roosevelt didn't tarry at Balaklava. It was dusk and there wasn't much to see. There was a long slope. Swale grass and other growth had replaced the gallant dead. He moved on to Sevastopol, a sizable city. As they drove through the rubble of the streets, Mr. Roosevelt's mouth hung open as he swung his head from side to side, studying the destruction. It was complete. Of the thousands of buildings in the port city, six were intact. The others yawned at the darkening sky. The party, somewhat depressed, motored out to the dock. The supply ship *Catoctin*, fat and lazy, was dressed for the President. The ship's complement stood on the forepeak in rows. A small deck gun fired a monotonous salute. Mr. Roosevelt, wheeled up the gangway by two Secret Service men, was piped aboard by a boatswain's mate. He was introduced to the officers and said he hoped there were some good Texas steaks in the ship's refrigerators. There were.

Stettinius and Steve Early remained at Livadia, busy working over the absolutely final drafts of the final drafts. When the last word of the last despatch had been sent on the land lines to the *Catoctin,* Freeman Matthews asked the Secretary of State, "Our last message has been sent. Can I cut the connections to the ship?" "Yes," said Stettinius. He smiled benevolently at the press secretary. "The last work of the conference has been finished." It was complete; the last servant had been tipped; the last repast would be devoured by the State Department group within the hour; the lights at Livadia, Vorontsov and Koreiz would wink out one by one; the last automobile would turn away from Yalta.

Churchill would sup in the main dining room aboard the old Cunarder *Franconia,* regaling Sir Alan Brooke and Sir Hastings Ismay with intimate observations of the conference. At midnight J. V. Stalin and his entourage would be aboard the huge armored train which would spin its drivers northward through the snows. Harry Hopkins, pale and bent, waited on the Simferopol railroad platform for someone to unlock the ornate coaches and permit him to hide under blankets from the freezing wind. Aboard the *Catoctin,* General Pa Watson was warm, but he was in sick bay, still depressed and suffering over Hopkins' demand that he give up his room to Winston Churchill. And the Prime Minister, shaking his head sadly as he sipped brandy, said, "Poor Neville Chamberlain believed he could trust Hitler. He was wrong, but I don't think I'm wrong about Stalin." In his cabin, the President was scribbling on a sheet of paper:

Dearest Babs: We have wound up the conference—successfully I think and this is just a line to tell you we are off for the Suez Canal and then home but I doubt if we get back till the 28th. I am a bit exhausted but really all right.

I do hope all goes well. It has been grand hearing from you and I expect another pouch tomorrow.

Ever so much love.

Devotedly,

F.

The twelfth was Lincoln's birthday. If it occurred to anyone in the President's party, it was not noted. The Chief was a man in a hurry. He was opposed to flying, but he was even more adamant about flying at night. Today, he said, he would reach Egypt, and by "today" he meant daylight. He was out of bed early, tired and elated. His valet bathed and dressed him. Dr. Bruenn examined FDR. The physician was too much of a professional to say that he was surprised that the President had sufficient strength to live through the interminable debates, the impossible dinners and the enervating hours. At breakfast Steve Early told him that the final words of the Yalta Communiqué had left the *Catoctin* at midnight. The amended time for simultaneous release in the three capitals was 4:30 P.M. The President guessed it would be well received. The three powers had worked with energy and some conciliation to reconcile the affairs of the world in eight days. Admiral McIntire said he didn't see how the Free World could greet it with anything except prolonged applause.

Admiral Brown, naval aide, brought Mr. Roosevelt up to date on the day's events. The coast road between Sevastopol and Saki had been bombed by the Germans when they left and there was danger of rockslides. They would have to motor inland to Simferopol, then back out to Saki—about 70 miles. At Saki the Russians advised Brown that there would be a guard of honor and a band. The President would be expected to ride up and down the rows of soldiers. The C-54s were fueled and ready. They would fly south, no higher than 9,000 feet on Admiral McIntire's orders, across the Black Sea, into Turkey, on a course near Ankara, then across the Mediterranean to a U.S. military airport 18 miles south of Ismailia in Egypt. The distance would be a thousand miles, flying time about five hours. Admiral Hewitt had provided picket ships on the route across the Black Sea and the Mediterranean. Everything had been prepared

The first faint streaks of light were on the wreck-strewn harbor when the President was carried down the gangway at 6:55. He took the salute of Vice Admiral Batistii and shook hands with the Russian as he was lifted into his car. The drive over the cold and damp mountains endured for three and a half hours. FDR sat huddled in his great Navy cape, glancing at the scenery, leaning back against a corner of the car to close his eyes now and then. At 10:25 he was at Saki. The royal train stood nearby. Harry Hopkins, who had nearly frozen to death on the platform at Simferopol the night before, appeared before the drawing room occupied by Edward Stettinius. He was in pajamas and barefoot. "If I ever see a foreigner on a station platform in America again," he said owlishly, "I'll show him the washroom and give him a drink." Ed, who found it easy to laugh at any joke, shook his head sadly. He could see the wretched condition of the President's adviser; Hopkins couldn't. McIntire had kept Hopkins in bed throughout the Yalta Conference, except for plenary sessions and private conversations of the Big Three.

It was obvious that he was weaker and sicker. So was the President. And Pa Watson. They were like wraiths conscious of historic roles, unwilling to rest in the wings. Roosevelt had three four-engine planes. One loaded with cargo and two Secret Service men was off at 8:00 A.M. When the formalities and salutes had been concluded, the President said he would like to board the Sacred Cow at once. The rear cage was lowered; his chair was backed on; and, waving, he was raised into the belly of the ship. He had made his farewells to Stettinius, the Harrimans and Ed Flynn. The boss of the Bronx had accepted FDR's tip to fly to Moscow with the others to see what he could do to help those who believed in God and wished to worship. "We," the President had told him, "are anti-Atheist."

At 10:55 A.M. two American planes were at the head of the runway. The Russian band was still playing, but the roar of all the engines smothered the music. The President's Sacred Cow started rolling. Aboard were Anna, Admiral Leahy, Admiral McIntire, Admiral Brown, General Watson, Commander Bruenn, Chief Steward Arthur Prettyman and two Secret Service men.

Mr. Roosevelt was buckled in his seat. In a few minutes, the plane was almost out of sight, climbing, as the Number 2 plane rolled down the runway. Aboard this one were Harry Hopkins, Steve Early, Chip Bohlen, Lieutenant Commander Fox, Lieutenant Rigdon, some cooks and stewards and six Secret Service agents—Rowley, Beary, Hipsley, Dorsey, Campion and Hanam.

Roosevelt was out an hour when the man who was chasing him was hunched in fear. Samuel Rosenman was flying from Marseilles to Naples. He had orders to join the President and help him with his Yalta speech, but he didn't know where Roosevelt was. Orders had been out for him to fly from London to Marseilles, and from Marseilles to Naples. The C-47 was a twin-engine plane with a cruising speed of 180 miles per hour. His two pilots were young. Sammy the Rose told them he didn't fancy being in the air. The co-pilot said that he didn't mind being in the air; he didn't care much for being knocked out of it. He pointed below. "Corsica," he said. "German fighter plane bases are to our left." The judge tried to think of something to say. "Today is my birthday," he shouted. The pilot smiled. "Today is my wedding anniversary." Nervously, Rosenman said, "Let's celebrate." He got some chocolate bars from his bag, the pilots found some bottles of soda. All three chomped and swigged, looking nervously toward mainland Italy.

The judge thought it was a happy birthday when he landed. He reported to Admiral Hewitt and showed his orders. "The most convenient way for you to join the President," Hewitt said, "would be to join me aboard *Memphis.* We're sailing for Algiers to wait for him."

At 2:30 P.M. American Lightning fighters picked up the President's plane at sea off Beirut and formed arrows above and flanking the C-54. They escorted it to Deveroir Field, which was being dismantled. It was located near the Suez Canal. Roosevelt was met by S. Pinckney Tuck, American Minister to Egypt, and a party of Air Force officers. On orders, honors were sparse. The President and Mrs. Boettiger were driven to the Suez Company landing. An admiral's barge with lace curtains bobbed at the dock. The President was carried aboard and his face lighted with interest as the boat cruised across the canal to Great Bitter Lake. There, the huge great hulk of *Quincy* stood at anchor against a background of desert sand. For Roosevelt, and for all those with him, including Mike Reilly, it was good to be safely aboard the heavy cruiser again.

No one in his party pretended to know why he wanted to meet the three kings—Farouk of Egypt, Haile Selassie of Ethiopia, and Ibn Saud of Saudi Arabia. In an offhand way, he had said he was doing it because he believed in "personal diplomacy, and I may not get over here again." He did not tell his Secretary of State what he proposed to discuss—to ask or to give. It could not have been a desire to go sightseeing, because FDR expressed increasing anxiety about the long time he had been away from Washington. He spent a few minutes talking to Captain Senn about the other ships at anchor, H.M.S. *Virago* of the British Navy, and two captured Littoria-class Italian battleships.

The President retired to his cabin. Far to the south, the U.S. destroyer *Murphy* was in the Red Sea heading for Great Bitter Lake at flank speed. The *Murphy* was on a presidential mission: to pick up King Ibn Saud at Jidda, the port nearest to Mecca, and bring him to Roosevelt aboard the *Quincy*. The Navy considered the voyage top secret and referred to it as *"Murphy* Mission to Mecca." The commander of Destroyer Squadron Seventeen, Captain John S. Keating, was aboard to give the ship some rank. On the surface, it was a routine assignment. There were some complications, however. Ibn Saud was old, infirm and arthritic. At Jidda the *Murphy* officers visited the American Minister, Colonel Eddy, Marine Corps Retired, and had to make a call on Sheikh Abdullah Sulayman, Minister of Finance, to detail the courtesies to be extended to His Majesty. Captain Keating said that the King could have his cabin; the commander of the *Murphy* surrendered his; four wardroom staterooms were vacated by junior officers—all of whom would sleep on deck on fold-ing cots. The Minister was pleased.

When Ibn Saud arrived at the pier, he was too weak to walk up the gangplank. A genius suggested lowering the whaleboat, putting the King in it and hoisting him to the deck. This was done. His Majesty, turbaned in checkered cloth with a braided band around his forehead, wearing a deep blue cloak, was hoisted up amid the salutes of 40-caliber guns, answered by Arab shore bat-teries. The King walked slowly around the deck and asked if a large tent could be erected on the forecastle, where he and his officers could eat and pray in privacy. The tent was brought from shore. Some native barges approached. Live goats were hauled up the fantail. An Arab slave tied them to stanchions. None of the petty officers could speak Arabic, but with the aid of sign language, it was made clear that the goats, one by one, would be strung from the jackstaff, where their throats would be slit and the animals eviscerated before cooking. It was obvious by the manners of the goats on the deck that they were apprehensive.

The King, it seems, did not plan to travel alone. In the boarding party were Emir al Saud, brother of the King; Mohammed al Saud, son of the King; Emir Man-sour al Saud, son of the King; the Minister of Finance; the Deputy Minister of Foreign Affairs; the Privy Coun-sellor; the King's physician; an astrologer and fortune teller; the leader of the palace prayers; commander of the King's guards; Mohammed Abdul Djther, radio op-erator to the King, who tried to take over the *Murphy*'s radio shack; an interpreter and personal monitor of all English broadcasts; Sirag Dhahran, official food taster; a chamberlain; a valet; a purse bearer; chief server of ceremonial coffee; an assistant chief server; ten guards with daggers; three valets, one for each prince; nine slaves, porters and scullions.

The *Murphy* cast off from Jidda, heading north looking as though she had grown a great white boil on her bow. Ibn Saud told Captain Keating that this was his first trip away from his country. The captain assigned a petty

officer to point out the sights as the ship hugged the
Hejaz coast. A special track chart was made for the
King, so that he could see where he had been, where
he was, and where Roosevelt was. After he was aboard
a few hours, His Majesty became bored, and said he
was a warrior, nothing more. Keating had the 40-caliber
guns fired for the King's "amusement," dropped depth
charges, launched explosive cans from K guns, and gave
the King a personal tour of the torpedo mounts. Goats
were slain; guts dried on sunny decks; the tent blew
down; the rancid odor seemed to come forward to the
bridge faster 'than the *Murphy*'s speed could blow it
back.

Ibn Saud was a vaguely suspicious man. He had ten
ranking members of ten Arab tribes aboard, and it was
difficult to say whether they were guests or hostages.
Mohammed Abdul Djither manned a radio circuit on
the ship and manned the *Murphy*-to-Mecca circuit. The
man in charge of Saudi Arabia in the absence of the
King was Prime Minister H.R.H. Prince Faisal. Every
half hour, day and night, he was asked in international
code, "O.K.?" A few minutes later would come the response, "O.K." There were five occasions for prayer each
day. Each time one was due the Deputy Minister of
Foreign Affairs would ask the navigator of the *Murphy*,
"Which way Mecca?" The officer would point. The King's
party would squat on rich rugs, face in the right direction
and utter their lamentable prayers. Two days later, when
the huge bulk of the *Quincy* was seen to starboard, the
officers of the *Murphy* murmured their own prayers.

The President was asleep on his darkened cruiser
when, at 10:30 P.M. Egyptian time, the air waves around
the world began to crackle with the message of Yalta.
It was late afternoon in the White House when Jonathan
Daniels passed out mimeographed copies of the agreement to press correspondents. It was late night in London
when *The Times,* the *Daily Mail* and BBC began to
study copies of the agreement. At a half hour before
midnight a condensed version was given to *Pravda* in

Moscow. Radio Berlin picked up the radio messages, but remained silent until the State Propaganda Department could find a way of ridiculing it and, at the same time, terrifying German citizens into a realization that unconditional surrender would mean dismemberment of the nation and enslavement of its manpower in subhuman Siberia.

Two hours before the worldwide release, American Ambassador Jefferson Caffery waited in an anteroom of the Élysée Palace for a personal interview with General Charles de Gaulle. His was the sensitive assignment: to acquaint the proud and aloof Provisional President with the accomplishments of Yalta and at the same time invite him to participate in world affairs as a fourth great power. Earlier, a message from Stettinius to Caffery had been sent from the *Catoctin* to Paris. In sum, it stated that the following message came directly from the Big Three for de Gaulle:

1. Quote: You will observe that the communiqué which we are issuing at the end of this conference contains a Declaration on Liberated Europe. You will also see that, in the last paragraph of the Declaration, we express the hope that your government may be associated with us in the action and procedure suggested. Had circumstances permitted, we should have greatly welcomed discussion with you of the terms of this Declaration. The terms are, however, less important than the joint obligation to take action in certain eventualities; and we feel that it is of the highest importance, in the interests of Europe, that the Provisional Government of the French Republic should agree jointly with her three allies, to accept such an obligation. Signed Winston Churchill, Franklin D. Roosevelt and J. V. Stalin. Unquote and end of first telegram.

2: Quote: We have been considering the question of the control of Germany and have come to the conclusion that it will be highly desirable for the Provisional Government of the French Republic, if they will, to accept responsibility for a zone of occupation and to be represented on the Central Machinery of Control. We should be glad to learn that the

French Government are prepared to accept these respon-
sibilities. Signed Winston S. Churchill, Franklin D. Roose-
velt, and J. V. Stalin. Unquote and end of second telegram.

The tender nature of Caffery's job was of time and
association. He was ordered to coordinate his efforts
with the British and Soviet ambassadors, and to bring
them with him if they desired. Second, he was to carry
his olive branch at precisely the moment that the doves
of peace were twittering in the communiqué. Caffery
did his work well. He read both the communiqué and
the Big Three telegrams in tandem, as de Gaulle sat
in his office behind a desk. The sensitivity was further
increased by the knowledge that two of the Big
Three—Roosevelt and Stalin—felt that France, by not
fighting valiantly in May 1940, had almost lost the
continent of Europe to the Germans. Both had little
respect for the French. In addition, they knew in advance
that de Gaulle would express no gratitude for France's
elevation to Permanent Member of the Security Council
as the "fourth great power"; nor was it at all certain
that he would accept a zone of occupation in Germany
and membership on the Allied Control Commission.
Because he had not been invited to Yalta as an equal
member, he could, in pique, turn France's back to the
future.

Caffery, however, did well. De Gaulle nodded throughout the reading, and seemed mildly gratified that France's
great role in history had been recognized. He would
not assent to the proposals at once; he would like to
discuss them with his Cabinet. On the other hand, he
softened his intransigent attitude toward Roosevelt.
He told the Ambassador that he presumed the President
would go home by ship. If so, he hoped the vessel would
stop at Algiers or Oran. He would like to confer privately
with Roosevelt. Caffery sent the good news to the map
room of the White House the same night. It was not
a *rapprochement;* perhaps *détente* approximates the
truth.

The world, with the exception of Axis countries, was

gladsome with the news of the great conference. The applause was deafening and almost universal. One of the slight exceptions was aboard the Cunard liner *Franconia*. Winston Churchill was staging a long, expansive lunch with Sarah, Anthony Eden, Sir Alec Cadogan and Field Marshal Alexander. The guests ate. The host talked. "P.M. in very good form," Cadogan wrote, "making a frightful noise at lunch." Alexander, a tall, mustachioed general in charge of the American Fifth and British Eighth armies in Italy, was pleading with Churchill that, as provinces were liberated, "we must do the best we can to help the Italians." The Prime Minister disagreed. Alexander recited the sense of the Declaration on Liberated Europe. For a mild man, Alexander became belligerent. This, he said, is what we are fighting this war for—to secure liberty and a decent existence for the peoples of Europe. "Not a bit of it!" shouted Churchill. "We are fighting to secure the proper respect for the British people!"

World opinion was at variance with the Prime Minister's. Commentator Raymond Gram Swing burbled: "No more appropriate news could be conceived to celebrate the birthday of Abraham Lincoln." The influential New York *Herald-Tribune* noted editorially: "the conference has produced another great proof of Allied unity, strength and power of decision." The Philadelphia *Record* called it "the greatest United Nations victory of the war." Soviet officers in Moscow lamented, "But for Britain and America, the whole of Europe would now be ours." *The New York Times* claimed Yalta would "justify and surpass most of the hopes placed on this fateful meeting." The Washington *Post:* "The President is to be congratulated on his part in this all-encompassing achievement." The Baltimore *Sun:* "The decisions justify high hopes for the future." Former President Herbert Hoover said, "It will offer a great hope to the world." Radio commentator William Shirer called it "a landmark in human history." H. V. Kaltenborn said, "A complete success." Republican Senator Arthur Vandenberg was dazzled to the point of stating that the communiqué "reaffirms basic principles of justice and undertakes for the first time to complement them by direct action." *Time* magazine, which had almost a week to reflect, crowed: "All doubts about the Big Three's ability to cooperate in peace as well as in war seem now to have been swept away." Comment around the world represented a majestic sweep of triumph and security. Statesmen and editors were too war-weary to ask themselves if there were any problems unmentioned in the communiqué, or if, perhaps, it was a crude soldering of three antagonistic ideologues which would fall apart when the weight of peace fell upon it. In the White House, William Hassett wrote: "The fly in the ointment is the acceptance, obviously at the insistence of Stalin, of the Curzon Line as the boundary between Russia and Poland. Stalin also takes over Yugoslavia and thereby will control Europe from the Vistula to the Adriatic. Here is woe enough for the President. However, the communiqué is commended widely by press and radio and in the Congress."

Stettinius, who, in concert with Roosevelt and Hopkins, considered the Yalta Conference to be a resounding success, jotted what he regarded as Russian concessions: she accepted the American formula for voting in the United Nations, thus breaking the Dumbarton Oaks impasse; backed off from a demand for 16 votes in the Assembly to three; agreed to allow nations who did not declare war on the Axis until March 1, 1945, to become original members; agreed to closer cooperation between military staffs; surrendered on the matter of French participation in a German zone of occupation, membership on the Control Commission, and permanent status in the Security Council; allowed settlement of Poland's western border to be postponed; agreed to "free and unfettered elections" in Poland; retreated from her demand that $20 billion be mentioned in the German settlement. Returning to the Polish situation, the Secretary of State reiterated that it was not a question of what Churchill and Roosevelt would permit Russia to do, but "what they could persuade the Soviet Union to accept. . . ."

Ed was not willing to concede that, when FDR said, "I got what I came here for," he was referring to the pledge of a Soviet attack on Japan, or that the acceptance of the U.N. organization was Roosevelt's monument to himself. These things, as Stettinius and others in the President's party agreed, were "most important." The victory lay in drawing the warriors together around a table to discuss, to concede. Everything else was negotiable. FDR kept the main goals in sight at all times, and paid exorbitant prices for them. He did not appear to realize that Churchill as well as Stalin was his ideological enemy. He had force-fed Britain for so long in food, munitions, and men that FDR looked upon Churchill as a dependent relation. Winston Churchill at all times was willing—as he had displayed in Moscow—to subvert his patron's political philosophy by dividing the European states with Russia. The Prime Minister never considered himself to be a citizen of the world. He was an Englishman.

At Yalta the Soviet Union, for the first time since 1917, was a "have" nation. With the exception of a final drive on Berlin, it had everything it needed in territory and influence which ranged through Hungary to the Slavic nations south. When Germany surrendered, Stalin's divisions could have traveled to the Far East and gobbled all of Manchuria without consulting Chiang Kai-shek. As the Japanese government had once organized a puppet government in Manchuria, so too could Stalin have made the same move—as he was engineering in Poland—and no power was strong enough to stop him. One of the subjects all three men feared to discuss was the European Advisory Commission, which was setting up zones of occupation in Germany. Russia had already been assured the largest slice, and had nothing to gain by bringing the matter to the table. Great Britain feared the Russian Bear, and was powerless to tame it; thus France, in a state of collapse, became important to England's continental ambitions. Churchill also feared that the United States would withdraw its military presence from Germany, leaving Great Britain alone. At no time did anyone, except the generals, mention how far each nation was to advance inside Germany. The Elbe River was used as an informal rendezvous point only because Generals Marshall and Eisenhower did not believe they could reach that point before the Russians invested it. Thus, when Germany collapsed, the Russians would have to retreat from their advanced positions to accommodate the Americans and the British. No one thought that, when defeat was inevitable, Germany would mass its remaining forces against the vengeful Russians, leaving the back door open to Eisenhower. For that matter, when the American admirals and generals said that the best estimate for victory in the Far East would be eighteen months after the collapse of Germany, no one weighed the value of the atomic bomb.

Roosevelt admirers called Yalta a triumph; his enemies referred to it as a defeat. It was both. He won a little, gave a lot. Personally, he was far removed from the vigorous champion of 1933. Fatigue and fear made him mellow and malleable. He made an error in seeing himself as the supreme arbiter between Stalin and Churchill; he was the rich target of two impoverished men. At moments when sparks were struck, he lapsed into stories which had but the barest relevance to the issue; at others he bargained shrewdly until he saw Stalin stand and rip the back of a chair—then he backed down a little at a time. In a childish way, he delighted in proving to Stalin that there could be no collusion between FDR and Churchill because he opposed and lectured the British Prime Minister at every opportunity. He was a man who despised treachery and deceit, and yet he permitted the Soviets to claim that the Big Three had no power to form a Polish government without consulting the Poles, while, on the other hand, he disposed of property belonging to a member of the Big Five—China. Even the final communiqué was designed to lull the watching world into believing that there was noble unity among Russia, Great Britain and the United States.

The *Quincy* swung at anchor in the late morning. The cruiser maintained radio silence, but operators were busy intercepting incoming messages for the President. All of them had been routed through the White House map room, and all had a similarity of superlatives. The congratulations and appreciation—even quotations from influential newspapers—were piled on the President's desk. At breakfast he smiled and sometimes chuckled. A few were read aloud by FDR to Admiral Leahy and Anna. After all the hard bargaining, he enjoyed the prolonged applause.

At 11:30 A.M. in weather chilly for the 31st parallel, Leahy and Mike Reilly met an incoming plane from Cairo. An honor guard of U.S. Marines stood to attention as the portly figure of Farouk, King of Egypt, descended, followed by the Royal Chamberlain and U.S. Minister Pinckney Tuck. Farouk, a round young man unblinking behind large sun glasses, wore the uniform of an Admiral of the Fleet. He was twenty-five, and spoke British English.

Roosevelt received him sitting behind a five-inch gun mount. There was a small round table, some wicker chairs and Persian rugs scattered underfoot. His Majesty seemed as eager as his Chamberlain to learn the purpose of the visit. He was cordial, almost deferential. The President smiled, waved his cigarette holder and spoke of future trade. Farouk seemed bewildered. Egypt, said FDR, was a grand and ancient land. He would like the King to know that Egypt had been in his thoughts often. He mentioned how much long-staple Egyptian cotton the United States had bought from Egypt in the war. The King nodded. He knew. Grow more of it, FDR said. The conversation became a monologue. Roosevelt said that, when the war was over, there would be a great deal of tourist travel to Egypt. Millions of Americans would want to see the great Nile and the great pyramids, not to mention the Sahara Desert. Farouk looked to his Chamberlain for guidance. He agreed that tourism would be good for his country, and Egypt would welcome the Americans.

After an hour lunch was served in the President's cabin. Conversation was animated and friendly. At 1:30 P.M. FDR said he would sit in the sun while naval officers escorted the King and his party on a tour of the *Quincy*. Once again Roosevelt was exercising his right to his man-to-man diplomacy, but he could not think of much to say to Egypt except about long-staple cotton and tourism. At 2:30 the two men were again on deck speaking about their countries. Again Roosevelt did the talking; the youthful King did the smiling and nodding. At 3:30 Farouk took his leave. FDR gave the King copy number 14 of his inaugural address, suitably framed, and told him that the United States would, in the near future, give His Majesty a twin-engine C-47 plane as a memento.

From 3:30 until 5:00 P.M. Mr. Roosevelt was in his cabin, responding to pouch mail, dictating letters to Rigdon. At 5:30 he was again sitting in his deck chair as Emperor Haile Selassie of Ethiopia, Lion of Judah, came aboard with a party of six. His Imperial Majesty was five feet three inches tall, a dark, woolly-haired man with strong dark eyes and a solemn dignity. He had been flown 1,400 miles from Addis Ababa by the American Minister, John K. Caldwell, and it was obvious that he was anxious to learn the purpose of the meeting. The President began the conversation by observing that the Emperor was wearing an off-white cape while he was wearing a dark blue one. The little man sat stiffly on the edge of his chair waiting. He spoke French and English, but chose to speak to the President in his native tongue, Amharic, through an interpreter. This slowed the conversation.

Roosevelt said that the speed of the airplane had brought Ethiopia closer to the outside world, and he hoped that "our two countries will get to know each other better." Had the Emperor been of a bitter turn of mind, he might have mentioned that his experience with planes was confined to Mussolini's Italian bombers, which had wrecked his capital and killed many Ethiopians. It was not mentioned. The President thanked the Emperor for donating land and buildings for an American Legation in Addis Ababa. Haile Selassie said that great improvements had been made in his country throughout the war. He would like to see relations between the two countries improve, and he would do whatever he could to further this ambition.

After thirty minutes of cordiality, His Imperial Majesty and party were taken on a tour of the cruiser. This one lasted twenty minutes. Roosevelt entertained the party at tea in his quarters. Again the conversation was diplomatically innocuous. At 7:00 P.M. Haile Selassie prepared to leave. He presented the President with a solid gold cigarette case and a gold-plated globe. FDR thanked him and, smiling, said he had gifts for His Imperial Majesty but could not deliver them by hand; they consisted of four command and reconnaisance cars. The Emperor bowed, thanked his host gravely and left ship under a night sky.

In Berlin Adolf Hitler sat in the Führerbunker reading digests of German reports on the conference at Yalta. He summoned Lorenz, his press secretary. He said he was disappointed in the German reaction to the Yalta Conference. It was too weak. "Those warmongers in Yalta must be denounced," he said loudly, "so insulted and attacked that they will have no chance to make an offer to the German people." Albert Speer sat, listening in silence. "Under no circumstances must there be an offer," Hitler said. "That gang only wants to separate the German people from their leadership. I have always said: 'Surrender is out of the question.' History is not going to be repeated."

In Washington pundits pronounced the United States happy over the Yalta Conference, mainly because the peace-keeping machinery of a United Nations had been organized. The White House released the names of the American delegation to the first meeting: Cordell Hull as Senior Adviser; Edward Stettinius, Chairman;

Republicans Arthur Vandenberg and Harold Stassen as delegates; Democratic Representative Sol Bloom, educator Virginia Gildersleeve and Republican Representative Charles Eaton of New Jersey as delegates. Roosevelt was being mentioned as a truly great President, one who would rank with George Washington and Abraham Lincoln. Stories of FDR's suspected illnesses disappeared from the press. To scores of millions of Americans, his well-remembered struggle against the economic depression; his arming of the Army and Navy before America was attacked; his superb leadership in a war beyond two vast oceans, leading to victory, made him more than a man. He was close to sainthood in the public eye, and, when Sunday rotogravure sections published his smiling face, it was pasted on stiff cardboard and framed, to hang in many a living room.

On the morning of Saint Valentine's Day Roosevelt breakfasted with Anna. A deck officer knocked, came in and said the U.S.S. *Murphy* was approaching from the south. The President smiled. He gave Anna a choice: she could confine herself to her stateroom, or she could go to Cairo and shop for some gifts. She chose shopping. She asked her father why she couldn't remain aboard to meet King Ibn Saud. "This king," he said, "is a Móslem, a true believer. He has lots of wives. However, the Moslem will not permit women in his presence when he is talking to other men. Sis, when he sees such a woman, he confiscates her." The President slipped a spoonful of peaches and cream into his mouth. Mrs. Boettiger was properly shocked and left the *Quincy* within half an hour.

At 11:30 FDR was taking his leisure behind the gun turret when Mike Reilly and Harry Hopkins asked him to "come around the other side and take a look." The President rolled his wheelchair over the rugs, and, with cigarette holder jutting, navigated around the mount. There, crouching like spies, were Hopkins and Reilly. They pointed. The President peeked carefully and saw the destroyer *Murphy* inching to port-side against the

big cruiser. The *Murphy* was indeed a strange sight.
The destroyer's forward deck was covered with rich
oriental rugs. A tent flapped idly on the bows. King
Ibn Saud sat high on the superstructure in a gold chair,
his robes swirling in the breeze. His guard, armed with
rifles and scimitars, manned the rail. A dead goat hung
from the jackstaff. Others bleated on the aft deck. A
radio officer on *Quincy* emerged to heliograph to the
Murphy: "Going nuts here. What does 'O.K.? O.K.'
mean?"

Roosevelt retreated. He did not want to be seen spying.
"Boss," said Reilly, wiping his eyes, "that's a sight to
see." The President wheeled back to his proper station
and waited. The King and seven princes and sheikhs
came aboard. U.S. Minister Eddy served as interpreter.
The gentlemen sat for an informal conversation, with
Hopkins sitting by to listen. Ibn Saud said that he was
old and infirm, but that he admired the aluminum
wheelchair the President was using. FDR said he was
delighted; he sent a Marine Corps officer to fetch the
spare he carried aboard. It was given to the King, who
tried it out at once and was impressed with its lightness
and mobility.

Two sick men faced each other. Roosevelt led off
by wondering if all the arid land in Saudi Arabia and
Egypt could not be made to flourish and bloom. The
King, in a most respectful manner, said he wasn't interested in the subject. He explained, with many gestures
of his right arm, that Mr. Roosevelt must understand that
he was a warrior—nothing more, nothing less. He had
spent a lifetime fighting tribes; now he was near the end of
his days. The thought of making deserts bloom was
a good one, but shouldn't there be a place for deserts?
The President said that the King had brought all the
dissident tribes together and had fashioned a great
kingdom; thought should be given to raising and selling
crops. The older leaders, such as we, Roosevelt said,
should point the way to a better standard of living to
the young. It was apparent, as the conversation gained
momentum, that Ibn Saud's reserve began to melt beneath

the charm of his host. The only strain imposed on
Roosevelt was that he knew he could not smoke, nor
could he serve a cocktail at lunch. The menu consisted
of rice, lamb stew and grapefruit. Ibn Saud enjoyed it.
He asked for two helpings of the rice and the grapefruit.

The party returned to the deck breezes. Roosevelt
said he was particularly interested in the Palestine question. The King leaned forward on his elbows and said,
"You mean Jews?" FDR nodded. It seemed shameful
to him, he said, that these unwarlike people had been
driven from many lands and had no country of their
own. The voice of the King was as soft as though he
were speaking of exporting sand. When peace comes,
he said, the Jews should be returned to the lands from
which they had been driven. This would keep them
separated from each other, Roosevelt said. He had information, he said, that three million Jews had been
killed in Poland. Ibn Saud nodded. In that case, he
said, there should be room in Poland for the resettlement
of three million Palestinian Jews.

To Harry Hopkins, the President appeared to be startled. He also felt that Roosevelt was naive in Arab-
Jewish problems. FDR said that the total number of Jews
was small compared to the number of Arabs, and, if the
Jews settled Palestine, they would present no problem
to the Moslem world. Ibn Saud looked him in the eye
and uttered one word, "No." It did not stop the President.
He said the Jews were industrious and would make good
neighbors. At no point did the King become rancorous.
He said that was precisely the trouble. The Jews wanted
to occupy a strip of land along the edge of the Mediterranean and, with the help of millions and millions in
American dollars and British pounds, would build farms
and cities. "Give the Arabs that much money and they
will do as well," he said. The President tried to speak.
Ibn Saud kept talking. The Jews are buying land all over
Palestine, he said. They have a Palestinian army "armed
to the teeth, not to fight Germans, but to fight Arabs." The
British, he said, had made a land commitment to the
Jews. The Arab world could not block it. However,
if the Jews moved beyond that promise—if they extended

their land holdings—the whole Arab world was watching. Jews would establish a culture entirely different from the Arabs, and eventually the Moslem world would have to fight it. As a true believer Ibn Saud would have to fight with the Arabs.

The further Roosevelt pursued the subject, the worse he fared. Once more he was appealing for simple justice in an unsympathetic atmosphere. Hopkins said later that Roosevelt was committed publicly, privately and by conviction to the cause of a Jewish homeland, but that old Ibn Saud had arrived prepared for the argument. The King said that the Jews had no more desire to "get along" with the Arabs than the Arabs wanted to live with Jews. Arabs preferred to die rather than live in proximity with Jews. The President said he had not explored the question of whether Jews desired to live with Arabs. In any case, His Majesty said, the hope of the Arab world lies in the sense of justice among the Allies, and particularly the United States. If the Jews confined themselves to the small area specified by the British, he thought that war could be avoided. If the Jewish underground army killed Arabs, war could not be prevented.

At this point, Roosevelt the professed Zionist seemed to reverse himself. He promised that the United States would do nothing to assist the Jews against the Arabs. It would be impossible, he pointed out, to prevent pro-Jewish speeches in Congress and in the American press, but, as Chief Executive, he would not interfere. Ibn Saud thanked Roosevelt and said the Arabs proposed to send a mission to the United States and England to explain the cause of the Moslem world. The President shocked Hopkins when he said he thought this would be "a very good idea because so many people in England and the United States are misinformed." The King dropped the subject. What was the American attitude toward French influence in Syria and Lebanon? Well, Roosevelt said, the French had given him a guarantee of independence for both areas and he would hold de Gaulle to his word. And if, Ibn Saud said, France should not leave these small countries? Then, FDR said, the United States would support Syria and Lebanon all the way, short of war. At Yalta he had reached an emotional plane where, against his earlier judgment, he found himself in agreement with whoever had his ear with the strongest argument. The great strong sense of righteousness was gone. When he listened to speeches in opposition to his view, he found merit in them.

He changed the subject, telling the King that he was a farmer. FDR was interested in farming and water resources. This had been his opening gambit, and he was back to it. He spoke of desert irrigation, tree planting and water power for vast Arab lands. He said he liked Arabs, and that His Majesty had the power to cultivate arid holdings and feed an increasing population. The King frowned at his interpreter. He said to tell the President that he appreciated the sentiments, but that he was a warrior all his life and understood little about agriculture. In fact, he felt no enthusiasm for it. Further, he said, why cultivate land if "this prosperity will be inherited by the Jews"?

The conversation wound down to an exchange of compliments and gifts. The King had the extra wheelchair, to the consternation of Arthur Prettyman. FDR gave His Majesty a fourth-term gold medallion and said he was sending a Douglas two-engine plane complete with American crew for His Majesty. Ibn Saud clapped his hands once. An aide gave him two large leather cases. Inside were four sets of Arabian attire for Roosevelt, a solid gold knife and a vial of perfume. He said he was sending separate gifts to the President's wife and daughter—complete harem attire. Admiral McIntire stepped forward with a small box and said, with the President's permission, he would like to present it to Ibn Saud's doctor. The Admiral explained that it was a new antibiotic called penicillin. Ibn Saud's physician asked if it was any good for venereal disease. "Yes," said McIntire. King and physician seemed impressed.

As the party reembarked on the *Murphy,* FDR advised His Majesty to use the destroyer to return to Jidda. Ibn Saud said he had a message from Churchill, who wanted to talk to him "tomorrow." As the *Murphy* cast off and backed down from the *Quincy*, the President told Harry Hopkins that he had learned more about the Arab-Jewish situation from Ibn Saud in five minutes than he had understood all his life. Later, Hopkins grinned his lopsided smile and said, "The only thing he learned was what all people acquainted with Palestine know, the Arabs don't want any more Jews."

The *Quincy* weighed anchor at 3:58 P.M. and her helm was swung north to clear the Suez Canal and Port Said on an overnight run to Alexandria. The President surprised the ship's company by asking to be carried below decks to shop in the ship's store. He was anxious to buy souvenirs. Afterward he asked to be wheeled to sick bay. There he sat beside the bed of General Watson. It was a sad meeting for two old friends. Roosevelt assured Pa that he was going to be all right, and Watson shook his head negatively. He reminded the Boss that he had often thought of being converted to Catholicism. Pa wondered if it was too late. Roosevelt expounded on the beauties and mysteries of all religions and advised his cherished friend and court jester to call the Catholic chaplain and do it at once. He reminded the General that this notion had been lurking in the back of his mind for a number of years. Why not do it now? Roosevelt was a practicing Episcopalian, a vestry-man at Hyde Park, and he felt comforted by the spiritual solace he derived from it. Why hesitate? The General said that Mrs. Watson was Catholic, and he would not want to rest in a place apart from her. That, the President said, was not a strong enough reason to convert. A man had to believe in a faith. The patient said he had always been attracted to Catholicism. As Roosevelt left, he patted his friend's arm, told him he would be all right, and, if he wished, Roosevelt would use his influence with the chaplain to speed up Watson's conversion. When FDR got back to his sea cabin, the smile had fled; the listlessness returned. A White House pouch of mail was on his desk, but he did not read it. He seemed engulfed in some secret meditation. He asked an orderly to request the ship's Catholic chaplain to see General Watson at once.

In Athens Winston Churchill stood on a platform in Constitution Square and addressed 50,000 Greeks who appeared to have been pacified by British soldiers. He spoke of darkness rolling away, a bright dawn coming. The essence was: "Speaking as an Englishman, I am proud of the part which the British Army played in protecting this great and immortal city against violence and anarchy. Our two countries have for long marched together along hard, dusty roads in friendship and in loyalty. . . . Greece forever! Greece for all!" The stout statesman remained for the ovation, then flew at once to Egypt to meet Roosevelt, and to have subsequent conferences with Farouk, Haile Selassie and Ibn Saud, in case the President had inflicted damage on their attitude toward the British Empire.

It was late at night when the *Quincy* sailed out of Port Said into the Mediterranean. The destroyers *Frankford* and *Baldwin,* which had been ordered to form an antisubmarine screen ahead of the cruiser, were not on station because the *Quincy* was early. Roosevelt was asleep when a response arrived by radio to his invitation to Eisenhower to join him at Alexandria: "Although I deeply regret my inability to meet you at the point suggested, I am sure that my absence from here at this time would be most unfortunate. Floods have held up an important plan and some changes will probably have to be made that no one except myself can authorize. I truly appreciate the courtesy of your invitation."

Nor was that the only disappointment. In Paris Ambassador Caffery was angry. Foreign Minister Bidault had informed him, in the afternoon, that General de Gaulle would like Roosevelt to understand that "it is not convenient for me to meet him at Algiers." Caffery bristled. He reminded Bidault that de Gaulle had sought the invitation to Algiers and had accepted it. "Yes," the Foreign Minister said, "I know he did. I have been doing everything to make him go but he has changed his mind and you don't know how stubborn he is." Caffery committed a forgivable indiscretion. He told Bidault that he knew why de Gaulle was sulking. It was because he had read the Yalta communiqué and "it did not mention him personally." The Ambassador returned to the American Embassy and sent a coded message via the White House map room to Roosevelt. De Gaulle had declined the invitation.

The *Quincy*'s log noted that, at 10:52 A.M. on February 15, a harbor pilot at Alexandria brought her to Buoy B–2. She swung silently on the tide amid heavy traffic. Oilers and cargo ships, in wartime gray, moved in and out of the submarine nets. Battleships, aircraft carriers and small destroyer escorts replenished fuel or hung high and exposed in drydock. The President was on the bridge early. Whistles and horns were blowing. Tugboats and barges chuffed between the anchorages. Ashore there was a glistening city of almost 700,000 persons, many of whom did not know that Alexandria had been founded by Alexander the Great in 332 B.C. The President knew it and, with his appreciation of history, might have wished to touch his foot ashore, but he was not to do so. He expected to see Churchill for lunch. In the early afternoon the *Quincy* would fuel up for a run to Algiers, homeward bound. The light cruiser *Savannah* was refueling nearby. So were the destroyers *Laub*, *Frankford* and *Baldwin*.

FDR had planned an easy day. It wasn't to be. Ten minutes after the *Quincy* had been moored, a small craft pulled up to the gangway. The visitors were Secretary of State Stettinius, who had completed his visit to Moscow in two days, Assistant Secretary Matthews, Chip Bohlen and Ambassador to Great Britain John Winant. All were still in an aura of contentment over Yalta. Roosevelt sat on deck and completed his talk with the group in forty minutes. As they departed, Rear Admiral Allan Poland, British Port Captain at Alexandria, came aboard for a courtesy visit. Five minutes later U.S. General Giles was aboard to talk with Admiral Wilson Brown.

There was a parade of small boats drawing up beside

the *Quincy*, and casting off. American Consul General Doolittle, stationed at Alexandria, felt that he should pay his respects. This also applied to the Secretary of the Legation at Cairo, Mr. Lyons. These were followed by British Vice Admiral Tennant, senior to Admiral Poland, who came alongside in his own barge with embroidered curtains. W. A. Eddy, the U.S. Minister to Saudi Arabia, spent fifteen minutes telling the President what Ibn Saud had to say after his departure. Prime Minister Churchill, who had flown early from Athens to Alexandria, was aboard the cruiser *Aurora* and made the trip across the bay with his daughter and Commander Thompson, his naval aide. A half hour later, at 1:00 P.M., another boat idled up with Major Randolph Churchill, who wanted to join his father for lunch.

At 1:15 P.M. Lieutenant Colonels Henry Myers and Otis Bryan were aboard to be presented to the President; they were the pilots of his Sacred Cow. Mr. Roosevelt did not sit to lunch until 2:00 P.M. As he ate, an officer told him that Lieutenant A. L. Conrad, White House courier, was about to depart for Washington. There was some mail still to be signed. The "F" in Franklin and the "R" in Roosevelt were decipherable. The remainder of the signature was a series of waving lines. The Prime Minister monopolized the conversation, which did not appear to displease Roosevelt. Churchill asked what the President got from the three wise kings, and the response was "Nothing." They had exchanged views about peacetime trade, but not much more. The Prime Minister received a gift, an album of photographs taken at the Second Quebec Conference. It was close to 4:00 P.M. when the Churchill group departed, the Prime Minister grasping Roosevelt's hand in both of his. Six minutes later, Captain Senn signaled his task group to get under way. The destroyers led the majestic procession, followed by the sleek *Savannah*, with the big *Quincy* bringing up the rear. Whistles tooted, sirens wailed. The *Quincy* responded to the courtesies with three long blasts. Then she was gone. On the *Aurora* Winston Churchill turned away from the ship's rail.

He said, "He has such a slender contact with life." Later, he confided to friends that, at the farewell, he could not keep his mind from all the meetings and messages between them. The Prime Minister figured that 1,700 Top Secrets had passed between them; in addition to meetings of state at Argentia, Washington three times, Casablanca, Teheran, two at Quebec and one at Yalta. It was pointless thinking, but Churchill could not help it. Later, he would write of the last visit: "His face had a transparency, an air of purification, and there was a faraway look in his eyes."

At sea, Captain Senn disposed his squadron properly and set speeed at 21.5 knots through the night. The sea was flat, and the only sound through the ship was a faint hum, like a tuning fork. In the dimness of his room, Pa Watson's head began to sag. A pharmacist's mate called Dr. Bruenn. He examined the General. Pa had sustained a cerebral hemorrhage. He was comatose. Bruenn, McIntire and the *Quincy*'s physician had all the equipment they required to care for the patient, but the damage was extensive, involving the entire right side. It was further complicated by hypertensive heart disease, a problem the President shared with Watson. When FDR heard the news, he was discouraged from visiting the patient. "He probably wouldn't recognize you." From that hour on, the *Quincy* became a quiet, almost a sad ship. As though trying to avoid his own thoughts, the President insisted that he would mix cocktails each night and, after dinner, his party would attend a motion picture—any movie—in Admiral Leahy's cabin. The first film was *None But the Lonely Heart*.

After lunch on February 17 Roosevelt signed a presidential order authorizing the Secretary of War to seize and operate the American Enka Corporation of Enka, North Carolina. Afterward, he sat on deck slouching in his Navy cape. Anna and Hopkins sat with him. They watched a destroyer come up over the horizon, in the Tunisian War Channel, and heel in a sharp turn to deliver mail to the ships in the group. It was not a White House pouch, merely mail for sailors. The President said he was glad to see Harry the Hop, who had been confined to his cabin. Anna pointed to the thin stream of smoke from the cruiser's funnels. It was lifting straight to the sky, indicating that the ship and the wind were moving at 24 knots in the same direction.

"Chip and I are getting off at Algiers," Hopkins said. The President frowned. "Why?" he asked. "Well, I'm sick. I mean really sick. I want to stop off and go to Marrakech and rest." FDR said that anybody could rest much more wholesomely on a sea voyage. "No, no," Hopkins said. "I can't rest on a ship. That's the problem." Roosevelt slumped back in his chair. Mrs. Boettiger went to her cabin. Later, she rejoined her father behind the gun mount. "Harry and Chip are going to leave us tomorrow," he said. She knew. It irritated her because she knew her father depended upon Hopkins, and, to a lesser extent, Bohlen, for help in the forthcoming Yalta speech. He had made up his mind that he would address a joint session of Congress when he got to Washington, and this had better be a good speech. To his daughter, the President looked annoyed—not ordinarily annoyed, but deeply hurt. "I am going to need a lot of help with that speech," he said. "I kept no notes." Bohlen had, but he was the only person who could decipher them. Anna, trying to be helpful, reminded her father that Jimmy Byrnes had kept notes in shorthand. Byrnes was in Washington. The notes could be transcribed and flown to the *Quincy*. He shook his head no. "I can't work with Byrnes," he said. With filial devotion, Anna went to the Hopkins cabin to entreat him to remain aboard and help her father. He was kindly, but intractable. "Truly, Anna," he said, "I am too sick to work. I mean it. And Chip is overdue for a vacation."

Anna tried argument. It wasn't fair to leave her father to write the speech alone. Hopkins knew how many persons usually worked on speeches, and how many drafts were typed. Everybody seemed to be sick or disinclined to help. "Tell your father to call Sam Rosenman in. He's in London and can fly down to Algiers and work on the speech all the way home." Hopkins didn't know that Sammy the Rose was waiting in Algiers. Anna surrendered. It did not seem possible that these two men, who had worked together for so many years, could part so abruptly when one needed the other. She thanked Hopkins and went back up on deck. "Hopkins won't budge," she told her father. He nodded. "Let him go."

It was Rosenman's desire to leave the President almost before he arrived. The judge wanted to rejoin his care-and-feeding-of-Europe group in London. At Naples he had studied a newspaper copy of the Yalta communiqué and, assuming that this was the substance of what had happened at Yalta, wrote a first draft of a speech. By the time Rosenman was in Algiers aboard the flagship of Admiral Hewitt, the first draft was complete, revised, reshaped, polished and ready. If, when he joined Mr. Roosevelt, the two of them could work over it—line by line—it might be acceptable before they passed the Strait of Gilbraltar. Sam Rosenman could say farewell to the President, and catch a plane back to London.

Rosenman, accompanied by a suitcase and a briefcase, was being driven to Navy B.O.Q. at Algiers in warm sunlight. He looked at the mosques, the minarets, the slums with interest. As his car passed the Hotel Aletti, he noticed three men sitting at a table on the lawn. They were Robert Nixon of International News Service, Douglas Cornell of the Associated Press, and Merriman Smith of United Press. They had been shuttled all over North Africa, waiting for the President. They knew there had been a big conference, and had been told that the cruiser would pick them up here, but the *Quincy* might have passed, en route home, days ago. When they saw the chubby face and curly hair of Samuel Rosenman, they knew that the President could not be far off.

The judge told them that Roosevelt would be along soon, but he knew no more than they. In the morning the four men were surprised to see the task force inch through the Algiers breakwater. At 10:01 the *Quincy* was moored to the south side of the *môle de pas-*

sageur. The *Savannah* berthed on the north side. The three destroyers anchored out in the roadstead. Within the hour Sam Rosenman and the reporters were aboard. So were Mike Reilly, Jim Rowley, Major Greer and others of the advance party. They would depart for a flight to Washington later in the day. Their work in Europe was complete. Mr. Roosevelt was reading and signing mail when the customary port visits commenced. Captain Senn had a chart plotted for the dangerous passage of the Strait of Gibralter and told Admiral Leahy that he would like to cast off no later than 4:00 P.M.

Before lunch, Roosevelt penned another note to his wife:

Dearest Babs: Headed in the right direction—homeward! All well, but still need a little sleep.

A fantastic *week. King of Egypt, ditto of Arabia and the Emperor of Ethiopia. Anna is fine and at the moment is ashore in Algiers. Give John and Johnnie my love. I hope to come to Washington when you say you are going to be there—one of those eight days.*

Devotedly,
F.D.R.

Rosenman was in the presidential cabin for a few moments of conversation about the speech. He left, saving his opinion until he returned to Washington: "He had lost a great deal more weight. He was listless and apparently uninterested in conversation. He was all burnt out." Ambassador Caffery flew from Paris to report personally on the de Gaulle debacle. He told the President that he was convinced that the French Provisional President had accepted the offer of a visit, and then declined, because de Gaulle had not been invited to Yalta. Roosevelt wagged his leonine head and smiled. It was strange, he said, that he had gone out of his way in his last State of the Union message to include France and de Gaulle in a favorable light; he had agreed to give France part of the American zone of occupation in Germany; he had voted to put France on the German Control Commission as a full member; he had invited France to become the fourth great power sponsoring the United Nations. "This," he said confidentially, "is something that will have to be taken care of later."

After lunch those who were leaving the ship stepped up to say good-bye. Mike Reilly and the others had turned away when Bohlen and Hopkins appeared. The President looked up gravely, held out a hand, and said, "Good-bye." There was no encomium, no good wishes, no "till-we-meet-again." Mr. Roosevelt was studying a paper he had prepared for release to the press; it was scathing in its treatment of General de Gaulle and France. Harry Hopkins had read it in his cabin, and wrote a note along the margin pleading with Roosevelt to be temperate, and not to lower himself "to a petulant level." The message was in the process of being softened when the two men left. Roosevelt did not look up from the papers. Later, he said that Hopkins left because he was "bored."

At exactly 4:00 P.M. Captain Senn turned his cruiser over to an Algerian pilot, Captain A. C. Samony, and used his escort vessels to clear the breakwater ahead of the *Quincy*. Once outside, they churned the water white at high speed and made circles, using their sound gear detection as the heavy cruiser slipped slowly out behind them. Senn signaled his group to take station, and set speed at 20 knots, course 273. The late sun was far ahead and to port in a golden stream of light when the President sat with Sam Rosenman and told him that they would have to work his speech out together. "Just the two of us," he said. The Boss impressed upon the judge that there was a great deal more to say than was in the official communiqué; also there was a great deal which could not be mentioned. He was not in the mood to work on it now, but, from time to time, he and Leahy and Rigdon would think of occurrences which would find places in the speech. Rosenman abandoned the notion of disembarking at Gibraltar. This, he felt, was going to be a long voyage.

In the morning the Rock of Gibraltar was sighted. Speed had been increased to 27 knots. At 11:40 the presidential party was surprised to find that the *Murphy,* after rendering departure honors to Ibn Saud, had overtaken the task group. Her decks and rigging were bright and clean. The crew of the *Quincy* was still making jokes as the *Murphy* racked up flank speed to take station ahead. Senn's plot worked out well. It was Monday and at 1:09 P.M. a junior officer noted "*Quincy* in Strait of Gibraltar." This was the danger area. The Germans knew that anything going into or emerging from the Mediterranean had to pass through the narrow strait, and it would be easy for Admiral Dönitz to have a wolf pack of submarines waiting. Senn had asked for heavy air cover by day. Two Venturas flew low ahead of the group, circling and searching. A squadron of P-38 Lightnings roared back and forth over the column. A slow-moving American blimp seemed to float along not much faster than the *Quincy.* The light cruiser *Savannah* was two miles behind *Quincy,* building up a fury of white water. Ahead was a full complement of seven destroyers dashing back and forth. A slow-moving minesweeper reported that two ships had been sunk in the strait the day before (Sunday, February 18) and had a submarine contact one hour ago. Eleven minutes later, Captain Senn, somewhat tense on the bridge, ordered all vessels up to 29 knots. In fifty-seven minutes his lookout reported Cape Spartel light to port, five miles. The *Quincy* was out of the strait, into the broad groundswell of the Atlantic Ocean.

It was 6:30 P.M. and chilly when Roosevelt invited the three pool reporters to his cabin. He would hold a press conference, but the journalists understood that there would be no way of getting the news to the world until the *Quincy* docked at Newport News, Virginia. To the three men, the President looked thin and tired, a man whose voice had weakened in volume, but who could still smile, still tell a story:

Three years ago, when I was first talking about the United Nations [the President looked to his left to make sure that Lieutenant Rigdon was taking the words], Winston said to me, "Where will you put it?" I said, "Not Geneva. Geneva's unlucky, has an unlucky record. I don't want to hold it in any location. I want everybody pleased." Although I don't think I will get it, I want to get a building like Al Smith's Empire State Building, just for the records and the records staff, and then have the conference meet half the time in one of the Azores islands. I was there once. In front of my house—I knew a Portuguese on San Miguel— had a great big house. He used to like to take me out on the front steps. There, right in front of me were royal palms and Norwegian spruce growing side by side. It's a wonderful climate.

Q. Wouldn't it turn into a resort after a while?

A. Not on the little island. I wouldn't let anybody on it. Not even the press.

Q. How did you like Russia?

A. Very much. I will give you a story on that. Yalta was Hollywood and our South rolled into one. We lived in what used to be the Czar's palace. He and his family had any number of very beautiful villas in the Crimea.

Roosevelt was rambling again, in his soft, gracious manner, and the reporters, enchanted out of their calling, did not seem disposed to ask incisive questions.

And when the Czar went out in 1917, the Soviets took over all the properties, and they turned them into a series of sanitoria and rest places. And if you were a Communist —if you needed a rest, had a cold—you made application and you were sent down there and you would be given a rest period there. The place was always apt to be filled with people. They ran from the Imperial Palace down to the small villas. Town of Yalta itself is filled with villas, and when the Germans came in and put bombs inside the villas, and blasted everything inside and then set fire to everything, the buildings were all gutted.

Q. Did that indicate that when they did it they felt they would not stay?

A. Yes . . .

Q. What can they do about getting reparations in kind from the Germans?

A. Get all they can.

Q. Will they have much to pay off with?

A. Yes, I think so. Got a lot of German prisoners . . . I would give anything in the world to write a funny story about Farouk and Haile Selassie and, on the second day, Ibn Saud, but I don't dare do it.

Q. We have heard stories of that, about the tents and so forth.

A. I hope they got some pictures showing the destroyer coming alongside, with the guard lined up the length of the forecastle, the King, a great big whale of a man, big proportions, sitting in a Louis Quinze chair, up on the forward gun deck, on a great pile of Turkish carpets. Yes, I believe we've got pictures of them.

Q. Do you think they could be released? Don't you think it would be a good idea to show the movies at our annual dinner? They would be the hit of the show.

A. Yes, I think it would be all right. I think we have gotten a movie in color. . . .

I have not even said to Sam what he said about the Jews. It was perfectly terrible. He doesn't mind the Jews there now, but he does mind the situation of the Jews that come there from Paris, London and New York. He makes all the difference in the world between them. The general feeling is that the Arabs want to be let alone. Do not interfere with the Arabs. Very interesting point of view. He is afraid that the Arabs will be controlled by the foreign Jews that come in. Says there's no way of keeping them in the bounds of Palestine. . . .

The three reporters, Robert Nixon, Merriman Smith and Douglas Cornell, were among the best in the United States. For weeks they had been starved for news as the Army moved them from place to place in North Africa. Now, in the presence of FDR, they sat as friends rather than adversaries, and they smiled and made small talk as he wandered from subject to subject. It might have been expected that each would have at least a page of questions already prepared: the single most powerful man in the world had just completed the greatest historic conference and it was their job to probe to find out what could be told beyond the words of the communiqué. There was a whole world of interrogation; even FDR's health could be considered a prime subject.

Instead, they asked personal assessments of Haile Selassie, Ibn Saud and his ceremonial coffee and food taster, and why it was the Algerians had no coffee but were percolating "charred date seeds." They asked about the *Quincy*'s course, U-boats and whether "they were laying there for us." Minutes later, one asked if, after the conference, the President could give "any real assurance [to the] American people and the rest of the world."

"Yes, I think so, but we have to win the war first. That is tacked onto everything we say: that we have to win the war first." He had explained to the reporters, that, when he got home, "I am thinking of going up to Congress, to the well of the House, sit at the table in the well, and have the broadcast from there."

FDR was asked if there would be another meeting of the Big Three. He said it would depend upon what was done at San Francisco on April 25. He amended this to state that San Francisco would be an organizational meeting, not a work meeting for keeping the peace. Nothing would be done, really. "Then we've got to go to Congress to get what we need. After that, I think they will have to go to work organizing. Might take a couple of months . . ." They spoke of Senator Vandenberg's acceptance as a member of the United Nations committee, although he insisted he would not be bound by any U.S. decisions. "He wants to be free to saw his head off," the President said. The men spoke of de Gaulle and Steve Early's temporary assignment to Eisenhower's headquarters and what a good job Jonathan Daniels had been doing in press relations while the President was away.

Merriman Smith said, "Thank you, Mr. President." The press conference was over. It had been a pleasant, uninformative chat. No one asked what would happen to Poland; whether Germany would remain intact after the war; what had been planned and promised for France, Italy, Bulgaria, Romania, Hungary, Czechoslovakia, Lend-Lease; why he had sought separate conferences with three kings; what did McIntire and Bruenn have to say about the state of the President's health; why had Russia been allowed to swallow the eastern half of Poland; how well did the military chieftains of the three nations collaborate on the prosecution of war; how he proposed to prosecute the Japanese war after Germany collapsed; was there any truth to the widespread rumor that Roosevelt would resign as President to become head of the United Nations? All of it was as friendly and complacent as the questions at Hobcaw ten months earlier.

The *Quincy* was in a long deep groundswell approaching the Madeira Islands on the morning of Tuesday, February 20. She was a gray ship in a gray sea under a gray sky. Her flaring steel bows lifted slowly, steadily, until they were pointed above the horizon. They held there for a moment and then crashed swiftly into the next trough. The spray curled inward in white veiling, shining the anchor chains and the big gun mounts. Anna was a good sailor. The pitching didn't bother her, or her father. They had breakfast together.

She waited until he had finished a steaming cup of coffee. Then she said it as gently as possible, "Pa Watson passed away this morning." The President looked up through his bifocals, the eyes appearing larger than usual. The jaw hung open. "About eight o'clock, they say." Like the ship, the President fell into a deep trough, but, unlike the ship, he did not rise again. He wallowed in misery. Throughout the years he had lost close friends, each of whom owned a small piece of his great heart, and each time he had sustained his sorrow in silence and turned his mind from it. But not this time. He sat looking like a man in confused thought, unable to admit the truth. The big husky, uncomplicated military aide and friend, the man who could make a tired President laugh, would never tell another story.

Sis and Sam Rosenman knew that FDR always lifted his big chin after these blows. When his mother had died at eighty-seven, he had acted as though it was totally unexpected, and he tried to avoid those who offered long condolences with old memories. Louis McHenry Howe was his political navigator and devil's advocate. The President could not spare Louis to eternity and the loss was felt for years. Missy LeHand, the pale, adoring, protective secretary, died and she too was an important voice in his life. Marvin McIntyre was a press secretary who could be entrusted with any assignment; he departed suddenly. Once, Gus Generich had been his New York bodyguard, and Gus could lift Roosevelt in or out of a car, and even carry him piggyback up a flight of stairs. Gus died. Few thought that the death of headmaster Dr. Peabody of Groton would affect the President. But few realized that Roosevelt had used Peabody as the father image he needed so badly. Peabody not only taught Franklin Roosevelt; he officiated at Roosevelt's wedding, prayed with him at inaugurations and was ready on the telephone or in person when FDR wanted some sage Yankee advice. The President never mentioned Dr. Peabody in conversations. He was a man afraid to stir the sediment of the mind.

Now Pa Watson lay dead under the steel deck and it was too much to bear. It was not that Pa was more important than the others; he was just one too many. The effect on Roosevelt was noticeable. He told Sam Rosenman that he "didn't feel like" working on the speech. This would be true today, tomorrow, the day after that and the day after that. Unlike his reaction to the other tragedies, this time he felt it impossible to stop talking about Pa Watson. Softly, sorrowfully, he told Sis about Pa, his loyalty, his burly protection of the President, his cascade of sparkling stories. When he wasn't talking about Watson, the President was in bed, reading. He slept later and later; he remained awake late reading. In the afternoons he wheeled himself onto

the ship's elevator and sat alone with Anna on the wing
bridge. There, she noticed, he did not speak. He smoked
cigarettes and stared at the unmoving horizon.

Late in the afternoon of the day it happened, Vice
President Harry S. Truman was presiding over the U.S.
Senate. A rumor spread through the corridors and was
whispered in the well from desk to desk. "Have you
heard? . . . The President is dead." Have you
heard . . . ? Truman rapped his gavel and appointed
a president pro tem and left the Senate. He hurried to
the office of the Secretary of the Senate, Mr. Lester Biffle. "I hear the President is dead," Truman said. "What
will we do? Let's find out what happened." Biffle called
the White House. Jonathan Daniels told him it was not
the President; it was General Watson. The news would
have to be kept in confidence because Mrs. Watson
had not been told, and FDR had sent a message that
there was to be no press release until he returned. Truman
felt relieved. An hour later he received a message from
Roosevelt routed through the map room. In it Roosevelt
asked Truman's advice about appearing before a joint
session of Congress to report on the Yalta Conference.
Truman gave it a moment's thought. "Tell him I think
it's a great idea."

At sea the President wrote out his own press release
on the death of the General: "The whole trip coming
back from the Mediterranean was greatly saddened
for me and all the members of the party by the death
of General Watson. This comes as a great personal sorrow
for me. He has been my military aide for twelve years
and my secretary for five years, and aside from our
joint work he has been my close friend and associate.
His death came very unexpectedly. He was in excellent
spirits on the trip over and at the Crimea Conference. . . ." Except, of course, for a violent argument
over a bed with another sick friend, Harry Hopkins.

Daniels sent FDR a message urging that the news
of the passing of Watson be released at once; otherwise,
the press would claim he was stretching wartime security
too far. Besides, the story was all over Washington.

Roosevelt didn't bother to respond to the message. Instead he sent one expressing his deep personal sorrow to Mrs. Watson at her home in Charlottesville, Virginia. He also told her that Pa had received the last rites of the Catholic Church. For the President these were days of silent melancholy. Sam Rosenman made notes: "I could not get the President to go to work on the speech. . . . He would stay in bed most of the morning, reading the books he had brought with him or looking over official reports. After lunch . . . he would go above to sit with his daughter on the top deck in the sun, quietly reading or just smoking . . . Sometimes Admiral Leahy and I went above to join him. Most frequently, we left him alone with his book—and his thoughts. . . . Day after day, as the *Quincy* steamed westward, the same routine was followed. The President rested continuously through the day and went to the movies at night."

The morose mood continued until Friday, February 23. The task group was one day's travel from Bermuda running at 20 knots along the 30th parallel. At breakfast the President called Lieutenant Rigdon. "Bring the boys in for a press conference at twelve-fifteen," he said. "I want to see you and the pouch about five-thirty. We'll work on some mail." He asked Anna what the movie would be for tonight. *"Going My Way,"* she said. When the pool reporters arrived, FDR, without waiting for a question, decided to discuss the Yalta Conference. He had also decided to stretch the truth toward the optimistic side:

"The conference hours at Yalta were not bad. We met in the afternoons, sometimes at four, sometimes at five, and continued through until eight or eight-thirty. It was tiring, a bit of a strain presiding over a thing like that. You have to keep awake all the time. On the general run of the picture, I think the public was quite right; also the press at home—virtually unanimously good—saying that it was a great achievment. You get that not only from the first reading but from subsequent readings. It's an extraordinary thing that there was so much unanimity in the whole of the conference. . . ."

The press conference would continue for an hour. The reporters learned nothing new about the United Nations; they understood the structure. They asked if Germany and Japan could ever become members of the U.N. "I hope so." This was not the page-one blockbuster that the journalists needed, so Roosevelt was asked if Germany and Japan would ever be permitted to rearm. "No. I hope for armament to be decreased all along the line, including the Big Five." "How soon?" "I am not a crystal gazer."

He was asked if there would be long-term occupation of Germany by American troops. This was a newsworthy question, and FDR appreciated American sensitivity on this subject. However, he appeared to have forgotten the new zones of occupation with the advent of France as an occupying power.

'I suggest that the first thing for us to do," he said, "is to win the war. We cannot crystal-gaze. We have not won the war yet. The original zoning plan was, roughly—this is old, not true now—was that Russia would occupy eastern Germany, England would occupy western and northwestern Germany, and that we would occupy the area from the turn of the Rhine at Mainz, south to and including Baden, Bavaria, and Württemberg, with a supply corridor to the sea at Bremen. But that was complicated, and has not yet been settled . . ."

Would Russia be asked to participate in the talks about Pacific problems? "I don't know."

Q. As far as the record stands now, they have not been asked?

A. Nobody has. I won't go into that now.

The reporters were trying hard to find a peg. What was planned for the two beautiful Italian battleships in Great Bitter Lake? Roosevelt didn't know. He asked that they be used to transport food from Africa to Italy, but the Navy said no, they were battleships. Would they be permitted to say that he made his trip on the *Quincy?* No. They could say a cruiser. If the military staffs of the Big Three agreed on closer cooperation, did that mean that the Russians were now members of the Combined Chiefs of Staff?

"Yes and no. The situation is, Russia will be in any discussions affecting her troops, but not in anything against Japan. They will have nothing to do with anything in the Pacific. It is an obvious fact that Russia has been neutral, and we will respect that neutrality."

He moved into a monologue about the death of "poor old Pa." Roosevelt expected that Watson would be buried in Arlington National Cemetery the day they arrived in Washington; there would be a mass at St. Matthew's Pro-Cathedral the following morning. The President would attend the burial. He spoke of the possibility of addressing a joint session of Congress on Friday, March 2. However, he wished the reporters would not speculate about it because he had to discuss this with congressional leaders.

The three interrogators realized that they represented all of the American press, and this would be the first press conference after Yalta. They asked why de Gaulle had not flown to Algiers to meet Roosevelt.

"If you say anything on it, say I would be glad to see him at any time. Right off the record, the poor, dear man, I am inclined to think, has no knowledge of what to do. It was a very bad break for him. Not from my point, but from his. He was all tied up in engagements."

Q. Do you recall when was the last time you appeared in person before Congress?

A. Last year.

Q. Are you sure . . . ? Wasn't it just before you went to Casablanca?

A. Yes. There was the question about France's interest in Indochina.

Once more, Mr. Roosevelt launched into a story:

This is very much off the record. For two whole years I have been terribly worried about Indochina. I talked to Chiang Kai-shek in Cairo, Stalin in Teheran. They both agreed with me. The French have been in there some hundred years. The Indochinese are not like the Chinese. The first thing I asked Chiang was, "Do you want Indochina?" He said, "It's no help to us. We don't want it. They are not Chinese. They would not assimilate into the Chinese people." I said, "What are you going to advocate? It will take a long time to educate them for self-government." He said they should not go back to the French. They have been there over a hundred years and have done nothing about educating them. For every dollar they have put in, they have taken out ten. The situation there is a good deal like the Philippines were in 1898. The French have done nothing about it. With the Indochinese, there is a feeling they ought to be independent but are not ready for it. I suggested at the time, to Chiang, that Indochina be set up under a trusteeship—have a Frenchman, one or two Indochinese, and a Chinese and a Russian because they are on the coast, and maybe a Filipino and an American—to educate them for self-government. It took fifty years for us to do it in the Philippines.

Stalin liked the idea. China liked the idea. The British don't like it. It might bust up their empire, because if the Indochinese were to work together and eventually get their independence, the Burmese might do the same thing to the King of England. The French have talked about how they expect to recapture Indochina, but they haven't got any shipping to do it with. It would only get the British mad. Chiang would go alone. As for the British, it would only make the British mad. Better to keep quiet just now.

The press was onto a good story, but all of it was off the record. Still, they pursued the sputtering fuse leading to the dynamite.

Q. Is that Churchill's idea on all territory out there; he wants them all back just like they were?

A. Yes, he is mid-Victorian on all things like that.

However, the President moved off course again, this time citing the difference between the British grasping for all the real estate they could hold, while Queen Wilhelmina and the Dutch were planning to grant Java its independence. "The Dutch marry the Javanese and the Javanese are permitted to join the clubs. The British would not permit the Malayans to join their clubs."

Churchill, a reporter observed, "seems to undercut the Atlantic Charter. He made a statement the other day that it was not a rule, just a guide."

The President: "The Atlantic Charter is a beautiful idea. When it was drawn up, the situation was that England was about to lose the war. They needed hope, and it gave it to them. We have improved the military situation since then at every chance, so that really you might say we have a much better chance of winning the war now then ever before. And when I get back to Washington I suppose people like Krock will write nasty articles about how much I always get scooped. That is perfectly true. But I think it is much better to get scooped than to talk all the time. Then there's the time element. The Prime Minister goes before Commons the day he gets home—breaks loads of stuff. People like Krock don't like it."

The Boss looked tired. His lunch was at hand. Admiral Leahy sat in the cabin, listening. Roosevelt nodded. There was one more question. "Do you remember the speech the Prime Minister made about the fact that he was not made the Prime Minister of Great Britain to see the Empire fall apart?"

Roosevelt smiled and wagged his head slowly. "Dear old Winston will never learn on that point. He has made his specialty on that point. That is, of course, off the record."

The President could not brace himself to work on the speech until the twenty-sixth. The task group had passed Bermuda to the south and turned west by northwest for Newport News, Virginia. At 4:00 P.M., still reluctant but with a sense that the work must be done now, he called Sam Rosenman into his cabin. He was sorry he had delayed it so long, but he was prepared to work until dinner, have a recess, then skip the nightly movie and work until he and the judge had a meeting of the minds on the text. He riffled through some notes he had kept, emphasizing to Rosenman that his role at Yalta was "as a mediator between Stalin and Churchill." The two had broad differences of opinion, FDR said, and it was his task to devise a compromise, or postpone a settlement. Of one thing he was certain: Yalta was the birthplace of the world he had dreamed of, prayed and hoped for most of his life. It would be a world in which the strong imposed peace on all nations. Whatever differences there were between countries could be debated in the Assembly.

As they worked over one paragraph at a time, the President interrupted to say that he believed in Stalin's sincerity. A large part of the Soviet Union was in ruins; it was to the advantage of the Communists to help maintain a world without conflict, a time to rebuild cities and farms, and most of all, the millions of youths who had been cut down in the inferno. "I understand Stalin, and he understands me."

If FDR had a fear, it was that the strong, anonymous men of the Kremlin might try to undo the work of Yalta. He didn't think that any coalition of Russians was strong enough to confront Stalin and subvert his agreements. But what if Stalin should die, or be flung from the seat of power? Sam Rosenman listened, worked hard with a pen, and submitted sentences and pages to the Boss.

As Rosenman said later, he knew that the President enjoyed flattery and expected it. He made his position at Yalta different from that of the other two: he was the mediator. Sam also knew that FDR was jealous of compliments paid to others. He did not want to be told that Winston Churchill was eloquent; the President might say it, but he smiled indulgently when his audience disagreed with him. As Sam said, "He liked so much to excel that he took almost as much pleasure in being told that he was a better poker player than someone else as he did in being told that Willkie was not as good an orator as he was; or that he was a better politician than Jim Farley."

The President was, in effect, dreaming his way through the speech. Time was now of the essence, and Rosenman, whose first draft had been declined out of hand, wrote a second and third in one day. The Boss studied each word, each phrase, hen-tracking them with his pen and admitting, with a sigh, that when he got to the White House, he would ask his son-in-law to help with the final. John Boettiger was not known to be a writer, but he had been publisher of Hearst's *Post-Intelligencer* in Seattle. Robert Sherwood was out of the country; Harry Hopkins was too sick to help. It seems awkward that he would choose Rosenman and Boettiger, two men who had not attended the Yalta Conference, and would have to be briefed in each area of contention and accomplishment. Jimmy Byrnes, who had shorthand notes of almost everything said at the conference, had an office in the White House, but FDR, who invited the man to attend Yalta against Byrnes's will, said he could not work with him. He might have summoned Chip Bohlen, who had acted as interpreter and note-taker, but he didn't.

In the morning a message came from the bridge that the *Quincy* expected to dock at 8:30 P.M. The group of vessels, closing the Virginia shore, were in a situation no sailor enjoys. The cruiser was westbound at 22 knots when it reached the Gulf Stream, with a steady gale pouring from north to south. Cresting seas 12 feet high were hitting her on the starboard side, lifting her high, and dropping her sidewards as they ran under the keel. Captain Senn, who knew that the danger from U-boats was always highest near any port, ordered an increase of speed to 24 knots on a zigzag course. It was difficult for the vessels to accept. The cruiser *Augusta,* two miles astern, could be seen shearing her bows high out of green water and plunging straight down, engulfed in a foaming sea. The destroyers *Satterlee* and *Herndon* blinkered to *Quincy* that they could not maintain station. Senn ordered them to slow down and fall behind.

In four hours the temperature dropped eighteen degrees and a cold white beard formed on *Quincy*'s forecastle. None of it affected the President. He worked over his morning mail with Rigdon, holding on to two edges of his cabin table. Then he called Sam for another go at the speech. An hour later Mr. Roosevelt invited the three reporters in to join him at lunch. It was understood that no notes would be taken, and the conversation would be off the record. As the newsmen swapped stories with the President, news was being made in other parts of the world. None of it was coming aboard the *Quincy* by radio, but it was important nevertheless. In the House of Commons in London, Prime Minister Winston Churchill, in black jacket and bow tie, was trying to paint an attractive face on Yalta:

The Crimea Conference leaves the Allies more closely united than before, both in the military and in the political sphere. Let Germany ever recognize that it is futile to hope for division among the Allies and that nothing can avert her utter defeat. Further resistance will only be the cause of needless suffering. The Allies are resolved that Germany shall be totally disarmed, that Nazism and militarism in Germany shall be destroyed, that war criminals shall be justly and swiftly punished, that all German industry capable of military production shall be eliminated or controlled, and that Germany shall make compensation in kind to the utmost of her ability for damage done to Allied nations. On the other hand, it is not the purpose of the Allies to destroy the people of Germany, or leave them without the necessary means of subsistence. Our policy is not revenge; it is to take such measures as may be necessary to secure the future peace and safety of the world. There will be a place one day for Germans in the comity of nations, but when all traces of Nazism and militarism have been effectively and finally extirpated. . . .

The speech lacked the deep clarion harmonics of poetic bells which Churchill could induce in his audience, but Commons looked for facts this time and Churchill, aware of the suspicions of the Laborites, focused on these areas, and gave members only such truths as would mollify them:

The three powers are agreed that acceptance by the Poles of the provisions on the eastern frontiers, and, so far as can now be ascertained, on the western frontiers, is an essential condition of the establishment and future welfare and security of a strong, independent, homogeneous Polish state . . . But even more important than the frontiers of Poland, within the limits now disclosed, is the freedom of Poland. The home of the Poles is settled. Are they to be masters in their own house? Are they to be free, as we in Britain and the United States or France are free? Are their sovereignty and their independence to be untrammeled, or are they to become a mere projection of the Soviet State, forced against their will by an armed minority to adopt a communist or totalitarian system? I am putting the case in all its bluntness. It is a touchstone far more sensitive and vital than the drawing of frontier lines. Where does Poland stand? Where do we all stand on this?

Most solemn declarations have been made by Marshal Stalin and the Soviet Union that the sovereign independence of Poland is to be maintained—and this decision is now joined in both by Great Britain and the United States. Here also the World Organization will in due course assume a measure of responsibility. The Poles will have their future in their own hands, with the single limitation that they must honestly follow, in harmony with their allies, a policy friendly to Russia. That is surely reasonable . . . The impression I bring back from the Crimea, and from all my other contacts, is that Marshal Stalin and the Soviet leaders wish to live in honorable friendship and equality with the western democracies. I feel also that their word is their bond. I know of no government which stands to its obligations, even in its own despite, more solidly than the Russian Soviet Government. . . .

As Churchill was speaking in the House of Commons, and the President, 3,000 miles away, was grinding out a message of hope for the Congress and the American people, the Declaration on Liberated Europe was undergoing its first test. Andrei Vyshinsky, Deputy Foreign Minister of the Soviet Union, a man who was party to all the agreements of Yalta, had flown in below-zero weather to Bucharest, Romania. His skin and his eyes were gray and his expression grim. He refreshed himself at the Soviet Embassy and was driven downtown past the old Curtea Veche with its ancient spires pointing to heaven, along the banks of the Dîmbo Vita River to an enormous square where the royal palace, a long, colonnaded building framed in snow, stood ablaze with light. Mr. Vyshinsky was accompanied by Russian Army officers. He had demanded an immediate audience with King Michael. His purpose was simple: to order the King to dissolve the pro-Western government of General Radescu and replace it with a pro-Russian government headed by a Communist, Peter Groza.

By accident or design, Averell Harriman in Moscow learned of the flight to Bucharest. Russian armies had liberated Romania, so the United States and British members of the Allied Control Commission asked for a meeting with the Russian member. The appointment was refused. Harriman cabled the State Department. Stettinius radioed Comrade Molotov, asking for a three-power meeting in Bucharest. The British heard about the Romanian crisis and joined the Americans in demanding a meeting. This time there was no response from the Russians, either in Bucharest or in Moscow.

Vyshinsky and his entourage of generals shook the snow from their collars in the palace and were shown into a study where King Michael sat with his Foreign Minister, Constantine Visoianu. Andrei Vyshinsky showed small courtesy to the King. He had made this special trip from Moscow, he said, to explain that General Radescu was incapable of maintaining order in Romania. The Soviet government, he said, was unwilling to complain about the internal affairs of Romania, but the Russian Army, which had swept through the country and liberated it from the Hitlerites, now felt uneasy with an anti-Russian government in its rear. This was precisely the "argument of military necessity" which the Russians had used to bring Poland to heel. King Michael maintained that his kingdom was orderly. However, he would like to know what Comrade Vyshinsky expected of him. "Dismiss the Radescu government," the Russian said, "and replace it with a government based on the truly democratic forces of Romania." His Majesty made an error of judgment. He began to act like a King. The request, he said regally, would be given "consideration." Vyshinsky smiled. He would be back.

In the morning, Mr. Burton Y. Berry, American Representative to Bucharest, asked for an appointment with Vyshinsky. He sent a messenger with a letter, explaining that, under the Yalta agreement signed fifteen days ago, no decisive action could be taken by the Soviet Union without prior consultation with the United States and Great Britain. Vyshinsky did not respond. Instead, he had a subordinate phone the palace and demand another audience at once. Vyshinsky raced to the palace. This time he was pointedly unpleasant. He refused to sit in the presence of King Michael. Instead he paced the floor and, at times, pounded his fists on the King's desk. What had the King done? he asked. Michael said that he had communicated displeasure to General Radescu and had begun consultation with Romanian party leaders about the formation of a new government. Surely that was enough. The Soviet Minister stared at the King. It was not enough. "Your response is unsatisfactory," he shouted. He glanced at his watch. "You have exactly two hours and five minutes," he said, "to announce to the people of Romania that the Radescu government has been dismissed." The time was 5:55 P.M. Also, he said, the King must tell his people the name of the new Prime Minister.

Foreign Minister Visoianu appealed to Vyshinsky. Surely, he said, the Soviet Union knew that Michael was a constitutional monarch and must consult the various political leaders before forming a new government. Vyshinsky waved the words away. Only yesterday, he said, Radescu had dismissed ten general officers who had been friendly to the Soviet Union. Radescu was protecting Fascists. He expected Michael to reinstate those ten officers at once and dismiss Radescu. The King, frightened, said he thought the matter could be taken care of. Vyshinsky nodded to his officers. He was the last to leave. He slammed the door so hard that the plaster around the frame cracked. Michael tried frantically to form a government under Prince Stirbey. The Romanian Communists refused to join. Vyshinsky had little patience. He sent a message to Michael that Peter Groza was the choice of Moscow. The King truckled. He appointed Groza, but Groza couldn't get the democratic elements of Romanian parties to join him. His support consisted of Communists and leftist elements. The King, whose primary loyalty was to his throne, made another mistake. He said he would dismiss Groza's ministers. Vyshinsky, who was anxious to be done with Romanian affairs, sent a message to the palace that unless Michael accepted Groza and his ministers by noon of the following day, "I will not be responsible for the continuance of Romania as an independent state." The leaders of the peasant and industrial parties were summoned to the palace and the King begged that they accept Groza and his Communists. They refused. With stiff formality, they advised Michael to abdicate his throne. The Russians had guessed correctly: Michael would prefer to keep his throne. "I can best serve my people by not deserting the country," he said.

One of the least contentious of the Yalta agreements was the Declaration on Liberated Europe. This was its first test. In Moscow, Molotov assured Harriman that three-power conferences were going on in Bucharest.

At 8:20 P.M. Navy tugs had shoved the *Quincy*'s port side against the enclosed Pier Six at Newport News. The single lines were tossed ashore, whipping through the darkness like snakes. The heavy lines followed. At

8:25 the executive officer signaled the engine room, "All engines stop. Finished with engines." Lieutenant Rigdon sat in his below-decks stateroom adding the mileage traversed by the President in the one month and five days since he had left the White House. He was surprised to find it totaled 13,842. The cruiser was dark and silent, a ghost in silhouette. The only sound was the rattling of blocks and falls as the gangway was lowered amidships. Admiral Jonas Ingram, Commander in Chief of the Atlantic Fleet, came aboard followed by Admiral D. M. LeBreton, Commandant of the Fifth Naval District. They brushed shoulders with Mr. Edwards, the harbor pilot, who was leaving.

The President invited the two visiting admirals to join him and Admiral Leahy and Captain Senn for a farewell dinner. Arthur Prettyman had tidied the cabin and packed Roosevelt's belongings.

The *Ferdinand Magellan* was under the covered shed. The special gangway, built by the *Quincy*'s carpenters, was in place. At 8:45 P.M. the President, muffled in his Navy cape, was wheeled off the ship huddled deep under the gray fedora. Sailors in blue flanked the rails to render final honors. Aloft, the presidential pennant was hauled down slowly. The President had only one request before he departed. He asked that the body of Pa Watson be held aboard until he was on his train. On the train he picked up the special phone which connected with the White House. He was on it thirty minutes while, in the gloom outside the windows, U.S. Marines and sideboys rendered honors as the body of General Watson was carried from the ship. Ranking members of Roosevelt's party served as honorary pallbearers; six officers from the *Quincy* carried the box aboard the train.

The pale pristine color of the city of Washington was gray with cold pelting rain when the special loafed along the Fourteenth Street siding and stopped at the Government Printing Office. Mrs. Franklin Roosevelt was on the platform, holding Mrs. Edwin Watson by the arm. The Catholic chaplain of the *Quincy*, Lieutenant

D. A. Brady, disembarked first. He went to Mrs. Watson's side to comfort the widow. Mrs. Roosevelt was anxious to see her husband but was told that he was still sleeping. This was not true. He was up, bathed and dressed, behind lowered shades. He had left word that he would attend the burial service at Arlington at noon but, for personal reasons, he did not want to witness the removal of the casket from the train. He waited until everyone had left. Then he was carried to his car.

At the White House the President seemed momentarily cheered at the sight of familiar faces. Bill Hassett said, "The President has come home in the pink of condition—hasn't looked better in a year." The Roosevelts enjoyed a hot breakfast upstairs in the White House as the faces moved in and out for a moment to say hello. Eleanor pressed her husband with an endless assortment of questions; she was a woman with broad-ranging vital interests. She told him she was shocked that little countries like Estonia, Lithuania and Latvia had been abandoned to remain in the clutches of Russia. Her husband looked over the top of a cup of coffee and said, "How many people in the United States do you think will be willing to go to war to free Estonia, Latvia and Lithuania?" She said, "I don't suppose there would be many." The President nodded. "Well, if I had insisted on their being freed I would have had to consider what I would do to back up that decision, which might require war. And I concluded that the American people do not care enough about the freedom of those countries to go to war about it."

Adolf Berle, who had been a member of the President's brain trust, stopped in to shake hands and grimace as he said, "Yalta." The President threw up both hands in mock surrender and said, "I didn't say it was good, Adolf. I said it was the best I could do." Eleanor said to Malvina Thompson, her secretary, "We do go out to open the San Francisco Conference." Grace Tully came into the room with a big smile, took one look, and kept the smile frozen to her face. "The signs of weariness were etched deeply in his thinning face," she said. "The sea voyage had not brought out the ruddy tan and sparkle of eye we always expected."

At noon, on a hill near the Custis-Lee Mansion, Pa was buried. The cold rain ran in gulleys between the white rows of headstones standing to attention. The grave was covered by a canopy and the mockery of false grass. Mrs. Roosevelt and Grace Tully, with William Hassett and some friends, sat on camp chairs under the canopy as Chaplain Brady read the prayers for the dead. On the road below, the President's limousine stood alone. Roosevelt sat in the back seat, leaning forward, the lean face long with anguish. He remained until the final blessing over the casket, the consignment of Pa's soul to God, then he waited for Mrs. Roosevelt and Anna to tread softly down the hill, under umbrellas carried by funeral directors, to his car. A moment later two dear and cherished friends separated in silence.

At the White House Mr. Roosevelt was immersed in work and the greetings of stenographers, clerks and assistants who had not seen him in over a month. In her workroom, Eleanor was writing: "He says he felt well all the time & he feels evidently that all went well. He liked Stalin better & felt they got on better than before. He does not seem upset over de Gaulle." The President spoke to John McCormack, House majority leader, about making his address sitting. It seemed to worry him, and he wanted more endorsement than one. McCormack was a tall, slender man known for his unswerving loyalty to his party. The man from Massachusetts heard the question and appeared shocked. "Why, Mr. President," he said, "there's nothing to it. We'll have a good-sized chair ready and we'll keep the cameras out of the House until you're seated. No one is going to think anything about it. To us, what you have to say is important, and it doesn't matter whether you're standing, sitting or lying down." Roosevelt chuckled. "All right," he said. "All right, John. I'll stop thinking about it."

Secretly, McCormack left the White House feeling that he had been talking to a dead man. All the dynamism, the sparkle, the essence of life itself had left the outer shell of the man. What was left, McCormack said, was a soft hollow voice, and eyes which seemed larger in the cavernous face. The hands remained steady when the President left them on the edge of his desk. When he lifted them, to gesture or to polish his glasses with a kerchief, they trembled with agitation and he seemed to have trouble making them do as he wished. Vice President Harry Truman had stopped, informally and confidentially, to speak to Eleanor and Anna about the address to the joint Houses. Solicitously, he asked if they didn't think it would be too much of a strain. Mother and daughter glanced at each other. No, they didn't think so. Did he? Truman, one of the most forthright men ever to grace the Congress, fumbled for words. He reminded them that, for any President, Yalta represented a long strain on the human mind and body. The trip must have been enervating. The daily conferences of the Big Three, the meetings with aides, the readings of position papers, the monitoring of decisions by the Chiefs of Staff, the State Department group, in addition to all the material relative to internal affairs flown to him each day—all of it had to be drudgery.

Mrs. Roosevelt and Mrs. Boettiger were impressed with the Vice President's sympathetic understanding. However, "Pa" was still influencing his decisions, and he had decided to address both the Congress and the nation on Friday. If he did not feel strong enough, the ladies were sure he would send a message to Congress and read a digest of it as a radio broadcast that night. Truman left. As he passed the President's office, he learned that the Boss was sitting alone with Sam Rosenman and Grace Tully and would like to say hello. Truman went in. He said very little more than hello, assuring the President that he would learn all about the Crimean Conference on Friday. He returned to his palatial Senate office with his head down. He told aides that he had seen Roosevelt, and "was shocked. His eyes are sunken. His smile is missing. He seems like a spent man. I had a hollow feeling inside me . . ." Grace Tully, who was writing a fresh draft of the speech, noted that, for the first time in all the years she had been at his side, President Roosevelt "worked slowly and laboriously."

And yet, at 6:45, on his way "home," Mr. Roosevelt stopped at Admiral McIntire's office to complain again, as he had through the years, of "stuffy sinuses." Nose drops were given, and Bruenn made a cursory examination. There was nothing alarming to report.

March 1945

———————

SECRETLY, OR PERHAPS ABSENTMINDEDLY, THE PRESIdent had moved his congressional speech forward one day. White House aides were surprised, and some were caught unaware, when FDR said he would make his talk "today at noon." Senator Alben Barkley was in the upstairs bedroom with the Boss at 9:00 A.M. He knew about the change of plan; so did Truman and John McCormack. The flurry of busy assistants on the main floor was an indication that some projected events had to be moved back, a few hurried forward. This was not Friday; it was Thursday, March 1. The stenographers were still typing the fifth and final version, and these would have to be copied for the press.

Roosevelt was a man in a hurry. He was cramming important business into small segments of time. William Hassett, the newly appointed press secretary, a man of diligent conscience, was less worried about the obvious decline in Roosevelt's viability than he was in the tremendously accelerated speed of the decline. For the first time Hassett began to dwell upon the imminence of death. He cast it aside as an unworthy worry. He reminded himself that a few people thought FDR looked great. And yet, it was obvious to all that the weaker he appeared to be, the harder and faster he worked. Hassett thought that perhaps the President felt bleak about his future; but then, the press secretary reminded himself that Hassett was known around the White House as the worrywart.

Still, it seemed strange that Roosevelt sought no rest from the incessant workload at Yalta before giving an account of his stewardship to the nation. It wasn't like him. In other instances he took the pulse of the country first, studied its points of irritation and figuratively looked down its throat for inflammation before committing himself. He had been away more than a month, and things had happened, as they always do. The closer America came to victory, for example, the more the people grumbled about their messy little books of rationing stamps, which told them how much food and gasoline they could buy. Honorable and patriotic citizens were cheating, buying stamps in the black market. FDR was not aware for two reasons: (1) he had no time for it; (2) the intelligence groups of the various departments screened material from his eyes. He would not know, offhand, that almost 16 million men and women were now in United States military uniforms; that 290,000 aircraft had been built; that 71,000 naval ships, 102,000 tanks and self-propelled guns, over 5 million tons of bombs, in addition to 40 billion rounds of small ammunition, were either at the various fronts or on their way. He would not know unless he asked. It is doubtful—unless he left his card-table radio on—that he would know America was singing "This Is the Army, Mister Jones," "I Left My Heart at the Stage Door Canteen," "Der Führer's Face" and "Don't Sit Under the Apple Tree."

There was a time when he would have evinced an amiable interest in any of these matters, but the time was past. This morning Senator Barkley sat in a chair near Roosevelt's bed as Dr. Bruenn conducted the morning examination. He was still there at breakfast, watching the President drop bits of toast to Fala. FDR had wanted to discuss the speech with Barkley; instead he was talking about Pa Watson, and the mass that was being celebrated across town at St. Matthew's. Franklin Roosevelt had made important speeches; but this one would either place the United States on a course of action for many years, or it would leave FDR empty of purpose, a pariah in the darkening years. His agreements with Stalin and Churchill were just and proper, or the United States had been sold out by a doddering old man. Yalta could not be half endorsed. And yet he spoke of Pa as though, in a gentle manner, he were trying to resurrect a face, a tone of voice, a special story. Alben Barkley listened for an hour and thirty-seven minutes. Then he said he would have to hurry back to the Capitol to make some arrangements. Roosevelt waved a tired farewell and picked up his phone. He said he would like to be accompanied to the Capitol by Mrs. Roosevelt, Colonel and Mrs. Boettiger, the Crown Prince and Princess of Norway, who were house guests, Bernard Baruch, Mrs. Kermit Roosevelt, Mrs. Helm, Malvina Thompson, Mr. and Mrs. Sam Rosenman, Dorothy Brady, Grace Tully, William Hassett and Jonathan Daniels. He said he was reading from a list and should he repeat it. A White House stenographer said no.

The President had been home from Yalta twenty-eight hours when Mike Reilly lifted him into the back of the limousine. The Secret Service agent noticed that the Boss felt heavier. This was not possible, because Roosevelt had lost fifteen pounds, claimed all his food was tasteless and ate little. Mrs. Roosevelt smiled and moved away as the limp bundle was deposited beside her. It was a clear, chilly day and the glittering motorcade emitted plumes of white. At the Capitol, both Houses of Congress had been seated. The time was 12:08 P.M., and the doorkeeper of the House of Representatives bawled out, "The Supreme Court of the United States," as the Justices walked solemnly down the red-carpeted aisle. Vice President Harry Truman, neat and birdlike, sat in his lofty chair staring at the distinguished gallery. Speaker Samuel Rayburn was not in Washington; Speaker pro tempore John McCormack sat in a chair next to Truman; he was frowning at the ambassadors and diplomatic group. At 12:29 the Cabinet was announced. Glancing at the gallery, Truman found his wife and daughter. He saw Mrs. Roosevelt lead the White House contingent to the last group of empty seats.

At 12:31 Ralph R. Roberts, the doorkeeper, stood in the aisle and announced the President of the United States. A wheelchair without arms started slowly down the aisle. Roosevelt was escorted by Senators Barkley of Kentucky, White of Maine and McKellar of Tennessee, in addition to Congressmen Ramspeck of Georgia, Doughton of North Carolina and Martin of Massachusetts. It was a solemn moment in a solemn setting. The arena was hushed as the President slipped from his wheelchair into a soft deep chair facing a desk and an assortment of silvery microphones. He was, for the first time, not standing behind the lectern in a position above the well; he was on the floor below the Vice President and Speaker pro tempore on a level with the first row of seats.

McCormack banged his gavel once. "Senators and Representatives," he said, "I have the great pleasure, the high privilege, and the distinguished honor of presenting to you the President of the United States." A thunderous wave of applause swept the well, and Roosevelt nodded as he assembled and reassembled a sheaf of white papers. He lowered his head, glanced around owlishly, and waved to a well-known face here, or grinned at another. Some in the galleries and in the well stood as a mark of respect. Mr. Roosevelt began his speech too soft and hollow of voice:

Mr. Vice President, Mr. Speaker, Members of the Congress, I hope you will pardon me for the unusual posture of sitting down during the presentation of what I wish to say, but I know you will realize it makes it a lot easier for me in not having to carry about ten pounds of steel around the bottom of my legs [laughter] and also because of the fact I have just completed a fourteen-thousand-mile trip. [Applause] First of all, I want to say it is good to be home. It has been a long journey and, I hope you will agree, so far a fruitful one. Speaking in all frankness, the question of whether it is entirely fruitful or not lies to a great extent in your hands, for unless you here in the halls of the American Congress, with the support of the American people, concur in the general conclusions reached at that place called Yalta, and give them your active support, the meeting will not have produced lasting results. And that is why I have come before you at the earliest hour I could after my return. I want to make a personal report to you and at the same time to the people of the country.

The voice was a pale copy of the vigorous tone Americans had come to know. And yet the words had that highly personal quality, that confidential "you and I know" manner which had enchanted a nation for twelve years. "I am returning from this trip that took me so far refreshed and inspired. I was well the entire time. I was not ill for a second until I arrived back in Washington, and here I heard all of the rumors which occurred in my absence. [Laughter] We seem to thrive on it." [Applause]

Sam Rosenman crouched in silent agony in the gallery. He knew now that the President was going to ad lib; that he would, at times, lose his place and repeat a sentence or a phrase. Rosenman also suffered because the Boss had ordered him not to mention that the Soviet Union was to get three votes in the U.N. Assembly. The judge had told Roosevelt that the bad news would be leaked to the press before that. But the President had said no, and no, and no. He did not want this first splendid day to be marred with a controversial truth. The speech droned on, and Rosenman was surprised to hear the President go into a dissertation of how small the world is, and of how communications kept him abreast, in Russia, of everything going on in the United States. In a moment, he was back to the written word:

I come from the Crimean Conference with a firm belief that we have made a good start on the road to a world of peace. There were two main purposes in this Crimean Con-

ference: the first was to bring defeat to Germany with the greatest possible speed, and the smallest possible loss of Allied men. That purpose is now being carried out in great force. The German Army, the German people, are feeling the ever-increasing might of our fighting men and of the Allied armies; and every hour gives us added pride in the heroic advance of our troops in Germany on German soil toward a meeting with the gallant Red Army. The second purpose was to continue to build the foundation for an international accord that would bring order and security after the chaos of the war, that would give some assurance of lasting peace among the nations of the world. Toward that goal a tremendous stride was made.

He digressed for a time on the lapse of cummunication among the Big Three after Teheran. Arrangements had been made at Yalta, he said, so that the Secretary of State could meet regularly with the foreign ministers so that each would understand the plans of the other two. He said he would like to explain some of the many problems which had been debated and settled at Yalta. There was the question of joint occupation of Germany after the war so that neither Nazism nor Prussianism could again threaten the peace of the world. The Big Three wanted to settle the arrangements made at Dumbarton Oaks for a United Nations Organization. "As you remember, and afterward, I said that we had agreed ninety percent. That is a pretty good percentage. I think the other ten percent was ironed out at Yalta." There was also the problem of Liberated Areas in Europe. "We over here find it very difficult to understand the ramifications of many of these problems in foreign lands, but we are trying to."

Roosevelt decided not to let the Polish problem stand alone. So he linked it with Yugoslavia:

Days were spent in discussing these momentous matters, and we argued frankly and freely across the table. But at the end on every point unanimous agreement was reached. And more important even than the agreement of words, I may say we achieved a unity of thought and a way of getting along together. [Prolonged applause]

At this point, President Roosevelt achieved the status of hero, even to those who loooked upon him and his administration with suspicion. Unanimous agreement, unity of thought and a way of getting along together moved even his most caustic critic, Senator Robert A. Taft of Ohio, to applaud. The President said that Adolf Hitler's forlorn hope was that there would be a "crack" in the unity of the Big Three . . . "a crack that would give him and his fellow gangsters one last hope of escaping their just doom. This is the objective for which his propaganda machine has been working for many months. But Hitler has failed."

He was carried away by the continued and deafening applause. "Never before have the major Allies been more closely united—not only in their war aims but also in their peace aims. And they are determined to continue to be united, to be united with each other—and with all peace-loving nations—so that the ideal of lasting peace will become a reality." They were heady words indeed, flamboyant mists of perfume designed to cover the rancid odor of separate interests. The military staffs held daily meetings to plan knockout blows, he said. The Russians were fighting on eastern German soil; the Americans and British were on western German soil. The time had come for daily liaison, for unifying plans of attack. He moved on to "unconditional surrender." He asked the German people, individually or in groups, to surrender. It would be a matter of common sense, he said. "They must realize that only with complete surrender can they begin to reestablish themselves as people whom the world might accept as decent neighbors." The Nazis were trying to equate unconditional surrender with enslavement. "I now repeat—that unconditional surrender does not mean the destruction or enslavement of the German people." He chose not to mention that it would mean slave labor in Russia for German men. "We do not want the German people to starve, or to become a burden on the rest of the world. It will be removing a cancer from the German body politic, which for generations has produced only misery, only pain, for the whole world."

The President had seen the "senseless fury" of the Germans at Yalta. Years ago, it had been a retreat for the Czars. Since then it had been used as a rest area for the sick and afflicted. It had no military significance at all.

When the Red Army forced the Nazis out of the Crimea almost a year ago last April, it was found that all of the palaces were looted by the Nazis, and then nearly all of them were destroyed by bombs placed on the inside. Even the humblest of homes of Yalta were not spared. There was little left of it except blank walls, ruins, destruction. . . . there is not room enough on earth for both German militarism and Christian decency. But, to go on with the story which I hope to do in under an hour . . .

Reporters with copies of the speech were ticking off the digressions. There were a dozen, and the number was growing. The President reverted to the United Nations, this time scanning the voting procedure lightly. He began to slur his words; he was fumbling.

There was one point, however, on which agreement was not reached. It involved the procedure of voting, of voting in the Security Council. I want to try to make it clear by making it simple. It took me hours and hours to get the thing straight in my own mind—and many conferences. At the Crimean Conference, the Americans made a proposal, a proposal on the subject which, after full discussion, I am happy to say was unanimously adopted by the other two nations. It is not yet possible to announce the terms of it publicly, but it will be in a very short time. When the conclusions reached with respect to voting are made known, I think and I hope that you will find them fair, that you will find them a fair solution of this complicated and difficult problem. They are founded in justice, and will go far

*to insure international cooperation for the maintenance of
peace.*

There he sat, resurrecting his own political father,
Woodrow Wilson, trying to explain the inexplicable.
When he "hoped" the Senate would find the procedure
to be fair, Roosevelt aroused suspicions. If it was so
fair, so just, why could he not explain that the Security
Council would consist of five permanent members, and
that any one of them could exercise a veto to render
action by the United Nations impossible? This was too
memorable a day to risk disenchantment. He admitted
that the charter "has to be and should be approved
by the Senate of the United States under the Constitution. . . . The Senate and the House will both be represented at the San Francisco Conference. The congressional delegates will consist of an equal number of Republican and Democratic members. The delegation is,
in every sense of the word, bipartisan because world
peace is not exactly a party question. I think that Republicans want peace just as much as Democrats." Those
who knew him well—Hassett, Rosenman, Daniels—
understood that the President was trying hard, and futilely, to treat a complex historic situation in the simplistic storytelling manner he used with newspaper
reporters. He was giving it much more substance than
the newsmen got, but Rosenman knew that the Boss
was wandering too frequently into what Roosevelt liked
to think of as "asides."

He came closest to revealing what was in his mind
when he said:

*It cannot be just an American peace, or a British peace, or a
Russian, French or Chinese peace. It cannot be a peace of
large nations, or of small nations. It must be a peace which
rests on the cooperative effort of the whole world. It
cannot be a structure complete. It cannot be what some
people think—a structure of complete perfection at first. But
it can be a peace, and it will be a peace, based on the
sound and just principles of the Atlantic Charter, on the*

conception and dignity of the human being, and on the guarantees of tolerance and freedom of religious worship.

It was a high note of idealism, if not of practicality. The Big Three, he said, were unanimously agreed that there is bound to be confusion in newly liberated countries. "They will endeavor to see to it that interim governments—the people who carry on interim governments between the occupation of Germany and the day of true independence—will be as representative as possible of all democratic elements in the population, and that free elections are held as soon as possible thereafter." Having said it FDR decided to hedge a little.

Final decisions in these areas are going to be made jointly, and therefore, they will often be the result of give-and-take compromise. The United States will not always have its way a hundred percent, nor will Russia, nor Great Britain. We shall not always have ideal solutions to complicated international problems, even though we are determined continuously to strive toward that ideal. . . . The United Nations must also begin to help these liberated areas adequately to reconstruct their economy—I do not want them to starve to death—so that they are ready to resume their places in the world.

At this point the President reached the sensitive and dangerous point of the speech: Poland. He understood American suspicions of Soviet intentions and he knew that the press was referring to the Lublin government as a Soviet satellite. There had been unconfirmed stories about Russian Army repression of the Polish people and the expropriation of territory up to the line that Hitler had given to Stalin in 1939.

One outstanding example of joint action by the three major Allied Powers [he said] was the solution reached on Poland. The whole Polish question was a potential source of trouble in postwar Europe, and we came to the conference determined to find a common ground for its solution. We

*did. We know everybody does not agree with it—obviously.
Our objective was to create a strong, independent and
prosperous nation—that is the thing we must all remember
—those words agreed to by Russia, by Britain, and by
me . . . There are, you know, two governments; one in London, one in Lublin, practically in Russia.*

*Accordingly, steps were taken at Yalta to reorganize the
existing provisional government in Poland on a broader
democratic basis, so as to include democratic leaders now
in Poland, and those abroad. This new, reorganized government will be recognized by all of us as the temporary government of Poland. Poland needs a temporary government in
the worst way—an interim government is another way of putting it. However, the new Polish Provisional Government of
National Unity will be pledged to holding a free election
as soon as possible on the basis of universal suffrage and
a secret ballot. . . . The decisions with respect to the
boundaries of Poland were frankly a compromise. I did not
agree with all of it by any means. But we did not go as far
as Britain wanted in certain areas; we did not go as far
as Russia wanted in certain areas; and we did not go as
far as I wanted in certain areas. . . . While the decision is
a compromise, it is one, however, under which the Poles will
receive compensation in territory in the north and west in
exchange for what they lose by the Curzon Line in the east.
The limits of the western border will be permanently fixed
in the final peace conference. Roughly, this will include in
the new, strong Poland quite a large slice of what is now
called Germany.*

The President was determined to make a solid case
that what the Poles would get from Germany would be
better, richer than what the Russians took. "It was
also agreed that the new Poland will have a large and
long coastline and many new harbors; also that East
Prussia—most of it—will go to Poland. A corner of it
will go to Russia; also—what shall I call it?—the anomaly
of the Free State of Danzig—I think Danzig would be
a lot better if it were Polish." It is well known, he added,
that most of the people east of the Curzon Line are

White Russians and Ukrainians, not Poles; and that people west of the line are mainly Polish. A final admonitory note to potential critics: "You must remember also that there was no Poland or had not been any Polish government before 1919 for many generations."

He moved on to recognition of France as a world power, even though France had not been invited to Yalta. Then, almost lamely, he said: "There were, of course, a number of smaller things I have not time to go into on which joint agreement was had. We hope things will straighten out . . . We have to remember that there are a great many prima donnas in the world all wishing to be heard before anything becomes final. So we may have a little delay while we listen to more prima donnas." There was a heavy surf of laughter in the House well. FDR turned to the war in the Pacific, and divorced Russia from it by stating that the talks took place at Malta, and were between the Combined Chiefs of Staff of Britain and the United States. "The Japanese warlords know that they are not being overlooked. They have felt the force of our B-29s and our carrier planes. They have felt the naval might of the United States and do not appear very anxious to come out and try it again. The Japs know what it means," he said, wagging his head vigorously, "that 'the United States Marines have landed.'" The succeeding words were drowned by applause. "And I think I may add, having Iwo Jima in mind, that the situation is well in hand."

The difference between what a statesman says and his knowledge of the facts is often marked by broad divergence. It was so in the case of Iwo Jima. The Third, Fourth and Fifth Marine Divisions had battled for a small island of volcanic ash from February onward. The United States needed it as a port in a storm for crippled bombers en route home from Japan to Saipan. It could also be used as an airport for P-51 Mustang fighters to meet and escort big bombers on the final 700-mile run into Japan. When the President arrived at his desk after returning from Yalta, he was given the news that Iwo Jima had cost 27,000 American lives and had not yet been secured. It was the first time in the war, through bad news and good, that anyone had seen the President gasp in horror.

Next he extolled the great work of General Mac-Arthur, then Admiral Nimitz. "But, lest somebody lay off work in the United States I can repeat what I have said, a short sentence even in my sleep, 'We haven't won the wars yet,' with an *s* on wars. It is a long tough road to Tokyo; it is longer to Tokyo than it is to Berlin in every sense of the word. . . . we must be prepared for a long and costly struggle in the Pacific."

The President looked up at the clock stuck to the ornate balcony. He hurried on, mentioning that he had stopped, en route home, to speak to three kings. Admiral Leahy, who had been at his side all the way, still did not understand what the President was trying to accomplish by chatting with Farouk, Haile Selassie and Ibn Saud. No one did. And yet, in his speech, he said:

Our conversations had to do with matters of common interest. They will be of great mutual advantage because they gave us an opportunity of meeting and talking face to face, and of exchanging views in personal conversation instead of formal correspondence. For instance, from Ibn Saud of Arabia I learned more of the whole problem of the Moslems and the Jewish problem in five minutes than I could have learned by the exchange of a dozen letters.

He had been speaking for over fifty minutes when he reached the peroration. The President would not have wanted it known that, for him, it had been an agony of effort to make the speech, to face his political friends and enemies—and the world—to marshal his attention span so that he would say the right words and enunciate the best thoughts so that his colleagues would see the world as he ached so much to see it.

The Conference in the Crimea was a turning point, I hope, in our history and, therefore, in the history of the world. There will soon be presented to the Senate and to the Ameri-

can people a great decision that will determine the fate of the United States—and, I think, therefore, the fate of the world —for generations to come. There can be no middle ground here. We shall have to take the responsibility for world collaboration or we shall have to bear the responsibility for another world conflict.

His voice became raspy. The words were hurried and hoarse. FDR came to a complete stop, poured part of a glass of water from a carafe and drank. Then he continued:

No plan is perfect. Whatever is adopted at San Francisco will doubtless have to be amended time and again over the years, just as our own Constitution has been. No one can say exactly how long any plan will last. Peace can endure only so long as humanity really insists upon it, and is willing to work for it, and sacrifice for it. Twenty-five years ago, American fighting men looked to the statesmen of the world to finish the work of peace for which they fought and suffered. We failed them. We cannot fail them again and expect the world to survive. . . . And that, my friends, is the only message I can give you. I feel it very deeply as I know that all of you are feeling it today and are going to feel it in the future.

With some agility, the President slid onto his armless wheelchair. The applause was indeed prolonged; the standing ovation from such a distinguished audience might sustain a man who had given the final ounce of strength for the cause of peace; the gray head nodded as the rear doors were held open by attendants. The wispy hair on top lifted and fell in the crescendo of sound. A few were misty-eyed, thinking that—even if he lived—he would not be back again; that he had worked hard and well and had passed the test of reporting to his peers, but he had used the last of his reserves and he had nothing left to give. They said he would not be back, and so, with sentiment, they watched him leave.

In the gallery Sam Rosenman sat with a pen. He had a copy of the speech before him. He told Mrs. Rosenman that Roosevelt had departed from the text forty-nine times. He looked upon the talk as close to a disaster. Harry Truman followed Roosevelt out into the anteroom. The Vice President said it had been a great speech, a fine piece of statesmanship. Truman was being kind. He told his cronies that he was shocked when the President left the text of his talk to discuss "prima donnas . . . all wishing to be heard." Roosevelt looked up at his Vice President and grabbed his hand. "As soon as I can," he said, "I will go to Warm Springs for a rest. I can be trim again if I stay there for two or three weeks." Grace Tully left the gallery saying, "Sam and I were just sick. He wasn't himself at all."

Some, like author John Gunther, who sat in the White House a few days earlier talking to members of the family, reflected a hopeful attitude. He was told that Roosevelt had an assortment of ambitions after he left the White House. He planned to be Secretary General of the United Nations; he aspired to be editor of a country newspaper; he would enlarge his lumber holdings and grow more trees at Hyde Park; he wanted to build a hurricane hut on the Florida Keys where he could spend his days fishing with his friends. Others, like Hopkins (who was in a hospital) and Steve Early (who was in France), turned their backs to the hoarseness, the weak voice, the slumped figure, and recalled that Roosevelt enjoyed a hilarious game of poker in which there were plenty of wild cards; he liked to go to baseball games, especially if he could boo the umpire; he enjoyed pejorative stories at the expense of his closest friends, and would tell them interminably; how he could work himself to a pitch of electrifying excitement at his twice-weekly press conferences, where he sparred genially with his adversaries. Once, he told Eleanor that he would like to retire someday and go to Egypt and Arabia and teach those countries how to create and harness water power, thus making the desert bloom.

His friends were humming at midnight. Dean Acheson

said, "It was an invalid's voice." On the way back to
the White House, Rosenman shook his head sadly. At
one point he said to his wife, "Some of his extemporane-
ous remarks bordered on the ridiculous. His statement
about the Moslem-Jewish problem—talking with Ibn
Saud for five minutes—this was a thought that must have
popped into his head because I never heard him say
anything about it on the way home from Algiers." Admiral Ross McIntire, who had insisted to the press and
to the President himself that his health was basically
sound, wrote of the speech: "A doctor's discerning eye
could see signs of weariness before the end of the hour
required by the length of the address. His voice sagged
and every now and then he passed his hand over his eyes
as if to clear his sight."

After lunch the President returned to his office. Grace
Tully, worried as only the spiritually frightened Irish
can worry, told the Boss that a lot of work had accumulated in his absence, "but we can chop away at it from
day to day." In the first session of dictation Miss Tully
discovered a new and discouraging President. Usually,
he lifted the mail, a letter at a time, from a pile on
his desk blotter, and, scanning it with lofted chin through
bifocals, would dictate a terse response with cordial
greetings. On this day he chatted amiably about a lot
of things not relevant to his work. This, she and Dorothy
Brady soon learned, was the new Boss. He spoke of
his trip; he scanned letters and remembered things about
"poor Pa." He talked of going to Hyde Park "to get
a *lot* of sleep." Without preamble, he recalled, in the
middle of a letter, that Grace Tully's mother was ill.
"Why don't you take some time off and spend a few
days with your mother . . . ?" The secretary sat with
her notebook on her knees. Her eyes dimmed with sorrow
as the man she revered prattled on and on about things
which had little relevance to anything at hand—thoughts
which appeared to pop into his mind at random; thoughts
he uttered with an indulgent smile. The new Roosevelt
upset everyone who worked near him.

The press reaction pleased the President. He was up early, propped on pillows, reading bits and pieces of newspaper stories and editorials. From Salem to San Diego, from Sioux Falls to San Antonio, editorial applause rang out for a job well done. *The New York Times* said FDR looked "tanned, well-rested." He was reading, smiling, and breaking crisp bacon into small pieces with a slice for himself and a slice for Fala when Judge Sam Rosenman was announced. "Come in, Sam. Come in." Leahy came in, too. So did McIntire, Bruenn, Hassett and others. Everyone congratulated the Boss on the good press reception. He wasn't ready for his morning medical examination; he wanted to make a few changes. From now on, he told Hassett, you will fill in as Acting Appointments Secretary for Pa Watson. Press relations can be the province of Jonathan Daniels until Steve Early returns. Rosenman interrupted to say that he was packed and ready to return to London, where his committee was ready to begin work on the needs of liberated peoples. "Do you have any instructions for me, Mr. President?" "The only further instructions I have for you, Sam, are these. It is very rainy and wet in London the early part of March. Be sure to take your rubbers with you."

Late in the morning, the President called a press conference, but the news, after the speech of the day before, was minuscule. The high point, if there was one, was in response to a question about the status of Jesse Jones. Roosevelt had always been delicate and tender in discharging employees, but Jones, fired five weeks earlier, remained in the personal office of the Secretary of Commerce and was still making noises as the head of the big Federal Loan Agency. This time the President put his words on the press record. He said that Jones was "ex-Secretary of Commerce. He is also out as head of the Federal Loan Agency since he held that office by virtue of being Secretary of Commerce." Roosevelt reminded the reporters that he had appointed Wayne Taylor as Acting Secretary in place of Jones. Jesse Jones, therefore, no longer worked for the government. Jones had been writing letters on the stationery of the Secretary of Commerce as recently as the day Roosevelt returned from Yalta, asking for an appointment to discuss department matters. Jones was unabashed, making his personal humiliation a public matter. He also told his friends that he had sufficient clout in Congress to retain his job in the Federal Loan Agency. When the press left Roosevelt's office, he put in a personal call to Harry Truman and asked him to corral enough votes to confirm Henry Wallace in both jobs. Truman wasn't sure he could do it. Jones had done favors for a number of senators and had a credit balance with many of them. The Vice President said he would confer with Alben Barkley and others and see what could be done. Henry Wallace, "the dreamer," had few votes.

The feeling in the White House was one of triumph. For the first time, both war and peace had been minutely defined and implemented by the will of the peoples of the world. The fire fights in Europe might flicker for months, but they were blueprinted to die in a dusty silence. The masses of men and guns in the Far East had, presumably, a long road ahead, but, as surely as sunrise, the Japanese Empire would fall and American soldiers would one day stand near the imperial moat taking snapshots of the palace. The work of peace had been accomplished by the winners before the losers surrendered. The President smiled, perhaps with relief, from the recesses of his wheelchair. The body may have been tired beyond its years, but the heart was light—as though he had completed a great and lasting work. His life's work, the ghostly ambition of the young man, had been realized by the old one.

Political philosophy is often no more than a translucent mirage standing between a statesman and reality. In London Sir Alexander Cadogan was writing the opposite of what Roosevelt had been saying. The President, at one point in his speech, said that "the Crimean Conference spells the end of the system of unilateral action, exclusive alliances, spheres of influence and balances of power—all the expedients which have been tried for centuries and have always failed." Sir Alec, the Foreign Office cynic, wrote: "It would have been nearer the mark to say that Yalta spelled a renewed lease of life for these expedients." He knew of the gentlemen's agreement between Churchill and Stalin regarding spheres of influence over Greece, Bulgaria, Romania and Yugoslavia. FDR had been told they were "ninety-day wonders"; they were permanent. Nor did he learn, on this bright morning of accomplishment, that Vyshinsky had at last forced King Michael of Romania to form a Communist government. Clark Kerr had cabled Churchill that Molotov refused to invite any democratic Poles except those approved by the Lublin government. Outraged, Prime Minister Churchill puffed his pink cheeks and growled, "I have not the slightest intention of being cheated over Poland, even if we go to the verge of war with Russia." There was no free election, no secret ballot in Romania; there would be none in Poland. The Polish government-in-exile, commenting on Roosevelt's speech, announced the "fifth partition of Poland, now accomplished by her Allies."

Anthony Eden advised the Prime Minister to appeal to the President to ask Uncle Joe to live up to the Yalta agreements. The P.M. wagged his head no. "I am no longer being fully heard by him," he said. "Roosevelt's devoted aides are anxious to keep their knowledge of his condition within the narrowest circle—various hands are drafting the answers which are given in his name." There was a superior reason for waiting. Churchill had fashioned a personal *cul de sac* and he was in it. At Moscow he had divided parts of Europe between the Russians and the British. Stalin had not interfered in the Greek battle against communism; the Prime Minister feared that if he challenged Stalin on Romania the Marshal had a right to ask, "I did not interfere in your action in Greece; why do you not give me the same latitude in Romania?" No, it would be better to wait. And yet the wise old Briton assured his associates that, with each passing day, Red Army troops and tanks were obtaining a harder grip on Warsaw and Bucharest. It would be impossible to pry those steel fingers loose.

All was not well, in spite of the feeling inside the White House. Ambassador Patrick Hurley, alarmed, had left China with General Albert Wedemeyer to rush to Roosevelt with a personal report. Chungking was heavy with rumors that their friend Franklin D. Roosevelt had sold China out to the Russians at Yalta, and Hurley hurried to ask FDR what had happened, and how he might placate the suspicious Generalissimo. Besides, Hurley had to admit that he had failed in his mission to unify China. He had brought the Communist Chou En-lai to Chungking to talk with Chiang about the formation of an all-China coalition government. The Generalissimo refused to negotiate; he said Hurley had been seduced by the Reds. In actuality, Chiang knew that a coalition, any coalition, meant the decline of his personal power and his Kuomintang. The best he could offer Chou was recognition of the Communists at Yenan as "a political party," in return for which he, Chiang, would command all Chinese armies, Communist and Nationalist. Chou En-lai smiled. "All we are asked," he said, "is to surrender." The talks were terminated.

Hurley now realized that he was gripped in the coils of the dragon. Not only was Chiang opposed to any compromise, but many of the Americans—military as well as State Department officers—were opposed to Chiang and called his government "corrupt, reactionary, and insensitive to the misery of the people." Although these Americans were not Reds, their sympathies gravitated toward Yenan. In Washington officials in the State Department's Far Eastern Office were out of sympathy with Chiang, and with Patrick Hurley, too. On this day, March 2, General Shang Chen of the Chinese Military Mission to Washington sought an appointment with the President. His government wanted to know what part of the Yalta discussions concerned China. Roosevelt said he was leaving for Hyde Park, but turned Shang over to Admiral Leahy. The Chinese General asked many questions, and received soft, amiable responses. Leahy repeated over and over all the published material about Yalta and said, "I am sorry that I cannot give you any more information."

As Churchill surmised, the President was indeed being shielded from unpleasant news. For example, the Soviet Union was asking for naval vessels. The request came from Gromyko through the State Department. The Russians would appreciate some Italian battleships and any American cruisers and destroyers not in use by the United States. Edward Stettinius had departed on a trip which would take him to Mexico City. In his absence Acting Secretary of State Joseph Grew, one-time Ambassador to Japan, did not advise the President. He relayed the request to Admiral Leahy with a suggestion that the United States "act slowly" on it so that the State Department might bargain for cooperation in European problems, such as Romania. Leahy told Grew to tell the Russians that Italian warships were too "thin-skinned" to be operated in northern waters. The shield of insulation which began to form around the President's person was not an act of collusion; the secretaries, aides and members of the Cabinet seemed to feel that their man was depleted in physical and mental resources. Each felt that he could help by making more of the decisions—especially nettlesome, irritating ones—referring only the highest policy matters to FDR.

The President, on the other hand, acted like a boy on vacation from school. For a time he would be free to work on his stamp collection; entertain visiting royalty, a situation which always enthralled him; run off to Hyde Park to oversee the establishment of his library; enjoy a secret lunch with Lucy Mercer Rutherfurd while the Secret Service and Brady and Tully guarded all the doors to the office and cut off phone service. A large amount of free time should have restored the President's spirits, but, except for a few odd days, he chose to see more people, read more state papers and congressional bills, forgo the after-lunch nap, and entertain friends at small dinners in "the house" rather than eat alone in bed.

One of the "easy" days was March 3, 1945. He arrived in the office late in the morning, worked awhile, returned to his private quarters for lunch, and was back in the office signing mail at 2:30. With a flourish, he signed the order commissioning his son Elliott as a Brigadier General. Then he dictated a note to Elliott, the one child out of five who could be called a Roosevelt maverick. This was the nonconformist, the one who refused to follow the Rooseveltian footsteps through Groton and Harvard; the one who had dared to marry a motion picture actress; the wild one who had no profession, no trade; the big-hearted, rough-talking, generous man who gave money away.

Dear Bunny:

It is grand to be able to address you as Brigadier General!

I am enclosing copy of a letter from Arthur Morris [an official of the New York Trust Company] for your information. Will you be good enough to let him know whether the suggested arrangement is all right?

I shall have lots to tell you about my trip the next time I see you.

I am off to Hyde Park for a few days.

Mother joins me in sending much love.

Affectionately,

F.D.R.

Hyde Park was a tranquilizer. He was home again, even though he had always thought of it as "Mother's house." The air was chill and bright with yellow sun; the old trees looked smaller bare and stark; there was a rime of ice around the pond near the New York Central tracks; the village pursued its daily tasks as though he had never been away, as though no one had ever sold a house or built one. The only business of moment was Jimmy Byrnes's phone call, saying that it might be necessary to seize the Chrysler plants to stop a crippling strike. FDR said, "If it becomes necessary, let me know." Mrs. Roosevelt was home with him. The Henry Morgenthaus were across the river. One of the stenographers found a fistful of pussywillow. On automobile drives Franklin surprised Eleanor by asking her to drive. She too was becoming acquainted with a new Roosevelt. She maintained her cheerful, toothy smile even though the new FDR caused her heart to sink.

She told her intimates that it was not merely the thought of addressing Congress sitting down. That, to her way of thinking, was an index to the fact that he was now surrendering to invalidism; he would not fight it anymore. There were other things. He turned away from serious conversation. Sitting by the big living room fireplace, she tried to draw him out on the parts of the Yalta agreements which he had not made public. He turned her away softly. On one occasion Colonel Hooker was advising Roosevelt to continue the draft law after the war, until peace was assured. Eleanor spoke against it with passion. At some point in the dialogue, she told her friends, she realized her husband had been hurt by her remarks, and had lapsed into silence. He no longer goaded her to act as the devil's advocate; it was as though he could no longer sustain her dissident vote.

A woman friend told Mrs. Roosevelt that Franklin looked "terribly thin and worn and gray." It did not help. The words confirmed Eleanor's observations. The friend said that Franklin's hands shook horribly. Mrs. Roosevelt said that she had noticed the tremors. Her husband refused to drive his specially built automobile; he rolled his chair away from serious discussions; he had trouble pasting stamps in albums; lastly, he gave up his old-time pleasure of mixing cocktails before dinner. The President asked Mrs. Roosevelt to do it, or Colonel Boettiger. To keep from worrying, Eleanor kept reminding herself that the President talked of going to the Middle East when he left the White House: "I believe I could help to straighten out the Near East." He told her he would like to "get into" straightening out Indochina and Thailand and India after the war. She preferred to believe his hopeful words rather than the vague medical nonsense she got from Admiral McIntire. Bruenn was practically inaccessible to her because of the Admiral's orders. And McIntire, with the eye of a physician, must have noted that the "new" Roosevelt was a dying man. He contented himself with warning Roosevelt that he had stopped taking his afternoon naps and he remained up too late. Again and again, he admonished the President against working too hard, entreating him to "take it easy."

Long ago Roosevelt had chosen not to be told the true state of his health. The isolation now included his wife and children. Within a few days, the despair of Mrs. Roosevelt would manifest itself in one sentence of a letter she penned: "I say a daily prayer that he may be able to carry on till we have peace & our feet are set in the right direction." Bill Hassett, the professional worrier, felt optimistic on Monday, March 5. Usually, he saw his President as enfeebled, dark cavernous circles around his eyes, gray of skin. This was a day of no appointments, no work. With cheer, Hassett sat in his quarters over the big Vanderbilt stables and wrote:

Grace and I together to the President's—no mail pouch this morning, but checked with him the roster of his forthcoming foreign visitors: Mackenzie King, Prime Minister of Canada, next Friday; Princess Juliana of the Netherlands, March 17–19; the Earl of Athlone, Governor General of Canada, and his consort, Princess Alice (Queen Victoria's granddaughter) March 22–25; and the Regent of Iraq for a state dinner on April 19, lodging for the night and exit next morning to Blair House. The President said he would leave on April 20 for San Francisco to open the United Nations Conference on April 25th; added he would come back to Hyde Park for weekend of March 24–26; returning to Washington, could leave afternoon of Tuesday March 27th, for a two weeks' stay in Warm Springs.

Insulation induces isolation. No pouch meant no news. The world outside the stately white building at Hyde Park was still moving inexorably eastward and, while the President felt almost pleasantly sedated inside the Big House, unpleasant events were occurring in the world.

On the day of "no pouch," for example, Averell Harriman, in Moscow, sat in the office of Foreign Minister Molotov and presented a letter to him protesting Soviet unilateral action in Romania. Harriman's grace was that he could speak rationally when his feelings were ruffled. He said that, in the name of the government of the United States, he was formally protesting Vyshinsky's crude threats to King Michael and the dissolution of the Radescu government under Soviet guns. He reminded Molotov that the British and American members of the Allied Control Commission had been present in Bucharest, but they had been advised of events at the whim of the Soviets, and had not, at any time, been consulted. Further, Harriman said, if there was disorder in the rear of the Soviet Army, it was created by the Soviet Army, which clanked tanks and guns and troops through the capital while Vyshinsky was slamming doors. What good was an Allied Control Commission, he asked, if the power which invested the country would make its own decisions without regard to the wishes of its friends? Molotov thought that the matter was not serious. He insisted that the Americans and British had been kept informed of Soviet action. Not so, said Harriman, and he had personal reports from the Americans to prove it. Molotov reminded Harriman that Romania had been a satellite of Germany, that Romanian divisions had killed Russian soldiers. It was, in effect, an enemy state near the Russian border. This, to Harriman, was specious. There was an Allied Control Commission which would function as a triumvirate in all cases, or it would function in none.

Far away, in Mexico City, Secretary of State Edward Stettinius made a speech and chose this day to reveal the voting formula of the United Nations Security Council. It is difficult to concede that Stettinius would do this without the approval of Roosevelt. Ed was the Boss's pawn. The President's proponents could not figure out why the trump card—the veto—was "secret" in the speech on March 1 but was a public matter on March 5. If FDR thought that all the critical bricks would fall on Ed, he was wrong. They fell on him. After a moment's hesitation, the big newspapers editorialized about a Yalta "sellout to Stalin." The heaviest criticism came, not from the isolationist right wing of the Republican party (where FDR expected it) but from the liberal group which had supported him for twelve years. They demanded to know why he had given power to the Russians to nullify action by the United Nations if, indeed, it was to be a permanent peace-keeping organization. Of course, the power to veto extended to the other members of the Security Council, but suspicion focused on Moscow. The discerning editors asked an additional question: had President Roosevelt made any other "secret" agreements at Yalta—if so, the American people were entitled to know and pass judgment on them.

Bill Hassett was on his bed, reading a book called *Anna and the King of Siam,* when the White House pouch arrived. He drove at once to see the President, who had chosen to remain in bed. From his pillows in the second-floor room FDR could look out the French doors across the little porch he enjoyed, to the slow-sailing chunks of ice in the Hudson River. He studied the mail quickly. Then, without calling Grace Tully, he disposed of it to Hassett. A warning memorandum from Harriman regarding Romania received no more attention than other missives. Hassett left, and McIntire came in. He had heard from Bruenn that the President had a gastrointestinal upset. The Admiral would like to have a "frank" talk about it. Years later McIntire would insist: "I did not mince words or pull a single punch. . . . I repeated my warning that he was no longer a young man able to take liberties with his health. *Admitting that tests proved him organically sound,* I stressed the dangers of lowered resistance—pointing out that a rundown condition opened the door to every variety of ill." Thus the Admiral and the President continued their charade. McIntire never told his distinguished patient that, eleven months earlier, he had called in some of the best physicians in America for a "panic" consultation. The frank talk wasn't frank. McIntire knew that Roosevelt was down twenty pounds from his normal weight of 187. He knew, from Bruenn's reports, that the Boss suffered from hypertensive heart disease. He knew that the blood pressure was chronically high. Even though there were no medical tests to measure hardening of the arteries, McIntire knew that Roosevelt had the classic symptoms. According to McIntire's account of the frank talk, the President finally "confessed" that he had been working too hard, and "he gave his solemn promise that he would be a good patient, neither playing hooky nor running out on a single rule."

If there was a tangible result of the talk, it was that FDR decided to stay in bed and postpone leaving Hyde Park until the next day, Wednesday, March 7. His stomach distress lessened, but the mail pouch was so heavy with work that he remained in bed all day, dictating to Grace Tully and issuing directives to Hassett. The train was standing in the station at Highland, New York, all afternoon. It was not until 11:00 P.M. that Roosevelt sat in his *Ferdinand Magellan* and had a glass of orange juice with his assistants before retiring.

On the same day, in Moscow, Molotov summoned Harriman. The crisis in Romania was over, he said. A new and friendly government had been formed. Therefore, he would regard the American protest as "now pointless." Harriman displayed no anger. He doubted, he said, that his government would recognize the new regime.

The deadly little game which McIntire and Roosevelt played with each other began anew the day the President arrived in the White House. There was no afternoon nap, no rubdown by Fox. In addition, it was a busy day. Nor did he sleep enough. The President was off the train and into the White House limousine at 8:30 A.M. He went to the upstairs office at once and summoned Jonathan Daniels and William Hassett. He said he would see Senator Barkley and Congressional Leader McCormack first. After that, he wanted to study the daily mail and find some time for dictation. Then he would receive General Joseph Stilwell. Two new ambassadors were to present their credentials. Major General Patrick

Hurley and General Albert Wedemeyer were waiting. He might see them after lunch, but asked, for some mysterious reason, to see them separately. He would like to see Admiral William Halsey just before lunch. There was a special message from MacArthur. FDR said it could wait until after lunch. Ditto Winston Churchill. "When I find the time," the President said.

For Roosevelt, this was a day on which nothing happened. But it was choked with the multitudinous duties of a Chief Executive as fatiguing, in its way, as the Yalta Conference. The frank talk, as both men knew, concealed more than it revealed. He wore a bright smile for Barkley and McCormack. He told them he had proposed a manpower bill, but it was still in committee. He wanted it out, unemasculated, and on the floor of both Houses for a vote. Barkley said it wasn't that simple. McCormack told the President that many congressmen, including "some on our side of the aisle," were opposed to the bill. Roosevelt wanted a "work or fight" bill; Congress, and their constituencies, could think of nothing but victory and peace. It was in the mood of the nation; the President's Yalta speech made it the more poignant. Roosevelt waved his snowy hands in protest. He had warned America that the "wars," plural, were not over. Too many men were drifting away from wartime plants to peacetime jobs. Something would have to be done to stop the tide. Barkley and McCormack had a dozen parliamentary reasons why it would be dangerous to bring the bill to a vote "right now." The President observed bitterly that some legislators were hoping that a quick knockout of Germany would obviate the need for any law.

The mail came next. Tully and Brady were summoned in tandem to take replies. To both women, it seemed as though the Boss was reading mail quickly, tossing off deft, terse responses, and leaning back in inertia. Vinegar Joe Stilwell brought with him twelve Philippine Rangers, in boots and whipcords. He introduced each man to the President of the United States. The General said that these were in a group which had stormed the notorious Japanese prison camp at Cabanatuan in January and had freed 500 starving American captives. Roosevelt was impressed. He remarked that they were very young—like boys. He was interested in a new ribbon they wore, one he had never seen, called the "Philippine Liberation."

It was lunchtime, but FDR sandwiched one more visitor in his schedule—or, rather, two: Ambassadors Baron Robert Silvercruys of Belgium and Alberto Tarchiani of Italy. He enjoyed their presence because both represented newly liberated European countries. In his customary informal manner, Roosevelt told them of the decision at Yalta regarding helping liberated nations to find a fresh footing, to bring them to full independence and a healthy peace. He had just dispatched Sam Rosenman to London to find out the needs of such nations, and to lend assistance.

The ambassadors left, the silvery steam table was wheeled in. The President asked that it be removed. He would have lunch in a half hour. That was the amount of time he could give to Hurley and Wedemeyer to find out what was going on in China. Hurley was admitted first. Afterward, he said that he was so stunned at the sight of Roosevelt's drawn face and drooping jaw that he could not speak. When he sat, Hurley went into a monologue about the intransigence of Chiang Kai-shek and the impossibility of drawing Mao's Communists and the Kuomintang into a single group to fight the Japanese. The President's mind was elsewhere. He listened with apparent attention, but when he spoke, it was not about China, but about Indochina. Hurley tried to keep him on Chungking, but he was in Hanoi. The people of Indochina, he insisted, deserved their independence. He wanted them to be free of France. De Gaulle was going to send forces to Indochina to subdue those people, and Roosevelt wanted to thwart that. Regarding China, the President said that Hurley's mission remained unchanged. Knock those Oriental heads together until they could see that they must coordinate their strength against the Japs, or be defeated separately.

General Wedemeyer, whose report on China echoed Hurley's, came in. The General did not get far. The President ordered him not to hand over any supplies—any supplies at all—to French forces operating in Asia. He wanted that clearly understood, because he and Stalin had agreed that Indochina required a United Nations trusteeship, not colonization. The French were determined to get back in there, and FDR would keep them out. In the Big Three, only Winston Churchill was opposed to a trusteeship, and that was because he had inherited an empire and wanted to protect all colonies from independence. Look at the Dutch, he said. Queen Wilhelmina told him that Holland was planning to give Sumatra and Java their independence after the war. This was the wave of the future—not empires, not spheres of influence. General Wedemeyer left with no orders about what to do with China.

Admiral and Mrs. William Halsey arrived next. Roosevelt greeted them effusively and said he expected them to remain for lunch. Then he presented the Commander of the gallant Third Fleet with a gold star instead of a third Distinguished Service Cross. He signed the citation and gave it to "Bill." However, the presidential hands were hardly controlled enough to pin the gold star so he handed it to Mrs. Halsey, who pinned it to the D.S.M. ribbon. As lunch arrived, Roosevelt remarked happily that he well remembered giving Halsey a gold star years before "for being a very good destroyer skipper." The Admiral smiled. The event had never occurred. After lunch the two men excused themselves and left Mrs. Halsey. Roosevelt took Halsey aside and revealed a lot of secrets about Yalta. Later, the Admiral said, "I would have preferred not to know them." FDR even told him the circumstances under which Russia would attack Japan.

Basil O'Connor was ushered in. Roosevelt's old partner in the Warm Springs Foundation and the annual March of Dimes was now President of the American

Red Cross. "Doc" said he wanted to acquaint Roosevelt with some of their fund-raising methods. The President said he was surprised, happy to see Doc in any case. O'Connor said he had been on the morning calendar of appointments, but someone had taken his name off, and he had waited in the West Wing until the President had a few minutes for him. Tully brought a presidential order for signature. It established a federal emergency board to prevent a strike on the Denver & Rio Grande Western Railroad.

It had been a grueling day. Roosevelt had listened and talked and listened through most of the morning and afternoon. General Marshall sent a MacArthur position paper to the President. The General, who was supposed to be under the direction of the Chiefs of Staff, often gave them advice on how to run the war. He wanted Roosevelt to read them, too. This one, summarized, read:

> As to Russia, General MacArthur pointed out that politically they want a warm water port which would be Port Arthur. He considered that it would be impracticable to deny them such a port because of their great military power. Therefore, it would only be right that they would share the cost in blood in defeating Japan. From the military standpoint, we should make every effort to get Russia into the Japanese war before we go into Japan; otherwise we will take the impact of the Japanese divisions and reap the losses, while the Russians in due time advance into an area free of major resistance. General MacArthur suggested that the President should start putting pressure on the Russians now.

It was read wearily. General MacArthur knew nothing of what had transpired at Yalta. The President pressed his desk button. Dorothy Brady came in. "Child," he said, "ask General Marshall to acknowledge receipt of this, and put it in your file." He left the office, and stopped in to see his doctors at McIntire's office. They were in professional attendance twice a day since the homeward voyage, and at times he was digitalized; at others, he was not. Whatever was happening inside the once magnificent body, the President surrendered without a fight to deterioration. As he became confirmed in the habit not to ask questions, he now appeared resolved to circumvent doctor's orders and do as he pleased. It became common for him to appear at the little clinic around 5:45 P.M. and ask for nothing more than nose drops.

He must have slept well and deeply because, in the morning, the President's mood was ebullient when Anna, Hassett and Daniels entered the bedroom. His face seemed so much more animated that the warmth of it reflected itself in the spirits of the visitors. Hassett drew FDR's attention to another heavy schedule, and counseled canceling some of it. No, no, the Boss said. I want no appointments Saturday; let me see them today. The benevolent smile was hardly expected because FDR had lost half the fight in behalf of Henry Wallace. He preferred to think that he had won half. Wallace was confirmed as Secretary of Commerce, but the Senate refused to allow him to become Federal Loan Administrator. Instead, they confirmed the President's second choice, Fred Vinson. The beaming visitors were told that, when they left, Mr. Vinson was expected to call at the bedroom. The three left almost precipitously.

He would not forgo the usual press conference, even though he had little news to disseminate. A reporter, who observed that the morning headlines said that Eisenhower's forces had crossed the Rhine at Remagen and that the Russians had crossed the Oder, asked FDR whether the war had reached a point where Germany might collapse overnight. "That," said the President, "is a crystal-ball question." He was asked if he would go to the conference at San Francisco and replied, "I don't know." The only thing he had to worry about, he said, was that Congress had failed to enact a work-or-fight law. It was much more important than people realized, he said. The press knew, he guessed, that the Canadian Prime Minister, William Mackenzie King, would be a White House guest this evening. Some had heard rumors. The reporters found the Canadian to be a colorless, terse man who never gave them news. Jonathan Daniels told Roosevelt that the press had a jingle:

> *William Lyon Mackenzie King*
> *Never tells us a goddam thing!*

FDR said he would recite it to the Prime Minister—it was funny. He worked hard on papers and mail. Governor Herbert H. Lehman, dear friend and political ally from New York, waited in the West Wing an hour before, at 11:45, Roosevelt could see him for fifteen minutes. As Lehman departed, National Democratic Chairman Robert Hannegan and New York Chairman Paul Fitzpatrick arrived. They had been marked for twenty minutes of time, and they were present to speak of spoils. A half hour later Bill Hassett entered the office noisily, but the gentlemen acknowledged no hint. They stayed. They talked. At 1:00 P.M. they were still with the Boss. Again Hassett came in and shoveled papers from the President's "In" box to the "Out" box, and back again. The Boss had invited Secretary of the Navy James Forrestal and Fleet Admiral Chester Nimitz to have lunch at 1:00. The politicians did not arise from the comfortable chairs until Roosevelt glanced at his watch and said, "Well, Bob. I guess that's about it." They left at 1:20, slightly irritated to learn that FDR would not attend the annual Jefferson Day Dinner, a Democratic gala staged each year. The best he could do, he said, would be to try to send a message which could be read to the distinguished diners.

He was back from lunch at 2:40, a half hour late to greet Prime Minister King, but the two men were friendly sons of Harvard and could forgive each other lapses in time. Nor could he remain long with King; a Cabinet meeting was scheduled. The secretaries gossiped among themselves about how energetic the President was today. Miss Tully saw it in another light; he was working hard and recklessly; he was a man, unable to walk, running at top speed, Roosevelt, as Governor and as President, had always been able to deputize authority. The team of men with whom he surrounded himself were able and efficient, in the main. The ladies in the secretarial office agreed that what the Boss had today was "bounce." These unobtrusive, loyal females had long become accustomed to Roosevelt's "down" days as well as the "up" days. This March 9 was an "up."

The next day, Saturday, FDR planned another long rest at Hyde Park. He would once more ride the slow, slow train to New York and up the Hudson River Valley. He had been studying reports from Harriman and Stettinius about Poland, and he could not credit what he was reading. In spite of solemn agreement to the contrary, Molotov would not permit Harriman and Clark Kerr to speak to Polish candidates, refused them permission to visit Warsaw and announced that members of the new, broadly based Polish government would consist solely of men invited by the Lublin Poles to become candidates. All others need not apply. Roosevelt kept his own counsel on this grave situation. When he mentioned it at all, it was to say that, when Stalin got back to Moscow, the Politburo may have felt that he had been too soft in his agreements; they may have attacked him and stiffened his attitude toward his allies. At least, FDR *hoped* this was the situation. The only other option would be to think that the Soviet Union had committed itself to liberal, far-reaching agreements, knowing that when Stalin returned to Moscow he could disavow those which did not support Russian expansionism. If this were true, Stalin's word was worthless and he had gone to Yalta smiling and offering flattering toasts knowing that he had betrayed the Big Three.

On Saturday, the tenth, a long cable arrived from Churchill, who was truly at wits' end. Reports from Clark Kerr repeated what Harriman sent to the President, and added that Poland was now in a state of convulsion because the Red Army, with the connivance of the Warsaw government, was rounding up herds of anti-

Communists who were being beaten, robbed of their land, tried and summarily executed as "Fascists." Any citizen of prominence in any city or village who did not meet the approval of the Warsaw group was tarred with the word Fascist, even if he could prove he fought the Germans in the Polish underground.

Churchill's Top Secret to FDR said that two members of his War Cabinet had resigned over the Polish situation, "four others abstained" from voting. "The Lublin Poles may well answer that their government can alone ensure the 'maximum amount of political tranquillity inside,' that they already represent the great mass of the 'Democratic forces in Poland,' and that they cannot join hands with *émigré* traitors to Poland or Fascist collaborationists and landlords, and so on, according to the usual techniques. Meanwhile, we shall not be allowed inside the country or have any means of informing ourselves upon the position. It suits the Soviets very well to have a long period of delay, so that the process of liquidation of elements unfavorable to them or their puppets may run its full course." Churchill referred to the venom between Poles of varying political hue "whose hatreds would eat into live steel."

The Prime Minister and the President were sick to their souls of Poland. They could bear the ravagement of Romania, even though that too was ashes in their mouths, but the sovereign independence of Poland had triggered World War II; it was the reason Britain and France, in obvious reluctance, declared war on Germany. In the summer of 1939 Poland had been free, and defiantly independent of both her huge neighbors—Russia and Germany. For either the United States or Great Britain to acquiesce in Russia's plan to crush Poland, to enslave it politically and economically, to steal her eastern provinces on the premise that Germany would pay Poland in the west was, in effect, to say that the entire war had been an exercise in futility.

Appended to this Top Secret was another. Churchill suggested that he would send this message to Stalin (provided he had FDR's approval) and he hoped the President would send a similar warning:

. . . I am bound to tell you that I should have to make a statement of our failure to Parliament if the Commission in Moscow were not, in the end, able to agree on the following basis: (a) M. Molotov appears to be contending that the terms of the Crimea communiqué established for the present Warsaw Administration an absolute right of prior consultation on all points. In the English text, the passage of the communiqué in question, which was an American draft, cannot bear this interpretation. M. Molotov's construction, therefore, cannot be accepted. (b) All Poles nominated by any of the three governments shall be accepted for the consultations unless ruled out by the unanimous decision of the Commission, and every effort made to produce them before the Commission at the earliest possible moment. The Commission should ensure to the Poles invited facilities for communicating with other Poles whom they wish to consult, whether in Poland or outside, and the right to suggest to the Commission the names of other Poles who should be invited to its proceedings. M. Molotov has raised objections to inviting M. Mikolajczyk, but his presence would certainly be vital . . . The Soviet Government should make arrangements to enable British and American observers to visit Poland and report upon conditions there in accordance with the offer spontaneously made by M. Molotov at an earlier stage in the Commission's discussions. We must not let Poland become a source of disagreement and misunderstanding between our two peoples. . . .

For the first time in a long and cordial relationship, Roosevelt did not reply. It amounted to more than bad manners; it was fear. Before Yalta and throughout the conference, he had hedged and retreated a little before Soviet greed. He needed the Russians for the larger good, active participation in his United Nations. They were fundamentally suspicious of the organization and might seize on any excuse to withdraw. If they did, the United Nations would be a Western World peace organization. One of the most powerful nations in the world would not be bound by its strictures. A hungry wolf would be prowling outside the corral. The President could not afford this. He could not challenge Stalin to honor the Yalta agreements; and, dismally, he could not fail to challenge him.

The President asked John Boettiger to find Robert Murphy at once and invite him to a dinner *en famille* with Mackenzie King. Murphy, like Sumner Welles and Hiss, was one of the intelligent and sophisticated diplomats with whom FDR surrounded himself. Murphy was a troubleshooter—a man to be sent to the danger zones. Six months earlier the President had told Murphy that he would be appointed United States High Commissioner in Germany. Murphy was also told that FDR felt certain that the occupation and administering of Germany would turn out to be the true test of Soviet-American cooperation. The diplomat wanted to hear more, but he was turned away, and whiled much of his time at the Army-Navy Club. Six months can be a long time. Robert Murphy was astounded to be paged at the Army-Navy Club and be told by Hassett that the President expected him for dinner—informal dress —around eight o'clock. The linkage of events, the Prime Minister's anguished cable about Poland, and Harriman's distressing notes from Moscow, make it appear that the President needed his favorite troubleshooter at once to ask what course to take regarding Poland.

To Murphy, the evening was a shocking disappointment. He made notes of his impressions:

When Roosevelt was wheeled into the second floor oval study his appearance was a terrible shock; he was a mere shadow of the buoyant man who had talked so confidently to me the previous September. He was aware of how badly he looked and mentioned that he had lost thirty-six pounds. . . . Stettinius told me the previous summer that Roosevelt's health was a matter of grave concern to his friends. Stettinius said that a few of Roosevelt's most trusted supporters had made an agreement among themselves to call upon the President in a body, to beg him not to run for a fourth term because he was so near collapse. The next time I saw Stettinius was after the election, and I asked him how Roosevelt had received the group's suggestion. Rather shamefacedly Stettinius admitted that all of them had lost nerve and nobody had mentioned the President's health to him before the election. Now Roosevelt's decline was so obvious that I was startled when he exclaimed: "Well, it's almost over!" But he was referring to the war in Europe, not to his own life.

After dinner Mackenzie King departed. The President said he would like to have a private chat with Murphy. "But," wrote Murphy, "the man who sat across from me that night was unable to discuss serious matters. He talked for an hour, but aimlessly." It was a study in pathos to watch one of the great men of history flounder in monologue, filling in his own silences with pointless asides and a small smile. It may have been the President's ardent desire to present the Polish problem and to ask an able diplomat for his best thinking, but he never mentioned Poland. He barely mentioned the Russians, but tottered from there to the subject of Germany. He told Murphy in detail about his student days in Germany, and of the arrogance and belligerence of Germans when they donned uniforms. The important thing, he insisted, as Murphy gave the President his full attention, is to keep the Germans out of uniform. "The uniform does something bad to them, especially to the young men."

Murphy used several of the aphasic silences to bring the subject around to his work in Germany; for instance, how to reconcile the divergent interests of the occupying powers; how best to utilize Germany's natural resources; in what light did the President see the future of Europe? The gentle, almost childlike responses of the President forced Murphy to regret condemning General George Marshall for making decisions in Germany which Murphy thought were the President's prerogative. Within the hallow precincts of the State Department, Murphy had been saying that Marshall had no right to decide who should take Berlin or where the Allied armies should meet. On this night he felt that he understood, as Winston Churchill asserted privately, that the President's subordinates were making decisions and writing Top Secret messages over Roosevelt's signature.

In the morning Dr. Bruenn began a rigorous examination. The eyes of the young Commander told him that his patient appeared to be slipping away, but his instruments denied it.

The President began to ignore his rest regimen [he wrote]. In addition to a heavy schedule during the day, he began to work much too late in the evenings. His appetite had become poor, and although he had not been weighed, it appeared that he had lost more weight. He complained of not being able to taste his food. There was no nausea. Because of the anorexia, digitalis was withheld for several days, although no digitalis toxicity was discernible in the electrocardiogram. There was no cough or cardiac symptoms. Heart size was unchanged. The sounds were clear and of good quality. The rhythm was regular, and the apical systolic murmur had not changed. Blood pressure values were somewhat lower. Despite the withdrawal of digitalis, he was still troubled with his lack of appetite. Otherwise, he insisted that he felt well. Digitalis therapy was resumed.

Late in the morning FDR changed his mind about responding to Churchill's message. He seemed to fear that, if he did not stop the Prime Minister, he might force Stalin into a confrontation from which neither side could retreat with grace. "I feel that our personal intervention would best be withheld," he radioed, "until every other possibility of bringing the Soviet Government into line has been exhausted. I very much hope therefore that you will not send a message to Uncle Joe at this juncture, especially as I feel that certain parts of your proposed text might produce a reaction quite contrary to your intent. We must, of course, keep in close touch on this question." It was almost, not quite, a do-nothing entreaty. The President expected Harriman and Clark Kerr to fight it out on Molotov's level. Churchill feared that his old sailor friend did not appreciate the true situation; that time was on the side of the Lublin Poles; that they would entrench themselves with Russian help and decimate all the democratic elements in Poland with impunity. And yet, as Churchill told Eden, he would have to remain in unity at Roosevelt's side because Great Britain no longer had the power to confront Russia—it would have to be the United States *and* Great Britain. The despairing truth seemed to be that the United States had the power, but its Chief Executive no longer knew how to exercise it.

The first thing the reporters noted at the 995th press conference on Tuesday, March 13, was that FDR was in a convivial, almost jocular mood. In the press room later some said he was "on top." Others said the Boss was "himself again." Health became a mercurial matter; the President vacillated between intellectual acumen and a vacuous attitude which was impossible to penetrate with ideas and conversation. These extremes presented themselves within hours of each other. Physically, Mr. Roosevelt slid downward without remission; in his wheelchair he looked like an assortment of wrinkled clothing with a freely nodding head. Bruenn had an accurate appreciation of the situation. He had been deeply concerned for a year; now he was worried. He made his daily reports to McIntire, but it was akin to reciting a theorem to a professor in medical school. The heart muscle became enlarged trying to pump blood nourishment to billions of body cells. The arteries became harder, less elastic as blood was squeezed through them at higher speed in narrowed walls. The most damaging aspect of generalized arteriosclerosis is that when brain arteries harden, they bring less sustenance—especially sugar—and this reduces the patient's ability to think, to concentrate and to absorb fresh knowledge. With it comes impatience, irritability, at times a dreamy euphoria and, sometimes, a sudden return of intellectual capacity.

The President felt well on this morning. Mackenzie King sat beside him, silent, as Mr. Roosevelt read a statement to the press announcing the presence of the Prime Minister of Canada and the unflagging friendship of the two nations. He said that he had met with the American delegates to the United Nations and that they discussed "the physical arrangements" of the first conference, not the political aspects. It had been known that Roosevelt was a political ally of the fusion mayor of New York, Fiorello H. La Guardia. Now, the reporters said, a Democrat named William O'Dwyer was to run against him. Who would the President support? The conference broke into laughter when the President said he had read two views in two New York newspapers: "One was right. One was wrong." The gentlemen asked about the U.N. voting procedures of the Big Three. FDR recognized the danger and flapped his oratorical wings without ever leaving the ground: "That, of course, is the trouble with answering the question at all. People will line up and say that is a victory for Mr. Stalin, or for Mr. Churchill or for me. I should say it was a common agreement. Well, that means it wasn't a victory for anybody, because they were all agreed. Honestly agreed as being what—what we all thought it was the best thing to do. In history, the question of who proposed it is the smallest end of it. If anybody has a better idea, we would be glad to consider it."

The press expected the President to explain and justify the statement of Edward Stettinius in Mexico that there was a veto power. This time, instead of permitting Roosevelt to disengage in laughter, several men began to press him with questions simultaneously. One asked if it was true that two powers could overrule discussion "on any proposal that might be brought up, not only force but anything else?" At this point, the President became confused. "As I remember the thing—the easiest way of putting it—on everything that is procedural, not the actual use of force, you have to have a majority of eleven. It sounded as though eleven votes would be required.

Q. Any six? ...

A. No, in other words you can look into things, anything you want, and go through all the preliminary procedures by a majority vote. You don't have to have unanimity at all— the majority vote of the eleven. When it comes to the use of power or sanctions, that requires a unanimous vote of the five larger nations.

They understood very little more than they had before the press conference. He would not spell out the use of the veto, and there was no point in pursuing it. One man said, "Mr. President, would you care to commit yourself on the subject of night baseball?"

Bill Hassett and Grace Tully kept the appointment calendar to a minimum. Once, when the President asked his acting appointments secretary whom he would see today, Hassett said, "Nobody, Mr. President. The only date I have is on Saturday the seventeenth. It's your fortieth wedding anniversary." The President smiled. There was a small dinner scheduled to celebrate that event. From March 11 to 17 he had no appointments. The doctors, in concert with the secretariat, turned many people away. The President was not told because his reaction would be, "Oh, let them stop in for a minute or two." There was no question in the minds of those who worked with him that Roosevelt was now aware of the alarming and deteriorating state of his health. Who was more aware that he could no longer bathe himself, or trust his fluttering hands to shave himself? Who understood more poignantly that his signature on documents had become almost indecipherable; that he, and he alone, asked again and again what he had been talking about; that after a long night's rest he awakened exhausted; that, in listening to a conversation, his mind wandered so that he lost the thread of the topic. His bathroom mirror told the President a story he did not wish to hear. If he had reflections on death, he told no one.

All his official family knew was that, in the past year, the Boss had become "a man in a hurry."

If . . . if . . . if only Poland would blow away. If only those three votes for the Soviet Union could be engulfed by good news. If only Russia would honor her signature under the liberated-areas paragraph. If only he could make Churchill and Stalin see that spheres of influence, expansionism, far-flung empires were important structures in a twentieth-century world. If . . . One of the "ifs" Mr. Roosevelt did not wish to discuss was his generous spirit of compromise, his proclivity for surrendering to demands which involved high principles. "If" he had stood his ground on Poland and the liberated area of Romania, would Stalin have capitulated? He would never know, because the President assured Harry Hopkins and Stettinius that he must keep the ultimate goal in sight: a permanent peace-keeping organization, in addition to Russia's willingness to come into the Japanese war at a price.

His impatience and irritation surfaced on the thirteenth when he received another Top Secret from the British Prime Minister:

At Yalta we agreed to take the Russian view of the frontier line. Poland has lost her frontier. Is she now to lose her freedom? That is the question which will undoubtedly have to be fought out in Parliament and in public here. I do not wish to reveal a divergence between the British and the United States governments, but it would certainly be necessary for me to make it clear that we are in the presence of a great failure and an utter breakdown of what was settled at Yalta, but that we British have not the necessary strength to carry the matter further and that the limits of our capacity to act have been reached. The moment that Molotov sees that he has beaten us away from the whole process of consultations among Poles to form a new government, he will know that we will put up with anything. . . .

The President was hopping mad. He saw the message as a threat from a friendly quarter. Churchill conceded that England did not have the power to force Stalin's hand, but, if the United States didn't, he would be forced to reveal a split between Great Britain and the United States. FDR was in favor of responding to it defiantly, but he was persuaded to wait, to "sleep on it." Neither the Prime Minister nor the President could see Stalin's side of the situation, which was that Russian blood had freed Poland at a fearful price, and, acknowledging the long-term suspicions between the two nations, the stronger had no intention of permitting the weaker to establish an independent regime which, on some far-off tomorrow, might plot against the Soviet Union.

On Friday, the sixteenth, Roosevelt canceled his customary press conference to work on a response to Winston Churchill. It was completed and sent "top priority" in the late morning:

I cannot but be concerned at the views you expressed in your message of the 13th. I do not understand what you mean by a divergence between our governments on the Polish negotiations. From our side there is certainly no evidence of any divergence of policy. We have been merely discussing the most effective tactics, and I cannot agree that we are confronted with a breakdown of the Yalta agreement until we have made the effort to overcome the obstacles incurred in the negotiations at Moscow. I also find puzzling your statement that the only definite suggestion in our instructions to Harriman is for a political truce in Poland. [Note: Churchill made this statement in an earlier message.] Those instructions, of which you have a copy, not only set forth our understanding of the Yalta agreement, but they make the definite point that the Commission itself should agree on the list of Poles to be invited for consultation, and that no one of the three groups from which the reorganized government is to emerge can dictate which individuals from the other two groups ought to be invited to Moscow. . . . Our chief purpose remains, without giving ground, to get the negotiations moving again.

The tone of personal irritation and affront moved Churchill, in spite of the late hour in London, to fire off a placating radio message to Roosevelt:

I am most relieved that you do not feel that there is any fundamental divergence between us, and I agree that our differences are only about tactics. You know, I am sure, that our great desire is to keep in step with you, and we realize how hopeless the position would become for Poland if it were ever seen that we are not in full accord. . . . At present all entry into Poland is barred to our representatives. An impenetrable veil has been drawn across the scene. This extends even to the liaison officers, British and American, who were to help in bringing out our rescued prisoners of war. According to our information, the American officers as well as the British who had already reached Lublin have been requested to clear out. . . .

On a hilly side street in Berne, Switzerland, there was a neat house with a small, overly precise garden in front. It looked like other houses except for beamed ceilings on the ground floor. The man who lived in it was the epitome of the retired, conservative businessman. He wore rubbers and carried an umbrella. None of the neighbors knew him except for a nodding *"Gutentag."* He was an owlish American who lived quietly. His name was Allen Dulles, and he was chief of the Berne branch of the Office of Strategic Services, America's first central intelligence agency, a hypersecret arm of the United States Joint Chiefs of Staff. The director of all operations was General William J. Donovan.

Dulles had radio transmitters and agents who worked for him, ferreting information about the Germans and transmitting it to Washington. In the code books Dulles was known as OSS/Berne. He was depressed about his work when, in 1943, President Roosevelt issued a proclamation about "unconditional surrender." Dulles felt that this hamstrung him. He could not bargain for group German surrender if the terms were unconditional. He was certain that the President had made a monumental mistake. And yet, every now and then, information reached him through underground sources that certain German generals would like to make a deal. Dulles could offer nothing in return for surrender.

Life became monotonous. A trickle of information passed through Berne to the Pentagon, but all it proved was disaffection for Adolf Hitler. No one felt strong enough to publicly oppose the Führer. A break in the monotony occurred on February 25, 1945. A Swiss Intelligence officer told Dulles that an Italian industrialist, Baron Luigi Parilli, would like to discuss the surrender of German forces in Italy. Dulles arranged a meeting and learned that Parilli represented a Nazi general, Karl Wolff. This man, who was an SS general under Himmler, sent word that the German forces under Field Marshal Albert Kesselring in northern Italy were tired of losing battles and retreating. They would like to arrange an armistice, perhaps a surrender. Dulles was suspicious. He told Parilli to go back to Wolff and ask him to show evidence of his good faith by releasing two well-known Italian prisoners: Ferruccio Parri, an underground leader, and Major Antonio Usmiani, who, besides working for the Italian Army, was Dulles' key agent in Milan. Three days later Mr. Dulles was summoned to a hospital in Zurich. There he was introduced to Parri and Usmiani. They had been blindfolded, taken to a car with drawn curtains and driven from Milan late at night. General Wolff had met the test. The Nazi sent word that he would like to meet Dulles in Switzerland to discuss surrender terms.

Dulles was uncertain. He arranged to meet Wolff at a Swiss café, without informing his superior, General Donovan. The Nazi turned out to be slender, a man with a scissored nose, one who fancied himself the darling of the drawing rooms and art galleries. He admitted that he had stolen King Victor Emmanuel's coin collection. Getting to the business at hand, the General said that further bloodshed would be a crime. Hitler had lost the war. He understood that the surrender of Kesselring's forces in northern Italy would have to be "unconditional." The Field Marshal, he said, could be "won over" to it. Wolff, however, as an SS general, was acting independently, without informing his superior, General Heinrich Himmler.

A meeting was arranged for March 19, at a small villa on Lake Maggiore, near Locarno. When Wolff left, Allen Dulles sent word of the prenegotiation talk to Field Marshal Alexander, chief of Allied forces in Italy. He detailed each step that he had pursued. The British Field Marshal was sufficiently impressed to send U.S. Major General L. L. Lemnitzer and British Major General Terence Airey, both disguised as Army sergeants, to Berne. They brought with them an OSS agent with the unlikely name of Davy Crockett. The mission was dangerous for the men of both sides. Wolff arrived, looking like a man destroyed. He said that news of the release of the two prisoners reached Himmler, who phoned and angrily ordered Wolff not to leave his post under any circumstances. As an afterthought, Himmler told his subordinate that he had located Mrs. Wolff and their children at St. Wolfgang on the Tyrol and had confined them to their home. Nervously, the Nazi General had spoken to Field Marshal Kesselring several times about surrender. Kesselring was "willing to listen" when Adolf Hitler's personal plane arrived with orders that the Field Marshal was to be transferred at once to the western front. The vacancy in top command was assumed by an unknown, Colonel General Heinrich von Vietinghoff. General Wolff said he would need two more weeks to speak to the new commander. To prove that he was trying to accommodate Dulles, he agreed to hide an OSS radio operator in Milan. A young Czech named "Wally," who spoke German fluently, was chosen for the post.

The talks were now under way. Wally, who was quartered in an attic at 22 via Cimarosa in the center of Milan, sent his messages regularly to Dulles in Berne. Mr. Dulles, however, made no report to the White House or the Pentagon. The whole matter, he felt, was in Alexander's hands. One of the secret meetings was postponed because Wolff flew to Kesselring, on the western front, to ask for a personal note to Vietinghoff, assuring him that he would be doing the correct thing in surrendering. Kesselring would not write a message; he gave one orally. Wolff brought it back to Italy. Vietinghoff said he would think about it. The decision was in delicate balance.

Meanwhile, on March 12, Alexander notified the Combined Chiefs of Staff in Washington of the pending negotiations. They approved the sending of Lemnitzer and Airey to Berne, but advised Alexander to wait until the Soviet government was informed. In Moscow, Harriman passed the word to Molotov, who said that the Soviet government would be interested in this spy-thriller and would dispatch three Army officers to take part in the negotiations. Harriman relayed the word to the Pentagon. The response was instantaneous: there would be no point in sending three officers to Berne, because nothing would be accomplished except to arrange a meeting between Allied and German staff officers at Caserta, Italy. There the Russians could join the others. In addition, the Combined Chiefs of Staff asked Harriman to make it clear to Molotov that, if serious negotiations became a reality, Field Marshal Alexander would conduct them and "make the necessary decisions." The Soviet High Command sent a message to Harriman that, if their officers were to be witnesses and not participants, they chose not to send anyone. Also, in the light of Big Three agreements, which clearly stated that all three would be parties to surrender on any front, the Soviet Union "insisted" that the surrender negotiations stop at once.

Their fear was a real one. Since June 1944, when Eisenhower launched his attack on *Festung Europa,* the Russians had suspected that Hitler would give ground to the Americans and British, while using his main strength on the Russian front. This suspicion was valid. Hitler had plucked divisions from in front of Eisenhower and sent them in long troop trains to fight in Poland. Secret negotiations on the Italian front could mean that German divisions would "melt away," to be found later facing the Russians on the Oder. Churchill, who was aware of the Dulles dilemma, was conscious of the Russian view at once. If the German Army in Italy surrendered, all available German soldiers, guns and tanks would be rushed to the Oder; also, the gate would be open for Alexander and his Fifth American Army and Eighth British Army to race across the undefended land to Vienna, perhaps to the Elbe River in Germany.

What had begun in Berne as a test of intentions was now out of control. In Moscow Molotov conferred with Sir Archibald Clark Kerr and handed him a diplomatic note dripping with bitterness:

In Berne for two weeks, behind the backs of the Soviet Union, which is bearing the brunt of the war against Germany, negotiations have been going on between the representatives of the German military command on the one hand and representatives of the English and American commands on the other.

Clark Kerr protested that there were no "negotiations," merely attempts to test the credentials and authority of an SS general named Wolff. Foreign Minister Molotov's response was insulting: "In this instance," he said, "the Soviet government sees not a misunderstanding, but something worse." Churchill, who was at the western front with Eisenhower and Montgomery watching the crossing of the Rhine, received the coded dispatch from Clark Kerr and showed it to the generals. Eisenhower became angry. His pink face reddened. The whole thing, he insisted, was a military matter, not a political one. On his front, he would accept the unconditional surrender of any body of troops from a company to an army, and he had "full authority to do this without asking anybody's opinion." He would merely insist that they lay down their arms and stand where they were. Then he would run his divisions through them to the east.

The Big Three dispute was flaring toward the loudest and highest on Saturday, March 17, but the insulation

of the White House from world events is best depicted
in the daily diaries of two members of Roosevelt's
team—Admiral Leahy and Bill Hassett. Leahy's jottings
follow:

*Major General Hull called to discuss a statement of the
War Department's attitude toward Russian objection to
proposed negotiations for the surrender of the German
Army in Italy. The War Department's attitude, prepared by
Secretary Stimson, is, in my opinion, a splendid statement
for the information of the State Department. The Soviet Government has taken the stand that negotiations for the surrender of German troops on the Italian Front should not
be undertaken until Soviet Representatives are permitted to
participate in the negotiations.*

*Dined with the President and Mrs. Roosevelt at a dinner
of 18 given in celebration of their fortieth wedding anniversary. The guests included Juliana, Crown Princess of
Holland, the Dutch Ambassador Dr. Loudon and his wife,
Madame Vantets, lady-in-waiting to the Princess, with
her husband, Assistant Secretary of State Nelson Rockefeller, War Food Administrator Jones and Mrs. Jones, and
Colonel and Mrs. Boettiger. Following the dinner we saw a
moving picture of the Crimea expedition at which I sat on
the right of Princess Juliana and found her interesting and
attractive.*

Had Admiral Leahy conferred with the President
about the Russian situation, it would have been a major
entry in his diary. The fact that General Hull took his
War Department position paper to Leahy indicates that
FDR was circumvented. Hassett, who had a keen appreciation of standing on the edge of history, waited
until bedtime to pen in longhand his observations. Hassett
kept few secrets from his diary. If the schism between
Russia and her allies had been brought to the President's
desk, Hassett, Leahy and Tully, among others, would
have been aware of it. However, a photo-facsimile of
Bill Hassett's diary depicts no hint of a storm:

March 17   Saturday   St. Patrick's Day and the fortieth wedding anniversary of the President and Mrs. Roosevelt, complete contrast in the position of the principals to the scene forty years ago when the bride was given away by her "Uncle Ted"—President Theodore, in New York where the ceremony of the marriage was performed. T.R., in the very heydays of his popularity, stole the whole picture . . . Having racked my brain for a suitable wedding present for a couple with so many possessions, finally fell back on two dozen yellow roses—Mrs. Roosevelt's favorite.

The President received Senator Elbert Thomas—to talk about work or fight legislation—in the oval study of the White House this morning and afterwards conferring with Senator Magnussen. Had asked him to get these appointments out of the way today in order to relieve the heavy pressure of callers next week. He did not go to the Executive Office today. . . . After dinner, which was good although scant in accordance with war restrictions, a very good movie was shown. The party dispersed soon after eleven o'clock. The President went to bed saying he would sleep until noon . . .

The old sailor at last saw the dark squall line growing in the east but he declined to take a reef in his sails. The political weather was so good that he invited two probing, questing writers to the White House. Edgar Snow, a competent journalist and sometime China-watcher, was surprised to find that FDR did not share his suspicions of Russia's intentions. "I got along absolutely splendidly with Stalin this time," the President said. "I feel I finally got to know the man and like him." Mr. Snow pointed out that the Bear's paw was heavy on Poland. Mr. Roosevelt leaned back in his chair and waved all pessimistic questions aside "with airy optimism." The Russians, he admitted, were "going to do things in their own way in the areas they occupy. I got the impression that the Russians *are now fully satisfied* and that we can work out everything together. I am convinced we are going to get along." In sum, the President was condoning Soviet injustices and cruelties to date, certain in his heart that they had grabbed all they wanted and would behave in the future. He sincerely saw himself as having played a strong hand at Yalta. Even in his private conversations with Stettinius and Byrnes, Roosevelt did not see that he had exposed his jugular vein to the Soviets by his repeated passionate pleas for the formation of a United Nations. When Stalin, Molotov and Vyshinsky saw it for what it was—the culminating triumph of his life work—they began to use it as a weapon to see how potent it might be. They asked for sixteen votes in the Assembly, and were declined. They reduced the demand to three votes, and got them. They refused to join if the Security Council could vote sanctions against the Soviet Union for any belligerent act in the future. They were appeased only when they were given an implacable veto over the Council. The Kremlin knew that, as long as FDR was in office, they could use the U.N. jugular as a pressure point. The President did not suspect it, nor, if the private papers of Jimmy Byrnes and Stettinius are examined, did they. Both men appeared to be convinced by the Boss's euphoric vision that "everything will be all right." Russia could be trusted.

Author John Gunther was also invited to the White House; the difference between him and Snow was that Gunther had an eye for small sentimentalities, whereas Snow's interest lay in the countermoves of international diplomacy. Mrs. Roosevelt invited Gunther to the President's private study on the second floor, and the author scribbled notes on the indexes to Roosevelt's character: a photo of his mother on a wall facing the desk; a picture of his wife behind it; "dozens of naval prints" on all walls; a wall shade of maps which could be pulled down individually; some books reposing on the desk with their covers closed—*Palestine, Land of Promise; How to Win at Stud Poker; Guide to the U.S. Army; A Dictionary of International Slurs;* a paperweight marked "Penalty for Removal, $250. F.D.R." Later, Gunther wrote that he saw Roosevelt as "obviously an extrovert; a man with sharp and eager curiosities; a restless man who liked ships, travel, his family, games and hobbies; a man with a strong sense of both past and future; a practical man who liked to do things with his hands and who loved life." And yet, as Gunther's eyes frisked the room, he saw piles of loosely tied bundles, heaps of old books and documents on the floor; old and yellowed government reports; a "tower of old phonograph records"; many packages tied with cheap string. Gunther had a second thought: "It seemed to be the room of a man who was packing up, who was going away."

The first false softness of spring brought warm breezes and cherry blossoms to Washington; government clerks ate their lunches in the parks, holding chins up to the sun; rhododendron hugging the south walls of the White House were in outrageous flirtation with the tall, naked oaks and elms. It was a moment for a migrating bird to stake out a home on a high branch close to the seat of power; a time for the thoughtful to ask themselves if this indeed might be the final spring of a long convulsion a day for lovers to think of unutterable poetry.

It was on such a day that President Roosevelt, frowning with anger, studied a Top Secret message of protest from Josef Stalin. He would like to know why the Americans and British had been holding bilateral peace talks with Kesselring without notifying their allies, the Russians. If the situation had been reversed, he would have no objection to the participation of British and American representatives in the discussion. He hoped that Roosevelt realized the military effect these secret negotiations would have on the eastern front.

The President "got his Dutch up." First, he called Leahy and Marshall to find out what was going on. This time, no note-taking secretary was permitted into his office. None of the three men discussed or wrote about the conference later. The Boss had a right to be angry over his lack of information. Leahy and Marshall insisted that there was nothing to talk about—there had been no surrender negotiations. Dulles had made a few preliminary contacts with a German general. It was Field Marshal Alexander, on the scene, who suggested that the Russians not be notified until a true negotiating

peace conference had been arranged to take place at
Caserta. Until that time, there was nothing to discuss.
Besides, the Combined Chiefs of Staff had endorsed Alexander's action by suggesting that, if the Russians were
invited to the preliminary arrangements, something
which might materialize in "four hours would take four
months."

FDR sent a message to Stalin, with a copy to Churchill.
There was a misunderstanding, he stated. The meetings
at Berne and Locarno were "preliminary talks," not
negotiations for peace. The discussions were concerned
with the "mechanics of a meeting." The President insisted
that neither Great Britain nor the United States was
violating the letter or the spirit of the Yalta agreement. This was purely a military matter which had not
yet matured; he would have to support his officers in
the field. As a military man, he said, Stalin knew "there
can be in such a surrender of enemy forces in the field
no violation of our agreed principles of unconditional
surrender and no political implication whatsoever." The
President might have taken into consideration Russia's
primary concern, which was that German forces would
leave the Italian front for the eastern. Although the
State Department and the ranking military men were
at his side when the reply was drafted, nothing in the
message assuaged Soviet fear; nor did it invite Russian
participation in the Berne negotiations.

A separate message was sent to Harriman asking
him to ascertain if it was Stalin who was sending the
messages, or the Politburo over the Marshal's name.
This, ironically, was the question Churchill was asking
himself about Roosevelt. Harriman sent a terse message
that the words and reasoning were Stalin's. It was a
cruel blow to FDR, who was certain that he could win
the cordial trust of any man, if he could talk to him
face to face. He was stunned. "All this proves one of
two things," he said. "Either Stalin has been deceiving
me all along, or he has not got the power I thought
he had."

In Moscow the President's message did nothing to

soften the Soviet attitude. To the contrary, Soviet Intelligence reports made it appear that Roosevelt was brazenly deceiving his friends about his intentions. All the latent suspicions in the Slavic mind surfaced. Stalin fired another message to Roosevelt. It was his understanding, he said, that no member of the Big Three could discuss German surrender alone. Even then, such talks would be allowed only if there was assurance that the Germans would not use the talks to transfer troops to other fighting areas—above all, to the Soviet fighting front. The Russians, he said, should have been asked to attend the preliminary conversations. It might interest the President, Stalin wrote, to know that the Germans had already used the secret talks to transfer three full divisions from Italy to the Soviet sector. Stalin demanded to know what had happened to the military agreement of the Big Three to hold the enemy "on the spot," not permitting him to move. The Soviet marshals were living up to this agreement, but Alexander was not. In addition, Alexander appeared to be stalemated; there was no Italian offensive at a time when increasing pressure should be applied to the Germans on all fronts.

As the Russians raised their tone of voice to an angry pitch, so too did the President. He waited only one day to reply. He denied all the charges with indignation. He repeated to Stalin that there "have been no negotiations." The reason Alexander had not mounted an offensive was because some of his forces had been transferred to Eisenhower on the western front. Besides, those three divisions of Germans were taken from the Italian front before Dulles had heard of General Wolff. Couldn't Stalin see that the Germans were desperately trying to sow suspicion between the Big Three? "Why let them succeed?" The next message from Moscow displayed clearly that the Soviets felt they had been betrayed.

Stalin said that if Roosevelt insisted that no negotiations had taken place, then he could only assume that the President was not "kept informed by your military advisers." Stalin's Red Army High Command reported to him that negotiations were not only under way, but had been completed. Kesselring was about to open the whole north of Italy and the south of Germany to the British and Americans. In return for this assistance from Germany, the United States and Great Britain had already agreed to soften the peace terms for the Nazis. The President exploded. He tried to compose a statesmanlike reply, and couldn't. His hands shook; his lips trembled. He asked for assistance. The State Department, the Chiefs of Staff, and a speech writer were called in. As they wrote, the Boss rewrote. He demanded strong language. As the message was finally written, it asked that Stalin have faith that the President was honest and truthful. None of the field commanders, including Eisenhower, would enter into any negotiations with the enemy without "informing me." The negotiations which Stalin described had not taken place. In addition, from the moment of the first preliminary meetings, Molotov had been informed by Harriman. Far from not being informed by his generals, the President wrote, he "deeply resented the vile misrepresentations" of the Marshal's "informers." The untruths they had relayed to the Marshal indicated to FDR that they were trying, for a reason indecipherable to him, to destroy the grand alliance of the Big Three.

The distrust may, at this point, have been beyond repair. Stalin replied that he would not question the personal honor or truthfulness of the President. That was not at issue. Moscow had received certain information from Soviet Intelligence, and it believed this information to be accurate. He had to place his trust in his own advisers, not only because it was sensible, but because it was more accurate than the information of Russia's allies. Cutting hard and deep, he said that General Marshall sent word to a Russian general to expect a German attack at a certain point in the lines. Russian officers insisted to Stalin that the attack would occur somewhere else. The Red Army concentrated its strength at the place where it believed the attack would occur, and had stopped a German drive. Of course, he said, the Germans may have deliberately misled Marshall.

The correspondence stopped as suddenly as it began. The pressure continued. Molotov told Harriman and Clark Kerr that the Poles would be represented at the United Nations by the Lublin government. It was not a question, it was a declaration. When the western ambassadors said that this was impossible because their governments did not recognize the Lublin group, Molotov became harsh. He said that if the ambassadors reread the Yalta agreement they would find that the Big Three agreed to "add a few Poles" to the Lublin group, and that the Soviet Union had been willing to abide by this except that when he studied the list of names suggested by Clark Kerr and Harriman, "we found we had insufficient information about these men and their whereabouts." What about Mikolajczyk? they asked. The Soviet Foreign Minister said he felt he had a right to veto that name, and he had. Harriman said he doubted that the Lublin Poles would be admitted to the San Francisco Conference. The Foreign Minister said he had intended to tell the British and Americans that he could not attend the April meeting; Stalin was sending Ambassador Andrei Gromyko instead. As Churchill observed, "This threatens to make all progress at San Francisco, and even the Conference itself, impossible." The President felt discouraged. Too late, he realized that he had exposed the jugular to Stalin, and, if he wanted a peace conference, he would have to pay Russia's price. In the third week of March 1945 FDR saw his great dreams dissipated by acrimony. It was as though Adolf Hitler had been right all along. He had predicted, again and again, that the British and Americans would come to blows with the Russians; their ideologies opposed each other. All along he had told Keitel and Jodl and Propaganda Minister Josef Goebbels that it would happen, and he hoped it happened in time to help Germany. On the surface, the Big Three were still unified. They would remain that way only so long as the United States and Britain submitted to the ultimata of the greatest land power in the world—Russia.

Roosevelt felt depressed. Dorothy Brady and Grace

Tully knew it; when he had work to do he dropped the mask. He showed no anger. His manner was that of a man to whom very little is important. Everything can wait. He saw fewer and fewer people; those he allowed to sit and chat for a moment (Anna Rosenberg, Frances Perkins) saw the pasted-on smile, heard the witty story. In the White House he sat at lunch and at dinner listening to the Earl of Athlone rumble through old stories as Princess Alice nodded approval. Some who watched thought his mind was elsewhere. His skin no longer seemed gray; it had a sheen, a translucence, like a meerschaum pipe well rubbed. The eyes appeared to be larger, but this may have been caused by loss of weight in his face. Sometimes he spoke with animation, but no one could detect whether he felt it, or felt it was expected of him. He ate little. His recurring topic was, "Soon I shall be off to Warm Springs for a good rest." The President felt an assurance about Warm Springs; it was his personal Shangri-La. The wits in the West Wing said that when he went to Warm Springs it was like a salmon spawning. This time he yearned for it and counted the days.

A week before leaving, the President looked chipper in bed as he read a three-page single-spaced schedule of his train, POTUS, Washington to Warm Springs. It was technical railroad jargon, but he read it all:

Special train will leave 14th Street, Washington, 4:00 P.M. Thursday, March 29th, 1945, en route Warm Springs, Ga., with following consist, train to be made up in order named:

1 Auto Car (B & O 748)
1 Southern all-steel Baggage Car
2 1-2 Sleeping Car for crew
1 Radio Car   (1401)
1 8-section lounge (Hillcrest Club)
1 6-compt., 3-DR, Sleeping Car
1 Southern Railway Dining Car (3155)
1 7-Compt. Lounge Car   (Conneaut)

1 Private Car   (No. 1)

—

9   *Cars*

The report gave all the orders in sequence—how much ice, air conditioning, food; the train to be ready to leave no later than 2:00 P.M.; the minuscule problem of having Superintendent DeButts contact Superintendent Henry of the Pennsylvania Railroad to "work out details covering movement of train from Washington Union Station to 14th Street." Even though Car Number 1 had its own elevator built into the rear platform, the report ordered a ramp to be brought aboard in case of emergency. Southern Railway believed that the passengers would spend about a month in Warm Springs. Therefore "all equipment released at Warm Springs is to be returned to Atlanta and Pullman equipment handled as directed by Pullman Company." On page three one note stated: "There must be no excessive speed at any point, and no publicity should be given the movement." It was signed R. K. McClain.

His prolonged interest in railroading and sailing were products of a sheltered childhood on the edge of the Hudson River in the 1880s. There, from the lofty perch of a claybank which looked down on the New York Central tracks, he watched wood-burning locomotives chuff noisily along the edge of the river, spitting steam and hissing plumes of sparks and smoke. Two hundred yards farther out, he watched the majestic river boats, their side paddles fashioning trains of white foam, moving majestically up river to Albany with pennants snapping in the breeze. To a boy alone, they were the fanciful mysteries which moved past Crum Elbow on their way to places found only in his geography book. A big-eyed boy with a head whirling with imagination and adventure, one forbidden to leave the confines of the estate, might vow someday to be on that train, to sail on that boat, to see those places beyond all the hills in sight. To the

President, the three-page railroad report was a promise which quickened the heart.

He had six days to wait before boarding that train. It was becoming more tiring to endure those days, but he knew he could do it. To make up for not keeping his promise to have a post-luncheon nap, the President remained in bed late each morning. He had his breakfast conferences, and he remembered which slices of bacon belonged to Fala (if by chance he forgot, Fala sat on the floor facing his master and whistled through his nose until he got some attention), and he read more of the newspapers than usual. Normally, he scanned everything, the eyes pausing only on articles which were of interest to him; that, and the obituary page. In late March, as Arthur Prettyman drew the bath and set out the clothing for the day, Mr. Roosevelt seemed intent on reading everything, including some advertising.

The New York Times and the Washington *Post* gave him a lot of intrinsic information: President Roosevelt said that the question of penalizing workers who refused to remain on war jobs depended a great deal on "the individual cases. We have to get manpower or jeopardize the war." The temperature was 77 degrees. Bonwit-Teller had a sale on hats fashioned of strawlike cellophane, each designed with ribbon and pert veil for $10.50. In Cuba the legislature approved a bill authorizing men to serve in the armed forces of the United Nations. The wreckage of Berlin was estimated at 87 percent.

There were early advertisements for Mother's Day: "He'll be thinking of you on Mother's Day—May 13th. Next best thing to being with you, he'll want a good, true-to-life photo of you and baby. $8.95. Saks." At Newport News, Virginia, Mrs. Bradford Ripley II smashed a bottle of beribboned champagne on the steel bows of the mightiest of all aircraft carriers, the 45,000-ton *Midway*. It will use 1945-model Navy fighters so new they haven't seen action yet. There is an acute shortage of fats; salvage them for your country by turning them in to your butcher for red points. *A Tree Grows in*

Brooklyn began its fourth week at the Roxy Theatre. Watch for the opening of Judy Garland in *Meet Me in St. Louis*. In golf, Byron Nelson and Sammy Snead tied for the $10,000 Charlotte Open, played an extra 18 holes, and ended deadlocked again. In Wall Street Greyhound closed at 24; McGraw-Hill 30⅜; Standard Oil of New Jersey 60; Food Fair 17½; Boeing Aircraft 18⅝. In Amsterdam, Queen Wilhelmina returned for the first visit to her people since the Nazis overran Holland in May 1940. A West Coast labor leader, Harry Bridges, was ordered to pay his wife $450 a month alimony.

John David shops were offering gray flannel single- and double-breasted suits for $35. The classified ads listed plenty of jobs: legal steno. $45-50; receptionist-typist $30; comptometer operator $35; hotel night auditor NCR experience $165 mo.; bank clerks, all depts. $30-40; mail clerks $30. On the radio, an instrument Roosevelt enjoyed when he played solitaire or worked on his stamp albums, he had a wide range of choices: Bob Burns, with guest Leo Gorcey; Dinah Shore with Eddie Cantor; Abbott and Costello Comedy; March of Time with George Romney & others; the Rudy Vallee Show with Monty Woolley; Arthur Godfrey; The Fitzgeralds; John J. Anthony; The Make-Believe Ballroom and, for a news report, Prescott Robinson.

The President thought that food prices were too high, and he used federal price controls whenever possible, to bring them within range of income. The newspaper told him that chuck steak was 29–30¢, beef liver 37¢ leg of lamb 35¢, veal breastbone 17¢, codfish 39¢; large eggs 48¢ a dozen; broccoli 19–39¢, tomatoes 25–39¢ a lb., spinach 9¢, snap beans 17¢, cucumbers 17¢. He was, innately, as much a penny pincher as any housewife, and it annoyed him that eggplant, which he enjoyed, was up to 14¢ a pound. A figure on page two was not related to food, but it caught his eye and, as he told the morning conferees, saddened him: "Dead, Wounded, Missing in Action since Pearl Harbor 859,587." The

President said he saw that figure as the cream of American youth.

The Boss was wheeled into the big office on the main floor at noon on March 23. Nine persons were in chairs, fanlike around his desk. He radiated good cheer as he refused Prettyman's assistance and moved himself to his big leather chair. "Going to stop up and see the judge at Bethesda this afternoon," he said. The judge was Cordell Hull. The people facing him were his choices as United States representatives to the United Nations. Democratic Senator Tom Connolly, big-nosed Texan and loyal to FDR; Republican Senator Arthur Vandenberg, a balding critic within bounds; Democratic Sol Bloom of New York City; Republican Congressman Charles A. Eaton, and Virginia Gildersleeve, erudite educator. With them, more or less as witnesses or adjuncts, were Acting Secretary of State Joseph Grew, Bohlen, Dunn and Admiral Leahy.

First, the President said, this must be regarded as a secret meeting. Nothing uttered within the walls could be repeated to anyone. There would be no public announcement of their visit, or its purpose. He would like to discuss the forthcoming United Nations meeting at San Francisco. This was to be an organizational meeting; a gathering to form an enduring structure—nothing more. He supposed there would be a temporary chairman and perhaps a nominating committee for U.N. posts. All of those present, he assumed, had read the little blue book labeled Charter of the United Nations and Statute of the International Court of Justice. Heads nodded. Then they understood the voting procedure, and the status of the five permanent members of the Security Council.

In confidence he discussed some of the agreements and some of the snags at Yalta, but, he said, he felt that the British and the Russians were now full partners in the United Nations and it was only a matter of time until all the nations of the world would seek membership. One of the things he especially hoped the members would not reveal was that the Soviet Union had insisted on two extra votes in the Assembly for White Russia and the Ukraine. On the face of it, he admitted, it sounded inequitable, but it wasn't. The British and their dominions had six votes. In addition, Stalin had told him personally that, if the United States wanted three votes, the Russian delegation would endorse it. So a few votes this way or that would not mean much in a big Assembly. Besides, if any nation got out of line, the subject had to reach the Security Council. There, the United States had the same veto power as Russia, England, France and China. "At a later date, perhaps, the United States may ask for three votes—I'm not sure."

Looking at the faces around him, he chuckled and said, "I'm not making the same mistake Woodrow Wilson made—this is a bipartisan group." He said that he wished he had a government policy he could give to them, but it was all nebulous at this stage. He hoped that some small nations might be represented on committees; it would be a good example to the bigger nations. He had dreamed of the United Nations for a long time, he said, and he was always a firm believer that if men can get around a table and talk out their differences, no one will be inclined to resort to guns. The group left as Mr. Roosevelt held out a hand to shake. He did not tell them much that they did not know—except for the three Russian votes—but the five delegates were glad to have seen FDR to get his blessing on their efforts. As they left, he reminded them once more that they were not to discuss anything he had said.

He held a short press conference after lunch, then motored up to Bethesda to see the judge. Hull was in bed, looking stronger, and the two old politicians talked of many things. Roosevelt left, saying that he was going to Warm Springs for a month of sleep. He would see the judge when he got back. A short while later James A. Farley stepped into the hospital room. Hull spoke of Roosevelt's kindly visit. "I was shocked by his appearance. He looked like death. He himself mentioned that he was not feeling well. I asked him, then, what was the matter and he said it was a sinus condition which caused him to have repeated nausea. He told me about the Yalta Conference. He was general and vague. Now and then he lost the thread of the conversation . . ."

In the late afternoon, the President asked Lieutenant General Albert Wedemeyer to call, and he asked Leahy to sit in. Roosevelt told the General that he had read numerous reports from ambassadors and generals about the situation in China, but he still did not understand it. Or, worse, he could understand the disunity but couldn't comprehend why the United States missions could not do something to correct it. Wedemeyer began to explain, and FDR cut in and said he wanted to hear about Indochina. The General said he felt less qualified to talk about that little nation, but he would tell what he could. The President wanted to know what Wedemeyer could do to arm the resistance groups opposed to French rule. Wedemeyer was an able and handsome man, and he spoke a good military jargon, but Roosevelt did not seem to draw much from the conversation except that Wedemeyer and Patrick Hurley, by wheedling, might stop the opposing Chinese forces from fighting each other and begin to fight the Japanese. FDR said he was interested in that. The General said he could almost promise that the Japanese would at least be stopped; that they would not be able to advance deeper into China. However, he had to reason with an assortment of warlords. Leahy wrote in his diary that Wedemeyer was "a resourceful soldier of particularly high ability."

The calendar was flipping pages from its face lightly and airily, but the President was stubbornly dragging his body through every one of them. He insisted on not only reading the important mail, but a daily sample of random letters sent by average citizens. On the afternoon of the twenty-fourth, even though he planned to leave for Hyde Park and had appointments with adviser Bernard Baruch and Patrick Hurley, the Boss insisted on dressing up so that he and Mrs. Roosevelt could escort the Earl of Athlone and Princess Alice to Union

Station. There was a pile of mail still on his desk, and Dorothy Brady tried to remove it. "Leave it there, child. I'll be back in an hour," he said. On the official calendar, this was a "nothing" Saturday. He also wanted to see Robert Sherwood, playwright and speech writer, who had just returned from a visit to General MacArthur in the Philippines. The two men and Anna sat sipping coffee on the portico over the south grounds, looking down to the cascading fountains and the white admonishing finger of the Washington Monument.

As a writer, Sherwood was rare, he could articulate. He said that getting to MacArthur's headquarters was about as easy as getting inside the Kremlin. He had never seen so many officers detailed to do nothing but turn visiting Americans away. However, he managed to see Douglas MacArthur for three hours. His headquarters was in the midst of the desolation of Manila. The President had asked Sherwood to find out from MacArthur what kind of occupying government Japan should have when the war was over. The tall, spare playwright scissored his legs and told FDR that the proper type of occupation government would evolve in time; what he was worried about was who would be the Supreme Commander, American Forces, when MacArthur reached the Japanese mainland and Admiral Nimitz's warships anchored in Tokyo Bay. The President asked what he thought. Sherwood said MacArthur. "He's the ideal choice, I feel." FDR nodded. The playwright said he was surprised at MacArthur's broad knowledge of the Orient, and the General said that the war would end sooner than the Joint Chiefs planned in Washington. At this point, the President looked wistfully at Sherwood and said, "I wish he would sometimes tell these things to *me*."

Sherwood rapped out a confidential report for Roosevelt's eyes:

1. General MacArthur's intelligence service on the enemy and enemy-held territory is superb, due largely to the

Filipino guerrilla organization which was organized and directed under his command.

2. On the other hand, I was shocked by the inaccuracy of the information held by General MacArthur and his immediate entourage about the formulation of high policy in Washington. There are unmistakable evidences of an acute persecution complex at work. To hear some of the staff officers talk, one would think that the War Department, the State Department, the Joint Chiefs of Staff—and, possibly, even the White House itself—are under the domination of "Communists and British imperialists." This strange misapprehension produces an obviously unhealthy state of mind, and also the most unfortunate public relations policy that I have seen in any theatre of war.

The General had detailed a modern history of Japan for Sherwood, invoking the god-myth of the Emperor, who would, said the General, retain his sacred aura only so long as a strong Army and Navy kept winning. The Japanese believe that might makes right—ergo, if Japan loses the war, the people will think that the United States has been right. If the United States can refrain from occupying Japan in an imperialistic manner, treat the people justly and liberally, then "we shall have the friendship and cooperation of the Asiatic peoples far into the future." It was, FDR thought, a sensible report, one worth weighing when victory arrived. Unaccountably, the President began to speak about his Jefferson Day speech, obviously forgetting that he would be in Warm Springs and had already told the Democrats that he could not attend. His conversation moved from there to San Francisco, and a second speech. "You know," he said, "Steve doesn't think I ought to open that conference—just in case it should fail." He chuckled. "He thinks I ought to wait to see how it goes and then, if it is a success, I can go out and make the closing address, taking all the credit for it. But I'm going to be there at the start, and at the finish, too. All those people from all over the world are paying this country a great honor by coming here and I want to tell them how much we appreciate it."

Sherwood took his leave of the President. He was so distressed that he walked to the Carlton Hotel. There Mrs. Sherwood opened the door and said, "What's the matter?" Sherwood told his wife that the President was "in much worse shape than I have ever seen him." He had seemed unnaturally quiet, even querulous. Never before had Sherwood found himself in the position of having to carry on most of the conversation without reply. "He perked up a little at lunch under the sparkling influence of his daughter Anna. I left the White House profoundly distressed." The sun was far down as Sherwood spoke his dismal thoughts; in the White House FDR was back at his desk, reading and signing mail. At 5:45 P.M. he usually stopped at the clinic. After 6:00 P.M. Bill Hassett found him still bent over the desk, reading under a shaded lamp and signing mail. In the past month the Boss was given to scanning legislative bills and important mail. His dictated letters had become shorter. What he had to say could be done in two or three lines, followed by a cheerful greeting and his scraggly signature.

In the early evening the President was carried aboard his train. He asked to be placed in bed at once. He did not want dinner. Prettyman and Mike Reilly helped him to undress and get into his pajamas. He fell back on the pillows and nodded to extinguish all except the tiny night light. Presumably, as POTUS rolled out of the Washington yards onto the Pennsylvania mainline, he was asleep. In the mail he had read that day was a disturbing bit of news. The President had had so much of it that he acquired the habit of pretending that it didn't hurt. Jimmy Byrnes said he would resign in a month. Personally, these two men did not match or mesh. Byrnes was a perfectionist who was stubbornly independent. The excellence of his work was such that FDR didn't care if they seldom agreed on anything. He needed Byrnes; Byrnes had quit a good post as Associate Justice of the Supreme Court to marshal America's war resources. Now, like Pa and Harry the Hop and Louis the Howe and all the others, he was gone. Not dead, but gone. FDR had dictated a letter, which carried the date of the twenty-fifth, stating that "I was, of course, knocked off my feet yesterday when you wrote that you ought to resign this spring . . . It will be, of course, next to impossible to find anyone to substitute for you . . . I just hate to have you go. I shall miss you and Maude more than I can tell you, but be sure before you take up anything else to get a real bit of rest. . . ." He would not ask Byrnes to stay.

Hyde Park was an illusory haven. The President found little time to rest. He worked Dorothy Brady hard on Palm Sunday. Mrs. Brady would not admit to fatigue. If he could keep going, she would stay with him, her pencil dancing in the dervish motions of shorthand as his voice whispered hollowly. A Dutchess County farmer had written to FDR reminding him that, in 1912, he campaigned on the size of apple barrels, but now he was deciding the fate of the world with Churchill and Stalin. "I still say," the Boss whispered, "thank God for those good old days and for old and tried friends like you." He added, gratuitously, that he and Mrs. Roosevelt were planning to visit England after the United Nations Conference in April. Someone in the room said it would be dangerous to travel by ship in British waters. "The war," he said softly, "will be over by then."

The pool reporters, whiling away time in a motel room, spoke about the mystical aspects of the President's attitude. One minute he seemed to be up; the next moment he wasn't even present. The Gridiron Dinner had been held the previous Thursday night. There, all the White House correspondents had a chance to observe FDR. Allen Drury was saddened as he watched Roosevelt wheeled into the formal dinner. He looked old, thin, scrawny-necked, and he stared at the crowded tables with a vacant expression. He didn't even respond to the ruffles and flourishes of the band and the deafening applause. Leahy was there. So were Marshall, Byrnes and Ickes. There were Biddle and Morgenthau, Vice

President Truman, Senators Morse, Austin and Ball; Justices Douglas and Jackson. Danny Kaye and Jimmy Durante performed. The place was in an uproar of laughter. Mr. Roosevelt sat sipping wine all evening and smoking cigarettes.

When laughter engulfed the room, the Boss suddenly cupped his ear and asked a table companion to repeat the joke. A moment later, he would stare out at nothing; the vague expression in his eyes, his mouth hanging open. At the close of the entertainment, he was expected to say something. Microphones were placed before him. It was embarrassing. "I will say something," he said brightly. "I will speak about humanity. We all love humanity. You love humanity. I love humanity. In the name of humanity, I will give you all a headline story: I am calling off tomorrow's press conference." The gentlemen remained at their tables as the President was wheeled out. Drury thought he saw a spark of the old Roosevelt at the moment his wheelchair passed through the curtains: he saw "the head going up with a toss, the smile breaking out, the hand uplifted and waving in the old familiar way." The pool reporters talked about it in the motel room. Was he truly sick? Was it overwork? How could he bounce back if something was wrong? Should they ask for another report from McIntire? Would it do any good at a press conference if someone said, "Mr. President, how are you feeling these days?" No, that would do no good. He would say fine, fine, fine, except for lack of sleep or something. If there was a story in the President's health, they couldn't get it.

The following day FDR asked his cousins, Margaret Suckley and Laura Delano (Daisy and Polly) to join him on the trip to Warm Springs. He enjoyed their company at all times; they were a family tonic. Daisy was a knitter, and a recollector of old family stories; Polly was the gay gossip who pretended she knew all the naughty secrets of the Hudson River Valley. Mrs. Roosevelt wouldn't go; she had appointments in Washington and New York—a full schedule. But she was glad to hear that Daisy and Polly would accompany her husband.

They possessed the kind of conversation he needed. He had not slept well in his upstairs bedroom at Hyde Park and he said, "It's no good. I must go to Warm Springs." He tried to sign mail and Grace Tully saw his hand shake so badly that he could not control the pen. She stood and took a chance. The secretary grabbed the President's wrist. "I meant to tell you that this stuff can wait until we get to Warm Springs," she said. Her voice was choking. He looked up as she removed her hand, and said, "Thank you." Upstairs, Mrs. Roosevelt was catching up on her diary. Hassett too had a diary: "The President weary this morning," he was writing. "Hope he responds to the good air and quiet."

The President looked better on the morning of Tuesday, March 27. It wasn't much better, but he seemed able to concentrate on conversation and work. A Top Secret was in from Churchill. He begged the President to do something in concert with him regarding the Russian rape of Poland. Soon, he said, he would have to make a statement to Commons about the situation—failure in Poland, failure in Romania:

In other words, Eastern Europe will be excluded from the terms of the Declaration on Liberated Europe, and you and we shall be excluded from any jot of influence in that area. Surely we must not be maneuvered into becoming parties to imposing on Poland—and how much more of Eastern Europe?—the Russian version of democracy . . . There seems to be only one possible alternative to confessing our total failure. That alternative is to stand by our interpretation of the Yalta Declaration. But I am convinced that it is no use trying to argue this any further with Molotov. In view of this, is it not the moment now for a message from both of us on Poland to Stalin? I will send you our rough idea on this in my immediately following telegram. I hope you can agree.

Roosevelt was too sick to sustain a crushing blow, or to bear a confrontation with Stalin which might destroy his cherished hopes. And yet, after reading the second

cablegram, he buckled down to it manfully. He called
Tully in and gave her the message, ordered a copy sent
to Winston Churchill, and asked that both be sent on
Thursday, the twenty-ninth:

*Roosevelt to Marshal Stalin Top Secret March 29, 1945
I must make it quite plain to you that any . . . solution
which would result in a thinly disguised continuance of the
present Warsaw regime would be unacceptable and would
cause the people of the United States to regard the Yalta
agreement as having failed.*

It was done. The gauntlet had been thrown. The old
man knew that the reaction in Moscow could be severe.
Stalin could claim that it was the Americans and British
who had betrayed the Yalta agreement. He could pretend
betrayal and, with his huge relentless armies, move to
Berlin and beyond, gobbling up everything Russia
needed. He could "go it alone," as many of his ranking
officers had advised. He could scorn the unborn United
Nations and effectively kill it or weaken it by withdrawing Soviet participation. On the other hand, he
would forgo all Lend-Lease, without which the momentum of his armies might stop. Sometime soon his forces
would reach a point where they would face British and
American armies in German towns and across German
streams. What would happen then? The Soviet Union
had many enemies and few friends in the west. Could
he take the gamble? And what about the war against the
Japanese Empire? There, the Americans had the greatest army and the most powerful fleet ever assembled.
Could the Americans, in victory, take the Kuriles and
Sakhalin and Port Arthur? It was up to Stalin to ponder
the imponderables.

The President was in bed, wide awake, on the morning
of the twenty-ninth. He did not work and did not appear
to be thinking. His former law partner, Basil O'Connor,
walked the long narrow hall to the bedroom, knocked
and entered. A breakfast tray was on the bed. O'Connor
said he had to leave, had to get back to New York.

The President smiled and nodded. O'Connor looked at the white embroidered bedspread and the snowy hands lying on top. "I came to say good-bye," he said. "We're going to need you when the war is over. But unless you go away for ninety days and do absolutely nothing, so that you can get your strength back, there's a good chance you're not going to be around that long."

The President looked up at his old friend and murmured, "If I could only put on some weight . . ." O'Connor thought there was a "faraway look in his eyes." And yet at noon Mr. Roosevelt was dressed and downstairs, issuing orders for a return to Washington in the late afternoon. To Hassett, the Boss seemed "in a happy mood when he signed his mail." FDR was speaking about leaving for Warm Springs tomorrow. It was a sporadic topic. He referred to it as though it was a spa, a secret cave where an animal might find refuge and restoration. His mood was up. Word came of many landings on Philippine Islands. The American flag was snapping in the breeze over Iwo Jima. The fire-raid photos from Tokyo showed that much of the metropolis had burned in the high winds. The American Third Army was advancing so fast on German soil that it was low on fuel. Okinawa had been invaded. The Japaese High Seas Fleet—except for a few large units—was at the bottom of the Pacific Ocean.

Good news, bringing with it a feeling of well-being. In the afternoon, the President and his party drove to Highland Station and boarded the train which would bring them to Washington in the morning. Then, in the afternoon, they would be off to Warm Springs at last.

The President's Appointments

Appt.   Day: March 29, 1945
11:00   Hon. James F. Byrnes
11:30   The Secy. of State
         The Under Secy. of State
         Asst. Secy. Archibald MacLeish
         Asst. Secy. James C. Dunn

Asst. Secy. William L. Clayton
Mr. Charles E. Bohlen
12:00   The British Ambassador
Mr. Oliver Lyttleton
Col. J. J. Llewellyn
12:30   Sen. Alben W. Barkley
Sen. Elbert D. Thomas
Hon. James F. Byrnes
12:55   Presentation of Commission to Hon. Jonathan
Daniels
1:00   Lunch
4:00   (Lv. for Warm Sp.)

The President was at his desk at 10:30, anxious to be off in wartime secrecy on his special train. He could not help but hope that the desk calendar with its appointments would be the last he would see in a long time. He feared that he would not be able to remain in Warm Springs much longer than two weeks—leaving the piney hills for Washington possibly on April 14. He had two speeches to work up—one to be read at the Jefferson Day Dinner, the other a welcoming speech to the world delegates at San Francisco. Those things, in addition to a daily pouch, would constitute all the labor he expected at Warm Springs—not counting the occasional important visitor who would need a personal decision.

At breakfast in bed he had seen a copy of the New York *Herald-Tribune*. The President had read the story alleging that a highly placed Washington source said that the Soviet Union would get three votes in the U.N. Assembly. He had thrown the crumpled paper to the floor. The leak had to come from one of the five delegates. He rang bells, called Daniels and Hassett and got on the phone to the State Department. It was a dastardly thing, Roosevelt felt, for someone to abuse his confidence like this, but the genie was out. It could not be rebottled. Reporters in the West Wing were crying for confirmation or denial. FDR said that he was off for Warm Springs—too busy to see them, and disinclined to let Hassett or Daniels juggle the story. He suggested that Stettinius call a press

conference and confirm the voting situation. Ed said
that some of his assistant secretaries hadn't known about
the three votes until they read it in the *Herald-Tribune.*
The presidential word was, "Do the best you can." He
reminded his Secretary of State that the United States
had been promised three votes "if we want them."

Mr. Roosevelt, who was seldom guilty of a political
miscalculation, made a sizable one in his fear of telling
America about the three votes. Perhaps he underes-
timated the general intelligence. The *Herald-Tribune,*
which published the story first, rationalized the consequences in an editorial:

> While an Assembly packed by as many as sixteen Rus-
> sian votes would obviously be inadmissible, a difference of
> two or three, one way or the other, in an international assem-
> bly of sixty or seventy members could have no practical
> significance. Even as matters stand, the United States will
> be able to count on the sympathetic votes of the Philip-
> pines, Cuba and others as surely as the United Kingdom will
> be able to count on those of the dominions, and almost as
> surely as the Soviets will be able to count on White Russia
> and the Ukraine. To make a tortured issue out of such in-
> consequentialities would be to endow them with an alto-
> gether fictitious importance.

It was a sensible analysis, but did not go far enough.
The Western World, fearful of the inexorable might
of the Soviet Union, would, in most cases, cause Great
Britain and her dominions to follow United States leadership, to say nothing of South American countries which
had long-standing economic and political alliances with
the United States. Of the so-called Big Five on the Security
Council, Stalin was aware that America, Great Britain
and China would vote en bloc. Patently, this is why
Russia required the insurance of the single veto—to forestall the ganging up of the Western powers.

Mr. Roosevelt's self-imputation of guilt about the
three votes created a flood of suspicion which eroded
the foundations of the Yalta Conference. Huge question

marks began to appear in the press, the radio and news magazines. What else was Roosevelt hiding? they asked. How much did this tired old man give away in the secret agreements with Stalin? In fact, could Yalta be regarded as a sellout? How could the President, for example, reconcile the brutal suppression of democratic voices in Romania and Poland with the Declaration on Liberated Countries? What caused the abrupt silence of the most voluble statesman in the world—Winston Churchill? Commentators demanded from the President a "full disclosure" of what went on at Yalta. Random street interviews depicted the average American as worried, suspicious, almost hostile to the word "Yalta." The Kremlin, the White House and 10 Downing Street refused to acknowledge that there were any secret agreements, or codicils. It is of passing interest to note that the admiration of the people for Roosevelt was not impaired by the uproar. The scores of millions of citizens who believed that he was the greatest President since George Washington held fast in their faith. The few who despised him and referred to him as "that man" lifted the decibels of their contempt to a high pitch, insisting that, in communism, FDR had been a "fellow traveler" all along.

On the twenty-ninth this storm was beginning to darken the political skies. Grace Tully wrote: "He was wheeled into his office about 11 A.M. and I went in immediately to chat with him. At first glance, I could see that the four or five days at home had failed to erase any of the fatigue from his face. 'Did you get any rest at Hyde Park, Mr. President?' I asked. 'Yes, child, but not nearly enough. I shall be glad to get down South.'" At noon, press secretary Jonathan Daniels phoned Miss Tully and said that he *must* see the President before his departure. Miss Tully suggested that he try 3:00 P.M. At that time, he was outside the office, with Assistant Secretary of State Archibald MacLeish. The State Department had written a press release—belated and defensive— about the three votes:

Soviet representatives at the Yalta Conference indicated their desire to raise at the San Francisco Conference of the United Nations the question of representation for the Ukrainian Soviet Republic and the White Russian Soviet Republic in the Assembly of the proposed United Nations organization. The American and British representatives at the Yalta Conference were requested by the Soviet representatives to support this proposal when submitted to the conference of the United Nations at San Francisco. They agreed to do so, but the American representatives stated that if the United Nations organization agreed to let the Soviet Republics have three votes, the United States would ask for three votes also.

The British and Soviet representatives stated that they would have no objection to the United States and its possessions having three votes in the Assembly if it so desired. These conversations at Yalta related to the submission of a question to the San Francisco Conference where the ultimate decision will be made.

The statement proved Churchill's fear that the President was no longer in command of his own statements. The State Department had become FDR's department of clarification. Daniels and MacLeish waited in the President's Oval Office with Grace Tully. Her observation was:

We had been waiting for the Boss in the Oval Study and when he was wheeled in I was so startled I almost burst into tears. In two hours he seemed to have failed dangerously. His face was ashen, highlighted by the darkening shadows under his eyes, and with his cheeks drawn gauntly. Both Daniels and MacLeish looked at him closely and I could see that they also were struck by his appearance. They showed him the proposed statement, however, and drew him into a discussion of its meaning and exact wording. He read it with evident care but suggested only some minor changes before indicating his approval. Then he turned to the great pile of mail and bills which I had already laid on his desk.

All his life, FDR had gloried in triumphing over the tedium of trivia. On this day, he surrendered and turned away from the work. It was more than health; White House intimates had the impression that his spirit, his will, had been crushed.

In the pile were three handsomely bound copies of his D-Day prayer. They were birthday presents for Anna's three children: Sistie, Buzzie and Johnny. He studied them and smiled but seemed unable to inscribe them. Miss Tully reminded the Boss that, of the three, little Johnny was in Bethesda Hospital, dangerously ill with a streptococcal throat. The child was so sick that Anna, torn between her allegiance to her father and her duty to her son, had decided not to go to Warm Springs. The Boss pulled the bound prayer close to him and wrote a cheerful message to his grandson. Grace Tully noted that this would be his last White House signature for some time; the rest of the work could go on the train with him. He could flash his smile, but it was vacant. Also the long, optimistic monologues seemed to have been sealed in silences.

At 4:00 P.M. the motorcade was at the Government Printing Office platform. At the White House, Eleanor Roosevelt sat in the East Wing chatting with a dear friend from Albany, Margaret Fayerweather. The visitor had seen the President earlier in the day, and said she found it painful to see him "terribly thin and worn and gray" and that she could not bear to watch the way his hands shook, even when they reposed on his lap. Nor could Mrs. Fayerweather comprehend the calm of Mrs. Roosevelt. The First Lady thought about the subject for a moment, and said: "A loss of muscular control is noticeable. He no longer wants to drive his own car at Hyde Park. He wants me to drive—which he never did before—and he lets me mix the cocktails." And yet, as the President was now insulated against the candid stares of the world, his wife had insulated herself against worrying about his health: ". . . Franklin said to me last Sunday, 'You know, Eleanor, I've seen so much now of the Near East, when we get through here I believe I'd like to go there and live. I feel quite an expert. I believe I could help to straighten out the Near East.'" This dreamy projection into the faraway future was sufficient to steady her frightened heart. If Franklin was able to think so far ahead, there was no reason to worry. It did not occur to Mrs. Roosevelt that the President had no conception of Near East problems except that the Arabs were violently antipathetic to Jewish immigration; further, they had no interest in Roosevelt's notion of irrigating their deserts.

On the train the President sat in the big chair behind his desk, looking through the big picture windows as friends boarded. In his car he had Cousins Daisy and Polly; Mr. Leighton McCarthy, who had been associated with him in the Warm Springs Foundation; his law partner, Basil O'Connor. In other cars were the Three Musketeers of the press: Merriman Smith of United Press, Robert Nixon of International News Service, and Harold Oliver of the Associated Press. They had been muzzled by Jonathan Daniels, who set up the "ground rules —no press releases unless the President holds a press conference, or gives me something to give to you." Dorothy Brady and Grace Tully arrived together. Hassett brought his secretary, Alice Winegar; Dr. Bruenn was already on the train with his medical equipment; George Fox sat at the window of a compartment. The statuesque Louise Hachmeister, the President's chief telephone operator, was on the platform with suitcases. She and Dorothy Brady were the sparkle, the laughter of these trips.

The train was ready to depart as Anna kissed her father farewell and hurried the length of the car to get off. She saw Grace Tully and said, "Grace, I'd like to speak to you a moment—outside." They stepped onto the platform. "Grace, I wish you would try to have Father work a little bit each day on his mail. If he doesn't, he will get terribly behind and I think it is good to keep him busy." Miss Tully did not agree. "I will try to keep things moving," she said, "slowly at first." The women noticed that Dr. Ross McIntire was not aboard. The

Surgeon General of the United States had gratuitously promised a congressional investigation committee to testify. Bruenn had, in fact, taken over all of McIntire's presidential duties except the administration of nasal drops. Considering the mounting cardiovascular difficulties, Howard Bruenn was the ideal physician for the President. And yet, as though two doctors may be considered better than one, Anna and Grace felt that McIntire's place was at FDR's side.

The sun was still bright when two massive steam locomotives yanked the nine gleaming steel cars to attention and moved slowly out of the yards. The President, talking to his cousin, had a sudden thought and asked Arthur Prettyman to summon Hassett, Brady and Tully. When they got to his car he said that the thought had just occurred to him that "tomorrow is Good Friday. You three are the Catholics around here. Don't you think you ought to get off the train at Atlanta and attend services?" The three looked at each other. "You can join the rest of us at Warm Springs," the Boss said. It was one of the acts of consideration which endeared him to those around him. Tully, Hassett and Brady took turns explaining that Good Friday is not a Holy Day of Obligation, and it was not compulsory to attend services. In fact, there would be no services except what was called the Three Hours of Devotion—more a matter of meditation and silent prayer honoring the Three Hours Jesus spent on the cross than a sermon by a priest. The President did not insist, but he thought that they should go.

He left a secret in Washington. It reposed in the Gaelic breast of Leo T. Crowley, Administrator of Foreign Aid. Mr. Crowley had been summoned to an off-the-record conference with FDR. He was known as a self-made Wisconsinite who was both taciturn and garrulous. He had been in charge of Lend-Lease. On the day Roosevelt left for Warm Springs, his deep and almost mortal disappointment in Marshal Stalin surfaced. He asked Crowley how much Lend-Lease had been given to allies since the start of the war. "Over forty billions of dollars' worth," Crowley said. How much, Roosevelt asked, do the Russians owe us? "About eleven billion." FDR said that Henry Morgenthau was pushing a proposal to lend the Soviet Union $10 billion more for reconstruction. This, according to the Secretary of the Treasury, could be amortized at 2 percent interest over a twenty-five-year period. Crowley said that no one had asked his opinion, but he was opposed. The President smiled ruefully and shook his head. "I have yet to get any concessions from Stalin," he said. The features hardened. "Leo," he said, "we are getting down to the tail end of the war. I do not want you to let out any more long-term contracts on Lend-Lease. Further, I want you to shut off Lend-Lease the moment Germany is defeated. Don't wait for any further orders. Just cut it off the day Germany surrenders."

Lend-Lease was one of the great historic innovations of the twentieth century. To schedule its demise secretly, almost as an act of revenge, seemed perilously close to irresponsible statesmanship. The President did not even make it a written order. The one extra person who was privy to the order was James F. Byrnes, who heard it from Leo Crowley. The Secretary of State was not aware of it; nor was Harry Truman, General George Marshall, Admiral Leahy, Senator Alben Barkley; nor the leaders of the House, Sam Rayburn and John McCormack. The President must have known that, when Germany sued for peace, two of the victors—the Soviet Union and Great Britain—would be close to bankruptcy. When it happened, whether the President was at home or abroad, alive or dead, the cancellation of material assistance would be a crippling blow. But then, it was no more bizarre than what had happened to the secret agreement with Russia to go to war with Japan at a price. No one but President Roosevelt knew what had happened to that document. It was in a small safe in the White House. This, however, is hardly at variance with his disparate filing system. FDR had literally staked his life on an honorable, equitable peace structure for

the world. Exactly forty-nine days after the great conference at Yalta, the President, in a personal agony,
was prepared to admit that his man-to-man talks with
Stalin had failed. The Russians had betrayed him and
had violated their signatures. Secretly he called Crowley;
secretly he arranged a monumental revenge. The Lend-
Lease administrator was not told that when the European
war ended, the Soviet Union had agreed to make war
on Japan for a price—and part of the price was a continuance of Lend-Lease. Crowley left FDR with the
impression that he was to carry out the order whether
Roosevelt was in Washington or not.

Aboard POTUS the President ate early and asked Prettyman and Reilly to help him to bed. The train was
rocking easily between the Virginia battlefields of the
Civil War when he tucked the bedclothes under his arms
and said, "Now don't let that engineer set any speed
records. Tell him to take it easy." Reilly would take
care of it. He and the valet, as well as Bruenn, had
seen that big frame nude and they knew it was gaunt
and flaccid; there wasn't even a cushion of muscle on
the buttocks to protect the President from pains in the
hipbones as the train moved slowly around curves.

After lunch the crowd began to collect around the
tracks in little congealed groups. It was warm, sunny.
Looking up the long single track, the people of Warm
Springs could see the faint green of grass growing in the
stone ballast. On the hill overlooking the left side of
the tracks, the wisteria was fading from long arching
fingers of yellow to green. They knew he was coming.
They always knew in plenty of time, and they congregated
quietly, not as gawking tourists, but as old friends who
saw him only in the spring and the autumn. Dr. Neal
Kitchens, half past eighty, stared down the curving
emptiness, smiling a little. Once he had entertained his
friend at dinner. Ruth Stevens, manager of the white-
washed hotel across the tracks, wiped her hands on an
apron and hung it up. The salesmen had been fed their
lunch; the dishes had been done. She was going to stand

at the tracks. Frank Allcorn, the Easter egg who owned the hotel and was mayor of Warm Springs, mopped his shiny head and took his place along the tracks. A woman turned the key in her ladies' emporium and locked it for the day; Minnie Bulloch hurried to the little gabled railroad station. The Methodist minister stuck his long legs from his old car and said smugly, "Well, he's here again," but he wasn't. Not yet.

A car almost hit Mabel Irwin, wife of a physician. She had had to park a few blocks away, around a corner, and had hurried down the middle of the street, fearful that she would be late. Turnley Walker, a patient at Warm Springs, watched it all from his wheelchair. In the tiny depot C. A. Pless sat jetting tobacco juice into a can. He did not have to hurry with the others; Pless was *the* railroad official. He would know, before the mayor did, when those huge locomotives began to make the old tracks sing with their six-foot drivers. He was present for all the arrivals of branch-line trains; he had heard the brakes squeal to a stop as the cars tilted a little on the curve. The man who was coming was an old friend who waved to the crowd, but he gave an individual salute to C. A. Pless.

It was three o'clock and after when C. A. Pless lowered the crossing gates and stood on the tracks with his lantern. There were 600 people lining the right-of-way and they knew the train was coming. They heard nothing; they saw nothing. The crossing light winked red and a steel hammer hit the railroad bell repeatedly. Everybody pressed a little closer, to get toward the back of the train, because that's where he would be. They wouldn't crush for space; there was a native dignity about saying hello to an old friend, no matter how high his office. They would say "howdy" if he waved. A boy with his bare foot on a track said he could hear the train coming. Someone saw a black plume rising straight up in the hot sky behind the hill. He was here.

They watched the big green locomotives, in tandem, slide by the station hissing steam, the brakes squealing.

One car passed. And two. Three. Long, beautiful Pullmans. Up ahead, iron-wheeled luggage wagons waited where the baggage car would pause. The last car came into view, barely moving. The train stopped. On the main street, clerks hurried out to stand on the sidewalk above the station and watch. People—distinguished-looking people—got off the train. The Secret Service men stepped off the last car and formed an ellipse, all looking outward at the people. They saw a sea of smiles. The rear door of the last car opened and a wheelchair emerged. "There he is," they whispered. "That's him." The chair was pushed onto the little elevator and it came down to the track level slowly. Mike Reilly ordered two Secret Service agents to open a path to the big car parked ten feet away. Everybody craned. This is where he always waved. He didn't.

Those closest saw a figure slumped in the wheelchair. A gray hat was pulled over his eyes. The hands were clasped on the lap. Some old friends waved tentatively. The figure did not move. C. A. Pless, carrying his lantern, pushed his way through. He looked down at the figure and said nothing. He pushed his way back to the crossing. "Just like setting up a dead man," he said. Merriman Smith, short, dark, mustached, happy to be at Warm Springs again, swung down from another car. Ruth Stevens grabbed him. Her eyes were big with fear. "Honey, is he all right?" Smith smiled. "Tired to death. But he'll pull out of it. He always does."

Mike Reilly reached down into the wheelchair and put his arms around the bundle. He had been doing it for years. The back door of the automobile was open; the jump seat was waiting. Mr. Roosevelt always reached back to the door with both arms and, as Reilly held him, yanked his body toward the door and onto the jump seat. His arms were always herculean. Then, with a twist of his body, he would swing himself onto the back seat of the car. It was easy, an old act. Reilly tugged and lifted. There was no response. He used all his resources to get the President free of the chair. Then he carried him to the car, straining and puffing. Mr. Roosevelt had to be lifted and helped into the back seat. "I never remember him being that heavy," Reilly said. Frank Allcorn, the official welcomer, stepped forward. "Welcome home, Mr. President," he said. The gaunt face, half covered by the hat, came up. "Why," said the soft voice, the face tilting into a smile, "His Honor the Mayor." He lifted a palsied hand to move the hat upward. The hand missed and struck his pince-nez. The glasses fell off. A Secret Service man picked them up. The President snapped them on his nose peevishly. The hand was extended weakly to the mayor. In the car, he was above the crowd. The gray flickering eyes scanned the faces and paused on the face of old Neal Kitchens. There was a moment of recognition, then it faded. Dr. Kitchens turned toward home. Mabel Irwin stepped forward. She took his hand in both of hers, and searched the tired features.

The old charm began to sparkle. "I saw you back there, Mabel," he said. He gestured in the direction from which his train had come. She had not been back there. "I was looking out of the train and I saw you in your blue Buick—back there along Raleigh Road." He tilted his head back and turned on the Roosevelt smile. "I guess the old eyes aren't so bad." She stepped away, swallowing repeatedly. The chief of police got in his car and led the way. The motorcade crossed the tracks and disappeared on the lower dirt road. The people looked puzzled. C. A. Pless thought it was strange; the President always waved.

The Boss was at Warm Springs for the customary miracle. Pine Mountain had never failed him. Here, both health and spirits soared. He insisted on being driven past the swimming pool and Georgia Hall, waving greetings on both sides. Then past the chapel and up the winding clay road through the brisk pine trees to the Little White House, with its three fluted columns and the neat spare guest house on the far side of the circular garden behind the flagpole. Inside the front door, beside the umbrella rack, was the wooden armless wheelchair. He would wheel himself around the rooms, smiling at the barkentine ship models, the naval prints on the walls, all the shiny hardwood American furniture, his bedroom with its single bed and thin mattress to the left of the living room, Mrs. Roosevelt's to the right. He never paused until he had rolled out on the back portico, where a table and chairs waited for the hot sun. The black cook, the gardener, his blue Ford convertible, his big leather chair near the smoke-stained fireplace were always waiting. Beyond the guest house was the white fence with its "bump gates" for his car, and the two sentry boxes—one square, one five-sided. He would have to see all of this, every bit of it, before he would loosen his tie and sit back to breathe the goodness of the high Georgia air.

He did none of these things. Vaguely, he asked that he be carried to bed. Reilly emerged from the bedroom to tell Bruenn that the Boss "is very heavy." Dr. Bruenn entered the bedroom and made his post-trip examination. He found nothing unusual organically. In the living room there was a direct line to the White House. McIntire ordered Bruenn to phone and report if there were any physical changes. The phone remained on its cradle. The newcomers spent the rest of the afternoon sorting luggage and hanging clothes. They had early dinner at Georgia Hall. It was a cool, quiet evening, without the usual bite of chill. The night breeze was soft. Hassett left the table and found Bruenn outside, leaning against one of the columns. The White House worrywart said, "He is slipping away from us and no earthly power can keep him here." Dr. Bruenn looked away from the night scene to his friend. "What makes you think so?" Hassett interpreted the question to mean that the doctor would not commit himself; this was accurate inasmuch as Bruenn was the only person who had been a member of the "Roosevelt family" for a year and had been refused permission to discuss any aspect of his work. Hassett said he understood the doctor's position—"you have an obligation to save life, never to admit defeat. But remember, I gave you the same warning last December."

The doctor nodded. He remembered that Bill Hassett felt that the Boss was dying.

The secretary was, on the surface, a composed man. Underneath, he was emotional, a sentimentalist. "I know you don't want to make the admission, Howard, and I have talked this way with nobody except one. To all the staff, to the family, and even the Boss himself I have maintained the bluff, but I am convinced that there is no help for him." Bruenn, who had been conversing in an offhand manner, became solemn. Like Hassett, he had a subterranean vein of sentimentality, coupled with an emotional fear for the patient. "Who did you tell?" Hassett did not answer. "Doc O'Connor?" "Yes, Doc O'Connor." Hassett said that the Boss's law partner and he had come to the conclusion that the President was dying—both felt that way before the November election.

"How long have you had this feeling?" Bruenn said. "A year. At least a year. Look at the Boss's indifference after the Chicago convention. He didn't act like a man who cared a damn about the election. Then he allowed himself to get mad at Dewey for those low attacks and the Boss came back strong at the All-American boy in the Statler speech. He got his Dutch up. That did the trick." It was a rarity for Hassett to prattle. "In spite of a cold October rain in New York—which I admit he completed without a cold or even a sniffle—I noticed his increasing weariness as I handled his papers with him—particularly at Hyde Park, trip after trip. He was always willing to go through the day's routine, but there has been less and less talk about all manner of things— fewer local Hyde Park stories, politics, books, pictures— the old zest is going."

The meeting of the two men ended in unspoken sorrow. Hassett returned to his room to write:

I told Bruenn I had every confidence in his own skill; was satisfied that the Boss was the beneficiary of everything that the healing art can devise. I couldn't suggest anything which should be done differently, but that it was my belief that the Boss was beyond all human resources. I mentioned his feeble signature—the old boldness of stroke and liberal use of ink gone—signature often ending in a fade-out. He said that was not important. Reluctantly admitted the Boss in a precarious condition, but his condition not hopeless. He could be saved if measures were adopted to rescue him from certain mental strains and emotional influences which he mentioned. I told him that his conditions could not be met and added that this talk confirmed my conviction that the Boss is leaving us. . . . We said goodnight with heavy hearts.

In the morning, the last day of March, Bill Hassett drove up the hill with the White House pouch. He waved to "Hacky," standing in the doorway of the little room where she had her switchboard, nodded to patients and parked on the side of the Little White House. He had a good morning for the Secret Service agents who stood outside—Hassett noticed that they had installed a telephone in the shrubbery almost under FDR's bedroom window—and he was more than pleasantly surprised when he stepped inside and found the President cheerful and conversational. With him, Margaret Suckley and Laura Delano shared coffee. To Hassett, this was a startlingly different man from the one he had seen yesterday. Roosevelt called Brady; he fixed his glasses, read the mail, dictated responses and, shortly after noon, signed it. He literally waded through a mountain of work.

At 5:00 P.M. Hassett was back with one unsigned letter. He saw Dr. Bruenn sitting on a couch. Hassett was surprised twice in one day, this time "shocked at his appearance—worn, weary, exhausted. He seemed all right when I saw him in the morning. Told me he has lost 25 pounds. Tires so easily. All too apparent when you see him after midday. Later observed this to Dr. Bruenn. He admits cause for alarm." It was Bruenn who, a year ago, had frightened McIntire and an assortment of noted medical specialists into holding secret meetings about the health of the President. The young

Navy Commander was alone this time. He phoned his concern to Admiral McIntire; the patient seemed to be failing in an erratic manner. "He began to look bad," Bruenn reported. "His color was poor, and he appeared to be very tired, although he continued to sleep well. Heart and lungs were unchanged. . . . The physical examination was unchanged except for the blood pressure, the level of which had become extremely wide, ranging from 240/130 to 170/88. There was no apparent cause and effect." The life of the President of the United States had been hanging in the balance for a year. He had used all the palliatives and specifics known to cardiology and his unremitting care had kept the wasted body functioning—perhaps beyond what could be expected. The Commander, for the first time, admitted to being worried because the decline in health was accelerating. Bruenn could think of nothing to do which had not been done. Sometimes his eyes told him more than his instruments. Roosevelt was an animated human being from 9:00 A.M. until 1:00 P.M. Each day, at lunchtime, he appeared to shatter into helpless fragments. The good nature seemed intact, but the body and the mind faded in function toward a smiling helplessness.

Under the rules, Dr. Bruenn was not permitted to call in additional medical help, had he felt so disposed. The best he could do was pick up the phone and ask Hacky to get Admiral McIntire so he could make his daily report. That, and nothing more.

April 1945

THERE WAS A RAIN-RUTTED ROAD MOVING DOWNHILL from the Little White House like a healing scar through rhododendron and hawthorn bushes and the overbearing maples and pines to the chapel at the bottom. The house

of worship was small, a white brick edifice with a steeple
and a bell, purposely designed to be quaint, as though
the venous ivy and flowering mimosas might endear
the supplicants to God. Inside were five pews with a
broad center aisle for wheelchairs. The altar was small
and severe, holding a crucifix and gold candelabra. The
chapel assumed unusual importance on the first day
of April because this was Easter Sunday. It was an extraordinarily bright and warm morning with a cheek-
touching fingertip of breeze. It was a day made for
dwelling on all sorts of resurrections.

The children who lived in Georgia Hall, across the
street, were out early hunting colored Easter eggs in
their wheelchairs. There were shouts of elation and groans
of disappointment. The adults sat in their chairs or leaned
on crutches watching from the porch. People from the
Lovett Cottage, the Carver Cottage and the Pierson
Cottage—all around the chapel—had been attracted by
the noise. A few older patients, unable to think of a
reason to be grateful, had been wheeled by nurses off
the back porch of Georgia Hall to the swimming pool.
Through the woods and on the far side of Pless's railroad
tracks, three reporters scraped the grits off the country
ham and eggs at the Warm Springs Hotel and discussed
the first news event of the trip, a visit by President
Osmeña of the Philippines. Although the purpose of the
visit had not been revealed, Mr. Roosevelt expected to
use the sick little man as a propaganda showpiece; he
would promise the Philippines their independence from
the United States as a gesture to Stalin and Churchill to
grant freedom to "liberated countries."

At 10:00 A.M. Arthur Prettyman had finished bathing,
shaving and dressing the President. The Boss asked
for his gray suit and a blue-figured tie. Prettyman, who
was completely devoted to the Boss, would not reveal
all the little services which the President could no longer
do for himself. He would not volunteer to Bruenn that,
for months, Mr. Roosevelt had been unable to wield
a razor, button a shirt, move his body from wheelchair
to toilet or, unless he pressed himself, spin the wheels

of his chair. The Chief Petty Officer and personal valet was as eager to assist the President as he was to hide the progressive weakness he saw so clearly. On the train Prettyman had watched Basil O'Connor chatting with FDR, and he listened with deepening sorrow.

"How are things with the Red Cross these days, Doc?" FDR had asked. Good, O'Connor had said. Hectic, but good. "And the National Foundation? Warm Springs?" Good, too. Over $10 million had been raised in the annual March of Dimes. As always, half had been left in communities to fight infantile paralysis; the other half went to Warm Springs. "We gave half a million to research," O'Connor said. "Warm Springs itself is in good shape. We'll treat six hundred fifty patients this year." The President shook his head sadly. "Doc," he said, "I want to apologize." "What for?" "Look what I've got you into." "All I ever wanted—" "I know, I know. To be a lawyer." The President leaned forward and grabbed O'Connor's knee. "There's this to be said for your life, Doc. Most men just go down the middle of the street, doing their chosen work. You've done that with the law. But you've also gone down the sides—working for the advancement of an important science, and spending every spare hour you've got helping take care of the other fellow who's had some trouble. It's not a bad way to make the journey and I take back that apology." Leighton McCarthy had walked in, and the men spoke of getting rid of the big swimming pool—it wasn't helping polio patients. The President seemed saddened. Some of his most hopeful days, he said, had been spent in that big pool, moving his legs a little and playing furious water polo with children. McCarthy and O'Connor said that the trustees agreed the pool should be abandoned, left to dry its walls in the Georgia sun. O'Connor stared at the President and frowned. His head was sagging, his mouth hung wide open, the shoulders hung forward. O'Connor glanced at McCarthy. "Bedtime," O'Connor said loudly. The President did not move. He seemed not to have heard. Arthur Prettyman hurried to Roosevelt's side. The President's law partner watched him taken away. "Our friend is dying," he said softly. Prettyman heard it.

At 11:00 A.M. on Easter Sunday the little chapel was full, except for a couple of aisle seats. The patients could hear the squeak of the President's wheelchair, but no one turned. With him were Daisy and Polly, brightly attired. Three Secret Service men were behind the Boss. He would not sit in the aisle. One man helped him to the pew. The two cousins got inside first. The agents knelt in the pew behind. A minister emerged from the sacristy and began the service. Easter lilies were in two vases on the altar. The President appeared pleased, as if this place too evoked old and pleasant memories. The congregation knelt to pray. The President sat, bowing his head. He reached for a hymn book and his glasses clattered to the floor. Silently, a Secret Service man stepped forward and crouched. He found the glasses, unbroken. Mr. Roosevelt seemed to be irritated. This too dissipated into a warm smile when the organ notes pealed an introductory bar or two of "Open the Gates," and his old friend Fred Botts sang it. His lips formed the lyrics of the psalm. Afterward, he read the prayers with the congregation.

At the cottage the President engaged in a little work and a lot of bright chatter with his cousins. He said he might go for a drive to the top of Pine Mountain after lunch. In addition to the morning pouch—flown daily from Washington to Fort Benning, near Columbus, Georgia, thence by U.S. Army car 40 miles north to Warm Springs—the President coaxed all the local gossip from cooks, maids, Ruth Stevens and therapists at Georgia Hall. Someone said that there was going to be an old-fashioned minstrel show with banjos and end-men and an interlocutor on Thursday, April 12. FDR said, "Count me in. I'll go." His favorite musician, Graham Jackson, played swift and bright music and slow sad songs on an accordion. He would be there. Jackson was a black recruiting officer in the Coast Guard office at Macon. Whenever the President was in a mood for music, Jackson shut up shop and took the day off.

Hassett was on the front porch of the Warm Springs Hotel loafing with the reporters. Ruth Stevens, bustling, busy, joined the group. Merriman Smith said, "Stevie, will you please make me a big pot of Brunswick stew?" Everyone knew that this was FDR's favorite dish. "Honey," she said, lying, "I just happened to buy a three-hundred-pound goddam hog so let's have a barbecue." Smith wasn't joking. "You mean it?" he said. "I'll sure get one," she said. "Who's coming?" "Everybody," Hassett said. Miss Stevens disappeared into the Pine Room where the big bald mayor was having breakfast. "Frank," she said, "how about having a barbecue at your place?" He nodded; a great idea. Nixon said, "How about a week from Saturday?" Ruth said no; on weekends soldiers came up from Fort Benning and the hotel was busy. Someone else suggested Friday. Bill Hassett said the President would be sure to attend if there was Brunswick stew, but he couldn't make it Friday the thirteenth; his calendar said he'd be working on a final draft of his Jefferson Day speech.

"How about the next Thursday?" The group on the porch counted on their fingers and agreed that this would be Thursday, April 12. Hassett felt that the Boss would be caught up in his work by then. He couldn't be sure, he'd have to ask. But Thursday the twelfth sounded good. Miss Stevens wrapped both arms around the tall Hassett. "Bill, honey, I'd give anything if that man would come." Mock-seriously, Bill said, "But my dear, he is not accepting engagements on this trip." The woman looked sad. "Lady Ruth," he said, "I'll tell him you will give him an old-fashioned Brunswick stew and plenty of it. You know he loves that more than any other Southern dish."

The reporters and Ruth Stevens agreed that if all who wanted to attend gave $2.50 apiece, it would cover all expenses. Neither the taste nor the recipe for the stew would appeal to everyone. Miss Stevens used 3 hogs' heads, 25 pounds of stew meat, 12 five-pound hens, 18 cans of corn, 18 cans of tomatoes, 6 medium-size onions, 1 pint of mustard, 1½ bottles of Worcestershire, salt to taste, red pepper to taste, black pepper to taste, 2 gallons of catsup, ½ gallon of homemade catsup. It required a great deal of running through a food chopper, a heavy pot, and simmering and stirring over a slow fire. "The secret to the Brunswick stew," Ruth Stevens said, "is the homemade catsup. If you don't have time to make the catsup, you can use a good grade of chili sauce."

It was this type of activity, intense rural concern about small events, which made of Warm Springs a presidential Shangri-La. In this atmosphere, where Mr. Pless, spitting tobacco in a can at a railroad station, was the community's contact with the rest of the world, FDR felt at home. Even more important, it made him feel far removed from that sophisticated, scheming world aflame with the thunder of falling shells and bombs where scores of millions of the finest youth struggled to kill each other in the sacred name of patriotism and honor. As Chief Executive, he could not divorce himself from it absolutely; he would still receive information grave and good; he would still make decisions; but, in all the other hours he could sit among friends before a crackling fire and engage in small talk and sip a cocktail. Or he could get in his old blue Ford and drive to the top of the highest hill on a clear afternoon and gaze down at a carpet of trees, or mares' tails in a blue sky, or watch slate-blue smoke climb from cabins in lofty apostrophes; or he could lie in that plain hard bed, reading or dozing. He was like an animal too old for the hunt, dragging what was left of the prey back to a hidden lair, a protected place.

To some, this was Easter Sunday; to others, it was April Fool's day. In the afternoon the President sent a Top Secret to Stalin. There is no record that he wrote it. Increasingly, the President was signing messages devised by Stettinius, Leahy and Marshall. FDR said he was disappointed at the "lack of progress made in carrying out, which the world expects, of the political decisions we reached at Yalta, particularly those relating to the Polish question." He had said this before. So had Churchill. What moved him to send one more plea to the Marshal, especially one which contained no new arguments and no threats, is a mystery. It was essential "to settle the Polish question for the successful development of our international collaboration." He mentioned Romania and said he could not understand why these matters did not fall under the Yalta agreement regarding the "Declaration on Liberated Europe." For a month, he had fretted about Stalin's peremptory unilateral actions. He wanted to believe that the Soviet chief had been pressed toward a harsher attitude by the Politburo. But Harriman had an audience with Stalin; his report indicated that the Marshal was making the decisions. The deep emotional lassitude which beset the President—with occasional flashes of viability—dates from that report. This is not to say that he was unable to work; he was unwilling. With a few day-to-day exceptions, his interest in world affairs flagged.

On the same day Winston Churchill dispatched a message to Stalin endorsing Roosevelt's message, which he had seen, and added: "The President has shown me the messages which have passed between him and you about V. M. Molotov's inability to be present at San Francisco. We had hoped that the presence there of the three foreign ministers might have led to a clearance of many of the difficulties which have descended upon us in a storm since our happy and hopeful union at Yalta. . . ."

At Moscow, identical mirrors reflected other images. Josef Stalin, V. M. Molotov, the Stavka and the Politburo were unanimous in seeing portents of grave danger from their Western friends. Eisenhower's First and Third armies were breaking through German lines and could, theoretically, engulf Germany before Koniev and Zhukov could reach the great prize, Berlin. Stalin had erred in ordering his commanders to hold their armies on the Oder. The men of the Kremlin were aware that the United States and Britain were less anti-Russian than Germany only in degree. Whether the American OSS had come to an agreement with the Nazi High Command or not, the Germans seemed determined to hold the Russians off with their last strength while retreating before Eisenhower and Montgomery.

The Soviet Intelligence reports were firm that the secret actions in Berne and Locarno were "bargains" with Kesselering, who could, they were certain, surrender northern Italy to Field Marshal Alexander, permitting his forces to run eastward toward Austria, while Russian armies were stalled 20 miles from Vienna. Both Churchill and Roosevelt knew that Russia required the buffer of Poland between her and a militaristic Germany, and yet they kept demanding a new democratic government in addition to "free and secret" elections, so that Poland could protest her traditional antipathy to Russia. The Stavka argument was that the Soviet Union was, for the first time, in a position of strength to take what she needed, without bargaining with her friends. It was agreed that Stalin wanted more, not fewer, vassal states on her borders: Romania, Czechoslovakia, Hungary and Bulgaria. Nor could the Politburo understand why Stalin had placated that genial old gentleman, Franklin D. Roosevelt, by agreeing to participation in the United Nations. A look at the proposed member nations showed a preponderance of Western votes. It is one of history's ironies that, while FDR and Churchill feared that they had given too much to Stalin, he and his advisers were certain that it was Stalin who had given too much. Overall, the pervasive feeling in the Kremlin was that the West was only a friend of convenience; each side needed the other temporarily. The strong opposing currents of ideology induced Moscow, London and Washington to believe that communism and democracy could not live side by side.

The mirror reflected opposing images. On the morning of April 1 U.S. Marine and Army divisions swept ashore at Okinawa, the island which sat astride the Japanese trade routes on the East China Sea. It was only 350 miles southwest of the big Japanese island of Kyushu. This would try the strength of the Americans, who had proved that they could fight two successful wars, one in the east and one in the west. This time, the desperate Japanese were flying manned bombers called Kamikazes into U.S. vessels of war. General Marshall had a secret report from General Leslie Groves at Alamogordo, New Mexico, that scientists believed the first atom bomb would be ready soon for testing; a second would be built in summer; a third could be expected early in 1946. If Moscow was aware of the atom bomb, it was not mentioned at Yalta, and this would heighten Russian suspicions about the United States. Stavka fed Stalin's distrust by sending a report: "There remains no doubt whatsoever that the Allies intend to capture Berlin before us, even though, according to the Yalta agreements, the city falls within the zone designated for occupation by Soviet troops."

On April 1, Stalin called an emergency meeting of Marshal Koniev and, from the State Defense Committee, Marshals Antonov and Shtemenko. Russian armies were within 50 miles of Berlin's Brandenburg Gate. Stalin, sitting at a board table, assumed the attitude of an amused schoolteacher. "Are you aware of the way in which the situation is developing?" he asked the two marshals. Zhukov and Koniev were rivals, each in command of separate Army groups; both were first-class soldiers. They said the situation was clear to them. Stalin nodded to Shtemenko, Chief of Operations. Military information sources, he said, showed that the Anglo-American group in the west was preparing an operation which would take the city of Berlin in a series of lightning strokes. Field Marshal Montgomery would advance against light German defenses north of the Ruhr Valley and arc east on a direct route to Berlin through Osnabrück and Hannover. General Bradley's Twelfth Army Group, led by Patton's Third Army and Hodges' First, would follow a more southerly route, probably from Frankfurt am Main to Erfurt and Leipzig. The effect would be a giant claw, snapping shut on the capital city.

Shtemenko assured Zhukov and Koniev that the Soviet Union had men at Eisenhower's headquarters, and that the plan was not only "entirely feasible" but "preparations for its execution are under way." "So," said Stalin, who was addicted to rolling his thumbs together on a table, "who is going to take Berlin, we or the Allies?" Koniev said, "We." "That's just like you," said Stalin paternalistically, "and how will you be able to carry out the necessary regrouping? Your main forces are on the southern flank. Obviously, you have to carry out large-scale regrouping." Koniev gave it some thought. "Comrade Stalin," he said, "you may rest assured that my Army Group will take all the necessary steps." He had thought that, in the war in the west, Stalin had favored Zhukov's forces, ordering Koniev to institute diversionary attacks while Zhukov fought the big battles. Zhukov, a broad man with the grin of a growing boy, said that his Army Group required no time to step off. "My armies are closer to Berlin and ready."

Stalin wanted Berlin. He, who admitted to Winston Churchill that he had killed three million Russians to solidify his personal power, was prepared to pay a high price in lives to take Berlin in a furious dash. So, against his customary policy, he invited both Koniev and Zhukov to take it. "Then both of you," he said, dropping the smile, "must prepare your plans in the Stavka and, as soon as they are ready—say, in a couple of days—submit them to Supreme Headquarters and return to your Army groups with the plans approved."

In a sense, both Army groups would be pitted against each other as much as against the Germans. There was further discussion, and Stalin said he would want the operation to begin no later than dawn on April 16. The fury of the attack would sweep the weak German *Volksturm* ahead and roll it up like an old carpet. Four days before the Moscow conference, Montgomery had radioed Sir Alan Brooke in London: "My intention is to drive hard for the line of the Elbe," he said. "The situation looks good and events should begin to move rapidly in a few days. . . . My tactical headquarters moves will be Wesel-Münster-Herford-Hannover—then via the autobahn to Berlin, I hope."

If Soviet Intelligence intercepted this message, which is possible, it explains the summary decision in Moscow to drive on Berlin. Montgomery was subordinate to Dwight D. Eisenhower and could not execute any plan of action without the concurrence of Eisenhower and SHAEF. Two days later, General Eisenhower sent a message directly to Stalin. He told the Russian that his immediate tactical plan was to isolate the Ruhr and to make his main attack southeast along the line Erfurt-Leipzig-Dresden. He showed no interest in taking Berlin. However, when Ike's southern claw was coupled with Montgomery's proposed northern pincer, Moscow saw it closing on Berlin. If Eisenhower worried about any part of his plan, it was that Adolf Hitler and his government would flee to the Bavarian Alps—the so-called southern redoubt—and, with the aid of elite troops, postpone German capitulation. To eliminate this possibility, he told Stalin, he proposed to open a secondary attack far south to join up with the Russian Army at Linz, Austria. Montgomery, he stated, would use his forces to open up the northern German ports to the Allies. That, and nothing more. He had, in fact, told Montgomery that he no longer felt an interest in taking Berlin. "That place has become no more than a geographical location," he said, "and I have never been interested in these. My purpose is to destroy the enemy's forces and his powers to resist."

Stalin, lying to a man he regarded as a liar, replied that Eisenhower's plan coincided entirely with the plans of the Soviet High Command. Berlin, he said, "has lost its former strategic importance. The Soviet plans to allot secondary forces in the direction of Berlin." Sir Alan Brooke studied a copy of the messages and told Churchill that Eisenhower had no right to make such decisions without first conferring with the Combined Chiefs of Staff. The Prime Minister agreed. He sent a tart message to Eisenhower stating: "The fall of Berlin would have a profound psychological effect on German resistance in every part of the Reich. While Berlin holds out, great masses of Germans will feel it their duty to go down fighting. . . ." Critical flak began to fly around Eisenhower's head. He appealed to General George C. Marshall for support: "The message I sent to Stalin was a purely military move taken in accordance with ample authorizations and instructions issued by the Combined Chiefs of Staff. Frankly, it did not cross my mind to confer in advance with the Combined Chiefs of Staff because I have assumed that I am held responsible for the effectiveness of military operations in this theatre and it was a natural question to the head of the Russian forces to inquire as to the direction and timing of their next major thrust, and to outline my own intentions."

There is nothing in the President's papers or in any diaries to indicate that this information reached Warm Springs. On the evening of Monday, April 2, Hassett wrote:

The President in good spirits when he signed his papers this morning. Weary and tired when, just after lunch, I carried him a message received over the phone from Ed Stettinius. He approved issuance of a statement by the S. of S. saying that the United States will not press at San Francisco for three delegates in the Assembly of the United Nations Organization. After lunch the President took a nap and later went for a drive. The fight over the Yalta agreement waxes, but he is determined not to postpone the San Francisco Conference, due to open on April 25. He is also determined to attend the opening session.

Nor was there any excitement over Eisenhower's solitary decision in Washington. Admiral William Leahy, privy to all military matters, made a note that French Admiral Fenard had called "again." Fenard told Leahy that France wanted to utilize her "naval and military" forces in the war against Japan. Leahy viewed the visit as a patent device to permit France to reclaim Indochina as a colony after the war, and also to make France, as a "participant" in the war, eligible for Lend-Lease. Leahy promised Fenard nothing.

Strategically, it was important for Marshal Stalin to keep FDR on the defensive in their correspondence. In the realization that the Soviet Union had made plans to execute unilateral decisions in Europe—decisions which contravened the Yalta agreements—Stalin could justify his deeds only by accusing the Americans and British of betrayal. On April 3 he sent a long message to FDR restating his accusation that the Berne negotiations "have developed an atmosphere of fear and distrust deserving regrets." In case Roosevelt didn't know what his subordinates were doing, Stalin would tell him. "Marshal Kesselring has agreed to open the front and permit the Anglo-American troops to advance to the east, and the Anglo-Americans have promised in return to ease for the Germans the peace terms." He said he could not understand the

silence of the British, who have allowed you to correspond with me on this unpleasant matter, and they themselves have remained silent, although it is known that the initiative in this whole affair with the negotiations in Berne belongs to the British. . . . The Anglo-American troops get the possibility to advance into the heart of Germany almost without resistance on the part of the Germans, but why was it necessary to conceal this from the Russians, and why were your Allies, the Russians, not notified? As a result of this at the present moment the Germans on the western front in fact have ceased the war against England and the United States. At the same time, the Germans continue the war with Russia, the Ally of England and the United States. . . .

Roosevelt read it. To the small group in the living room, he said he would refuse to permit it to depress him. He was angry; he was irritated; yes. But he would not be depressed. The message reflected two possibilities: the first was that Stalin believed his spies, and was as badly misinformed as he accused the President of being. On the other hand, Stalin didn't believe a word of what he was saying, and was using the accusations as a justification for backing off from his agreement about San Francisco. In either case, FDR was not going to succumb to melancholy. To prove it, he moved the message from his desk and spent an hour with Jonathan Daniels, newly appointed press secretary, discussing details of the visit to Warm Springs of President Osmeña.

The Stalin message was sent to Leahy. The Boss asked him to prepare a reply. Leahy wrote: "I prepared for the President, and sent to Marshal Stalin, a sharp reply to his message that approaches as closely to a rebuke as is permitted in diplomatic exchanges between states." Once upon a time the scurrilous words of Marshal Stalin would have aroused the President to fighting pitch. He would have called in Robert Sherwood, Sam Rosenman and Harry Hopkins and, after delivering himself of his angry sentiments, would have asked them to write a number of drafts in reply. He might even have brazened it out to the point of demanding an immediate conference of foreign ministers to go over all the Yalta agreements word by word and phrase by phrase to interpret the responsibilities of each of the Big Three. One step further, and he might have said that Russia, Great Britain and the United States must honor the letter and spirit of each of the agreements, or else the entire instrument was invalid. But he didn't. He repeated softly that he would not permit Stalin to depress him, and the response was given to Admiral Leahy to phrase and send. The Admiral, a highly qualified military man and a most honorable personage, was hardly an intelligent choice. FDR still had Secretary of State Stettinius, Charles Bohlen, and Dean Acheson—each one able and qualified. The State Department wasn't notified about the exchange of messages until carbon copies were distributed.

Hassett wrote "quiet day at Warm Springs" on April 4. The villagers did not enjoy quiet days when the President was among them. They sustained too many quiet days with the sun coming up and setting on time, shops opening and closing at predictable hours, a rare train clanking into the station with no passengers getting off or getting on, absorbing local gossip in the barbershop or the beanery; waiting for a newspaper from Macon to find out what was happening. The inhabitants of Warm Springs fell into two categories: those who worked themselves into a state over any unusual occurrence; those who had no interest in anything that did not impinge on their personal lives. Ruth Stevens of the hotel and Mayor Frank Allcorn enjoyed any excitement which might relieve the tedium of life in a backwoods village.

April 4 was quiet for FDR, but it wasn't for Stevens and Allcorn. A few minutes before 11:00 A.M. two transient salesmen on the hotel porch rose from the rockers when they saw three sleek cars pull up. An army colonel emerged from one. A half-dozen Secret Service men trotted into the lobby. The hotel was old, a place of potted ferns and slow-moving ceiling fans, but they examined everything, including the upstairs rooms. At a signal, car doors opened and a captain, a lieutenant, a man who turned out to be a physician, and a short, molasses-skinned man with a big streak of gray hair got out. He was Sergio Osmeña, new President of the Philippines. The news raced up and down the main street, and across Mr. Pless's tracks to the restaurant and the boardinghouse. The gossips said that he had not only signed the hotel register himself, but had added his mother's name after his own. He would not be seen again until his visit with President Roosevelt the next day, but, for the moment, Warm Springs had two Presidents.

In the morning the President was cheerful. The Soviet Union had renounced its neutrality treaty with Japan. He told Hassett and Bruenn he thought it indicated that, after all, they "meant business." It was a public step toward war; Tokyo and Moscow understood the implications. The President admitted that it was a bold step for Stalin; his heaviest forces were still engaged against the Germans. Japanese forces fighting in China could be turned northward through Manchuria to the

Russian border. Reports were coming in from American commanders deep in German territory, and from American observers with Russian forces, that millions of people had been put to death in ovens and gas chambers. There had been reports from military Intelligence sources two years earlier that this was so; in April 1945 photographs arrived of huge mounds of bones; photos of shower baths with deadly gas jets; huge ovens with bones still lying inside the doors; eyewitness stories of emaciated survivors. It was a crime beyond the realm of credence. At the prison camps, ranking United States officers became ill.

Hastily, FDR sent a note to King Ibn Saud: "Your Majesty will recall that on previous occasions I communicated to you the attitude of the American government toward Palestine and made clear our desire that no decision be taken with respect to the basic situation in that country without full consultation with both Arabs and Jews. Your Majesty will also doubtless recall that during our recent conversation I assured you that I would take no action, in my capacity as Chief of the Executive Branch of this government, which might prove hostile to the Arab people." The letter was pointless, the product of disorganized thinking. It did nothing for the Jews; nothing for the Arabs except to assure them that President Roosevelt was not hostile. Stettinius saw the note (or a copy) and said it was prompted by Roosevelt's fear that there would be bloodshed between Arabs and Jews. "Some formula, not yet discovered, would have to be evolved to prevent this warfare," said the Secretary of State, quoting the Boss.

And yet, April 5 was not a day for a discussion of genocide. The President sat at lunch with Sergio Osmeña and a physician. The President of the Philippines had recently undergone a prostate operation and was in a weakened state of convalescence. Roosevelt was interested in all the little man had to say about the Japanese occupation and the destruction of Manila. He sent Jonathan Daniels to summon the pool reporters. At 1:00 P.M. they were lounging in the lobby, with nothing to do after lunch except await dinner. A half hour later they were on their way to the Little White House. The Boss was sitting in his big brown leather chair, with sunbeams spilling across the back of his head from the rear porch. Dorothy Brady sat in a corner with a note pad on crossed knees. At Roosevelt's side sat Osmeña, who seemed intent on smiling himself to death. Fala, overweight, waddled like a dark specter around the floor, sniffing at shoes and garments.

It was Roosevelt's 998th press conference, unusual inasmuch as it was called on a Thursday (instead of a Tuesday or Friday). No one but Daniels knew that the motive behind the conference was that Roosevelt could find no other way to be rid of the Filipino President. The two had been together since late morning. At 2:00 P.M. Osmeña seemed no closer to a farewell than at his arrival. Leighton McCarthy, FDR's Canadian friend, had heard about the dilemma and phoned Hassett that, if the Boss agreed, he would walk right in and take the Filipino "off the President's hands for two hours—but not more than that." The offer had been declined with thanks.

Daniels managed to repress a chuckle as Roosevelt said, "President Osmeña and I have been having a nice talk, and I thought you would come up and write a story for release when we get back to Washington. It may be another week or ten days." FDR jammed a Camel in his cigarette holder and the reporters noted that the tremor was so violent that he missed the mark. He said that he and Osmeña had been discussing the future of the Philippine Commonwealth when the news of the fall of the Japanese Cabinet came in. Both thought that was good news. Roosevelt also received a firsthand account of the terrible destruction wrought by the Japanese—"about three-fourths of Manila is destroyed." There was still much fighting to be done "in the center of the islands. . . . We are absolutely unchanged in our policy of two years ago, for immediate Filipino independence." The United States, which had a predilection for rebuilding countries damaged by war, would help to restore Manila and other Philippine cities to their former greatness. "It was not the fault of the Filipino people that the Japanese attacked Pearl Harbor, but they have been terribly hurt by the result of the war."

The reporters knew that, at some point, Roosevelt would wander into his storytelling routine. He did not disappoint them. "In Manila there is this famous old cathedral—which is one of the oldest cathedrals in the Far East. I think this country will want, as a gesture of sentimentality, to restore the Cathedral of Saint Dominic. Other things, like wrecks and harbors with Jap ships—it certainly is our duty to take those wrecks and blow them up, so commerce at different ports will be able to function again." As far as trade and commerce were concerned, FDR thought that the Philippines should enjoy the same preferred customer status after independence as before. He spoke of policing Japan, internally as well as externally—"in the same way Germany is prevented from setting up a military force which would start off again on a chapter of aggression." The Congress had set a date for Philippine independence, he said, "July 1946." It might be sooner; "it all depends on how soon the Japanese are cleared in the islands."

A reporter asked, If the Japanese mandated islands were to be taken from them, which would be the new controlling government—the United States? Roosevelt was in one of his sharper mental moods. "I would say the United Nations," he said. The reporters showed no further interest in the Philippines. They began to run away with the news conference. When could they speak to Roosevelt about the three-votes-for-Russia issue? Any time before San Francisco? "I think you will see me several times before I go. Some of the boys cannot get their facts straight. It would really be fun if I went on the air and simply read the things which have appeared in the paper. Of course, you know that it is not true, factually." The three men said they had read so many interpretations—

FDR: As a matter of fact, this plea for votes was done in a very quiet way. Stalin said to me—and this is the es-

*sence of it—"You know there are two parts of Russia that
have been completely devastated. Every building is gone,
every farmhouse, and there are millions of people living in
these territories—and it is important from the point of view
of humanity—and we thought, as a gesture, they ought to be
given something as a result of this coming victory. They
have had very little civilization. One is the Ukraine, and the
other is White Russia. We all felt—not any of us coming
from there in the government—we think it would be fitting
to give them a vote in the Assembly. In these two sections,
millions have been killed, and we think it would be very
heartening—would help to build them up—if we could get
them a vote in the Assembly." He asked me what I
thought. I said to Stalin: "Are you going to make that request of the Assembly?" He said: "I think we should."*

*I said: "I think it will be all right. I don't know how the
Assembly will vote." He said: "Would you favor it?" I
said: "Yes, largely on sentimental grounds. If I were on
the delegation, which I am not, I would probably vote yes."
That has not come out in any paper. He said: "That would
be the Soviet Union, plus White Russia, plus the Ukraine."
Then I said: "By the way, if the conference in San Francisco should give you three votes in the Assembly—if you
get three votes—I do not know what will happen if I don't
put in a plea for three votes and insist on it." It is not
really of any great importance. It is an investigative body
only. I told Stettinius to forget it. I am not awfully keen
for three votes in the Assembly. It is the little fellow who
needs the vote in the Assembly. This business about the
number of votes in the Assembly does not make a great
deal of difference.*

Q. They don't decide anything, do they?

The President closed his 998th press conference with
one word: "No."

It was early evening in London. Sir Alexander Cadogan
had summoned Polish Count Raczynski to the British
Foreign Office. Cadogan said that sixteen Polish leaders
had left London for Moscow to assist in forming a new
Polish government. They had been gone a full month.

The British Ambassador had reminded Molotov that the Poles had gone to Moscow under a written Russian guarantee of safety. It was Cadogan's sad duty to inform Count Raczynski that the Russians now maintained that they did not know what had happened to the sixteen men; in fact, they claimed never to have seen them.

The days became monotonously good. The sun was strong, the air warm; the breeze at night had a sufficient chill to make a blanket feel good. Bruenn, Brady and Hassett became addicted to the big swimming pool. The President's after-lunch drives in the open blue Ford had tanned his skin. The loner, Lieutenant Commander George Fox, was present for rubdowns, but he spent most of his time at his quarters. Margaret Suckley was crocheting or knitting something. Laura Delano took walks from the guest house through the woods, or sat chatting with FDR. Louise Hachmeister, close to the switchboard in a cottage, sometimes mixed Manhattans and waited for the President to pass by to offer refreshment. Grace Tully was grievously worried. She alternated with Dorothy Brady working with FDR in the mornings. Miss Tully, beset by Irish foreboding, seemed to some to become overbearing.

He was "coming back," she felt, but not fast enough this time. The bounce was missing. She mentioned it to Polly and Daisy. They agreed. He looked better after six days in the sun, but he was weaker than any of them remembered. All the extra work she had brought from Hyde Park and the White House was added to the pile of daily pouches. When the President nerved himself to work, Miss Tully felt that he worked too hard. On other days he ignored urgent papers to work on his stamp collection, or the big box of books he had sent to Warm Springs. These were bound volumes of speeches and important papers which he proposed to inscribe for the Roosevelt Library, his personal Hilltop Cottage, his mother's Big House and the White House. Often, there were four copies of one book to autograph. Tully shivered within herself when FDR pointed to the box and said to Prettyman, "Move the coffin a little closer to my chair." The phrase unnerved her, even though she realized he was joshing. She begged him to rest. His patience was thin, and he showed no irritation other than a frown—but he revenged himself by asking more and more of Dorothy Brady. As he could not abide warnings from Dr. Bruenn, so he would not be mothered by Tully.

On Friday, April 6, FDR puttered. The only record of anything which might be called work was the reading of a dispatch from Averell Harriman about Russian foreign policy. It could be digested in thirty seconds: "(1) Collaboration with the United States and the United Kingdom in a world organization; (2) Creation of a security ring through domination of the border countries; (3) Penetration of other countries through their Communist parties." It gave the President no additional insight into the mysterious and implacable decisions of the Kremlin.

In the first week at Warm Springs the President had strengthened an old trick he had often used. This was an effort to make himself appear to be in better spirits and health than he was. He had tried it out at the Osmeña press conference and it had worked well. The reporters left the Little White House telling each other that he appeared to be "tired and weak—but not sick." On Saturday, the seventh, he phoned Mrs. Roosevelt at Hyde Park after donning the cloak of sparkling levity and a stronger tone of voice. It worked. Mrs. Roosevelt was so relieved, so touched by his phone call that she wrote (speaking of herself and "Tommy" Thompson at Hyde Park, unpacking cases and barrels of china and glass): "We ache from our unwonted exercise, but we've had fun too! In May I'll finish the job. . . . I'm so glad you're gaining, you sounded cheerful for the first time last night & I hope you will weigh 170 pounds when you return. Devotedly, E.R."

He could not fool Tully, Hassett, Bruenn, Prettyman and Fox. The first had premonitions which were bad; Hassett saw his beloved Boss as "slipping away"; Bruenn knew that medical science could not fight hypertensive

heart disease, an enlarged heart and a suspected generalized hardening of the arteries. The best he could do was
to try to slow the process. Prettyman knew that, in the
privacy of his room, the President was unable to do
things for himself; he required the assistance one would
accord a heavy infant. Commander Fox had once mas-
saged that skin into a pink glow; the legs were always
flaccid—now it had spread to the arms. To keep from in-
ducing pain, the rubdowns had to be more tenderly administered.

There was a small amount of cheer in a new message
from Stalin. It was received by Roosevelt late on Saturday, April 7, while he was working over procedural
plans for the San Francisco Conference. Condensed, it
said:

*The point at issue is not that of integrity and trustworthi-
ness. I have never doubted your integrity and trustworthi-
ness or Mr. Churchill's either. My point is that in the course
of our correspondence it has become evident that our
views differ on the point as to what is admissible and what
is inadmissible as between one ally and another. We Russians think that in the present situation on the fronts, when
the enemy is faced with inevitable surrender, if the representatives of any one ally ever meet the Germans to discuss
surrender, the representatives of another ally should be af-
forded an opportunity of participating in such a meeting. . . .
The Americans and British, however, think differently and
regard the Russian standpoint as wrong. They have, accordingly, refused the Russians the right to join in meeting the
Germans in Switzerland.*

The Soviet Marshal was placing the onus on FDR
but, instead of shouting, he was now whispering. He
soon reached the crux of his hurt:

*It is difficult to admit that the lack of resistance by the
Germans on the western front is due solely to the fact that
they have been defeated. The Germans have 147 divisions
on the eastern front. They could, without prejudicing their*

own position, detach 15 to 20 divisions from the eastern front and transfer them to reinforce their troops on the western front.

Yet the Germans have not done and are not doing this. They are continuing to wage a crazy struggle with the Russians for an insignificant railway station like Zemlyanitsa in Czechoslovakia which is as much use to them as hot poultices to a corpse, and yet they yield without the slightest resistance such important towns in the center of Germany as Osnabrück, Mannheim and Kassel. You will agree that such behavior on the part of the Germans is more than curious and unintelligible. . . .

The tone, the words, were much softer than before. FDR had barely savored them when a second message arrived from Stalin. This one dealt with the Polish problem. If the first was soft, the second was harsh. The matter of Poland, Stalin said, was at a dead end because Averell Harriman and Clark Kerr had departed from the language of the Yalta agreement. They insisted that the original Lublin government should be completely disbanded, "liquidated," and that they would form an entirely new government. Mr. Harriman stated at a meeting of the commission that it was possible that no member of the Lublin group would become a member of the new government. (Harriman denied making such a statement.)

Stalin said that, as he understood the Yalta agreement, five persons were to be invited from Poland and three from London, these to be added to the Lublin government. Harriman and Clark Kerr had insisted on the right to invite as many "outside" Poles as they pleased. It was now impossible to form a new government because of the disruptions of the American and British ambassadors. So far as admitting American and British observers to the coming Polish elections, Stalin said he could not consent to it because the Poles would "consider this an insult to their national dignity." FDR sent an urgent note to Churchill not to respond to this attack at once; to wait. Then, still fearful that Russia might withdraw

from the United Nations, he dictated a short message
to Churchill. "I would minimize the general Soviet
problem as much as possible," he counseled, "because
these problems, in one form or another, seem to arise
every day, and most of them straighten out as in the
case of the Berne meeting. We must be firm, however,
and our course thus far has been correct." He studied
the desk calendar. "Don't send this message today. Send
it next week—Thursday the 12th."

The small presidential desk—or end table—was littered
with charts and digests about San Francisco. The seating
of member nations, and the opening agenda for organization of the United Nations, was a chore for Alger Hiss
of the State Department, but FDR had taken it from him
and decided to play midwife down to the last detail. He
overlooked nothing, even matters of security at the airport and the railroad terminal. It is hardly speculation to
state that Roosevelt was about to succeed where his old
Chief, Woodrow Wilson, had failed. The extra work,
for FDR, was a joy. At long, long last many men of
many tongues and divergent ambitions would meet to
find a way of living together as Good Neighbors. As he
labored over the minutiae all Sunday afternoon, it was
Hassett who had to bring him up short and remind the
Boss that the Jefferson Day speech was only five days
away—Friday the thirteenth. The President did not want
to drop the one for the other, but something had to be
done about that big Democratic Party rally.

The first draft had been prepared by "someone" on
the Democratic National Committee, an indication of
how low the speech stood on the list of presidential
priorities. Roosevelt read it and wrinkled his nose. He
asked that it be sent to Sammy the Rose; Hassett said
that Rosenman was still in London conferring with the
British about reallocating some American food from
Great Britain to liberated Europe. Send it to Bob, he
said. The speech went to Robert Sherwood, who burnished the phrasing and made the philosophy gleam. The
President read it and was not satisfied. He said he would
like to send it to Harry Hopkins at the Mayo Clinic,

but Hopkins was "out of the picture." His alter ego was undergoing ulcer tests and was in pain. The United Nations papers and charts were taken away and Roosevelt buckled down to writing his own speech. He crossed out phrases and sentences and paragraphs and wrote, in his own shaky hand, between the lines. Nor was he satisfied with his work. He told Tully and Hassett that it required at least one more full draft.

On the last page, he found room for a closing idea. He gave it some thought, glanced around the room, blinking behind the burnished glasses. Then, dipping a pen into the well, he wrote:

Today, as we move against the terrible scourge of war—as we go forward toward the greatest contribution that any generation of human beings can make in this world—the contribution of lasting peace, I ask you to keep up your faith. I measure the sound, solid achievement that can be made at this time by the straight edge of your own confidence and your resolve. And to you, and to all Americans who dedicate themselves with us to the making of an abiding peace, I say: The only limit to our realization of tomorrow will be our doubts of today. Let us move forward with strong and active faith.

That would remain in the speech. He moved it aside and decided to take a ride through the rutty lanes of Pine Mountain. In the past week Mike Reilly had noticed that the Boss wanted to be driven to the highest spot, there to park and search the distances for the pale greens and ruddy wild berries which always herald birth in the springtime. He seldom asked to be driven down to Georgia Hall, or the swimming pool, or even to take the low road into the village to exchange greetings with old friends. The cousins who sat in the back seat did not seem to notice that Franklin always drove to the same eminence. They were happy that he was in a mood to take a sunny drive.

Sam Rosenman was at Chequers. The judge was impressed. There was nothing in San Antonio, where he was born, and less in New York, where he practiced law, to match the vast sweep of formal gardens, the cascading lawns, the subdued splendor of the Prime Minister's home with its high ceilings and glittering chandeliers. The cordiality of the cherubic Churchill was almost effusive. Rosenman wanted to talk about food for starving Europe. The Prime Minister responded by going into his "poor England" speech. Thanks to the Americans, he said, the British had sufficient calories to sustain life throughout the war, but the diet was deadly dull. The judge agreed. He had been living on it since the arrival of his group in London.

However, President Roosevelt wanted to send food to those liberated areas of Europe where malnutrition was common. The judge had a sheaf of reports of starvation in Holland, Belgium and France. In other areas, the retreating German Army had scorched the earth and sowed poison in the soil. In still other sections, Rosenman said, the crops were intact in the rural sections, but there was no means of getting the food to the cities. Besides, the farmers no longer trusted the value of their currency. Winston Churchill puffed on a cigar, and listened, nodding to Lord Cherwell, his economist. Rosenman was deferential, but firm. There was just so much food that the United States could send, and it would have to be spread around to keep populations at a bare level of subsistence.

Churchill waved his cigar at Cherwell. His Lordship read a list of statistics of how much foodstuff had been shipped from the United States to England, how much had been shipped out of England to the Continent, and how much had been left in the British Isles. It became obvious that, while Churchill was a world statesman, he was first of all an Englishman. Again and again, he hoped piously that President Roosevelt was not thinking of diverting food from Great Britain. He was close to God-knows-what-will-become-of-us when he switched the topic to something closer to his heart, the summary execution of Nazi leaders. It was not part of Rosenman's commission to discuss such matters, but Churchill knew that Sammy the Rose had FDR's ear, and he wanted to convince the judge that it would be wrong—terribly wrong—to try Adolf Hitler and his leaders and then kill them. They should be executed on sight. His reasoning was sound for any victor: "A long drawn-out trial is going to provide a sounding board for Nazi propaganda."

Rosenman understood the difference between being a winner and a loser. There was also a difference between summary execution and justice. The judge repeated, as closely as he could quote it, the Boss's view: "If those men are shot without any trial, there will soon be talk stimulated by Nazi adherents about whether they were guilty of any crimes at all." Instead of dead murderers, the Germans would have heroic martyrs. The most important thing, according to Roosevelt, was not to permit Hitler's guilt to be open to future debate. He wanted an open trial, with permanent records of prosecution and defense, and he wanted those records to be accessible to future generations.

The Prime Minister shook his head negatively. The best thing, he said, would be to capture and shoot a half dozen of the top men—Hitler, Goering, Ribbentrop, Goebbels, Himmler, Streicher—and then announce to the world that they were dead. Rosenman noted that he had been pressured in London on the same subject, with the same views, by Anthony Eden and members of the War Cabinet. He had to tell Churchill: "I am sure the President will never agree to that." At once, the Prime Minister skipped blithely to another subject, the visit of Mr. and Mrs. Roosevelt to England in May. It occurred to Judge Rosenman that they were getting further and further away from food for Europe, but there was little he could do about it. Somewhat lamely, he suggested that the subject of Nazi war criminals might be properly placed on the United Nations agenda. The P.M. was already on the subject of the President's visit—something which Rosenman knew nothing about.

"Will you tell him," Churchill said, "that he is going to get from the British people the greatest reception ever accorded to any human being since Lord Nelson made his triumphant return to London? I wanted you to tell him that when he sees the reception he is going to get, he should realize that it is not an artificial or simulated one. It will come genuinely and spontaneously from the hearts of the British people; they all love him for what he has done to save them from destruction by the Huns; they love him also for what he has done to relieve their fear that the horrors they have been through for five years might come upon them again in increased fury."

Churchill put on a small, sheepish smile, a rare expression for him. "Here is the second thing I want you to tell him," he said. "Do you remember when I came over to your country in the summer of 1944 when your election campaign was beginning? Do you remember that when I arrived I said something favorable to the election of the President, and immediately the associates of the President sent word to me in no uncertain terms to 'lay off'. . . . ? Do you remember I was told that if I wanted to help the President get re-elected the best thing I could do was to keep my mouth shut; that the American people would resent any interference or suggestion by a foreigner about how they should vote? Now, what I want you to tell the President is this. When he comes over here in May I shall be in the midst of a political campaign myself; we shall be holding our own elections about that time. I want you to tell him that I impose no such inhibitions on him as he imposed on me. The British people would not resent—and of course I would particularly welcome—any word that he might want to say in favor of my candidacy."

At Warm Springs the ladies were in the living room when Prettyman wheeled the President out of the bedroom and left, cheerful, bowing, remarking that the warm weather was holding. They were sipping coffee —Daisy, Polly and Franklin—speaking in a confidential manner across the table when Bill Hassett arrived with his "laundry" and Grace Tully with her notebook and pencils. The President wheeled himself to his desk and seemed in better humor, or loftier spirits, to Hassett. Mail was signed and Hassett set each letter on the floor to dry ("no blotter should ever touch a President's signature") when he mentioned the barbecue again. It would be held Thursday afternoon at 4:30 on Columbus Highway up near Henry Toombs's old place. The mayor and Ruth Stevens wanted to make sure the President would attend, and they wanted a guest list.

Fine, the President said. Fine. He had heard about the pig, but he didn't care for barbecued pork. He'd prefer Brunswick stew preceded by an old-fashioned. Hassett said it had already been arranged. Ruth Stevens had told him she was combing Merriweather County for the exact ingredients. Roosevelt ordered Hassett to kiss her on both cheeks for him. How about the guest list? Hassett asked. The Boss said for Bill to make it up; "keep it to our crowd, you know, Secret Service and all. I'm not up to greeting a lot of strangers." Mayor Allcorn said he was going to have to send five Negroes up to the old Toombs place to clean up the leaves and the undergrowth. Major DeWitt Greer said that the Signal Corps would have to lay some land lines there so that the White House switchboard could keep in touch with the President. The whole mountain was alive with flowering dogwood and a carpet of blue violets. There was a heady fragrance of wild honeysuckle.

Hassett left. Grace Tully took dictation. She felt an aura of suppressed excitement in the room. It was as though someone had a secret, and wasn't telling. The letters were few in number. Outside the front door, a Secret Service agent stood near the bush where the telephone was hidden. Black maids were sweeping the porch of the little guest house, and one was inside, singing. Two Secret Service men stood outside the white bumper gate near the two sentry boxes, talking to two Georgia state troopers. Down in the deep glen behind the Little White House a platoon of armed U.S. Marines stood among the heavy bushes. It was a day, a replica of all the other days, but Miss Tully could sense an excitement in that sitting room.

She walked down the incline to chat with Hacky. Then on to her typewriter and the White House letterheads. Hassett stopped in after lunch and tried to goad the President into purchasing *The History of the Rebellion and Civil Wars in England* by Edward Hyde, the first Earl of Clarendon. Hassett reminded the President that Hyde Park had been named for the Earl's grandson. No, FDR said, he wouldn't buy the set. It consisted of three volumes, and he would like to read it, but the dealer wanted $17.50, and FDR said he couldn't afford it. Later, the President's secretary wrote: "The Boss feeling the pinch of poverty today."

If there was excitement within the room, it climaxed at 3:00 P.M. when Mike Reilly wheeled Mr. Roosevelt out front to his Ford. A Secret Service car was in front, and another behind. Mr. Reilly sat with FDR. The three cars moved off, through the bumper gates, and out onto the main road. The motorcade disappeared. It turned right on old Route 41 and down the old narrow road, between the low-slung clay cliffs and the fields of wildflowers to level ground, the road full of sudden turns between hummocks of tall trees. Then the road fell away again, swinging to meet the little towns of Manchester and Woodland, then straight down to Talbotton. The motorcade slowed to low gear where 41 met 208. There the men in the front car saw the Cadillac convertible. It was parked.

Drivers of passing cars saw the President's head tilt back, saw the cheerful wave. The three cars stopped. A tall, smiling woman got out of the Cadillac. Reilly left the President's car. The tall woman got in. The President kissed her fervently. He was with his beloved Lucy Mercer Rutherfurd again. Behind her came Madame Elizabeth Shoumatoff, portrait painter, watercolor artist. She squeezed into the front seat with Mrs. Rutherfurd. Reilly got into the Cadillac with Nicholas Robbins, a photographer with a Russian accent. Mr. Robbins drove. He had the women's suitcases and the easels and his cameras in the trunk.

The drive down from Warm Springs was only twenty miles. For a sick and tired man, it was a special nosegay. The President had been on the phone with Mrs. Rutherfurd several times since his arrival at Warm Springs. He wanted to see her; he had to see her. The question was—what day, what hour? Two years earlier, the President had commissioned Madame Shoumatoff to make a watercolor of him in his Navy cape for Lucy. This time, Mrs. Rutherfurd paid Madame Shoumatoff to execute another one—this one for her youngest daughter, and the President's favorite, Barbara.

Dusk was on the road when they started back to Warm Springs. Daisy and Polly were beside themselves with excitement, because they knew that Lucy was joining the group. No one revealed the conversation in the little Ford. Surely it was animated. The presence of Lucy was a more exhilarating lift of the heart than FDR could get from Bruenn's medication. And yet, in retrospect, this long-term romance was a study in sorrow—a continuum of things which could never be. Lucy Mercer was the sealed secret of the West Wing of the White House. She was the gentle butterfly in a jar; when the President lifted the lid, she appeared; when he dropped it back in place, she disappeared. It had to be that way, if he was to keep his career and his family. A romance which endures for thirty years is not an affair. This one had begun as a flirtation between a handsome young Assistant Secretary of the Navy and his wife's social secretary; the Episcopal father of five and the tall Roman Catholic society girl with the small pursed smile, the lovely whose family had high social station and had lost its money.

No flirtation is harmless; it has a winner and a loser. In a manner of speaking, this one had two losers—they fell in love. And love too has its price, usually set at a little more than the lovers can afford. Perhaps the true tragedy of love is that it survives its tests. This one began with summer picnics and buzzing bees and the smell of honeysuckle. It began with a wife taking the children to Campobello. It began with weekend sailings down the Potomac with Franklin's dear friend Nigel Law of the British Embassy pretending to be Lucy Mercer's escort.

Did anyone on that slow night ride from Talbotton to Warm Springs remember these long-ago boat rides? It is doubtful. Who would think of the snowy tablecloths on the grass and the wicker hampers of sandwiches and the cold beaded bottles of wine at Harpers Ferry? Would a religious father divorce a good wife to give his name to a Catholic girl who faced certain excommunication? At what point does love, this most illogical of emotions, concede death? Why would Elliott, eight years of age, cower in his nighties as his mother stood in his room waving a packet of scented letters under her husband's face, shrilling the accusations of the good woman as her husband begged, "Please, Babs. Please. The dinner guests are downstairs." Would a little boy listen wide-eyed, and wonder at the ungovernable anger of his mother? His mother was noted as a self-contained woman. Then why, as his father left the room, did his mother fall on his little bed and bury her face in his pillow to sob like someone smothering for so long a time? A little boy might remember but never quite understand.

Can love survive a confrontation? Yes, it can. And more. It can live through a showdown at Hyde Park, a wife offering a divorce again and again, and a dowager umpire, a towering majesty of righteousness, begging her son never, never to see that woman again. The promise was wrenched; the vow was made. And when the re-criminations died in their own sparks, the wife exacted her personal price—she would never, never sleep with him again. For her, the manifestations of love were easy to dispense with. She was incapable of appreciating the embrace of a man, and this was peculiar, because this very proper wife found it easy to give all of her heart to suffering millions she never met. Her innate dignity cloaked the shame of betrayal until her girl child became adolescent. Then, speaking of women's business, she said, "Sex, my dear, is a thing a woman must learn to endure." The proper lady did not see in this a confession of her own failures. Nor was she above telling the child about Father's "affair." Anna could not contain herself. She said she knew about it.

Mother was stunned. How could the teen-age girl be aware of the family shame? "Aunt Polly told me." Aunt Polly? Eleanor repeated. Aunt Polly? How did she know about it? Mrs. Roosevelt, young, honorable and unaffectionate, did not know that her husband's love for Lucy Mercer was a teacup topic on Embassy Row—nor would she understand it if someone told her. Alice Roosevelt Longworth, a cousin, was immersed in the subject of Franklin and Lucy—further, she befriended them. When Franklin told Lucy about the discovery of the packet of letters, Miss Mercer was in panic. She confided her despair to her sister, and her cousins the Cottons of Carolina. The story was told *entre nous* in many places. It is a certainty that Franklin Roosevelt told Nigel Law, because Law had been his stalking horse. Those who savored the delicious gossip appeared to agree in one respect—that it was beyond the power of Franklin and Lucy to break the relationship.

And yet, if either of the two who shared the chill night breeze of age on the ride back to Warm Springs was given to meditation, he would have to admit that fear of exposure caused Lucy to run away. It was as though distance could silence the sound of a second heart. She took a job as governess for old Winthrop Rutherfurd at a beautiful and spacious estate called, of all things, Tranquillity. It was situated in northern New Jersey near a small Erie Railroad station called Allamuchy. Mr. Rutherfurd was a flinty old man of enormous resources, social and economic. His wife was chronically ill; his children were growing. The tall, demure Lucy was ideal as a governess. In winter she moved with the family to Ridgley Hall, a huge Georgian home among the horsy set of Aiken, South Carolina. Did the lovers communicate? If they did, someone without wings played cupid and acted as a secret mail drop and message center for both.

There is no evidence to indicate that Franklin Roosevelt had any intention of honoring the vow he made to his wife. And yet his respect for Eleanor was more than perfunctory. When Mrs. Rutherfurd died, the governess married the boss. He was thirty-one years older than she. The marriage restored the fortunes of the Mercers and gave Lucy a haven. Eleanor read about it and wrote to her mother-in-law: "Did you see where Lucy Mercer married old Wintie?" A book of suspicion slammed shut. The handsome young man with the pince nez, gifted with flirtatious double entendres, contracted infantile paralysis. Could he cry out for Lucy? He could do nothing but endure the solicitous ministrations of Eleanor and his mother. Paralysis made the prisoner.

He might have quit; perhaps should have. Franklin Roosevelt could have played the heir-apparent to Hyde Park, fretting over books of stamps, watching the children grow, sitting in the sun dreaming of crime and punishment. But he didn't. He believed Louis McHenry Howe and Alfred E. Smith when they said he had a political future. He wanted with all his heart to believe it because, in a real sense, it would mean emancipation. FDR made it—State Senator, Governor, President of the United States. At the inauguration as President on March 4, 1933, there was a private Secret Service car off the edge of the crowd and the cheers. In it was a tall woman who sat back, half-concealed, watching. She would attend every inauguration.

Lucy cultivated a new friend. It was Miss Marguerite LeHand, longtime personal secretary to Roosevelt, so close to his needs, so possessive, so domineering that politicians regarded her as his general manager. The Roosevelts regarded her as a pseudo-adopted member of the family. It was "Missy" LeHand who arranged the details so that the lovers could meet. When she used her private phone to call Georgetown, she told Mrs. Rutherfurd where to park her car so that the President could meet her. When Roosevelt spoke to his love on the phone, while Grace Tully or Dorothy Brady sat with notebooks on their laps, he spoke in French. Love was alive, and the fact that it was may be the best proof that it was never dormant.

Louise Hachmeister, at the White House switchboard, took the first "open" phone call in the autumn of 1941. A sweet voice said, "Ann Rutherfurd calling the President, please." Hacky went through her list of names of those who could be put through to FDR. There was no Rutherfurd. She told the woman she could not speak to the President and yanked the plug. In a minute the voice was back on the line. Hacky, irritated, called Missy. "I have an Ann Rutherfurd on the phone who wants to speak to—" "Put the call through," snapped Missy. Two days later Miss LeHand drew the inner circle of confidants together and said: "Whenever you get a call, or a letter, or a message—anything—from a Mrs. Rutherfurd, put it straight through to the President. Understood?" It was understood.

The phone calls were frequent when Mrs. Roosevelt was away from Washington. Also the private luncheons. Missy arranged to meet Lucy at the southwest gate and escort her directly to the big French doors of the President's office. At such times, a lunch tray for two was sent in, and Secret Service agents were ordered to permit no one into the President's office—no one. Later, FDR would ask Anna, "Would it be all right if I asked an old friend to dinner?" Anna did not ask what friend. She knew. "Yes," she said. With trepidation, she played hostess to her mother's archenemy. As a grown woman, she knew that there was no way to stop it; just as there was no way that Mrs. Roosevelt would relent in her insistence on her own bedroom. Anna, watching at various dinners, came to the same conclusion as the Secret Service men who had met Lucy: "Ladylike to her toes." When Anna was away, Missy was hostess at the private dinner parties in the White House.

The President went a step further. On his trips from Washington to Warm Springs, Georgia, the long train pulled off the main line of the Southern Railway onto a rusty spur at Union Street, in Aiken. It seems impossible to hide a train, or keep it secret, but it was done. The Army Signal Corps laid land lines all the way through Aiken to Ridgley Hall; the Secret Service blocked both ends of the clay road leading to the Rutherfurd estate and the country club across the street. The President of the United States was visiting the Winthrop Rutherfurds. It could not have been done without an invitation from old Wintie. And he was a jealous man; so jealous that when painters were doing the center hall in a flat off-white, he pounded his cane into the floor and ordered them to keep their eyes on the wall and off his wife.

Sometimes the President remained there three days. The pool reporters could not understand the stop in Aiken, and no one explained it to them. On the third day the Southern Railway had to take the cars back up to the Raleigh yards for re-servicing, re-icing. This happened many times. The joy there might have been in old lovers glancing surreptitiously across a dinner table is easy to comprehend. The President manifested great personal interest in all the Rutherfurd children—he got military commissions for two sons—but his deepest affection was reserved for the only child Lucy gave birth to—Barbara. He sent personal messages to her, shopped for birthday gifts and admonished her when she did not stop at the White House to see her "Godfather."

Time was on Eleanor's side. Everyone was growing older. Franklin's time was taken up with a world conflagration. Lucy's time was taken up with a husband who sustained a stroke and who placed himself in a small upstairs bedroom where, in aging irritation, he clumped on a cane to the bathroom and left indentations in the cork floor. For a reason known only to Mr. Rutherfurd, he placed Barbara's bedroom between his and Lucy's. Mrs. Rutherfurd used a huge square one on the north side, one with a private porch looking out to pines which hummed in the breeze.

Winthrop Rutherfurd died, but it was too late. Time had run out. Lucy was an aging lady with a wisp of gray in her brown hair; Franklin was enfeebled in a wheelchair. In the latter days of the war, when his wife was away somewhere on a speaking engagement, he would wheel himself to a phone. In a moment, Lucy, at her sister's house in Georgetown, would be listening to the voice of a lonesome man. Could she—would she—meet him in Rock Creek Park? She could. The President of the United States restored the telephone to its cradle. "Mike," he would say cheerfully, "I'll be ready in fifteen minutes." On winter nights of 1944, he would sit in the back of the big seven-passenger car; a Secret Service car was ahead, another behind. They made noiseless plumes of steam as they went through the gate. The cars moved up Sixteenth Street toward Walter Reed Medical Center, left on Military Road into the park.

They moved slowly, looking for a sedan parked on the right. When they reached it, they stopped. A lady got out and stepped into the back seat with the President. He pressed a button and a glass wall slid up between them and the driver. The procession was funereal. It moved slowly up and around the curving roads for an hour. They chatted; they held hands; they spoke of many things. They were in the same city where they had met so long ago. Perhaps—although no one knows—they might have discussed what might have been; what kind of a life it could have been if, in those days when Woodrow Wilson was still the vigorous Chief Executive they had accepted the challenge of discovery and he had told Eleanor, "Get a divorce. I want to marry Lucy Mercer." It's a dubious subject, even in speculation, because Franklin Roosevelt was a man unable to look in any direction except ahead. Would he make a promise that, when he left the White House in 1948, they would share the Hilltop Cottage he had built? This too is to be doubted, because he was spent and he knew he was spent. He had nothing left to give.

After an hour, Reilly would bring the slow motorcade back to the parked car. The lady would be helped out, and into her own car, saying a soft "Good night and thank you." Before she left the curb, the three cars would move off for the trip back to the White House. There, Prettyman would undress the President and help him into bed before the dinner tray arrived. Some of these things may have flitted across the minds of Franklin and Lucy as they sat in the front seat of the Ford with Madame Shoumatoff on the way back to Warm Springs. This was not April 1915. They braced themselves against the chill of sundown.

The successive days reserved their brightest colors for Warm Springs. It was too warm and good to remain in bed. Grace Tully was out early, trudging up the hill to the Little White House, paying little attention to the shrill calls and chatter of the birds. At the door a Secret Service man nodded good morning. The Boss was still in his room; Laura Delano, dressed and ready to share hot coffee, sat on the sofa. Within a few moments, Madame Shoumatoff was there. Her chatter was like that of the birds. "Oh, Miss Tully," she said, "I am so happy. I stayed awake most of the night thinking and praying. I am so anxious to get the President in a good pose. I think it has just come to me." Polly and Grace listened, as Lucy Rutherfurd slipped quietly through the front door. The artist said she wanted a "different pose" from the watercolor she had done in 1943. She would like FDR to wear the same Navy cape "but somewhat differently," and she would like him to hold a rolled scroll in his right hand, representing the "peace that will come soon, we hope."

A Secret Service man was sent to the hotel to get Nicholas Robbins, the photographer. It would be his job to shoot an assortment of photos of the President in various poses, to be used as references for features and cape when Madame Shoumatoff completed her sketches. Mr. Robbins and his camera were in the sitting room, and Shoumatoff and her easel, when the bedroom door opened and FDR emerged, smiling and good-natured, with Prettyman behind him. He said he had had his breakfast, but would have another cup of coffee with the ladies. Daisy Suckley arrived to find him out on the elliptical porch as Robbins made his photographs, and Madame Shoumatoff arranged the old cape this way and that. A sheet of paper was rolled up and placed in his right hand. The women stood on the porch or in the doorway, offering suggestions and comments. The President sparkled with bright chatter as though, for a moment, he enjoyed being moved about by the ladies.

Hassett arrived with the mail. He enjoyed the spectacle on the porch, but he had already gone on record telling the President that he did not appreciate Shoumatoff's work. The Boss asked why. The Secretary said the work was "too pretty," that Shoumatoff had "missed the soul of the man in the cape. I refer to her watercolor as one of the President *wearing* a cape, not as the President with a cape on." FDR laughed heartily and said, "Capon! Don't you just love it!" When the posing was done, the President asked Robbins if he would make a photo of Mrs. Rutherfurd. Lucy appeared to be flustered. The picture was made, a closeup of Lucy smiling, her eyes "lit," as Roosevelt said, "by a certain quality of reserved warmth."

Everyone came inside; the President gave his cape to Prettyman. The women sat around the room speaking softly as Roosevelt phoned Anna to ask how little Johnny was doing. The doctors said that he was recovering; the swollen glands were diminishing in size, but he was still a sick boy. Anna said she wished she could be with her father. He understood, but he said her place was with Johnny. In any case, he'd be "home in less than a week."

After lunch he received a phone call from the White House advising that Senator Taft, Republican of Ohio, had tacked an amendment on a bill ordering the government not to use Lend-Lease when Germany surrendered. Although this was what, in pique, the President had ordered Leo Crowley to do, FDR saw it as a threat to his authority and his power to bargain with Russia and Great Britain. The Senate well was quiet as the roll was called. Thirty-four Republicans voted "yes," to stop Lend-Lease. Four Democrats and one Progressive, Senator Robert La Follette of Wisconsin, voted with the GOP. Opposed were thirty-seven Democrats and two Republicans. The clerk announced a tie vote—39 to 39. The bow-tied Vice President stood, smiling happily, and shouted, "The chair votes no." It was a close call.

The team of persons who worked with the President understand that he would like to spend as much time as possible chatting with Mrs. Rutherfurd. There were many questions to ask before they would "catch up" with each other. They had been on the phone several times, but the last time Lucy had seen Franklin was on that cold January 20, his hair wisping and flying as he took the oath of office on the south portico for a fourth term. As always, she had seen him, from a car at a distance; he had not seen her. There was much to talk about, but the interruptions were merciless. Daisy brought her knitting basket, and sat. Polly wanted to know all and tell all. Tully was in and out with whatever required the President's attention. Hacky gave the phone three short rings when the call was important. Hassett asked how many guests the Boss wanted at the barbecue and when he would be ready to attend the minstrel show down at Georgia Hall. The answers were "less than fifty" and "about five or a little after." Madame Shoumatoff had been in the guest house; she stopped over to display the first "roughs." Mr. Roosevelt said he liked them. The final embers of love brightened and died every time the front door was opened.

Dr. Bruenn had been in early. He had learned to enjoy the 88-degree water of the big pool. "By April 10," he wrote, "improvement had continued. His color was much better, and his appetite was very good; he asked for double helpings of food. Although he had not been weighed, it was apparent that he had begun to gain a little weight. Had been resting very well, and he began to increase his activities." In the late afternoon the President received a long Top Secret from Churchill, citing the "desperate" plight of Holland. Between two and three million persons were starving to death as the Germans retreated slowly. "I fear we may be in the presence of a tragedy." Eisenhower had food for the people, but the German Army had requisitioned every scrap of food and potables and had blown up dikes and flooded the land. The Prime Minister thought that he and Roosevelt should appeal to the Germans through Switzerland to permit food and medical supplies to get through to the Dutch civilian population.

Nor was April 11 going to be less busy. If anything, it would be worse. On Wednesday Madame Shoumatoff was in the Little White House early to set up her easel and mix some colors. Fortunately, the President could hold a conversation while holding his chin up. Shoumatoff had barely adjusted the cape to the morning light when an invitation arrived from Major Dickinson, in charge of the detachment of U.S. Marines at Warm Springs, asking the President of the United States to honor them with his presence at noon dinner on Sunday. He said yes, he would be glad to eat with them. Leighton McCarthy stopped to ask the President not to go to San Francisco. He said he would go come hell or high water. In fact, he summoned Bill Hassett at once to lay out an itinerary. His neck hurt, he said, from holding his head in one position and he would rest awhile. Madame Shoumatoff didn't mind; she would flesh out some colors while waiting.

Hassett, less worried about the Boss than usual, observed some of the old verve when the President consulted his desk calendar. He would leave Warm Springs on Wednesday the eighteenth, arriving Washington Thursday the nineteenth. He wanted word to go at once to the White House that he would give a state dinner for the Regent of Iraq on the evening of the nineteenth. He would leave Washington for Chicago on Friday the twentieth. He preferred to travel by the Baltimore and Ohio Railroad. Out of Chicago westbound, he said he felt indifferent, just so long as he didn't have to go through the Royal Gorge. He assured Hassett he had seen it twice. He said Mike Reilly felt the terminus should be the Army Embarkation Reservation at Oakland, California. He expected to be taken across the bay to

San Francisco, reaching there no later than noon. He would make his speech of welcome to the delegates of many nations, and be back on the train by 6:00 P.M. of the twenty-fifth. He expected Mrs. Jimmy Roosevelt to travel part of the way on the train; he would drop her off at Los Angeles. He might go on to San Diego to see Mrs. John Roosevelt and his grandchildren. Either way, he wanted that train to leave California by sundown on April 26, heading slowly—repeat, slowly—back to Hyde Park. He would rest there for a few days. And by the way, FDR said, "Mrs. Roosevelt will be going with me to San Francisco."

The women came and went to the guest house. When he worked, they sat quietly, whispering. At noon, he called the "child"—Dorothy Brady—to dictate the first complete draft of the Jefferson Day speech. When he finished that, he told Mrs. Brady to tell Tully that, in the morning, he would start work with her on his address to the United Nations. The President had elected to work hard at a time when his assistants counted on his enjoying some relaxation. Mrs. Brady was picking up her gear when the President said, "Child, stay for lunch. Be our hostess." The secretary was surprised. While taking the Jefferson Day speech, she had felt that there was tension between the women who sat awhile, left and returned. Her intuition told her that the surface conversation was polite, but that there was some stiffness between them. She guessed that the Boss was aware of it too. If he asked her to stay for lunch, it probably meant that he would direct his conversation toward Brady. She did not learn what the problem was, but guessed that an old envy, or jealousy, that Daisy Suckley felt toward Lucy Rutherfurd had popped up in a remark. Females, all the way from royalty to relatives, vied for the President's favor. It had always been this way. Miss Suckley, Franklin's cousin and librarian, the one who had been granted her own room at Hilltop Cottage "when I leave Washington," appreciated the President's affection for Mrs. Rutherfurd (and lent herself to the secret meetings) but seems to have made the mistake of allocating for herself a place in Roosevelt's heart behind Anna and in front of Eleanor. Now and then, she was prone to disagree sharply with the mild Lucy and, although it seldom brought a retort from Mrs. Rutherfurd, it brought a deep frown to the face of FDR. Mrs. Brady guessed this was what had happened. Just guessed.

At lunch the women spooned soup almost silently. Mr. Roosevelt put on his cheerful expression and said, "There are some pretty good farms about ten miles from here. Not expensive. Dorothy and her husband always wanted to go down to a farm." No one responded. "I think that will happen sooner than she thinks." Tasty sandwiches were passed from place to place. FDR spoke of San Francisco. The women looked up as he spoke of the birth of the United Nations. They had heard him lay out his railroad schedule with Hassett. Everyone looked surprised when he said, "You understand what I'm telling you, don't you, Dorothy? I don't want to go to San Francisco." Some asked why, but he had turned his attention to food. He did not want to go—but he insisted on going. A senseless monologue.

Mrs. Brady knew that his mood was not as high as it had been. When he was mischievous, he enjoyed telling his favorite Dorothy Brady story, about the day when the young lady was first assigned, on temporary duty, as secretary to press secretary Steve Early. As FDR told it, the innocent Brady told Early that a former secretary of his, Wilma Meredith, was in the outer office with her husband's instrument, and wanted to show it to him. Early, whose expression in repose was akin to smelling decay, said, "Come here." He took her by the arm into Roosevelt's office. "Mr. President," he said, "you know Dorothy?" The President nodded. "Dorothy, tell the President what you told me." "Mr. President," she said, frightened at the excessive attention, "I was only trying to tell him that Wilma Meredith is outside with her husband's instrument in a big black box, and wants to show it to him." FDR stared at the ceiling. "Her husband has a patent on it. It's outside on the filing cabinet if you want to see it." Steve Early's face was close to exploding. The President said, "Steve, I think you'd better go get it." Mrs. Brady said, "It has a handle on it." The men burst into uproarious laughter. The Meredith invention was a weigh-and-balance machine.

The President didn't tell the story, and Brady was glad. Instead, he said he would go for a short drive with Daisy and Polly. Prettyman passed the word to Mike Reilly, who decided to use the big presidential car, with one Secret Service vehicle in front. Miss Suckley asked if everyone would please wait a minute; she wanted to take snapshots. She handed the camera to agent Jim Beary and asked if he would run ahead, and get on something high enough to make a photo of the three of them in the back seat. The Secret Service agent stood on an embankment and snapped the shutter as the big car slowed near him. As he handed the camera back, Beary thought that there must be ten thousand photos of the President.

The ride wasn't a short one. The President signaled to get on Alternate 27 and go north. At Greenville they turned left and went on through attractive rural hill country. He talked a little, glanced about a lot. His love of trees and running streams was everlasting. Near La Grange, the lead car stopped at a small wooden bridge. A sign said: "Load Limit 4,000 pounds." Mike Reilly came back to the President's car. "I'm sorry," he said, "but your auto has a lot of steel armoring and weighs 7,500 pounds. This bridge can only take half that." The President agreed. "Okay, Mike. We'll turn around." Daisy Suckley looked imploringly to FDR. "Oh, Franklin," she said, "don't you think if we go real fast we can get across?" Reilly looked at the President. The Boss tipped his head back, squeezed his eyes shut, and laughed almost with a roar. The Secret Service agent recalled he hadn't seen the Boss laugh like that in a long time.

The night air was brisk. Through the lacy pines, a confetti of stars stood still in the sky. The President sat on his wheelchair on the small front porch. He saw the Secret Service men pace, but he said nothing. His old friend, his Secretary of the Treasury, Henry Morgenthau, had phoned that he would stop down for dinner if he was invited. "You're invited, Henry," the President had said. He waited alone for his guest. The kitchen was small and oblong. The stove was hot; soup simmered on it. Lizzie McDuffie, the housekeeper, sat chatting with Daisy Bonner, the cook. There was little to do until Mr. Morgenthau arrived. The women shared a room over the President's pine garage. It was always hot up there under the bare eaves in summertime. There was a white basin, a big pitcher of water standing in it, and a creaky closet near narrow stairs. It was a spare and cheap abode; the automobile below had the cooling benefit of being on the ground floor.

Daisy Bonner said she was making waffles for the President for dinner. It was not because he liked them, adorned with pure maple syrup and butter, but because Mr. Morgenthau had given him the waffle iron the previous Christmas. Lizzie McDuffie could see the President by squeezing her face diagonally against the window screen. Daisy Bonner said, "You think the President looks feeble?" Lizzie nodded. "Yes, but he looks better than when he came here." Like most women who were close to Roosevelt, Mrs. McDuffie and Miss Bonner loved the President. Daisy was possessed of the magical nostrums of cooks; if you feed a "peek-ed" man right, he will recover. "I know what I'm going to do," she said. "I'm going to give him the things he likes to eat." She said he liked turnip greens, hush puppies and a dish called country captain, which approximated chicken curry. She would feed him these things. Not tomorrow, of course, because he would be at the mayor's barbecue. Miss Stevens would have plenty to eat for everybody. But, from now on . . .

Daisy cooked; Lizzie served. When relatives maneuvered the menu, Miss Bonner obeyed, but she passed a whispered word to Mrs. McDuffie to take the platters to the table and whisper to the President "that I say don't eat any." Mr. Roosevelt never disobeyed the admonition of the cook. Sometimes, guests like Miss Suckley and Miss Delano would say, "Franklin, aren't you going to eat what Daisy made?" Mr. Roosevelt would say, "I will eat some of that tomorrow." The headlights of a car stopped at the bumper gate. The Secret Service waved it in to the elliptical gravel drive. Daisy Bonner tapped some lard onto the brand-new waffle iron and started dinner.

FDR was glad to see Morgenthau. The Roosevelt team could not understand the friendship betwen two old Hudson Valley neighbors. The President was genial, anecdotal, and enjoyed a funny story. Mr. Morgenthau was humorless, often grim, and was dedicated to hard work. In the past year he had been especially dedicated to goading FDR to breaking Germany into small pastoral states. The President sent Prettyman to the guest house to tell the ladies that dinner was near ready, and that they would be having waffles. Madame Shoumatoff came in, then Margaret Suckley and Laura Delano—last, Lucy. Morgenthau gave the women perfunctory attention, then directed himself to FDR, asking if his attitude toward Germany had softened. The President shook his head vigorously. No, his attitude hadn't changed. Germany was going to have to be broken down to a powerless state before it could be built sufficiently to join the family of nations. Of one thing he was certain: the German people would never become aggressive again.

The Secretary of the Treasury wanted to continue the conversation. Mr. Roosevelt, enjoying the soup and waffles, said he preferred to talk about "old times." He spoke about Pa Watson and how much he missed him. Then he moved off to ask Henry if he remembered the days when the Hudson River froze solid and the ice boats were flashing up and down the opaque ice between the snowy hills. Morgenthau remembered. Henry began to lose interest as the President, with evident relish, began to dwell upon all the people they knew who were gone with the old times. It wasn't intended to be morbid; it seemed to Morgenthau as though his old friend had an understandable desire to be a boy again. The Secretary, who wanted to speak of war and politics, was vetoed. For a reason which Morgenthau couldn't understand, Franklin was using him on this particular night to resurrect his boyhood. Henry Morgenthau said later that this may have been the reason why he was invited, with such enthusiasm, to stop for dinner. The Boss had even waited out front for his arrival.

When the two shook hands good-bye, the President said that he was feeling a little stronger. Tomorrow he would attend a big barbecue, then be off to witness a minstrel show. He didn't like to say good night so early, but he needed the sleep. Henry would understand. Henry did.

At the Capitol, Speaker of the House Sam Rayburn dined late with cronies. He had the face and head of a shaved bulldog. "The President," he said at one point, "is not a well man." The congressmen around the table understood the Texas understatement. Rayburn meant that Roosevelt was dying. He looked at his watch, saw how late it was, and said, "I think I'll have a talk with Harry Truman tomorrow. He's got to be prepared to carry a terrible burden."

Carver Cottage was at the bottom of the hill. William D. Hassett was in the bathroom at 7:45 A.M. The poetic side of his nature had already asserted itself; he had looked out upon Georgia Hall, across the way, and the sweep of green which went up the successive small rises to the Little White House, over a mile away. He had already noted that the aggressive finches and robins had frightened the low-sweeping cardinals from the breakfast areas and the air was shrill with unfriendly cries. The early sun was strong and warm over the mountain and etched long blue pointing fingers from the trees. April 12 would be a good day for a barbecue.

The bathroom stifled the poetic meditations of Hassett. He shared it with the occupants of the other two bedrooms—Grace Tully and Dorothy Brady—and their precise agreement with him was that he would be out of it no later than eight every morning. And so, with a face half lathered, and less than fifteen minutes left, he was not happy to hear the living-room phone ring. He fumbled in his robe for the steel-rimmed glasses, slipped them over the soapy ears and said, "Hello." It was the White House in Washington. Steve Early was back from Europe. The news was not earth-shattering: the capital had been fog-bound most of the night and the pouch had been rushed by train. It should arrive at Atlanta around 9:00 A.M. and be in Hassett's hands by 11:00. Steve Early suggested that the Boss be permitted to sleep a little later. Hassett agreed that FDR could use the extra hour or two; he could have used it himself. The important thing, now that he was up, was to get out of the bathroom before the timid knocking began.

When Hassett got off the phone, Grace Tully was up. He told her the news. This altered her morning schedule. The President would dictate the first draft of his United Nations speech today. If the pouch was late, Miss Tully could spend the morning at the swimming pool. Tully phoned Hacky. She was alone in a small cottage, a place where she could handle the switchboard and wave from the doorway to passing friends. Yes, Hacky would go swimming. Miss Hachmeister phoned the solemn young Navy Commander—Howard Bruenn. He was up and dressed in his khaki slacks and shirt. Yes, he too would enjoy a swim, but a little later. He expected to examine the President around nine-thirty.

If there was a busy bee on this warm, lazy morning, it was Ruth Stevens. At 8:00 A.M. she was up on the hill at the barbecue site, her short hair flying, supervising everything and nothing. The mayor and his wife were moving chairs into place. The long pit had been dug into red clay; the kindling was on the bottom and the logs on top. A long steel rod that looked like an axle from a freight train hung the length of the pit. Allcorn, with the assistance of Jess Long and Len Williams, impaled two hundred-and-fifty-pound hogs and a lamb on the rack from mouth to tail. The fire was lighted; a black woman friend of Miss Stevens watched. Ruth, walking and trotting to her tasks, shouted: "I already cooked twelve five-pound hens and twenty-five pounds of the best stew meat you ever saw. Plus two hogs' heads in that pot." She pointed to a black caldron.

The place seemed high up in the bright morning sky. The quince were flowering; the dogwood were dropping petals of different colors. The mayor set out an assortment of hammocks under hickory nut trees. There were dozens of canvas-striped folding chairs. The bald-headed mayor had a special chair for the President of the United States—a large wooden armchair with a good backrest and a fluffy cushion. It was placed in shade, under hanging purple wisteria. From that chair he could look down the green slopes to the tall stands of timber far below. The tables, each seating four, were grouped in the shape of a capital U. There was a portable bar. "The reporters will open that," Miss Stevens said. Some of the women went hunting with shears and came back with white azaleas, huckleberry branches and wisteria. They decorated the tables. Off to the side was an ancient two-gallon coffee pot. An old black woman sat beside it. She had served coffee to Roosevelt from that pot when he was young and first came to Warm Springs. She wanted to do it one more time.

When Merriman Smith suggested the barbecue, he said it would be about a dozen people. A week ago the list numbered forty. This morning it was sixty-four. Some of the names were unknown to the Warm Springs crowd. Elizabeth Shoumatoff was one. Nicholas Robbins was another. And who was Lucy Rutherfurd? President Roosevelt had never permitted her name to adorn any list. This time, he told Hassett, he wanted her name on it. The women were still exclaiming over the names on the list when Monty Snyder drove up. He was FDR's chauffeur and he drove the big Lincoln in off the road up the driveway and turned it toward the lawn where the barbecue would be held. He backed it down again. Then the car came up backwards. Mr. Snyder was still "rehearsing" the big automobile when the first four Secret Service agents arrived. With small fixed smiles and affable nods they began the intricate business of "sanitizing" premises to be graced by the President. They looked over, into, and under everything, including the huge coffee pot.

It was only 9:00 A.M. when Major DeWitt Greer, chief of communications for the President, arrived with a detachment of the U.S. Army Signal Corps. Greer located a clapboard barn adjoining the table area. This would be communications headquarters for the late afternoon. There was a short-wave radio transmitter, an assortment of walkie-talkies and a land line which was run on huge wooden wheels spinning down hills into glens to form a solid telephone line to the Little White House and to Hachmeister's switchboard. Bun Wright arrived with his fiddle and everybody paused to grin. The old man was very early. He lived on a nearby farm, and he had been old when he first sawed a square-dance tune for Roosevelt years ago. He had rasped those old resined strings, done a small clog dance and announced gravely to the President, "I'm the best damn breakdown fiddler you ever heard." FDR had tipped his head and roared with laughter. Since then, on festive occasions, he would intone, "Mr. President—giving you 'Cackling Pullet.'" He would play it at top speed, then announce, "Mr. President—giving you 'Fiddler's Dram.'" The President enjoyed the presence of the lively old man.

Mr. Roosevelt could sleep. But he didn't. Arthur Prettyman told him there would be no pouch until noon, but FDR asked for fried eggs and bacon and a piece of toast. He looked down toward the hooked rug and exchanged greetings with Fala. Prettyman got some extra pillows and propped them behind the Boss. He adjusted his pince-nez and began to read the Atlanta *Constitution*. The news was good. The Associated Press said that the final offensive of the war in Europe had begun. Vienna had fallen to the Russians. The U.S. First Army was at Nordhausen. The Twelfth Army Group had taken 1,018,000 prisoners since June 6, 1944. Germany was fragmented and, as Stalin had insisted, the Nazis were surrendering to the Americans and British in the west and fighting with their final strength against Zhukov and Koniev in the east. The Russian armies were within 40 miles of Berlin, having gained only 10 miles in two weeks. In Italy the British and Americans under Alexander were pounding the outskirts of Bologna. On Okinawa, U.S. Marines fought to the death for one more ditch, one small open field. In London 2,000 bombers took off to darken the cold sunny skies on the Prussian plain.

Although the President did not know it, the U.S. Ninth Army had reached the banks of the Elbe River. There was a British "official" story that Adolf Hitler was dying in his Chancellory bunker and had appointed Heinrich Himmler as the new Führer. Simpson's Ninth Army was 57 miles west of Berlin; Zhukov had a division of mounted Cossacks 30 miles east of the German capital. Mr. Roosevelt turned on his portable radio and listened to the morning music. It was soft in tone, unobtrusive, as he continued to read. If he was surprised by anything in the paper, it was that none of Jonathan Daniels' White House releases were in print. When FDR was absent, they usually arranged a succession of presidential announcements to cover the time he was away; this was designed to make the White House press corps believe that FDR was still in Washington.

In the kitchen Lizzie McDuffie, armed with old dust rags and an oil mop, was arguing with Joe Esperancilla, the President's Filipino messboy. Mrs. McDuffie said that she believed in reincarnation, and no boy was going to reconvince her. Mr. Esperancilla tried logic. He could not dent the credence of the stout black maid. She weighed two hundred pounds and, if she had a neck, no one had seen it. "If there is such a thing," she said loudly, "when I come back to this world I want to be a canary bird." Esperancilla, teasing, said, "You'll sit in a cage and eat."

She stomped out of the kitchen, flicking a feather duster at books on shelves, ships on chocks and woodwork and lamps. She raised the venetian blinds on the big rear windows leading onto the porch, and the buttered sunlight poured in. She was so angry about the allusion to her eating that she was puffing hard without working hard. The President called from his bedroom, "Lizzie!" She stopped, and looked frightened. Lizzie McDuffie, in common with so many women, adored the President, but she felt afraid when he called her. She inched over to the half-open bedroom door and looked in. FDR smiled at her over the tops of his glasses. The newspaper was spread on the counterpane.

"Lizzie," he said, "you have been having a grand time out there." It was a mock accusation. The President was nosy; he wanted to know what prompted the loud voices. "Oh my!" she said, stepping into the bedroom. "Did we disturb you?" "No, no. What in the world were you talking about?" The stout Mrs. McDuffie was embarrassed. "Well," she finally said, "do you believe in reincarnation?" He sat up. "Do I believe in *what?*" "Reincarnation." "Well, tell me, Lizzie. Do *you* believe in reincarnation?" She became sheepish. "I don't know if I do or not. But that's what Joe was trying to find out. I told him I don't know, but if there is such a thing, I want to be a canary bird." The President looked stunned for a moment. His bright eyes studied Mrs. McDuffie's figure. He picked up the newspaper and threw it down and burst into roaring laughter. "A canary bird!" he shrieked. "Don't you love it? Don't you just love it?" When he subsided, Lizzie asked the President how he was feeling this morning. He put the palm of his hand on the back of his neck and pulled his head from side to side. "I don't feel too good, Lizzie," he said. Lizzie thought that anything the President said was sheer gospel. Many times, he had fingered his nose and his forehead, indicating that his sinuses did not feel well. This was the first time he had rubbed the back of his neck. Maybe it was all the posing for the painter.

Mrs. McDuffie left when Dr. Bruenn arrived. The cardiologist sat on the edge of the bed, exchanged greetings with the President and, as he unpacked his instruments, asked how his patient had slept. He had a good night, but there was this slight headache and a sort of stiffness in the neck. As is the case with all physicians, Bruenn did almost as much work with his eyes and his ears as with his stethoscope and blood-pressure cuff. There was a slight cyanosis of fingernails and lips; sometimes the mouth was slack, sometimes not. The eyes looked larger when the patient was losing weight. Once in a while he seemed to have a hearing problem, leaning forward with a slight smile to make certain of what the doctor said. If FDR felt chipper, Dr. Bruenn knew it at once. When he was deeply fatigued, he leaned back on his pillows in abject apathy, not caring about the procedures.

In a talking mood, the President voiced his innermost feelings about people and events. Recently, he had been disconsolate about Stalin not sending Foreign Minister Molotov to the United Nations. Other countries were sending their foreign ministers. Stalin, in a pique over Poland, was downgrading the United Nations. Molotov was too busy to attend; Ambassador Gromyko would represent Russia. The Boss was hurt. He felt that Stalin was deliberately hurting *him*. This morning the subject did not come up. The pain in the neck bothered him. He bent his head forward as Bruenn brought his thumbs down the flanking muscles. A little massage made a lot of difference. Roosevelt said he felt better, as he turned his head this way and that. The conspiracy of smiles between the old man and the young was still intact. No questions, no volunteered information.

Dr. Bruenn made his daily notations and took his leave. Outside, as always, he phoned the White House and made his daily report to McIntire. It was a common story. Blood pressure was 180/110–120; the heart action was the same—an enlarged organ limping along with a murmur. He seemed to have gained a little weight, a few pounds at least. There was the usual evidence of advanced arteriosclerosis, but there was nothing medical science could do about it. Bruenn's professional despair was offset by McIntire's optimism. After the young doctor's report of steady deterioration, with a slight un-measured gain in weight, McIntire would write:

When Dr. Bruenn telephoned on Thursday, April 12, his report was most optimistic. The President had gained back eight of his lost pounds and he was feeling so fit that he planned to attend an old-fashioned Georgia barbecue in the afternoon and a minstrel show that evening for the Foundation's patients. Every cause for anxiety seemed to have lifted.

It was eleven o'clock when the President summoned Prettyman to fix his bath and help him to shave and dress. He had dawdled over the *Constitution* because the pouch was late, but he forgot that Elizabeth Shoumatoff would be waiting in the living room with her easel and watercolors. He folded the newspaper carefully and placed it on the small bare night table next to a small book. The book was *The Punch and Judy Murders,* by Carter Dickson, and was opened to page 78, the beginning of a chapter headed "Six Feet of Earth." He startled Prettyman when he said, "I want to wear my dark gray suit and vest. Get me my red-striped Harvard tie." He never wore a vest; he was partial to bow ties. The valet thought that the artist may have suggested the attire.

The women were in the living room when Arthur Prettyman pushed the wheelchair over the bedroom door-sill. He was bright with good mornings, but they felt he had no color. The deep oyster pouches were again under the eyes. Laura Delano was fluttering back and forth from the living room to the bedroom she shared with Margaret Suckley. She was getting fresh water for vases. After that, she was busy getting flowers for the water. Miss Suckley sat on the couch, busy with her interminable crocheting. She could crochet and listen better than she could crochet and talk. The painter was setting her easel, a busy woman who kept talking even when others were trying to speak. On the couch facing the fireplace, which faced the big leather chair in which the President sat, was Lucy. Of the four, she spoke the fewest words. She sat erect, hands entwined on her lap. She had a little more than the small smile so often attributed to her; she had the bright expectant eyes of a child who has been promised a doll if she will remain quiet.

The painter, in her fourth day of work, was less awed in the presence of the President. Her Russian accent was sharp; he would please hold his head a little more to the right; the chin must be lifted a little. As FDR chatted amiably with the women, Madame Shoumatoff smoothed her smock and went to the President and measured his nose. She wanted his chair moved a trifle, so that the shafts of morning light would come across the right side of his cheeks and highlight his forehead.

In Washington the heavy night fog had dissipated. The streets glistened damply. The Senate convened; the chaplain delivered himself of a long political prayer asking the protection of the Almighty for the President and a blessing on American arms and American senators. There was debate scheduled on a water rights treaty with Mexico; many senators answered "Here!" to their names and shuffled out the back doors. The Vice President, Harry S. Truman, was still in his office. Nothing of imperative importance was on the agenda, and he left the presiding officer's functions to Senator Alben Barkley on a pro tem basis. The White House was as close to being empty as it could be. The ushers and cooks were present. So were the clerks. On the ground floor, Steve Early and Edward Stettinius were in the West Wing chatting. Admiral McIntire was in his dispensary, writing notes. On the second floor, Anna was dressing to go to Bethesda Hospital to see Johnny. Her mother, who had a predilection for being in her quarters when the President was away, and vice versa, was holding a press conference for women. They were in her sitting room; all of them were aware that the First Lady would rather discuss political matters than social affairs. She impressed everyone as a thoroughly honest and honorable person, much more interested in going to San Francisco with her husband than what she might wear.

She told the women that, in a day or two, she would be off again to make speeches, this time in New York. A journalist asked what the United States would propose to do with Germany at the United Nations Conference. This was precisely the type of question Mrs. Roosevelt hoped for. The proper authorities, she said, would make all the decisions when the time came, but the important thing for Americans was to stop thinking in terms of "we":

We must accustom ourselves to remember we are one of three great nations with a responsibility for waging war, and once there is a United Nations organization, countries once occupied have a right to express their opinions too. We will have to get over the habit of saying what we as a single nation will do. When we say "we" on international questions in the future, we will mean all the people who have an interest in the question. A United Nations organization is for the very purpose of making it possible that all the world's opinion will have a clearing house.

Mrs. Roosevelt was asked if there was anything important on her calendar today. She asked Malvina Thompson for a copy, adjusted her spectacles far down her nose and shook her head no. There was nothing earth-shattering. She would have lunch at one with Mr. and Mrs. Grosvenor Allen and Mrs. Nila Magidoff; at three she would chat with Mr. Charles Taussig about United Nations trusteeships; at four she would go to the Sulgrave Club for the annual Thrift Shop party—something she wouldn't miss—and, at seven-thirty, she would have dinner at the Arthur Davis home to hear a report on subsistence homestead communities. It wasn't much. Reporters could attend the Thrift Shop party if they chose; there would be some prominent women speakers, and Edith Wilson, widow of President Woodrow Wilson, would be sitting with Mrs. Roosevelt on the dais.

In the Senate, the chair recognized Senator Raymond

Willis of Indiana. He asked unanimous consent to insert in the *Congressional Record* an article current in *The New York Times,* datelined Havana, which stated that America's wartime ally, the Soviet Union, was sending an inordinate number of Russian diplomats to Cuba. The Senator admitted that he did not comprehend the possibly sinister purpose behind it, but it should be published in the *Record*. There being no objection, it was so ordered by the chair. Harry Truman came into the well, grinning over a polka-dotted bow tie, a caricature of himself. He shook hands with Barkley and replaced him on the chair. The Vice President handed a sheaf of papers to the reading clerk. There was a Treasury Department report on the Exchange Stabilization Fund; a resolution by the legislature of the State of Pennsylvania announcing a welcome home celebration at the end of the war for General George S. Patton—the President of the United States was hereby invited. There was a resolution from Alaska asking that the U.S. Senate help to preserve reindeer by removing restrictions on the killing of timber wolves and coyotes; there was an embossed resolution from the Saturday Lunch Club of Minneapolis praising President Roosevelt for his efforts in behalf of victory, peace and unity.

These were read, and more senators drifted out. Looking down, Truman saw a scimitar of gleaming desks. This, he knew, would induce someone to propose that a quorum was not present and bells would ring with urgency in the corridors and in the Senate Office Building. Albert Hawkes of New Jersey stood to present a petition from the Sons of Italy in America asking President Roosevelt to invite Italy to San Francisco. When the Senate fell into intellectual doldrums, it always fell deep and dark. Scott Lucas of Illinois reported that the Committee to Audit and Control Contingent Expenses of the United States Senate had approved the continuation of the fund for "the purposes stated in said resolution." Lucas sat. Kenneth Wherry of Nebraska popped to his feet to ask Lucas to explain what "said resolution" encompassed. He sat. Lucas stood and said he didn't have the remotest notion. He turned to Tom Connally of Texas to ask if he knew. Connally got to his feet and said the fund was designed to pay for the lunches of distinguished foreigners so that the senators would not have to pay out of their own pockets; the committee in charge of such matters had found a surplus in the fund at year's end and had voted to continue using it until it was spent.

Wherry said he had a right to know how much lunch money was left. Connally said he didn't have the figure at hand, but Lucas might know. Scott Lucas stood and said he had no idea. Connally got to his feet and said that there might be two, maybe three hundred dollars in the kitty. Wherry sat. Senator William Langer of North Dakota suggested the absence of a quorum. Bells began to ring. Senators dogtrotted from offices and committee rooms to obey the bell. The clerk called each name deliberately, slowly, and marked present or absent with circular flourishes of his pen. Some senators yelled "Here!" as they burst through the rear doors. Fifty-two of ninety-six senators were present—a quorum. When the roll call was completed, senators began to disappear again, before the greatest deliberative body in the world could buckle to the task of administering to the needs of the Republic.

Truman drew some paper and a pen. When proceedings were dull, he found that, in his lofty chair, he could apply himself to writing a folksy letter to his mother and sister in Independence, Missouri, without disturbance from the rhetorical exercises in the well. The one-time Army captain had an acute appreciation of history, and, as Vice President, he was almost as awed to be a part of it as his mother was when she received those letters. He had been pleasantly surprised, this morning, to receive a call from Sam Rayburn's office. It was an invitation to join him, after recessing, in a little-known room called the "Board of Education." Mr. Sam maintained this room in the House Wing for the solace of his cronies who drank good bourbon and branch water and "struck a blow for liberty." A free drink or two seemed of small importance, but the "Board of Education" was limited to a select knot of professional Democrats whose party loyalty and political ingenuity were prized. This was Mr. Truman's first invitation; he said he would be happy to attend.

"Mr. President," said the small, dark-skinned Dennis Chavez of New Mexico, "I ask permission to leave the chamber." Truman emerged from his reverie and gave permission. He was holding a pen when the bulk of Tom Connally got to its feet and announced that, as Chairman of the Foreign Relations Committee, he considered that it was time to begin debate on the Mexican water treaty. The Vice President nodded. Senator Ernest McFarland, whose state of Arizona abutted Mexico and was vitally interested in the business at hand, said he hoped that the treaty would be ratified without delay. It had already gone through the White House and won approval; the State Department could find no error in it; the Senate Foreign Relations had reported it out of committee favorably. . . .

It was close to noon and the President tired of holding his position for the artist. He waited for the pouch and made small talk. When Polly Delano had completed arranging all the flowers in all the vases, she sat. "I understand," said FDR, "that men often take complete vacations before they resign their jobs." Polly knew a joke was coming. She knew Franklin. He didn't smile—just held his position and stared at his favorite cousin. "I'm going to resign from the Presidency," he said. Daisy Suckley and Lucy Rutherfurd looked up. "You are?" Polly said, not believing. "What will you do?" He maintained his serious expression. "If I can get the job, I'll head the United Nations." The women waited for his laughter. He didn't smile. They said nothing. He added nothing. It was one of a series of dead-end reversals in his thinking. He insisted that he wanted to open the first meeting of the United Nations. At lunch only yesterday he had told Dorothy Brady that he didn't want

to go. Today he appeared willing to resign the Presidency
to administer the United Nations.

Mr. Roosevelt wanted to know how the barbecue
was coming along. Also the evening minstrel show. He
told the ladies that they would enjoy themselves at both
events. The President looked at his watch. It was shortly
after twelve. He could stop posing any time he chose,
but, as long as the pouch wasn't in, he chose to please
Elizabeth Shoumatoff. Hassett came through the front
door with a heavy load of mail. The President seemed
glad to see him. Hassett greeted the women in turn,
and noted that FDR's countenance "registered great
weariness." He had said, to Bruenn and others, that
the Boss was at his brightest when he got out of bed
and that his strength declined rapidly after high noon.
He also thought that Mrs. Shoumatoff was "too aggressive." As FDR was reading the mail, tilting his head,
she got up from her easel and placed his head in its
original position.

The small desk was placed in front of his chair. He
read letters and signed others. Dewey Long came in.
He showed the President a detailed study of the railroad
itinerary to San Francisco and back to Hyde Park.
Roosevelt nodded. He said he wasn't interested in a
scenic route this time. For the first time, he did not
admonish Mr. Long to make sure the train moved slowly.
Arthur Prettyman, en route from bedroom to kitchen,
heard the President say, "Let's have lunch around one."
He did not like to sign appointments to postmasterships,
but there were several. Hassett took the sheets and placed
them on the floor to dry the signatures.

There were some additional signatures required for
citations for the Legion of Merit. There was a bill, passed
by both Houses, to extend the life of the Commodity
Credit Corporation and to increase its borrowing power.
He glanced up at Hassett, smiling through the glittering
pince-nez. "Here's where I make a law," he said. He
wrote "approved" and the date. Then he signed it. The
President's secretary smiled back. The sheaf was placed
on the floor to dry. Had Hassett studied the signature,

he might have been surprised. It did not read "Franklin D. Roosevelt." It was one word formed into a small arched bridge, almost indecipherable.

A stack of state papers was left within the grasp of the President on another table. These were to be read later. Hassett was slow picking the signed papers from the floor. Before him, Roosevelt had a message which he proposed to send to Stalin. It was, he said, his last attempt to maintain cordial communication with the Russians. He could not hide his hurt over the contemptible action of the Soviets in not sending Molotov to San Francisco, nor could he countenance Stalin telling him that, as President, his subordinates had not kept him informed about peace negotiations in Berne. He had received a polite message from Stalin; now he proposed to return one, but he could not refrain from touching it with a schoolteacherish tone:

Thank you for your frank explanation of the Soviet point of view of the Berne incident, which now appears to have faded into the past without having accomplished any useful purpose. There must not, in any event, be mutual mistrust, and minor misunderstandings of this nature should not arise in the future. I feel sure that when our armies make contact in Germany and join in a fully coordinated offensive the Nazi armies will disintegrate.

The President passed it to Hassett. "Send it," he said. The Boss told him to pick up Leighton McCarthy and drive him to the barbecue. "I'll be there at four-thiry," he said. He had one more order. Hassett was to phone Postmaster General Frank Walker that the President approved the new issue of stamps to commemorate the United Nations meeting. FDR said to tell Walker to put the stamps on sale April 25, and that the President would stop at the post office in San Francisco on that day and buy a sheet of them. He glanced at a letter he had signed for the State Department. His head wagged woefully. "A typical State Department letter," he murmured. "It says nothing at all." Lugubriously,

Hassett said, "I'm glad I didn't write it." The President chuckled because on occasions when he had asked Hassett to write a note, he had studied it and said, "Bill, this says nothing at all."

As the secretary departed, frowning at the artist, Mrs. Shoumatoff rearranged the folds of the heavy Navy cape. The President became engrossed in state papers. Mrs. Shoumatoff tried to engage him in conversation, possibly to restore the serene expression he had worn before. But, when he glanced up, it was to smile at Lucy, who sat to his right near the French doors leading to the porch. "I saw a new Florida centennial stamp," the artist said in her Russian accent. "It's a pretty stamp. Did you have anything to do with that one?" "I certainly did," the President said. He was still smiling in Mrs. Rutherfurd's direction when he saw Joe Esperancilla come out of the kitchen with place settings. "Now," he said, "we have about fifteen minutes. . . ." The Filipino went about his work silently. Mr. Roosevelt slipped some surplus stamps into an envelope and wrote on it "To Give Away." He glanced through his wallet, found a card and slipped the wallet into his inside jacket pocket. He tossed the cardboard into a wastebasket. It was the draft card he had carried throughout the war.

Noiselessly, the President pulled to him the small straightback chair with the casters. He braced his strong arms; quickly, he went from the big leather chair to the movable one. Daisy Bonner came from the kitchen with a round silver tray. On it was a steaming cup of gruel. The Boss did not like it, but Daisy and Lizzie had been ordered to make it and serve it every day before lunch. He took a spoonful or two and replaced the spoon. Out front, Secret Service agent Jim Beary stood leaning against his car. The only sign of life he had seen all morning had been the two women coming from the guest house to the Little White House. Now he watched stout Lizzie McDuffie move in the opposite direction. She was going to make the beds of Mrs. Rutherfurd and Madame Shoumatoff. Lizzie turned to look back. Through the window, she could see the Presi-

dent in majestic profile. She could not hear him but
he seemed to be speaking to Mrs. Rutherfurd. She saw
him twist a cigarette into a holder and light it.

Hacky emerged from the pool. Bruenn was lying face
down in wet shorts on a bath towel. Brady and Tully
climbed the pool ladder, dripping. They asked the doctor
if he would join them for lunch. He lifted his head and
thanked them. No, he said, the sun was good and warm.
He would lie at poolside awhile. He asked Hacky to
"reserve" a sandwich and a bottle of milk for him at
Georgia Hall. He had promised to compete in a golf
tournament after lunch. Hassett was already in the
Georgia Hall dining room. He confined his lunch to
a plate of soup; at the barbecue there would be a great
deal to eat. Besides, he was still annoyed at the behavior
of the artist. He hoped he could see Doc Bruenn and
ask him to restrain that woman from ordering a sick
man to hold his head this way and that.

Lunch was almost ready. Mrs. Shoumatoff could not
get the attention of the President. He kept glancing from
one set of papers on a bridge table to a set on the opposite
side. Then back again. The cigarette holder was at a
jaunty angle. The artist began to fill in the red and blue
striped tie on her painting. Mr. Roosevelt took the cigarette from his mouth and placed it on an ashtray. Daisy
Suckley was obviously tired of crocheting. She was rubbing her hands. Polly came out of Mrs. Roosevelt's bedroom. She had forgotten one vase of flowers—the one
for the room she shared with Daisy. Only Lucy Rutherfurd sat watching the President. Shakily, he raised his
left hand to his forehead as he perused the papers.
He seemed to press against the temple. Mrs. Shoumatoff
looked up. The hand went down at his side, then came
up again. This time the fingers encompassed the front
of his forehead. He seemed to be squeezing. He said
softly, "I have a terrific headache." The hand dropped
clumsily. Miss Suckley smiled at Franklin. "Did you
drop something?" She stood to help him find whatever
it might be. The sweet, composed smile of Lucy

Rutherfurd died suddenly. She looked shocked, alarmed.

The President, leaning forward to study the papers on the table, settled back in his chair. His eyes were full on the only person straight ahead: Lucy. Then the eyes dropped half closed and he slumped to his left. Polly placed the vase on the fireplace and said loudly, "Franklin, are you all right?" There was no response. The body, slumped in the regal cape, was motionless. The mouth began to open slowly, an imitation of a long, slow yawn. Mrs. Shoumatoff jumped to her feet. She screamed. It was sufficiently piercing to bring Prettyman out of the bedroom and Esperancilla out of the kitchen. Mrs. Shoumatoff ran out the front door of the house. Her features were distorted. She saw agent Beary. "Call a doctor!" she shouted. "Something terrible has happened to the President!" Beary used the radiophone in the car. He tried to get Hachmeister. There was no answer, but the Warm Springs operator came on the line. "Find Dr. Bruenn," he said, "and get him up here right away. The Little White House. Yes." He hung up and phoned the Secret Service gate. "Beary," he said. "Doc Bruenn is on his way up. Let him through right away." He contacted Guy Spaman, supervising agent. "Something happened up here. I called Doc Bruenn. No, I don't know."

Arthur Prettyman, dark and strong, looked down at the collapsed body. "Joe," he said softly, "help on the other side." They locked arms behind the President's back, and held hands under his knees. Slowly, the sleeping President came out of the chair. Carefully, step by inching step, they carried him around the living room furniture toward his bedroom. The Navy cape was flowing out behind him, sweeping the polished floor. The head lolled with each step. Mrs. Rutherfurd stood in frozen horror, her fist against her mouth. Polly was shouting something about a doctor. Mrs. Shoumatoff was sobbing. Margaret Suckley picked up a phone and said, "Get a doctor up here quick. Who? This is Daisy." She had never referred to herself as Daisy. The operator thought it was Daisy Bonner.

In the bedroom Franklin D. Roosevelt was lowered onto the counterpane. Joe Esperancilla stood back. Whatever was to be done, he knew, was Prettyman's privilege. Tenderly, the valet loosened the Harvard tie and opened the button of the collar. Then he pulled each shoe off by the heel and set them under the bed. The half-opened eyes didn't appear to be looking at anything. Arthur closed them. The President began to snore. There was unconsciousness, no pain. There had been a "terrific headache," then lights out, the cool refreshing darkness, peace. Jim Beary stood in the bedroom doorway. He moved no closer. The thing had happened; he would do the things he had to do and he would do them at once. He loved this man—loved him—but tears never approached his eyes. An unseen hand throttled his throat and he drew the breaths one at a time. In a moment, he knew, hell would be bursting in this little house.

In the living room a woman was shouting that Lucy had better go. "Hurry!" the voice said. Mrs. Rutherfurd was dumbfounded. A moment ago she had been exchanging secret smiles with the man she had loved for so long. He was sick, hurt—maybe even dying—and they were yelling to her to flee, to go home. Madame Shoumatoff had the easel under one arm, and the painting at arm's length. She was trying to drag Mrs. Rutherfurd. It must have seemed unfair to Mrs. Rutherfurd that, whenever he sorely needed her—at Campobello or at Warm Springs—she was not permitted to approach his side. Still, in the agony of fear, she hurried out with the painter and walked swiftly across the street to the guest house. Nicholas Robbins was called. He was at the Warm Springs Hotel. All Mrs. Shoumatoff said was, "Pack everything quick and bring the car up. We're leaving right away."

Five minutes later, Hacky said that before going to lunch she would like to check her switchboard. Tully and Brady stood outside the cottage as Louise Hachmeister plugged a line into Georgia Hall. "Hacky," she said. "Anybody calling me?" "Yes," the operator said. "Do you know where Dr. Bruenn is?" "Who wants him? We just left him at the pool." "The Little White House." "Thanks. I'll take care of it." She plugged the Little White House and rang. Daisy Bonner answered. "Does the President want Dr. Bruenn for lunch?" "No," the cook wailed. "He's sick. The President is sick."

Like Beary, Hacky wasted no time. "The President is sick," she said to her friends. She rang the pool dressing room. When Bruenn got on the phone she said, "The President's sick. They want you right away." The doctor asked her to call George Fox. She rang another extension. There was no answer. She looked out the cottage door. George Fox was taking a stroll in the sun. "George," she shouted, "Doc Bruenn wants you to go to his place, pick up his bag and meet him at the Little White House." Grace Tully felt ill. Brady wrung her pale hands tight. There was a dreadful sensation that this was not a stomach upset. This was serious. They decided to get into the car and drive up to the cottage. Guy Spaman located Mike Reilly down near the pool area and told him the President had some sort of seizure. Hassett received an emergency call from Reilly. "Get up to the Little White House. The Boss is sick."

Bruenn dressed at speed. Guy Spaman drove a car down the rutted road, whipping the berry bushes as he hurried to the pool. He got Bruenn and headed back up the hill. In the guest cottage, two women tossed garments into suitcases, weeping as they hurried. They took turns looking out the window for Robbins, but he had not left the Warm Springs Hotel. He had cameras, lenses and tripods to pack, in addition to clothing. As they looked out the window, they saw isolated persons running breathlessly toward the Little White House across the crushed stone driveway. Now and then an automobile would pull up, skidding to a stop with stones rattling against the fenders. The President had fainted at 1:15 P.M. Central War Time. It was now 1:30.

Beary was standing out front when Spaman's car pulled

up. "It's the Boss," he said to Bruenn. The doctor got inside just as Fox arrived with the medical bag. They moved fast. "Get Admiral McIntire on the phone and hold him," the doctor said to no one in particular. Daisy called Hacky. The bedroom was small. The noise of the snoring could be heard all the way to the kitchen. Polly paced the floor. "I'll have to call Eleanor," she said. Daisy held the phone, waiting for Dr. McIntire. Grace Tully came in with Dorothy Brady. Both sat on the edge of the couch without exchanging greetings with anyone. They too could hear the deep snoring from inside. Tully's lips began to move in prayer.

Bruenn peeled the eyelids back one at a time. There appeared to be no dilation. Respiration was deep, stertorous. Wrist pulse was shallow and fast. The heart action was swift. Systolic blood pressure was 300 and probably more; the cuff only registered 300 at the top of the gauge. The doctor asked Fox for heavy shears. He unbuttoned clothing wherever he could; he cut the shirt, undershirt and trousers off and cast them on the floor. The shorts were peeled down; the socks taken off. The pallid body was exposed for examination. To the medical mind there were several possibilities—infarction, aneurism, cardiovascular accident—but Bruenn saw only one: CVA, a stroke, a cerebral hemorrhage. The body stopped breathing. Bruenn lifted the shoulders and dropped them to the bed. The body began to breathe. At the same time, it urinated. The pupil of the left eye began to dilate. Pulse was 104. Bruenn brusquely asked for a syringe. The doctor injected aminophylline and nitroglycerine directly into the arm. This would expand the arteries and lower the blood pressure. "Get his pajamas," Bruenn said, and went out and made a terse report to Admiral McIntire. The President had fainted, he said, and was still unconscious. It looked like CVA to him, but he couldn't be positive. He explained the dilation of the left eye and the treatment. Asked for his personal opinion, he said: "It's serious."

McIntire said he would call Dr. James Paullin in Atlanta and ask him to hurry to the President. Paullin, a top-flight internist, was 70 miles away. The battle would be won or lost before he could get to Warm Springs. The women sat listening to the professional jargon of the doctor. But they knew, they knew. So did Bill Hassett, who came through the front door, looked around at the silent, stony faces and heard the horribly rhythmic snore. "I knew then," he said, "that it was the last of earth." He sat. Joe Esperancilla sat in the kitchen. Lizzie and Daisy sat with him; there was fright on the features, but no words. In the bedroom, George Fox managed to get striped pajamas on the patient. Bruenn returned, and went through the examination again. It had to be a stroke; probably a massive hemorrhage in the occipital area, caused by a clot, or else a hardened artery had broken, spilling venous blood in a pool between the inside of the skull and the brain. The skull would neither bend nor break; the brain would be depressed by the weight of the blood. Bruenn found the Navy cape and placed it over the patient.

He went out on the elliptical porch to stand in the sun and think. He spoke to Hassett. "A long siege," he said. "A long siege." Bruenn returned to the bedroom and tried a series of reflex tests. "So far as I can see," he said to George Fox, "there is no paralysis." He was fighting an unseen, almost unknown enemy which does its damage quickly and silently, coming without warning, leaving without a visible trace. Mike Reilly, so upset that he looked angry, strode into the house and looked into the bedroom. In a manner of speaking, that man was his baby. For many years, Reilly had lifted him, carried him, knew his secrets, kept them, shielded him from the world when he was helpless, served him with selfless devotion. "Mike," Bruenn whispered, "this is serious." Reilly didn't need the words. The big cape, worn across the front of the body, backwards, the thin face of gray stone, the open mouth with the pivot tooth missing, the snowy feet, the spasmodic tremors of the whole frame—Mike Reilly required no words to tell him what any layman could surmise—that Franklin Delano Roosevelt, thirty-second President of the United

States, age sixty-three years and two months, was about
to lose a great battle.

The doctor left the bedroom to tell Reilly that McIntire
had sent for Paullin. The Secret Service chief phoned
Spaman and told him to send men out along the roads
between Warm Springs and Atlanta to meet the doctor
and help him through the speed traps. There was a wartime limit of thirty-five miles an hour, designed to save
gasoline. At the gate, agents hopped into automobiles
and moved out fast. The quickest way would be Route
85 to Woodbury, then 85-W up into the hills. The men
didn't know the man they were looking for, or what kind
of car he would be driving. Spaman asked someone to
phone Paullin's office in Atlanta to get the information,
which would be sent out on shortwave. Reilly sat on a
couch with Grace Tully. It occurred to him that they
were whispering, like people in the presence of death.

Secret Service agents saw Nicholas Robbins and the
Cadillac convertible coming up the hill. They opened
the gates and nodded. He pulled up in front of the guest
house and was suprised to see both women carrying
their own bags. They seemed to be in disarray. As they
hurried off the porch, a Secret Service man ran by.
"Please," Mrs. Rutherfurd shouted, "can you tell me
something about his condition?" The man stopped and
looked at the tall, distraught woman. "Grave," he said.
"It doesn't look good." He ran on. She began to weep
again as she got into the front seat. Robbins didn't understand the excitement. Lucy couldn't talk about it. Mrs.
Shoumatoff told the photographer that she had been
painting the President's tie and suddenly he had an attack;
he just slumped in the chair. Robbins couldn't understand
why, at a time like this, they had to run. The artist
told him to head for Aiken, South Carolina. Robbins
knew it was going to be a long ride.

Bruenn was the professional. His step in and out
of the room was steady and easy; his voice was never
raised; he worked quietly, looking, probing, testing, administering. He acted like a man who could win the
contest between God and him. Lungs were still clear;

breathing remained stertorous, but regular. Blood pressure, which had been over 300/190, was coming down. Perspiration was profuse; hot water bottles and blankets over the extremities and neck had been applied. One grain of papaverine was injected. Amyl nitrite was given to relieve intense vasoconstriction. Reflexes were not obtainable in the legs. At two o'clock the doctor called Admiral McIntire again. Softly, rapidly, he repeated his diagnosis, enumerated methods of treatment, said that paralysis was present, and blood pressure down to 210/150. He repeated the phrase, "A long siege." McIntire was calm. Paullin was on his way, he said. He might be of some help. The Admiral would tell Mrs. Roosevelt and Anna the situation.

McIntire hung up. He walked to the door of his dispensary as Anna got off the White House elevator. The Admiral called her inside. "What is it?" she asked impatiently. "I want to be out there when Johnny gets his penicillin shots." McIntire was the epitome of unction. "I wanted to tell you that your father has had some sort of seizure." he said. "He's unconscious." Mrs. Boettiger was pulling gloves on her fingers. She paused. "What kind of a seizure?" she said. "Howard Bruenn has been calling from Warm Springs. Whatever it is, we don't believe it will affect his brain." Anna would remember the words the rest of her life, because she was torn between love of her father and duty to her son. She didn't know how to evaluate the word, "seizure." It could be one of many things. And yet, if the doctor said it would not affect her father's brain, his thinking, his functions— "I'm going to Bethesda," she said. "I have to go." She backed out of the door. "Please keep in touch with me." The Admiral asked her not to mention the seizure. If he had any news, he would phone her.

McIntire's phone rang. Mrs. Boettiger waited a moment. The Admiral listened to a message from Dr. Bruenn. The President's daughter asked to speak to Bruenn. "This thing," she said, "will it mean any further paralysis for my father?" The young Navy Commander was in a difficult position. His boss had been minimizing the President's poor health for a year. What could he say? "If that were so," he said haltingly, "it would not be paralysis which would affect the brain." She placed the phone on a desk blotter and left for her son.

In the sitting room upstairs, Eleanor Roosevelt shook hands with Charles Taussig and asked him to be seated. He was to be an adviser to the American delegation at San Francisco and, as he explained his mission, his field was to be United Nations trusteeships of small nations and islands unprepared for self-government. He had tried to get an appointment with the President, but, he said smiling, everybody knew that her husband ran a busy office downstairs, and he had been unable to see Mr. Roosevelt. He said he hoped that, by seeing Mrs. Roosevelt, perhaps she could ask her husband about his wishes in the matter of trusteeships— She said she was sorry, but that if it would help, she would put in a phone call to her husband. At that point, Malvina Thompson opened the study door and asked Mrs. Roosevelt if she would speak to Laura Delano. The First Lady excused herself and picked up a phone. Her hello was hearty but, after listening a moment, her voice softened. Polly's voice was under control; she had to tell Eleanor that Franklin fell into a faint just before lunch. How did he faint? Well, he was just sitting in his chair looking over some papers and he just passed out. He had been carried to the bedroom. Dr. Bruenn was with him right now. Mrs. Roosevelt was conscious of Mr. Taussig's presence. She whispered her questions guardedly, but Polly did not sound alarmed. Mrs. Roosevelt thanked Polly and asked her to phone again later. She hung up and excused herself. "Mr. Taussig, I will speak to my husband about this and get back to you. At the moment, I have some pressing business—" He understood. Taussig shook hands and left. Eleanor phoned McIntire.

The Admiral told her that he had been in touch with Warm Springs. He wasn't sure what the problem was. Mrs. Roosevelt asked if she shouldn't cancel her Thrift Shop date and fly to Warm Springs at once. Oh no, the Admiral said. She said she got the impression that

McIntire was not alarmed. To the contrary, he counseled Mrs. Roosevelt, if she canceled her daily appointments rumors would start flying, and she knew what that would lead to. He had been planning a visit to Warm Springs to see the President over the weekend. Why not keep her appointments, and then, in the evening, they could fly down together? Mrs. Roosevelt said she would do it. This was contrary to McIntire's inner feelings. As he wrote later:

Dr. Bruenn went on to tell me that he had rushed in to find the President pale, cold, sweating profusely, and totally unconscious. Making no effort to conceal his alarm, he reported that the pupils of the eyes were equal at first, but that the left had become widely dilated in a few seconds. Paralysis was also present. . . .

In the Senate well, Senator Alexander Wiley of Wisconsin was expatiating on the Mexican water treaty. Surreptitiously, Vice President Harry Truman began to write:

Dear Mamma & Mary: I am trying to write you a letter today from the desk of the President of the Senate while a windy Senator . . . is making a speech on a subject with which he is in no way familiar. The Jr. Sen. from Arizona made a speech on the subject, and he knew what he was talking about. . . .

We are considering the Mexican Treaty on water in the Colorado River and the Rio Grande. It is of vital importance to Southwestern U.S. and northern Mexico. Hope we get it over some day soon.

The Senators from California and one from Utah and a very disagreeable one from Nevada (McCarran) are fighting the ratification. I have to sit up here and make parliamentary rulings—some of which are common sense and some of which are not.

Hope you are having a nice spell of weather. We've had a week of beautiful weather but it is raining and misting today. I don't think it's going to last long. Hope not for I must fly to Providence, R.I., Sunday morning.

Turn on your radio tomorrow night at 9:30 your time, and you'll hear Harry make a Jefferson Day address to the nation. I think I'll be on all the networks, so it ought not to be hard to get me. It will be followed by the President, whom I'll introduce.

Hope you are well and stay that way.

Love to you both.

Write when you can.

Harry

Merriman Smith had helped to open the barbecue bar. If there was to be an inaugural drink, it belonged to him because the barbecue had been his idea. Ruth Stevens, still flashing from log pit to pot and back again, said she knew all along that the newspapermen would open the bar. She asked Merriman Smith to go back to Georgia Hall and get some special spices. He said okay. It was strange, he said, that the only thing that could keep this affair from being successful would be if the President found out that everyone except him had chipped in $2.50 for the food and drinks. The Boss wouldn't like that. Everyone had been sworn to secrecy. FDR didn't appreciate the idea of wage earners putting up money for his amusement. He might even get his Dutch up and stay home.

Smith got in his rented car and ran down to Georgia Hall. Music came from the big main room. The minstrel show was in its final rehearsal. Chief Petty Officer Jackson was inside with his accordion. The short black man with the skittering fingers could fascinate the President. Merriman Smith got out of his car and got the spices. He placed them on their sides in the front seat and got back in. Just then he saw Alice Winegar running across the street from Georgia Hall. She was Hassett's secretary. "Hey!" he yelled. "You folks better be getting ready." She didn't respond. He yelled, "What's the matter?" She looked over her shoulder as she disappeared into the Hassett cottage. "Nothing," she said. "Nothing." "Something," Smith said later, "was brewing. I knew it." He had a sharp instinct. There was something abou the way Alice Winegar hurried into that cottage that told him something important had occurred. Smith could speculate: maybe Germany had surrendered; maybe someone had killed Adolf Hitler; Stalin was coming to San Francisco; Japan was suing for peace; Stettinius resigned; food stamp rationing was being suspended—the possibilities were infinite. He turned the car back up the hill. When the Boss was ready, he'd release the news.

At 2:45 P.M. (Central Time) Dr. Bruenn noted that the patient's complexion improved. Blood pressure was down to 240/120. The heart sounds were good and the pulse was 90. However, respiration was becoming irregular, with deep breaths followed by pauses. Now and then, the body snapped into rigidity. Then it relaxed. Commander Fox, taciturn as always, stood watching with the doctor. Both men felt that they were looking at the last act of a long play; the final curtain was descending slowly. The doctor felt that there was no use calling the Admiral again. Except for slight changes, the situation remained the same—bad.

The time was one hour later in Washington—3:45—when Mrs. Roosevelt bustled out on the south grounds of the White House and got into a black limousine. The Secret Service car moved out ahead, and she was at the Sulgrave Club within a few minutes. A society reporter made a note: "Mrs. Roosevelt sat at the head table, between Mrs. John A. Dougherty, chairman, and Mrs. Woodrow Wilson. The First Lady looked unusually smart and in soaring spirits." Each of the ladies brought a carefully wrapped "white elephant" to be sold for the benefit of the Thrift Shop. One by one, the women at the head table were introduced to make brief remarks. Mrs. Roosevelt paid tribute to Mrs. John Williams, one of the most indefatigable workers, who was home ill.

Mrs. Roosevelt was still speaking glowingly of others when, at Warm Springs, Bruenn examined the unconscious patient again. In Georgia, it was 3:15; the President had been stricken two hours. It is possible that Bruenn, secretly, marveled that there was this much fight in the old man. All indications were of massive occipital hemorrhage, but the Boss kept battling the odds. Blood pressure was down to 210/110; the heart rate was 96. One eye, moderately contracted, dilated suddenly. The lips and fingernails were markedly cyanotic—concord blue. The end could not be far off, and yet there was no way of telling how much strength and struggle were left.

The white Cadillac slowed as it passed Lizella and on into the city of Macon. Mrs. Shoumatoff had reached to switch the radio on; Mrs. Rutherfurd said, "Please." Robbins had turned the driving over to the artist; she knew the roads between Aiken and Warm Springs. There were long meditative silences, and sudden swimming of tears. Whatever the news was, Lucy did not want to know; Elizabeth feared not to know. The wind whipped around the corners of the windshield; farms and villages appeared small and insignificant ahead of the car, passing by a few minutes later in a blur of freshly turned earth and a half dozen streets of wooden buildings pasted together around a brick church. "All right," Lucy said, nodding toward the radio. She clenched her hands. Madame Shoumatoff turned it on. The sound was soft sweet music. Robbins tried a few other stations. There was nothing except music and terse weather reports. The thing which froze Lucy with fright could not have happened; she shut the radio off.

Hassett was beset by peculiar, most sentimental, notions. Because Franklin D. Roosevelt's wife and sons and daughter were not present, he felt that it was wrong to stand at the bedside of the dying President. With the others, he had been sitting listening to the breathing for almost two hours. There was nothing except the long shafts of sunlight pointing diagonally down to the floor of the living room, and that breathing. Hassett believed that, even if Doc Bruenn closed the bedroom door, the dead snore would have been heard through the wall. He could bear it no longer. The phone in this room had always been busy. Now, except for Bruenn's reports to MacIntire, it reposed on its cradle. Hacky, who knew only that the President was sick, turned all call away at her switchboard. Bill stood. The act of standing drew the attention of the others. He walked to the bedroom door, swung it open and looked in. George Fox was standing against the wall. Bruenn sat half on the edge of the mattress, facing the President. ". . . the Greek nose and the noble forehead were as grand as ever . . . the awful breathing. . . . I knew that I should not see him again."

He returned to the vigil of the women. Bruenn came out, picked up the phone and asked Hacky for the direct wire to McIntire. The doctors were engaged in their medical terminology when Fox shouted, "Doc Bruenn!" The doctor dropped the receiver and hurried into the bedroom. The respiration had altered its cycle. The President was gasping, then lasping into a deadly quiescence. Bruenn ordered Fox to get on the bed astride the President and begin artificial respiration. The doctor injected caffeine sodium benzoate. In the living room the telephone had been forgotten. It swung loosely on its wire, an eccentric pendulum. The sound of breathing, dreaded by Hassett, Brady, Tully, Polly and Daisy in its labored snore, now became welcome as an audible sign of life.

The front door swung open, loud enough to slam against the umbrella stand, and everyone stiffened. It was Dr. James Paullin. He had made the trip from Atlanta in an old wreck of a car in an hour and forty minutes, whirling along the two-lane country roads he knew so well, never meeting a waiting Secret Service man. He went directly to the bedroom without nodding to anyone. Later, he wrote his thoughts:

The President was in extremis when I reached him. He was in a cold sweat, ashy gray, and breathing with difficulty. Numerous rhonchi in his chest. He was propped up in bed. His pupils were dilated and his hands slightly cyanosed. Commander Bruenn had already started artificial respiration. On examination, his pulse was barely perceptible.

The two doctors spoke in low tones. Paullin removed his jacket. Fox looked up from his labors. "He stopped breathing," he said. Both doctors looked for life signs. Paullin reached into his bag and drew a glass syringe and put Adrenalin in it. Fox backed off the Boss's chest. Paullin counted down the rib interstices and jabbed the needle directly into the heart. The Atlanta doctor listened. He heard two or three contractions. Dr. Bruenn listened with stethoscope for a minute or more. Paullin tried a blood-pressure cuff. He got no reading. Bruenn heard no sounds from the heart.

He nodded to Fox. "This man is dead," he said softly. He looked at his watch. The time was 3:35 P.M. Lieutenant Commander Fox got off the bed. Bruenn used his thumbs to press the tired eyes closed. It would not occur to him that the last living image reflected in those tired eyes had been the smiling face of Lucy. It was at that moment that darkness had come. Dr. Paullin stood aside as Fox bent over one side of the bed and Bruenn the other. Tenderly, they composed the body, closed and buttoned the pajama top, and composed the hands across the stomach. They straightened the legs, and rolled the counterpane up and up, until it covered the face and wispy gray hair.

Dr. Bruenn went into the living room hall and picked up the hanging phone. As he passed his sitting friends, he hung his head and shook it from side to side. He spoke softly into the phone. Hassett got up and asked to speak to Steve Early. Dr. Paullin and Fox came out of the bedroom. No one sitting there had to be told. The hoarse, sucking noise of the breathing had stopped. Bruenn gave the final news to McIntire, then gave the phone to Hassett. Steve Early was stunned. He who was quick with hard opinions had none. Everybody knew the Boss wasn't feeling well, but this— He trailed off. Hassett said he had the three pool reporters. Should he announce the death? No, Early said, no. Mrs. Roosevelt is at the Sulgrave Club and she must be notified at once and first. Bill could make the public announcement in Warm Springs at four o'clock Georgia time, and Early would make a White House announcement at the same time—unless, of course, he couldn't reach Mrs. Roosevelt. "Go ahead with the announcement," he said, "unless you get a call from me."

Hassett felt the full tragedy of the event. So did Grace Tully, who had worked with the President seventeen years. So did Dorothy Brady, who had been sent from a government office to the White House years ago for "three days of temporary duty." It is possible that, although all felt the sudden absence of the father image, the jokes, the joshing, the masterful orchestration of a leader of government, perhaps Mike Reilly felt it most poignantly. He was the only one present who, throughout the two-hour-and-twenty-minute vigil, kept assuring himself that the "Boss will make it. He's made it before when they thought he was down. Watch—he'll bounce out of the room." The blow may have been more crushing to him.

Hassett was still standing, pulling on his lower lip when a snapping, snarling series of barks was heard. No one had paid any attention to Fala. He had been dozing in a corner of the room. For a reason beyond understanding he ran directly for the front screen door and bashed his black head against it. The screen broke and he crawled through and ran snapping and barking up into the hills. There, Secret Service men could see him, standing alone, unmoving, on an eminence. This led to the quiet question: "Do dogs really know?" No one believed it. Bruenn shrugged and went out on the porch with Paullin. In the kitchen Daisy and Lizzie were sobbing. Arthur Prettyman arose from a kitchen chair and spoke to Laura Delano. "Could you please ask Mrs. Roosevelt to bring down a nice dark suit of clothes?" Aunt Polly said that nobody really cared how he would look because the family believed in closed caskets.

Prettyman went back to the kitchen. Grace Tully got up, sighed and walked into the President's bedroom. She turned the counterpane down and kissed his forehead. Lizzie McDuffie was shivering, saying she remembered a strange white bird which flew around inside the house

while she was waiting for the arrival of the President.
There was a pine wall over the drainboard. Daisy Bonner
took a pencil and printed on it: "In this room for the
President, Daisy Bonner cooked the first meal and the
last." Quietly, Mike Reilly came into the kitchen and
claimed all the unwashed plates and cups and saucers
used at breakfast. He ordered Jim Beary to send them
off for chemical analysis. It was a routine thought.

Bruenn was out on the back porch, smoking a cigarette.
Until now, he had been the professional physician. He
was conscious of a new dimension: he had lost a friend.
For a year he had been as close to Franklin D. Roosevelt
as his heartbeat. No questions asked; no answers volunteered. It was the end of a strange and intimate relationship. Young Bruenn knew more about the President
as a vital personality than he did as a human body with
a medical history. The little he knew about the frailties
of Franklin Roosevelt could be encompassed in a paragraph: 1937—systolic hypertension; 1941—systolic and
diastolic hypertension; 1944—congestive heart failure;
one episode of coronary insufficiency with no evidence
of myocardial infarction; 1945—deceased by reason of
a massive cerebral hemorrhage. That was the total record.
There was X-ray evidence of an inflamed gallbladder
and the presence of gallstones. There was nothing to
show the rapid wear and tear on arteries, the fatty plaques
inside which diminish the size of the artery and cut
down the flow of blood; nothing in medical science could
point a warning finger at an artery plugged by a thrombus,
or even a ballooning aneurism. Bruenn stomped on his
cigarette and went inside. He had to ask his boss how
much he could tell the reporters. Bruenn was still in
the Navy, still under the orders of his Admiral.

Up on the sunny hill, Ruth Stevens began to smile.
The barbecue was almost ready. At four o'clock she
had worried because so few had arrived. Everyone was
to be there at four. The President and his party would
arrive in a half hour. Old Bun Wright began to saw
"She'll Be Comin' Round the Mountain." The pigs and
the lamb, turning slowly over the ruddy pit, dripped

grease as their tan became deeper and deeper. Ray Hoover of Western Union showed up grinning. The reporters decided to have one more drink before FDR arrived, probably to insist on shaking a cocktail mixer. Some telephone linesmen arrived. A new radio commentator, Don Fisher, who would introduce the President tomorrow night at his Jefferson Day address, walked into the circle, introducing himself as from the National Broadcasting Company. Major DeWitt Greer walked toward the barn, where he had his shortwave operators waiting, and observed that he had never seen so many old-fashioneds in one group. Mayor and Mrs. Allcorn, greeting all arrivals, were as nervous as Ruth Stevens about the President. They wanted everything to be exactly right for him.

In Washington, the time was a few minutes after 5:00 P.M. A waiter approached the head table at the Sulgrave Club and whispered to Mrs. Roosevelt that the "White House was calling." Her heart sank. She had spent all her life exercising control. The First Lady had succeeded so well—except for the sobbing on the pillow in 1918—that her children felt that she had lost the knack of exuding emotion. She felt the deep, unspeakable dread now, but she excused herself for a moment and went "backstage" to the phone. It was Steve Early. Unthinkingly, he did not tell Mrs. Roosevelt the news. His voice sounded choked. "Mrs. Roosevelt," he said, "I wish you would come home at once." She did not ask why. She said, "Thank you, Steve," and hung up. Then she returned to the head table, turned on her toothsome smile, and took the microphone. "Ladies," she said. "Ladies. I must ask you to excuse me. Something has come up and I must leave at once." She heard the lamentable sound "Ohhhh" through the room. But she had made her speech and lived up to her obligations to the Thrift Shop. Now she must depart, and, when she got into the back of the big black car, the First Lady was alone and she could allow the clenched fist tension to assume command of her being. She wrote, "I knew what had happened, but one does not actually formulate these terrible thoughts. . . ." The streets, the traffic, moved past her vision, but she saw none of it. All she knew consciously was that she was going to her sitting room and put in a call for Admiral McIntire and Steve Early to come to see her at once.

A new edition of *Yank,* the soldiers' periodical, was going to press. Buried inside was a pertinent quotation from an anonymous G.I. in battle: "It's almost over and I'm almost home and I'm scared that maybe just a lucky shot will get me. And I don't want to die now, not now it's almost over. I don't want to die now. Do you know what I mean?" Aboard the aircraft carrier *Randolph,* a work party on deck was shouting its cadenced contempt of the President: "Ah hate wah! Ah hate wah! But I'd rather be in wah than be in Eleanor!" The United States Senate adjourned without taking action on the Mexican water treaty. The Vice President walked to his office and dropped his letter on the desk of a secretary. "Mail this to my mother," he said. "If anyone wants me, I'm at the Speaker's office." He began the long walk along the polished marble corridors. He nodded pleasantly to Capitol tourists, who thought that Truman looked just like his photos wearing the snappy double-breasted gray suit and the polka-dotted bow tie.

Merriman Smith was becoming irritated. His watch said it was 4:20, and none of the Little White House group had arrived at the barbecue. Smith was, first of all, an old-line newshawk who would scoop his best friend if he could; secondly, he was an extroverted party-goer, who enjoyed the food, the drinks, the casual conversation and the relaxing atmosphere. He walked into the barn. The fiddling music and the buzz of the locals was so loud that he pulled the big door closed behind him. "What's holding up the staff?" he said to Major Greer. The major listened in on his headset. "I don't know, Smitty. I don't understand the double-talk I'm getting." Sergeant Wayne Shell was on the direct line to the Little White House. "Wayne," he said, "let me call and see if the Boss is on the way." Shell picked up his transmitter. "Indiana to Pine," he intoned. "Indiana to Pine. Come in, please." A voice said, "Pine to Indiana—go ahead." "Is there any sign of movement?" "No. No sign of movement."

Merriman Smith grabbed the transmitter. "Pine—who is this?" The voice said, "This is Anderson." He was a Secret Service agent. "This is Smitty, Andy. What the hell is going on down there?" "Smitty, I don't honestly know, Smitty. I don't understand the double-talk I'm posed to be here in a few minutes." "I know. But there's nothing moving. Want me to give you a call?" "No, thanks. I'll call Hacky." To do this he needed a regulation telephone, not a shortwave set. Smith strode into the home of Mayor Allcorn and asked daughter Janet to let him use the phone. She pointed to a wall phone with a crank handle. He was becoming angry without knowing why. He called Georgia Hall and asked, "Ring the White House switchboard." Louise Hachmeister answered. "Yes, please?" "Hacky, this is Smitty. Why aren't you people on the way? What's holding things up?" "I don't know, Smitty. I just don't know. I'll call you back." Smith knew Hacky. As he hung up, he said, "That doesn't sound like Hacky."

Smith stood thinking. The wall phone rang. "Smitty? Hacky. Get the boys and go to the Hassett cottage right away." He found Bob Nixon of INS and Harry Oliver of AP together. "Hacky called; said to see Hassett at his place." They borrowed an Army Signal Corps car and hurried down the mountain. As always, the newsmen speculated about what it might be. All of them agreed that it was a poor time for a White House news release; Hassett and the Boss knew about the barbecue. If, on the other hand, it was spot news—something which just occurred somewhere around the world—then it would be announced in Washington, too.

In Washington Steve Early was having trouble rounding up reporters in the West Wing. Earlier, a woman clerk had passed the word that there would be no further announcements from the White House and almost all of them had left. Steve was going to make some direct phone calls.

At Hassett's cottage, the three men pulled up. Their recollection is that they stopped "in a cloud of dust and dashed inside." Bill Hassett said they drew up slowly, and got out dragging their feet. The press secretary, tall and solemn, stood near the fireplace. Tully and Brady shared a couch. Both were crying. Merriman Smith moved to the only phone in the room and stood beside it. It was on a radiator, leaning against a wall. Smitty lifted off the receiver.

"Gentlemen," Hassett said slowly, "it is my sad duty to inform you that the President—" Smitty held the receiver against his ear. He heard the Warm Springs operator say, "Number, please?" He whispered, "Priority One—Washington, D.C." "—died at three thirty-five this afternoon." "Executive three four three oh," Smith said. "My name is Merriman Smith." Nixon and Oliver stared at Hassett in disbelief. Grace Tully was wiping her eyes. The act was an endorsement of what Hassett was saying. Smitty heard the operators passing the call. Then a voice said, "United Press." "Flash!" Smitty said. "President Franklin D. Roosevelt died at Warm Springs this afternoon. More to come." The operator said, "Who is this?" Smith yelled, "Give me the desk!" Oliver and Nixon began to yell about Smith using the only phone out. Hassett showed them the bedroom phones. Merriman Smith had cleared his original flash when Howard Bruenn walked into the cottage.

The three got off the phones to ask questions. They made notes. They didn't expect it at the time, but they would be interrogating people all night long, writing quick takes and dictating them over the phones. Bruenn told them it was a "massive cerebral hemorrhage." He mopped his face with a kerchief as though hot and fatigued. "It was like a bolt of lightning," he said. "One minute he was alive and laughing. The next minute— wham!" "Did you see this thing coming?" "It isn't the sort of thing you can forecast. He was very tired when he got here. You saw him the other day—wasn't he in fine spirits?" The question led Smitty to recall that, two days ago, he had rented a horse and was riding through the brush when the President's car went by, moving slowly. President Roosevelt had removed the cigarette holder from his mouth, grinned and said loudly, "Heigh-o, Silver!"

"Bill, did you see the President today?" "Yes, around noon. He signed some bills and some mail." "Was he ill then?" "He seemed to be fine. He joked as usual about all the 'laundry' I had to dry." "Who was with him when he was stricken?" "Madame Shoumatoff says he reminded her that 'We have just fifteen minutes.'" "He said that?" "He was referring to lunch." They wanted to know who was present at the Little White House. They were told Laura Delano, Margaret Suckley and Madame Shoumatoff. There were the servants, of course: Prettyman, Esperancilla, Daisy Bonner and Lizzie Mc-Duffie. No one else? No ane else. Bill said he expected that Mrs. Roosevelt would fly to Warm Springs tonight with Admiral McIntire and Steve Early. Funeral arrangements would, of course, await the arrival of Mrs. Roosevelt.

At Georgia Hall, Mabel Irwin was rehearsing the minstrel show. Someone said, "The President died." "This is no time for jokes," Mrs. Irwin snapped. Up at the barbecue, a signalman came out of the barn to tell Ruth Stevens that the presidential party would arrive in six minutes. Someone asked why he was taking so long. Major Greer shrugged. "He has been held up, possibly by a phone call. It happens." A minute later a call came from Hacky for Greer to report to the Little White House at once. He got into his car and sped down the hill; it seemed no more than a few minutes when he was back up, skidding in dust. He walked over to Ruth Stevens. "Stevie," he said, "stop the music." Allcorn approached, frowning. Major Greer put his hand on the mayor's shoulder. "Frank," he said, "I guess we won't be able to have the party. The Boss died." Stevens bent her head down to her apron and began to sob. Greer tried to console her and burst into tears. Old Bun put his fiddle under his arm and removed his funny hat. "What a good man to leave us," he said. "What a good man to leave us." A Filipino messboy burst into tears. "He promised to send me to the Philippines so I could see my mother. He promised."

Mabel Irwin, who refused to believe the news, stood in Georgia Hall looking out at an audience of grinning faces and wheelchairs. Graham Jackson, the accordionist, was funny. He had on a battered silk hat, a swallowtail coat with the tails too long and the sleeves too short, a necktie flowing to his knees and a giant rubber cigar in his mouth. Tears made shiny lines down his cheeks. Hazel Stephens, acting as stage manager, said, "What's wrong with you, Graham?" His accordion was folded under his arm. "Mr. Roosevelt is dead," he whispered. The audience began to murmur. Miss Stephens asked for a minister to make an announcement. None stepped forward. She stood in the glare of the lights at stage center, and murmured twice or three times, "The President just died." She heard no sound except small crippled children crying. Everyone else stared as though waiting for the rest of the story.

In the House wing of the Capitol, Harry Truman walked down a flight of stairs and reached the "Board of Education." Sam Rayburn was pouring drinks. House Parliamentarian Lew Deschler sat on a chair leaning against a wall; a correspondent of *The New York Times,* William S. White, a Texan, sat sipping. James M. Barnes, former Representative from Illinois, stood to shake hands. The men sat to indulge their favorite hobby: inside politics. It had been in the Speaker's mind to discuss the Presidency with Harry Truman this afternoon. Rayburn was a man who led to important points of discussion with the slow precision of a cotillion. It could wait. For the moment, while pouring, he forgot to tell the Vice President that a phone call from the White House had been routed from the Truman office to the "Board of Education." That too could wait.

In the upstairs study, Mrs. Roosevelt dropped into a chair and asked an usher to ask Mr. Early and Admiral McIntire to come up. When they entered the room, the Admiral's round face was sad and silent. Steve Early took a breath and said, "The President slipped away this afternoon." Slipped away; the gentle touch. Eleanor Roosevelt, who had feared this moment a long time, felt the crushing finality of the words. She sat straight, a touch of valiance. She said "Thank you" in an almost formal tone. After a moment she said she must get off some telegrams to the boys. Then she asked Steve to please call Harry Truman to the White House.

Mrs. Roosevelt's secretary, Malvina Thompson, stood by in distress. The First Lady wrote something on a sheet of paper and gave it to her. "See that this gets out top priority to the boys." It read, "Father slept away. He did his job as he would want you to. Love, Mother." At Bethesda Hospital, Anna was sitting beside Johnny's bed stroking his tousled hair as he dozed. A nurse said there was a phone call. She too knew. It was Admiral Ross McIntire. "My car is outside the hospital waiting to bring you to the White House," he said. He did not say that her father had died. But then, neither did Steve Early tell Mrs. Roosevelt at the Sulgrave Club. Anna, who was her father's love, did not sob. Tears welled on her eyelids. She returned to her son. "I must go for a little while," she said. "I'll be back." She mentioned something about Grandpa. The boy said, "Did Grandpa die?" He did not like his grandfather because he felt that the old man took his mother away from him. "I think so," Anna said softly. "But Mr. Truman will carry on for Grandpa." The little boy burst into tears. "I don't have to have *him* as my Grandpa, do I?" he wailed.

The first drink had been finished; the four men had fallen into a discussion of bills. Rayburn said, "Harry, there was a call for you from the White House." The Vice President picked up a phone. He got Steve Early. Truman was told: "Leave the Hill quietly and come to the main entrance of the White House." The Vice President told the others he had an errand, but would be back. He accepted Steve Early's use of the word "quietly" as meaning "secretly." For the first time, the Vice President dodged his Secret Service agents, departed by a back entrance, and hailed his car and driver. The *de facto* President of the United States had no protection. White House police were surprised to see Mr. Truman sail through the west gate and up to the front portico.

Steve Early took him to Mrs. Roosevelt's study. The First Lady was explaining to "Tommy" Thompson that most people freeze in a situation such as this, but that one moves automatically to do the things which must be done. She wanted a funeral service in the White House; she didn't know yet what day or hour, but she wanted Anna and Tommy and Edith Helm to work it out. She would leave the details to them. Mrs. Roosevelt had not wept. Dry-eyed, she turned to face the Vice President. She placed her hand on his shoulder. "Harry," she said, "the President is dead." He blinked behind his glasses. It was as though he could not comprehend the words, and yet the sense of it had occurred to him frequently. McIntire came into the room and saw the stunned expression on Harry Truman's face. The county politician from Missouri had come to the ultimate glory. Everyone in the room had detected the possibility of death for a year; they had learned to live with it and to lie to each other hopefully. There was, they learned, a difference between the possibility and the stunning actuality. It was death and much more than death. The man lying on the bed under the Navy cape had been the power and the repository of individual leadership for a longer span of time than any other American. A world had expired at 3:35 P.M. in Georgia; the consummate politician, the main fuse, the idealist, the jolly father who spanked and rewarded had ceased to function, and all of the strength and might was now in the hands of the dapper man in the bow tie; the man who knew so little about Roosevelt's plans that he could recall but two private chats since the election—and those were concerned solely with pending legislation. Truman's ignorance of grand strategy was monumental, only because the President chose not to take him into his confidence.

It was possible that, in the small group in Mrs. Roosevelt's study, Harry Truman was the most bereft because, while death deprived the others of a person, a powerful presence, it had the opposite effect on the Vice President, throwing the future and the hopes of the United States to a man politically and militarily blind. "Is there anything I can do for you?" he said to Mrs. Roosevelt. She smiled and looked down at the figured rug. "Is there anything we can do for you?" she said. "For you are the one in trouble now." The second sentence contains an essence of cruelty; a man newly elevated to the Presidency does not appreciate being told that he is "in trouble." And yet this too was truth. Few, even those in the Senate who admired Truman, felt that he had sufficient stature for the Presidency. The very first order of business in the transfer of power would be that he would have to learn and learn and learn from many sources. To cite one small aspect—it would require months to locate the secret codicil agreed at Yalta between the Soviet Union and the United States. It was in a small White House safe. Franklin Roosevelt put it there and told no one. In time, it would be located by Admiral Leahy, but, long before that event, President Truman would have to appeal to the British to reveal the ramifications of an agreement between the United States and Russia.

A question of propriety struck Mrs. Roosevelt. "I have asked Steve and Admiral McIntire to fly with me to Warm Springs," she said. "Do you think it would be all right to use a military airplane?" She was no longer the First Lady. Privileges and rights expire with the final breath of the man. "Of course," Truman said. "I will arrange it myself. Whatever you need . . ." Later, Truman would say, "I kept thinking, 'The lightning has struck. The lightning has struck!'" Behind him two men entered the room. Les Biffle, Secretary of the United States Senate, was a Truman friend. Behind him strode the handsome Secretary of State, tears wandering down his face. For the moment, everyone forgot that Edward Stettinius, by virtue of his position, was the keeper of the Great Seal of the United States, keeper of all official government papers, and the man who must ascertain the death of a President and so notify the

Vice President. Truman turned away from the tears. He had made his first official decision. "Please call a meeting of the Cabinet as soon as possible," he said. Steve Early said he would take care of it, but suggested that Truman be sworn in first. "Locate the Chief Justice," the new President said. "Have everybody meet me in the Cabinet Room." The inert wheels, cogs and gears of the government of the United States made their first squeaky motion.

Steve Early was in his office. "Conference call," he said to his secretary. She got the Washington bureaus of the International News Service, Associated Press and United Press. "White House calling," she said. The President's secretary forgot to announce who was calling. He said, speaking fast, "The President died this afternoon at—" A telephone operator cut in: "Do you mean President Roosevelt?" "Christ!" Early shouted. "There's only one President. Of course I mean President Roosevelt . . . at Warm Springs, Georgia." As Early spoke, his listeners were frantically nodding to bureau managers to hook into the line. ". . . death resulted from a cerebral hemorrhage."

Newsmen scurried from desks to the night wire operators. At INS Charles Sparenbaugh pressed his bell key four times. In newsrooms all over the United States and in radio stations, this gave him a clear line for news of momentous importance. Then he tapped out the shortest story ever sent:

FLASH
      WASHN—FDR DEAD
            INS WASHN 4/12/547 PPH 36

The newsmen, who cultivate cynicism as a professional virtue, began to question the story. Bill Hutchinson of INS looked at the words and roared, "How the hell do you know?" He phoned a reporter in the Capitol building. "Go find Harry Truman," he said. He forgot to tell the reporter why. The time was 5:47 Eastern

War Time, 4:47 at Warm Springs. The United Press bells began to ring all over:

FLASH. WASHINGTON. PRESIDENT ROOSEVELT DIED THIS AFTERNOON.

5:48 P.M. One minute later the Associated Press bell rang four times and the message read:

FLASH—WASHINGTON—PRESIDENT ROOSEVELT DIED SUDDENLY THIS AFTERNOON AT WARM SPRINGS, GA.

New York City was indulging its molten flow of people hurrying homeward on sidewalks; rivers of automobiles being dammed by red lights and loosed by green ones. At 485 Madison Avenue, John Charles Daly, young and perspicacious CBS news commentator, sat in the newsroom editing material for the 6:15 P.M. broadcast. His ears heard, without understanding, the soft loudspeaker which introduced a radio serial called *Wilderness Road*. Two minutes later, he heard a more commanding sound: four bells from the INS teletype. Lee Otis ripped the copy from the machine, looked stunned, dropped it on Daly's desk. His impulse was to get the attention of the control booth, make a cut signal across his neck and ask for the whole Columbia Broadcasting network. Caution stopped him. Suppose it was a rumor? Suppose it was a joke perpetrated by an office boy working a teletype machine? Suppose . . .

The UP bell jangled four times. John Daly took the sheet, ran into the main studio, and made a cut signal. Then, with no copy, he waited until *Wilderness Road* fell into a roaring silence, then spoke:

"We interrupt this program to bring you a special bulletin from CBS World News. A press association has just announced that President Roosevelt is dead. All that has been received is that bare announcement. There are no further

details as yet, but CBS World News will return to the air in just a few minutes with more information as it is received in our New York headquarters. We return you to our regularly scheduled program."

A stone dropped into a large still pool. One minute later NBC stopped *Front Page Farrell* to make the announcement. At the same time the ABC network cut into *Captain Midnight* with the news practically no one wanted to hear. The story would be monumentally tragic for scores of millions of people; it would arrest them in their daily pursuits and they would remember this moment always; they would mark it on the cave of memory as though it were an intimate personal loss; a relative; family.

The three reporters at Carver Cottage were two minutes late with their flash. The Washington bureaus ordered them to "stay on the story all night"—"keep sending." For a moment the reporters and editors dwelled only on the stark truth of death: ". . . massive cerebral hemorrhage . . . Steve Early . . . Mrs. Roosevelt notified her four sons . . . Truman was called to the White House in secrecy . . . emergency Cabinet meeting . . . The widow will fly to Warm Springs . . . Admiral Ross McIntire . . . Interment Hyde Park . . . He went to Warm Springs for a rest . . ."

It is outlandish to ask what death means to the deceased. No one wondered. To Franklin D. Roosevelt, it represented the final frustration. It was more than the end of life, the darkness of eternity with its promise of bright redemption; it was a vicious act of fate to allow a man to lead his country from the despair of economic catastrophe up and up until it was forced to confront the world of fascism and fight amid a world in flames toward the final, the ultimate, victory. To the man who had drafted the grand design of twelve years, the man who was planning the peace while awaiting the victory—if he had been permitted a last thought after murmuring, "I have a terrific headache"—such a man must depart in bitterness. He would feel cheated. The most powerful man in the most powerful nation in all history was destined to slump in his own prison, his wheelchair, and expire inside a body he had not trusted since he was afflicted at Campobello. The United Nations was thirteen days away.

To many men, the death of Franklin D. Roosevelt was not assessed in terms of what it did to him, but in terms of what it did to them. He was of sufficient stature so that they could afford to wonder what it would mean to their lives. William D. Simmons, White House usher, was one of many summoned from home to hurry to the Executive Mansion. He did not know why until, driving across the Fourteenth Street bridge, he heard the flash on the radio. He was a big broad man with a leonine head. His automobile kept rolling to the White House, but his stunned mind was aboard a campaign train in 1936. FDR, sitting at a picture window, said, "Bill, how would you like to be President for a while?" Simmons thought it was a joke. Roosevelt moved his wheelchair away from the window, put Simmons in a chair, leaned across him and placed the pince-nez on his nose. The Boss grinned. "Fine, fine. Now take this cigarette holder. That's it. Every time we pass a little town, wave the cigarette holder like this. You be President. I'm going to take a nap."

Margaret Truman had a date. She was applying makeup in the Vice President's apartment at 4701 Connecticut Avenue when the phone rang. It was her father, asking to speak to "Mother." Truman's voice was under control. He told Bess that the President had died; he would be sworn in as President of the United States in a few minutes. A White House car was on its way to pick her up—Margaret, too. It was heady, dizzying news. Margaret had a date with Marvin Braverman. Now she had a date with the new President. In the "Board of Education" room Speaker Sam Rayburn accepted the news in silence. He was a tough Texan who never had more than two emotions: solicitude and anger. On this one day he found a third. He walked to a window

and wept. In a dental office Henry A. Wallace had settled
back in a big chair and resigned himself to some pain.
He was called to the phone. The White House wished
to inform him that President Roosevelt had died suddenly. He placed the phone on its cradle and returned to
the big chair. If the Boss had had his way, Henry Wallace
would have hurried to the White House to be sworn
in. He sat back and resigned himself to pain.

Mrs. Rutherfurd asked Mrs. Shoumatoff to stop the
car. It was in downtown Macon. It was obvious that
Lucy could no longer bear the agony of not knowing.
The last she had seen of that great face was when he
looked full at her, then encompassed his brows with
his left hand. It could have been a fainting spell; it could
have been worse. The fear of bad news had kept her
rigid in the car. She asked Elizabeth to use a public
phone and call Warm Springs. Ask to speak to Grace
Tully; nobody else. Just Grace. And find out how the
President was doing. Elizabeth Shoumatoff got some
silver. She dropped a nickel in the box. An operator
asked, "Number, please?" She said she wanted Warm
Springs, Georgia. "Just a minute for long distance,"
the operator said. "You hear about President Roosevelt
dying there?" Mrs. Shoumatoff hung up. She walked
slowly back to the car.

The remainder of that night ride back to the big estate
outside of Aiken, South Carolina, is misted in secrecy.
A few things are known. Lucy Rutherfurd fell into uncontrollable hysterics. Nicholas Robbins tried to soothe
her. So did Mrs. Shoumatoff. But there was no consolation. The car was full of wild wailing and deep sobs.
Even time could not seem to stop it. The car was stopped
again. A call was placed for Father George Smith, pastor
of St. Mary Help of Christians Church in Aiken. The
priest, a native of Toms River, New Jersey, had been
confessor and friend to the Rutherfurds. He had a painting
of the stately Lucy on a rectory wall. Years later,
remembering that wild night, he would say, "Please
don't make it a sordid affair. It wasn't sordid." As Lucy's
confessor, he was in a position to know. Now, when

hysteria wracked her soul, she turned to Father Smith. Whether he drove out in the night with a curate to meet Lucy and drive her home is a guess. Her love, her only love, was gone and she who was inconsolable needed consolation. Father Smith would never forget that ride —"worse than a night ride," he said, "an all-night ride." And yet the distance between Macon and Aiken was only 150 miles. Lucy refused to believe that Franklin was dead. She could not convince herself that she would never look upon that face again—never again feel the warmth of the smiling eyes, the touch of a hand. It was gone, gone, gone, and she would not even be permitted to attend the funeral. It was a wild all-night ride with many stops.

In the West Wing reception hall, Admiral McIntire and Steve Early faced the returning press at 6:00 P.M. Early wore the deep frown, the sniffy nostrils, which he always presented to reporters. The Admiral was as bland, as unctuous, as he had been upstairs when he broke the news to Mrs. Roosevelt. He looked neat, slightly portly in his khaki uniform with the shoulder boards and the three stars. "This is a tough one for me to have to give you," he said. He was always apprehensive in the presence of the press; he would not speak until a White House stenographer was prepared. The Admiral weighed his words so carefully that he was prone to error.

He said he had a call from Warm Springs at 3:05, stating that the President had fainted. The call was at 2:31. He said he called George Fox this morning. Howard Bruenn phoned the Admiral. "Everything was fine. In fact, I was going to run down there and play a little golf and come back with them. . . . This came out of a clear sky . . . I asked Dr. James Paullin of Atlanta, one of the most prominent men in this country in the field of medicine—I called him and asked him to go down to Warm Springs, which he did." McIntire gave Paullin a leading role in the final illness of the President. He overlooked the fact that Dr. Paullin arrived five minutes before Mr. Roosevelt expired, in spite of a breathtaking drive from Atlanta. Howard Bruenn had been McIntire's dark secret for a year. The Admiral, still bland, still waving his arms benevolently as he spoke, had no intention of revealing Bruenn as a qualified cardiologist who had been summoned originally in desperation and who had been in daily attendance on the President of the United States. McIntire went on to state that Paullin had made a "rather remarkable trip down there." Then: *"They* called me to say this was a very serious thing. Dr. Howard Bruenn told me it was a very serious thing—undoubtedly a cerebral hemorrhage. Dr. Bruenn is a Commander. Then I notified, of course, everyone here and got hold of Steve who came in at once. Steve and I were talking over plans about what we should do about getting down. A phone call came in again. This was at four-thirty our time. At the start of the conversation Dr. Bruenn told me things were just about the same. Then he asked me to hold the phone as he was called away. He hung up. Then he called back in a few minutes telling me that at four-thirty-five—three thirty-five their time—the end came very suddenly. They are positive it was a cerebral hemorrhage. The whole picture was apparently very clear at that time."

"Who was at the bedside?" "Dr. Bruenn and Dr. Paullin—no members of the family. The President appeared in good health this morning. He has been carrying on at Warm Springs just about as he usually does when he goes there. There was no apprehension about him at all." The proof of that was that the Admiral had not been with his chief at Warm Springs. McIntire would have been there, as physician to the President, if he had been worried. No, it was a sudden, stunning surprise—one which no one could have foreseen. He had been in reasonably good health for a man of his years—flaring sinuses, a hacking cough. If a reporter asked for an explicit medical history of the President—now that there was no further reason for secrecy—it wasn't answered. The Admiral knew that Commander Bruenn would be asked questions in Warm Springs, but McIntire could depend on the Commander to say no more than that the President died of a cerebral hemorrhage.

The reporters asked Early about Mrs. Roosevelt, and he told the story of the Sulgrave Club and the Thrift Shop. At one point he added a little shine of his own. "She said—I think she would let me quote it—'I am more sorry for the people of the country and the world than I am for us.' " It was a courageous quotation. Mrs. Roosevelt did not say it. Later, when she read it, she said she wished she had. President Roosevelt's Chief of Staff, Admiral William D. Leahy, would not appear in public to comment on the passing of his chief. He was alone in his office at 6:00 P.M. bending over a sheet of paper, writing:

This world tragedy deprives the nation of its leader at a time when the war to preserve civilization is approaching its end with accelerated speed, and when a vital need for competent leadership in the making and preservation of world peace is at least seriously prejudiced by the passing of Franklin Roosevelt, who was a world figure of heroic proportions. His death is also a personal bereavement to me in the loss of a devoted friend whom I have known and admired for thirty-six years, since we first worked together in the first world war. . . . The captain of the team is gone. . . .

For a reserved, contained personality such as Leahy, the words were an excess of emotion. But, like most diarists, he was convinced that they were written for his own eyes. At a U.S. Army post at Rome, New York, an early dinner dance for officers was in progress. The war was almost over, the music was sweet, couples glided over a small polished floor. The commanding officer took the microphone, waved the band to silence and shouted into the instrument: "Ladies and gentlemen, news had just come over the radio that President Roosevelt is dead." The dancers stood awkwardly in each other's arms. "Now," the commanding officer said, "I won't have to call that son of a bitch Commander

in Chief anymore." There was a pause. A few giggles.
The music started up.

The stone, once dropped, spread its ripples evenly
around the world. At 6:05 P.M. (11:05 P.M. European
time) the German News Agency DNB cut in on a musical
program to announce that news received in Amsterdam,
Holland, stated that the American President, Franklin
Roosevelt, died suddenly. Two minutes later the British
Broadcasting Company announced: "It is with deep
regret that we report the death of President Roosevelt.
He died suddenly this afternoon from a cerebral hemorrhage." At about the same time, a long convertible
Mercedes with bulletproof windshield crept through the
fallen masonry of the streets of Berlin. The big saffron
lights picked out the bomb craters and the car moved
slowly to the Wilhelmstrasse. Josef Goebbels, chief of
German propaganda, was returning to his office across
the street from Adolf Hitler's Chancellory. He was
back from a visit of desperation to the headquarters
of General Busse on the Oder River at Küstrin. Until
now, it was considered to be treason to mention defeat.
Official Germany would not use the word, and yet, crouching in its own ruins, the government was terrified at
the propsect of being overrun by the "barbarian Slavs."
The Wehrmacht had extended no mercy to the Russians in 1941 and 1942; they anticipated nothing less
if the Soviet tidal wave engulfed Germany. Busse had
assured Goebbels that a Russian breakthrough along
the Oder was "impossible. We will hold out until the
British kick us in the ass," he said. The propaganda
minister felt reassured because, barring some miracle,
Greater Germany would be invested by the forces of
the West, or the hordes from the East. It became an
unspoken policy of Germany that light forces would
retreat before the British and Americans; her main
strength would face the Russians.

The word "miracle" had respectable status in the
Hitler bunker. Staff officers wondered aloud about it,
citing the last-minute miracles which would have saved

Frederick the Great from defeat; a miracle would come. Goebbels reached his darkened office, depressed because he had watched the Adlon Hotel light the night sky with flames; the above-ground portion of Hitler's Chancellory was reduced to broken stone columns by an RAF air raid. A secretary came into Goebbels' office grinning. "Roosevelt," he said, "is dead." The propaganda minister could not believe it. The DNB teletype sheets were placed before him. Herr Goebbels was an intelligent man, but he hugged the news to his breast as an omen. "Bring our best champagne," he ordered happily, "and get the Führer on the phone." Having convinced himself that the death of one soldier would alter the course of history, he infected Hitler at once. "My Führer!" he shouted "I congratulate you. Roosevelt is dead. It is written in the stars that the second half of April will be the turning point for us. This is almost Friday, April thirteenth. It *is* the turning point!"

Goebbels did not record the Führer's response. It is certain that he was pleased. That he subscribed to the naive notion that the death of a leader will halt the progress of armies and air forces is difficult to credit. He may have felt elated that he had outlasted his crippled tormentor. Both men had assumed positions of leadership at about the same time in 1933. In the early years Hitler had mocked the impotence of Roosevelt to enforce peace. Later, he saw the President as the main obstruction to German expansion. Russia had been on the verge of final defeat when American Lend-Lease had given Stalin tanks and guns and planes and bullets. The Führer was certain that, as his armies were unable to cross the English Channel to defeat England, so too the British and Americans could not cross it to fight on Continental soil. He had misgauged American intentions, American strength and, most of all, the American will to win. Whatever Hitler's reaction to the death of the American leader, joy infected the personnel in his bunker. Count Schwerin von Krosigk wrote: "This was the angel of history! We felt its wings flutter through the room. Was this not the turn of fortune we awaited so anxiously?"

The bunker, at one time so hyper-efficient, had become an asylum for the practice of self-mesmerization.

Seventy-five miles northwest of the bunker, near Wittenberg, the lean, exhausted body of Lieutenant General George Patton slipped between blankets. He was sleeping in a command trailer on the banks of the Elbe. But sleep came hard. He and Generals Dwight D. Eisenhower and Omar Bradley had inspected a river crossing won by the 83rd Infantry. There had been two crossings, but the Germans had battered one back across the stream. Caches of gold ingots hidden by the Germans had been discovered. Two huge munitions dumps had been detonated by the Wehrmacht. Eisenhower had to make a decision: whether to widen the single bridgehead and fight on to Berlin, or whether to conserve strength and lives by standing on the west bank and waiting for the Russians. It was a political as well as a military decision. The three generals were tired after a long day of work. Patton turned on his trailer radio. The announcement came quickly and repetitively: "President Roosevelt died suddenly at Warm Springs, Georgia." The General got out of bed, buckled his belt and went to the other trailers. The news depressed Eisenhower and Bradley. The minds of the three commanders began to recollect personal experiences with FDR. They would sit and talk until 2:00 A.M. They would wonder what kind of man Harry S. Truman was. So few seemed to know. He was mistakenly regarded as a small-town politician. The notion was so pervasive that Herr Goebbels asked Hitler to order Reichsminister Albert Speer to fly "to the West to talk to Truman." The Germans were imbued with the notion that Truman could "be talked to." It involved Hitler's old notion that, sooner or later, the West would have to fight the East. If the British and Americans were willing "to come to their senses," they could join Germany in the struggle and beat the Russians in final battle.

Like General Patton, Judge Sam Rosenman had completed a difficult day and was sliding between the sheets at Claridge's in London. The phone rang. It was from

Bernard Baruch, who had a suite on the same floor. "Put on your robe and come down right away." Baruch was in bed when Sammy the Rose arrived. "Now, Sam," said Baruch, "steady in the boat. Brendan Bracken just phoned. He said the radio had announced that the President died." They sat listening to the radio. Baruch, with presidential permission, had flown to London in the Sacred Cow. Earlier, he had invited Rosenman to join him on the return trip in the morning. "Bernie," he said, "I guess I will be going back after all. . . ." Baruch was thinking. "Let's see whether Ed Flynn and Elliott Roosevelt would like to join us. There's plenty of room." The phones in Baruch's suite were busy for hours locating Roosevelt and Flynn, making arrangements for the pilots to fuel the plane and start for Washington at noon.

Although the sun had barely set in Washington, the hour was past midnight in Moscow. Averell Harriman had been host at an American Embassy party. Half-empty stem glasses reposed on the fireplace mantel under the Great Seal of the United States. A minor official handed Harriman a sheet of paper. He read it; the mandibular muscles of his jaw flexed; the party was over. In spite of the lateness of the hour and the unearthly emptiness of the great metropolis, Foreign Minister Molotov arrived, signed an Embassy guest book, and said that he had come to offer his condolences to the American people on their great loss. Harriman was surprised. Death had seemed a cheap commodity in Russia. Within a few hours, attired in morning coat, Harriman was inside the Kremlin chatting with Josef Stalin. The dictator, for a reason known only to him, had displayed marked respect for Roosevelt, even when they were in disagreement. Sometimes he was deferential. This time he said that expressions of commiseration from the Russians would not be enough. What could the Soviet Union do to show its appreciation of the President? Without hesitation, Harriman said, "Send Molotov to the San Francisco Conference." Stalin nodded. "The Foreign Minister will go," he said.

It was night when the phone rang in Harry Hopkins'

room at the Mayo Clinic at Rochester, Minnesota. The caller was Chip Bohlen, at the State Department. The President was dead. There was an interminable silence. Then the tired voice of Harry the Hop came back. "I guess I getter be going to Washington," he said. On Rivington Street in New York a Jewish woman dispensed soda and ice cream from a small shop. A customer asked why she didn't turn her radio on. "For what do I need a radio?" she said. "It's on everybody's face." On Fifth Avenue well-dressed men and women walked erectly, without speaking, with tears sliding down their faces. In Warm Springs Ruth Stevens and Frank Allcorn had all the barbecue food trucked into the hotel lobby for anyone to eat. Residents on the side streets picked early flowers from their gardens, fashioned them into bouquets and walked with them in their hands, not knowing where to leave them. In Lafayette Park people gathered to stand and stare at the simple majesty of the White House as their forebears had done on an April night in 1865. In a Capitol corridor a tall young Congressman stood alone, leaning against a granite wall. Someone said hello. Lyndon Johnson looked up. "He was the one person I ever knew," he said, "anywhere— who was never afraid." At Mount Sinai Hospital in New York a premature baby, born at the time President Roosevelt was stricken, expired. The young father crushed the brim of his hat. "The baby is gone," he said, "but I'm mixed up. I feel that my father died, too."

In front of the U.S. Embassy in Buenos Aires, a legless cripple who sat at the fence, with his overturned hat on his stumps, raised himself backward to stand upright as a girl clerk departed. He placed the hat on his head, then removed it. He marshaled his best English: "Madame," he said, "I am desolated." Newspaper makeup editors in disparate parts of the United States penciled a small notation and asked that it be placed in the list of local soldiers and sailors killed or missing in action:

*ROOSEVELT, Franklin D. Commander in Chief U.S.
Armed Forces, at Warm Springs, Georgia.*

Signs began to be pasted in shop windows: "Closed. FDR Died." A few, more sentimental than others, scrawled: "Closed—Death in the Family." At Fire Department Headquarters in New York a switch was closed and, in all fire houses throughout the five boroughs, the slow toll of five bells repeated four times was sounded. To firemen, it meant a comrade had died in the line of duty. In a hotel elevator a man broke the thick silence saying, "So he's dead. Isn't it about time?" A woman passenger slapped his face. The evening chill at Hyde Park was broken when the solemn bell in the tower of St. James Episcopal Church began a slow toll. A senior warden had just died. Afternoon newspapers got out extra editions. Printers reversed the rules, marking newspaper columns to show thick black mourning borders. In Harlem, a black man stood with a crowd in front of a radio store. "Don't worry," he said. "He was a great man with great ideas and he didn't let any grass grow under his feet. His plans are made and somebody is gonna carry them out." A teen-age boy in Jersey City stood in the street in front of the *Jersey Journal:* "I don't believe it," he said, "but if it has happened, then God bless him!"

At *The New York Times,* a graying editor was rapping out a first draft of a lead editorial for tomorrow's editions:

A great and gallant wartime leader has died almost in the very hour of the victory to which he led the way. It is a cruel and bitter irony that Franklin D. Roosevelt should not have lived to see the Allied armies march into Berlin. It is a hard and stunning blow to lose the genius and the inspiration of his leadership in this decisive moment of the war. The people of the United States, our comrades in the Allied Nations, the cause of democracy throughout the whole free world, have suffered a heartbreaking loss.

History will honor this man for many things, however wide the disagreement of many of his countrymen with some of his policies and his actions. It will honor him above all else because he had the vision to see clearly the su-

preme crisis of our times and the courage to meet the crisis boldly. Men will thank God on their knees a hundred years from now, that Franklin D. Roosevelt was in the White House....

The great personages of the American government arrived in small groups and stood in the Cabinet Room with their coats on. They were birds of dark plumage standing close to the pale walls. Everyone, it seems, knew that he was working himself to death; they knew he could not last, but the shock of unexpected death was on their faces. The new President was behind that small door, in Franklin Roosevelt's Oval Office. Some knew the man; others had a handshaking acquaintance with him. The wall clock clicked to 7:00 P.M. as Chief Justice Harlan Stone came into the room. He glanced around and slipped his coat on the Cabinet table. A Secret Service man escorted Mrs. Truman and Margaret through a door leading from the mansion. They had been with Mrs. Roosevelt and Anna. Frances Perkins nodded to them. There was a pervasive sensation of a crowded room in which people were unable to speak. It could be called mourning, but it was more acute. It was shock, disbelief, the whirling of many minds wondering what to do. The little white door opened and Harry Truman entered the room. The groups around the table turned in silence. The man from Missouri did not look like one capable of wearing the shoes of the departed giant. The small frame, the enlarged snapping eyes behind thick lenses, the almost lipless mouth, the slick hair reassured no one. He kissed his tearful wife and daughter and seemed unable to say anything.

He looked at the Chief Justice. Harlan Stone said that the chief receptionist had gone to look for a Bible. Truman nodded. The clock on the wall pointed to 7:05. The waiting time was an embarrassment. Bill Simmons came back, saying that he had searched everywhere and had found a Roman Catholic Bible in William Hassett's desk. Mr. Truman said it would do. The Chief Justice motioned for the Truman women to come closer.

Harlan Stone intoned: "I, Harry Shippe Truman . . ."
This was wrong; the Chief Justice had been told that
the S stood for Shippe, Truman's grandfather's name.
It stood for nothing. The new President had no middle
name. He said, "I, Harry S. Truman . . ." Less than
two minutes later, it was over. No one, including the Trumans, looked joyful. The handshaking was solemn.
Steve Early asked permission to bring the news photographers in. The event, he thought, should be preserved
for posterity. Truman had an appreciation of that word.
The cameramen came in. The photos they made show
the wall clock at 7:09 P.M.

The President told Mrs. Truman that he had some
things to do, but he would be "home" as soon as possible.
The group dissipated. The people who remained were
members of the Cabinet. There was a high-backed leather
chair in the middle of the table facing the windows.
This was Roosevelt's chair. Truman sat. The others
took their accustomed places. One person was absent,
Postmaster General Frank Walker, who was ill. Truman
was about to utter his first words as President. Jonathan
Daniels, in an almost comedic manner, came into the
room and said the Press wanted to know if the United
Nations Conference at San Francisco would open on
schedule. The question was, at best, ill-mannered. Mr.
Daniels stood waiting. The members of the Cabinet
glanced at the President. He was about to make his
first decision. *Of course* the conference would open as
scheduled, he said almost petulantly. It was important
to the peace of the world. Daniels withdrew. Truman
then asked the Cabinet members to remain at their several
posts. In time, he said candidly, he expected there would
be some Cabinet changes, but he needed the assistance
of experienced hands now. The only other thing he could
tell them was that he expected to follow "the Roosevelt
Policy." At the same time, he assured them, he would
be President of the United States in his own right, making
his own decisions.

He looked up and down the table. No one spoke.
Truman stood. The Cabinet meeting was over. Madame

Secretary Perkins and the gentlemen shook hands with Truman and wished him well. One remained. Secretary of War Henry Stimson moved to a chair adjoining the President's. He waited until the two were alone. Stimson, who wore his hair parted in the middle, said he had waited because there was something that was, properly, the business of the President. Truman listened. The Secretary of War said that the United States had a secret war project. A small group of men were aware of it. The President urged Stimson on. The man's tone, according to the President, was "urgent" but what he had to say made little sense. The government had been devising a super-bomb; an explosive of "exceptional force." It was not quite ready for testing, but no one in Congress and few in military circles knew about it. Truman tried to display proper interest. But Stimson stopped. He could not say more, he said; at least not now. It was strange that the man who was President of the United States could not be told simply that this country was about to split an atom, releasing forces of energy beyond anything man had ever seen. The Secretary of War stood. He would like to make an appointment to speak with the President, and perhaps bring General Marshall with him. They could discuss the explosive and await the President's orders for its use. Truman nodded amiably.

Under the big portico at the front of the White House, Eleanor Roosevelt stood talking to her daughter. The widow wore a black dress and accessories and a black coat. Anna was in a two-piece red suit. Steve Early and Admiral McIntire stood at the bottom of the steps, waiting beside a black limousine. These women, who had been competitive for the President's affection, were suddenly bound by belated understanding. Anna put her arms around her formal mother and kissed her. Eleanor Roosevelt said that Anna's place was with her living son, not her dead father.

Official Washington—which includes the Roosevelt family—rose above the initial stunning shock within three hours after the death. The lamentations, the tears, the torrential tide of memories were alive in the streets in many towns and cities. At 7:30 Washington time the United States government was functioning. The things which had to be done quickly were being done. Steve Early phoned Hassett and asked him to consult with Bruenn and select a suitable casket for the President. George Catlett Marshall sat under lights in his office with aides from Fort Myer. They planned the stiff-legged funeral for a departed chieftain. Admirals and generals were hurrying from southern posts to Warm Springs to arrange a formal ceremony for bringing the body to the train. Ushers at the White House began to prepare the big East Room for a church service. Soldiers from Fort Benning were in trucks, bouncing northward over rutted roads to encamp at Warm Springs for the parade in the morning. The guard of U.S. Marines in the dell below the Little White House put a crease in its dress blues, to lead the parade.

The Roosevelt crowd had always been a drinking group—not a drunken group, but an official family which believed that evening cocktails were as important as the setting of the sun. On this evening, the Warm Springs group drank seriously. Alcohol, they knew, had the power to shove the deadly realities of the situation to the back of the mind, and to bring forward the rusted flowers of sentimental memory. They drank from cottage to cottage, hardly realizing that, when each said, "Remember the time he said this"—or "Remember the time he did that"—they were resurrecting the body for a moment. One off-duty Secret Service man got sodden drunk and stood out on the ellipse beneath the flagpole shouting that "the Boss is going to have the best Goddamn funeral anybody ever saw in history," and, as he enumerated the number of cannon and tanks he expected to see in the morning, his voice trailed off and he staggered into a bed of flowers.

At Warm Springs there was a reluctance to let the man die. Laughter over some amusing recollection was followed by sobbing. Hassett phoned Southern Railway in Atlanta to order the train to be at Warm Springs no later than 7:00 A.M. It was an afterthought. C. A. Pless could have left his shack at the tracks, but he was fascinated at the action on the main street. Cars and trucks were running back and forth, long black cables were being strung; the engineers of a radio network set up shop in the "Colored" waiting room. The two-lane roads leading into Warm Springs were choked with news media and tourists. Someone passed the word that Mrs. Roosevelt had arrived and was viewing the body. Ruth Stevens was passing out food to anyone who wanted to eat. Many of the locals were in the lobby when the mayor said, "This food was for the President at a barbecue. You can come and eat it if you wish." Nobody moved. Some government men had their bags packed and were checking out. Strangers questioned strangers. A stout woman said, "It's the greatest thrill of my life."

It was a warm starry night in Sakishima Gunto. The old battleship *Tennessee* had turned south from the Okinawa picket line to bury her dead. Dawn was dangerous and her captain used TBF (Talk Between Ships) to ask for extra escorts as the chaplains prayed over the blistered bodies before they slid from under the American flag on the lee rail into the sea. *Tennessee* had been hit by a kamikaze. The clerics were still praying when the loudspeakers opened. "Attention! Attention! President Roosevelt is dead. Repeat, our Supreme Commander, President Roosevelt, is dead." The speakers became silent. The men who were holding the boards on which the bodies reposed began to weep. Everybody told everybody else they didn't believe it. But the young shiny faces were shedding tears, not for the bodies under the flags, but for a man they had never met.

Dawn was an outrageous assortment of pink and pale yellow spears stuck in the vase of the horizon. *Tennessee* was still busy burying. Task Force 58 had taken a beating at the time the Commander in Chief murmured, "I have a terrific headache." General Simon Bolivar Buckner's Army forces had captured two airfields on Okinawa—

Kadena and Yontan—but it appeared as though Imperial Japan had decided to make its suicide stand here, rather than on the main islands. The Navy, supporting Buckner's forces ashore, had 13 fast carriers, 14 jeep carriers, a British task force of five aircraft carriers, in addition to battleships, cruisers, and the thin ready line of radar picket destroyers in a tight fan around Okinawa. As the President lay dying in the snoring sleep, the Japanese staged 17 raids on the fleet. A suicide plane landed in the engine rooms of the *Cassin Young; Jeffers* was in flames from a near-miss; the new 2,200-ton destroyer *Mannert L. Abele* had her back broken by a kamikaze. As she lay dead in the water, the Japanese introduced the first *baka.* This was a small glider, loaded with 2,645 pounds of high explosive, released near a target from a bomber. Inside the *baka,* a patriot guided his small craft to the biggest ship he could find. The first *baka* hit the *Mannert L. Abele.* Eighty men were killed or missing in action. Two hours later, the fast-reacting Japanese had planes in the sky dropping leaflets printed in English: "We must express our deep regret over the death of President Roosevelt . . ."

Aboard the carrier *Hornet* Lieutenant John Roosevelt stood watch on the flag bridge. His function was to keep voice contact with other ships. The loudspeaker blared some fuzzy sound as morning flushed the sky with color. It sounded like something roaring. Then it was turned down and the voice became lucid. More than that, it sounded familiar. In code, the ship was identified as the destroyer escort *Ulvert M. Moore,* on the picket line. The two voices exchanged phrases which could be familiar only to John Roosevelt and Franklin D., Jr. Then the voice from the picket line said, "Are you making it home, Old Man?" "No," replied John. "Are you?" "No. Let's clean it up out here first. So long, Old Man. Over." "So long. Out." In England, the sad news had reached General Elliott Roosevelt. He had an appointment with Bernard Baruch and a plane home. On Leyte, in the Philippines, tall, slender James Roosevelt, Colonel, U.S. Marine Corps, lazed himself through the first hour of another day on a cot. He was awake, but not up. An orderly was at the door. He had a message. It was the bulletin originating from Admiral Turner's flagship announcing the death of Franklin D. Roosevelt. Jim was the arm on which the President had leaned for so many years. His ties of love for his father were as close in his way as Anna's were in hers. The Colonel set an impossible task for himself. He was going to get permission to start flying home to "Pa." He and his dead father were half a world apart, but he would fly on whatever priorities the military would grant him to close the gap. Young Roosevelt would be content if he could get to Hyde Park before the funeral.

President Truman left the White House at 7:30 P.M. and went home. He was depressed when he saw the number of Secret Service agents and the care which accompanied him. He had lived simply in a five-room apartment at 5701 Connecticut Avenue for years; all he asked was to go home, get something to eat and get to bed. The noise of his guardians would attract the neighborhood. Truman didn't like it. The little spring flower beds around the apartment lawn looked as bright as usual, but the people on the sidewalk were unusual. Behind the glasses, Harry S. Truman thought of himself as Harry S. Truman. On the other side of the spectacles, a world of people stared in awe at the President of the United States.

Three of the men even followed him up to the apartment door. Duty, they said. Truman didn't want them standing outside the apartment door. When he tapped the bell, there was no response. The apartment was empty. The President—slightly stiff, somewhat formal—found Mrs. Truman and Margaret in the apartment of General Jefferson Davis, next door. They were unnerved by the afternoon events; the Davises had a bronzed turkey and a baked ham. They had been friendly with the Trumans; now they were different. Truman was not asked in. The General and his wife would bring some sandwiches and milk to the Truman apartment. The President thanked them. He sat in a stuffed dining room chair with both arms hanging down the sides. He was hungry and tired. As he ate, he kept glancing at his red-eyed wife. No one had congratulated him; it is to be doubted that Truman congratulated himself. He phoned his mother in Grandview, Missouri. She had heard the astounding news. At the age of ninety-one she did not want to talk to reporters, but the front door bell and the phone were ringing. "Mamma," he said, "I'm terribly busy." She spoke for a minute. He said, "You probably won't hear from me for some time." Except, of course, for the letter he had mailed that afternoon.

State police, Marines and the Secret Service ringed Warm Springs Foundation. An entire side of Pine Mountain was off-limits to all except a few. At 7:40 P.M. the officious Dr. James Paullin thought that Hassett ought to make a phone call for a funeral director. He nodded his head toward the bedroom. It would require time, he said, to get funeral directors and embalmers to Warm Springs, and more time to prepare the body and put it in a casket. Hassett was too upset to make the call. He and Dr. Bruenn asked the Atlanta doctor if he knew a reputable mortician. Yes, he said, H. M. Patterson & Sons, who were in the Spring Hill section of Atlanta, would be a good choice. Bill Hassett asked Bruenn to make the call. Paullin said he would phone first—to make sure that Fred W. Patterson was in.

Patterson was out. He had spent the day playing golf. After a shower, he heard that Roosevelt had died. He had dinner and went home. Mr. Patterson, sixty-two, did little of the work at his dignified stone establishment. Brannon Lesesne, who had grown up in the business, was the technical expert. However, there had been nothing in the funeral home to require his attention, so he had gone to an afternoon movie and then to a bowling alley. The match was betweeen the Atlanta Kiwanis and the Optimists. A bowler asked if the match would be postponed because of the death of the President. Lesesne was eating a sandwich. "What president?" he said. He was sure that the executive of one of the contending clubs had died. "President Roosevelt," the bowler said. "It was on the radio. He died in Warm Springs." It is strange that Lesesne hurried back to Patterson & Sons, although he had no reason to believe that his firm would be called to Warm Springs. Mr. Patterson was at home, where he received a call from his friend Dr. Paullin. When he hung up, the old man hurried to his establishment to await a phone call from a Dr. Bruenn or a Mr. Hassett. Patterson and Lesesne were surprised to see each other hurrying from the parking lot. Patterson decided not to wait for the call—he called Warm Springs.

Bruenn took the call. His voice was calm, subdued. He and Hassett had consulted Grace Tully. She thought the President would want something simple, but rich. His mother had been buried, she remembered, in a solid mahogany casket with a copper lining. The President had selected it. The doctor said he wanted a casket about seventy-six inches long, made of solid mahogany with a copper lining. Patterson said he was sorry; it was impossible. No copper had been used for linings since the war started. There were a few around, but they were rare. The doctor said that time was short; the body was to leave Warm Springs for Washington at 10:00 A.M. "What do you have?" Fred Patterson said he had a solid mahogany casket—just one—but it had been promised to Preston Burgess of Madison, New Jersey. Besides, it had no copper lining. Suddenly, Hassett decided that he could discuss this matter. He spoke to Mr. Patterson and said he wanted "one solid bronze coffin." Patterson said he had a solid mahogany with no copper lining, but it had been promised. "Bring it," Hassett said. "Just make sure it measures six feet four inches."

The funeral director, sensing the distress at Warm Springs, made the decision. The mahogany casket, destined for New Jersey, was at the Atlanta Casket Company plant. Patterson phoned, explained the situation and asked if workmen could be called from home to hammer a solid copper liner under the satin lining. They could.

By 8:00 P.M. the men were working on it. They made
only one request: that they not be paid for the work
and not be mentioned publicly. Lesesne said he would
wait for the work to be finished, and would take Cannon
Young of the casket company with him. The old man
phoned George Marchman and Haden Snoderly, two
embalmers, and asked them to meet him in the embalming
room at once. It was close to 9:00 P.M. when Fred Patterson, with the two men and their equipment, departed
for Warm Springs.

The White House was almost empty. Few lights were
on. On the second floor Anna Roosevelt worked hard
with Edith Helm and Malvina Thompson trying to find
modern records of a White House funeral. The situation
was impossible. The only President who had been buried
from the White House in many years had been Warren
G. Harding. The files were ransacked for the records
of procedure. They were gone. Someone with a touch
of solicitude had given them to Mrs. Harding after the
funeral. Anna did not want to go all the way back to
McKinley, Garfield and Lincoln for guidance. They
phoned General Marshall and began to establish their
own guidelines. On the ground floor of the White House,
the President's office was in darkness except for the two
guards outside the doors. Jonathan Daniels was in his
office. He had promised to advise the press if any fresh
news came from Warm Springs, but none had come.
Besides, he was tired. He sat in a swivel chair with
his head back and his eyes closed. For the first time,
Daniels was the senior person in the White House.

He gave little attention to the official messsages of condolence which trickled to his desk like a paper cascade.
General de Gaulle wrote: "It is with great emotion and
deep sadness that the French Government and the French
people learn of the death of the great President Roosevelt.
. . . He was, from his first to his last days, the faithful
friend of France." The small, dark, taciturn man, Soviet
Ambassador Andrei Gromyko, said, "It was a terrific
shock for me to learn the news of President Roosevelt's

death. . . . One of the greatest statesmen the world has
ever had as well as a great person has been lost. . . ."
The Polish Ambassador, Jan Ciechanowski, hit a tragic
chord when he said, "The name of President Roosevelt was held in love and respect by the people of Poland,
who laid their fervent trust for Poland's independence
in his spirit of justice and democracy. . . ." In London,
Prime Minister Winston Churchill had slept awhile, then
returned to his "war office" near Admiralty Arch. His
secretary handed him a sheet of paper and said, "Sir,
President Roosevelt died a short time ago." Churchill
sat slowly slumping behind his desk. The secretary
fidgeted. Several minutes later, the Prime Minister looked
up and whispered, "Get me the palace." A director
of Lloyd's of London issued an order that the famed
Lutine Bell should be tolled, a sound heard only when
a great ship sank in the deep.

Before the U.S. Embassy in Moscow, a white-gloved
Marine stood guard against the empty streets. A group
of Russian citizens approached, removed their hats,
and said: *"Jhalko!"* (I have pity.) In China the wall
signs went up in many cities. Workers and soldiers looked
at each other, and asked, "But who killed him? Who
killed him?" Radio Tokyo surprised the U.S. Pacific
Fleet by broadcasting in English: "We indeed grieve
to learn of the death of President Roosevelt. We didn't
expect that he could pass away when the whole world
is in such a state of chaos . . ." As expected, Churchill
penned his own note to Mrs. Roosevelt:

I FEEL SO DEEPLY FOR YOU ALL. AS FOR ME, I HAVE LOST
A DEAR AND CHERISHED FRIENDSHIP WHICH WAS FORGED
IN THE FIRE OF WAR. I TRUST YOU MAY FIND CONSOLA-
TION IN THE GLORY OF HIS NAME AND THE MAGNITUDE OF
HIS WORK.

                                        CHURCHILL

Simmons, the White House usher who had been FDR's
double on a campaign train, walked into the office of
Jonathan Daniels because he saw a light under the door.

Upstairs, he said, Anna and her husband and "Mrs. Roosevelt's people" were drawing up a list of persons to be invited to the funeral services on Friday. The East Room would hold 250 people. One of the first names agreed to by all was James A. Farley, the politician who had engineered the first two successful campaigns for the Presidency, but who had broken his friendship with FDR on the third term, and had opposed him on the fourth. Bill Simmons suggested to Jonathan Daniels that, having nothing better to do, they should both go to the President's Oval Office and "clean up." The big, impressive room belonged to Harry S. Truman. It seemed strange, and yet eminently correct, to pack FDR's twelve-year accumulation of trinkets in the dark of one night. They found packing cases and cardboard boxes. There were donkeys, crystal paper weights, personalized pen and ink set, ship models on desk and wall, toy elephants and a spare set of glasses.

It was a night when people did not retire early. There were families in Salem, Seattle, Sacramento and San Antonio who sat at their radios for hours, sometimes in meditation. Night clubs, motion picture houses, restaurants and Broadway shows were closed temporarily, even though such a respectful observance could accomplish nothing of substance. At the Kremlin in Moscow a soldier made a mistake; he ran up the huge Red Banner with black border—an honor accorded to a few Soviet heroes—in the night sky. In Atlanta, Fred Patterson sat at the wheel of his car and drove away from the mortuary with Snoderly and Marchman, embalmers. At the same time, the clang of train bells could be heard in the Southern Yards as the presidential special—POTUS—left Atlanta slowly and majestically, headed for Warm Springs. A short time later two scrubbed black hearses left the Patterson Funeral Home. Lesesne was driving one; he said he was no longer sure of the tires. Beside him sat Young, his assistant. John Shrader drove the second. One carried a mahogany casket; one held one with a bronze finish.

It was the night of the long silence. Secret Service

agent Jim Beary drove the President's car out of the bumper gate at Warm Springs, and the guards didn't even nod. He was on his way south to pick up Mrs. Roosevelt, McIntire and Early at the airport near Columbus. An editorial writer in Chicago was moved to inspiration when he wrote: "It would be the most natural and characteristic thing on earth or in heaven if Franklin D. Roosevelt were to be saying at the Bar of Judgment exactly what he said in beginning the very last speech he made to the American people, the time he returned from Yalta last month and began his report—'It is good to be home. It has been a long journey. I hope you will agree that it was a fruitful one.'" In Spartanburg, South Carolina, Jimmy Byrnes answered the phone to find Navy Secretary James Forrestal calling. "I have talked to President Truman and we both think you can be of service in the next few days. My plane is on its way to pick you up. Besides, I know you would want to attend the funeral."

The sorrowful sentimentalist, William Hassett, was on the phone with Basil O'Connor. "You and I knew it was coming," FDR's law partner said. He must get to his office, O'Connor said, and find that will. He wasn't so much interested in the provisions of who was to get what; the burial instructions were important. Hassett said it wouldn't be necessary. Five years before, he had been standing beside Missy LeHand when the burial instructions had been dictated by the President: a simple service, and burial in the Rose Garden surrounded by the hemlock hedge of the estate. O'Connor asked if any arrangements had been made for Warm Springs. Some, Hassett said. Army and Navy commanders from the Southern Area had taken over, and they planned to line the road from the Little White House to the railroad station with 2,000 uniformed men. There would be a line of march, a military band, an honor guard, the hearse and funeral cars for the family. The train was on its way from Atlanta; some of the people, including Dr. Bruenn, would board it and go to sleep when it arrived.

Roosevelt was guarded with greater security dead than alive. Rings of troops paced posts on the perimeter of the Warm Springs Foundation. The military held the outer ring, the Secret Service the inner. Patients over a mile away at Georgia Hall could not leave or enter the grounds without challenge. The funeral director and his embalmers arrived at the grounds at 10:40 P.M. Fred Patterson was challenged three times on the way in. He was a proud man who imputed dignity to his calling and resented stopping the car to present his credentials. He did not appreciate waiting for a guard to phone the Little White House to find out "if it is all right to let them through." He was on the most august mission of his career, but he thought of the dead President, as he explained to friends, as a body which had been deceased seven hours. The longer he was kept waiting, the more difficult the embalming and dressing of the body.

An additional rebuff awaited him at the Little White House. As he strode in with Snoderly and Marchman and their equipment, Bill Hassett asked them to take chairs near the center hall. "We can't do anything until Mrs. Roosevelt arrives," he said. "We need her permission." Mr. Patterson was ruffled. Hassett asked about the "bronze" casket. Two were on the way, Fred Patterson said; one with a "bronze finish" and one of pure mahogany. He had already computed the cost, in case anyone asked. The casket and embalming would come to $3,300. That would not include the extra cost of accompanying the body on the train to Washington, where the body would have to be reset in the casket after a train ride and additional embalming fluid would have to be used. No one asked.

The room was rull of sibilant whispers. Polly and Daisy were debating how much to tell Eleanor when she arrived. Bruenn and Hassett stood near the bedroom door with Paullin. The funeral director recognized a friend in the Atlanta physician. If he had to wait, he said, could he just look at the remains? This induced a conference. It was decided that he could take a look, for whatever professional reasons he had in mind. Mr.

Patterson tiptoed into the bedroom. He saw the small bed, a lumpy mass under a counterpane and a sheet. Patterson drew them back to the waist. The President was in pajamas and a dressing robe. The funeral director's first thought was, "He's awfully thin." A flexing touch of the wrist and neck showed that rigor mortis was advanced. The mouth hung wide open. He knew that there would be quite a bit of work on this case. He asked how long it would be before Mrs. Roosevelt arrived. "Soon." Patterson sat. Fifteen miles from Warm Springs, Lesesne was having problems, too. A tire on the leading hearse blew out. He and his assistants were trying to repair it in the dark.

All of them were sitting around the Room of Whispers when Mrs. Roosevelt came in with McIntire and Early. The black dress and somber expression made Eleanor look unapproachable. She nodded to the strange faces and was embraced by Polly and Daisy. They wept on cue; Mrs. Roosevelt looked pale and preoccupied. In passing, she said, "I will go inside for a minute." She went into the bedroom alone. Did she break down in the presence of the remains of the man to whom she had pledged her life? No one saw reddened eyes or the use of a kerchief. In the living room, McIntire drew Bruenn and Paullin toward the porch to discuss arrangements. He saw no reason to perform an autopsy. Nor did they. Paullin, a somewhat dominating man, had no doubt that there had been a "massive intracerebral hemorrhage which had ruptured into the subarachnoid space." The cardiovascular accident had been induced, he felt, by hypertensive heart disease and generalized arteriosclerosis. The young Commander was outranked. For a year he had been as close to the President as his skin. But he too could see no purpose gained by an autopsy. He subscribed to what Paullin and McIntire had said.

Mrs. Roosevelt surprised everyone by remaining five long minutes in the bedroom. When she returned to the living room, McIntire asked if she had a choice of caskets. Mr. Patterson joined the group to explain that his men had brought two. The subject seemed distasteful to Mrs. Roosevelt, who clasped and unclasped her hands. Dr. Bruenn advised that a choice be made. Admiral McIntire glanced at Mrs. Roosevelt and said, "Bronze." She nodded. The word passed to Lesesne, and his men brought the casket inside. Fred Patterson asked if his people could "go to work." He was nodded toward the bedroom. For the first time in hours, Arthur Prettyman moved from a chair barely inside the kitchen doorway. He went to the bedroom with Patterson. So did a U.S. Marine guard, who stood inside the door.

An operating table, a Turner portable pump, and other equipment went into the bedroom. Patterson glanced at his watch. It was 12:25 A.M. Mr. Roosevelt had been dead almost nine hours. When the body was placed on the table and stripped, the embalmers knew that old man Patterson was right—this was going to be a difficult job. Besides, the room was too small for efficient work. Prettyman shoved the foot of the bed away from the table. Medical science had no means of diagnosing with certitude generalized hardening of the arteries, but the embalmers knew a way. They made carotid incisions in the neck and the pulsator pump clicked with formaldehyde. In an average case, they use 24 ounces of formaldehyde in three gallons of water. The arteries were so severely plugged with plaques that the pump strained and stopped. They tried axillary punctures under the arms with the same result.

In the closed room, the men began to perspire. They tried two femorals in the groin. The results were poor. They worked and spoke in whispers. Patterson said it was impossible to embalm the body properly. He and the embalmers would have to follow the funeral on the train to Washington. There they would use hypos—individual syringe injections in many parts of the body. Mr. Patterson told Haden Snoderly and George Marchman to phone their families that they would be gone for a few days. Arthur Prettyman seemed unable to bear watching the pain-wracked body submitted to further indignities. He left for his solitary post in the kitchen. Mrs. Roosevelt sat on the couch chatting with her cousins. Grace Tully came up from her cottage, and, in spite of her resolve to the contrary, started crying again. Hassett stood on the porch looking at the bright night sky, listening to the muffled rhythmic tramp of many boots. Mrs. Roosevelt sent word to the Secret Service agents that, duty or not, all of them were invited to attend the funeral. Dr. Paullin told McIntire he must leave; it would be close to dawn when he got home. He received the thanks of Mrs. Roosevelt. He told her she must be strong.

The Marine guard came out of the room and asked Prettyman to come back. Patterson and his men had done whatever they could to compose the features and the limbs. Someone had thrown the Navy cape over the nude body. The valet drew a freshly pressed blue suit from the closet. Snoderly was smoothing the President's features and kept asking Prettyman if "this is the right expression." Roosevelt's manservant said, "Yes. It looks like him now." He went to the bathroom and returned with FDR's comb. Tenderly, he parted the hair, and combed it back. When he finished, he stepped away. For an instant, the deep grief disappeared. He seemed pleased. Mrs. Roosevelt was called in. She looked at the body, nodded, and thanked each one of the workers. Lesesne brought the casket in and the body was lifted into it. Prettyman approached Mrs. Roosevelt. Although the President seldom carried cash, the valet had found $133 in his pocket. He gave the money to her. He smiled sadly. "I'm back in the Navy now."

The day, to those who had a part in it, seemed interminably long. The night, conversely, was short. In Washington as at Warm Springs, some remained abroad through the dark hours to drink, to talk, to reminisce, to remind themselves that history had turned a notable corner. At 2:15 A.M. the long train began to back into Mr. Pless's little wooden station. A big steam locomotive was pulling the rear car. Two locomotives were at the front end, pushing. Some county farmers sat on the curb hugging their knees, watching. They made no noise. They seldom spoke. The word went up the hill and soon Admiral McIntire came down with Dr. Bruenn and Steve Early. They chose to sleep on the train. It was a poor choice. Army trucks began to grind down the hill in low gear loaded with baggage. They were guided slowly up the right-of-way to the baggage car, with men shouting in the night. William Hassett walked up the steps of the hotel. He saw Ruth Stevens, still chipper in her yellow linen dress, the one she had selected for the barbecue. "Lady Ruth," he said gravely, "no one knows what he meant to me—and he thought you were such a princess!" He turned back.

Fred Patterson pressed a glass lid on the lower half of the casket until it locked. He pulled the metal lid down a third, and left it that way. He looked around to no one in particular and asked if a bier had been built for the train. No one seemed to know what he meant. "A bier and a ramp," he said. "This casket weighs six hundred pounds. We need a carpenter fast." A Secret Service man held up a finger. "Let me see if I can help." he said. He drove down to the Foundation and got Hoke Shipp out of bed. Also Al Moody. Mr. Shipp was the executive housekeeper of the Foundation; Moody was an expert carpenter. Patterson drove down to the train with them. The last car was the *Conneaught*. The big rear compartment had been stripped of every piece of furniture except a mirror on the wall.

The funeral director explained to two sleepy men that the big rear window on the hotel side of the car would have to come out. That would be step number one. When it was out, the men would have to build a ramp inclining upward, so that ten military men could lift the casket up to the empty window. Ten men would have to be stationed inside the car to receive the casket. Shipp and Moody began to assess a big hurry-up job. In addition, Mr. Patterson said, a bier would have to be built inside the car to hold the casket and keep it from sliding. This would require a wooden frame about twenty inches tall with a half-inch lip all around it. The casket, he said, was 84 inches long and 26 inches wide. The lip should measure 86 by 28. Shipp scratched his head. He had some prime pine well seasoned that he had been saving. He could start work at once if he had enough men who knew how to use hammers and saws. Mr. Patterson was a "take charge" man. At 4:00 A.M. a dozen men were at the station working on carpenter's horses under a single blazing street light. Some were building a long ramp to the window. Others were taking the window out without breaking it. Shipp and Moody were inside, building that precise bier. The noise of the workmen hammering and sawing, the trucks grinding up and down the hill, the hoarse voices of men in the night and the chuffing of the locomotives kept the small village awake.

In the Little White House, Arthur Prettyman washed and shaved and put on his Chief Petty Officer's uniform. He sat up with the body. Mrs. Roosevelt, exhausted, went to her own bedroom to the right of the living room to indulge in whatever retrospection she chose. When she asked Polly and Daisy who was with the President when he fainted, the answers tumbled over each other. If Mrs. Roosevelt sensed fear or hysteria in the confused response, she did not contest it.

Sleep was beyond price. No one was permitted to pry into the thinking of any of the people who were close to Roosevelt. Some lay across beds in dresses and suits trying to "get a little rest." But the carousel of the human mind was in high gear. Some were sober. Some were maudlin drunk. Some wept. Some murmured prayers. Some thought of him; others thought of themselves and the bleak future. Edward J. Flynn, personal friend of FDR, was on a night train bound for Washington—ostensibly to attend the funeral, but actually to achieve political rapport with President Truman. Jimmy Byrnes, in retirement less than a week, was flying north to assist in the transition of power, but unknown to him, to become Secretary of State. Jonathan Daniels, the lonely man in the White House, knew that he was unfair when he dwelled on how small Harry

Truman looked swinging in the President's swivel chair. To Dorothy Brady, the world had ended. Grace Tully, like a cloistered nun, had devoted her life to her god, but the god had died and there would be no political hereafter. To Bill Hassett, the melancholy tone of the deep bell was in his ears; the United States had had a President—it could not have another. Mike Reilly, who had protected him from all danger, could not surrender him to death. He could say to Jim Beary, "The Boss is gone," but he didn't believe his words. Lucy? The long night ride, the sobbing, the consolation of a priest to the inconsolable—most of all, hardest of all, the knowledge that she alone would not be permitted to approach the funeral; she would not be allowed to say good-bye. The final moment would belong to Eleanor. Would she know how to encompass a cold face with warm hands?

No matter how troubled, how inconsolable the thoughts of many people, the inevitability was dawn. At Warm Springs, it was cloudless, breezeless and hot. It is possible that Mrs. Roosevelt did not sleep because, as soon as the first light filtered into the bedroom, she was up, washing, dressing, combing, smoothing the black dress and slipping her feet into those "practical shoes." Hassett was waiting on the couch. The casket, on the other side of the room near the President's bedroom, was the biggest item in the Little White House, but Bill refused to approach it. He asked Mrs. Roosevelt who would be invited on the train.

The two went down a list in no particular order: Mrs. Roosevelt, Hassett, Louise Hachmeister, Steve Early, Fala, Admiral McIntire, Dr. Bruenn, Grace Tully, Laura Delano, Margaret Suckley, Dorothy Brady, Michael Reilly, James Rowley, Guy Spaman, James Beary, a military honor guard and three pool reporters. The secretary explained that the military had arranged a solemn parade to the railroad station. If Mrs. Roosevelt could be prepared to leave about 9:00 A.M.— She could. In the glen behind the Little White House a loud argument was in progress between Hoke Shipp and a

U.S. Marine supply sergeant. The work at the train was almost complete. Shipp learned that the casket was copper colored, and he wanted two Marine green blankets to place under it, hiding the wooden platform. The sergeant was demanding to know who would sign for the blankets and when he could expect their return. Shipp was losing his temper.

He asked if the sergeant knew that they were for the President of the United States. The sergeant said he didn't care who was going to use them, he had a responsibility for government property. Shipp demanded to speak to the commanding officer. "Impossible," said the sergeant. "He's asleep." "Then, by God," said Shipp, "he's about to wake up." The sergeant was mollified. No use getting excited, he said. He could sneak two green blankets out of the supply room. Shipp said he didn't want them "sneaked." He walked back up to the hot clay road with them under his arm.

Down at Georgia Hall, Dewey Long and Mike Reilly worked out the special schedule of the funeral train. R. K. McClain, assistant vice president of Southern Railway, had been up all night getting POTUS down to Warm Springs and making arrangements for bringing it back up to Washington. At 5:00 A.M. he had sent orders to divisional chiefs at Warm Springs, Knoxville, Tennessee, and Charlotte, North Carolina. R. H. Hamilton, S. S. Brooks and T. C. Blackwell had been awakened to study them. The wires up and down the right-of-way were chattering, and operators at the way stops were listening. The regular schedule would have suffered less dislocation if McClain had been permitted to allow the train to run at high speed. The White House people insisted that there would be "thousands of people" along the tracks in small towns and big cities to say farewell to Roosevelt; the big picture window in the *Conneaught* would make the casket visible, and the train would have to move slowly.

McClain had spent lunch hour the day before studying a final schedule of the President's return trip to Washington on Wednesday, April 18. When he heard news of the death, he had invalidated the first and started a second one. Then the word came to slow the train; he worked out a third one. Briefly, it advised:

Lv Warm Springs, Ga. 11 A.M.; *arrive Williamson‾ Ga 12:01 (take on water); arrive Atlanta Ga. 2* P.M. *(change engines and crews); Gainsville, Ga 3:40* P.M. *(Water); Greenville, S.C. 6:50* P.M. *(Change engine crews and water); Hayne, S.C. 7:55* P.M. *(Coal and water); Salisbury, N.C. 11:10* P.M. *(Change engine and crews); Danville, Va. 1:50* A.M. *April 14th (Ice and Water); Monroe, Va. 4:15* A.M. *(Change engine crews and water); Applegate Va. 5:40* A.M. *(Let No. 30 Pass); Charlottesville Va. 6:20* A.M. *(Use telephone); Weyburn, Va. 6:55* A.M. *(Coal and water); Bealton, Va. 8:15* A.M. *(Let No. 48 Pass). Arrive Washington Union Station 10* A.M.

One of the most formidable steam locomotives made was Southern's huge 1400 series. These had been especially assigned to Roosevelt's POTUS for a number of years. Today, except for the first leg of the trip, the 1400s, all painted brilliant green with silvery wheel rims, would be waiting to haul him on the last journey.

Harry S. Truman sat at breakfast with some newspapers brought in by the Secret Service. He told Mrs. Truman that he had slept well, but that he had awakened without realizing he was President of the United States. He said it required a few minutes for him to remember. As he ate his breakfast, he glanced at *The New York Times.* The unsmiling photo of the handsome face of Roosevelt with the black borders seemed to make his death official. The headlines were big:

PRESIDENT ROOSEVELT IS DEAD:
TRUMAN TO CONTINUE POLICIES:
9TH CROSSES ELBE, NEARS BERLIN

It was strange that Truman had been President over twelve hours, and no one had phoned him from Warm

Springs to explain what had happened. He was interested; he idolized his President. The bits and shreds of information he had came from Steve Early in the White House. He studied the columns and columns of copy, but most of it was concerned with Roosevelt's biography. Truman knew that story. The little he gleaned about what happened at Warm Springs was contained in a paragraph:

The Associated Press announced that the President was posing for an artist named Nicholas Robbins of New York when he became ill. The only others present in the cottage were Commander George Fox, White House pharmacist and an attendant on the President, William D. Hassett, presidential secretary, Miss Grace Tully, confidential secretary, and two cousins, Miss Laura Delano and Miss Margaret Suckley.

The other item of interest was an Official German War Communiqué, which, to the new President, displayed venomous desperation:

The Fortress of Koenigsberg was surrendered to the Soviets after several days of strong attacks by the fortress commander, General of the Infantry Lasch. Despite this, parts of the garrison who remained faithful to their duty split up into several battle groups and are offering bitter resistance to the Soviets. General Lasch was sentenced by court-martial to death by hanging for his cowardly surrender to the enemy. His kin will be held responsible.

It is doubtful that the new President had time to peruse the newspapers He ate, he glanced, he flipped a few pages, and he was gone "to the office." Other people died on April 12. The one which editors later agreed epitomized all was the demise of George Andrew Farrant. He was seventy-one, a retired reporter of the *Jersey Journal* in Jersey City, New Jersey. He had spent a leisurely day at home and, at 6:30 P.M., he had stepped out on the lawn to lower the American flag. Carefully, he folded the banner and walked to the front porch with it. As he opened the door, the radio blared that President Franklin D. Roosevelt had died suddenly at Warm Springs, Georgia. Mr. Farrant, still holding the flag, fell forward, dead. It was a small item on the obituary page.

At Warm Springs, Fred Patterson was affronted. As the hour of nine approached, many people were in the living room of the Little White House, but no one seemed able to make a decision. Mr. Patterson had worked hard all night, and at age sixty-two none of it was easy. A Secret Service man had followed him, insisting that "By Christ, the President is going down to that railroad station on a caisson." The funeral director pointed to the rutty clay roads and said that the body would be jostled out of position in the casket. It made no difference to this man. There was going to be a caisson. Patterson mingled among the notables in the living room, requesting that a Cadillac funeral car be used, but no one could approve his request. A field artillery caisson would be a desecration, he thought. Everyone referred him to someone else. His dignity began to fray when he asked that Snoderly be given room on the train with embalming equipment. "You see," he said quietly, "the family has two funeral directors waiting, according to what I hear. One is Gawler in Washington; the other is Mrs. Ralph Worden in Hyde Park. The remains are going to require additional embalming, and Snoderly will offer his assistance without interfering with the others."

His request was referred upward from Bruenn and Hassett until it reached the man who enjoyed taking charge—Admiral Ross McIntire. He listened and said, "Sorry. No room." Patterson assured the Admiral that Snoderly wouldn't require much room. "No room on the train." McIntire said. Patterson hurried outside into the hot sun to ask an Army general where the casket flag might be. The general didn't know. "We thought the Marine detachment took care of that," he said. The casket had to have a flag. Patterson was hurrying too fast on too many errands. He waved to Marchman to drive the hearse up the driveway to the front door. He found the Marine major, who said that the flag had been given to a Secret Service man. No, he didn't know which Secret Service man. The old man puffed up to Lesesne, his bright young assistant. "See that flag up on that pole?" he said. "Put it on the casket."

The military looked startled when they saw the flag come slowly down the flagstaff in the center of the Little White House driveway. No one objected. They may have thought it was part of the ceremony. Lesesne took it to the side of the house and shook it thoroughly for loose dust. Then he carried it inside. Lizzie McDuffie was saying, "Oh, he looks handsome. You wouldn't think he was sick a day." It was nine o'clock, and a few minutes past. Patterson was puffing and trotting. Where, he begged, are the pallbearers? The search began. Someone found them up at the white bumper gate. The ten, four Army men, four Marines, two sailors, marched in file to the front door. They were young and strong and unaccustomed to marching together. Lesesne asked them to wait outside the door in two open ranks.

Laura sauntered over to the casket and looked in. The President looked younger and had a better complexion than Miss Delano had seen in a long time. His double-breasted blue suit appeared to be old-fashioned. The blue and white tie was one he had worn at his third inauguration. Looking down, Miss Delano could see the socks on the feet—no shoes. Mr. Patterson leaned over and brought both glass lids down tight. He looked around. Mrs. Roosevelt was at the door, chatting with Daisy Suckley. If no one wanted to see the body a last time, Patterson would close the metal lid, but not seal it.

Hassett felt ill at ease. He wrote later in the day that he had been engulfed by the eternity of eternity—he kept thinking, "I worked with him in this room twenty-four hours ago." Less than twenty-four hours. There would be no pouch this morning; no drying of Hassett's laundry. Few people are conscious of the last time for any repeated event. Yesterday, in this room, he had jokingly said, "Here's where I make a law." He would joke no more, make no more laws. Already man had begun, on a gigantic scale, his pagan honors to the dead with none but the living to draw joy from it. It was a ritual, with all the actors in place and in proper costume, prepared to ride slowly, to gaze at those who gazed, to stand, to kneel, to pray, to whisper, to dwell upon the awesome difference between the living mobility and the stillness of clay.

Lesesne and Snoderly wheeled the casket on the roller table to the door. The mourners stepped back. One of the President's armless wheelchairs was near the umbrella stand; it was taken away. Patterson whispered for the young men to squeeze in and lift the casket. They found it to be heavy, and they grunted as they carried it to the black Cadillac and carefully slid it inside on rollers. Mr. Patterson arranged the flag, and placed a mixed bouquet on top. The hearse moved forward. When Mrs. Roosevelt was called to the next car, she asked Daisy, Polly and Grace Tully to ride with her. Outside in the sunshine, she held her veil up over her hat and squinted and smiled in the sun. The driveway ellipse was ringed with military, rifles and bayonets gleaming at present arms. She maintained the smile, and, seeing ranking officers of different services, she walked to each one, shook hands and thanked him for "helping us at this time." She called Fala to follow her. Mr. Lesesne assisted her into the car. She sat near the window. The cars moved ahead and stopped. In the second car were McIntire, Bruenn, Early and Hassett.

No one could see ahead. Far down the hill, a U.S. Army band, led by ranking officers, prepared to play the dirges. Behind them 2,000 soldiers closed ranks to fit within a narrow road. The sun was hot, windows were lowered. From the tall scraggly pines came a cool cascade of song. On both sides of the road, soldiers stood guard every twenty feet. As the hearse inched past each one, he snapped to attention and presented arms. When the cars had been loaded, Patterson nodded to Lesesne, Snoderly and Young, and the four got into a Patterson automobile, kicked up dust as they passed the standing procession and all the soldiers downhill and hurried to the depot. Patterson looked at his watch. It was 9:25 Eastern Time; the train would not leave at 10:00.

The procession began in slow march. The soldiers at the side of the road looked so very young. Tears were rolling down some cheeks. Some faces were frozen in comic grimace. One young man stood with his rifle held straight out toward the hearse, and, without a cry, slowly tumbled in a faint. G.I.'s nearby saw him go; no one moved out of line to help him. The band walked in measured slow cadence, the shiny instruments under their arms. Only the drums fought the cheerful gossip of the birds. The drums were deep and muffled, a deadly beat. The procession moved at a slow walk all the way back down to Georgia Hall, behind which the big swimming pool gleamed blue. Here, before he left Warm Springs, he always drove by the Hall and Carver Cottage, waving farewell, the gray fedora snapping in the breeze, the cigarette holder jaunty. Today, the patients waited for the farewell. They were on wheelchairs in sunlight and shade; some were on trundle beds which had been pushed out of rooms; some leaned against walls on crutches. The old, the young, the children. The world had lost a leader; the nation had lost a President; these had lost a protector, a father.

The tears started. Mrs. Roosevelt turned away. Cameras clicked. They saw the ranks of helmeted and high-booted paratroopers and they heard the crunch of gravel. Out of the darkness the black face of Graham Jackson emerged. He was in his recruiting officer's uniform and his eyes begged Marchman to stop the hearse for a moment. It stopped. He took the accordion from under his arm and began to play the sweet slow strains of "Going Home." His weeping left shiny scars. In spite of the hot day, Mrs. Roosevelt pulled her black fur cape tighter and, as though to escape watching the distressing sentiment, reached to the rug on the floor and lifted Fala to her lap. She petted the dog and whispered to him. The cortege began to move while Jackson was still playing. The raucous cries of young lieutenants for "right turn

—hut!" stilled the birds. The slow hearse followed the soldiers, down the tawny clay road between thick hummocks of pines. The distant drums were a disconcerting heartbeat.

On the main road to the station, villagers stood aside to see, to remember, to boast someday. They wore cotton prints and open shirts and some of the more practical may have worried about what would become of the village now that its chief patron was departing. The line of march was less than four miles, but it required almost an hour of time; a long period for a dolorous display. At the railroad station, C. A. Pless held his warning gates up, but stood on the track with a lantern. On the far side, the porch of the hotel was jammed with sightseers who enjoyed an elevated view. A county deputy held all cars from driving down the main street toward the tracks. Black cables snaked up and down the street as radio announcers, summoned from the important centers of information, tried to acquaint themselves with the village and its people so that they would have "sidebar" fonts of information before the arrival of the cortege. The cadre of ranking officers, with their shoulder stars and eagles, led the troops across the tracks and on up the main street, the drumbeat now harmonizing with heavy boots on macadam. They kept marching on and on, until at last the hearse passed Mr. Pless, who raised his railroad cap and watched it turn right until it was adjacent to the sloping ramp.

There, an honor guard of picked troops stood at parade rest. Mr. Patterson was waiting. He had studied that ramp with a cautious appraisal. Shipp had done well. It was sturdy enough to support ten men, in addition to a casket which now weighed 760 pounds. Inside the car, almost out of view of the brightness of the sun, ten more men waited to carry that casket inside the *Conneaught* and set it at rest on the twenty-inch bier. The green and gold Marine rugs covered the interior structure. He asked Snoderly for the sealing gun and the embalming equipment. His purpose was to set them on the bier, under the casket, for Gawler in Washington. A Secret Service man said no. Patterson was tired of interference, in short temper at being thwarted. No objects of any kind could be placed under the casket, the Secret Service man said. Patterson said they would have to go there, so that Gawler's men could find them. They would be needed in Washington. The funeral director, mopping his forehead, said that the Secret Service could examine the material. Reluctantly, the man said, "Okay." Mrs. Roosevelt's automobile moved up the siding to the next Pullman, the President's armor-plated *Ferdinand Magellan*. She boarded without looking back. The transfer of the casket proceeded as smoothly as though it had been rehearsed. The men in front crouched and held onto the rounded bottom. Those in back held it on their shoulders. The casket remained level. From inside, hands and arms emerged from the big empty window to grasp, to lift. On the crushed stone right-of-way, the pool reporters scribbled their last notes before boarding. Guards from various branches of service were posted around the casket as railroad men reinserted the big picture window, screwing and sealing it firmly. Pless and a few other privileged persons took a last look through the window. From up on the main street the casket and the honor guard were easy to see. The eleven cars were standing on a looping curve, on a downgrade of one percent. Conductor E. E. Whittle stood halfway up the track, trying to see both ends of his train.

At 10:13 (11:13 Eastern Time)—thirteen minutes late—he received a slow wave of the arm from flagman S. A. Wallace that all were aboard. He waved H. E. Allgood, engineer of the lead locomotive, to be on his way. Allgood would remain a half mile ahead on the route to Atlanta. Whittle waited a minute or two, then signaled O. B. Wofford, the engineer of POTUS, to move out. He hopped aboard a middle car as Wofford released the brakes. In the back of the train, the people gathered at the crossing for a last look. Most of them would have liked to pay their last respects to the President by filing silently by his body at the Little White House, but they hadn't been invited. He had been a part-time neighbor, and they didn't like to see him go. They heard the small shrieks of the brakes as the wheels began to turn, but engineer Wofford had not opened the throttle. He was inching downward on the grade, and the last car moved so slowly that people jogged each other and said, "It's moving"; "He's going."

It was going. The military band blared a funeral march. Squeaking, squealing, the *Conneaught* followed the other cars around the big curve, edging off in a profusion of hillside sassafras and weeds. Then it was gone, and the people stood looking up the empty tracks. It was a Friday, and everybody knew that the President never traveled on Friday.

The morning walk on Connecticut Avenue was a failure. Harry Truman was addicted to post-breakfast strolling in good weather and bad. It was a constitutional and more than that; it was a fixed, unbreakable habit. He was accustomed to striding briskly, almost militarily, at 7:45 A.M., usually alone. On the morning of April 13 he was dismayed to find that a group of Secret Service agents strode ahead of him, and there were three behind him. Washington neighbors who were accustomed to crossing the street to ask "Harry" what he thought of this public question or that were blocked politely and firmly. Nor was the new President the only one who was disappointed with the walk; the Secret Service could appreciate a Chief Executive who might stride up and down the south grounds of the White House, but not one who merged with pedestrian and vehicular traffic.

He looked glum and smiley by turns as he strode with Hugh Fulton, who had been counsel to the Truman Senate Committee. The President felt that he was in the middle of a crowd. He returned to his apartment. A big limousine with the seal of the President of the United States was at the front door. He forced a smile for the people who watched. Among them was Anthony Vaccaro, Associated Press correspondent assigned to the Congress. "Hop in, Tony," said the President. Stunned, Vaccaro occupied a jump seat. The ride was quiet. Until last night Vaccaro would have felt free to ask almost anything of Truman. The reporter enjoyed the easy, almost familial atmosphere of the white-domed Capitol. He had no trouble relating to Truman, Rayburn, McCormack, Barkley, Martin and other congressional leaders. Since last night, his friend had been elevated to a remote, almost holy status: President. The broad chasm between Vice President and President was seldom symbolized as sharply as on that short ride to the White House.

"There have been few men in history the equal of the man whose shoes I am stepping into today," the President said quietly. "I pray to God I can measure up to the task." Vaccaro wasn't certain whether it was ethical to quote a President. "I know I'm ready to give it all I have." The car approached the White House. Truman sensed the reason for the reporter's silence. "I just want the folks I love to know that if we can't get together in the old informal way, it is not my choosing. Tell them that, will you? You know, if I could have my way, I'd have them all come in without knocking." Tony understood. A lot of things died yesterday and a lot were born. Helplessly, Vaccaro asked when the President would move into the White House. As Truman dropped his friend off, he said, "I want Mrs. Roosevelt to stay just as long as she pleases. I'm comfortable where I am."

The new President was charitable and generous, and yet acutely conscious of his rights. He could have requisitioned any office in the White House, but he walked directly to the Oval Office and seemed to be disturbed in the presence of packing boxes and crates laden with Roosevelt memorabilia, and of some FDR objects still on the President's desk and in the drawers. He walked to the door and spoke to a Secret Service man on the far side. "Get someone in here to clean this up," he said. An usher and two workmen came in to make the office acceptable. Truman had his secretary, Matthew J. Connolly, in the White House, but it was not enough. He needed more help. He called William Simmons, the receptionist. The man who had once impersonated FDR was asked if he knew the White House routine—whom to see, when to take which phone calls, how to get people in and out without offense—and Simmons nodded. "Good," said Truman. "You be my appointments secretary until I can find one."

No officer of the United States government is kept purposefully ignorant as much as the Vice President. It has always been the American way. Abraham Lincoln did not call Andrew Johnson in for a chat about policy and politics until April 14, 1865, the day he was assassinated. William McKinley was affronted by the presence of Theodore Roosevelt, whom he regarded as brash and bold. Warren G. Harding's relationship with Calvin Coolidge was almost nonexistent. FDR had had three: John Nance Garner, Henry A. Wallace and Harry S. Truman. To none did he confide his policies, his aspirations for his country, or his personal relationships to other world leaders. There were White House press secretaries, such as Steve Early, William Hassett and Jonathan Daniels, who might have made more efficient Presidents in the first week of the Truman Administration. Mr. Roosevelt reposed confidence in each of them, and each knew a part of his mind—just as Missy LèHand, Grace Tully and Dorothy Brady each understood a third of his correspondence.

Truman had two items in his favor. As little as he knew about the intricacies of the Presidency, he could announce loudly that he was prepared to pursue the Roosevelt doctrine inside and outside the United States. This could, it was hoped, keep the governmental gears from grinding to a stop. The second thing was that Truman had dedication and energy. He was an old-fashioned patriot who was willing to make decisions. And yet he was as much in awe of his lofty position as a bumpkin tourist looking at White House public rooms from behind plush cords. He realized that many of the sophisticated Roosevelt officials looked upon him as an accidental President; a political "lightweight." It is possible that Truman's greatest virtue was his lack of imagination:

he believed that hard honest work and a no-nonsense attitude would make him an acceptable successor to Roosevelt.

At 10:00 A.M. Edward Stettinius was in the Oval Office. The President was cordial; each respected the office of the other, but not the man. The Secretary of State told Truman that there would have to be a proclamation of the death of Roosevelt. By tradition, it would be signed by the new President and the Secretary of State. Truman said he would dictate it at once. Second, Stettinius said that his department had been accustomed to drawing up a position paper for the President. Would Truman like to have one prepared? The new President smiled. He would indeed; he had no notion of the United States' position in many matters, foreign and domestic. Truman said he would send the proclamation of death to the State Department as soon as it was typed. He called a stenographer. It seemed impossible to work because Matt Connolly walked in to advise him that certain people were waiting in an anteroom to speak to him; Jonathan Daniels was in and out to report important visitors and phone calls; the receptionist, Simmons, was trying to find out which persons Truman was willing to see and which ones could be deflected to someone else.

TO THE PEOPLE OF THE UNITED STATES:

It has pleased God in His infinite wisdom to take from us the immortal spirit of Franklin Delano Roosevelt, the 32nd President of the United States. The leader of his people in a great war, he lived to see the assurance of victory but not to share in it. He lived to see the first foundations of the free and peaceful world to which his life was dedicated, but not to enter on that world himself. . . .

Truman signed it, and executed his signature with satisfaction. He said that the document expressed what he felt deeply. At 11:00 A.M., a short time before the Roosevelt train left Warm Springs, the President called his military leaders in. He had an office full of braid:

Admiral William D. Leahy, Secretary of War Henry
Stimson, Secretary of the Navy James Forrestal, General
George C. Marshall, Admiral Ernest J. King, Lieutenant
General Barney Giles of the Air Forces and a
stenographer to take notes. The faces were sober, almost
stony. Truman prefaced the chat by running up the same
flag he was going to hoist to win the support of his
predecessor's advisers; he intended to follow Franklin
D. Roosevelt's domestic and foreign policies to the letter.
He admired Roosevelt as much as they, and he was
going to require a lot of assistance to carry the burden
dropped so abruptly by the champ. The gentlemen began
to soften. Briefly, they estimated that Hitler would hold
out for six months; that Japan would surrender in a
year and a half. In turn, each man detailed a certain
phase of operations in a given theater. Truman was
a fast reader. His questions were concise and intelligent.
The meeting closed when Truman said that he thought
he should send some word of encouragement to the
far-flung forces, but he felt that first he should address
Congress. On his fingers, he ticked off the priorities:
the Congress, the people, the armed forces, the Allies.
As the military leaders departed, with a slightly better
opinion of the new man, he asked Leahy to remain.
Truman's assessment of the Admiral was that they were
alike: direct, blunt, independent. Leahy was asked to
remain as "the President's Chief of Staff."

The Admiral looked surprised. "Are you sure you
want me, Mr. President?" he said. "I always say what
is on my mind." "I want the truth," Truman said, "and
I want the facts at all times. I want you to stay with
me and always to tell me what's on your mind. You
may not always agree with my decisions, but I know
you will carry them out faithfully." Leahy was no smiler.
He grinned and stuck his hand out. "You have my
pledge," he said. "You can count on me." He had won a
friend. Truman was pained to learn that old political allies had been kept waiting in the reception room. Senator
Alben Barkley came in, shook hands, and said, "Have
confidence in yourself. If you don't, the people will lose

confidence in you." Sam Rayburn came in glowering. He was the first to lecture the new President. "Stop shooting from the hip," he said. "You don't stop to think how some things will look in print. Your biggest hazard is in this White House," the Speaker said with emphasis. "Some of the people here are going to try to do to you what they've tried to do to every President since I've been here. They are going to try to build a fence around you, and, in building that fence, they will be keeping the very people away from seeing you that you should see." Roosevelt's dear personal friend, Edward Flynn of the Bronx, stopped by and tried to discuss new political appointments with Truman. "I don't think this is the time or place for this kind of talk," Truman said rudely.

At Williamson, Georgia, the train was out of the hills of western Georgia. It moved along slowly, almost sedately, through the furrowed farm country. Children hurried to fence rails to sit and gape. Sweaty farmers behind plows stopped their mules in midfield to watch the slowly spinning green and silver drivers, the chuffing of black smoke against blue sky, and the passing of the last car with its immobile guards and flag-draped casket. At chiming crossings, sheriffs' cars waited. The radio had told them it was on its way to Atlanta. At road crossings lonely soldiers stood leaning on carbines, to present arms as the last car drew abreast. Someone in authority had dispersed soldiers all along the right-of-way to Washington. In small towns whole populations stood on the freight platforms, waiting under the eaves from the sun, saying monotonously, "Here it comes." It was a personal matter with each of the half million or more people who would wait along the right-of-way to say good-bye to a man they knew, but had never met; someone who, they were certain, had protected them and whom they could not protect. It was admiration, respect, love and curiosity. Above all, it was a feeling of having known this man—his big winning smile, his reassuring voice, his sly asides, most of all the intimacy of his repeated phrase, "You and I know . . ."

The three pool reporters were in the communication's car. They had copies of Roosevelt's Jefferson Day speech, something which, undelivered, would live for a day in the newspapers. Oliver, Nixon and Smith seemed surprised, during respites, that they could think the right thoughts and hit the right keys after working all night. They would also have to file stories about the last train ride. One said that they could get enough material between Atlanta (2:00 P.M.) and Greenville, South Carolina (6:50 P.M.), to file night stories. After that, they could go to bed. Mrs. Roosevelt was too busy to mourn. Whatever personal sorrow she reserved for herself had been expressed when she sat beside the bed in the little pine room the night before. Lesesne remarked that the First Lady spent about five minutes with the body. He remembered it had seemed a long time to wait for permission to embalm. She wasn't in an amiable frame of mind this morning, but she seemed extra considerate of those who had worked with her husband. She asked Tully if she would mind coming into the President's big comfortable lounge to help work out some problems. She wanted suggestions about a card of acknowledgment for condolences. They worked over the wording until they resolved a simple response. Miss Tully worried about what questions Eleanor might ask. There was a distillation of fear. Mrs. Roosevelt said, "Did Franklin give you any instructions about his burial?"

This was a safe question. The President had once told Tully that if he died at sea he would like to be buried at sea. "It has always seemed like home," he had said. Grace Tully said she was outraged at the thought. "I do not like it or even the thought of it," she told Mrs. Roosevelt she had responded. "And I believe the people of the country feel as I do." Death and thoughts of it were a sometime thing to the President. The day after Christmas, in 1937, he had addressed a note in pencil to his son James detailing his burial wishes. There was another on file with Basil O'Connor.

And his expressed wish to Grace Tully to be buried at sea. Mrs. Roosevelt said that, in the long ago, she and her husband had discussed death and both were opposed to embalming and both were opposed to lying in open caskets with people staring.

When Miss Tully left, Aunt Polly and Daisy came in to keep Eleanor company. Somewhere in the conversation, the explosion occurred. Laura Delano said that Lucy Mercer had been with Franklin. No one made a record of the conversation, except to whisper that it occurred. It was a vicious, cutting bit of news, totally unexpected by Eleanor. She made it shockingly plain that she would not have lived with Franklin if she had thought he had not kept his vow of 1918 never to see that woman again. The scene in the train was of such towering anger that Aunt Daisy refused to relate it to relatives; Aunt Polly referred to it in guilty whispers; Eleanor resolved that she would mention it to one living person—Anna. Polly's excuse was that "Eleanor would have found out anyway." Her story was that Eleanor must realize that it was no secret—Franklin met Lucy at the White House, went for automobile rides, even had dinner with Anna serving as hostess. The Cottons knew all about it; almost everyone who worked with Franklin knew that the President had lunch with Mrs. Rutherfurd when Mrs. Roosevelt was out of town. It wasn't as though Polly were telling something which everyone didn't know. When Franklin fainted, he was posing for a painting for Lucy.

The scene is lost to history. The wound was deep. The revelation, coming on the edge of sudden death, may have been too much for Mrs. Roosevelt to bear. Did she weep? Polly wouldn't say. Her defense was that someone was bound to tell. Even Alice Longworth was aware of it. Laura Delano may have thought that her manner of telling could lessen the shock. This is to be doubted. She was on Franklin's side of all family arguments; she was never an intimate of Eleanor. Daisy, with her incessant crocheting, was too secretive to do more than listen. She was another favorite cousin; she

was also Franklin's librarian. Grace Tully had been
a party to the long liaison. So had Steve Early, and
Dorothy Brady, Miss LeHand, Louise Hachmeister,
Bill Hassett, Jonathan Daniels, Pa Watson, Mike Reilly,
the Secret Service—many men in high places who never
discussed it. The person most concerned, the one who
had punished him by removing her intimate person
from his presence so many years before—she did not
know. Nor could tears of rage supplant tears of grief.

Much later, speaking to author Bernard Asbell, she
would recall this train ride and her feelings, but the
words would be veiled, as a lady might wish to remember them: "At a time like that, you don't really feel your
own feelings. When you're in a position of being caught
in a pageant, you become part of a world outside yourself
and you act almost like an automaton. You recede as
a person. You build a façade for everyone to see
and you live separately inside the façade. . . ."

The long train eased through the slums and shacks
outside Atlanta, the groups standing along the track
growing larger. Children playing in fenced yards stopped
to glance, to return to their games. At the station, train
crews in striped overalls and caps stepped down from
locomotives to watch the deadhead locomotive idle
through with the long string of coaches a minute behind it. Mayor William Hartsfield held a spray of
flowers. The important people of Atlanta were around
him and behind him. Police held others back from the
platform. Men sat on billboards overlooking the station.
Surface trolleys stopped. Passengers gawked down at
the tracks. The train stopped, emitting a long sigh. Arthur
Prettyman, wearing his Navy uniform, led Fala out on
the platform. Steve Early emerged to talk to the mayor.
The flowers were not for Mrs. Roosevelt. They were
to be placed on the casket. Early said they could be put
at the foot of the bier.

The railroad officials were busy. The two locomotives
were to be replaced; new crews were to take charge.
The cars had to be iced. There was a steady sound
of running feet, and the bumping of coupling links. The

mayor told Mrs. Roosevelt how he felt. She said, "I understand." Two big engines, hooked in tandem, backed into the cars. All the engineers were seniors, men with whitening hair, like C. E. Blackman, who was at the throttle of 1409. The crowd near the rear of the train could see the casket, the expressionless faces of young men in the service of their country. Some bystanders burst into tears. A few fell into fits of sobbing, and it seemed contagious. A reporter scribbled that it must have been like this in April 1865—exactly eighty years ago—when Mr. Lincoln's train made the long, slow journey to Springfield, Illinois. At 2:15 P.M. conductor F. K. Fry flagged his arm and stepped aboard. The train began to move again. It was going to be like this all day and all night. The people on the train stared moodily at the stricken faces which slid silently by the big windows.

Hassett spoke to Mrs. Roosevelt and returned to his compartment. He wrote: "Two hours or so after we were under way I sought Mrs. Roosevelt. I could say little. She was very gracious—expressed gratitude and appreciation of all the arrangements I had helped to make—very generous in her words and calm and composed." It must have been a difficult role for her to play. The expressions of condolence seemed to embarrass her; her response was to sympathize with the person expressing the words of grief. She could not bear to be the person to be pitied. And yet within a span of less than a day, she had lost her husband to eternity, and learned that he had been in love with another woman for at least twenty-seven years. The burden must have been crushing. Still she maintained the ladylike qualities she had been raised to cherish, and masked the emotions which boiled inside. She asked a porter to bring her knitting basket from the President's bedroom. Then she called Dorothy Brady and Grace Tully to sit with her. Aunt Polly came too—unbidden. The women chatted about a host of trivial topics. Mrs. Brady, young and attractive, worried that at any minute the casual question might arise, "Who was with Franklin when he died?" Neither Brady nor Tully knew how to answer, because they didn't know whether she knew or not. If she didn't know, they did not want to be the ones to tell; if she did know, their evasiveness could nail them to blatant lies. Eleanor spared them the question.

Both Houses of Congress convened at noon, and resolved "with profound regret and sorrow . . ." The House majority leader, the thin Bostonian John McCormack, stood to make a solitary statement: "President Roosevelt was one of the great men of all time, a builder of human values. He loved the people. He will go down in history as the savior of democracy throughout the world. I have lost a dear friend." Similar messages from all over the world were in a pile on Truman's desk. They came from Pius XII, Stalin, Churchill, Senator Arthur Vandenberg, Harriman, Eden, Mackenzie King, Princess Juliana of the Netherlands, the Lublin government, Eisenhower, Admiral Halsey, Bernard Law Montgomery, Vargas of Brazil, Thomas Dewey, the governments of Ireland, India, Italy, Mexico, Bolivia, Colombia, Australia, China—a geography of personages. Most of them followed the diplomatic pattern of citing the sorrow of the people at the passing of Franklin D. Roosevelt; generalizing his greatness and immortality in history; pledging friendship and cooperation to the government of Harry S. Truman.

Of them all, only Winston Churchill would regret an error of decision. At dawn, he had a long-range Lancaster warming up at Gatwick Airport. He was going to attend the funeral of his great friend. He sent a Top Secret to Ambassador Halifax asking if he would be welcome. The response was swift: Harry Hopkins was in Washington and thought it was a great idea; President Truman had been told of it *ex officio* and said he would welcome the chance of spending a day or two with the British Prime Minister after the funeral. There was much he wanted to know about Yalta. Churchill sustained a mental lapse which cannot be explained, and which he regretted for years. He fell into a personal argument with Anthony Eden about whether the Foreign Minister should also attend the funeral;

then he changed his mind and said Eden should go but the Prime Minister should not; at last, puffing with irritation, he penned a second message to Truman, opening: "I very much regret that it is impossible now for me to change my plans, which were approved by the King and the Cabinet this morning, and upon which all arrangements have been made for the conduct of the debates in Parliament next week, including my tribute to the late President on Tuesday. . . ." Later, the P.M. wrote: "In the after-light, I regret that I did not adopt the new President's suggestion. I had never met him . . . It seemed to me extraordinary, especially during the last few months, that Roosevelt had not made his deputy and potential successor acquainted with the whole story."

Harry Hopkins, pale, weak and candid, sat beside Truman's desk and dispensed with a discussion of their mutual great loss. He got into the complexities of the agreements and disagreements between the Soviet Union, the United States and Great Britain. He placed a call to Les Biffle, Secretary of the United States Senate, and asked him to round up the leaders of both Houses for an informal lunch with the President. Biffle wasn't sure he could find everybody. "Find them," Truman said. "And tell them I'll meet them in your office." "My office?" A President summons people; he seldom visits. "In your office at one o'clock." He hung up. On the rare occasions when a President goes to Capitol Hill, arrangements are made in advance, committees are selected to greet him and escort him; the Secret Service arrived to "sanitize" the area; ruffles and flourishes are *de rigueur*. The President astounded Congress by entering through an underground passage and walking alone, except for protective agents, directly to Biffle's office. He asked that some lunch trays be brought in.

Thirteen senators and four representatives sat, somewhat abashed in the presence of a man they had known as "Harry." The President said that he had a hell of a lot of work to do, and he must organize his priorities. The funeral, he said, would be held Sunday at Hyde Park. Nothing could be done publicly until after the fifteenth. He wanted to address a joint session on Monday, because that was priority number one. A few of the gentlemen thought the speech would be crowding the funeral. Truman disagreed; the transfer of power was smooth, but it was necessary for him to have a forum to express his ardent desire to pursue the Roosevelt policies. He wanted to make it plain and loud that there would be no changes whatever at home or abroad. He proposed to make that speech Monday. A congressman grinned and told Truman that he would come whether "we liked it or not." Truman nodded, but said he would prefer to come with the assent of both Houses.

He finished his lunch and he walked down the familiar corridors to the press room. The reporters stood. "Boys," the President said, standing close to the door, "if newspapermen ever pray, pray for me now. I don't know whether you fellows ever had a load of hay fall on you, but when they told me yesterday what had happened, I felt like the moon, the stars and all the planets had fallen on me. I've got the most terribly responsible job a man ever had." It sounded modest, but the reporters knew the stubborn determination of this man to make good at any post thrust upon him, whether it was county judge or President. The journalists knew him as one who always did his homework. He was stepping, blindfolded, into the shoes of a champion. He knew practically nothing of the Roosevelt commitments and plans; he wasn't even the Boss's choice for Vice President, but he did understand constitutional law and he had an appreciation of the separation of powers. There were areas of his new home, the White House, which Harry Truman had never seen, but he was considered to be an expert on how to work with both Houses of Congress, So he chose, this once, to visit them rather than summon them. The leaders of both parties were pleased. Most of all, he needed a honeymoon period with Congress; they were ready for the unexpected marriage. He left the press room and returned to the White House.

On his desk were two sheets from the Secretary of

State. These spelled out the official position of the United
States in foreign affairs. President Truman polished his
glasses, placed his elbows on the desk and digested the
document which, he told Byrnes, spawned more fresh
questions than it answered:

UNITED KINGDOM: *Mr. Churchill's policy is based fundamentally upon cooperation with the United States. It is
based secondarily on maintaining the unity of the three great
powers but the British government has been showing increasing apprehension of Russia and her intentions.
Churchill fully shares this government's interpretation of
the Yalta Agreements on Eastern Europe and liberated
areas. He is inclined, however, to press this position with
the Russians with what we consider unnecessary rigidity
as to detail . . .*

If this was Churchill's crime, it was also Roosevelt's.
There was more—Britain's consciousness that she was
no longer a first-class power; her desire to dominate
western Europe while permitting the Russian Bear to
masticate eastern Europe.

FRANCE: *The best interests of the United States require
that every effort be made by this government to assist
France, morally as well as physically, to regain her strength
and influence. It is recognized that the French people are
at present unduly preoccupied, as a result of the military
defeat of 1940 and the subsequent occupation of their country by the enemy, with questions of national prestige. They
have consequently from time to time put forward requests
which are out of all proportion to their present strength and
have in certain cases, notably in connection with Indo-
China, showed unreasonable suspicions of American aims
and motives . . . Positive American contributions toward
the rebuilding of France include: present and future rearm-
ing of the French Army; support of French participation
in the European Advisory Commission; the control and
occupation of Germany; the Reparations Commission and*

other organizations; and the conclusion of a Lend-Lease Agreement.

SOVIET UNION: *Since the Yalta Conference the Soviet Union has taken a firm and uncompromising position on nearly every major question that has arisen in our relations. The more important of these are the Polish question, the application of the Crimea Agreement on liberated areas, the agreement on the exchange of liberated prisoners of war and civilians; and the San Francisco Conference. In the liberated areas under Soviet control, the Soviet Government is proceeding largely on a unilateral basis and does not agree that the developments which have taken place justify application of the Crimea Agreement. Permission for our contact teams to go into Poland to assist in the evacuation of liberated prisoners of war has been refused although in general our prisoners have been reasonably well treated by Soviet standards. The Soviet Government appears to desire to proceed with the San Francisco Conference but is unwilling to send their Foreign Minister. They have asked for a large postwar credit and, pending a decision on this matter, have so far been unwilling to conclude an agreement for the orderly liquidation of Lend-Lease aid. In the politico-military field, similar difficulties have been encountered in collaboration with the Soviet authorities.*

POLAND: *The present situation relating to Poland is highly unsatisfactory with the Soviet authorities consistently sabotaging Ambassador Harriman's efforts in the Moscow Commission to hasten the implementation of the decisions at the Crimea Conference. Direct appeals to Marshal Stalin have not yet produced any worthwhile results. The Soviet Government likewise seeks to complicate the problem by initiating and supporting claims of the Warsaw Provisional Polish Government to represent and speak for Poland in international matters such as the San Francisco Conference, reparations and territorial questions. Because of its effect on our relations with the Soviet Union and other United Nations and upon public opinion in this country, the question of the future status of Poland and its government remains one of our most complex and urgent problems both in the international and the domestic field.*

The report continued, in misty specifics, to cover the "Balkan Area," where Hungary, Yugoslavia, Bulgaria and Romania were in the grip of Soviet forces, democratic elements in those areas driven into hiding, and Communist-inspired governments flowering and flourishing. United States protests were: (1) unanswered; (2) denied. The problem of what to do with Germany was dispensed in one long sentence:

> . . . *destruction of National Socialist organizations and influence, punishment of war criminals, disbandment of the German military establishment; military government administered with a view to political decentralization, reparation from existing wealth and future production, prevention of the manufacture of arms and destruction of all specialized facilities for their production, and controls over the German economy to secure these objectives.*

Austria would be disengaged from Germany and become an independent nation. Italy was a political janissary; a defeated Axis partner now a "co-belligerent" against Germany. "We have been unable to end the anomaly of Italy's dual status as active co-belligerent and as a defeated enemy." An extra paragraph was added dealing with SUPPLIES FOR LIBERATED AREAS. Without mentioning countries, the State Department asserted that some were facing "chaos and collapse," then, with commendable subtlety, warned that "political stability and the maintenance of democratic governments which can withstand the pressures of extremist groups depend on the restoration of a minimum of economic stability . . . It is essential that we organize ourselves at once to meet this problem. The Department is prepared to play its full role in this matter."

The new President was less than candid regarding his respect for the State Department. As he was jamming this report in his briefcase, he extended a warm welcoming hand to Jimmy Byrnes. Both were consummate politicians. Truman asked Byrnes to tell him *everything* he recalled about Yalta. The Justice complied. He recalled

facets of the meetings at random; the President asked
questions. A half hour later, Truman nodded. He now
understood something of Yalta. He told Byrnes he knew
that no official minutes had been made of the conference,
but he had heard Byrnes made his personal stenographic
notes. "I want them," he said. The Justice said it would
require time to transcribe them. Truman asked Byrnes
to do the work as soon as possible. One more thing
was on the President's mind: he asked Jimmy Byrnes
to consider becoming the new Secretary of State. It
was an impressive offer, although it could hardly be
expected to overwhelm a man who thought he would
have made a better President of the United States. Harry
was still the "junior" who had promised to place Byrnes's
name in nomination for the Vice Presidency. Like some
Southern politicians, Jimmy Byrnes had a longer memory
for an affront than for a fact. And yet, Byrnes appreciated
that, less than twenty-four hours after the death of Roosevelt—the man who had casually permitted him to retire
—he was offered a high and powerful post in government.

As Byrnes departed, promising to think about the
offer and above all to keep it confidential, Truman, vis
à vis Roosevelt, was still energetic. He asked the stenographic pool to bring some mail in. He signed a few
documents. At 3:30 Stettinius had returned, this time
with Chip Bohlen. The Secretary of State was bracing
himself for questions with the presence of Bohlen, the
department's expert on Russia. Briskly, the President
asked the same questions he had asked of Byrnes. What
about Yalta? What about Poland? Stettinius brought
with him the Top Secret messages between Roosevelt
and Stalin, and Roosevelt and Churchill. Truman
scanned them chronologically, as the two men sat staring
at the pale scars of pictures removed from the walls.
From the notes, Truman drew one accurate conclusion
and one inaccurate. Russia, the President noted, "was
imposing her will on smaller nations around her." And
"because of the activities of the anti-Communist Poles,
both in Poland and abroad, what we actually face in

Poland is not merely a political situation but one that *seriously threatens civil war*. This had been clear, I now learned, even at the time Roosevelt, Churchill and Stalin met at Yalta." It is impossible to discover who, or what set of documents, gave him the second impression. With Russian armies and army rest camps all over Poland, there was no threat of civil war or an uprising. Poland was as tractable under the Russian heel as Austria had been under the German.

A long message was composed, revised, and sent to Churchill suggesting that he not discuss the Polish problem in public, and that another joint message be sent to Stalin offering to reestablish the Polish provisional government with more Lublin Poles than London Poles, and with the Soviets being granted the opportunity to select and name one member of the new Polish government. Stettinius and Bohlen must have seen it for what it was—another palliative which would be declined by the Kremlin. Truman was also in favor of explaining, point by point, the charges of the Russian government that the British and American ambassadors in Moscow were responsible for the future of the Yalta agreement. It is remarkable that Stettinius and Bohlen did not tell the President that neither of his notions would be productive.

The President was reading reports when he turned his chair around to look out of the big French windows to the south grounds. It was dark. He hadn't realized the time. In the new job, no one would have the temerity to suggest that he quit and go home. He looked at his watch. It was after seven. As he wrote later, he wondered—not at the number of people he had seen in one day—but that "I did more reading than I ever thought I could. . . . I was weary."

The train was a tired thing clicking tediously across the bridge below Lake Keowee. What was left of the sun was behind Persimmon Mountain. Many of the people aboard were having dinner when the cars pulled into the station at Greenville, South Carolina. One of the reporters clocked it as it stopped and computed that it had averaged 24.5 miles per hour since it left Warm Springs. There was a big crowd at the station, and to those inside it seemed strange to see nothing but worrisome expressions outside the window, whereas, on many other occasions, there had been wreathy grins and applause. The faces at crossings, on bridges, leaning from overhead walks, on tracks and station platforms seemed never-ending. At one small-town stop, a group of uniformed Boy Scouts stood to attention near the rear car and sang "Onward Christian Soldiers." If Mrs. Rutherfurd had to say good-bye, Greenville would have been the place. There is no record, no voice to testify that she did, and the chances are that she would have been afraid of being seen and identified. It would have been a 100-mile run up 19 to Route 25 to get there. Of necessity, she would have buried herself in the crowd toward the rear of the platform. Then she would see only a huge oblong glass, a well-lighted lounge, some soldiers and sailors standing at corners of the casket, and a slightly wrinkled American flag. It is almost certain that, if she wanted that last long look, that silent farewell, her daughter Barbara would have dissuaded her. Or perhaps Father Smith. Anyone could have reminded Lucy that it would be better to remember the last look he turned in her direction, just before the frown and the hand embracing both temples. Much better to conjure that vision than this one.

Within fifteen minutes the train was slipping out of the station. Night had fallen and the two locomotives throbbed and pulsed as they got the right-of-way and firemen confirmed the signals engineers looked for: "Green over green!" Fifty minutes later, it stopped at Hayne, South Carolina. In the *Ferdinand Magellan* a great and unusual fatigue overcame the indomitable frame of Eleanor Roosevelt. She ate dinner and asked to have the President's bed prepared. Polly and Daisy would have sat with her, but Mrs. Roosevelt wanted to be alone. If she hoped to sleep, to forget for a few hours, she could not court unconsciousness. Whatever

grave thoughts there were to think, they prodded her
awake. So, as she told Anna, she extinguished all the
lights in the room, lowered the window shade halfway,
leaned on an elbow, and looked out into the night. There
was a big crowd waiting at Charlotte, North Carolina.
In dim silhouette behind the shade, she saw the faces
on the brightly lighted station; she heard the hoarse
shouts of conductors and the mournful whistles of donkey engines in the yard. Then the train moved again,
creaking at first, and the young buds on brave saplings
trembled in the night as the train split the air to make up
time for Salisbury, North Carolina, and on to Danville,
Virginia. She stared out that window, a woman alone.
What she thought about, how much she saw, she would
not reveal. If she roused from the reverie, it was probably to marvel that, in the late hours, farmers and their
families waited at the crossings, hats over hearts, to
watch a train fly by.

At some point, Mrs. Roosevelt was overtaken by
sleep. She would not remember what hour, or what place.
Somewhere along the right-of-way, the big drivers clanked
as they slowed. Inch by inch, the forward locomotive
pulled up to a swinging water pipe. Then the train
stopped. It was down between two cliffs of farmland. Far
below, the lighted cars looked like fireflies. A fireman
stood on the tender with a long iron hook. He swung the
pipe over and turned the gushing water on. The night sky
was spangled with stars. The engines stood panting.
Unseen, the face of a black man appeared on top of
one of the cliffs. Soon, he was back with other faces,
sleepy faces. They had not been able to vote for Roosevelt, but they felt he was their father, too. A deep
voice began to sing the sad sweet notes of "Hand Me
Down My Walkin' Cane." Other voices, some shrill,
picked up the words. At the cliff on the opposite side,
dark faces appeared. They too disappeared and ran back
to the shacks in the fields, awakening the very young
and the very old. They looked down and saw the beautiful train and heard the breathing of engines which
had come a long way. They saw the brightly lit last car,

and the flag. They too picked up the song coming from the opposite cliff. They thought they were in time with it, but the sound required part of a second to traverse the space between. The firemen shut the water down, swung the pipe away, and wondered why the Negroes did not sing together. The train inched forward until the second locomotive was in position.

The pipe returned, gushing clear cold water into the hot tender. The people so high above sang another chorus of "Hand Me Down My Walkin' Cane." Oh, how he would have loved that. For almost a quarter of a century he had fought to reach the stage where he would require no assistance other than a walkin' cane. He never made it. In some instinctive divination, the singers were hoping that he had made it now. The pipe was slammed away a second time. The throttles opened. There was a roar of sound, and showers of sparks climbed in the night. Those who would work the fields tomorrow had seen enough tonight.

The upstairs corridors of the White House were quiet on this Saturday morning of April 14, 1945. No ushers, no maids walked the polished floors with breakfast trays. The Roosevelt clan had been gathering, and Anna had been assigning rooms for late arrivals. James's wife arrived a little after midnight. So did Elliott's wife, the actress Faye Emerson. Then Mrs. John Roosevelt was announced, and at 2:05 A.M. Mrs. Franklin Roosevelt, Jr., was in. Small chintzy rooms had been assigned. There was time to chat, to rediscover the sadness of the occasion, to hope that he had departed without pain, to speak of children and husbands who were far away. At 3:15 A.M. General Elliott Roosevelt checked in, debonair in his uniform, grim of expression. Of the sons, he had made it in time. James was halfway across the Pacific, sleeping in an Air Transport Command plane.

They slept late. This too was its own anesthetic. They would not be interested to know that this was the prettiest day the Virginia countryside had seen in a long time. Washington looked whiter in the warm, sparkling air.

Azaleas and lilacs and rhododendron lifted suede faces of several colors all the way down through the Potomac Valley in the fields. The few clouds were dollops of snow. The breeze was so timid that it barely lifted the banner from its half-staff position on top of the White House. Even the old bronze equestrian statues in the parks captured the brass of sun on horses' flanks. It was not an ordinarily nice day. It was special in its beauty, as though nature was dressing to go to church.

Mr. Truman was at his apartment, carving sturdy phrases as he worked over his speech to Congress. The hour was too early, even for him. The weakness of the strong man is that he courts exhaustion. There were good speech writers in the Executive Branch. As he said later, thoughts of Roosevelt walked unbidden on his thinking and he felt the deep, engulfing sorrow of losing a President. But Truman was a practical man and a practical man seldom debates the immutability of death. It is the flame-out of a star; the crash of a wave on sandy shore, to recede forever under other waves; the melting of a flake of snow as it lights on a running brook.

The President was at his desk at 8:05 A.M. On it reposed a foot-high sheaf of telegrams and departmental communications. Truman began to tear through them impatiently. He was dismayed to learn that his job consisted of a great deal of paper work. Unlike Roosevelt, he was a good reader and was blessed with a good memory. Like Roosevelt, the new President was fundamentally a people-meeter. He preferred to sit with experts, discuss a problem and get to the point, rather than read the carefully couched sentences with their interjectory clauses.

The President asked that the Secretary of the Treasury be sent in. Henry Morgenthau looked forward to this interview because, as he explained to his assistants, he wanted to size up the new President. He planned to ask Truman a number of questions about policy—foreign and domestic—literally to assess a stranger. Morgenthau, somewhat remote, sat before the little man from Missouri with the ease of a person conscious of his superior knowledge and his seniority. He was stunned when Truman said that he did not want to take up the Secretary's time; he wanted a comprehensive report of America's financial situation as soon as possible. Truman was not on trial; Morgenthau was.

The Secretary of the Treasury was hardly out of the chair when the President asked Simmons to "send in Mr. Byrnes and Mr. Wallace." As they chatted, they represented a most unusual trio: Byrnes, who thought he *should* have been President of the United States; Wallace, who *could* have become President; Truman, who *was* President. If there was any uneasiness, it was concealed. Mrs. Truman and Margaret, the President said, would accompany him on the train to Hyde Park "tonight." The ladies had a great deal to do. He would be obliged if Byrnes and Wallace would ride with him to the train this morning and accompany Roosevelt's body back to the White House. The men glanced at each other, and agreed. Mr. Truman had accomplished a minor miracle. In the Sunday newspapers, he was going to be seen in an open car riding with his two principal rivals; the question of party unity with the new, almost unknown President would be dramatized by a news photograph.

At Bealeton, Virginia, the train moved more slowly. C. R. Yowell, engineer of the first locomotive, saw that the switches were turned, so he pulled the long train onto a siding. Forty-five miles ahead was Union Station, Washington. He and H. D. Hansborough, his fireman, glanced at their watches. It was 8:15 A.M. If the schedule was right, a Washington express called "Number 48" should pass in five minutes. Mr. Yowell had the most sensitive part of the long journey, the final leg. For years, POTUS had been taken out into the Washington Yards, then backed down to the Printing and Engraving Platform at Fourteenth Street. Today, he would take it out into the yards, then back down carefully, slowly, probably on track one, into Union Station. A wooden ramp had been built for the removal of the casket in the last car. Yowell, at the head of the long train, would depend upon Trainmaster J. W. Shelton to signal him to the exact foot, so that the big window would stop directly over that ramp.

Number 48 roared past the standing train as the mourners aboard finished breakfast and packing. Hassett was in the communications car. A message had come in from Edith Helm at the White House asking what Mrs. Roosevelt's wishes were regarding hymns at the afternoon service. She didn't take long to dwell on it. She told Bill Hassett to radio a response that she would like "Eternal Father, Strong to Save" and "Faith of Our Fathers." Also, she said, she wanted to have an inscription added to the headstone at Hyde Park: "The only thing we have to fear is fear itself"—the words of her husband at his first inaugural. The train was back on the main line at 8:27, moving slowly toward Manassas. It was woodland, green dells, small streams hurrying to help the Rappahannock, dogwood dropping petals like a flower girl at a wedding, and always the neat, terraced farms with bursting barns and faded Bull Durham signs.

The train loafed onward to the broad basin of the Potomac, and across to Washington, the wheels creating a roaring sound inside the cars as the shiny green Pullmans brought the hero to the bastion of his triumphs. Those inside looked out the window at the familiar sights. None of them, including the widow, realized that the nation was in mourning. In their intimate knowledge of the man, they too sorrowed but, in less than two days, they had learned to live with it. It did not occur to Hassett or McIntire or Mrs. Roosevelt or Aunt Polly or Grace Tully or Dorothy Brady or Arthur Prettyman that, as on another April 14 a long time ago, scores of millions of people had a compelling desire to see him, to touch him, to say thank you. No one on the train knew that thousands of small shops, movies and restaurants had been closed. No one knew that some newspapers refused advertising until after the funeral; that radio sta-

tions from coast to coast were talking of little else except
the death of the President, filling the time between talks
with Brahms and Beethoven, music they never played.
All the mourners knew was that there was to be a fitting
observance—a parade to the White House, suitable honors
for the dead chieftain and a train tonight to Hyde Park.
There would also be a period of mourning. They knew
these things, but they did not feel the intense bereavement
of the whole land, even though they had seen farmers
in the fields of Georgia and South Carolina drop the reins
of mules and kneel on furrows.

At 9:40 A.M. the train had stopped in the yards near
Virginia Avenue. The yardmaster had ordered "red over
red" signals for all other traffic. Even the donkey engines
waited on sidings. The signal came back slowly into the
station. Yowell moved it at a walk, the springs creaking
as the eleven cars moved down track number one. A flagman was on the lower step of the *Conneaught* waving
his free arm slowly ahead. The platform, he saw, was
full of fashionable people. Any man with a knowledge
of faces would recognize the entire Supreme Court, the
members of the Cabinet, the Roosevelt family, President
Truman, the fifteen appointed congressmen and the fifteen appointed senators. At 9:50 the coupling hoses at
the rear of the *Conneaught* were close to the big bumper.
The flagman held his arm straight out. The train stopped.
He shoved some Secret Service man aside to jump off
and ascertain if that big window was abreast of the heavy
wooden ramp. It was. He stood on his toes and waved
his lantern. The whole train sighed. Capital police cleared
a way for Anna Roosevelt. She was with her husband,
Colonel John Boettiger. Anna looked pale in black, pale
and older. Behind her were General and Mrs. Elliott
Roosevelt and Franklin's wife and John's wife. None
of them approached the *Ferdinand Magellan,* where
Eleanor Roosevelt waited in the lounge. They climbed
to where the casket was, where the military guards stood
straight and still. They were followed by an old family
friend, Major Harry Hooker, Mrs. Roosevelt's secretary,
Miss Malvina Thompson, and Edith Helm.

All of them could be seen from the platform, pausing to look down at the casket. One or two wept. They saw Arthur Prettyman. He led them through the car into the *Ferdinand Magellan*. Behind them came Harry Truman with Byrnes and Wallace. The President explained why Mrs. Truman and Margaret were not at the train. Eleanor was gracious. She had an especially warm handshake for Henry Wallace. To those who remained at her side, Mrs. Roosevelt radiated an aura of sympathy toward those who were trying to commiserate with her. She was, as always, bigger than her personal sorrows. Some of the visitors sobbed. The widow added to her small smile, her ladylike phrasing, timid pats on the shoulder. She was embarrassed. This was going to be an ordeal.

Smartly uniformed soldiers and sailors stood high on the ramp after the train window had been removed. The casket emerged slowly. Men standing on the platform lifted their hats and held them. Again, the strong young men managed to hold the casket level, and carry it to a black caisson. The elite unit of Fort Myer, in white gloves and braided fourragères, snapped the big straps tight across the casket and the flag. Three pairs of white horses led the caisson into the sunshine. An extra white horse served as guidon. Between the railroad station and the White House, 350,000 mourners lined the curbs. In the gutter, spaced at six-foot intervals, stood soldiers at stiff attention. At a signal, sixteen motorcycle policemen in a phalanx from curb to curb moved off slowly up Delaware Avenue. Behind them marched ranking officers of the branches of military service; then a company of armored troop carriers rattling their steel treads on the pavement like chains. The United States Marine Band struck up Chopin's "Funeral March." An arm-snapping battalion of Annapolis midshipmen walked behind; motorized infantry in huge trucks which hugged all the space between curbs followed. A full complement of Women's Army Corps marched; so did a company of WAVES, followed by the United States Navy Band, and women Marines.

There was a space in the line of march. Three riders

urged the six horses forward. A hoarse military command could be heard. Somewhere in the distance, three field guns started firing their slow salvo salute and leaves on the poplar trees shuddered. Fourteen motorcycle policemen inched their vehicles beside the caisson, as though the dead President needed extra guarding. An officer marched behind the casket. Behind him, two flagbearers bore the American flag and the presidential standard. Then came the black limousines moving noiselessly between the tremendous crowd. There was a strangeness, an eerie quality. All these people, often seven deep on both sides of the street, and no sound. It was so quiet that the clopping of hooves and the distant thunder of guns were the only sounds. Suddenly, frighteningly, twenty-four huge bombers roared low over the buildings up the line of march and past the White House. At windows and on rooftops, radio commentators described the melancholy scene as it came into view, each saying essentially the same things; each one seeing someone—often a black woman—crouching behind a soldier in tears, waving good-bye with a handkerchief.

If the parade was designed to rend a nation's heart, it was done well. The clank of the caisson wheels as they crossed the trolley tracks was loud. The parade was two miles long from start to finish, but it required one hour and twenty minutes to pass a given point. A squadron of P-51 planes tore the blue sky with speed and executed a slow roll over the cortege. The military bands played dirges and a man in a window of the old Post Office Building said, "It's too sad for tears," and turned away. Those in distant cities, on farms, in factories and shops stood close to radios, listening.

At the top of Fifteenth Street the caisson turned left. The White House was in view. The oaks, the beeches and the elms were in sedate green. In the late morning sun the white building seldom seemed more blinding in its beauty. The man who had resided there longest—twelve years, one month, eight days—had returned for a few hours. He would rest here, and then go home, and this was strange because he had said he could get no rest in

the White House—for surcease he had to go to Hyde
Park or Warm Springs. The military parade with its contingents kept marching past the Executive Mansion.
Somewhere a band was playing "Onward Christian Soldiers." Opposite the White House a huge crowd stood
with bared heads in Lafayette Park, watching. When the
white horses reached the northwest gate, they turned in.
The cars containing the family and close friends followed. "Thank you," "Thank you," Mrs. Roosevelt
whispered as bereaved ushers assisted her and her family to the gravel driveway. Another squadron of
bombers roared low over the White House. The normally busy gray squirrels seemed frozen halfway up the
trunks of trees. Master Sergeant J. Bowder, barking
commands to eight husky noncommissioned officers,
watched them unsnap the great straps on the caisson.
Anna and Mrs. Roosevelt stood with Grace Tully near
the bottom step of the portico as the men drew the casket toward them, lifted and grunted in unison and
filed slowly past.

Inside, Gawler's had erected a bier and covered it with
rugs. It was placed, peculiarly, not in the center of the
great East Room under the crystal chandelier, but close
to the east wall, near the Stuart portrait of George
Washington. Red runner rugs had been placed from the
front door through the foyer into the big room. This was
one duty the U.S. Army did not share with other services.
Bowder's soldiers carried the heavy casket slowly, toe
and heel, along the runner, into the room, across the
parquet floor and, showing no strain, set it gently on the
bier. No one said. "In this room exactly eleven weeks
ago, this man knelt in prayer to ask God's help as he
began his fourth term of office." Nor did anyone say,
"This man's booming laughter rang in every room and
corridor of this building. Strange, I hear no echo." No.
Whatever was said was whispered. Mrs. Roosevelt was
surprised to see half the east wall around the casket
banked with flowers, dominated by lilies. She had asked
his friends to please omit flowers. Her attention was dis-
tracted as four military guards, representing the branches

of services, marched into the room with rifles, took their place on command at the four corners of the casket, and thumped the stocks to the floor.

Sadly, silently, Dorothy Brady walked to the Oval Office and looked in. It was empty. She stepped inside timidly. Mrs. Brady didn't want to disturb anyone, but the haste with which a great President was being hurried offstage seemed indecent. All of her young and good years had been spent here, between the secretarial office and the big Oval Office. She felt disturbed, almost resentful. At Union Station, as she and Grace Tully stepped off the train, a young Secret Service agent had stopped them and asked for identification. They knew the whole White House detail—knew their families, in fact—and overnight they who had labored far into the night hours at the side of the President were asked, "Identification, please." She looked around the office. She nodded. Then she opened the desk drawers. It did not hurt to know that his desk had been emptied, but she was offended to see that Roosevelt's prized John Paul Jones painting was off the wall. She rubbed her arms. There was a chill in the office.

Dorothy Brady was back in the mansion when President Truman walked into the office with Harry Hopkins. The President had a lot of faith in politicians. He believed they would tell him the truth succinctly—bitter and sweet. A long time ago, the man behind the desk had been presiding judge in Jackson County, Missouri, and had worked closely with the Federal Works Progress Administration. The head of it, in Washington, was Harry Hopkins. This time, the President was the supplicant; he wanted to know so much of what FDR thought of this situation and that, how he regarded Churchill and Stalin and Eisenhower and Nimitz and Wallace and scores of others. He had no time for the niceties. Neither did Hopkins.

The two Harrys sat. The President said, "How do you feel?" "Terrible." "I hope you don't mind my calling on you again, but I need to know everything you can tell me about our relations with Russia—all you know about Stalin and Churchill and the conferences at Cairo, Casablanca, Teheran and Yalta." The dying man crossed his skinny shanks and pulled his lower lip away from his teeth in a lopsided grin. "One reason I'm glad to be here and glad to offer all the assistance I can is because I'm confident that you will continue to carry out the policies of Franklin Roosevelt. And I know that you know how to carry them out." The President fired the questions. The responses were candid. The President ordered two lunch trays. The men barely disturbed the food. "Stalin is a forthright, rough, tough Russian. He is a Russian partisan through and through, thinking always first of Russia. But he can be talked to frankly." "Roosevelt and Churchill have had a strong influence on each other in world affairs." "Did you know I plan to retire from the government on May twelfth?"

Truman hoped not. He realized that, in dealing with Hopkins, one had to begin by stating, "If your health permits . . ." He asked Harry Hopkins to stay, but the frail and fading friend and counselor to FDR did not respond to the entreaty. Rather, he preferred to open his warehouse of confidential information now—in a two-hour talk. The President, who was forced to beg for information in both domestic and foreign affairs, did not seem to be frightened by his lack of knowledge; he was gobbling successive "briefings" by Hopkins, Stettinius, Stimson, Bohlen, Leahy, McCormack—anyone who held a key to a presidential problem. There was, as he put it, "a whole world going on outside this office" and he was determined to learn as much as possible as quickly as possible.

There was indeed a "world going on." Nor would it slow its spin to accommodate the new man. Events great and small were occurring with tremendous acceleration as the war in Europe drew to a close. Yesterday, Vienna had fallen. In the map room arrowheads were drawn to show Allied armies curving across the heartland of Germany with such speed that the Russians, the Americans and the British must meet within a week, cutting the Reich into pockets of resistance. The suspicion of the Russians, that Hitler would, at the end, draw divisions away from Eisenhower's front to contain the Soviets, was true. A message was in from Churchill stating that Allied armies from east and west would meet at any time, and would President Truman like to join him in broadcasting a triumphant message with Marshal Stalin? Truman responded at once that he would be willing to study a draft of such a message, "if Stalin agrees." A second message from the Prime Minister asked Truman to postpone the use of pilotless bombers, loaded with explosives, against the Germans. London had survived the V-1 and V-2 terror bombings, but he was hesitant about giving the Germans an excuse to start a third wave of senseless slaughter. The President phoned General Marshall, asked a few questions and advised Churchill that he agreed such bombing should be discontinued.

A major general of the Third Army advised General George S. Patton that he was no longer certain "where the front is." The Third and Ninth armies had been racing against diminishing opposition, in addition to coping with disorganized German troops from the Russian front who turned to surrender to Americans. The line of formal resistance was vague. This was also true of Montgomery's British and Canadians in the north, and Americans Simpson and Hodges in the center. At sea, U-boats were still sinking merchantmen as they operated in wolf packs in the Far East the big island of Okinawa was proving to be the most costly victory in American history. Matt Connolly advised the President that there were only eleven days left before the United Nations would meet in San Francisco. He also had to find out how many of the "Roosevelt people," if any, would be willing to continue their work—the Hassetts, Daniels, Earlys, Tullys, Bradys, even Mike Reilly, who could ask for a transfer.

On the second floor, Mrs. Roosevelt spent time having lunch and going over funeral plans. One of her strong wishes was that none of the grandchildren should be present at the White House or at Hyde Park. She insisted that she and her husband shared an old-fashioned belief that they would like to be remembered as they were in

life, not in the stiff, shocking rigidity of death. To the
daughters-in-law who were present, Eleanor Roosevelt
seemed older, more remote, one who walked clumpily.
She was reminded, at one point, that she had something
special to do. She excused herself and said she would
return in a few minutes. In the East Room a Secret Service agent saw her in the doorway near the casket. Mrs.
Roosevelt held a few small flowers. Two hundred chairs
had been set up in rows, facing the bier. A few members
of the White House staff were on their knees. A Gawler
man talked to Mrs. Roosevelt, then he led her to the
casket and opened both the metal and the glass lid. She
gazed down at her husband, shook her head sorrowfully,
and placed the few flowers where his hands were composed. Then she whispered to the funeral director. As
she left, two men sealed the lid forever.

Gawler, in his office on Wisconsin Avenue, phoned
Mrs. Ralph Worden in Hyde Park to tell her that there
was no further work to be done. The sealant had been
applied. Mrs. Worden wondered why the Roosevelt
family had not asked for a burial permit. She pointed
out that it would require a special permit for the President
to be buried on the estate. This could be granted only
by the selectmen of the village, and they would not meet
for a week. Mr. Gawler was alarmed. He said he hoped
that no one would try to stop the interment, but he
begged Mrs. Worden to see if she could obtain the permit
tonight or, at the latest, in the morning. Mrs. Worden
thought that she and her manager, Henry Page, could
try to round up the selectmen at their homes. It would
be a violation of law to bury the President in the Rose
Garden without the permit.

The funeral director decided not to alarm Mrs. Roosevelt with the news. At Hyde Park, the grave had already
been dug at the prescribed place and was covered with
a matting of false grass. Death, in any family, spawns
problems and enigmas. Had Mrs. Roosevelt thought to
open the small safe in the President's bedroom, she would
have found the burial wishes he had addressed, in pencil,

to James. It was to be used, the President wrote, only
if he died in office. His wishes were:

1: ". . . a service of utmost simplicity in the East Room
of the White House.

2: "No lying in state anywhere."

3: That the Army bring his body to the Capitol for
a "simple service" in the rotunda for the Congress, the Ju-
*diciary, and the Diplomatic Corps. He asked a twenty-min-
ute service with two hymns, "no speaking."*

4: A funeral train to leave for Hyde Park at "1 P.M. ar-
*riving there at 8 P.M." That the Navy have charge of this
part of the burial.*

5: A simple service in St. James's Church be held at
once "for old neighbors."

6: "The casket be taken from the church to the house and
placed in front of the East fireplace in the big room for
the night."

7: That burial occur the next morning where "the sun
dial stands in the garden" and the casket be carried by men
who work on the nearby estates.

8: "That a gun carriage, not a hearse, be used throughout."

9. That the casket be of absolute simplicity, "dark wood,
that the body be not embalmed or hermetically sealed." In
addition, FDR asked for a white marble stone to be used
as a marker. "It is my hope," he wrote, "that my dear wife
will on her death be buried there also, and that the monument contain no device or inscription except the following . . .

FRANKLIN DELANO ROOSEVELT
1882–19—
ANNA ELEANOR ROOSEVELT
1884–19—"

Mrs. Roosevelt did not think of looking in the bedroom
safe. In the morning, someone else (unidentified) would
open it and give the envelope to Eleanor. She had a right
to open it, but wouldn't, because it was addressed: "To
James Roosevelt—Burial Instructions." Nor did the widow

wonder how much money was left in the estate, or to
whom it would go. In time, she would learn that all of
it had been left to her and that, on her death, it was to
be given to the five children. The gross estate was
$1,940,999, in addition to insurance policies totaling
$562,142, with the Warm Springs Foundation as bene-
ficiary. Of the almost $2 million, $920,115 had been
left to FDR by his mother, and he had not spent a penny
of it. A small income was assured for Missy LeHand,
but she died before he did. Investments ranged from 800
shares of General Electric down to 1 share of Safeway
Stores. Listed among the President's liabilities were bills
for $8.88 owed to a Hyde Park pharmacist for news-
papers; $48.53 to a Hyde Park bakery; a telephone
bill of $44.86; $786.07 owed to workers on the
estate; $46.20 which Mrs. Roosevelt had itemized as
expenses at Campobello; $72.96 to a stamp collector
in England; $368.58 for books.

The White House services were to begin at 4:00 P.M.
A half hour early, the Blue Room was filled with distinguished guests and their wives. The high bald head
of James A. Farley could be seen in a corner. Later, he
said that he had peeked toward the East Room and had
seen one of the President's armless wheelchairs. Although
the two men had been political enemies for five years,
Farley said he was obsessed by the thought that the
wheelchair had shackled the wasted body, but that the
mind of the man had been in soaring flight through a
dark day in history. Thomas Dewey was there. So was
Mrs. Woodrow Wilson and members of former Roosevelt
cabinets. There was Crown Princess Martha of Norway,
on whom the President had often honed his charm. There
were more ranking military officers than anyone remembered seeing in one place. And members of the Supreme
Court, in addition to a delegation from both Houses of
Congress. There were personal friends, such as Harry
Hopkins and Louise Hopkins. And Anthony Eden, Andrei Gromyko, Harold Stassen, and President Osmeña
of the Philippines. There were many ambassadors.

White House ushers guided the guests to their chairs.

The room seemed hot, the smell of flowers was over-powering. When all had been seated, some had to stand. A group of men remained in the doorway of the Blue Room. under a loudspeaker. Others, including stenographers, stood in the east doorway near the casket. Except for a cough here and there the room was quiet. At five minutes of four, President Truman, holding his wife at one elbow and his daughter at the other, entered the room and sat in the front row left. No one, it seemed, remembered that it is proper to rise when the President of the United States enters a room. Nor did Truman notice. Two minutes later, Mrs. Roosevelt entered the room and there was a noisy shuffle as everyone got to his feet. Elliott placed her in the aisle chair. Anna sat next to her mother. Two chairs away, Elliott sat with his wife. The daughters-in-law used the remainder of the row of chairs.

It was one minute of four when three cassocked and white-surpliced figures strode into the room and stood, hands clasped, before the casket. The one in the center was the Right Reverend Angus Dun, Bishop of the Episcopal Diocese of Washington. At his sides were the Reverends Magee and Wilkinson. They looked at the ranks of chairs solemnly. Bishop Dun said, "Eternal Father, Strong to Save." Behind the mourners, someone struck a chord on the concert grand piano. The mourners began to sing. Harry Hopkins, standing, leaning on the chair where Louise sat, looked angry. He burst into sobs and bent forward, clutching the chair. At this moment —4:00 P.M. Eastern War Time—the United States of America came to a two-minute halt. Telephone service stopped. Newspaper teletype machines tapped out in capital letters: SILENCE. New York subway trains came to a stop with sparks flying from brake shoes. Church bells tolled from Salem to Seattle; rabbis recited *kaddish* to minyans; all radio stations went silent. In Times Square some pedestrians fell to their knees. In great cities fire bells tolled brassy gongs for the dead. A commercial DC-3, landing at the New York airport, turned off the runway and stopped a half mile from the passenger terminal. In Pittsburgh, Chicago, Omaha, Dallas, Denver and San Francisco and all the small places between, a nation paused to meditate upon a man. In many cities, traffic lights turned orange and remained that way. In ships at sea, chaplains stood before off-duty work parties on the quarterdeck to say a prayer for a departed sailor; in Warm Springs, neighbors stood one by one in a hot, crowded hall to say, "I remember the time he . . ." Ocean liners at piers emitted the three blasts of recognition and salute. It was a time when the honored man, had he been able to witness it, would have lifted his big jaw, jutted his cigarette holder up, roared with laughter and shouted, "Don't you love it! Don't you just love it!"

"I am the resurrection and the life, saith the Lord: he that believeth in Me, though he were dead, yet shall he live . . ."

The mourners sang "Faith of Our Fathers." Afterward, the bishop looked down at the familiar faces, and began his prayer for the deceased: "Oh God of peace, who hast taught us in returning and rest we shall be saved . . . remember Thy servant, Franklin Delano, Oh Lord, according to the favor which Thou bearest unto Thy people." The room was stifling. The sobbing was contagious. "In his first inaugural address," the Bishop said, "the President bore testimony to his own deep faith: 'Let me assert my firm belief that the only thing we have to fear is fear itself.' As that was his first word to us, I am sure he would wish it to be his last; that as we go forward to the tasks in which he has led us, we shall go forward without fear of the future, without fear of our allies or of our friends, and without fear of our own insufficiency."

The service was simple. At 4:23 P.M. Mrs. Roosevelt stood slowly. The Bishop blessed Franklin Delano Roosevelt and blessed everyone in the room. She turned, as Elliott took her arm, and left. The family did not wait to say farewell to the guests. They went up the grand staircase alone. A few minutes later, they were met by President Truman and his family. Small, awkward talk was exchanged in the hall. Outside, the world was in bustling motion again, going where it had to go, doing

what it had to do. As the radios started their intelligible
noise, station WQXR in New York introduced William
R. Benét to read a memorial poem written by the late
Stephen Vincent Benét:

We remember, F.D.R.
We remember the bitter faces of the apple sellers
And their red cracked hands.
We remember the gray cold wind of '32
When the job stopped, and the bank stopped,
And the merry-go-round broke down,
And, finally,
Everything seemed to stop.
The whole big works of America,
Bogged down with a creeping panic,
And nobody knew how to fix it, while the wise guys sold
    the country short,
Till one man said (and we listened)
"The one thing we have to fear is fear."
Well, it's quite a long time since then and the wise guys
    may not remember.
But we do, F.D.R.

We remember some other things.
We remember the home saved and the crop saved and the
    courage put back in men's faces.
We remember you said from the start,
"I don't expect to make a hit every time I come to bat."
We remember that.
And sometimes you've struck out and we know it
But we know the batting average too.

(Not we the-Wall-Street-people but we the people)
It's written in our lives, in our kids growing up with a
    chance,
It's written in the faces of the old folks who don't have
    to go to the poorhouse
And the tanned faces of the boys from the CCC,
It's written in the water and earth of the Tennessee Valley
The contour-plowing that saves the dust-stricken land,

*And the lights coming on for the first time, on lonely
farms. . . .*

*A country squire from Hyde Park with a Harvard accent,
Who never once failed the people
And whom the people won't fail.*

In the East Room the mourners formed a ragged queue.
They passed the casket one by one, pausing to think or
to pray. Some blessed themselves; some knelt. The tall
playwright Robert Sherwood, with a longing glance at
the metal casket, turned to the living. "Come on out to
our house for a little while," Harry Hopkins said to him.
Sherwood looked at his wife. Harry the Hop wiped his
eyes and said, "I'll lead the way." Admiral Ross McIntire
followed Admirals Leahy and King to the West Wing.
Harry Truman said he was going home to lie down and
rest for a while. Arthur Prettyman stood in a doorway,
staring fixedly at the bronze casket. Former Chief Justice
Hughes bowed gravely left and right as he threaded his
way toward the portico. Morgenthau studied the face
of Edward Stettinius as though he found something new
and interesting there. Eleanor Roosevelt was told that
Foreign Minister Anthony Eden would like to come up
for a moment. "In a few minutes," she said. "Just a few
minutes." She walked with a strong gait down the
corridor to Anna's room. Mrs. Boettiger had checked
with Johnny's nurse to see that he was doing well. Her
mother burst into the room. This was a different woman
from that lady of restraint. Her eyes were blazing; she
slammed the door behind her; the black dress looked
frumpy as she whirled and shrilled: "Did you know that
Lucy Mercer was at Warm Springs? Did you?" Anna
had seen this venomous shrieking woman before—not often—but she had not seen the distorted accusatory face.
"No," Anna said with composure, "I did not."

"Well," Eleanor said, "I understand that she's been
here for dinner and that you have been here!" Anna
swallowed carefully. It hurt to hang the deed on the dead,
but she told the truth. "Father asked me." *"He* asked

you?" the mother shrilled, as though it was beyond credence. Mrs. Roosevelt studied the rug on the floor. She twisted her hands together. If there were going to be tears, they would not be in sorrow but in helpless rage. "Momma," Anna said softly, "I had a husband and children. I tried to fill Father's gap of loneliness. But I couldn't. I just couldn't." Her mother took a long cold look at her only daughter. "Well," she said in a more reasonable tone, "I am sorry." She left. Later in the evening Mrs. Roosevelt said that she planned to move out of the White House as quickly as possible.

In Georgetown, Harry Hopkins went to bed. Then he sent for Robert Sherwood to come upstairs and talk to him—or perhaps to listen. The room was small; there was an end table with a sizable lamp on it. The light tossed shadows onto the saffron skin and sunken sockets of Hopkins in such a way that he looked better to the playwright than he had at the funeral services. It seems strange that Hopkins would vent his innermost political thoughts to an intellectual who had no weight in Washington. He sat up in his pajamas, arms clutched around knees, and lit a fire under his emotions. "God damn it," he said, "now we've got to get to work on our own. This is where we've really got to begin. We've had it too easy all this time because we knew he was there and we had the privilege of being able to get to him. Whatever we thought was the matter with the world, whatever we felt ought to be done about it, we could take our ideas to him, and if he thought there was any merit in them, or if anything we said got him started on a train of thought of his own, then we'd see him go ahead and do it. And no matter how tremendous it might be or how idealistic, he wasn't scared of it. Well—he isn't there now, and we've got to find a way to do things by ourselves."

He had stiff, unelastic opinions about everything. But then, this is what endeared him to Roosevelt. Hopkins, in an ironclad way, was akin to Truman; he required little time to think an idea down to its worthiness, its feasibility and the cost. Having taken a stand, he was a difficult man to move. The rueful, cockeyed smile came to his face. "I'm pretty sure that Jimmy Byrnes and Henry Wallace, Bill Douglas and Harold Ickes are saying right now that they would be President of the United States today if it weren't for me. But this time I didn't have anything to do with it. I'm certain that the President had made up his mind on Truman long before I got back to the White House last year." He thought for a moment. "I think he would have preferred Bill Douglas, because he knew him better and he always liked Bill's toughness. But nobody really influential was pushing for Douglas. I think he'd gone off fishing out in Oregon or someplace." The smile flared again. "Bob Hannegan was certainly pushing for Harry Truman and the President believed he could put him over at the convention. People seemed to think that Truman was pulled out of a hat, but that wasn't true.

"The President had his eye on him for a long time. The Truman Committee record was good; he'd got himself known and liked around the country. And above all he was very popular in the Senate. That was the biggest consideration. The President wanted somebody that would help him when he went up there and asked them to ratify the peace." Sherwood posed few questions; he was in a mood to listen. He might have asked why the Boss saw Truman but once since the election. Why hadn't Roosevelt confided the secrets of Yalta to the man who, theoretically, had enough Senate votes in his pocket to win endorsement of the United Nations? Why hadn't Roosevelt told him of the impasse on Poland; the secret agreement to give to Russia lands and ports belonging to an ally—China? In the 1944 campaign, FDR divorced himself from Truman except to advise him not to fly, and to counsel him on the administration's stand on campaign issues Thomas Dewey would raise. It is also doubtful that, in 1944, Senator Harry Truman could generate enough votes to alter the outcome of the election. Assuming that the victorious FDR could have won alone, what was he saving Truman for? If, as Hopkins said, it was to gain acceptance of FDR's peace in the Senate—and this means the United Nations—why didn't he cultivate his Vice President? What Truman heard of the United Nations he listened to as he sat behind the President in the House well on March first. That, and nothing more.

Hopkins began to tire. He said he was going to quit. He told Sherwood that the whole Cabinet should get out en masse, except for Navy Secretary Forrestal and War Secretary Stimson—"they should remain at their posts until the end of the war." The playwright rose to shake hands and depart. "Truman has got to have his own people around him," Hopkins said, "not Roosevelt's. If we were around, we'd always be looking at him and he'd know we were thinking, 'The *President* wouldn't do it that way.' "

It was time to go. An hour after dinner, the caisson stood outside the White House in darkness. Behind it was a fleet of automobiles stretching the curving length of the White House grounds, out the northwest gate, and far up on Pennsylvania Avenue. Armed soldiers stood again on both curbs all the way to Union Station, but the crowds had diminished. The sight of the six white horses, at a slow clopping walk, and the strapped casket rocking gently on its black wooden bed had become American's self-inflicted wound. The country was fascinated by its own melancholia. There was pity for the dead, and self-pity for the living. He had been dead fifty-three hours, and no voice anywhere was heard to inquire why the obviously sick man had been permitted to run for a fourth term. No enterprising journalist asked Mr. Roosevelt's physician for his health records—now that they were no longer a matter of secrecy. No editor pointed out that FDR had served less than three months of a four-year term, and that the public had a right to know the medical diagnostics and prognostication and history of disease.

The national mood would not permit it. The pool reporters had the word of Dr. Howard Bruenn that the cause of death was a cardiovascular accident, and that

medical science had no means of predicting one. This
was the truth. The whole truth reposed in the secret
records of Dr. Ross McIntire, and he was not inclined,
now or later, to state: "For a year I had a dying patient
with irreversible heart and vascular damage. Under the
laws of medical probability he could not live but I kept
hoping for the best." Dr. McIntire would not reveal that
the State Department had passed on to him a secret
message from Stalin requesting that an autopsy be performed on the President because the Russians suspected
that he had been poisoned. McIntire read that one, and
decided it wasn't worth a response, except to say thank
you.

The final official White House calendar of the Roosevelt era states:

*9:30. To Hyde Park with the body of the late Presi-
dent a/c by Gen. and Mrs. Elliott R., Col. and Mrs. John
Boettiger, Mrs. James R., Mrs. John R., Mrs. F.D.R. Jr.,
Major Harry Hooker, Miss Laura Delano, Miss Marg.
Suckley & Mrs. Price Collier.*

It was the last of 4,399 White House calendars and
it had been drawn up by Mrs. Roosevelt and Malvina
Thompson. The aged and infirm Mrs. Price Collier,
FDR's maternal aunt, had arrived in the afternoon solely
to "ride home with Franklin." It is a small list, but it
does not reflect the size of the group of notables which
had joined the widow. It was so huge that POTUS had
been expanded from eleven Pullmans to seventeen and,
on track three, a second train of eleven cars was waiting
to board congressmen and department and bureau chiefs.
The Secret Service and the U.S. Army fretted about the
situation because practically all of the United States
government was in that first train—the President, the Cabinet, the Supreme Court and the leaders of Congress.
The timetable of the train had been published. An accident or act of sabotage could severely disrupt America's
ability to govern itself.

Hastily, the Army posted guards along the Pennsylvania Railroad main line to New York, and the New York Central up the Hudson River to Hyde Park and beyond. The railroads sent urgent messages to all divisions to double-check all closed switches and to sidetrack anything that moved on rails near POTUS. Two of the heaviest locomotives at the head of the train were given the departure signal. They spun their drivers until heels of sparks came from the rails. The train did not move. They tried again. This time it jerked and stopped. On the third attempt a coupling broke. A reporter from a Republican newspaper lifted a drink in salute and said, "My editor told me we'd have trouble getting FDR out of Washington." In another car Grace Tully walked into the *Ferdinand Magellan* and was stunned to find herself in the presence of President Truman and his family. Jimmy Byrnes, saying something, looked up and stopped. Miss Tully excused herself. It seemed strange to her for Truman to take the Pullman designed for Roosevelt. The car, as Mike Reilly told the Boss, was designed for "the President." Harry Truman held that office. It was his privilege and his *duty* to assume all the prerogatives and responsibilities of the office as quickly and efficiently as possible—FDR's office, desk, phone, armor-plated car, files, safe, assistants, secretaries and stenographers and, indeed, to expect loyalty from the Roosevelt team until he had time to organize his own.

There was enough liquor aboard both trains to control overnight grief. More liquor than food was consumed. In the Pullman where members of the Cabinet sat, some drank heavily, some watched. The worn mask of politeness was in tatters. Harold Ickes, Secretary of the Interior, irritated his wife by denouncing Truman in loud and acerbic tones. The train had not reached Baltimore when he was in heated argument with her, and Mrs. Ickes left the Pullman to find Grace Tully. For a reason no one could fathom, Treasury Secretary Morgenthau remained aloof from the others. He told Mrs. Morgenthau that Stettinius seemed "nervous as a witch." A few, such as Commerce Secretary Wallace and Postmaster General Frank Walker, continued to mourn for the fallen chief, and appeared to be unconcerned about the future. The hour was still early when Bill Hassett retired. He walked back to Mrs. Roosevelt's car and said good night to her and the ladies who sat with her. She again thanked him for "all that he had done." When he got to his bedroom, he found he was sharing it with Leighton McCarthy, the Boss's Warm Springs friend. McCarthy insisted that Hassett use the lower berth. Hassett refused. It was resolved when Hassett vaulted up to the top berth, and McCarthy murmured, "Okay. Thanks."

It was a long, slow night for two trains in tandem. On the congressional train, leaders drank and talked of Truman and the possible directions of the new government. Everyone tried to remember off-the-cuff remarks of Harry Truman concerning whom he liked and disliked. The gentlemen were busy deciding who would be dropped, and who would remain. A mile and a half ahead of them, POTUS meandered through Wilmington, Delaware. There were people on the platform, though the hour was late. As the last car passed, they saw the bright lights, the casket and the guards rocking gently as it passed to diminish in size to a pinpoint of light, and disappear forever.

Dawn is the daily miracle. Henry Wallace, sitting alone in the dining car, was eating a hot cereal. The train had been standing an hour in the Mott Haven Yards in the Bronx. Secret Service men walked the tracks beside the train. Deputy Chief Inspector John J. O'Connor posted his New York City policemen around the train, on the trestles, on flatcars. The man who might have been President watched the shiny blackness diffuse to an opaque gloom. As he sorted his random thoughts, the timid flush of pink etched a halo over the filth of the smoky metropolis. The bands grew brighter and, below him on the tracks, a man tossed a pail of water up at his window. Mr. Wallace ducked, then smiled. He sat quietly over coffee as the broad brush cleaned the window, and moved on to the next. The train had come to a jarring, bucking stop and the few who had managed to sleep were awake.

Flagmen hurried through the corridors. Some asked why the train had stopped. Because the schedule called for the congressional train to move ahead of POTUS and unload at Hyde Park before the President's body arrived. A simple question, a logical reply.

The train moved again, starting in noisy protest. A mile ahead, a dead-head locomotive cleared the way on the New York Central tracks. The Secret Service men made the high hop from the roadbed to the lowest car step. Soon, the seventeen cars were moving along the edge of the Hudson, through Spuyten Duyvil, clicking loudly on the Harlem River Bridge with the sheer green of the Palisades on the other shore. There was High Tor, Sugar Loaf and the forbidding eminence of Storm King. Would the President have been flattered to know that a small group of men stood at the crossing at Garrison, holding their hats over their hearts? Perhaps. He would have been one of the few *littérateurs* who could say that, exactly eighty years ago, men stood at the crossing, heads bared, to watch a crepe-decorated, wood-burning loco-motive go by.

The sentimental loyalist, Bill Hassett, was up early, walking back through the cars to ask if he could be of service to Mrs. Roosevelt. He excused himself as Secret Service men okayed his passage through the Truman car. Hassett noted in his diary: "Have not met the President nor any of his staff as yet." The vague line of demarcation between the Truman people and the Roosevelt people was growing sharper. It was not accidental. The outs were in and they recalled poignantly that the Roosevelt crowd paid scant attention to the Vice President except to relay messages from the President. The Truman people were seldom "consulted" or "invited." When Harry Tru-man walked into the Oval Office on that first morning—with little knowledge of what to do or say and in almost total ignorance of pending projects—Jonathan Daniels was in an office down the hall, available for infor-mation; Steve Early at Warm Springs was no farther away than Truman's phone—but the President appointed a receptionist to be his temporary appointments secretary.

Truman's personal executive secretary, Matthew Connolly, and his military aide, Colonel Harry Vaughn, were free to solicit as much information as required to begin their new functions—but they didn't. Whatever rancor was husbanded for the Roosevelt crowd did not extend to the late President's family. To them, Truman was cordial, solicitous, helpful. The fact that he had resurrected Jimmy Byrnes overnight was viewed by the Roosevelt Cabinet as a threat. Truman was an honest, gut politician; he could relate to Byrnes, Hopkins, Hannegan, Edwin Pauley (treasurer of the Democratic National Party), even old Cordell Hull, but he could not and would not seek the counsel of the "elite idealists"—Stettinius, Morgenthau, Attorney General Francis Biddle, Secretary of Agriculture Claude Wickard, or even the innocuous hard-working Postmaster General, Frank Walker. Truman would jettison all of them before the year was out.

As Hassett apologized his way through the Truman car, the President was in deep thought listening to Jimmy Byrnes translate his shorthand notes on the Yalta Conference. Hassett found Mrs. Roosevelt sitting at a window staring at the passing rails. She emerged from her reverie to accord her cheerful good morning and to say that she had nothing at present for him to do. Tonight, she proposed to have dinner with Elliott and her daughters-in-law at the White House. She would tell Hassett more about it later. William Hassett thought that the scenery across the Hudson was beautiful, breathtaking, but Mrs. Roosevelt apparently did not see it. She returned to watching the silvery tracks slide by her vision.

Anna and Colonel Boettiger breakfasted early. She was cheerful, almost vivacious. To some, she seemed to have made a long, long trip the length of the seventeen cars, saying hello, maintaining a smile and trying to keep the conversation away from her father's death. She also sought the Truman people and exchanged greetings. At Poughkeepsie station the engineer plucked a message from a metal arm. It said that the congressional train had arrived at Hyde Park, disembarked its passengers and backed off the siding. The news was welcome because he had only nine miles to go.

Hyde Park, in personality, was always slightly aloof. The descendants of Dutch burghers and British colonials maintained a clean and quiet village of shops between the prongs of the Roosevelt estate to the south and the Vanderbilt estate on the north. Hyde Park wasn't even a postillion stop on the old Albany Post Road when the ornate carriages required five days to travel between Nieu Amsterdam and Albany. It was purposely small and proud, a place where a grog shop made of ancient smoke-darkened timbers would flourish and a motion picture house would not. Quadrennially, the villagers allowed themselves an unseemly act; they marched to Crum Elbow in a body to cheer the election—or reelection—of their neighbor, Franklin Delano Roosevelt, as President of the United States of America. Some of the older people could not understand how he occupied such a high office, but they were not resentful; Roosevelt was one of the few Presidents who carried his home town on election day.

This morning, very early, they had done another alien thing. Black crepe was tacked around the doors and windows of shops. A sexton dressed in formal black stood under the bell tower of St. James Episcopal Church ready to yank the thick rope when the funeral train pulled onto the siding far below. Some, not invited to the services, brought clutches of wild flowers and presented them to Will Plog inside the Rose Garden. Mr. Plog had worked for the Roosevelts fifty years—exactly fifty years. With reluctance, he had agreed that he was too old to dig the grave, so he supervised it. Gray and slender, he stood beside it, accepting the flowers, muttering thank you and placing them down front before the two huge carloads of blooms which banked the freshly turned earth. They had done what they thought proper, and he had done what he thought proper. These people would not intrude. A little later, when the casket came up the hill, they would represent self-isolated people at the top of

the hill—watching, studying, whispering behind their
hands. Later many would be at St. James's because this
was Sunday. In the 134-year-old churchyard all of them
knew the simple Roosevelt lid of stone, under which it
stated that James died in 1900 and Sara in 1941.

The old-fashioned virtues with their concomitant
restraints were not peculiar to Hyde Park. Far off in
Grandview, Missouri, Harry Truman's mother donned
her Sunday dress to go to church. Her daughter Mary
had counseled against worship, reminding the ninety-two-
year-old woman that reporters were waiting outside on
the sidewalk. The lady had remained indoors since
Thursday evening; she would go to church early. The
reporters had but one question: "How do you feel about
your son being President of the United States?" She
stopped tapping her cane and leaned on it. The bent
white head under the old straw hat came up smartly.
"I can't really be glad he is President," she said, "because
I'm sorry that President Roosevelt is dead. Now if he
had been voted in, I'd be out waving a flag, but it doesn't
seem right to be happy or waving a flag now." Far off
in the opposite direction, the afternoon light was dimming
when Lieutenant General George S. Patton, trim and
grim in battle decorations and pearl-handled revolvers,
hurried to the head of his Third Army at Chemnitz, 115
miles south of Berlin. He had found an intact bridge
across a river. Standing in a jeep, he saluted the bridge
and shouted, "This structure will be known as the
Franklin D. Roosevelt Bridge. Now, move it!"

The train pulled onto the siding below Crum Elbow
and stopped. The last part of the train was still on the
main track. Iron stools were placed on the cinderbed
so that passengers could step down. It was 8:40, too
early for the 10:00 A.M. burial on the hill, so some
remained aboard, others left. Funeral cars stood around
the earthen cliff where the boy Frank Roosevelt used
to lie on his belly and watch the trains. The automobiles
ran a shuttle serivce a mile and three-quarters up the
steep hill to the estate, and back for more passengers.
Bill Hassett found himself with a most unlikely pair

Mrs. Nesbitt, the White House cook, and Edwin Pauley, the Democratic treasurer. It was another in a succession of fair days, the river dimpled by a westerly breeze, the road up the hill canopied with old elms and edged with wild violets. Soldiers and Marines stood at parade rest all the way. Behind the hedges on both sides, pale apple blossoms trembled on boughs.

A little after nine, the guests began to assemble in the Rose Garden. New York State troopers assisted the Secret Service in admitting guests to Crum Elbow and pointing to where they should stand. Admiral Ernest King stood in silence with his staff; so did General George Marshall, and General Barney Giles, who represented the Air Forces. Admiral Leahy stood alone. On the far side of the plot he recognized Canada's Prime Minister, Mackenzie King, Anthony Eden and the Earl of Athlone. James A. Farley stood bareheaded near Edward Flynn. Hundreds of soldiers, shoulder to shoulder, looked small against the tall hemlock hedge. The members of the Cabinet and the congressional leaders stood in their formalized place. The distinguished personages stood well away from the grave. There were close to three hundred of them waiting in silence. The only sound was the westerly breeze in the old trees, and the cheerful gossip of birds over the bounty of another spring.

Down at the river, the Roosevelts and Trumans waited in cars as the casket was lifted once more from that broad window. An officer fired a Very pistol. There was a small snap and the arc of a white interrogation mark of smoke in the pale sky. High up near the estate, a field piece fired the first of twenty-one salutes. In the silence, the crashing sound was earsplitting, and it carried across the Hudson and rolled back to Crum Elbow like old thunder. In the village the sexton grabbed the bell rope with both hands and backed up as he pulled. The deep bronze sound rattled through the village like a trembling tongue. Some birds fled. The warbling, the trilling, stopped. The larger birds swooped from the trees and high eaves in coveys and flew low over the Rose Garden. There was sunshine and silence. The hundreds who stood heard a growing hum. Out of the grove of leafy trees came thundering bombers, passing over Crum Elbow as silent mourners squinted into the light.

At the river edge soldiers slid the casket into a hearse. It started up the hill slowly, rocking in the freshet gullies of the road. Behind came the few limousines with the select mourners. The crashing sound of the big gun, every fifteen seconds, became something the mourners braced against. Halfway up the hill the hearse stopped. The road ahead was blocked by a caisson with six brown horses, a seventh horse caparisoned in black with boots reversed in stirrups, 600 West Point cadets immobile in their pale uniforms and crossed white belts. Far in front was the West Point Band, instruments and shoes sun-spangled, and two rows of drummers with cloth covering their instruments. At terse military commands, the Army pallbearers opened the back of the hearse, waited for a second command, slid the casket back, heard another sound and the gloved hands lifted the remains of the President, and marched forward to the caisson. The ammunition carrier was on a steep slope, so care had to be taken to strap the casket tight. A signal was given and the drummers began the hollow beat for the slow step. The cadets marched stiffly, the ranks of knees all bending at the same time as they led the last slow climb. On signal, the band lifted their instruments and opened the minor notes of Chopin's "Funeral March."

In the Rose Garden the dirge could be heard on the westerly breeze, and the sound died with the whisper of air. The element of poignant personal sorrow, which had been absent in the cheerful morning sunlight, came alive with the drums. The bell at St. James's was a distant solitary sound. The members of the United States Supreme Court, mostly aged and alone on their piece of sod, seemed to flinch as the field gun continued its deafening sound, followed by several lesser echoes returning from the highlands. All of it amounted to the cumulative conspiracy of the living to punish the living in behalf of the dead. On the far side of the estate, across Route 9, the manager of a filling station had said, three days ago, that he had never seen Roosevelt and felt no allegiance to him. He had remained open this Sunday morning, but he could not shut out the doleful tone of the bell, the heartbeat of the muffled drums, the crack of cannon. He said, "It's no use," and locked the pumps and went home.

The line of march made it to the top of the hill. The villagers were congealed. None were seen to weep. They were close enough so that the band thundered as it marched in hesitation and played "Nearer My God to Thee." In their silence, they appreciated the 600 scrubbed faces of the white-gloved cadets and the creaking of the caisson hinges and the scrape of the wheels. These people knew him and respected him and their interest in the grandeur of the moment dissipated the depressing thought that they would not see him again, leaning out of that silly old car to chat with the butcher, a senior warden of the church, or a woman who had once worked for his mother. There were a few among them who had been schoolboys when Frank had been taught at home by his mother and a governess. It had taken time for them to like the rich, secluded boy of Crum Elbow, but when he showed them that he could hand-fashion a good muskrat trap, could sail an iceboat at speed over the cold opaque mirror of the wintry Hudson, knew birdcalls as they knew birdcalls and was not above the mischief and vallainy of the village boys, he had made friends. And so, as some said later in the day, they looked at the taut flag on the caisson and did not think of a President or a Commander in Chief, or even a landed lord of Hyde Park—they recalled a gawky boy who believed that if he could speak personally to another boy, he could make a friend. To those few, it seemed fitting that he should come home to stay.

Through the east hedge a young crucifer came holding a gold cross on a staff. Behind him, head bowed, strode Reverend Dr. George W. Anthony, rector of St. James's. He was old and gray, a cavernous-faced man with a goatee and a skullcap. He wore a black cassock and a white surplice. The music was loud, growing louder. The

West Point Band was outside the hedge, playing the triumphant strains of "Hail to the Chief." This was the final formal accolade to the dead President; it was the first to a new President. The cadets melted into ranks of two and came through the hedge marching, each unit taking its place in the big square behind the mourners. When they stood at attention, all the mourners, without being obvious, could see the widow, in dull black, being led through the hedge on the arm of her son. Behind them were Anna and her husband, the dutiful daughters-in-law, and then President and Mrs. Truman and Margaret. To some, it was executed with such perfection, without hesitation, that it seemed to have been rehearsed. A squadron of fighter planes crashed the ears in low flight. The Reverend Dr. Anthony watched the casket as it was carried in and placed on a rug of false turf. He lifted his skullcap.

The big gun had stopped shattering the spring breeze. In the village the bronze bell fell silent. The bandsmen stood with their instruments under their arms. The heartbeat of the drums was stilled. But the birds did not chatter again. It was possible for mourners to hear people standing behind breathing. The gentlemen of the press darted glances here and there and scribbled notes. The three pool reporters who had known him better than the others—Smith, Nixon, Cornell—wore masks of personal grief, a license seldom granted to the good reporter.

The Reverend Dr. Anthony, standing to the east of the graveside, glanced at the bright pale vault of sky. At the age of seventy-eight, he knew that the words which now trembled on his lips would soon be said by someone over him. "Unto Almighty God we commend the soul of Thy brother departed," he said loudly, in quavering tone. President Truman removed his gray fedora and held it limply in his left hand. A small private plane, possibly owned by a newspaper and used for aerial photography, passed noisily and some of the words were lost. " . . . and we commit this body to the ground; earth to earth, ashes to ashes and dust to dust, in sure and certain hope of the resurrection unto eternal life . . ."

Margaret Suckley stooped to reassure Fala and pet him. He crouched at her feet. "Uncle Fred" Delano and Mrs. Price Collier, Sara's surviving siblings, were not strong enough to stand. They sat precariously on chairs which sank in the soft grass. A blooming lilac bush peeked over the tall hedge beneath the old stable with its big numbers "1886." The building of it was Franklin Roosevelt's earliest memory; it had survived the age of the horse; it survived him, too.

"Blessed are the dead who die in the Lord. Lord have mercy on us. Christ have mercy on us. Lord have mercy on us." The aged rector lifted a hand. Eight non-commissioned officers eased the straps which held the casket. It was lowered slowly as the Reverend Dr. Anthony's voice penetrated the edges of the Rose Garden: "Now the laborer's task is o'er; Now the battle day is past; Now upon the farther shore Lands the voyager at last . . ." It was so quiet that everyone could hear the creaking of the straps. "Father in Thy gracious keeping, Leave we now our brother sleeping . . ." The clergyman stepped back from the grave. A single file of West Point cadets marched smartly to the grave and took positions on both sides of it. A cadet lieutenant, sword sparkling in the bright light, brought it up toward his lips. His commands were sharp and swift. "Attention! Should-d-der arms! Ready! Aim! Fire!" The rifles canopied the grave and they fired as one. Fala howled and rolled over and over in the grass. The second command was given. Then a third. A wisp of powder-blue smoke hung in the air. The casket was in the bottom of the grave. A sergeant lifted a silvered instrument to his lips. Agonizingly slow, the lingering notes of "Taps" hung on the air. It was over. Military commands were shouted. Mrs. Roosevelt, slightly stooped, turned to leave the garden. The battalion of cadets left in precise formation, and the people—some shaking hands, some pressing kisses on cheeks, some nodding curtly—dispersed in slow disorder.

The garden, empty, looked bigger. Old Bill Plog shuffled forward and told the workmen to use their shovels. The heavy moist earth thundered onto the box below. Within a few minutes, it seemed, Plog saw Mrs. Roosevelt return alone. She did not approach him. She stood in the opening near the main house and watched the shovels and heard the thumps. Somewhere, perhaps in her room at the house, she had found something she wanted to wear. Above her heart on the black dress, she had pinned the small pearl-decorated fleur-de-lis Franklin had given her as a wedding present. She watched for a moment, and then walked away. Much later, reporters would surround her to ask questions. For them she reserved a smile of pity.

"The story," she said, "is over."

Bibliography

Allen, Frederick Lewis, *The Big Change: America Transforms Itself, 1900–1950*. New York, Harper & Row, 1952.

American Heritage Pictorial History of the Presidents of the United States. New York, American Heritage Publishing Company, 1968.

Asbell, Bernard, *When F.D.R. Died*. New York, Holt, Rinehart & Winston, 1961.

Baldwin, Hanson W., *Battles Won and Lost: Great Campaigns of World War Two*. New York, Harper & Row, 1966.

Bernstein, Barton J., and Matusow, Allen, eds., *The Truman Administration: A Documentary History*. New York, Harper & Row, 1966.

Biddle, Francis, "The Wartime Cabinet," *American Heritage,* June 1962.

Bohlen, Charles E., *Witness to History, 1929–1969*. New York, W. W. Norton & Company, 1973.

Burns, James MacGregor, *Roosevelt: The Soldier of Freedom*. New York, Harcourt Brace Jovanovich, 1970.

———, "FDR: The Untold Story of His Last Year," *Saturday Review*, April 11, 1970.

Byrnes, James F., *Speaking Frankly*. New York, Harper & Brothers, 1947.

Churchill, Winston, *The Second World War:* Vol. VI, *Triumph and Tragedy*. Boston, Houghton Mifflin Company, 1953.

Clemens, Diane Shaver, *Yalta*. New York, Oxford University Press, 1970.

Congdon, Don, ed., *The Thirties: A Time to Remember*. New York, Simon and Schuster, 1962.

Daniels, Jonathan, *The End of Innocence*. Philadelphia, J. B. Lippincott Company, 1954

————, *The Time Between the Wars*. Garden City, New York, Doubleday & Company, 1964.

Dean, Vera Micheles, *The Four Cornerstones of Peace*. New York, McGraw-Hill Book Company, 1946.

Dilks, David, ed., *The Diaries of Sir Alexander Cadogan, 1938–1945*. New York, G. P. Putnam's Sons, 1971.

Di Salle, Michael, *Second Choice*. New York, Hawthorn Books, 1966.

Eisenhower, John S. D., *The Bitter Woods: A Comprehensive Study of the War in Europe*. New York, G. P. Putnam's Sons, 1969.

Farley, James A., *Behind the Ballots: The Personal History of a Politician*. New York, Harcourt, Brace, 1938.

————, *Jim Farley's Story*. New York, McGraw-Hill Book Company, 1948.

Ford, Corey, *Donovan of O.S.S.* Boston, Little, Brown & Company, 1970.

Friedel, Frank, *Our Country's Presidents*. Washington, National Geographic Society, 1966.

Gardner, Brian, *The Year That Changed the World, 1945*. New York, Coward, McCann, 1963.

Geddes, Donald Porter, *FDR, A Memorial*. New York, Dial Press, 1945.

Graff, Robert, and Ginna, Emmett, with Roger Butterfield *FDR*. New York, Harper & Row, 1963.

Gunther, John, *Roosevelt in Retrospect: A Profile in History*. New York, Harper & Brothers, 1950.

Hassett, William D., *Off the Record with FDR, 1942–1945*. New Brunswick, New Jersey, Rutgers University Press, 1958.

————, Diary. National Archives, Washington, D.C.

Hunt, Frazier, *The Untold Story of Douglas MacArthur* New York, Devon-Adair Company, 1954.

Hurd, Charles, *The White House Story*. New York, Hawthorn Books, 1966.

Hyde, H. Montgomery, *Stalin: The History of a Dictator* New York, Farrar, Straus & Giroux, 1971.

Jensen, Amy, *The White House and Its Thirty-four Families,* new enl. ed. New York, McGraw-Hill Book Company, 1965.

Krock, Arthur, *Memoirs: Sixty Years on the Firing Line.* New York, Funk & Wagnalls, 1968.

Lash, Joseph P., *Eleanor and Franklin.* New York, W. W. Norton & Company, 1971.

Leahy, Fleet Admiral William D., Diary. Manuscript Division, Library of Congress, Washington, D.C.

Liddell Hart, B. H., *History of the Second World War.* New York, G. P. Putnam's Sons, 1971.

Loewenheim, Francis, L., ed., *The Historian and the Diplomat: The Role of History and Historians in American Foreign Policy.* New York, Harper & Row, 1967.

McIntire, Vice Admiral Ross T., *White House Physician.* New York, G. P. Putnam's Sons, 1946.

Macmillan, Harold, *The Blast of War, 1939–1945.* New York, Harper & Row, 1968.

Mahoney, Booth, *The Politicians, 1945–1960.* Philadelphia, J. B. Lippincott Company, 1970.

———, *Roosevelt and Rayburn.* Philadelphia, J. B. Lippincott Company, 1971.

Morison, Samuel Eliot, *History of United States Naval Operations in World War II:* Vol. XIII, *The Liberation of the Philippines . . . 1944–45;* Vol. XIV, *Victory in the Pacific.* Boston, Atlantic–Little, Brown & Company, 1948–62.

Morris, Edwin Bateman, compl., *Report of the Commission on the Renovation of the Executive Mansion.* U.S. Government Printing Office, 1952.

Murphy, Robert D., *Diplomat Among Warriors.* Garden City, New York, Doubleday & Company, 1964.

Nesbitt, Henrietta, *White House Diary.* Garden City, New York, Doubleday & Company, 1948.

Reilly, Michael F., *Reilly of the White House.* New York, Simon and Schuster, 1947.

Rigdon, William M., *White House Sailor.* Garden City, New York, Doubleday & Company, 1962.

Rollins, Alfred B., *Roosevelt and Howe.* New York, Alfred A. Knopf, 1962.

Roosevelt, Eleanor, *The Autobiography of Eleanor Roosevelt*. New York, Harper & Row, 1961.

———, *This I Remember*. New York, Harper & Brothers, 1949.

———, *You Learn By Living*. New York, Harper & Row, 1960.

Roosevelt, Franklin Delano, *F.D.R.: His Personal Letters*, ed. Elliott Roosevelt, 4 vols. New York, Duell, Sloan and Pearce, 1945–50.

———, *The Public Papers and Addresses of Franklin D. Roosevelt*, ed. Samuel I. Rosenman, 4 vols. New York, Harper & Brothers, 1950.

Roosevelt, James, and Shalett, Sidney, *Affectionately, F.D.R.* New York, Harcourt, Brace and Company, 1959.

Rosenman, Samuel I., *Working With Roosevelt*. New York, Harper & Brothers, 1952.

Sann, Paul, *The Lawless Decade: A Pictorial History of the Roaring Twenties*. New York, Crown Publishers, 1971.

Schlesinger, Arthur M., Jr., *The Age of Roosevelt:* Vol. 3, *The Politics of Upheaval*. Boston, Houghton Mifflin Company, 1960.

Sherwood, Robert E., *Roosevelt and Hopkins: An Intimate History*, rev. ed. New York, Harper & Brothers, 1950.

Shirer, William L., *The Rise and Fall of the Third Reich: A History of Nazi Germany*. New York, Simon and Schuster, 1960.

Smith, A. Merriman, "Death of a Leader," in *Fabulous Yesterday*, ed. Lewis W. Gillenson. New York, Harper & Row, 1961.

Snyder, Louis L., and Morris, Richard B., eds., *A Treasury of Great Reporting*. New York, Simon and Schuster, 1949.

Speer, Albert, *Inside the Third Reich: Memoirs*. New York, The Macmillan Company, 1970.

Stettinius, Edward R., Jr., *Roosevelt and the Russians: The Yalta Conference*. Garden City, New York, Doubleday & Company, 1949.

Stevens, Ruth, *"Hi-Ya, Neighbor."* New York, Tupper & Lowe, 1947.

This Fabulous Century: Vol. 4, *1940–1950.* New York, Time-Life Books, 1969.

TIME Capsule, 1945. New York, Time-Life Books.

Toland, John, *The Rising Sun: The Decline and Fall of the Japanese Empire, 1936–1945.* New York, Random House, 1970.

Truman, Harry S., *Memoirs:* Vol. I, *Year of Decisions.* Garden City, New York, Doubleday & Company, 1955.

Tugwell, Rexford G., *The Democratic Roosevelt.* Garden City, New York, Doubleday & Company, 1957.

———, *F.D.R., Architect of an Era.* New York, The Macmillan Company, 1967.

Tully, Grace, *F.D.R., My Boss.* New York, Charles Scribner's Sons, 1949.

U.S. State Department, *Foreign Relations of the United States, Diplomatic Papers: The Conferences at Malta and Yalta.* U.S. Government Printing Office, 1955.

Walker, Turnley, *Roosevelt and the Warm Springs Story.* New York, A.A. Wyn, 1953.

Werth, Alexander, *Russia At War, 1941–1945.* New York, E. P. Dutton & Company, 1964.

Wharton, Don, *The Roosevelt Omnibus.* New York, Alfred A. Knopf, 1934.

White, Theodore H., and Jacoby, Annalee, *Thunder Out of China.* New York, William Sloane Associates, 1946.

Willoughby, Charles A., and Chamberlain, John, *MacArthur, 1941–1951.* New York, McGraw-Hill Book Company 1954.

Periodicals

Congressional Record, March 1, 1945.
Life, April 23, 1945.
The New York Times, 1944–45, various editions.
Southern Funeral Director, May 1945.

Interviews

Frank Allcorn, mayor, Warm Springs, Georgia; Howard Anderson, U.S. Secret Service; James Beary, U.S. Secret Service; Dorothy Brady, personal secretary to the President; Howard G. Bruenn, M.D., physician to the President; Benjamin V. Cohen, Counselor of the Department of State, 1945–47; William F. Geeslin, Southern Railway System; Louise Hachmeister, White House telephone operator; Anna Roosevelt Halsted, the President's daughter; Alger Hiss, Office of Special Political Affairs, Department of State, 1944–47; Lyndon B. Johnson; Brannon Lesesne, Patterson Funeral Home, Atlanta; John McCormack, majority leader, House of Representatives; Michael Reilly, Chief, White House Division, U.S. Secret Service; William M. Rigdon, Lieutenant j.g., USN, secretary to the President; Elliott Roosevelt, the President's second son; James Rowley, U.S. Secret Service; Reverend George Smith, St. Mary Help of Christians, Aiken, South Carolina; Ruth Stevens, manager, Warm Springs Hotel; E. L. Thompson, Baltimore & Ohio Railroad; Grace Tully, personal secretary to the President.

Index

How to do almost everything

What are the latest time and money-saving shortcuts for painting papering, and varnishing floors, walls, ceilings, furniture? (See pages 102-111 of HOW TO DO *Almost* EVERYTHING.) What are the mini-recipes and the new ways to make food—from appetizers through desserts—exciting and delicious? (See pages 165-283.) How-to-do-it ideas like these have made Bert Bacharach, father of the celebrated composer (Burt), one of the most popular columnists in America.

This remarkable new book, HOW TO DO *Almost* EVERYTHING, is a fact-filled collection of Bert Bacharach's practical aids, containing thousands of tips and hints—for keeping house, gardening, cooking, driving, working, traveling, caring for children. It will answer hundreds of your questions, briefly and lucidly.

How to do almost everything

is chock-full of useful information—information on almost every thing you can think of, arranged by subject in short, easy-to-read tidbits, with an alphabetical index to help you find your way around —and written with the famed Bacharach touch.

SEND FOR YOUR FREE EXAMINATION COPY TODAY

We invite you to mail the coupon below. A copy of HOW TO DO *Almost* EVERYTHING will be sent to you at once. If at the end of ten days you do not feel that this book is one you will treasure, you may return it and owe nothing. Otherwise, we will bill you $7.95 plus postage and handling. At all bookstores, or write to Simon and Schuster, Dept. S-52, 630 Fifth Ave., New York, N.Y. 10020

VOLUME TWO

Over 1,000,000 copies of Volume one sold)

THE WAY THINGS WORK

From aerosols to video tape
recording. 1,057 two-color drawings.
Clear, concise explanations.

How do aerosols work? (See page 20 of THE WAY THINGS WORK, VOLUME TWO.) How is foam plastic made? (See page 52.) How can the performance of your automobile's engine be improved? (See page 260.) How does the color get into TV? (See page 288.) What is inertial navigation? (See page 374.) How do safety bindings on skis protect you? (See page 444.) What are the different methods of video tape recording? (See page 560.)

This remarkable book will answer hundreds of your questions (and the "hows" and "whys" your children ask) about theories and their practical application in machines that, seen or unseen, are part of our everyday lives.

Now you can know *The Way Things Work*

Here are concise, carefully detailed descriptions of the principles and the working parts of musical instruments, industrial metallurgy, ballistics, wing geometry, ship stabilizing, automotive engineering, computers, generators—in short, of hundreds of things small and large, simple and complex, that make you wonder, "How does it work?"

And those who *didn't* read Volume One will surely want to take advantage of our offer to obtain *both* of these invaluable reference books that explain the marvels of technology that daily fill our world.

The books that satisfy the curiosity most of us feel when we push a button, throw a switch, or turn a knob on any one of the hundreds of appliances and machines that surround us with their mysteries.

Send for your free examination copy today

We invite you to mail the coupon. A copy of Volume Two of THE WAY THINGS WORK will be sent to you at once. If at the end of ten days you do not feel that this book is one you will treasure, you may return it and owe nothing. Otherwise, we will bill you for $11.95 plus mailing costs. At all bookstores, or write to Simon and Schuster, Dept. S-54, 630 Fifth Avenue, New York, N.Y. 10020.

LOOK FOR THESE GREAT POCKET 🦘 BOOKS BESTSELLERS AT YOUR FAVORITE BOOKSTORE

THE PIRATE	Harold Robbins
HARLEQUIN	Morris West
THE SILVER BEARS	Paul E. Erdman
MURDER ON THE ORIENT EXPRESS Agatha Christie	
SPY STORY	Len Deighton
THE JOY OF SEX	Alex Comfort
FORBIDDEN FLOWERS: MORE WOMEN'S SEXUAL FANTASIES Nancy Friday	
MY SECRET GARDEN	Nancy Friday
AN AMERICAN LIFE	Jeb Magruder
JOURNEY TO IXTLAN	Carlos Castaneda
THE TEACHINGS OF DON JUAN Carlos Castaneda	
A SEPARATE REALITY	Carlos Castaneda
ALONE	Rod McKuen
SHADOW OF EVIL	Frank G. Slaughter
BODY LANGUAGE	Julius Fast
TEN LITTLE INDIANS	Agatha Christie
RETURN JOURNEY	R.F. Delderfield
YOU AND ME, BABE	Chuck Barris
THE HAVERSHAM LEGACY	Daoma Winston
HOW TO IMPROVE YOUR MAN IN BED Lynn Barber	
THE MERRIAM-WEBSTER DICTIONARY	